Antisocial Behavior by Young People

Written by a child psychiatrist, a criminologist, and a social psychologist, *Antisocial Behavior by Young People* is a major international review of research evidence on antisocial behavior. The book covers all aspects of the field, including descriptions of different types of delinquency and time trends, the state of knowledge on the individual, social–psychological and cultural factors involved, and recent advances in prevention and intervention. The authors bring together a wide range of disciplinary perspectives in order to provide a comprehensive account of antisocial behavior in youth.

Sir Michael Rutter is Professor of Child Psychiatry at the University of London's Institute of Psychiatry. An international authority on child development and child psychiatry, Rutter's research has earned him numerous awards and honors, including the American Psychological Association Distinguished Scientific Contribution Award, the Castilla del Pino Prize for Achievement in Psychiatry, and the Helmut Horten award for research on autism. His previous books with Cambridge University Press include *Psychosocial Disturbances in Young People* as well as *Biological Risk Factors for Psychosocial Disorders* and *Stress, Risk, and Resilience in Children and Adolescents*.

Henri Giller is Managing Director of Social Information Systems, Ltd. After receiving his Ph.D. from the Institute of Criminology at the University of Cambridge, Giller has served as a Fellow at the University of London's Institute of Psychiatry and a Lecturer in Law at the University of Keele. His previous books include *Juvenile Delinquency Trends and Perspectives* (Penguin) and *Understanding Juvenile Justice* (Croom Helm). Giller is a founding member of the International Workshop on Juvenile Criminology.

Ann Hagell is Co-Director of the new Policy Research Bureau in London, where she specializes in policy research on young offenders, antisocial behavior problems, at-risk young people, and parenting problems. Previously she has been a Senior Fellow at the Policy Studies Institute, a Fulbright scholar at the University of North Carolina, and a Research Scientist in Professor Rutter's research team at the MRC Child Psychiatry Unit, where she also completed her Ph.D.

Antisocial Behavior by Young People

MICHAEL RUTTER

HENRI GILLER

ANN HAGELL

 CAMBRIDGE
UNIVERSITY PRESS

PUBLISHED BY THE PRESS SYNDICATE OF THE UNIVERSITY OF CAMBRIDGE
The Pitt Building, Trumpington Street, Cambridge CB2 1RP, United Kingdom

CAMBRIDGE UNIVERSITY PRESS
The Edinburgh Building, Cambridge CB2 2RU, UK   http://www.cup.cam.ac.uk
40 West 20th Street, New York, NY 10011-4211, USA   http://www.cup.org
10 Stamford Road, Oakleigh, Melbourne 3166, Australia

© Michael Rutter, Henri Giller, & Ann Hagell 1998

First published 1998

Printed in the United States of America

Typefaces Palatino 9.75/12.5 pt. & Optima   *System* AMS-T_EX   [FH]

A catalog record for this book is available from the British Library

Library of Congress Cataloging in Publication Data
Rutter, Michael, 1962–
Antisocial behavior by young people / Michael Rutter, Henri
Giller, Ann Hagell.
p.   cm.
Includes bibliographical references and index.
ISBN 0-521-64157-8 (hb)
ISBN 0-521-64608-1 (pb)
1. Juvenile delinquency.   2. Conduct disorders in children.
I. Giller, Henri.   II. Hagell, Ann.   III. Title.
HV9069.R93   1998
364.36 – dc21   98-36581
                                                                        CIP

ISBN 0-521-64157-8 hardback
ISBN 0-521-64608-1 paperback

Contents

Acknowledgments

This book is the result of a project, funded by the Department of Health, that was carried out between 1995 and 1998. We are grateful to the Department for providing the financial support for the project, and to the members of the advisory group (representing the Department and the Home Office) for their help and guidance – especially Carolyn Davies (the chair) but also Norman Duncan, Maggie Ferguson, John Graham, Jeremy Mean, Wendy Rose, and Chris Sealey.

We owe a large debt to the many other people who have helped us in a variety of ways over the last few years. We would like to specifically acknowledge the contributions of Mark Savin, who played a major role in bringing the book to completion, and also of Marina Arrendale, Julie Burnell, Simon Dupont, Rita Goldberg, Susan Johnson, Karen Langridge, Joy Maxwell, Sian Putnam, Gill Rangel, and Karen Wrench, who were helpful in innumerable ways. Although there are too many to list individually, we would also like to thank the numerous researchers who have generously provided us with material, particularly papers that were in preparation or in press at the time and that would have been difficult for us to include otherwise. Finally, we have been greatly helped by the detailed critiques of an earlier draft of this text generously provided by Avshalom Caspi, David Farrington, Josine Junger-Tas, Barbara Maughan, Terrie Moffitt, Andrew Rutherford, Robert Sampson, David Smith, and Eric Taylor, as well as the anonymous reviewers who provided comments to the Department of Health.

1 | Introduction

What Do We Mean by "Antisocial Behavior" and "Young People"?

This book is about young people who commit criminal offenses. They may not necessarily have been prosecuted – although many of them are. We are interested in a range of things about these young people, their behavior, and the system within which they offend. We ask: who they are, what types of things they do, whether their criminal activities are accompanied by other problems, how trends have changed over time, and what can be concluded about the backgrounds to those behaviors. Can anything be done to intervene or prevent young people from offending?

The question of terminology is always a difficult one, particularly when writing for an international audience, and we need briefly to discuss our use of the terms "antisocial behavior" and "young people" in the title of this book. Our focus is on acts that involve breaking the law and on the individuals who engage in such antisocial behavior. We might have referred to either "delinquency" or "crime" and will do so in the text occasionally, but both imply conviction (or its possibility) and, as we discuss, all studies have shown both that the majority of crimes do not result in anyone appearing in court and that many people who commit acts for which they could be prosecuted never appear in the crime statistics. Moreover, children below the age of criminal responsibility engage in antisocial behavior for which they cannot be prosecuted. If we are to understand the origins of delinquency, it will be crucial to consider antisocial behavior that is outside the realm of the law and also the illegal acts that do *not* result in prosecution as well as those that do. These are encompassed by the term "antisocial behavior."

Clinicians, both psychologists and psychiatrists, tend to write about diagnostic categories such as oppositional/defiant disorder, conduct disorder, and antisocial personality disorder, rather than crime as such. These disorders often involve engaging in delinquent behavior, but they are far from synonymous with crime. On the one hand, the criteria for their diagnosis involve many behaviors that do not involve breaking the

1

law. On the other hand, many individuals who receive convictions do not show the social impairment and psychological dysfunction that are required for a psychiatric diagnosis. We consider findings on those psychopathological patterns insofar as they are relevant to an understanding of antisocial behavior, but not otherwise.

Our use of the term "young people" is meant to indicate a focus on the age period preceding maturity or adulthood. In general, we have paid particular attention to those under the age of 20 years but, as other reviews have noted (see e.g. Rutter & Smith, 1995), development does not cease at 19 years and, in many respects, it is more appropriate to extend the term up to the age of about 25. Similarly, research findings are clearcut in their indication that antisocial behavior often begins in childhood before the age at which people can be prosecuted. Our review reflects this extension upward and downward, but we have paid most attention to the age period of 10 to 19 years.

We have not defined this in terms of the adjective "juvenile" because that word tends to carry the connotation that the lower limit is set by the age of criminal responsibility and the upper limit by the age when young people can be dealt with by courts for adult offenders. These ages not only vary across countries but also have changed over time and are not the same for all offenses (Justice, 1996; Pease & Tseloni, 1996; Snyder & Sickmund, 1995).

Why a New Review?

Two of us were responsible for a somewhat similar review some 15 years ago (Rutter & Giller, 1983), and it is necessary to ask why another review is needed. Three considerations predominate: a great increase in research findings, changing approaches to theory, and an altering pattern of questions deriving from policy and practice. Since the 1983 review, there has been a substantial increase in empirically based knowledge on the nature of delinquency, its causes, factors that influence its perpetuation into adult life, and its prevention and treatment. Theories of crime based on the notion of a single unifying set of causal factors have fallen into disrepute, and there has been increasing attention to both the origins of individual differences in liability to antisocial behavior and to the major differences in rates of crime over time and among groups, whether defined in terms of gender or nationality. Rising rates of crime, legislative changes, an increased international focus on the rights and needs of young people, and general concerns over child homicide and sexual offenses by young people have all altered the pattern of questions about antisocial behavior in young people. In our review we have tried to reflect, and respond to, these various changes.

The conclusions from the 1983 review were many and wide-reaching, including an implicit program for future research. Our general approach in this update of the field has been to take the earlier review as the starting point and then evaluate the extent to which recent research has built on or modified the earlier literature, met the identified research needs, or addressed issues not covered in the earlier review. We have not re-reviewed the research prior to 1983, but we have summarized the findings up to that point, fitting new evidence into the general framework provided by the earlier volume. This has involved a reassessment of the original conclusions, so the resulting review is an integrated update with a broader coverage and somewhat different set of concepts, and not just a revision.

A key strength of the previous review was its multidisciplinary approach; bringing together clinical, social, and criminological perspectives. The current review follows the same pattern. However, the field of antisocial behavior was already immense by the late 1970s and has grown greatly since then, so limits have had to be set on our coverage of the literature. As well as focusing on recent research, we have concentrated on empirical findings and on research published in English.

Of course, bald "facts" are of little use on their own. In order for them to have meaning and to be of value in planning policies or modifying practice, they need to be placed in a social context and to be integrated with respect to the light shed on the merits and demerits of competing explanatory hypotheses and theories. This we have tried to do, and have thus referred to approaches such as feminist sociology or sociology of deviance, or to social practices and institutions, where they provide useful context. However, our focus on empirical findings has meant that we have not sought to provide a comprehensive coverage of theoretical perspectives otherwise, or a very detailed description of cultural context, except in cases where there is empirical research or at least testable hypotheses. Similarly, we have not drawn on descriptive, ethnographic, or naturalistic data except where they have implications for testing postulates or mechanisms. The way in which research was judged for inclusion in the book is described in the next chapter, where it will become clear that the approach we have taken affects the balance of the research content of the book, because the studies most often meeting these criteria have tended to focus on individual and psychosocial aspects of antisocial behavior rather than on broader, societywide influences, although we consider these in some detail in Chapter 8, as well as returning to them in

Chapters 11 and 12. The more limited data on societal factors reflect, in part, the difficulties inherent in researching the broader questions; as we shall see, there is still a great need for more empirical data in a number of critical sociological areas.

Growth in the extent and quality of information on offending by young people in the late 1980s and early 1990s has occurred via three main routes: official statistics, research findings, and the development of international comparisons. First, there have been significant developments in the official criminal statistics. These are becoming more extensive and involve reports from a range of sources. The United States Bureau of Justice Statistics has conducted a National Crime Victimization Survey (NCVS) since 1973, based on interviews with approximately 49,000 households (Perkins et al., 1996). In 1982, the England and Wales Home Office followed suit and initiated the British Crime Survey (BCS) to complement the annually published *Criminal Statistics* (see e.g. Home Office, 1996). In England and Wales, the victim survey consisted of interviews with over 10,000 members of the general population. The BCS was repeated in 1984, 1988, 1992, 1994, and 1996 (see Mayhew, Aye Maung, & Mirrlees-Black, 1993; Mirrlees-Black, Mayhew, & Percy, 1996). In addition, the first International Crime Survey (ICS) took place in 1989 – followed by subsequent sweeps in 1992, 1994, and 1996 – and covered twenty European and other countries, including Japan (Mayhew, 1993; Van Dijk, Mayhew, & Killias, 1990).

These victim surveys contribute much information to knowledge about which crimes have been experienced and to what extent they were reported; they also provide a source of comparison for police-generated statistics (Bottomley & Pease, 1993). Moreover, crime surveys provide a useful corrective to simplistic "political" interpretations of rises (or falls) in recorded crime. The patterns emerging often differ from those evident in the police statistics and from country to country. Not infrequently, the trends shown in the victim surveys are less dramatic than those in the official statistics, with less change evident over time. Within the United Kingdom, for example, the rates of vandalism doubled in Home Office statistics in the 1980s but remained constant in the BCS. Conversely, the most recent crime survey (Mirrlees-Black et al., 1996) showed a recent rise in crime not reflected in official statistics. Analyses of these types of comparisons have meant that general understanding about the strengths and weaknesses of official statistics has developed considerably, including an unraveling of the biases to which they are subject and their relationship to the real world of crime (see e.g. Coleman & Moynihan, 1996; Walker, 1995).

Second, concurrent with these developments in official recording, the psychiatric, psychological, sociological, and criminological literatures have contributed substantially to the untangling of trends and perspectives on offending behavior by adolescents. Criminology itself has developed substantially over the last decade, as has child psychiatry, both of which were relatively new disciplines a few decades ago. They converge in their growing emphasis on the importance of longitudinal research for understanding patterns in development and for studying causal questions. Tonry, Ohlin, and Farrington (1991) argued a strong case for longitudinal research in criminology, as did Rutter (1988) for child psychiatry. This has been accompanied by advances in the clarification of the ways in which longitudinal data may be used to test causal hypotheses (Loeber & Farrington 1994; Rutter, 1994a). Major longitudinal studies begun in the sixties, seventies, and eighties have contributed a considerable amount of data to the investigation of antisocial behavior as cohort members develop into adolescence and early adulthood and continuities and discontinuities in behavior are better documented. Findings relate to the origins of antisocial behavior in preschool behavior (Campbell & Ewing, 1990; White et al., 1990), oppositional/defiant disorder (Lahey & Loeber, 1994) and hyperactivity (Rutter et al., 1997b), as well as to its desistance or persistence into adult life (Farrington, 1995a,b; Kerner, Weitekamp, & Stelly, 1995; Kratzer & Hodgins, 1996a; Quinton et al., 1993; Rutter et al., 1994; Tracy, Wolfgang, & Figlio, 1990). Reanalysis of older data sets has also contributed in a major way (Sampson & Laub, 1993).

As well as general developments in the literature, the last dozen or so years have witnessed specific advances in particular issues relating directly to antisocial behavior. These include recognition of its heterogeneity and advances in understanding causal processes. Recent research has suggested ways in which varieties of delinquency could be differentiated – for example, those associated with early-onset hyperactivity or those with early rather than adolescent onset (e.g. Hinshaw et al., 1993; Moffitt, 1993a,b; Patterson & Yoerger, 1997). In addition, there has come to be a better appreciation of the need to distinguish among the somewhat varied causal processes involved in *individual differences* in the liability to engage in antisocial behavior, changes over time in the overall *level* of crime, *situational* variations in delinquent activities, and *persistence/ nonpersistence* of antisocial behavior as individuals grow older (Clarke & Cornish, 1985; Loeber & Hay, 1994; Quinton et al., 1993; Rutter & Smith, 1995; Sampson & Laub, 1993).

A better understanding of the issues underlying comorbidity (i.e., the co-occurrence of two supposedly separate disorders) has also resulted in data relevant for unraveling the nature and origins of antisocial behavior. More is known on the associations between crime and substance abuse (alcohol and illicit drugs), between crime and reading difficulties, between crime and suicide, and between conduct disorder and depression (Harrington et al., 1991; Hinshaw, 1992; Ito, Miller, & Pollock, 1996; Liebling, 1992; Maughan et al., 1996; Moffitt, 1993b; Robins & Rutter, 1990; Sumner & Parker, 1995).

Third, the increasing emphasis on the importance of the international perspective (arising from significant worldwide developments such as changes in Eastern Europe, the end of the Cold War, the growth of the European Union, etc.) has both complicated the picture and helped to put national developments in context. Comparative studies are becoming more ambitious and are extending their gaze beyond the United Kingdom and North America, as shown, for example, by the first International Crime Survey (Van Dijk et al., 1990) and the first truly international self-report study (Junger-Tas, 1994a). Complications arise from the difficulties of trying to compare the underlying trends in antisocial behavior in different jurisdictions and cultures. For these reasons, one of the participants in the international self-report study has expressed doubt on the validity of drawing global conclusions from data from the individual countries (Graham, 1994). Putting national statistics into the international context helps, however, by highlighting particular outstanding findings in certain countries, such as the very low rate of delinquency in Japan and the striking growth of homicide by young people in the United States (Kelley et al., 1997).

Besides these three main types of development in the basic data, other reasons for an updated review of the delinquency literature include legislative and social changes. As this is a review of antisocial behavior, rather than of conduct disorder generally, legislative changes have potentially widespread effects on the overall picture. This is the case in terms of the definitions and recording of antisocial behavior and also in terms of the legal requirements relating to the treatment of children and young people. The 1980s saw significant European and international advances in the protection of children (e.g., the 1989 UN Convention on the Rights of the Child), but these have sometimes clashed with other areas of national policy relating to disposals for young offenders. In the United Kingdom, calls for a more integrated youth policy have become increasingly urgent, and critics have suggested that segmented approaches to offending and child care are based on service delivery and political expediency rather than on social or economic need or on research findings.

Changes in social trends that indicated the need for an updated review of antisocial behavior include transformations in family patterns, changes in education and the youth labor market, changes in the normative experiences of young people, and international social changes such as the growth of the information society and the explosion of multimedia. The most obvious changes in family patterns include a dramatic increase in divorce: between 1977 and 1992, both the number of divorces and the number of children aged under 16 of divorced couples increased drastically in the United Kingdom. The number of children aged under 5 affected by divorce in 1992 was 57,000, almost two thirds higher than in 1977 (Central Statistical Office, 1994). Relatedly, the proportion of lone parents has also risen. In the United States, the proportion of children living in two-parent families over a comparable time period declined from 85% to 73% (Snyder & Sickmund, 1995). As we shall see, the relevance of these changes for antisocial behavior has been the subject of much discussion in both the academic literature and the general media.

Successive sweeps of various national surveys have shown that, over this period, the proportion of young people staying on in education has increased dramatically and, in the United Kingdom and the United States, economic recession has had implications for the youth labor market. Young people are more likely now than they have ever been in the past to come into contact with, and experiment with, illegal drugs during the years of their compulsory education (Parker, Measham, & Aldridge, 1995). They also live in a society where new technologies play increasingly important roles, and where the commercialization of information and communication are resulting in a global cultural market (Featherstone, 1991; Wartella, 1995).

Another major social trend that has received much attention is the continued rise in crime rates, as evidenced in official statistics. There is no doubt that, in a number of countries including the United Kingdom, offenses recorded by the police have risen since the 1980s, although explanations for the rise – and its relationship to underlying behavioral trends – remain elusive. It is clear that the rise applies not just to crime but also to depression, suicide, and drug abuse (Rutter & Smith, 1995).

Coverage and Structure of This Review

Despite the fact that this review is loosely based on the structure of the 1983 book, we have made several critical changes in terms of the topics included, reflecting some of the major social changes just outlined. Thus, we have concentrated to a greater extent than previously on the significance of ethnic group membership. There are several reasons for this, although they vary nationally. In the United Kingdom, the primary concern in the 1960s and 1970s was on ethnicity in relation to immigration, but there are now well-established second and third generations of ethnic minority British nationals for whom the issues may be different. In addition, U.K. criminal statistics now record some data on ethnicity, and ethnic minority adolescents are increasingly the focus of high-profile programs of police action. In Europe, particularly Eastern Europe, migration remains a central issue, whereas the focus in the United States has generally been on black–white differences that have nothing to do with immigration. Moreover, in the United States, a striking recent feature has been the growth of the Hispanic population and the increasingly disproportionate representation of young black men in the murder (perpetrator and victim) statistics. Overall, on the basis of a number of surveys and studies of the experiences of ethnic minorities, it is becoming accepted that it is not sufficient to consider ethnicity as a unitary variable, and the importance of acknowledging the diversity of experience between different groups and in different places is now emphasized (see e.g. Modood, Beishon, & Virdee, 1994). We need to assess the importance of this emphasis for antisocial behavior.

A decision was also made to provide a short discussion of drug offending and of the role of drugs in crime. The original argument for not including these was that they were not common in the United Kingdom at that time, although increases in drug use had already taken place in America by the early 1980s. As we have already indicated, at least some low-level experimentation with drugs is now far more common in Europe than it was 15 years ago, and drug offenses are on the increase. There is also some limited evidence that rates have recently begun to increase in the United States again (Robertson & Skinner, 1996; Snyder, Sickmund, & Poe-Yamagata, 1996). Similarly, sexual abuse both of and by young people was originally excluded because it was thought to be uncommon. It is considered briefly this time, not because it has become common but because it has a higher public profile than it did, and public awareness of childhood sexual abuse and its role in development is greater than it was. This relates in part to a greater understanding of the overlap between victim and offender (Boswell, 1995) and to better data on perpetrators of child and adolescent abuse (Vizard, Monck, & Misch, 1995). In addition, because of the overall increase in psychosocial disorders in young people (Rutter & Smith, 1995), we have included mention of some research on the relationship between crime and emotional disorder or suicide.

It has long been apparent that the crime rate for males is several times higher than that for females. Despite this, there has been a paucity of research into male–female differences in antisocial behavior. Increasingly, however, it has become recognized that elucidation of the causes of this gender difference might throw important light on the origins of antisocial behavior more generally. Accordingly, although firm conclusions are thin on the ground, we have a separate chapter on the topic.

In many ways, the major growth area in studies of crime has been the focus on developmental patterns over the life-span, with analysis of criminal careers and with a study of the factors that seem to affect desistance from (or persistence in) antisocial behavior in adult life. Again, we have a separate chapter on this topic.

We start, in Chapter 2, by outlining some conceptual and methodological considerations that have guided our approach to this review. Chapter 3 sets the scene with a discussion of age, blame, and the age of criminal responsibility, and then looks at the picture of adolescent crime derived from criminal statistics, victim surveys, and self-report data. A number of factors that affect the coding and processing of information lead to some variation between sources of information, so we discuss these before looking at the differences thrown up by these sources of data between non-offenders versus offenders and infrequent versus persistent offenders.

Chapter 4 focuses on the major rise in crime that has taken place in most countries over the last half century, and Chapter 5 on what is known about heterogeneity in antisocial behavior. Chapters 6–8 bring together what is known about various sorts of causal factors; Chapter 9 discusses gender differences, and Chapter 10 considers life-span developmental issues. Chapters 11 and 12 review what is known about prevention and intervention, pulling together the conceptual and theoretical perspectives in order to look at policy and practice implications. The final Chapter 13 highlights a series of significant findings from the review as a whole and discusses the relationship of research to policy and practice.

We have intended that the book should have a broad and varied readership, although it has been a challenge to present such a range of different topics in a way that is accessible to everyone. No doubt we have not succeeded entirely, but we would hope that the book is treated as a whole, as we have considered its parts to be complementary, from the biological to the sociological.

2 | Identifying the Most Useful Research

As our Introduction indicates, in some respects this volume uses as a starting point the 1983 review written by two of us (Rutter & Giller, 1983). Nevertheless, the considerable expansion in empirical research over the last 15 years, together with the improved clarification of concepts, has meant that we have been able to tackle the task of reviewing the field with a rather tighter focus, and with somewhat higher standards with respect to the quality of the evidence on which we rely. In this introductory chapter we outline some of the main features of our approach.

First, we note the breadth of antisocial behavior and the need to take into account its various facets. Second, we consider the generally low agreement among informants and hence the need for multiple data sources. Third, the value of representative general population samples, especially when followed over time, is discussed. Fourth, we draw attention to the two-way interplay between psyche and soma. Fifth, we emphasize the variety of concepts of causation, moving on to the need for examining causal chains of both direct and indirect links, finishing with the steps needed to test causal hypotheses. We will refer to (or develop) many of these points later in the book, so they provide an important starting point for considering the studies described in later chapters.

Breadth of Antisocial Behavior

Numerous studies have now shown that individuals who engage in frequent delinquent or criminal activities tend to differ from other members of the general population in a host of ways that extend well beyond acts that break the law (see e.g. Farrington, 1995a,b; Jessor, Donovan, & Costa, 1991; Jessor & Jessor, 1977; Smith, 1995; Thornberry, Huizinga, & Loeber, 1995).

Some of the findings are reviewed in greater detail in subsequent chapters. In brief, they may be summarized as follows.

- When *very young*, people who subsequently engage in repeated antisocial activities tend to be overactive, disruptive in their behavior, oppositional, and have difficulties getting along with other children.

- Also *when young*, they tend to be impulsive and keen to seek exciting new experiences.
- As well as these characteristics, in *middle childhood and adolescence* they are more inclined than others to show feelings of misery, to have difficulties in reading, and to take illicit drugs.
- When these features persist in *later adolescence and early adulthood*, they often take the form of heavy drinking, an irregular employment record, difficulties in relationships with family and friends, a tendency to run up debts, gambling, and a tendency to respond to frustration and other difficulties with the use of violence.

Of course, the extent to which individuals who are delinquent show this broader range of behaviors varies greatly. However, that the range exists in the important way that it does means that any attempt to study the causes of antisocial behavior must consider the factors involved in the origins of this broader range – features of what is sometimes called an antisocial lifestyle.

It is also evident that the world does not divide up into those who are, and those are not, criminal. To a very considerable extent, antisocial behavior, and the committing of criminal acts, operates on a continuum as a dimensional feature that most people show to a greater or lesser degree. Accordingly, this must be taken into account in empirical studies. This need applies not only to studies of causal mechanisms but also to the effects of prevention or intervention. That is, the benefits (or otherwise) of interventions need to be assessed with respect to possible effects on the frequency or severity of delinquent activities, and also with respect to this broader range of antisocial life-style features. For all these reasons, we have paid most attention to studies that encompass this broader range of behaviors and which do so in a manner that allows for quantification.

Multiple Sources of Information

As discussed more fully in the next chapter, studies of delinquency have increasingly relied on a combination of official crime statistics and self-reports. On the whole, the two tell much the same story. However, they have a rather different set of advantages and disadvantages, so it is highly desirable to be able to use both in the same data set. This need for multiple sources of information is by no means confined to crime statistics. It has been a general finding in studies of all forms of emotional disturbance or behavioral difficulties that the level of agreement between different informants is moderate at best (Achenbach, McConaughy, & Howell, 1987; Eaves et al., 1997; Simonoff et al., 1995, 1997, in press; Verhulst & Koot,

1992). The correlations between parent reports and teacher reports are typically around the level of 0.3 to 0.4; those between parents and children are often still lower; and even those between fathers and mothers usually do not exceed 0.5 to 0.6. In part this relatively modest agreement between informants is a function of the inherent unreliability of measures; in part it is a consequence of the fact that people often behave differently in different situations; in part it reflects differences in the opportunities to notice particular forms of behavior; in part it may be a result of perceptual biases of various kinds; and in part it may arise because informants vary in the reference groups that they use.

Thus, for example, when rating children's behavior, teachers are likely to compare the behavior of one child with that of other children in the same class or in previous classes that he or she has taught. Parents, on the other hand, are likely to pay particular attention to the behavior of other children in the same family and, to a lesser extent, the children of friends and neighbors. Their reference group will thereby be both smaller and more selective than that of most teachers. Children, on the other hand, may make the same comparisons but, in addition, they are quite likely to pay particular attention, especially with respect to moods and feelings, to the way they themselves felt some time ago. In other words, when they say that they are particularly depressed, they may mean that they are feeling more miserable than they did a year ago rather than that they are necessarily more miserable than other people.

Particular circumstances may also bring about biases and consequent differences in the meanings of ratings. Thus, for example, parents who are themselves feeling depressed or irritable may thereby rate the behaviors of their children differently; teachers, in assessing the behavior of their pupils, may be influenced by the ways in which they respond to educational tasks and thereby be open to the influence of differences in the children's cognitive abilities. It is obvious that none of these sources of data constitutes any kind of "gold standard." Rather, it has become apparent that it is highly desirable, in any one study, to have multiple informants, to have data deriving from behavior in different situations, and to have repeated measures. We have therefore placed most weight on studies where such data have been available and have been used.

Samples

Much of the earlier criminological literature was necessarily based on specialized samples of one kind or another. Sometimes these were special in terms of the ways in which young people have been dealt with by the law. Thus, much research was based on young people in custodial care or those who had received some particular form of judicial action. Alternatively, the samples were special because they had been referred for a psychiatric report or psychiatric treatment, or because they were receiving some form of special schooling deriving from the fact that they had committed an offense and were thought to be in need of special help.

There is now very much less need, for most purposes, to rely on such specialized samples. In many different parts of the world, there are large-scale, prospective, longitudinal studies of general population samples spanning the age period from childhood to adolescence or adult life. Thus, such studies are available in the United Kingdom (Farrington, 1995a; Kolvin et al., 1990; Wadsworth, 1991), mainland United States (Elliott, Huizinga, & Menard, 1989; Loeber et al., 1993; Tracy et al., 1990; Weitekamp et al., 1996; Wolfgang, Thornberry, & Figlio, 1987), Hawaii (Werner & Smith, 1982), Canada (Soussignan et al., 1992; Tremblay et al., 1994), New Zealand (Bardone et al., 1996; Fergusson & Horwood, 1995, 1996; Fergusson, Horwood, & Lynskey, 1995; Henry et al., 1996), Germany (Kerner et al., 1995), Sweden (Elliott et al., 1989; Janson, 1984; Klinteberg et al., 1993; Kratzer & Hodgins, 1997; Magnusson, 1988; Stattin & Magnusson, 1995), and Finland (Hämäläinen & Pulkkinen, 1996). In addition, there are also epidemiologically based, longitudinal studies of a variety of groups with an increased risk of antisocial behavior for one reason or another (Farrington, Loeber, & Van Kammen, 1990; Harrington et al., 1991; Maughan et al., 1996; Nagin, Farrington, & Moffitt, 1995; Rutter et al., 1997b). Although the methods and measures are not identical across these studies, there is sufficient commonality for a realistic assessment of the degree to which the findings are comparable. Wherever possible, we have used such comparisons and have placed most weight on findings that do generalize across samples and across social contexts. This is not to say, of course, that we have necessarily expected the findings to be the same across all social situations, but rather that we have tried to determine whether there are systematic reasons why the findings vary in an explicable fashion across contexts. In addition, there are a few important large-scale studies (Kessler et al., 1994; Robins & Regier, 1991) that, although cross-sectional in design, have attempted to obtain retrospective data covering the age period from childhood to adult life. Also, there are some cross-sectional self-report studies that are informative (Graham & Bowling, 1995; Junger-Tas, 1994a). Where these data appear sound, we have made use of them.

Because of the much greater availability of high-quality epidemiological studies as compared with the situation some years ago (see Berk, 1983, regarding the importance of representative samples for drawing valid conclusions), we have not needed to pay as much attention to reports on clinical samples or other specialized groups, and we have paid less attention to anecdotal accounts or studies based on unstandardized measures, particularly where there has been a lack of adequate comparison groups. There are, however, two circumstances in which it has been necessary to rely, for the most part, on non-epidemiological data. This has been the case, first, with respect to delinquent activities that either are relatively uncommon or have not been adequately covered in most epidemiological studies. This would apply, for example, to juvenile sex offenders, to youth homicides, and to crime associated with emotional processing features characterized by the term "psychopathy." The second circumstance where epidemiological data have been scarce concerns at least some types of biological investigation. Thus, where these have involved rather invasive procedures, it has not been either acceptable or practicable to apply them on an epidemiological basis. On the other hand, this limitation is a fast-diminishing one as technological developments have made it possible to study chemical features based on samples of saliva, rather than blood samples, and as it has become possible to examine chromosomes from cheek scrapings rather than blood. Thus, we have placed particular reliance on biological findings based on epidemiological samples but we have, perforce, had to make some use of results on smaller, more specialized, groups of one kind or another.

Biology and Behavior

At times in the past – and (regrettably) occasionally still in the present – there has been a tendency to assume that, if some biological feature or abnormality can be identified and associated with a particular behavior, then the biological feature must have caused the behavior. It is now clear that this assumption is unwarranted because there is a complex two-way interplay between psyche and soma. Thought processes and emotions and behavioral tendencies do not arise outside the body. To the contrary, there are, and must be, biological accompaniments, at least immediately. That is to say, when someone is feeling anxious and frightened, this will be accompanied by a rise in the pulse rate, sweating, and an outpouring of particular hormones. In the longer term, too, the lasting effects of experiences will involve some change in the organism. Thus, animal experiments have shown that learning processes are accompanied by changes in the brain (Horn, 1990) and that the effects of stress are accompanied by structural and functional changes in the neuroendocrine system

(Hennessey & Levine, 1979). Alternatively, the carryforward of the effects of experiences may be through styles of thinking, or cognitive processing, or self-concepts, but in one way or another there will be some accompanying alteration in the biological substrate. Studies in both animals and humans similarly indicate the two-way interplay between hormones and behavior. If male sex hormones are raised artificially by one means or another, then this will have measurable effects on certain behaviors such as dominance. Equally, however, the outcome of social situations will alter hormone levels. Thus, for example, the winner of a closely fought tennis game or chess match tends to show a rise in sex hormones, whereas losers tend to show a fall (Mazur, Booth, & Dabbs, 1992; Mazur & Lamb, 1980). Or, again, the "abnormal" functional brain-scan findings associated with particular psychiatric disorders may be reversible when the symptoms are relieved by treatment (Schwartz et al., 1996). Of course, there are ways in which research may be used to determine just how the causal mechanisms operate (see e.g. Kruesi & Jacobsen, 1997), but the point is that this research needs to be done. There has been an upsurge in the last decade or so of biological studies of antisocial behavior, and there is no doubt that these are potentially informative on possible factors that may play a role in the genesis or persistence of antisocial behavior. On the other hand, it is essential to examine the findings critically in order to avoid jumping to premature conclusions about the nature of the causal processes involved.

Causality

Concepts of Causation

Traditionally, questions of cause have tended to be thought about in terms only of individual differences – why this person is delinquent and that person is not. It is important to appreciate that this constitutes a seriously misleading oversimplification of what is involved in causal processes. Thus, so far as antisocial behavior is concerned, at least five rather different types of cause need to be considered (Clarke & Cornish, 1985; Loeber & Hay, 1994; Quinton et al., 1993; Rutter & Smith, 1995; Rutter et al., 1997b; Sampson & Laub, 1993). Distinctions need to be drawn between the processes involved in:

(a) individual differences in the liability to engage in antisocial behavior;
(b) the translation of that liability into the actual committing of illegal acts;
(c) differences over time, or between places, in the overall levels of crime;

(d) situational variations in delinquent activities; and

(e) persistence or nonpersistence of antisocial behavior as individuals grow older.

The factors and processes that are involved in each of these may be similar or they may be quite different. Thus, for example, the factors associated with violent crime seem broadly comparable between Europe and North America. These include both adverse family experiences and particular personal characteristics. On the other hand, the reason why the murder rate in the United States is some dozen times that of Europe is not explicable on these bases. Not only would such an explanation be implausible, but the finding that the difference in homicide rates between these two parts of the world is largely confined to those involving the use of guns (Snyder et al., 1996) strongly suggests that the availability of guns constitutes the main explanation. Interestingly, however, variations within the United States in the availability of guns (variations that are on the whole rather small) do not seem to be related to individual differences in liability to kill. Similarly, the major rise of crime in Europe during the several decades after the Second World War cannot be attributed to poverty, economic hardship, and unemployment, because these years were ones that showed a major improvement in all of these features of society and also a reduction in social inequalities (Rutter & Smith, 1995). On the other hand, there is evidence that, at an individual level, personal experience of unemployment and all that it entails may have an important role to play in the predisposition to steal. The evidence suggesting that this is so derives particularly from longitudinal studies showing an increase in stealing when people become unemployed and a later decrease when they obtain work (Farrington et al., 1986; Sampson & Laub, 1993).

We need to emphasize that these differences among the various contrasting types of causal questions are in no way specific to antisocial behavior. Three rather different examples from other fields help to illustrate this point.

- *Height* is one of the most strongly genetically influenced of all human characteristics. It has a heritability of 90% or so, a finding confirmed at all times in Europe or North America when the matter has been examined. Nevertheless, over the first half of the twentieth century, the average height of London schoolboys rose by about 12 cm (Tizard, 1975). That rise had nothing to do with a change in the gene pool and almost certainly resulted from improved nutrition. Because the improved nutrition tended to affect the country as a whole, it made little difference with respect to individual variation in height but made quite a big difference to the average height in the country as a whole.

- Personal factors of various kinds play a substantial role in accounting for individual differences in *the likelihood of being unemployed*, particularly at times of relatively low unemployment. By contrast, these personal factors (level of skills, personality features, chronic ill health, etc.) have nothing to do with the huge rise in levels of unemployment that took place in many European countries during the 1980s (Rutter, 1994a).

- The detoxification of domestic gas in the United Kingdom had a marked effect in bringing down *the suicide rate among older people*, because coal-gas poisoning was a favored method of suicide and because the detoxification made that no longer lethal (Clarke & Mayhew, 1988). This removal of one means of suicide made no difference to the overall propensity to feel suicidal, but – in reflection of the fact that feelings of suicide come and go when people are feeling depressed, and that committing suicide is dependent upon opportunity as well as liability – it meant that the removal of this particular option was associated with a reduction in the number of successful suicides.

Causal Chains

A somewhat related conceptual point concerns the recognition that many causal processes involve indirect chain effects and not just one basic cause (see Chapter 11 for a more extended discussion of this point). These chain effects may involve either the processes leading to the commission of an illegal act, or the ways in which risk factors impinge on the individual, or both. Thus, as is implicit in the different concepts of causation, it is necessary to consider causation in terms not only of the individual liability to engage in antisocial behavior but also of how this liability eventually results in the commission of a particular illegal act in a particular place at a particular time (Farrington, 1995a; Rutter et al., 1997b; Tonry & Farrington, 1995). Again, this consideration is in no way special to antisocial behavior. For example, drug dependence involves a causal chain that is first manifest by a person taking drugs experimentally (but, in the case of heavy drug users, often with its origins still earlier in the form of antisocial behavior), proceeding to take them on a regular basis, becoming psychologically and pharmacologically dependent on their use, and not taking steps to alter this situation. Robins's (Robins, 1993; Robins, Davis, & Wish, 1977) studies of Americans serving in the armed forces in the Vietnam conflict showed that the factors involved with each of these stages were by no means the same. For example, inner-city African-Americans were the group most likely to take heroin in the first instance, but whites living in rural areas were the ones most likely to continue to be addicted to heroin upon demobilization from the armed forces. It is necessary, therefore, that causal chain processes be analyzed one link at a time rather than by attempting to find a set of factors that operate comparably across all phases.

Testing Causal Hypotheses

It is well accepted that the mere identification of a factor that is statistically associated with crime does not mean that it has played any role in causation. In our review, therefore, it has been necessary to consider the various steps that could be taken to test hypotheses about causal mechanisms (Farrington, 1988; Rutter, 1994a). The first requirement has been to determine whether the association postulated possibly to represent a causal mechanism is consistent across samples and across different types of measurement. Of course, a lack of consistency could mean that the mechanism operates only under certain circumstances but, if so, consistency across those circumstances needs to be tested for and not assumed.

The second requirement has been to differentiate between risk indicators and risk mechanisms. In brief, indicators are features that have indirect connections with causal processes but which, in themselves, are not part of the mechanisms that are directly associated with causation. The need to make this distinction is usually discussed in terms of taking account of so-called confounding variables. Usually, this means pitting one possible causal explanation against another. For example, many years ago "broken homes" were found to be statistically associated with crime, and the question arose as to whether the causal mechanism lay in the child's separation from one or both parents or rather from the discord, conflict, and family disorganization that tends to be associated with the breakup of the family (Rutter, 1971). This could be tested by comparing breakup that is not usually associated with major discord (such as parental death) with breakup that is more likely to be associated with discord (such as divorce). Findings have been consistent in showing that, on the whole, divorce carries the greater risk for antisocial behavior (Rutter, 1971). Thus, the breakup of the parental marriage is an indicator of risk but it does not constitute the main direct causal mechanism for crime. Alternatively, multivariate analyses may be undertaken to determine whether, within equivalent levels of conflict, separation or family changes are predictive of antisocial behavior or whether, conversely, within equivalent frequencies of separation, conflict is predictive (Fergusson, Horwood, & Lynskey, 1992). Again, the findings have indicated the greater predictive power of discord.

It is important to appreciate that what appears to be a confounding variable may nevertheless play a part in the causal chain, albeit at a point more distantly related to antisocial behavior. For example, poverty and economic stresses appear to have only a weak and inconsistent association with antisocial behavior, and they are therefore unlikely to play a major role in the proximal processes concerned with the genesis of antisocial behavior. On the other hand, poverty does seem to play a role by making it more difficult to sustain family harmony and adaptive patterns of parenting (Brody et al., 1994; Conger et al., 1994). There are also many variables that, by their nature, carry no meaning with respect to causal mechanisms until they are further specified. For example, as we discuss in Chapter 9, being male is accompanied by a much increased risk for antisocial behavior. But that is not very helpful in understanding causation until one can go on to determine whether this risk is mediated hormonally, through the Y chromosome, through differences in the ways that boys and girls are dealt with, or through cultural differences in the lifestyles of males and females.

There are several further steps that may be taken to put causal hypotheses to the test. As Farrington (1988) pointed out, there is considerable advantage in being able to test causal hypotheses through examination of changes within the individual over time in relation to alterations in the postulated risk factor. Thus, it is instructive to ask whether, say, the experience of unemployment (or imprisonment, or harmonious marriage) increases or decreases the risk of later antisocial behavior, having taken full account of the individual's prior behavior, social circumstances, and the possibility that the change reflects measurement error (Horney, Osgood, & Marshall, 1995; Sampson & Laub, 1993). It is particularly helpful to be able to use the test of reversal. That is to say, when the risk factor is lost (e.g., when the person who is unemployed finds a job), does the risk of antisocial behavior go down? There are many methodological hazards to be circumvented or overcome in undertaking tests of this kind, yet there is no question but that much can be learned from the systematic epidemiological testing of causal hypotheses.

Three particular alternative explanations always need to be borne in mind and tested for. First, there is the possibility that the causal arrow runs in the opposite direction – that the antisocial behavior has caused the supposed risk factor rather than the other way around. This is a very real possibility in many circumstances. There is much evidence that children's disruptive or antisocial behavior elicits negative reactions from other people (Bell, 1968; Bell & Chapman, 1986; Lytton, 1990; Rutter & Rutter, 1993; Rutter et al., 1997b). This has been evident using a variety of experimental designs as well as through naturalistic studies, and the reality of the effect is not in doubt. Thus, when it is found (as it often has been; see e.g. Reiss et al., 1995; Rutter et al., 1997b) that parental criticism and hostility are associated with children's antisocial behavior, it is necessary to ask whether the parental criticism has predisposed the children to antisocial behavior, whether the children's behavior has elicited negative responses from the parents, or whether there is a bidirectional circular process in operation. In that connection, it is important to appreciate that negative experiences that have been brought about by the young people themselves may nevertheless still have effects on their own behavior (Quinton et al., 1993; Rutter, Silberg, & Simonoff, 1993; Sampson & Laub, 1993). There are methods of analysis that can test the possibility that that is happening.

The second possibility is that the association reflects genetic mediation rather than an environmental risk process. It is only in recent years that this possibility has been considered seriously, but there is now quite a lot of evidence that genetic factors play a role not only in the origins of risk experiences but also in the risks that stem from such experiences (Plomin, 1994; Plomin & Bergeman, 1991). For example, it is obvious that parents not only pass genes on to their children but also help shape and select their children's experiences. Thus, for example, there is evidence that genetic factors play a role in the causation of family discord and that this effort is mediated in part through parental personality characteristics (Meyer et al., submitted). Because personality characteristics of the parents may be equivalent to those that play a part in the individual characteristics that predispose children to antisocial behavior, the possibility of genetic mediation is real. It is important to use genetically sensitive designs to determine the extent to which this is the case. On the other hand, just because genetic factors play a role in determining individual differences to environmental risk exposure, that certainly does not mean that such risks are without effects in the causal processes leading to antisocial behavior. Indeed, genetic designs, as applied to both antisocial behavior (Meyer et al., submitted) and alcoholism (Kendler et al., 1996), have shown the reality of environmentally mediated risks.

The third possibility that must always be considered is that the causation concerns not antisocial behavior as such but instead some other feature with which it happens to be associated. That "other feature" may be of several different kinds. Most obviously, it may concern whether or not the individual perpetrator of illegal acts is caught, prosecuted, and convicted. The association, therefore, may be with the response of society to the act rather than the act itself. Alternatively, because antisocial behavior is often associated with various other forms of emotional or behavioral disturbance, the causal process may apply to these correlates of antisocial behavior rather than to the delinquency per se. Finally, when dealing with special samples, such as those referred to psychiatrists, there is always the possibility that the causal process concerns that particular form of referral or method of dealing with the behavior rather than the behavior itself.

Strength of Effects

There are numerous different ways of expressing the strength of effects of a risk or protective factor on antisocial behavior (see Farrington & Loeber, 1989; Fleiss, 1981; Rosenthal & Rubin, 1982). That is so both with factors being considered in relation to their possible role in causation (Lipsey & Derzon, 1998) and with interventions being studied for their value in prevention or treatment (Lipsey & Wilson, 1998). Two points need to be emphasized in considering the relative merits of the different statistics. First, they often carry a quite different meaning of "strength of effect" (Rutter, 1987a). Second, they also give sharply contrasting impressions of "strength" (Lipsey & Derzon, 1998). With respect to the first point, Rutter (1987a) used the example of Down syndrome. One large-scale study found that it correlated only 0.076 with IQ, accounting for an absolutely trivial proportion of the variation of IQ within the general population: 0.6% (i.e., 0.076 squared). Yet, the children with Down syndrome had, on average, an IQ 60 points below the rest of the population – an absolutely huge effect! The explanation lies in the relative rarity of Down syndrome (12 per 25,000 in the population studied). At an *individual* level it has an extremely powerful effect in lowering IQ, but at a *population* level its effects are trivial because so few people have Down syndrome. The variations in IQ in the bulk of the population who do not have the syndrome must be due to other factors. Both conclusions are important, but they have entirely different meanings.

There are many sound conceptual and statistical reasons for preferring to measure both crime and its predictors in dimensional, rather than categorical, terms (see e.g. Fergusson & Horwood, 1995). The conceptual reason is that most variables function dimensionally. That is, there is a continuum both for predictors (such as family discord or IQ) and for antisocial behavior itself. In neither case does it make sense to regard such predictors as present or absent, because they may be present to varying degrees. The statistical reason is that precision of measurement is inevitably lost by forcing data into a dichotomy, and statistical power is also lost because no account is taken of variations across the range. Accordingly, many researchers (particularly psychologists) prefer to express their findings in terms of correlations. As we have noted, however, these do not represent the strength of effect at an individual level if the predictor applies to only a small proportion of the population. In other words, correlations are affected by the base rate. Moreover, they rely on consistency of association across the range (see Rutter, 1987a). If the effects are found mainly or only at the extreme, then the correlation will underestimate the strength of effect from that extreme.

The point about impressions is best demonstrated by making direct comparisons. Lipsey and Derzon (1998) did this for various risk factors for antisocial behavior. Thus, broken home showed a 0.09 correlation with subsequent serious or violent delinquency, accounting for only 0.8% of the population variance. This equated with an odds ratio of 1.98, meaning that a broken home roughly doubled the risk of serious or violent delinquency. The latter statement appears to reflect a much stronger effect than the former, but both are based on the same data. The contrast is perhaps even more marked with male gender, for which the correlation was only 0.26 (7% of the variance) but with an odds ratio of 18.55. For the most part, we have opted to present odds ratios because they provide a better intuitive impression of the strength of effect at an individual level, but we have been constrained by the ways in which findings have been presented in each study.

"Positivistic" Approaches

An entirely justifiable concern about the excessive focus on individual differences in considering causation, together with an appropriate rejection of notions that any factors can *determine* criminal acts (i.e., cause them directly), has led many criminologists to abhor what they term "positivistic" concepts (see e.g. Gilling, 1997). This has led to claims that the "scientific pursuit of cause . . . serves the political pursuit of legitimacy, to govern errant populations and allay the anxiety and uncertainty of the modern condition" (p. 205). This is a mistaken view, albeit one understandably fueled by the increasing preoccupation with surveillance, policing, and control (see Downes, 1992). The development of effective means of preventing crime requires an understanding of how causal mechanisms operate; throughout this book, we seek to use a range of research strategies to examine alternative possibilities. As the evidence shows, there is no one cause and there are several different kinds of causal question. Such questions require attention to a wide range of possible influences extending from the wider society and through the more personal social contexts (such as the family, school, and peer group) to the individual. Their investigation necessarily involves sociological as well as psychological and biological approaches, necessitating a broad conceptualization of possible influences. These approaches are considered in turn in Chapters 5–10 and are then brought together in Chapter 11, where we discuss approaches to prevention and intervention.

Conclusions

Naturally, no single study includes all the elements necessary to deal with this extensive range of considerations. Nevertheless, the quality of the relevant research has improved greatly over the last two decades and, taken together, it is often possible to take causal hypotheses much further than would have been feasible at the time of earlier reviews. Hence we have, whenever possible, attempted to go beyond statistical associations to possible causal mechanisms. That has usually meant reliance on quantitative measures of one sort or another. Because most postulated causal processes involve qualities of some kind (in relationships, behavioral features, or experiences outside the home), we have paid particular attention to research that has used discriminating detailed measures that reflect such qualities. Descriptive, ethnographic, and naturalistic data have often been very helpful in throwing light on the nature of possible causal mechanisms or, alternatively, on the particular social context within which the mechanisms may operate most powerfully. We have therefore used these when appropriate.

CHAPTER 2 – SUMMARY OF MAIN POINTS

❑ Antisocial behavior is a very *broad* term, which operates as a dimensional feature that most people show to a greater or lesser degree. We have concentrated on behavior by those aged between 10 and 19 years.

❑ *Multiple sources of information* are important because different sources of information about antisocial behavior and delinquency result in rather different pictures.

❑ Large-scale, prospective, longitudinal studies of *general population samples* are the most useful types of study for untangling the roots and consequences of antisocial behavior across the life-span. Other types of studies are useful for answering specific questions.

❑ There is a complex *two-way interplay*, between biological features and behavior, that must be acknowledged in any consideration of the evidence on causal pathways. Each influences the other.

❏ Understanding of *causality* has developed considerably, including: (a) consideration of at least five different types of causality; (b) appreciation that what works as a cause at one level of explanation may not work at another; (c) more exploration of indirect chain effects; and (d) better testing of causal hypotheses.

3 | Concepts and Measures of Crime

We start by setting the scene with a discussion of age, blame, and criminal responsibility, and we then look at the picture of adolescent crime derived from criminal statistics, victim surveys, and self-report data. A number of factors affect the coding and processing of information, leading to some variation between these sources of information. Hence we examine these factors before finally looking at the statistical differences generated by these data sources regarding non-offenders versus offenders and also infrequent versus persistent offenders.

Age, Blame, and Criminal Responsibility

Criminal justice is based on the premise that blame can and should be attributed. In a discussion of concepts of crime, the issue of age and criminal responsibility is thus a starting point because, without an attribution of blame and an acceptance that they are old enough to be responsible for their actions, young people cannot be said to have committed a crime. In order for someone to be guilty of a crime there must be one of two things and usually both: (1) a voluntary act (the *actus rea*) and (2) a mental element, an intention to commit a crime (the *mens rea*). For some crimes (e.g., drunk driving), the act is sufficient without proving the *mens rea*. More unusually, the *mens rea* might be sufficient without the crime (if, for example, there were an attempt to commit a crime that was in fact impossible). The attribution of blame has been called the "originating and vindicating activity" in the whole criminal justice process (Stephenson, 1992).

Even if the *actus rea* and *mens rea* are established, there are various reasons for not blaming a person for a crime; one reason would be their young age (Walker, 1991). This results, in essence, from distinctions between blame, guilt, and responsibility. We can blame them in that they committed the crime, but they were perhaps not responsible for their actions because of limitations in cognitive and moral development, or liability to suggestion. In practice, the age at which criminal responsibility is recognized in different jurisdictions varies greatly.

Table 3.1. National Variations in the Age of Criminal Responsibility (1995)

Criminally Responsible	Country
At age 7	Ireland, Liechtenstein, Singapore, Switzerland, United States[a]
At age 8	Scotland, Northern Ireland
At age 9	Jordan, Malta
At age 10	England, Wales
At age 12	Canada, Greece, Netherlands, San Marino, Turkey
At age 13	France
At age 14	Austria, Bulgaria, China, Germany, Hungary, Italy, Japan, Latvia, Lithuania, Russian Federation, Slovenia
At age 15	Czech Republic, Denmark, Estonia, Finland, Iceland, Norway, Slovakia, Sweden
At age 16	Andorra, Chile, Poland, Portugal, Spain
At age 17	Costa Rica, Fiji
At age 18	Belgium, Luxembourg, Peru, Syria, Romania

[a] The law in the United States also has specification of the minimum age at which a juvenile may be transferred to an adult court by judicial waiver. Several states do not have a specific age but, of those that do, the ages vary from 10 to 16 years (Krisberg & Austin, 1993).

Sources: Adapted from Pease and Tseloni (1996) and the National Association for the Care and Rehabilitation of Offenders (1995).

Table 3.1 shows how the commencement of the age of criminal responsibility varies among a sample of countries (National Association for the Care and Rehabilitation of Offenders, 1995; Pease & Tseloni, 1996). In most European Union countries, the median age at which children can be prosecuted is 14–15 years. The recent trend has been to raise the age: for example, from 14 to 15 in Norway and from 14 to 18 in Romania (Justice, 1996).

Variation in the age of criminal responsibility may also be exhibited *within* countries, especially where they comprise a federation of previously autonomous states. In Australia, for example, the age of criminal responsibility is 7 in the state of Tasmania, 8 in the Australian Capital Territory, and 10 in the other states (Queensland, Northern Territory, Victoria, New South Wales, South Wales, South Australia, and Western Australia) (Boss, Edwards, & Pitman, 1995).

International variations also exist with respect to the end age of *juvenile* criminal responsibility. Usually this upper age band is 18 years and marks the point at which young people will cease to be dealt with by procedures and tribunals modified to meet their needs as juveniles. At this age, the full adult criminal justice system and procedures may apply, although many jurisdictions modify procedures and tribunals for "young adult offenders" between the ages of 18 and 21 years. Many countries, however, have legislation that allows the procedures and jurisdiction of the juvenile justice system to be waived in certain serious cases (see Chapter 8).

Within these age bandings, many countries have a presumption of criminal incapacity for those of ages not regarded as fully responsible. In England and Wales, for example, children between the ages of 10 and 14 are afforded the limited protection of *doli incapax*, by which children are presumed not to know the full implications of right and wrong. The younger they are, the stronger the presumption. In order to secure a conviction, the prosecution must prove not only that the child committed the offense, but also that he or she knew it was seriously wrong† (Justice, 1996). Similar rules can be found in Australia, Germany, France, Spain, and the United States.

Although offenses cannot be sanctioned by the criminal law when committed below the minimum age for criminal responsibility, this does not mean that official intervention in the life of the child is avoided. Frequently the civil law and the social welfare system will be used to provide intervention and/or support. Proof of the commission of the offense (usually to the civil standard of the balance of probabilities rather than the criminal standard of beyond reasonable doubt) may be used to indicate that the child is beyond parental control and in need of compulsory measures of state care (Dunkel, 1991). The interface between criminal justice systems and welfare systems is important when attempting international comparisons of the extent to which children are under control of the state (Stewart & Tutt, 1987).

The existence of this range of ages poses particular problems for establishing the nature of adolescent offending from the official statistics. For example, it has sometimes been suggested that different types of offenses are more likely in certain age groups. For example, in a Swedish longitudinal study in which data were collected from individuals and from official records, crimes of theft were common at all ages, but violent offenses seemed to begin at age 15 (Stattin, Magnusson, & Reichel, 1989). If this is the case, then comparing official statistics across countries becomes complicated. We might expect a population of offenders aged between 7

---

† This assumption would be abolished by provisions of the Crime and Disorder Bill 1998 currently being considered by the U.K. parliament.

and 17 to have a different offending profile than a group aged between 15 and 18, regardless of cultural variations. At what age should children be held responsible legally and socially? In making this decision, what part is played by what is known about child development and what part by the social and cultural context? The topic is rather ignored in the literature. In a review of the issues, Dalby (1985) asserted that theories of child development could offer clear pointers to the appropriate age, but the fallibility of theories makes this a dubious basis for decision making. The need to pay attention, instead, to empirical research findings on children's cognitive capacities has been largely ignored by policy makers, with an inevitable arbitrariness in legislation.

There is extensive research evidence that important developmental changes continue through the teenage years (Justice, 1996; Keating, 1990; Rutter & Rutter, 1993). During early adolescence, young people's thinking tends to become more abstract, multidimensional, self-reflective, and self-aware, with a better understanding of relative concepts. They are better able to hold in mind several different dimensions of a topic at the same time and so generate more alternatives in their decision making. They become better able to monitor their own thinking for inconsistency, for its gaps in information, and for the accuracy of its logic. The greater intellectual sophistication that comes during the teenage years is accompanied by related developments in the way young people think about themselves. During adolescence, there is a marked increase in emotional introspection together with a greater tendency to look back with regret and to look ahead with apprehension. That is, not only do young people become increasingly able to consider the long-term consequences of their actions, they also tend to think about such consequences more in terms of their own sense of responsibility and with increased awareness of the effects of their actions on other people.

As would be expected, there are parallel developments in children's capacity to remember events, to recall the timing of happenings, to understand interrogation, and to be resistant to the influence of adult suggestions. It is not just that there is a gradual increase in children's mental capacities as such; there are also parallel decreases in children's suggestibility and susceptibility to being swayed in their views by how adults question them.

There are important developmental changes, too, in children's ability to feel guilt and shame. Guilt involves the appreciation of responsibility for negative outcomes, resulting from acts of either commission or omission; shame is associated with negative feelings about oneself on the basis of a self-perception of being unworthy or bad. Amongst other things, the emergence of guilt and shame as experienced by adults is connected to a growing awareness of when one has caused another person's misfortune, a capacity for self-evaluation, and a recognition that one has choice and control over one's own behavior. There is evidence that children's ability to express guilt increases with age. Young children are, of course, aware when they have done wrong, but the way in which they think about this alters as they grow older. Older children are able to use internal justice principles and have concern for victims or wrong acts, whereas younger children tend to be more governed by fear of punishment after detection.

The teenage years also constitute the age period when there are marked changes in emotional disorders. Depressive disorders become much more frequent at this age. Rates of suicide and attempted suicide increase dramatically. The reasons for the increase are likely to be complex and are, in any case, poorly understood. However, part of the explanation is likely to lie in age-related changes in young people's ability to experience guilt and self-blame and their propensity to think about the long-term consequences of their actions and their life situation.

These developments in intellectual capacities and in emotions derive in part from continuing brain development (which extends well into the teenage years) and in part from life experiences. During adolescence, there is also the important biological transition of puberty, together with the marked hormonal changes that are involved and their implications for behavior and feelings. There is no single age at which it can be said that physical and mental development has reached maturity. Moreover, there is marked individual variation in timing. This variation is most obvious with respect to the major differences in the age at which young people reach puberty, but it is characteristic of all aspects of development. Accordingly, any decisions on how young people should be dealt with must take into account this marked individual variation.

Children and adolescents therefore have a diminished capacity, as compared with adults, to think in terms of the long-term consequences of their actions, to reflect about their behavior and its effects on others, and to experience enduring feelings of guilt. This argues for a different approach when applying criminal responsibility concepts to young people.

Other arguments for raising the age of criminal responsibility are based on a welfare perspective leading to the belief that exposure of children to the workings of the criminal justice system does them harm in one way or another, or on sociological perspectives that argue that younger people are not fully integrated into society until they have joined the labor market or started their own families. The welfare perspective gained momentum in the 1980s through the increasing number of international regulations governing the treatment of children, such as the 1989 United Nations Convention on the Rights of the Child. The decade witnessed a period of intense codification of the rights of young people (Queloz, 1991). The UN Convention was supplemented by various other rules and guidelines on administration of justice for minors (1985), for prevention of juvenile delinquency (1990), and for the protection of children in care. In 1987 the Council of Europe produced the Recommendations of the Council of Ministers concerning social reactions to juvenile delinquency. Similar provisions are being introduced across the world (Dunkel, 1991; Sagel-Grande, 1991).

Underlying these tensions between crime prevention, the welfare of young people, and developmental capacities is a constantly shifting interrelationship between different arenas of social control, the nature of which might change considerably between the preschool and late teen years, and between cultures. The main arenas of control are (i) the family and peers, (ii) the school, (iii) the welfare aspects of state provision, and (iv) the criminal justice system. Younger children will be expected to be provided for and controlled by the first three primarily, young adults by the fourth. The age at which people move out of the first three spheres and into the last has been the focus of this discussion.

The Nature of Adolescent Crime

What do we know about the nature of adolescent crime, and where does that information come from? It is probably fair to say that it is common for most young people to be involved at some point in behavior that is not legally sanctioned – for example, underage drinking, minor shoplifting, buying cigarettes, or experimenting with "soft" drugs. It is not unusual for young people to get into trouble with the police for behavior of this type, although the majority of those who do so will have only informal or transient contact. A significant minority of young people, however, will go on to acquire a criminal record at some point in their adolescence. Recent Home Office analysis of two cohorts of people born in 1953 and 1958 showed that approximately a third of male adults (31% and 33%) had been convicted of at least one standard list offense by their thirties (Home Office, 1995d). Many of these convictions were as a result of offenses committed before adulthood. In their longitudinal study of 411 males in inner London followed from age 7 into adulthood, Farrington, Lambert, and West (1998) reported that the average criminal career began at some point between 14 and 21 years, lasted ten years, ended at about age 26, and (for those who committed more than one offense) consisted of 4.6 offenses leading to conviction. Overall, roughly equal proportions of all their offending was committed in the three age periods of 10–16, 17–20 and 21–32 years. It is also evident that criminal careers are more persistent than commonly supposed. This important investigation is (somewhat confusingly) called the Cambridge Study because the researchers have their offices in Cambridge.

In addition to the fact that many young people are involved in crime, it is also clear that there are different patterns of involvement. In addition to the young person who does not get caught, or who has only transient contact with the police, there are those who are convicted of one or two offenses and also those who reoffend more frequently. The early 1990s have seen a growing public debate in many countries about the possible existence of a relatively small number of young offenders who, because of their *persistent* involvement in crime, account for a large proportion of juvenile offenses.

We begin, so to speak, with the end. Despite the fact that only a minority of delinquent activities result in prosecution, the official statistics on the level and types of recorded crime committed by young people, and the processes by which they are dealt, are the most frequently used handles on adolescent offending. In this way, the study of juvenile delinquency differs from that of problem behavior generally. Rutter and Giller (1983) reported continuing controversy over the concepts and measures of delinquency, and especially over the question of whether it was justifiable to consider offenders as a meaningful group of individuals or to consider delinquencies as a valid group of behaviors. In the next sections, we look at developments in concepts and measures of delinquency and factors affecting official processes and statistics.

Criminal Offenses

The legal definitions of criminal offenses are the start of the process by which an individual (or sometimes collective) act becomes an official statistic. Definitions change over time and vary from place to place. Legislation can alter levels of crime overnight by introducing new offenses, by removing old ones from the statute book, or by reclassifying previously "nonserious" offenses as "serious," thereby inflating the index of such crimes recorded by the police in criminal statistics. In addition, laws may change and new offenses be introduced in ways other than by statute. In the United Kingdom, the courts frequently do this by applying common law.

The legal definitions can be categorized into four main types of offenses that could be committed by young people. First, there are grounds for court cases based on noncriminal but "risky" behavior (beyond the control of parents or authorities, etc.). In the United Kingdom, cases based on risky behavior have changed considerably in the last 15 years, especially since the passage of the 1989 Children Act. Two significant changes have been that neither offending nor truanting per se are now specific grounds for admission into the care of a local authority.

Second, there are status offenses, where it is simply the age at which an act was committed that makes it a crime. Thus, for example, in the United Kingdom it has been a crime for homosexual men to have intercourse if the participants are under 18 years of age, but not if they are over that age, whereas the age of consent for heterosexual intercourse is 16. Similarly, some laws relating to drinking and gambling are concerned with age rather than the act itself. In these examples, an implicit assumption about developmental maturity is made. At certain ages some acts are presumed to be damaging; at other ages they are considered not to be – or, at least, individuals are allowed the liberty to make that judgment themselves.

A third category of offenses consists of behaviors classified as crimes to protect the perpetrator but without an obvious victim; this includes, for example, possession of drugs. These behaviors are deemed to be inadvisable whatever the age of the perpetrator, but it is only the individuals themselves who are affected. Finally, there are crimes with an obvious victim, such as the majority of notifiable offenses like burglary, robbery, and shoplifting. The victim might be an individual, a corporate body of some kind, or the general public.

Criminal Statistics

Criminal statistics based on police returns are widely available for a number of countries, although the details of how offenses and offenders are broken down or categorized vary from place to place. Even within-country and across-time comparisons are not entirely straightforward, being subject to variations in policy and practice that may distort the figures (Pease & Tseloni, 1996). The main source of data on offenses committed in England and Wales is *Criminal Statistics*, an annual publication from the Home Office. *Criminal Statistics* gives a range of tables based on "notifiable offenses," of which there are about 70 types. These are notifiable in that the police notifies the Home Office of their occurrence, (almost) regardless of what happens next. Most notifiable offenses are "indictable," meaning they must be (or can be) tried by a judge and jury. A few are "summary" offenses, meaning they can be dealt with only in a magistrates court. Nonnotifiable offenses are either motoring offenses or fall into an "other" category. The police do not notify the Home Office of these, although if they end in a caution or conviction they will appear in *Criminal Statistics*. In addition, the British Home Office also publishes *Probation Statistics, Prison Statistics*, the Lord Chancellor's Department publication *Judicial Statistics*, the British Crime Survey, police force statistics, various specific data bases (e.g., The Offender Index), and the reports of audit agencies and inspectorates.

Similar central collations of official statistics are published by most Western governments. In the United States, these have been published by the FBI (Federal Bureau of Investigation, 1993) since 1929 as the *Uniform Crime Report* (UCR), which provides an overview of the 50 states but carries the warning that "These simplistic and/or incomplete analyses often create misleading perceptions which adversely affect cities and counties, along with their residents" (1993, p. iv).† The U.S. statistics are based on "index crimes," roughly equivalent to the British indictable offenses but more restricted in scope. The UCR findings for each calendar year are published in a preliminary form in the spring, followed the next year by a detailed annual report called *Crime in the United States*. The UCR program is being reorganized and extended to become the National Incident-Based Reporting System, which will provide more detailed information. In addition, the Office of Juvenile Justice and Delinquency Prevention (OJJDP), part of the U.S. Department of Justice, publishes very useful summary statistics on offending by young people that are based on the FBI figures (see e.g. Snyder & Sickmund, 1995; Snyder et al., 1996).

In addition, the United Nations Crime Survey, coordinated by the Secretary General and compiled from questionnaires sent out every five years to member states, started in the 1970s and is now a much larger enterprise than when it began. However, there are methodological weaknesses in the survey, and the data submitted tend to be rather fragmentary (Pease & Tseloni, 1996). The Council of Europe (1995) has sought to improve the situation by compiling a sourcebook comparing official statistics, victimization data, and self-reports in twelve European countries.

The official statistics reflect certain characteristics of offending by young people, which vary by nation but which also reflect some fairly universal patterns. We will use them to discuss four main topics: the proportion of crime accounted for by juveniles, the types of offenses committed, gender differences, and age trends.

---

† Despite this caveat, the report carried a "Crime Clock" asserting that in 1993 the United States recorded one murder every 21 minutes, one forcible rape every five minutes, and one property crime every three seconds. This gives the misleading impression that the risks of victimization are random and largely determined by time.

Proportion of Crime Accounted for by Juveniles. Estimates vary on the proportion of all crime committed by young people. The most recent English and Welsh statistics suggest that 26% of those cautioned or convicted of indictable offenses in 1995 were youths (aged 10–17) and 17% were young adults (aged 18–20). Analysis of the United Nations Crime Survey concluded that countries differ dramatically in the proportions of juveniles featured in their criminal justice processes, and the rates vary depending on whether the focus is rates of apprehension, prosecution, conviction, or imprisonment. According to these UN figures, which are available only for 1975, the ratio of juveniles to adults in prosecutions ranged from 0.03 in Bangladesh, through 0.30 in England and Wales, to 1.23 in Norway (Pease & Tseloni, 1996). However, the age of criminal responsibility differs substantially in these countries, and comparisons are rather futile for that reason. The ratios for apprehensions tend to be less variable since they are less affected by criminal responsibility, but in Pease and Tseloni's study these ratios were not available for either England and Wales or Bangladesh. In the United States the ratio was 0.35, and in Norway it was 1.01. Combining these figures and concentrating on England, Wales, and the United States, it would appear that approximately a third of those stopped and prosecuted tend to be juveniles. Of course, this estimate is rather vague because of the difficulties of comparison.

Types of Offenses Committed. Police figures lead to the conclusion that young people tend to commit more of certain types of offenses than they do of others. Thus, much of juvenile crime is seen to be theft, and it is fair to conclude that this is a universal finding (Netherlands – Junger-Tas & Block, 1988; Sweden – Wikström, 1990; England and Wales – Home Office, 1996; United States – Snyder et al., 1996; international review – Smith, 1995). The 1995 data from the most recently available English and Welsh *Criminal Statistics* (Home Office, 1996), show that 48% of males aged between 14 and 17, as well as 74% of female offenders in the same age group, were cautioned or prosecuted for theft-related offenses. This was largely shoplifting; if burglary is included in this category, the rates increase to 64% and 78%, respectively. Violent crimes form a very small proportion of known offending by young people, usually less than 10% (U.K. 1995 statistics presented in the figure show 10%), although many, perhaps most, very frequent offenders will have a violent offense on their record. This is also generally confirmed in official statistics from a range of countries.

It should be noted that the official statistics also show that crimes involving a weapon vary greatly among countries. Those involving a gun (committed by young offenders) are some 15 times higher in the United

States than in Europe. These differences can be reflected in a number of different ways. In the United States, for example, the number of juvenile homicide offenders tripled between 1984 and 1994, and the increase was almost entirely firearm-related (Snyder et al., 1996), whereas U.K. rates of homicide by young people have remained relatively constant over the decade.

Gender Differences. Official statistics always show a clear imbalance in offending by young men and young women, with the latter accounting for a far smaller proportion of recorded offenses. In 1995, of the 217,000 young people cautioned or found guilty between the ages of 10 and 20 in England and Wales, 80% were male. Theft formed a larger proportion of the offending by the young women than young men, the latter having relatively larger proportions of violence, burglary, and drug offending than the young women. Similar results were reported for the Netherlands by Junger-Tas and Block (1988), where almost ten times as many boys as girls had official contacts with the police prosecutor or juvenile judge. Wikström (1990) reported rates five times as high for young men in a Stockholm cohort. This ratio tends to differ by type of crime, with young women accounting for relatively higher proportions of less serious offenses. Basing estimates on scans of official records containing all offenders rather than just on cohorts of offenders also seems to make a difference: the former estimates tend to demonstrate a lower ratio than the latter.

Age Trends. In addition to the patterns concerning types of offenses and gender differences, official statistics offer certain conclusions concerning age trends in offending. Estimates of the peak age vary internationally and by year, but estimates tend to center on 17–18, with the start of the criminal career (first adjudication) usually being estimated to be around age 14 or 15 (Farrington, 1995a; see also Chapter 10). There is some evidence that the sexes differ in terms of the peak age of their offending. In the most recent British statistics, this was 18 years for boys and 15 for girls (Graham & Bowling, 1995; Home Office, 1996). On the other hand, Wikström (1990) reported a peak age of between 15 and 17 for young men, but between 22 and 24 for young women. The reason for this disagreement between studies is unclear, but it may be that there are two peaks in females; the matter requires further study.

Official statistics are invaluable for the study of juvenile delinquency, but it has long been acknowledged that they are affected by various types of bias – some known and some unknown – and thus can tell only part of the story. It is obvious that the true extent of crime will be underestimated, as not every offender is caught, for instance. In addition, a longstanding criticism of the official statistics on crime has been that they are distorted by many (often unmeasured) other factors apart from the true levels of crime. These include variations in reporting behavior, policing policy (e.g., targeting of certain groups), variations in police recording procedures, and variations in the response made by the judiciary.

We will discuss in more detail those variations in the processing of offenders and offenses that have been suggested as sources of bias in the official statistics. At this stage, in terms of the overall relationship or ratio between the crime figures and the underlying levels of crime, many of the conclusions of the 1983 review have been confirmed by more recent work. As Rutter and Giller (1983) explained, there are two main arguments regarding the study of the underlying "dark figure" of "real" crime. The first is that there is nothing given about crime, and no real level of crime exists independently of cultural and societal definitions. The second is that in some sense there *is* an absolute level of crime, and untangling the influences on various official statistics and empirical studies can eventually lead to greater understanding of the actual level. A slightly less strong version of the second argument holds that there is enough consistency in the collection of data around the socially constructed categories of crime to allow us to make useful observations, even if the real levels are unknown or do not exist. The emphasis on the importance of the social context in the construction of statistics has made an important contribution to criminology by highlighting the interdependence of offender and the culture in which he or she offends. Despite some conflict between these viewpoints, the empirical evidence in the early 1980s was relatively clear (see Maguire, 1997). It certainly pointed to much variation and discretion in the processing of offenders. Even though caution was needed in using official statistics, to abandon them entirely was unwarranted because they usefully reflected certain aspects of underlying behavior in the offending population. The most unreliable sections of the official data related to cautions, minor delinquent activities, and one-time offenders (see e.g. Home Office, 1996, p. 92).

One of the clearest commentaries on the use of British official statistics is that edited by Walker (1995), a collection of analyses based on government statistics. Walker highlighted the complications inherent in converting complex human events into objective statistics. She cited an example of a group of three men with knives attacking another group of five men, injuring two of them and robbing them of all their cash and credit cards. Confidence in crime statistics erodes considerably upon learning that this translates to one offense of robbery, one of wounding, and one of obtaining property by deception. Indeed, if the offenses are not reported or the police take no action, this situation will translate to no offenses whatsoever. However, the underlying argument in Walker (1995) was that useful information can be mined from the official statistics if the processes by which offenses are reported, collected, and collated are clarified.

In addition to the statistics collated annually by government departments, official statistics on offending can be collected from individuals' criminal records, although this route is closely monitored by the relevant departments (the Home Office in the United Kingdom, for example) and particular permissions are required, primarily in order to protect the individuals concerned. Police paperwork and detailed information often exist in these records, even for offenses that did not end in conviction, and information on the situation surrounding the incident as well as the initial charge (which is often altered later in the process) can be coded. A far better feel for the nature of juvenile delinquency can be achieved by reading such records than by scanning the collated figures.

Victim Surveys

Most of the information about crime derives from data on offenses and on perpetrators of offenses, but useful data can also be obtained by asking members of the general population about their experience as victims of crime. As we have already indicated, victim surveys, including the U.S. National Crime Victimization Survey (NCVS) (Perkins et al., 1996), the first International Crime Survey (Van Dijk et al., 1990), and repeated (usually biennial) sweeps of the British Crime Survey (BCS) (Mirrlees-Black et al., 1996) have added considerably to knowledge about experiences of offenses. The BCS, for example, asked questions of members of the general public about experiences of crime, although the survey was limited in terms of the people represented and the crimes covered. Its existence reflects a marked change in criminology in the late 1970s and early 1980s, years that saw a growth in attention to crime victims (Maguire, 1997; Mawby & Walklate, 1994). Initially a feminist movement, one major effect of this trend was to focus the interest of criminologists on the offense rather than the offender. Psychologists, however, still remained largely interested in the offender.

Figure 3.1 compares the estimated proportions of different offenses in England and Wales from the 1991 BCS and from the *Criminal Statistics*, illustrating the similarities and differences that depend upon the source of the statistics. The sum of the offenses in categories that can be compared between the two sources shows that the amount of crime actually

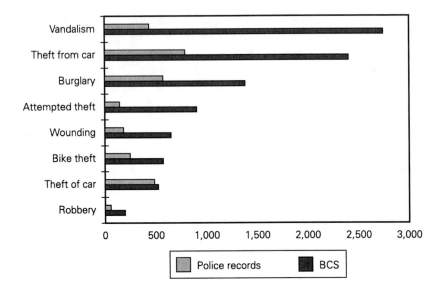

Figure 3.1. Comparison of the results from the 1991 British Crime Survey (BCS) with crimes recorded by the police (number of offenses, in thousands, for selected crimes). *Source:* Adapted from M. A. Walker, *Interpreting Crime Statistics* (1995, p. 12), by permission of Oxford University Press.

committed may be up to four times the number of crimes reported by the police. The extent of underreporting varies with the type of offense concerned. Thus, three times as many domestic burglaries were committed as recorded; four times as many bicycle thefts, thefts from vehicles, and woundings; seven times as many offenses of vandalism; and eight times as many robberies and thefts from the person. Only with respect to thefts of vehicles are the BCS and police figures similar, primarily because victims seek police assistance in recovering the vehicle and to meet the requirements of insurance companies.

Childhood Victimization

Until recently, little attention has been paid to the issue of the links between offending and victimization of young people. Certainly the official statistics illustrate the greater risk of (certain) recorded crimes among the young. In the United Kingdom, for example, recorded victimization rates for violence against the person show that, for both sexes, those in the 16–24-year-old age group are most at risk. The lowest rates are for those aged 0–9 and those aged 60 or over. In the United States, over one third of murder victims are young people below the age of 25; between 1980 and 1994, nearly half (46%) of the victims killed by juvenile offenders were 15–24 years old (Snyder et al., 1996). The NCVS collects information on victimization against household members down to the age of 12. Those 12–15 years old are generally less at risk of theft and most forms of violence than older teenagers, but both groups are at higher risk than adults of robbery and simple assault.

Some studies have examined the specific experiences of children with respect to sexual abuse (Baker & Duncan, 1985; Finkelhor & Dziuba-Leatherman, 1994; Russell, 1983) and how child sexual abuse victims are dealt with in the criminal justice system (Dent & Flin, 1992; Spencer & Flin, 1990). More broadly based inquiries into children's experiences as victims of crime (Morgan & Zedner, 1992) or harassment such as bullying (Farrington, 1993a; Olweus, 1978, 1991) have been limited.

Two recent Scottish self-report studies of 11–15-year-old school children in Edinburgh (Anderson et al., 1990) and Glasgow (Hartless et al., 1995) reported high levels of assault, theft, and harassment within the past 9–12 months of the investigation. Females, in particular, reported significant levels of sexual harassment and importuning by men, often over the age of 18 years. Given the breadth of definition of the behaviors recorded, it is somewhat problematic to determine if all such incidents constitute "crime." Both studies also recorded high rates of self-reported offending within the samples: 69% of the Edinburgh group and 76% of the Glasgow group admitted to at least one offense, with a high correlation between the experience of victimization and the commission of offending.

More detailed findings on the victimization of young people comes from an additional sample of 1,350 12–15-year-olds gathered for the 1992 BCS (Aye Maung, 1995). Information was collected on victimization (crime and other disorder), offending behavior, drug use, fear of crime, seriousness of crime, and contact with and attitude toward the police. Overall, 60% of the sample recalled at least one incident over the past six to eight months. A third said they had been assaulted on at least one occasion; a fifth said they had had something stolen, a fifth had been harassed by people of their own age and a fifth by someone aged 16 or over. Levels of victimization on the basis of those incidents considered a crime was as low as 18%. In comparison with older groups, 12–15-year-olds experienced more thefts of property, although thefts from the person and assault incidents were comparable with these of 16–19-year-olds. Self-reported offending was one of the strongest correlates of victimization – particularly assault, theft from the person, and harassment by other young people. Other factors that traditionally correlate with offending also seemed to

---

BOX 3.1. THE NATURE OF JUVENILE OFFENDING: THE PICTURE
FROM OFFICIAL STATISTICS

- Juveniles (under age 18) account for approximately a quarter to a third of offenses in England, Wales, and the United States, although rates vary around the world. Victim surveys confirm this finding. In the United States, 28% of "personal crimes" were attributed to juveniles.

- Most juvenile crime is theft-related. Studies based on official statistics in the Netherlands, the United Kingdom, and Sweden have all shown that approximately half of offenses by young men were types of theft (excluding burglary).

- Only a small proportion of juvenile crime is violent. According to official U.K. statistics, violence accounted for 10% of juvenile crime in 1995. In the United States, victims thought juveniles were responsible for about one in five violent crimes, compared with one in four of all crime. Arrest data suggest this proportion may be even lower.

- Young men commit a higher proportion of juvenile crime than young women. In the United Kingdom in 1995, young men under the age of 21 accounted for 80% of recorded offenses cleared up and attributed to this age group. The ratios vary by country.

- Crimes involving a weapon vary greatly among countries. Those involving a gun are some 15 times higher in the United States than in Europe.

- The peak age of offending is usually in the late teens. In the United Kingdom, for example, the official statistics suggest that it is 18 for young men and 15 for young women. These rates differ by country.

---

correlate highly with victimization: poor parental supervision, access to inner city areas, being out with friends – especially with respect to personal (as opposed to household) victimization (see also Gottfredson, 1984; Mayhew & Elliott, 1990).

Box 3.1 presents the main "headlines" about juvenile crime that can be gleaned from the official British and American statistics as well as from police and victim reports.

Self-Reported Offending

Given the limitations of official statistics and the problems (due to variations in the age of criminal responsibility) in comparing jurisdictions, self-report studies have a significant role to play in building a picture of the nature of adolescent offending. In this section, we review issues of prevalence of offending as described in this type of study, and we also address questions of methodology. (Time trends in self-report data are discussed in Chapter 4, where secular trends are considered.) Self-report studies usually aim to record nonpersonal and victimless acts, as well as the more usual forms of delinquency, and to make use of background information about the respondents.

The methodology employed in such studies is usually to give respondents a standard list of specified delinquent activities. These can be presented as interview questions or as a questionnaire for self-completion. Some recent studies have experimented with sophisticated new technologies such as respondent laptops, where data are entered directly by the subject (Ramsay & Percy, 1996). Rutter and Giller's (1983) conclusion – that, despite being open to a range of biases such as variations in memory and honesty, self-report methods were generally reliable and valid – has been supported by more recent reviews (Junger-Tas, 1994a; Junger-Tas & Marshall, in press). As part of an international study of self-reported delinquency (ISRD), Junger-Tas and her colleagues conducted a pilot study including reliability tests, repeating earlier questions at the end of an interview. Internal consistency of the answers to six questions ranged from about 90% to 75%, with the lower levels of reliability relating to higher-frequency events such as shoplifting. Various participating nations also conducted indirect validity checks, comparing results with other national studies or with official data. Generally, results from different sources that relied on rank ordering of offenses showed substantial similarity. In a separate study, Junger-Tas estimated that 11.5% of those interviewed gave inconsistent answers (Junger-Tas & Block, 1988).

Validity is often more of a problem than reliability. Despite expressing confidence in the reliability of its measures, the ISRD (Junger-Tas, 1994a) identified some unexplained and potentially problematic validity issues. One of these involved the self-reports of ethnic minorities. In three countries participating in the study (Switzerland, England and Wales, and the Netherlands) it was found that ethnic minorities reported fewer delinquent acts than their national counterparts, but no police arrest or conviction data were available to check these results. Such discrepancies have been found in earlier self-report studies in the United States (see Huizinga & Elliot, 1986), although the variety of reasons offered for such underreporting are by no means consistent – interviewer bias, feelings of discrimination leading respondents to hold back information on delinquency,

school underachievement, and socioeconomic factors. Klein (1994) noted
other problems common in self-report data, particularly the issue of over-
reporting of minor and underreporting of serious offenses. Loeber and
Waller (1988) raised the question of the significance of the number of answer categories in self-report questionnaires, systematically manipulating
the answer categories to demonstrate that this produced very divergent
results. Specifically, they suggested that evidence showing that generalized delinquency was more common than specialized delinquency may
be a methodological artefact of the number of answer categories respondents are allowed.

Sampling has also been raised as a serious methodological issue in self-
report studies. It has been argued that the burgeoning of self-report studies has led to an increased focus on representative populations of young
people rather than study of official and serious delinquents, thus failing to
ensure that enough of the more persistent offenders are included for separate analysis. An empirical study of the effects of drawing representative
and selected samples (Cernkovich, Giordano, & Pugh, 1985) concluded
that, in order to determine whether particular variables distinguish more
chronic offenders from the rest of the offending and non-offending population, self-report studies should be broadened to include more incarcerated or other officially defined samples. It also seems that – even if
the samples are adequate – self-reports may not be very satisfactory with
respect to the hard core of offending, because there is a tendency to down-
play: either by reporting the offense as less serious than it actually was or
by placing the crime further in the past than it actually occurred. Moreover, a low response rate is a problem in many self-report studies.

Despite these major methodological difficulties, it remains the case that,
as Rutter and Giller (1983) concluded, the results from a range of studies generally concur, particularly in terms of the frequency of delinquent
acts and of the differences between delinquents and nondelinquents. For
the ISRD, data were collected in 13 nations. In order to maximize comparability, only a few central crime categories were compared, and only
descriptive data on prevalence and frequency were accepted. In a preliminary attempt at comparing the contributing nations where the surveys
were based on national (or similar) random samples, Junger-Tas (1994a)
compared the Netherlands, England and Wales, Portugal, Switzerland,
and Spain in terms of rates of delinquency, excluding status offenses. The
results for ever having committed an offense, and for having done so in
the last twelve months, are compared in Figure 3.2, confirming the earlier
result that the great majority of young people admit having committed
delinquent acts at some time.

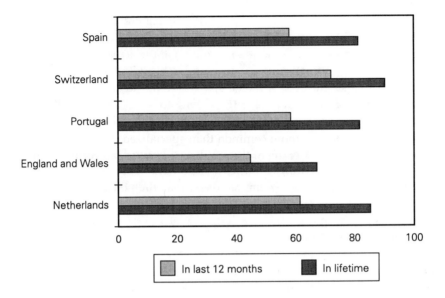

Figure 3.2. Prevalence rates in five countries: results from the ISRD (percentage having committed offense in last twelve months versus in lifetime). *Source:* J. Junger-Tas, *Delinquent Behaviour among Young People in the Western World* (1994), by permission of Kugler Publications.

Preliminary analyses suggested that the rates of property and violent offenses committed in the last twelve months were approximately similar in these five countries, with property offenses ranging from 16% to 33.5% and violence from 15.8% to 34.5%, although an alternative interpretation might draw attention to the fact that the rates in some countries were more than double those of others for these offense types. Drug offenses ranged from 11.3% to 25.9%; when seven city samples were included in the comparisons, the rates were found to be relatively low in southern European countries and higher in western Europe and the United States. The violence category, however, included a range of acts such as carrying an offensive weapon (a baseball bat or knife), vandalism, violence against objects, and interpersonal violence. Rates of actually hurting someone with a weapon were far lower, ranging from 0.7% in Switzerland to 1.4% in England and Wales.

The figures for the United States, however, are much higher (Elliott, 1994). In the National Youth Survey, the cumulative prevalence up to age 27 years for serious violent offenses (SVO) was 42% for males and 16% for females. In two thirds of reported SVO events, some medical treatment of the victim was required. The findings bring out three important methodological issues. First, the *annual* prevalence was much lower (below 10%) than the cumulative prevalence. Second, it may well be that the responses of individuals who have participated in multiple waves of a longitudinal study are not comparable with those seen for the first time in a single cross-sectional study. Third, the rate varies greatly by age: below 0.5% through age 11, peaking to 5% at age 16, and dropping to 1% or less in the 20s (figures for both sexes combined). Virtually all serious violent offending begins before age 20.

Reflecting the patterns already identified in the official statistics, young men in all the participating countries of the international self-report study admitted committing more delinquent acts than did young women, with the ratio varying by offense type. For property offenses, the male : female ratio was approximately 1.5 : 1 or 2 : 1; for violent offenses it was higher, ranging from approximately 2 : 1 to 4 : 1. The more serious the offense, in general, the higher the ratio between the sexes. More detailed national data from countries participating in the ISRD have also been published, including a full report on the English and Welsh contribution (Graham & Bowling, 1995).

Other national and smaller self-report studies tend to confirm the general pattern of results from the ISRD. The self-report measure used in the ISRD was developed from that employed in previous research, and was specially designed to measure official delinquency for comparison with official statistics. Respondents were asked whether (and, if so, how often) they had participated in criminal behavior (see e.g. Elliott, Huizinga, & Morse, 1986). Results are also available from the Adolescent Health Behavior Survey, conducted among Colorado junior and senior high school students using a ten-item scale to measure antisocial behavior (Donovan, Jessor, & Costa, 1988); Kandel, Simcha-Fagan, and Davies (1986) followed up a sample of high school students (but with a high attrition rate) in New York State, tracking their drug use and offending. Other self-report studies include further analyses from the Cambridge Study (Farrington, 1995a), the Dunedin study (Moffitt, 1990a), data from the Netherlands (Junger-Tas & Block, 1988) and the Pittsburgh Youth Study, which has been unique in including self-reports of younger children aged 7 (Farrington et al., 1990a).

These studies all confirm that over half of young men have been involved in some kind of delinquent behavior (54% in Junger-Tas & Block, 1988; 55% in Graham & Bowling, 1995; 96% in Farrington, 1989). For young women, between a quarter to a third (estimates are usually between 20% and 35%) have been found to be involved in delinquency (24% in Junger-Tas & Block, 1988; 31% in Graham & Bowling, 1995). Comparisons among studies are obviously difficult because of variations in definitions of offenses and in the age ranges covered. It is notable that estimates of participation by young women are much higher than the official statistics would suggest, and consequently estimates of the ratio for offending between young men and young women is lower when based on self-report studies. This may well be because the self-report studies have a tendency to concentrate on more minor offenses and do not succeed as well with more frequent offenders (Cernkovich et al., 1985). Offending by young women has been reported to be of a more restricted nature (a higher proportion being theft, also confirmed by official statistics), less frequent, less persistent, and less serious (Junger-Tas & Block, 1988).

Problems with external validity have already been mentioned, but where studies have included both official and self-report data the worst offenders according to official records are usually those who report the most offending when asked for self-reports (Farrington, 1997a; Huizinga & Elliott, 1986). In the Cambridge Study, 11% of the males between ages 15 and 18 admitted burglary, and 62% of these were also convicted of burglary according to the official records. The correlates of both types of record have also been claimed to be very similar. However, the relationship between self-report and official records is not simply a matter of higher estimates of offending being made in self-reports. As we have already noted, in self-reports of their offending, individuals tend to overestimate some crimes and underestimate others (Tarling, 1993). Reports also vary according to age: Farrington (1989) found that an average of 46% of all offenses admitted prospectively between ages 10 and 25 were denied retrospectively at age 32. Given the overlap with substance abuse, alcohol use, and low levels of schooling, memory problems are not unlikely, particularly for the most prolific offenders.

Aspects and findings of self-report studies are summarized in Box 3.2.

Variations in the Processing of Offenses

If the variation between self-report results and official data is to be understood, research on variations in the processing of offenses is crucial. Rutter and Giller (1983) outlined various stages in the processing of criminal behavior:

(a) legal definition of the behavior as criminal;
(b) recognition that a criminal act has been committed;
(c) decision to report it to the authorities;
(d) police decision about what to do about the report;
(e) identification of a suspect;
(f) decision on how to deal with the suspect;
(g) sentencing decisions.

BOX 3.2. FINDINGS ON THE NATURE OF ADOLESCENT CRIME
FROM SELF-REPORT STUDIES

- Self-report data and official statistics on the nature of adolescent crime match quite well, although there are some systematic variations.

- Self-report studies portray less serious offending overall, with the majority of detected and undetected offending by young people being theft-related.

- Self-report studies tend to suggest higher levels of delinquency among the juvenile population than would be anticipated on the basis of the official statistics, particularly among young women.

- While showing greater participation by young women than official statistics, self-report data also suggest that their offending tends to contain a higher proportion of theft-related offenses, less frequent offending, less persistent offending, and less serious offenses.

- Although violent offenses constitute a very small proportion of all offenses, over a third of all offenders have committed at least one violent offense at some time in their criminal career.

Figure 3.3 clearly illustrates the enormous discretion being exercised by different individuals and authorities at the various stages between the commission and ultimate sentencing for offenses.

How and why do variations in the sequences of processing arise? Rutter and Giller (1983) discussed evidence up to the beginning of the 1980s. In order to update, we have split the stages into three blocks: (1) recognizing and reporting (stages a–c), (2) police procedures (stages d–f), and (3) judicial procedures (stage g).

Recognizing and Reporting Crime

Only certain behaviors are recognized by the law as crimes, only some of those are then recognized by the public as crime, and only a proportion of *those* actually get reported. The legal definition of crimes varies (obviously) with new laws, with the size of the population at risk, and with inflation. In addition, the role of victims in reporting their experiences is crucial to the process. Reports of crime by the public are the source of 80% of all recorded crime (Maguire, 1997; Reiner, 1992). Seriousness of crime, and perceptions of whether the police will or could do anything, both affect reporting of crime. Requirements of other agencies,

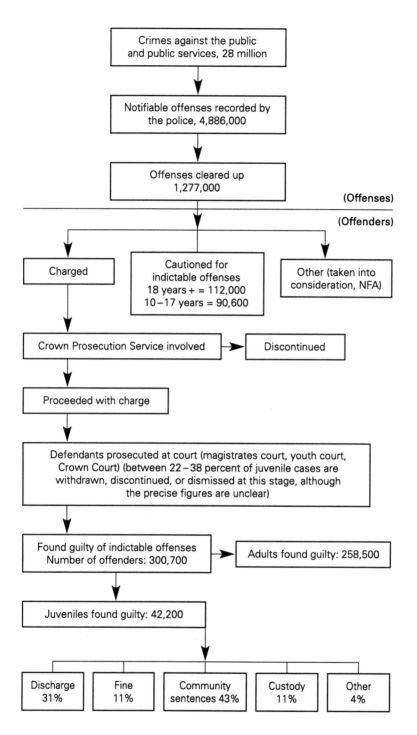

Figure 3.3. U.K. processing of offenses in 1995. *Sources:* Home Office (1996), Audit Commission (1996b).

such as insurance companies, also affect the process. For example, virtually all car theft in the United Kingdom is reported, because it must be if victims wish to claim on their insurance and all road-using vehicles must be insured (some are not, of course, but that is a separate offense) (Mirrlees-Black et al., 1996). It may be significant that in Japan, which has a very low crime rate, there is no insurance against theft. The various victim crime surveys already discussed have contributed considerably to the understanding of which crimes get reported. Webb and Marshall (1989) analyzed 44,593 reports of personal victimization and concluded that the following factors increased the likelihood of reporting: age (older people reported more), sex (women reported more), weapons present (increased reporting), multiple offenders (increased reporting), type of crime (e.g., armed robbery more likely to be reported), and bystanders present (increased reporting). (Other social psychological work suggests that having bystanders present leads to reduced feeling of responsibility for witnessed crimes and hence *decreased* stepping in; Stephenson, 1992). Of little importance were race, family income, educational level, age range of population, household head, unemployment, and poverty.

The reporting of certain types of offenses has received more attention than others. For example, there is a growing body of work on reporting of rape (e.g., Feldman-Summers & Norris, 1984; Grace, Lloyd, & Smith, 1992; Smith, 1989). Rape by young offenders is very rare, but the results of these studies may shed light on general reporting biases. A survey of 179 female rape victims (Feldman-Summers & Norris, 1984) who either did or did not report showed that their perceived outcome of making a report, social expectations, and certain situational characteristics predicted reporting behavior. Reporting behavior was not related to demographic characteristics, attitudes toward self and others, or attitudes and beliefs about the offense. However, the sample was self-selected (recruited from notices in clinics, newspapers, and media announcements), and a number of years could have elapsed since the incident; the average was 3.4 years, and of course recall could change over such a period. Combining the results of this study with the previous one suggests that perceptual and social psychological variables have more influence on the process than structural and socioeconomic variables.

There is considerable variation in the extent to which various crimes are reported. More detail about these variations is now available, and corrections could potentially be made to improve estimates of the actual levels of the underlying behavior (Mayhew et al., 1993; Mirrlees-Black et al., 1996).

The Police as "Gatekeepers" of the Criminal Justice System

Police procedures have an important part to play in both (i) variations in the exercise of police discretion, which determine the level and type of offending that is officially recorded, and (ii) recording procedures once a suspect is apprehended. In the former category, the police have a role to play in stopping suspects, deciding whether or not to arrest, and deciding whether to charge, caution, or dismiss the case after arrest. All of these can be affected by a number of factors. Policing policy, for example, might encourage the targeting of particular groups. Indeed, there is considerable discretion in deciding how to target finite resources in the first place. In addition, police discretion about what to do once targets have been stopped might be affected by features of the police officer or the defendant, by police "culture," or by broader societal influences (Reiner, 1997). This topic has been at the center of police research throughout the last three decades, and a great deal of evidence has been published since Rutter and Giller (1983). Reiner (1997) reviewed the history of discretion research, starting with its "discovery" in the United States in the late 1950s, including detailed discussion of developments in the 1980s and early 1990s. Most of the work starts from the assumptions that police discretion is inevitable, crime will always outstrip police resources, and translating laws into enforcement cannot be mechanistic and automatic but requires interpretation. The key question is: How might these variations in decision making affect what we see recorded in the official statistics?

Role of the Police. Three interrelated aspects are likely to structure the discretion of the police and in so doing influence the volume and nature of crimes recorded and processed (Sanders, 1997). First, there is the emphasis applied by particular forces on the goals of policing. Traditionally, these goals have been the tripartite elements of maintaining order, controlling crime, and catching criminals, with the emphasis particularly on the first two. More recently, government policy has been to emphasize the latter element as the "core business" of the police, with the private sector and community initiatives being encouraged to take up the first two roles (Hoddinott, 1994; Reiner, 1997).

Second, local force policy will be influential in shaping the local picture of crime along with the style of policing preferred – proactive (community policing) or reactive ("fire brigade" style). Different offenses will be locally targeted as a priority for processing, as will how the force places itself on this community-policing–fire-brigade continuum. The former will involve attempts to seek out incidences, the latter reacting once offenses have been detected (Audit Commission, 1996a).

Third, there is the impact of "cop culture" on individual investigation and recording practices – elements of sexism, racism, and stereotyping of certain individuals, groups, and areas that influence the identification of offenses, offenders, and victims (Reiner, 1985).

Despite the presence of centrally prescribed counting rules for recording crime and responses to it, local practices can and do have a skewing effect both on the volume of crimes recorded and the rate at which they are "cleared up." Farrington and Dowds's (1985) study, for example, showed that between two thirds and three quarters of the differences in crime rate between the two police-force areas reflected differences in police reactions to crime, with the remaining one third related to local differences in criminal behavior. Variations are also evident in how forces record offenses taken into consideration (TICs) and "prison write-offs" (i.e., police officers questioning convicted prisoners to clear the books of outstanding recorded offenses).

Using the "clear up" rate as a proxy for effectiveness is not without problems. Crimes known to the police may vary independently of actual levels of offending, for example, if a larger number of victimizations are reported by the public (Mayhew, Elliot, & Dowds, 1989). Improving communications, such as growing telephone ownership, may make it easier to contact the police. Between 1980 and 1994, recorded crime in England and Wales rose by 90% while police personnel increased by 8% and the number of offenses cleared up by 25% (from 1,056,000 to 1,320,000). However, the proportion of offenses cleared up relative to the number of crimes recorded by the police fell from 38% to 26%.

Little has changed in the recent literature on the impact of police deployment practices on crime rates. It remains the case that the vast majority of offenses recorded by the police (up to 80%) are reported by members of the public (Shapland & Vagg, 1988). In McConville's study of over 1,000 arrests, undertaken for the Royal Commission on Criminal Justice, the police themselves witnessed the offense, saw the suspect at the scene of the crime, or apprehended the suspect following a stop in only 25.6% of the cases (McConville, Sanders, & Leng, 1991). Increasing the number of police officers on foot or in car patrols to deter, detect, and apprehend offenders continue to be ineffective strategies. Increasing police coverage does not affect crime control beyond the baseline achieved by having a level of policing at all (Reiner, 1992). The enhanced speed of response provided by cars, radios, and computers does not change the apprehension rate (Clarke & Hough, 1984). Car patrols may even be counterproductive in that they cut the police off from contact with the public, thereby reducing the opportunity to receive information from them. Likewise, cars may exacerbate the negative aspects of police culture, leading to overreaction to incidents.

In the United Kingdom and the United States, renewed enthusiasm for foot patrols has arisen owing to the beneficial impact it may have on the fear of crime, community safety, and a positive identity for the police force. Moreover, police officers who foot patrol have more job satisfaction and are more community oriented in their role of policing (Audit Commission, 1996a; Reiner, 1992). These gains are valued over and above the neutral impact such policies may have on local crime rates.

Understanding police discretion at the investigative stages continues to be influenced by labeling theory: "suspicion, accusation, conviction and criminal self-identity are not objective characteristics of 'criminals' but are the products of law enforcers as well" (McConville et al., 1991). In recognizing that a crime has taken place, the police must make a primary decision as to whether to respond at all; increasingly, forces are adopting a graded response that depends upon the seriousness of the offense and the ability to secure an apprehension.

Information provided to the police by citizens is mediated through police values and priorities as part of a process of constructing a case. Research has begun to expose the working rules used by the police to inform their decision to recognize and respond to an event as a "crime." Among the factors to be taken into account are previous knowledge of the person suspected, the extent to which suspects show respect to the police in face-to-face situations, the context in which suspects are found, the detail of the information provided by members of the public, the demands of existing workload, and the extent to which the character of the victim is perceived as influential by the police (Maguire & Norris, 1992; McConville et al., 1991).

Police Stops. As we have noted, to a large extent the police respond to crime reports from the public. However, they can also pursue their own initiative in targeting particular groups for questioning, and they can decide how to follow up crime reports. Thus, it has always been clear that some groups are more likely to be targeted, and ethnicity, age, sex, and economic factors have all been identified as potential factors.

Offenders (or potential offenders) of different ages, gender, and ethnicity may receive different treatment from the police. For example, there is some evidence that teenage girls stopped for prostitution may be dealt with by the police in more diversionary ways, for various reasons including protective motives on the part of male officers (Brogden, Jefferson, &

Walklate, 1988; Dunhill, 1989). Overtargeting of racial minorities in police stops is now well documented (see the review by Smith, 1997a) and is
important because the vast majority of arrests of these groups result from
police stops.

Decision to Proceed to Arrest. Those from ethnic minorities may be
more likely to be picked up by the police, but there is also some evidence
that the ethnicity of the victim may affect police responses to calls from
the public. Smith, Visher, and Davidson (1984) analyzed arrests made
by officers on 900 patrol shifts in 60 different residential neighborhoods.
When there was a complainant involved, there was a marked tendency
for the police to be influenced by the race of the victim. Complaints by
white females were more likely to lead to arrests than were complaints by
black females. Winkel (1991) reported the results of an interesting Dutch
study on the interactions between the police and minority ethnic group
members. Nonverbal communication errors were witnessed in three experiments in which culturally determined nonverbal behaviors were systematically varied. The police seemed to be mistaken in their interpretation of these behaviors, being more likely to interpret them as suspicious.
Reporting the results of observations of over 550 prisoners received into
nine police stations, Morgan, McKenzie, and Reiner (1990; cited in Reiner,
1997) found that over half had no employment, most were young (59%
under 25), 87% were men, and 12% were black.

Interviews and Interrogations. Both policy and research have emphasized the need to protect the vulnerability of young people in the process
of the police obtaining evidence of crime from them, especially by way of
interview and interrogation leading to confession. At a policy level, the
U.K. Police and Criminal Evidence Act (PACE) of 1984 affords "vulnerable" people (including juveniles, the mentally ill, and those with learning
disability) the special protection of having an "appropriate adult" present
during such interviews. In practice, the police may not always ensure that
the right of such people to an appropriate adult is enforced; when they
are present, such adults may not always receive an adequate explanation
of their role (Evans, 1992a; Littlechild, 1995). Since the implementation of
the PACE legislation, there continue to be notorious instances of breaches
of the Codes of Practice, leading to subsequent court acquittals. The importance of these protections is heightened by the fact that the U.K. Criminal Justice and Public Order Act of 1994 allows courts to draw inferences
in certain circumstances if suspects exercise their right to silence during
a police interview.

A tendency for children to give unreliable evidence is presumed because of their immaturity and because the police station, with its routines and processes, is very much police territory. Research has identified three types of coercive strategies that may result in unreliable confessions. These are:

(1) coerced compliant confession – where suspects confess for some instrumental gain, such as release from custody (Gudjonsson & Clark, 1986);

(2) coerced internalized confession – where suspects are persuaded through influence that they have committed the crime (Gudjonsson & MacKeith, 1988); and

(3) coerced passive confession – where suspects adopt words used by the police which amount to a confession without understanding that they have made an admission (McConville et al., 1991).

This is not to say that any of these are common, but if they exist at all then they will have some effect, however minor, on the accuracy of police-derived criminal statistics.

Research undertaken for the Royal Commission on Criminal Justice into the conduct of police interviews (Evans, 1992b) confirmed that confession evidence is relied on by the police at a far higher rate for juveniles than for adults. In a sample of 367 juvenile arrests examined, 48.6% resulted in confession evidence, although in three quarters of these cases the interviews were perfunctory and routine with no evidence of unfair persuasive tactics being used. Evans showed that the strength of the police evidence was the strongest factor associated with obtaining a confession, leading to the paradoxical finding that confessions are most likely when least necessary to the prosecution process. The findings do, however, provide some concerns in that: (i) the police written record of the outcome of the interview did not always accord with the words spoken and recorded on tape (the Crown Prosecution Service rarely listens to the tape recording itself, relying more on the police written statement of the outcome and proposed action); and (ii) in some instances, denials or no clear admission by the interviewee led to cautions or informal warning (20% of the cautions or warnings given).

Decision to Charge. Having apprehended a suspect and having initiated the processing procedures, a certain amount of discretion exists over which incidents to proceed with. Many suspects are released from precharge detention with no further action – "NFA" (McConville et al., 1991). Centrally collated official figures are not available, but in a British study by McConville et al. (1991), researchers found that 26% of detained adults and 24% of detained juveniles in their sample were NFA'd; 14% of adults and 38% of juveniles were cautioned, with most of the rest prosecuted. Such figures can be estimated by looking at individual police records. In a survey of over 500 repeat offenders from two geographical areas in the United Kingdom (Hagell & Newburn, 1994), police files showed that of 3,690 offenses for which 531 offenders were arrested in one year (all of whom had been arrested at least three times in that period), 67% had resulted in a conviction and sentence, 11% in a caution, and the remaining 23% were still pending at the time of the research or were dismissed, discontinued, withdrawn, or resulted in a "not guilty" verdict.

The decision to caution or to take no further action is usually made by an inspector or more senior officer, but charge decisions are made by the arresting officer or custody officer. Sanders has commented that demeanor and the other factors influential at street level all play their part in the charge–caution decision, and the inconsistency revealed by research is, again, explicable in part by the operation of working rules. "The same factors apply with juveniles, despite relatively sophisticated juvenile liaison arrangements: many juveniles are still charged immediately, and even multi-agency juvenile bureaux still rely on police constructions" (Sanders, 1997, p. 1073).

The discretion employed in the decision to charge means that the police have a vital part to play in diverting young offenders from the criminal justice system, if they believe that is desirable. This is particularly the case with respect to the decision to give informal warnings in some cases, as figures for these will not then be recorded in official statistics nor on an individual's record (Home Office, 1996, p. 92). Giving an official caution also diverts the individual from the system, although it will be recorded on his or her record. Home Office commissioned research into the effect of Home Office guidance on cautioning in the 1980s found that police forces responded in markedly different ways (Evans & Wilkinson 1990). The authors drew attention to the need for more systematic recording of decisions, preferably computerized recording about precourt decisions, in order both to monitor the system and to develop information about best practice and management. They noted, for example, that NFA decisions could be made either because there is an obstacle to prosecution or because prosecution is possible but officers decide for one reason or another not to proceed with the case. To assess the influence of police discretion, these factors need to be untangled.

Thus, evidence relating to various police procedures such as stop and search, arrest, and the decision to prosecute all show overrepresentation of certain groups, particularly the young, men, and those from minority ethnic groups. This reflects a complex interaction between discrimination and disproportionate offending, and it poses a serious problem for interpreting the real level of crime from statistics derived from the criminal justice process. Explaining these variations in procedure is not easy, and it is probably true that most police targeting follows from a logical, empirically based, actuarial approach. In deciding on whom to stop for questioning, an actuarial approach would require a focus on males rather than females, on younger men rather than older men, on blacks rather than Asians or whites, and so forth. This is because there is evidence, to which we will return in the discussion of ethnicity in Chapter 8, that crime rates are higher in these groups. However, the approach is essentially discriminatory because individuals are being targeted as a result of their group membership. Moreover, the targeting will necessarily amplify the original group differences. That is, if males are picked up by the police but females are not, this will increase the likelihood of males being caught as compared with females. Thus, both the views – that targeting only arises through prejudice, and that targeting based on actuarial principles is never prejudicial – are wrong.

Variations in Judicial Procedures

The third stage in the processing of offenses involves the influence of the judicial and court procedures. In this respect, a major development in the United Kingdom since the publication of the Rutter and Giller review (1983) has been the establishment of the Crown Prosecution Service (CPS), recommended by the Royal Commission on Criminal Procedure in 1981. The CPS was set up by the Prosecution of Offenses Act in 1985. Under this Act, the police continue to charge, summon, caution, and NFA as before. Once charged or summoned, the accused then becomes the responsibility of the CPS, which decides whether to continue the prosecution. The CPS is headed by the Director of Public Prosecutions (DPP), whose office had previously been responsible for national prosecutions of particular importance and for the prosecution of police officers. Many Crown Prosecutors are former police prosecutors, the only difference now being their new power to drop cases (Sanders, 1997). Cases proceed only if they have a "realistic prospect of conviction" and if the prosecution is in the public interest (on which see Gelsthorpe & Giller, 1990). The DPP has published a code of practice that is intended to guide the discretion. The choice of charge may determine the level of court that will hear the case and the sentencing powers available to it (Ashworth, 1997). Consequences of introducing the CPS have included an increased proportion of cases ending in acquittals and a marked increase in discontinued cases (Sanders, 1997). In youth courts, some 14% of cases are discontinued and a further 11% dismissed (Audit Commission, 1996a).

In England and Wales, the legal framework for dealing with juvenile offenders in court has changed significantly over the past ten years with a succession of Criminal Justice Acts (1982, 1988, 1991) being passed by Parliament. These Acts sought both to restrict the courts' use of custody while expanding the noncustodial sentencing options available. This former policy intention has been revised with the implementation of the Criminal Justice and Public Order Act of 1994 and subsequent legislation.

Sentencing practice in the English youth court has shown a decline in the absolute and proportionate use of custody for juveniles over the past ten years. Over 50% of youth court outcomes continue to be the more traditional disposals of fines and discharges rather than the more recently introduced "mid-tariff" options. Whereas the powers to impose penalties on the parents of juvenile offenders have increased in the decade, these have yet to see a significant role in court outcomes. (The parents were ordered to pay their child's fine in 11% of 1995 cases involving 10–17-year-olds.)

Disparity in outcomes continues to be a feature of court sentencing. Official recognition of the need to secure a more consistent approach across courts has led to increased emphasis in the Home Office criminal statistics on sentencing disparity. In 1994, for example, the proportionate use of custody for 14–17-year-old males sentenced in magistrates courts varied from 4% in North Wales to 16% in Humberside.

Such sentencing patterns reflect the continuing research finding that different panels of magistrates adopt a distinctive ethos toward juvenile offenders (Parker, Sumner, & Jarvis, 1994). Such variations remain, despite enhanced training initiatives and even controlling for the different mix of offenses and offenders coming before the courts (Ashworth, 1997). Tighter controls have also been introduced by government in an attempt to reduce the effect of extraneous influences on sentencers. Monitoring of racial basis in sentencing outcomes, introduced by the 1991 Criminal Justice Act, is intended to affect the prevailing disparity in outcomes experienced by minority ethnic groups, particularly blacks (Hood, 1992). Research continues to show similar disparities in the sentencing of females, the overall picture of leniency in sentencing concealing a trend toward severity with respect to minority females (Farrington & Morris, 1983).

Significant changes have also been introduced with respect to the information routinely provided to sentencers on the background and history of offenders being sentenced. In contrast to traditional welfare approaches to dealing with young offenders in juvenile courts, where broad-based "social inquiries" would be made of their family, social, and educational environment (Morris & Giller, 1987), courts now focus on the offending behavior, past and present. "Presentence reports," as they are called, are accompanied with National Standards published by the Home Office that seek to ensure that report writers (social workers and probation officers) approach the construction of such reports more consistently in both form and content. Available evidence suggests that limiting the focus of the report may assist in minimizing the biases that may otherwise influence sentencers (Gelsthorpe & Raynor, 1995).

In conclusion to this section on the processing of offenses, it remains the case that, for a number of reasons, only an indirect relationship between delinquent behavior and official statistics exists. This is now widely acknowledged, but more is known about the various influences on this processing. We have focused, in the interests of simplicity, on the situation in England and Wales, but close parallels exist in other countries.

Differences between Offenders and Non-Offenders

Are there differences between offenders and non-offenders? This can be split into several related questions, to which we return throughout the course of this book. The first concerns the differences between those who offend at all and those who do not, regardless of who is prosecuted. A second concerns the differences between *official* offenders and those who do not get caught. A third (e.g., Cernkovich et al., 1985) concerns the differences between those who commit major and minor offenses, the assumption being that the salient feature is the seriousness of the offense rather than the offending itself.

A wealth of material exists relating to the task of differentiating offenders from non-offenders. We return to this in Chapter 5, where we explore the evidence for heterogeneity in antisocial behavior. In brief, there are particular problems with the question itself. One of these is the very high base rate of delinquent behavior in the general population. With some 80% of young men admitting to breaking the law to varying degrees, it may be difficult to identify key variables that distinguish them from the remainder. However, if offending behavior is treated as a continuum, with those who do not offend at all at one end and persistent offenders at the other, then there may be other points on this continuum where it makes more sense to seek to distinguish between groups. Indeed, it may not even be a continuum but, if there is a break in the distribution, it is likely to be at some point other than between the non-offenders and the remainder. Delinquency itself is thus unlikely to be the defining characteristic that distinguishes groups of young people. Other factors – such as age of onset, overlap with hyperactivity, or very persistent behavior – might imply more meaningful, discrete groups. Rutter and Giller (1983) concluded that it remained unclear at that time whether a categorical or dimensional approach made most sense. Recent research on different *types* of offending behavior and overlaps with other problems is beginning to suggest that certain categorical distinctions may be useful. Such distinctions are not, however, without controversy.

Turning to the distinction of offenders according to whether or not they have been caught, different concerns and conclusions are evident. Earlier in this chapter the evidence for the prevalence of offending was examined, particularly that from self-report studies. The subsequent section on variations in processing outlined various places within the criminal justice system where the discretion of its representatives can affect the process – from committing an offense to being sentenced. Putting together this information leads to a question concerning the ways in which official delinquents differ from the non-official delinquents. Rutter and Giller (1983) firmly rejected the view that official delinquents do not differ from official non-delinquents. For example, earlier research showed that official delinquents had been involved in more delinquent activities than those who had not been caught by the police. Recent evidence continues to suggest that some people are more likely than others to be caught up in any part of the criminal justice system – because they offend more and also for other reasons (e.g., being from a minority ethnic group). Thus, the chance of a young offender being processed by the police is not completely random. However, the overall correlation between self-report and official records suggests that, although some variations may exist, official records provide a sufficient approximation of underlying behavior.

Persistent Young Offenders

Much of what has been written in this chapter does concern persistent young offenders, but renewed U.S. and European public interest on the topic justifies a separate section specifically pulling together some of the issues raised. The majority of young offenders have only a few convictions, and it is widely accepted that the few who are very persistent account for a high proportion of offenses (Blumstein et al., 1985, 1986; Farrington, 1996; Graham & Bowling, 1995; Hagell & Newburn, 1994; Home Office, 1995d; Thornberry et al., 1995; Tracy et al., 1990; West & Farrington, 1973; Wolfgang, Figlio, & Stelim, 1972; Wolfgang et al., 1987). The issue is not that this group accounts for a disproportionate number of crimes, since that is what one would expect to be the case even if offending in the general population were distributed normally. The question concerns the size of the proportion, with the difficulties mainly involving matters of definition (Blumstein et al., 1985, 1986). Although studies specifically addressing the question of persistent offending are still relatively infrequent and tend to have major limitations of design, some conclusions can be drawn.

Identifying persistent young offenders at an early stage in their career remains a major difficulty, and considerable confusion about the cutoff for "persistence" remains. In their much-cited study, Wolfgang et al. (1972) used number of arrests as a method of identifying persistent offenders, although they referred to them as "chronic." In their study, the authors suggested that the chronic offenders, who had been arrested five times or more, represented 6% of their cohort of 10,000 boys in Philadelphia. Tracy et al. (1990) reported similar results in a different cohort. In the Cambridge Study of Delinquency, the more extreme group of offenders were also referred to as "chronic" – defined as having reported six convictions by the age of 18 – and this group constituted 5% of the cohort (Farrington, 1995a; West & Farrington, 1973). In a study based on police and legislative definitions of persistence and focusing on one year's offending only, Hagell and Newburn (1994) reported that approximately 1 in 250 young people aged between 10 and 16 (both males and females) were arrested three times or more, suggesting that this was a far harsher criterion than previous studies. However, Hagell and Newburn referred to this group as "reoffenders," preserving the term "persistent" for an even smaller (and still difficult to classify) proportion of the reoffenders. Graham and Bowling (1995) reported that 3% of offenders in their national random sample of 14–25-year-olds were responsible for 26% of self-reported offenses in one year. Magnusson, af Klinteberg, and Stattin (1994) used the term to suggest lifetime rather than adolescent persistence, and in their Swedish study used "persistent" to refer to those who had an officially recorded offense in both their teenage and adult years.

Not surprisingly, given the variations in definitions, estimates of the proportion of offenses accounted for by the persistent groups also vary. In his original study, Wolfgang's chronic offenders accounted for half of the offenses of the whole group of 10,000 boys (Wolfgang et al., 1972), as did the chronic offenders in the Cambridge Study (Farrington, 1995a). Graham and Bowling's 3% of offenders accounted for about one quarter of offenses committed by the sample. Hagell and Newburn's reoffenders, who are not unlike the Philadelphia and Cambridge "chronics," accounted for half of the offending in their areas in the year of study, but those defined as "persistent" (average 11–13 arrests a year) accounted for only about 10% (at most) of local offenses. Because young offenders may be responsible for anything from one offense to hundreds, it follows inevitably on statistical grounds that a small proportion of offenders will be responsible for a large proportion of offenses. The exact proportions may be in doubt, but the general conclusion is not. The key issue does not concern the reality of the phenomenon (which is clear-cut) but rather the two further issues of how to define "chronic" offenders and whether they differ meaningfully from one-time offenders.

What are persistent offenders like? Do they differ from less frequent offenders? Where studies have looked at persistent offenders, their patterns seem to suggest that they are broadly similar to other offenders but show their characteristics to a much greater degree (Blumstein et al., 1985, 1986; Farrington & West, 1993). Thus they are more likely to be male and more likely to have started younger (Junger-Tas & Block, 1988) but, on the basis of limited evidence, it does not seem that the profile of offenses committed differs much (Hagell & Newburn, 1994; Weitekamp et al., 1996). The general focus on frequency rather than severity of offending has thus been claimed to be misleading by overemphasizing the dangerousness of persistent offenders to the general public (Weitekamp et al., 1996). The picture emerging suggests that they will have more educational problems (Farrington, 1995a; Hagell & Newburn, 1994; Junger-Tas & Block, 1988), lower levels of social integration (Junger-Tas & Block, 1988), more disrupted family backgrounds and experience of institutional care (Hagell & Newburn, 1994), and are likely to have more developmental difficulties of one type or another, including hyperactivity (Magnusson et al., 1994), which we will investigate further in the next chapter. It has been pointed out that, like ethnicity, persistence is a self-perpetuating definition, since young people with more serious behavior run a higher risk of being officially recorded (Junger-Tas & Block, 1988). Nevertheless, the empirical findings are clear-cut in showing that chronic offenders are, in numerous ways, a much more deviant group (in both their individual characteristics and their experience of other factors) than one-time offenders.

The question of how to define "chronicity" is, however, much more difficult, as Hagell and Newburn's (1994) study showed. From a policy perspective, it might be tempting to think that a substantial proportion of crime might be prevented by locking up chronic offenders for long periods. We consider this issue in greater detail in Chapter 12, but the point to be made here is that it is much easier to identify the chronic offenders after they have been followed over time for many years (as in the longitudinal studies) than at the time they first come before the courts. With as many as a third of males receiving a conviction, and some half of those being convicted twice, it would not be feasible to incapacitate one in six of the male population. Also, as we have noted, by no means are all chronic offenders serious offenders, so that prolonged spells of incarceration would be difficult to justify.

Conclusions

In this chapter we have sought to clarify the main ways in which juvenile offending has been conceptualized, how such concepts vary from country to country and at different ages, the ways in which delinquency is measured, and the various influences on the procedure that produces the official and self-report measures. In the intervening years since the 1983 review, the volume of material published on the topic has grown considerably, and certain methodological advances have been made.

We have shown how both the quality and understanding of official published statistics have improved. However, the ways in which offenses are recorded, classified, and counted are far from intuitive and are open to various biases. Consequently, the relationship of these figures to the "dark figure" of offending in the real world remains not entirely clear, but the development of victim surveys has helped to identify certain areas of discrepancy between the original reports of offenses and the final pattern of official statistics relating to sentencing of young offenders. Different writers have varying perspectives on the question of an underlying reality, but the results from most studies tend to emphasize that official statistics reflect a process of perceptions, decisions, and social interactions as much as any underlying "real" event. This is not to deny that official statistics are a useful source of information. Police research has continued to clarify the effect of police and judicial discretion on the processing of young offenders, and it is obvious that there is a great deal of variation that depends on a range of individual, cultural, and structural variables.

Developments in self-report studies, particularly the initiation of the international self-report study, have clarified methodological problems inherent in this type of research and have begun the very difficult task of making cross-national comparisons. In many ways, the most striking findings from this study have been the similarities in national patterns rather than the differences, although the latter are very great with respect to the use of guns. International comparisons of offending rates are still in their infancy, but pressure to make such comparisons is on the increase and is likely to be a major headache in the near future.

Because young offenders do not always get caught, many crimes go unreported. Because the system treats some people differently, and because self-report accounts of offending will not be totally accurate, we cannot really be totally confident about the nature of adolescent crime. However, there are certain familiar patterns emerging with enough regularity from different sources that some conclusions can be drawn – most notably, that juveniles (under 18) account for approximately a quarter of offenses, that young men commit more offenses than young women and the majority of these are theft-related, and that the peak age (at least for young men) is about 15 to 18 years. The question of whether official young offenders are different from those not caught is a little more difficult. Certainly, a small group accounts for a disproportionate amount of crime, but estimates vary and descriptive information concerning more persistent groups is surprisingly rare. In subsequent chapters, we will return to the question of whether offending behavior by young people is distributed on a continuum or whether distinct groups exist within the distribution. We will see that the data suggest a continuum to some degree, but also suggest that the extremes – the most persistent, for example, or the most hyperactive – appear to be rather different.

CHAPTER 3 – SUMMARY OF MAIN POINTS

❑ Crime is a *moving target*. Establishing definitions, overall levels, and historical trends all involve estimates rather than facts. Each source of information is subject to different biases and distortions. The vast majority of antisocial behaviors do not become official statistics. Combining sources of information (official statistics, self-report data, victimization studies, etc.) helps to build a more complete picture of underlying behavior patterns.

Levels of Participation

❑ Official statistics and victim surveys show that *juveniles* (under 18) account for approximately one fourth to one third of offenses in England, Wales, and the United States.

❑ British official statistics indicate that approximately *a third of adult men* will have a criminal record by the time they reach their mid-30s, mostly acquired as juveniles. Self-report studies suggest higher levels of delinquency among the juvenile population: an estimated 50% to 80% of males participate in antisocial behavior at some time, but importantly most of these behaviors are less serious than those recorded in the official statistics.

❑ Most delinquency is minor and fleeting. Serious and persistent offending is shown by only a *very small minority* of young people. Identifying and defining persistent young offenders remains a major difficulty. That this group accounts for a disproportionate amount of juvenile crime is indisputable, but the exact proportion is unclear, ranging between 10% and 50% of juvenile offending.

Type of Participation

❑ Most juvenile crime is *theft-related*. Studies based on official statistics in the Netherlands, the United Kingdom, and Sweden have all shown that approximately half of offenses by young men were types of theft. Self-report studies suggest that this proportion is even higher, with the majority of detected and undetected offending by young people being theft-related.

❑ Only a small proportion of juvenile crime is *violent* (e.g., approximately 10% of all U.K. juvenile crime in 1995). Self-report data show that these offenses account for a small proportion of overall offending, but many offenders have committed at least one violent offense at some time in their criminal career.

❑ Crimes involving a *weapon* vary greatly among countries. Those involving a gun are some 15 times higher in the United States than in Europe.

❑ The *peak age* of offending is usually in the late teens. In the United Kingdom, for example, the official statistics suggest that it is 18 for young men and 15 for young women. These rates differ by country and by source: self-report data in the United Kingdom have suggested that the peak age is 21 for males and 18 for females.

4 | Historical Trends

Setting Out the Issues

Concern over growing levels of crime and the numbers of young offenders has been present for many years and is not abating. The problems inherent in tracking time trends in offending by young people remain, but they have proved soluble to a worthwhile degree. In this chapter we attempt to set out some of the main international developments in the rates and types of juvenile delinquency over the last 50 years, and to set these in the context of the broader picture of trends in psychosocial disorders. Is the current level of concern over increasing rates of juvenile crime justified? Have rates actually gone up over the last half century? Has crime committed by young people changed at all in terms of the types of offenses committed and, if there are any changes in overall level or types of crimes, to what can these be attributed?

We begin by describing the evidence on the time trends in crime rates both overall and for juveniles. We go on to look at contemporaneous changes in juvenile justice systems around the world in order to see how these relate to some of the trends in the official statistics. Crime is not the only indicator of rising rates of difficulties for adolescents, and developments in psychosocial disorders of young people generally are also described. The social context in which childhood and adolescence is played out has changed dramatically over recent decades, and the dimensions of this are examined. Finally, a description of the ongoing debate concerning the causes for any or all of these trends is provided.

Trends in Crime Taken as a Whole

We have already discussed, in the previous chapter, some of the problems inherent in relating trends in official or self-report statistics to the actual behavior of individuals. Official statistics are the main source of information on time trends (because they have been collected for longer), but we have discussed the ways in which these statistics might be distorted by factors other than levels of crime (such as reporting biases, the operation of police discretion, different legal definitions, and varying ages of responsibility). Nevertheless, we concluded that official statistics remain a useful indicator of underlying trends, and that increased understanding of the factors affecting them has clarified systematic biases and also provided the means of dealing with them.

However, even if the data are accepted as a reasonable reflection of underlying behavior, it remains the case that there are major problems comparing trends in crime across time and countries. For example, since 1950, statistics have been collated by the International Criminal Police Organization (Interpol); these were recently analyzed by David Smith (1995). Not only are the figures actually rather difficult to obtain, there are also several serious difficulties with their interpretation. First, they were based on replies to an official form circulated by Interpol, and each country reported on their own statistics – which are, of course, based on national legal definitions. Thus, for example, different countries might have different definitions and classifications of theft. Different countries certainly define juveniles differently, as we have already seen, and collating rates of crime for juveniles as a whole is not possible: in some cases this might refer to a group aged 10–16, in other cases a group aged 15–19. Second, countries have gaps in their returns to Interpol, and a continuous picture cannot be constructed without filling in data from other sources. Third, the crime classification by Interpol was changed in 1977, making a continuous time series difficult. The only solution to these limitations in official statistics is to check the direction and magnitude of the trends identified against trends in other types of related behaviors and events, such as the reports of victims or trends in psychosocial disorders generally. This does not provide a foolproof check, but it does ensure that we make the best use of the rather limited data available.

Starting with the official statistics and looking at data sources such as Interpol, there is little doubt that – at least until the last few years – crime rates have been on a steady rise over the last half of the twentieth century, with few national exceptions. Recent reviews (e.g., Farrington, 1992, 1996; Smith, 1995; Wilson & Herrnstein, 1985) have confirmed the earlier analysis by Rutter and Giller (1983) that the rise has occurred and also that the explanations for it are elusive and complicated. From his analyses of selected countries, Smith concluded that there was a huge increase for nearly all countries in the levels of crime, and that this continued up to the point at which he stopped collating data (in 1990). Over the whole 40-year period of his study, the greatest increases in total crime rate were in Spain (by a factor of 29) and Canada (by a factor of 27). Rises for Sweden and Norway were also high (the factors were 14 and 13, respectively), whereas

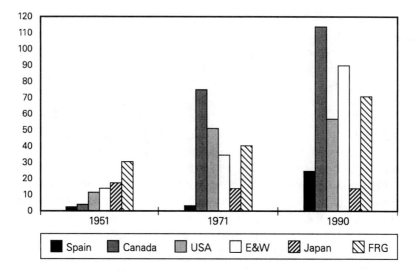

Figure 4.1. International trends in total recorded offenses, 1951–90 (rates per 1,000 population). *Note:* The 1971 U.S. figure represents 1977 data (1971 data unavailable); 1990 figure for Spain represents 1993 data (1990 data unavailable). *Source:* Adapted from Smith (1995, p. 401).

for all other countries (Australia, England, France, Germany, Italy, the Netherlands, and the United States) the increases were of a factor from one to six. There was one exception to this trend: in Japan, crime rates have remained fairly stable over the past 40 years. The country comparisons based on the Interpol figures for 1951, 1971, and 1990 are shown in Figure 4.1.

Looking at one example in a little more detail, the picture every year since the 1950s for England and Wales is shown in Figure 4.2. Notifiable (reasonably serious) offenses per 100,000 members of the population clearly and dramatically increased over the period, quadrupling between the early 1950s and the late 1970s, and then doubling again by the early 1990s.

However, as this graph indicates, trends began to look a little different in the late 1980s and 1990s. Crime has continued to rise, but perhaps more slowly, and in some instances has shown a decline. Overall, during the more restricted time frame of 1980 to 1990, Smith's (1995) international analyses showed that more countries recorded a slight fall rather than a continuing rise for these years. In the United States, Canada, and Australia, a decline was reported for the 1980s. Recent figures from the Home

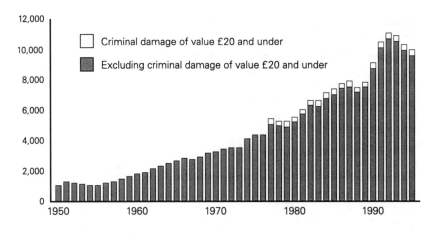

Figure 4.2. Notifiable offenses recorded by the police (per 100,000 population) in England and Wales, 1950–90. *Source:* Home Office (1996, p. 29).

Office criminal statistics (Home Office, 1996) show that the choice of time period can influence perspectives on change.

Table 4.1 shows an 8% decrease in recorded crime between 1993 and 1995 reported for England and Wales, which was accompanied by decreases of between 1% and 8% in Scotland, France, Germany, Austria, the Netherlands, Denmark, Greece, the United States, Canada, and Australia, despite the fact that all of these countries had reported increases for the longer seven-year period (since 1987). Rises for the 1993–95 period were still reported for Northern Ireland, the Republic of Ireland, Portugal, Italy, and New Zealand (Home Office, 1996).

The slightly different pattern noted in the Home Office comparisons for these most recent years was also confirmed in a report based on national responses to the Fourth United Nations Survey on Crime Trends (Kangaspunta, 1995). The author concluded that the amount of recorded crime had continued to increase in Europe and the United States over this period, but that the trend from 1986 to 1990 appeared to be less uniform than in previous years; more countries reported declines than increases for the crimes of theft, burglary, and robbery. However, they did also note that the amount of recorded crime increased dramatically in Central and Eastern European countries over this period.

For the more recent period, we can turn to victim surveys to check the trends seen in the official statistics. As we saw in Chapter 3, repeated sweeps of various crime surveys that interview members of the public about their experiences of crime (e.g., the BCS, NCVS, and ICS) have

Table 4.1. Percentage Changes in Crime
Recorded by the Police

Country	1987–95	1993–95
England and Wales	31	−8
Northern Ireland	8	4
Scotland	4	−7
Republic of Ireland	20	4
France	16	−6
Germany[a]	—	−1
Austria	24	−1
Netherlands	8	−4
Denmark	3	−1
Finland	21	—
Portugal	—	6
Italy	21	1
Greece	9	−8
United States	2	−3
Canada	12	−3
Australia	12	−2
New Zealand	25	1

[a] Comparison based on West Germany only.
Crown copyright is reproduced with the permission
of the Controller of Her Majesty's Stationery Office.

shown primarily that the official figures are a substantial underestimate, but also that fluctuations in the overall levels in the police statistics are less obvious in self-reported victimization. In the United Kingdom, for example, the British Crime Survey estimated that between 1981 and 1993, for those crimes that could be compared, the numbers increased by 77% – less than the 111% reflected in police statistics for this period. More recently, when the police statistics reported a fall in crime rates, this was not reflected in the BCS although the *rate* of increase did slow down in the crime survey over the same period. The most recent BCS analyses show that, between 1993 and 1995, when the number of crimes recorded by the police actually fell by 8%, reports of experiences of crime in the victim survey still rose by 2% (Mirrlees-Black et al., 1996). Victim surveys tend to reflect a higher overall level of crime (with many more offenses reported than in the official statistics), as well as a more even trend, than do official statistics.

BOX 4.1. POSTWAR TRENDS IN CRIME

- The postwar period has witnessed a general pattern of rising crime rates, which has been a pervasive phenomenon in most Western societies. The main exception to the trend has been in Japan, where crime has remained at much the same level since World War II.

- Comparisons between rates in 1980 and the early 1990s show a continuing overall increase in crime levels throughout the decade, particularly in Eastern and Central Europe.

- However, in the *late* 1980s, decreases were seen in the United States, Canada, and Australia. Most recently, falls in crime in the United Kingdom have been reported. Whether these are part of a long-term trend is unclear.

- Data from sources other than the official statistics are not widely available until the 1980s, but these support a continued rise during the decade. So far, however, they do not tend to support the most recent trends for a fall in crime. Overall, victim surveys have tended to show an *overall level* of crime that is higher than in the official statistics, but a less dramatic *pattern* of rise and fall.

In short, despite the fact that we must rely on official statistics for the longer time span, it is clear that the postwar period has been one of rising crime rates, a pervasive phenomenon in most Western societies. See Box 4.1. The main exception to the trend has been in Japan, where crime has remained at much the same level since World War II. However, more recently these trends have become less clear, with many countries reporting a slight decrease in crime since the early 1990s.

Does Juvenile Crime Reflect the Same Trends?

Analyses of the contribution of juveniles to the postwar rises in crime have concluded that, given the overall picture, it is most unlikely that offending by juveniles has fallen when the overall rises were so dramatic, since about a quarter of crime is committed by juveniles (Farrington, 1996; Home Affairs Committee, 1993; Smith, 1995). However, when we try to untangle the particular contribution of young offenders to this overall picture, it is obvious that the situation is more complicated than widespread reports of an ongoing (if leveling) rise in crime would suggest. Particularly in recent years, even where overall rises are reported, it seems that in some countries the numbers of juveniles going through the system has remained static or even fallen.

In exploring the relationship between juvenile crime and overall levels of crime, the focus has tended to be on the last 15 years, when alternative sources of data on behavior by young people are also available. Starting with the official statistics, and looking at the United Kingdom as an example, despite increases in recorded crimes over the 1980s, the figures for the numbers of all individuals convicted or cautioned for indictable offenses showed a *slight* fall (from 556,000 in 1980 to 540,000 in 1990). However, the numbers of juveniles found guilty or cautioned for indictable offenses per 100,000 population fell, between 1984 and 1994, by 44% for males aged 10–13 and by 19% for males aged 14–17.†

There are three potential reasons for the disparity between the juvenile and the overall statistics in the 1980s. First, it is possible that, in spite of an overall rise in crime, there was less committed by young offenders. Testing this suggestion is virtually impossible because police clear-up rates are so low (only a quarter of U.K. offenses were cleared up in 1995). It is true that, in the United Kingdom in the mid 1990s, young offenders (aged 10–17) represented 26% of all known offenders, compared with 36% of all offenders a decade earlier. The proportion accounted for by slightly older offenders (aged 18–20) remained the same (17%).

There is some limited evidence, to which we return later in the chapter, that the peak age of offending for males may be getting later – and that this might be related to trends in education, training, and employment – but in this case we would expect the proportion accounted for by offenders in their late teens to have risen more substantially. In addition, analyses of the U.K. offender index, where the criminal careers of successive cohorts are traced, does not indicate that later cohorts were more likely than earlier cohorts to start offending as adults. It is not possible to tell from the victim surveys whether the proportion of crime accounted for by young people has dropped, because the age of the perpetrator is not recorded and in most cases would be unknown. It should also be noted that, in North America, a reversal of the trends in Europe were witnessed. Whereas U.S. recorded crime fell overall between 1980 and 1990 (Smith, 1995), between 1985 and 1994 the proportion of arrests of juveniles (compared to adults) *rose* slightly in most offense categories (Snyder et al., 1996). It seems more likely that the disparities are due to differences in processing than to changes in the proportion of crime accounted for by juveniles.

---

† For females, the number for 10–13-year-olds fell by 11%, but the number for 14–17-year-olds rose by 28%.

Another way to tackle this first hypothesis (that offending by juveniles has fallen) is to look at the self-report data and data relating to trends in the underlying behavior problems associated with offending. As outlined in Chapter 3, in self-report studies of offending, individuals are asked in confidence whether they have committed crimes for which they have and have not been caught. Depending on various factors (age, location, social characteristics, wording of the questions), self-report studies have found that between 50% and 100% of samples will admit to having committed at least one offense during their lifetimes (Farrington, 1989; Graham & Bowling, 1995; Maguire, 1997). Unfortunately, statistics tracking trends over time are still not readily available from these types of study. Preliminary results from the first international self-report delinquency study (Junger-Tas, Terlouw, & Klein, 1994) confirmed high rates of self-reported offending, but that study was likewise cross-sectional.

American studies of trends in behavior problems have included the Epidemiological Catchment Area (ECA) study (Robins & Regier, 1991). This study measured conduct disorder generally, rather than juvenile delinquency specifically, but results did show a rise in conduct disturbances by comparing recall from different age groups. The youngest groups recalled the highest rates of behavior problems. In a study of successive cohorts of young people in Pittsburgh, Loeber et al. (1996) found that the boys in the youngest cohort were at a greater risk for developing serious delinquency at a younger age than were boys in the middle or oldest cohorts. This difference between cohorts in delinquency might reflect variations in sampling. Nevertheless, the studies do not support the hypothesis that the underlying trend is for a reduction in antisocial behavior by young people.

The second potential explanation, then, is that the disparity between the overall rise in crime and the decrease in juvenile offenders (seen in Europe, at least – Kangaspunta, 1995; Kyvsgaard, 1991) could be attributed to the growth of diversionary practices such as "prison write-offs" and "informal cautions," whereby minor crimes are cleared with a minimum of official fuss, or to other forms of reaction to juvenile delinquency, rather than to changes in the underlying behavior (Farrington, 1992, 1996; Maguire, 1997). Reporting on official statistics in the Netherlands between 1970 and 1982, Junger-Tas and Block (1988) faced distinct problems disentangling criminal justice effects from underlying rates. Thus, the numbers of children (per 10,000) who were adjudicated against remained constant between the two dates, but there were substantial increases in those who entered the juvenile justice system but were subsequently dismissed and not prosecuted. One possibility is that more offenses were officially reported. It is not clear whether more were committed. Later in this chapter we return to the relationship between criminal justice procedures and perceptions of crime trends. Although the two are subject to quite different external influences, it is obvious that they also interact in a way that distorts the picture of underlying behavior change.

Third, it has been suggested that the reduction in the number of juvenile offenders, set against an increase in crime, reflects a growth in the number of persistent or repeat offenders in the juvenile population (e.g., House of Commons Select Committee on Juvenile Offending, 1993). The data necessary to prove or disprove this theory are simply not available. Even if studies of repeat-offender cohorts existed, disentangling the effect of the rapidly changing criminal justice policies would be extremely difficult.

In conclusion, we cannot say for certain if juvenile crime has risen overall in the last few years, although it certainly did rise during the 1950s to 1980s. It seems likely – from the overall official crime statistics and from victim surveys – that there has continued to be a rise in the offenses for which juveniles are most often guilty, despite falls in the numbers of juveniles formally processed or convicted in some systems. Studies of behavior problems in young people suggest that these are rising rather than falling. Because of this, and owing to the likely impact of policy changes regarding the ways in which juveniles were treated by justice systems over the 1980s and early 1990s, it seems likely that neither the steepest increases (e.g., in the United States) nor the greatest declines (e.g., during the late 1980s in the United Kingdom) in officially recorded juvenile crime closely reflected changes in juvenile behavior (Farrington, 1996; Smith, 1995).

Has the Nature of Offending by Juveniles Been Changing?

A rather different issue concerns changes in the types of offenses being committed by young people, and changes in the development of offending behavior. In this section we look at the evidence (i) that some types of offenses attributed to juveniles are more common than they used to be, (ii) that the ratio of offending rate between the sexes is still falling, (iii) that there have been changes in the interaction between gender and offense type, and (iv) that the peak age of offending is increasing.

Changes in the Types of Crimes Committed

For these trends we must rely largely on offenses that have been cleared up and attributed to a known individual. Very few longitudinal studies have used multiple cohorts and have detailed enough measures of offending to allow comparisons across time for particular offense types. However, several trends are obvious enough to suggest they reflect a real change. The first of these is the rise of certain types of offenses and the fall of others. Many European countries reported a relatively small but clear rise in violent offenses (including robbery) over the 1980s and 1990s but decreases in burglary, theft, and criminal damage (Junger-Tas, 1995a; Kangaspunta, 1995). In the Netherlands, for example, rates of violence against persons committed by juveniles increased between 1978 and 1982 from 5.9 to 6.7 per 10,000 children aged 12–17 (Junger-Tas, 1995a). In an analysis of trends in assault offenses between 1913 and 1993 in Sweden, Hofer (1995) concluded that "it seems difficult to deny that the Swedish society in recent years has been hit by a breaker of juvenile violence" (p. 1). However, he also concluded that, in the past 10–15 years, the picture has become less clear and figures have been complicated by a wave of law enforcement and public panic about juvenile violence that may have disturbed the statistics.

There was a somewhat similar trend in the United Kingdom between 1985 and 1995 (Home Office, 1986, 1996). Whereas the 1995 juvenile offenders committed fewer offenses as a whole, more were found guilty of violence: some 9,000 out of 81,000, compared with some 8,000 out of 96,000 for the 1985 offenders. However, caution is needed in interpreting the difference because the 1995 figures included 17-year-olds whereas the 1985 ones did not.

The more dramatic recent rise in violent offenses committed by juveniles in the United States has received a great deal of attention. Analyses of the FBI statistics showed that, after a period of some stability in the early 1980s, the juvenile violent crime arrest rate soared between 1988 and 1994 by more than 50% (Snyder et al., 1996). Interestingly, trends in juvenile arrests for specific violent crimes showed different patterns, with the clearest rises for aggravated assault and murder and less clear increases in rape and robbery. (This pattern was also reflected in European countries over the same period; Junger-Tas, 1995a). Robbery rates actually declined for most of the 1980s (Snyder et al., 1996).

It is important, however, to keep the statistics on juvenile violence in perspective. Even though between a third and a half of frequent offenders have a violent offense on their records (Hagell & Newburn, 1994; Loeber, Farrington, & Waschbusch, 1998; Thornberry et al., 1995), it is still true that, overall, violence forms a very small part of the arrest profiles of juvenile delinquents (Home Office, 1996; Snyder et al., 1996). Whatever the baseline, however, the evidence does suggest that violence by young people is on the increase.

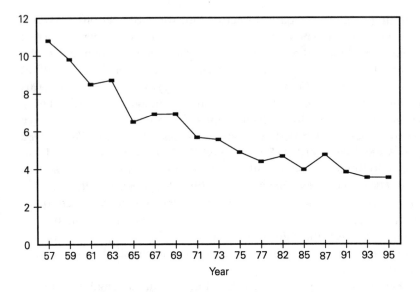

Figure 4.3. Male/female offending ratio (cautions and convictions) for 14–17-year-olds in the United Kingdom, 1957–95. *Sources:* Data from Rutter and Giller (1983); Home Office (1996). Crown copyright is reproduced with the permission of the Controller of Her Majesty's Stationery Office.

Changes in the Sex Ratios

Changes in the ratio between male and female young offenders can be clearly identified internationally over recent decades. Young women account for an increasing proportion of juvenile offenses, and this is reflected in, for example, official statistics from England and Wales (Home Office, 1996), the Netherlands (Junger-Tas & Block, 1988) and the United States (Snyder et al., 1996). The English and Welsh ratios for the years from 1957 to 1995 are presented in Figure 4.3. The very steep decline in the sex ratio in the postwar decades, which was noted by Rutter and Giller (1983), leveled off in the 1980s but began to decline again in the 1990s. It had fallen from approximately 11 : 1 in the late 1950s to approximately 6 : 1 in the early 1970s, and in 1995 it stood at 3.6 : 1. Similarly, using the Netherlands data, Junger-Tas showed the greatest increase in participation by young women to be in the 1970s (Junger-Tas & Block, 1988).

Changes in the Type–Gender Relationship

The question of an increase in violence by young women has been of particular interest recently, with several cases of girl gangs receiving widespread media attention on both sides of the Atlantic. It must be re-membered that the rate of participation by girls is minor when compared to that of boys. The U.K. official statistics do show a rise in violence by women (Home Office, 1996; they also show a rise in violence by young of-fenders generally), but the base rate is so low that a relatively small num-ber of cases can make a great deal of difference. A 250% increase between 1984 and 1994 in violence against another person in fact constitutes only an extra 4,000 or so cases per year by 1995, a tiny proportion of the female population. Many of these offenses were cases of assault (rather than rob-bery), and Junger-Tas (1995a) has suggested that female violence (result-ing in an offense) tends to be expressive – and less serious – than male violence, which has a greater tendency to be instrumental. In the United States, female juvenile violent crime arrests more than doubled between 1985 and 1994, constituting 11% of juvenile arrests for violent crime in 1985 and 14% in 1994 (Snyder et al., 1996). Thus, violence did not simply rise overall; the proportion accounted for by females also rose. Snyder and Sickmund (1995) also reported that a small proportion (6%) of gang mem-bers reported by law enforcement agencies in 1992 were female, but com-parative statistics were not available.

Changes in the Peak Age of Offending

One of the most interesting developments in offending by young peo-ple over recent years is the change in the peak age of offending. Despite long-held and rigidly adhered-to theories concerning the "invariant" na-ture of the relationship between age and crime (Hirschi & Gottfredson, 1983), there is recent evidence that the relationship is changing. This is obvious, for example, in a comparison of the peak age of offending in the United Kingdom in recent years (Home Office, 1988). As Figure 4.4 shows, the peak age of offending for young men rose from 14 in 1972 to 18 in 1995. For young women the trends are different, and in the United Kingdom the peak age has remained steady at around age 14 or 15. Some support for this comes from recent self-report studies. A recent Home Of-fice self-report study (Graham & Bowling, 1995) found the peak age for offending was 21 years for males and 16 years for females. However, these findings varied within and between the gender groups, depending on the type of offense admitted. For males, the peak age of expressive property offenses was 14, 16 for violent behavior, 17 for serious offenses, and 20 for drug and acquisitive property offenses. For females, the peak age of offending was 15 for property, expressive, and serious offenses; 16 for vio-lent offenses; and 17 for drug offenses. These self-report responses were elicited retrospectively and were not checked against official records, so

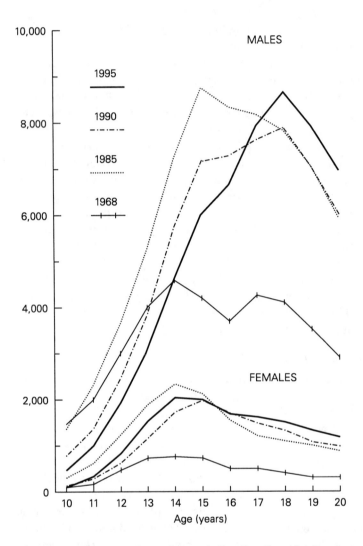

Figure 4.4. Changes in the peak age of offending (found guilty of or cautioned for indictable offenses) for persons aged under 21 in England and Wales, 1968–95 (per 100,000 population). *Source:* Home Office (1997a; line for 1968 data estimated from earlier Home Office graph). Crown copyright is reproduced with the permission of the Controller of Her Majesty's Stationery Office.

it is difficult to be sure of the extent to which they may be affected by factual and temporal distortion caused by recall or memory problems.

Several writers have suggested that the peak age of offending is related to adolescent milestones such as finishing full-time education. Setting offending within a life-course perspective, which emphasizes the social forces influencing development (a perspective most persuasively stated by Elder, 1994, 1995; see also Conger & Elder, 1994), it has been argued that the peak age of offending is closely related to the timing of events in the transition from dependence to independence, including the compulsory school-leaving age and transition into the labor market. As we have seen, the age at which this transition is reached in Western Europe has been increasing steadily, in a way that mirrors the peak age of offending for males. As part of an innovative attempt to set offending behavior in the context of the life cycle – that is, subject to changing intergenerational processes and social forces – two writers have recently documented the timing of and developments in delinquent behavior in Japan (Harada, 1995) and Germany (Schumann, 1995). Particular features of the Japanese educational system are held to be responsible, by Harada, for a sharp peak in offending behavior in early adolescence and a rapid decline thereafter. Based on a similar premise, Schumann argued that the system in Germany – which allows a very prolonged transition from education, through vocational training, and into the labor market – results in a later peak and longer tail for offending behavior by young Germans.

These changes in the peak age, like all other features of the crime statistics, will to some extent reflect changes in criminal justice policy and practice, such as changes in recording practices and "informal" actions with apprehended offenders (Farrington & Burrows, 1993). It is crucial to keep a close eye on these changes in the peak age, as they may reveal critical influences on criminal behavior, and to untangle the relative contributions of broader social changes and those within criminal justice policy.

To conclude, this section on trends in offending by young people has highlighted three main findings.

- Offending by juveniles must be set against a background of rising rates of crime in some countries over the period since 1980, but these trends were less clear and less pervasive in the 1980s and early 1990s than they had generally been in the postwar period. In particular, some falls have been noted in the countries of North America.
- After policy and practice variations are taken into account, it seems likely that juvenile crime has risen in most industrialized nations over the last five decades. Comparisons with trends in victim data and studies of successive cohorts support this conclusion.
- There is some evidence that in many countries a larger proportion of juvenile arrests are made for violent offenses, a larger proportion of juvenile crime is being attributed to young women, and the peak age of

offending reflects changes in the opportunities for education and employment, becoming progressively later in countries where education is prolonged and employment is less likely in the teenage years.

The Relevance of Recent Trends in Juvenile Justice

To what extent do the trends in juvenile offending outlined here reflect changes in the ways in which the criminal justice system chooses to deal with young offenders? In what ways did the criminal justice systems of different countries change over this period, and what is the evidence that ties these changes to patterns in the official statistics? Rutter and Giller (1983) identified several key juvenile justice policies and practices that may have been in some way related to the rises seen in official statistics of juvenile crime since the Second World War. Many of these examples came from the United Kingdom, but some reflected international shifts in criminal justice and suggested that at least some of the rise in crime was simply illusory. Diversionary tactics, intended to keep young offenders out of the criminal justice system, were adopted by many countries in the 1970s and 1980s. However, diversion may have led to a widening of the net, since informal warnings were likely to have been replaced by official cautions, meaning that the offender then appeared in the official statistics. Rutter and Giller (1983) reported some evidence that this was part but not all of the explanation for the trend in rising crime. Also, changes in the classification of offenses that followed both new legislation and alterations in police recording practice also had an effect on the apparent crime levels in the postwar period, again contributing to an impression that crime had risen faster than it actually had.

Significant changes have taken place in the philosophy and context of justice over the past half century; these changes have affected both the nature and types of interventions used to deal with offending once offenders have come to the notice of the authorities (Bottoms, 1995a; Gelsthorpe & Morris, 1994). In Britain, the immediate period after World War II was characterized by the establishment of what came to be termed the "welfare state," with the development of a greatly strengthened range of social, educational, and health services. This was accompanied by a merging, so far as social policies were concerned, of neglected children in need and young offenders. The approach was an explicitly welfare one, although at the same time there were strategies that focused on punishment. During the 1960s, the overall political consensus on welfare principles broke down, and the 1970s were marked by a move away from a welfare response to offending by young people. This shift was brought about by changes in political attitudes more generally, by an awareness that the crime rate was rising, and by the development of various social tensions in the country. Bottoms (1995a) identified four key conceptual developments in this period: a concern over "just deserts"; managerialism; a community focus; and a populist punitiveness.

Just Deserts

In all Western countries there was a shift from the welfare model of dealing with juvenile offenders to one that emphasized punishment for offending based on the concepts of just deserts and the recognition of human rights. The welfare model emphasized the rehabilitative and educative role of the legal system in responding to young offenders, often using offending as a diagnostic opportunity to initiate intervention to meet underlying need. Such interventions for juveniles were customarily (a) different from the interventions applied to adults; (b) unrelated in intensity to the seriousness or frequency of the presenting offending behaviors; and (c) indeterminate in duration, being subject to the offender's response to the treatment dosage.

The decline of the rehabilitative ethic in the 1970s (Allen, 1981) coincided with concerns over fairness, proportionality, and determinacy in the application of legal sanctions. This movement subsequently became enshrined in international obligations relating generally to human rights and specifically to the rights of young offenders. This led in 1985 to the United Nations Standard Minimum Rules for the Administration of Juvenile Justice, in 1987 to the Council of Europe Social Reactions to Juvenile Delinquency, in 1989 to the United Nations Convention on the Rights of the Child, and in 1990 to the United Nations Rules for the Protection of Juveniles Deprived of their Liberty. Each of these statements emphasized the requirements for procedural legality in the operation of national juvenile justice systems, and they promoted the principles of diversion, minimum intervention, and the use of custody only as a last resort (Dunkel, 1991). While the precise interpretation of these international obligations varies across jurisdictions, they have undoubtedly been influential in shifting current juvenile justice systems from their traditional welfare orientations.

Managerialism

From the 1980s onward there has been increasing recognition that the various agencies with responsibility for recognizing and responding to juvenile justice do so within an interacting, systemic context (Feeney, 1985). As a consequence, this has led to:

(1) an emphasis on interagency cooperation to fulfill particular goals of the criminal justice system;

(2) an emphasis on creating, wherever possible, an overall strategic plan for the system;

(3) identification of key performance indicators to evaluate the efficiency and effectiveness of the system; and

(4) active monitoring of the system by information technology collecting and aggregating performance indicator data.

Such an approach has tended to detach juvenile justice from its traditional normative values such as a focus on welfare and rehabilitation (Moxon et al., 1985; Tarling, 1979).

Community Focus

Three aspects of a growing orientation toward a community focus in sentencing policy are evident in: (i) the expansion of community-based penalties and diversion arrangements; (ii) the recognition of locally based interpretations of national legislation (Richardson, 1990); and (iii) the emergence of local arrangements for responding to youth offenders (e.g., reparation and mediation schemes, family group conferencing arrangements; Curtis, 1989).

Populist Punitiveness

Increasingly over the last 20 years, politicians have been tapping into (and using for their own purposes) what they believe to be the public's generally punitive stance on crime, especially youth crime. Nevertheless, although this belief has some relevance for how offenders should be dealt with, public opinion is mixed (e.g., Ashworth & Hough, 1996; Tarling & Dowds, 1977; Walker & Hough, 1988). Bottoms (1995a) identified three interrelated beliefs underpinning this strategy: (i) the belief that increased punitiveness will reduce crime through general deterrence and/or incapacitation; (ii) the belief that this may help to strengthen a moral consensus in society against certain kinds of criminality; and (iii) the belief that this approach will satisfy a particular electoral constituency.

These beliefs have led to changes that allow more stringent requirements within existing orders, such as (a) ordering financial penalties to be paid by the parents of juvenile offenders; (b) introducing minimum compliance requirements in supervision and probation orders that are sanctioned by breach arrangements enabling a return to court for resentencing; and (c) the use of electronic monitoring or tagging at the presentence (Mair & Nee, 1990) or postsentence (Jolin & Stipak, 1992) stage.

Table 4.2. Estimated percentage of the male population with a conviction, by age: England and Wales

Age	Year of Birth				
	1953	**1958**	**1963**	**1968**	**1973**
17	15	17	16	14	9
20	22	24	25	21	*
24	27	30	30	26	*
29	31	33	*	*	*
39	34	*	*	*	*

* Data not yet available.
Source: Home Office (1996, p. 206). Crown copyright is reproduced with the permission of the Controller of Her Majesty's Stationery Office.

Evidence on each of these methods suggests that increasing the level of coercive supervision in community penalties, in and of itself, has little effect on reducing recidivism (Audit Commission, 1996b; Junger-Tas, 1995a). Moreover, the commission of technical violations of orders is no indicator per se of future criminal behavior (Petersilia & Turner, 1993).

In England and Wales the main policy thrust of the 1980s continued to be diversion from both court and custody (Morris & Giller, 1987; Rutherford, 1992a, 1996). A series of Home Office circulars (in 1978, 1985, and 1990) continually encouraged the police to exercise their discretion to caution (i.e. formally warn) rather than prosecute juveniles. The 1990 circular included national standards for the exercise of police discretion and recognized the possibility of using cautions on more than one occasion. Similarly, the policy guiding the operation of the Crown Prosecution Service emphasized that prosecution for juveniles should be regarded as a last resort (Gelsthorpe & Giller, 1990). The impact of this policy seemed to be that the "net-widening" effect of diversion of the 1970s was reversed in the 1980s. Real diversion seemed to have been achieved, with substantial numbers of those who would otherwise have been prosecuted avoiding a court appearance (Farrington, 1993a; Morris & Giller, 1987).

Evidence of this point can be seen from Home Office estimates of the proportion of the male population with a conviction (Home Office, 1996), shown in Table 4.2. These estimates are derived from the conviction records of people born in four selected weeks of the years 1953, 1958,

1963, 1968, and 1973. The lower proportion of males born in 1973 who had a conviction by the age of 17 years probably reflects the increased use of cautioning during the 1980s.

More recently, however, there has been a U-turn in the policy on cautioning, with revised guidance from the Home Office seeking to limit police discretion (see Home Office circular 18/1994). The impact of this policy revision is only just beginning to be seen in the annual criminal statistics.

Contemporaneously, diversion from custody was a driving force in the juvenile justice policy of England and Wales (Allen, 1991). Monitoring by the National Association for the Care and Rehabilitation of Offenders (NACRO) suggested that the introduction and support of intensive intermediate treatment (IT) programs as an alternative to custody had some impact on the custodial sentencing of juveniles during the 1980s (Bottoms et al., 1990, 1995; NACRO, 1987). Contrary to predictions at the time (e.g., Allen, 1991; Burney, 1985), magistrates did not, after passage of the 1982 Criminal Justice Act, seem particularly attracted to the available "short, sharp, shock" detention center regimes. Rates of (male) custody as a whole dropped from a peak of over 7,000 in 1980 to fewer than 2,000 in 1990 (Hagell & Newburn, 1994).

Allen (1991) has identified several main reasons for the declining use of custody, including a declining population of juveniles and the diversion strategies of local welfare professionals who played a part in the court cases. However, once again, the latest policy development has been a shift back toward encouraging courts to use custodial remands and sentences – at least for certain subgroups of offenders, particularly the most persistent. Courts are already making more use of remands to custody and are passing more custodial sentences, given the relaxation of the eligibility criteria for such options. In essence, the English criminal justice system in the late 1990s is witnessing a movement from a diversionary to a retributive position.

The United States provides a similar example (Howell, 1997). Juvenile justice policies continue to vary from state to state, but some overall trends in the 1980s and early 1990s can be identified. Here, rises in the proportion of violent crime accounted for by juveniles (Kelley et al., 1997) were accompanied by a swing in the pendulum from diversion to retribution. Treatment models from the 1970s have given way fairly extensively to retributive justice in the 1990s as a result of failures and contradictions in the existing system (Bazemore & Umbreit, 1995; McGarrell, 1991). The 1980s saw the implementation of a "just deserts" approach to juvenile justice, intended to make the system more rational and less erratic. The result, however, was more punitive than anticipated, leading to increased incarceration and longer sentences. In both countries, policy making and academic commentary show signs of reflecting a schism. While federal and state politicians call for tougher sanctions and more custody for young offenders, academics suggest that ever-more severe options and sentences are inadequate to the task (Currie, 1996). Restorative justice and alternative sanctioning models receive academic support, although whether such models work in practice is still moot. We will return to the question of efficacy in later chapters of this book.

Of course, international comparative analysis tends to generalize processes and outcomes. For countries that are collections of individual states, for example, it may be difficult to identify unifying themes from the diversity of local approaches (see e.g. Boss et al., 1995, and Wundersitz, 1993, for discussion of the juvenile justice policies of Australia). Diversity might also be the case *within* countries on an even more local basis. Police-force cautioning policies, procedures, and outcomes in the mid-1980s in the United Kingdom varied considerably (Evans & Wilkinson, 1990; Laycock & Tarling, 1985). Policy does not, therefore, equal practice, and global directives may be operationalized in a variety of ways that may bear little resemblance to each other. Practices in very localized areas of different countries may resemble each other more than they resemble their own national policies. Finally, responses to different types of offenders or different offenses may vary, with some types of crimes considered as more worthy than others of welfare or noncustodial options (e.g., alcohol and drug offenders have tended to be treated somewhat differently in the United States; Schneider, 1988). As Bazemore and Umbreit (1995) have pointed out, American cities are distinctly different from those in Europe and the Antipodes, and different responses might be necessary. See Box 4.2.

Analysis of the interplay between criminal justice policy and practice is highly problematic, be it on a national or international basis. Little is known about the causal relationships between policies and practice or about the impact that intervening variables may have. In England and Wales, for example, the drop in crime figures in the 1980s pre-dated the official diversion policies subsequently introduced (Morris & Giller, 1987; Rutherford, 1992a). External factors, such as demographic changes, have also been contributory to the change, in addition to policy or practice initiatives (Pratt, 1985; Riley, 1986).

Trends in Psychosocial Disorders of Youth

The rise in crime rates generally over the last five decades have been accompanied by rises in a variety of other psychosocial disorders and

---

BOX 4.2. RELATING CRIMINAL JUSTICE POLICY TO TRENDS IN
JUVENILE JUSTICE

- In the United States, decreases in overall crime levels in the 1980s
  were accompanied by ostensible rises in violent juvenile crime and
  homicide. The same period saw more punitive, retributive forms
  of juvenile justice for persistent young offenders. Diversion-based
  approaches were still used to some extent for less serious or less
  persistent offenders.

- In the United Kingdom, overall crime figures rose in the 1980s, but
  there were ostensible falls in juvenile crime and actual falls in juvenile custody. This was a decade of experimentation with diversionary tactics to keep young offenders out of the criminal justice
  system.

---

problem behaviors in adolescents, which are relevant to inferences about
the nature of the these changes in behavior by young people. In a unique
collection of papers, Rutter and Smith (1995) reported the results of a European academic study group originally set up to establish whether certain
types of disorder had increased among the young (aged 16–26) in the last
50 years. Their conclusion was overwhelmingly affirmative, and the study
showed a marked increase in a range of problem behaviors. The conclusions of the study group for each different type of disorder considered are
summarized in Table 4.3, citing references for the direction of the trend.

The most striking findings were those relating to the increase in crime,
which we have already discussed. Several of the target disorders, including crime to a certain degree, reflected a profound increase in rates up
to the 1980s and a leveling thereafter. This was certainly the case for alcohol consumption, which showed a marked increase from 1950 to 1980,
when it reached a plateau (Silbereisen et al., 1995). By this point, there
was less between-country variation in rates than had been noted in the
earlier part of the century, with the rates in larger, industrialized nations
becoming more like each other. Similarly, the same 30-year period witnessed a massive increase in illicit drug use, particularly evidenced in the
United States. In Europe, the rise in drug use may have occurred slightly
later, and may not yet have leveled off to the same extent.

A range of epidemiological studies has shown a parallel (but lesser)
increase in depression and related affective difficulties during the period since the Second World War; data are not available before this point

Table 4.3. Trends in the Psychosocial Disorders of Young People

Disorder	Direction of Trends	References
Depression	Marked increase in recent birth cohorts, although the size of change cannot be estimated	Fombonne (1995a)
Suicide	Increase, particularly in young males in the 1970s; less clear pattern for females	Diekstra, Kienhorst, & de Wilde (1995)
Alcohol abuse	Marked increase in use 1950–80, followed by a plateau; patterns for abuse less clear	Silbereisen, Robins, & Rutter (1995)
Drug abuse	Marked increase 1950–80, possibly followed by a plateau; data are less clear	Institute for the Study of Drug Dependency (1994); Silbereisen et al. (1995)
Crime	Marked increase until the last few years, when the international pattern is less clear	Farrington (1996); Smith (1995); Wilson & Herrnstein (1985)
Anorexia	Lack of agreement between studies	Fombonne (1995b)

(Fombonne, 1995a). Rates of suicide among young people (aged 15–24) have increased, although a limited amount is known about the general pattern of increase in depressive disorders. It is known that the increase in suicide has been confined to adolescents and young adults, and that the rates are higher among young men than young women, typically by a factor of 2.5 to 3.0. Again, there is some suggestion that the rates for suicide have also leveled off somewhat in the period since the 1980s (Diekstra et al., 1995).

Eating disorders have also possibly shown an increase, although this is less clear than for other psychosocial disorders (Fombonne, 1995b). Both anorexia nervosa and bulimia nervosa are more common in females. Anorexia peaks earlier in adolescence than bulimia and both are more recognized now, which may account in part for the increase in reported cases.

Within this general pattern, there were differences in the prevalence of disorders for males and females and for different countries. Problems tended to have begun to rise in frequency between 1950 and the mid-1970s, when unemployment was low and living standards were rising, and show some signs of leveling off as the end of the century approaches.

This raises a number of questions about the causes of these increases in psychosocial disorders, which the next two sections address.

Changes in the Social and Economic Context for Young People

Undoubtedly, the lives and normative experiences of adolescents have changed dramatically over the last few decades of the twentieth century. Obviously there is much variation in what happens to different adolescents in different cultures, but some global changes (particularly in Europe and North America) provide a background for understanding changes in historical trends in offending. At the simplest level, the numbers of young people and the proportion they form of the general population have changed. The trends are not entirely straightforward but it is likely that, whichever way they are going in individual countries, the changes will be important to the experiences of young people in these age groups. At least in the more advanced countries, national populations have continued to rise over most recent decades, mirroring economic development (Smith, 1995). However, the sharp rises seen following industrialization in the nineteenth century have tended to slow down; in many countries, increases have been leveling off since the 1960s. Those with most recent economic growth have witnessed a greater rise in population (e.g., Japan) whereas some other countries witnessed a slight fall in population in the 1970s and 1980s (e.g., the United States; Snyder & Sickmund, 1995). Projections for early next century are quite varied. The juvenile (under-18) population of the United States is certainly predicted to rise, and it is expected to have reached 74 million by the year 2010 (Snyder & Sickmund, 1995). In Europe, falling fertility rates mean that total population is expected to fall in five of the twelve EU countries and to rise in the other seven (Northcott, 1995). The rises are likely to be due to increases in life expectancy, in many cases leading to a reduction in the proportion of these populations accounted for by very young people. Older juveniles are expected to continue increasing in the United States (Snyder & Sickmund, 1995); people under 16 currently account for 20.3% of the U.K. population, and this is projected to fall to 17.6% by 2041 (Northcott, 1995).

Family patterns have changed over the period, directly affecting the experiences of young people. The development of the "nuclear" family is actually a relatively recent phenomenon, though it is often treated as a more permanent and long-term feature of the past than it ever was. Hess (1995) showed how the industrial revolution heralded major changes in the basic roles of the family, ushering in the more isolated, traditional, nuclear or "bourgeois" form of family that we usually associate with the term. In this bourgeois form, a married man in full employment usually headed the household, while his partner had primary responsibility for maintaining the home and socializing the children (Hess, 1995). This type of family is thought to have reached its peak in Europe in the mid-twentieth century. The period after the 1960s has witnessed another transformation in family patterns, characterized by diversification of family forms and the decline of the nuclear version. How far any of these historical stages can be clearly delineated is, of course, open to debate, and the picture is never as clear as such a brief summary would suggest. However, there is widespread agreement that experience of family breakdown and changes is more common now than it was several decades ago. Between 1971 and 1991, the U.K. marriage rate halved, the divorce rate more than doubled, and the proportion of live births outside marriage increased threefold (Northcott, 1995), matching the proportion in the United States (30% in 1991; Snyder & Sickmund, 1995). Northcott (1995) concluded that these kinds of social changes were widespread throughout Europe but that Britain was experiencing more extreme change. In the United States, fewer children lived with both parents in 1990 than at any time in the past, and it has been estimated that half of all children will now spend some time in a single-parent home – the proportion being particularly high among African-Americans (Snyder & Sickmund, 1995). Hess wrote:

If current trends in Europe continue, more and more children and adolescents in the future can expect: to grow up as a single child or with very few siblings; to experience maternal employment; parental divorce and/or remarriage; to postpone leaving home (especially young people who are economically disadvantaged and unemployed); to live alone for a greater portion of their lives (either before uniting with a partner or in their extended old age); to cohabit as a transition to marriage; to have several cohabitations that break down; to postpone marriage or refuse to marry and have children; and to choose planned single-motherhood or parenthood outside marriage .... (1995, p. 173)

Most of the major industrialized nations – including those of Europe, North America, Australia, and New Zealand – have witnessed another major change in the experiences of young people over this period, relating to the length and nature of their transition from compulsory education into the labor market and independent living. As the economic and labor markets of developed countries have changed dramatically, so too have the experiences of young people trying to enter them. The introduction of new technologies has changed the nature of work, and as employment opportunities have been reduced, the length of the transition to adulthood has increased.

This has both positive and negative consequences. The rates for staying on in education have increased across Europe, and this is markedly the case in the United Kingdom. The proportion of those staying on after the conclusion of compulsory education has risen from approximately a third in the early 1970s to over 65% in 1992 (Youth Cohort Survey analyses by Payne, 1995a). Of those who left compulsory education in 1992, only 11% went directly into a job (Payne, 1995b). This figure is even lower in disadvantaged inner-city samples (Hagell & Shaw, 1996). In the United States, school dropout rates nearly halved between 1978 and 1992 (Snyder & Sickmund, 1995).

It is the effect of these social changes for more disadvantaged groups that is of primary interest to this review. Opportunities may have been opened up for some sections of the young population, but for others these changes may have led to marginalization and increased periods of dependence. There is growing evidence that, in the most advanced Western nations, society is becoming increasingly unequal. Comparisons across time of a standard measure of inequality based on income (the "Gini coefficient," where $0 =$ complete equality and $1 =$ complete inequality) show that it ranged between 0.245 and 0.276 from 1960 to the early 1980s in the United Kingdom; since then, however, inequality has increased it to 0.365 and it is still rising (Northcott, 1995). While many are doing well, even better than before, others – who have been excluded from the mainstream because of social factors such as ethnicity, geographical location, socioeconomic status, economic inactivity, and so on – are doing less well (NACRO, 1995; Wilkinson, 1995).

As an example of some of the social changes being experienced by young people, Box 4.3 presents a picture of recent changes in the United States. The evidence for a relationship between any of these trends and offending behavior will be discussed later in this chapter, and in subsequent chapters where issues of causality are examined. Although the links are unlikely to be clear or direct, it is undoubtedly the case that at least some of these trends will be found to be associated, and we might expect their effect to be largely exacerbating. There is evidence, for example, that later school-leaving ages may be associated with later ages for peak criminality (Blau & Hagan, 1995), and we might hypothesize that extending the period when young people are dependent on others through increased periods of education and lack of economic opportunities prolongs the period when young people are criminally active.

BOX 4.3. SOCIAL CHANGE: A SNAPSHOT OF THE EXPERIENCES OF U.S. YOUNG PEOPLE IN THE EARLY 1990s

- There are more of them. The juvenile (under-18) population declined during the late 1970s and early 1980s but has been growing since 1984. It stood at 69 million in 1995 and is predicted to rise to 74 million by 2010. They now constitute 26% of the whole population.

- Some are getting poorer. In 1992, 14.6 million juveniles lived below the poverty line, 42% more than in 1976. The increase was largest for white juveniles, but this group included Hispanic youth, whose population grew enormously during this period.

- A growing proportion are born to unmarried mothers: one in twenty were born to unmarried mothers in 1960, one in four by 1990. Divorce tripled over this period. The proportion living in two-parent households declined from 85% in 1970 to 73% in 1990. African-American families had the greatest decrease in these figures. Half of all children will spend some time in a single-parent home.

- School drop-out rates (leaving high school early) declined between 1978 and 1992, varying by family income level but not by type of community. In 1992, 11% failed to complete their high school education; this rate was highest for Hispanics.

Source: Based on statistics presented in Snyder and Sickmund (1995).

Possible Reasons for the Rise in Crime and Psychosocial Disorders of Young People

The evidence is clear-cut that overall crime rates, including crime by juveniles, have risen greatly over the last half century, and that this has been paralleled by increases in many psychosocial disorders among young people. The reasons for the rise in crime might be different from those for the rise in other psychosocial disorders, but it would be parsimonious to assume they were similar, or at least related, until we have evidence to the contrary. It is important to stress that explanations for overall trends may not be the same as explanations of individual variation (Rutter, 1997b). In the Academia Europæa study, Rutter and Smith (1995) used the example of height,which clearly illustrates the problem: individual differences in height are largely determined by genetic inheritance, while the secular trend of increase in average height is probably a result of improved diet. Bearing in mind this distinction between causes of individual differences and time trends, what then are the main candidates as explanations for the overall rise in psychosocial disorders or the specific rises in overall crime rates?

Four groups of explanations have been put forward. First there are explanations based on such individual risk factors as genetic influences, low IQ, and poor educational attainment. Here the distinction between individual-level explanations and explanations for secular trends are very clear. Whatever the importance of genetic factors in relation to individual differences in antisocial behavior, they cannot explain secular trends because changes in the gene pool could not possibly occur at the speed of the trends witnessed in behavior. Similarly, while there is some contradictory evidence that obstetric factors may constitute a contributory factor for some types of crime when combined with psychosocial risks (see Chapter 6), it is implausible that they play any significant role in the rise in crime. Babies are generally healthier at birth, survive longer, and have fewer health problems than at any other time in the past. This does not necessarily mean that the rate of perinatal damage has declined, because the fall in the rate of damage in some groups is accompanied by a rise in the survival of damaged babies who would have died in a previous era. However, the latter phenomenon applies primarily to very low–birth-weight babies, whose proportion of the general population is far too small to affect crime statistics. Again, while there is evidence that IQ and academic achievement have a part to play in explaining individual differences in behavior (to which we return in Chapter 6), overall levels of IQ and academic performance have actually improved in the periods and countries that witnessed the greatest increases in crime. Hence these factors can also be ruled out as explanations. However, it may be that – rather than absolute achievement levels – it is the social comparison processes and educational aspirations that are important; these factors could contribute to frustration and lack of social bonds in *relatively* disadvantaged groups.

This leads to the second group of explanations, which is based on changes in living conditions and socioeconomic factors. Worsening living conditions do not directly account for the rising levels of disorder because, using Europe as an example, soaring crime rates between the 1950s and 1970s were associated with a marked *increase* in the standard of living and low unemployment rates as well as steady or slightly reducing rates of inequality (Rutter & Smith, 1995). Increased affluence may be associated in other ways – for example, through rising inequality or more opportunity for theft. Increasingly consumerist societies may provide more situational opportunities (through new-style shopping centers, more shoppers, etc.), but the evidence on the role of such factors in causing crime is equivocal at best and methodologically very hard to test. In addition, these theories seem unlikely to provide the full explanation, since increases have been recorded in many different types of crime (including those involving violence) and not simply theft.

The third main class of explanation offered for the rise in psychosocial disorders and crime among the young is based on family and socialization factors, including the influence of the mass media. Increasing levels of family breakup over this period are indisputable, but if there is a risk associated for developing psychosocial disorders it is likely to arise from discord and lack of parental support and involvement rather than from family structure per se. It looks plausible that these family factors have had some role to play in the rise in crime, but it is impossible to be certain that a causal inference can be drawn without the test provided by either a reversal in family trends or large swings in rates of breakup and discord. Evidence to date on the role of the mass media (e.g. Livingstone, 1996) concludes that they are not likely to play a directly causal role but may reflect changing attitudes and thereby augment the effects of societal change.

Finally, the fourth class of explanations covers the changes in the role of adolescents in society and the nature of the transition from childhood to adulthood. A main contender for a possible risk factor has been a major change in the meaning of adolescence that has taken place over this century. This has consisted of an increasing commercialization of many aspects of youth culture such as music and fashion, changes in sexual behavior, increased periods spent in education, and a slower transition into full-time work and financial independence. In a Home Office self-report survey of young people and crime, for example, Graham and Bowling (1995) described a new type of "perpetual adolescence" caused by a lack of direction and security resulting from the economic situation and changing patterns of adolescent transitions. Many of these changes are ongoing, rather than occurring as discrete events, which again makes causal testing difficult, but it is possible that they may have been of relevance to the time trends.

Another significant change in the experience of adolescence relates to illegal drug use and increased alcohol consumption. The use of drugs among young people has undoubtedly increased, to the point (it has been suggested) of becoming "normalized" (see e.g. Parker et al., 1995). Both alcohol and drug use constitute a risk factor for each other (Kaplan, 1995; Rutter, 1996) and potentially a risk for antisocial behavior. This is probably an effect that is mediated through the deleterious effect of heavy use on employment and on relationships (cf. the research evidence presented in Chapter 6). It is likely that the increased use of alcohol and drugs has played some role in the rise of some sorts of crime, but it seems improbable that it constitutes the main cause of the overall rise in crime during the last 50 years.

We return to many of these factors in the subsequent chapters on causal factors in the development of offending behavior. However, in terms of their role in overall crime trends, there is no one clear factor that has a proven link. Because the rises in crime and other psychosocial disorders have been very great, it is obvious that some environmental factors are responsible, but exactly which ones is not known.

Conclusions

Crime has risen substantially over the last 50 years in developed nations, and this includes a rise in the rates of juvenile crime. In this respect, the current level of concern over increasing rates of juvenile crime *is* justified, although the very clear patterns of rising juvenile crime obvious between the 1950s and 1980s seem less clear for the last decade. In addition, crime committed by young people has changed in nature, becoming a little more violent, somewhat more likely to be committed by young women, and – possibly reflecting changes in the experience of adolescence in Western countries – something that peaks in later rather than mid-adolescence. We have seen how changes in trends in the official statistics are often accompanied by criminal justice policy change, although whether there is a causal connection between the two is uncertain. In the United States, a rise in juvenile delinquency in the 1980s was accompanied by increasingly punitive strategies; over the same period, an apparent fall in U.K. juvenile delinquency was accompanied by diversionary policies. The rise in crime and other psychosocial disorders of young people since the Second World War must be attributed to environmental influences of some kind. The prime contenders are the increased rate of family breakdown (together with the associated discord, conflict, and disruption that tend to be involved), the changing meaning of adolescence (with prolonged education and economic dependence on parents at a time of increases in autonomy in other spheres); a possibly increased disparity between aspirations and the opportunities to meet them; diminished surveillance and increased opportunities for crime (as a consequence of altered housing and shopping patterns, together with more goods to steal); a rise in the use and abuse of alcohol and drugs; and possibly changing public attitudes to what is acceptable behavior (with these enhanced by media influences).

CHAPTER 4 – SUMMARY OF MAIN POINTS

❑ Official statistics leave little doubt that *crime rates* have been on a steady rise over the last half of the twentieth century, with few national exceptions (Japan). In the United Kingdom, notifiable (and thus reasonably serious) offenses per 100,000 members of the population quadrupled between the early 1950s and the late 1970s and then doubled again by the early 1990s. Rises since then have been less dramatic and less uniform, with some countries reporting decreases. Victim surveys over the last two decades have also shown a rise, though sometimes a less dramatic one than suggested by police statistics.

❑ Given that crime has risen overall, and that there is no reason to assume that the proportion accounted for by juveniles has changed, we can assert that *crime by juveniles* has risen as well. However, in some countries, the actual numbers of juveniles going through the system has fallen over the same period for which crime rates are reported to have risen.

❑ Three *explanations* have been put forward: (1) that fewer juveniles are accounting for more crime; (2) that more juveniles are being diverted from the criminal justice system; or (3) that the peak age of offending is rising because adolescents are becoming less likely to desist from offending, so that young adults now account for a larger proportion than they previously did. There is evidence for more diversion for juveniles in the 1980s in particular, but apart from this, these explanations are either untested or the data are equivocal. Looking to other sources of information on the underlying behavior patterns, we saw that American studies of the trends in behavior problems have shown a rise.

❑ Both U.S. and U.K. official statistics reflect an increase in *violence* by juveniles – most dramatically in the United States, where the juvenile violent crime arrest rate soared by more than 50% between 1988 and 1994.

❑ A significant fall in the *ratio between male and female* young offenders can be clearly identified internationally over recent decades, most clearly in the 1970s. The U.K. ratio fell from approximately 11:1 in the late 1950s to 3.6:1 in 1995. There is some evidence that violence by young women showed a particular increase, although it is not clear to what extent this reflects processing changes (self-report trend data on violent offending are not available).

❏ The *peak age* for offending may reflect changes in the opportunities for education and employment, and it appears to be getting progressively later in countries where education is being prolonged and employment is less likely in the teenage years.

5 | Varieties of Antisocial Behavior

The previous chapters have analyzed the nature of antisocial behavior in young people from the starting point of official and self-report data, and they have thus set the judicial and social context. At this point we move on to consider a rather different set of arguments that concern whether or not we can distinguish different types of antisocial behavior. For this purpose, the sources of data are also rather different, relying on the psychiatric and psychological literatures as well as criminological sources.

There has long been a recognition that there is considerable versatility in delinquency (Hindelang, Hirschi, & Weiss, 1981) and also that the patterns may represent meaningful heterogeneity in varieties of antisocial behavior. This is obvious, for example, with respect to pervasiveness and persistence. Thus, the great majority of males in the general population engage in at least occasional delinquent activities at some time in their lives (so that, in a statistical sense, their behavior is almost normative). By contrast, only about 1 in 23 males and 1 in 150 females shows persistent antisocial behavior that is associated with such pervasive social malfunction that the diagnostic term "antisocial personality disorder" is applied (Robins, Tipp, & Przybeck, 1991). On the grounds of their widespread psychological and social dysfunction, this minority group is generally regarded as having a psychiatric disorder (Earls, 1994). The disorder is associated with a considerable morbidity and also an increased early mortality.

There would also seem to be heterogeneity with respect to severity and to pattern. On the face of it, stealing bottles of milk off doorsteps seems a very different activity from killing someone, which seems different yet again from sexual exhibitionism. Nevertheless, despite this acceptance of the reality of surface heterogeneity, until recently there has been uncertainty on whether the disparate nature of the acts reflected anything more than varied manifestations of the same underlying antisocial tendency. The uncertainty was increased by the widespread evidence that the legal definitions of types of crimes clearly did not provide a good means of grouping, if only because most chronic offenders commit quite a range of different crimes over the course of a lifetime. Even among those researchers who regarded the heterogeneity as meaningful, there was little agreement up to the 1990s on how best to subdivide either antisocial behavior or the individuals who engage in delinquent activities (Rutter & Giller, 1983).

Research in the last decade has, however, enabled substantial progress. The key requirements in the development of valid classificatory subdivisions is that the differentiations on patterns of behavior be validated by parallel differences on features *external* to those patterns (Cantwell & Rutter, 1994). Such validating features could concern causal influences, epidemiological correlates, response to treatment, or long-term outcome. Such evidence is now increasingly available. Ideally, of course, validation should be provided by several different criteria. The empirical evidence to date suggests the importance of two well validated differentiating factors – presence or absence of associated hyperactivity and age of onset – as well as three further factors with reasonably good supporting evidence: the presence or absence of associated violence, of psychopathy, or of psychosis. In each case, there are replicated findings that the differentiations matter. What is much less clear, however, is whether they serve to pick out valid meaningful subcategories or, rather, whether the differentiating characteristics operate as dimensional risk characteristics. Thus, for example, it remains uncertain whether the association with psychopathy is most appropriately conceptualized as present versus absent or rather in terms of the *degree* of associated psychopathic features. Nevertheless, what is evident is that it is no longer acceptable to discuss antisocial behavior as if it constitutes a homogeneous entity.

Key Valid Differentiators

Association with Hyperactivity

Probably the best validated differentiation concerns whether or not the antisocial behavior is associated with hyperactivity and attention deficits. Antisocial behavior that is accompanied by hyperactivity and/or inattention stands out from the rest in terms of: (a) an onset in early or middle childhood; (b) a strong association with social malfunction and poor peer relationships; (c) a high likelihood of persistence into adult life; (d) an association with cognitive impairment; (e) a beneficial response to stimulant medication; and (f) a strong genetic component.

Follow-up studies of children with hyperactivity/inattention in early or middle childhood have shown a much increased rate of antisocial behavior developing before adolescence (Campbell, 1997; Campbell et al., 1996; Taylor et al., 1996). Also, clinical studies have shown that early referred boys have higher hyperactivity scores than those referred later (Loeber et al., 1992). Conversely, longitudinal studies have shown that young people whose antisocial behavior did not begin until adolescence were less likely than those with early-onset antisocial behavior to have been rated by an independent observer as showing a "difficult temperament" at ages 3 and 4 years (Moffitt et al., 1996). This rating was based on emotional lability, restlessness, short attention span, negativism, and willful rough behavior (Caspi et al., 1995). These studies have also shown that individuals with the combination of hyperactivity and disruptive antisocial behavior tend to show a range of other problems, including difficulties in peer relationships.

However, the Pittsburgh longitudinal studies showed that, although hyperactivity was associated with an increased risk for all forms of antisocial behavior (e.g., authority conflict, covert delinquency such as theft and vandalism, overt delinquency such as fighting and assault), the main association was with the persistence of these behaviors rather than their severity (Loeber et al., 1997). The presence of hyperactivity is associated not only with early offending but also with an increased likelihood of recidivist offending persisting into adult life (Farrington et al., 1990b). This prediction of chronicity remains after taking account of concurrent conduct problems in middle childhood and has been found in several other longitudinal studies (e.g. Magnusson & Bergman, 1988, 1990; Schachar, Rutter, & Smith, 1981; Stattin & Magnusson, 1995).

The Swedish longitudinal studies (Stattin & Magnusson, 1995) emphasized the extent to which children with multiple problems (including hyperactivity but also lack of concentration, low school motivation, scholastic underachievement, and poor peer relations) accounted for criminality and alcohol abuse in adult life. Single problems carried little increase in risk. Moreover, variables (such as aggressiveness) that predicted adult outcome in the sample as a whole ceased to do so once the multiple problem group had been removed from the sample (Stattin & Magnusson, 1995).

Hyperactivity is associated with both specific and general cognitive impairment, whereas conduct problems in the absence of hyperactivity are not, other than to a mild extent (Fergusson, Horwood, & Lynskey, 1993; Frick et al., 1991; Hinshaw, 1992; Moffitt, 1990a; Rutter et al., 1997b).

In theory, a specific response to medication could constitute a validating feature, but in practice it seems not to do so. Stimulant medication tends to be thought of as a treatment for a particular psychiatric disorder – hyperkinetic syndrome or attention deficit disorder with hyperactivity. Treatment studies of more broadly defined groups have shown, however, that the beneficial effects are not diagnosis-specific. On the other hand, the benefits are a function of the degree of associated hyperactivity (Taylor et al., 1987).

Finally, twin studies have shown not only that the trait of hyperactivity involves a particularly strong genetic influence (Eaves et al., 1997; Simonoff et al., in press; Thapar & McGuffin, 1994) but also that antisocial behavior associated with hyperactivity is likewise strongly genetically influenced (Silberg et al., 1996a) and that there is a strong genetic overlap between hyperactivity and disruptive behavior, especially in middle childhood (Silberg et al., 1996b). The importance of this finding is underlined by the fact that the same research has shown that antisocial behavior which is unaccompanied by hyperactivity and which especially involves covert activities that may not be known to parents and teachers seems to be largely environmental in origin (Silberg et al., 1996a).

The empirical research findings are consistent in showing that antisocial behavior associated with hyperactivity is characterized by its early onset, accompanying difficulties in peer relationships, somewhat below-average cognitive skills, poor scholastic achievement, and a marked tendency to persist into adult life. The pattern is strongly influenced by genetic factors. What is much less clear, however, is where the cutoff should be applied (i.e., how much hyperactivity needs to be present for this category to be applied) and whether the distinction is categorical or dimensional. In other words, does this pattern constitute a qualitatively distinct diagnostic category or does it represent the (severe) end of a dimension or continuum? The evidence so far is inconclusive. However, it is clear that this pattern of antisocial behavior is particularly likely to be accompanied by widespread social malfunction, and that it carries a relatively poor prognosis.

Age of Onset

Moffitt (1993a), Nagin and Land (1993), Patterson (1995; Patterson & Yoerger, 1997), and others (Hinshaw et al., 1993; Stattin & Magnusson, 1995) have proposed the need to differentiate antisocial behavior according to its age of onset. The main distinction drawn has been between "life-course–persistent" and "adolescence-limited" antisocial behavior. There is also a subgroup whose antisocial behavior seems to begin only in adult life (Hämäläinen & Pulkkinen, 1995; Kratzer & Hodgins, 1996b) and a subgroup of "discontinuous offenders" who commit crimes irregularly at different times in their lives (Kratzer & Hodgins, 1996b; Nagin et al., 1995). It follows that there must also be a subgroup with an early onset of antisocial behavior but a lack of persistence into adolescence and adult life. Empirical findings confirm that this is in fact the case (Moffitt et al., 1996).

It is apparent from the terminology used that the age-of-onset differentiation is postulated to carry with it other implications. Thus, "life-course–persistent" has come to be preferred over "early-onset" because the former conveys the message that there is both an unusually early age of onset *and* a tendency to persist into adult life. Most of the research has therefore been based on longitudinal data that are used to pick out just such a subgroup: one whose antisocial behavior is distinctive in terms of an early onset and a high degree of persistence.

There is certainly good evidence from several independent studies that this subgroup is indeed distinctively different from a subgroup defined in terms of the dual criteria of adolescent onset and a lack of persistence into adult life. For example, Moffitt et al. (1996) used the Dunedin study longitudinal data to compare the 7% of boys with a life-course–persistent (LCP) pattern (i.e., antisocial behavior spanning both childhood and adolescence), the 24% with adolescence-limited (AL) antisocial behavior, the 6% who "recovered" from early-onset antisocial behavior, and the remaining 58% ("unclassified") whose antisocial behavior was approximately normative. The first two groups did not differ in their level of antisocial behavior at age 18 but, by definition, the LCP group showed higher levels from early childhood to adolescence. The two groups did *not* differ in their age at first arrest, despite the marked difference in their age of onset of antisocial behavior. It is probable that the association between age of onset and age at first arrest will be much influenced by the age of criminal responsibility.

The LCP group differed from the AL group in exhibiting (i) a higher level of adverse temperamental features (restlessness, inattention, negativism, etc.) at ages 3 and 5, and (ii) greater levels of both social alienation and a lack of social closeness as self-reported at age 18 (items such as feeling victimized, suspicious, callous, and socially distant). It is noteworthy that undercontrolled behavior at 3 years predicted antisocial personality disorder, recidivist crime, and violent offenses at 21 years, as well as suicide attempts (Caspi et al., 1996a). Despite the long time span involved, early temperamental assessments are associated with an increased likelihood that antisocial behavior will persist into adult life. It is clear from other reports based on the Dunedin study that stable and pervasive conduct problems that persist through childhood are characterized by cognitive, language, and motor deficits; associated hyperactivity and attentional problems; extreme aggressiveness; reading difficulties; impulsivity; adverse family contexts; and poor parenting (Henry et al., 1993; Moffitt, 1990a; Moffitt, Lynam, & Silva, 1994; White et al., 1990).

The findings from the large Swedish cohort studied by Kratzer and Hodgins (1996b) are broadly similar. In particular, the results confirmed the cognitive deficits associated with early-onset antisocial behavior and the high rate of associated individual and family problems, as well as the association with violence. This list of findings points to the likely importance of both family experiences and individual characteristics in persistence. It also makes obvious the overlap between persistent behavior and that associated with hyperactivity. In almost all respects, the two appear the same. Perhaps one difference may lie, however, in the association with violent offenses, which was much greater by age 18 in Moffitt et al.'s LCP group (25%) than in the AL group (8%), although both were much higher than the 2% in the normative "unclassified" group. Violence has not been a particularly marked feature in the reports of children with hyperactive behavior (although it has not been subject to much systematic study). It may be relevant that, unlike hyperactivity, violent crimes seem to involve only a weak genetic component (see the next section).

Additional evidence is provided by findings from the Christchurch longitudinal study (Fergusson, Lynskey, & Horwood, 1996b). Statistical analyses – focusing on the postulated latent construct in order to remove measurement error – indicated strong behavioral continuity across the age span from 7–9 to 14–16 years. Even so, 12% showed a discontinuous pattern: 5% with early onset but later remission, and 7% with later onset but no earlier disruptive behavior. Delinquent peer affiliations proved to be the key differentiator between these two subgroups, being absent in those who remitted and present in those with an adolescent onset of antisocial behavior. The early-onset persistent group stood out in terms of a very high level of both individual and family risk factors (such as lower IQ, poor reading comprehension, hyperactive behaviors, and family adversity). Thus, their mean IQ was 89 compared with 104 in the nonproblem group, their reading comprehension score 5 versus 11, their hyperactivity score 27 versus 19, and their family adversity score 12 versus 6. It is sometimes assumed that the adolescent-onset group is, by contrast, a near-normal segment of the population showing just an exaggeration of normal adolescent misbehavior. That view is somewhat misleading. Instead, the Christchurch study findings show this group to be intermediate in risk features between the nonproblem and LCP groups. Thus, their mean IQ was 98, their reading comprehension score was 7, their hyperactivity score 21, and their family adversity score 11.

Patterson's findings, based on intensive investigation of the Oregon Youth Study high-risk sample of boys followed from age 10 to 18, told a similar story (Patterson, 1996; Patterson & Yoerger, 1997). Early-onset antisocial behavior was defined in terms of first arrest prior to age 14 and late onset as first arrest between 14 and 18 years. The early-onset group

($n = 43$) differed markedly from the no-arrest group ($n = 89$) with respect to both family risk factors (such as parental antisocial behavior and poor discipline) and their own antisocial behavior in middle childhood, but on both domains the late-onset group ($n = 52$) was intermediate. As with the Christchurch study findings, involvement with deviant peers seemed to play a key role in fostering an escalation of delinquent activities in adolescence.

Magnusson's Stockholm longitudinal study (Magnusson et al., 1994) is informative with respect to the role of individual characteristics for persistence of antisocial behavior into adult life. Of the eleven males with a crime record both before and after age 18, nine had both a high level of hyperactivity *and* a low level of adrenalin excretion, a pattern found in none of the 46 males without a criminal record and in only 2 of the 13 with a crime record that did not persist after age 18.

Pulkkinen and Pitkänen's (1994) Finnish longitudinal study showed that antisocial behavior beginning before the age of 10 and continuing into adulthood is particularly likely to be associated with early-onset alcohol abuse. Also, individuals with a first arrest by age 16 had been more aggressive at age 8 than those whose first arrest came at a later age (Hämäläinen and Pulkkinen, 1995).

There are few findings on the early-onset group who cease to show antisocial behavior in adolescence, but it is noteworthy that in the Dunedin study this "recovered" group did *not* differ from the LCP group with respect to adverse temperamental features in the preschool years (Moffitt et al., 1996). Follow-up of Campbell's sample of children with hyperactivity in the preschool age period also showed that a good outcome in middle childhood was associated with positive family features (Campbell, 1997). The course of disruptive behavior is associated with both family and individual characteristics. Similarly, Taylor and his colleagues found that a good outcome for hyperkinetic disorders was associated with a lack of expressed negative parental feelings (Rutter et al, 1997b; Taylor et al., 1996). The findings caution against any assumption that the outcome is necessarily bad for children with either early-onset antisocial behavior or hyperactivity or both.

It is evident, too, that care must be taken in deciding just what constitutes early-onset antisocial behavior. As already noted, it cannot necessarily be equated with first arrest at an early age. That is because arrest is likely to be influenced by the age set for criminal responsibility (which varies across countries from 7 to 18 years; see Chapter 3) and by other variations in the ways in which delinquent activities in young people are dealt with. Equally, it cannot be equated with disruptive behavior in early and middle childhood, if only because so many children show this at some point. Moffitt et al. (1996) required for inclusion in the LCP group that antisocial behavior be elevated (at least one standard deviation above the mean) on at least three out of the four assessments at ages 5, 7, 9, and 11, *and* that it have been present at both home and school. Thirteen percent of the boys met these criteria for early onset and, of these, just over half persisted into adolescence, thereby meeting the criteria for LCP. It is evident, therefore, that this is not a distinction that can be made on the basis of a single assessment. It should be added that little is known on how well the differentiation applied to females.

The size of this life-course–persistent group is also uncertain. Moffitt (1993a; Moffitt et al., 1996) suggested that it probably applied to about 6% of the general population – a figure comparable to that for antisocial personality disorder in males (Robins et al., 1991). Using data from a Swedish longitudinal study, Kratzer and Hodgins (1996b) likewise found a rate of 6.2% for their early-starter group among males. However, the analyses of the West and Farrington inner London (all-male) sample by Nagin et al. (1995) put the figure much higher. They differentiated between what they called high-level chronics (with a very high rate of offending in the teenage years and early adult life but a marked peak in the late teens) and low-level chronics (whose crime rate was never very high but who persisted at much the same level of antisocial behavior right through their 20s). Between them, these two groups accounted for some two thirds of offenders (i.e., some 20% of males in the general population). The proportion of life-course–persistent offenders among women is even less clear, owing to the lack of studies with representative female samples. In a rare study of a female cohort (6,751 born in 1953 in Stockholm), Kratzer and Hodgins (1996b) estimated that 6% of the cohort were offenders; of those, 7% were "stable early starters" – the group that most closely resembled life-course–persistent offenders. This group thus formed only 0.4% of the general population of women, or 1 in 250.

There is some uncertainty still over the meaning of the predictive validity of an unusually early age of onset of antisocial behavior as such. Three main possibilities need to be considered. First, it could be just an epiphenomenon resulting from the association with hyperactivity, an association that arises simply because hyperactivity is usually first manifest in the preschool period. Second, it could merely reflect severity, with more serious disorders tending to begin at an earlier age. Thirdly, an early onset could be important in its own right because, perhaps, it sets in motion a reinforcing spiral between offending behavior and subsequent stigmatizing and labeling, with low expectations from families and targeting by criminal justice authorities. Data from the American National Youth Survey (Tolan & Thomas, 1995) suggest that it is both a marker of a more severe underlying antisocial propensity and an independent influence in its own right after controlling for propensity.

Those writers who have distinguished between life-course–persistent and adolescence-limited delinquency have noted that the prevalence of delinquent activities rises greatly during adolescence, a fact that is obvious from the official statistics (see Chapter 2). These studies have shown that the antisocial behavior arising *for the first time* during this age period shows a lesser male preponderance, tends to be unassociated with hyperactivity, and is less likely to be accompanied by major social malfunction and poor peer relationships; that it is less likely than early-onset antisocial behavior to persist well into adult life; that it is particularly likely to occur as part of delinquent peer group activities; and possibly that it involves a relatively weak genetic component. The last point is a potentially important validating criterion, but the evidence so far is inconclusive with respect to age of onset.

In some respects, this adolescence-limited antisocial behavior group seems not to differ from nondelinquent samples. Thus, Moffitt et al. (1996) found that they differed neither on temperamental features during the preschool years nor on antisocial activities during elementary school (age 5-11). On the other hand, at 18 years they were more likely to be unemployed, to show dangerous driving habits, and to be engaging in unsafe sexual behavior (the rates of each being two or three times that of the normative "unclassified" group). Kratzer and Hodgins (1996b) found that, on the whole, the AL group (in both males and females) was intermediate between the early starters and the no-crime group. As already discussed, the findings from the Christchurch (Fergusson et al., 1996b) and Oregon (Patterson & Yoerger, 1997) studies are similar.

The findings on the size of the AL group are contradictory. Moffitt et al. (1996) found that it accounted for the majority of offenders during the teenage period (24% of the population among males versus 7% with LCP antisocial behavior). By contrast, Kratzer and Hodgins (1996b), using Swedish data, found that AL was only slightly more frequent than early-onset offending in males (9.9% versus 6.2%); it was substantially more frequent in females, albeit at a very low rate (2.2% versus 0.4%).

Up to now, the adolescence-limited category lacks adequate defining criteria. Thus, to what extent should the definition be based on the age of onset or on its duration over the teenage period? When should be the cutoff for adolescent onset? Should a continuation into the early 20s be regarded as an exclusion criterion, or should this category instead be regarded as the remainder of teenage delinquency after excluding life-course–persistent antisocial behavior? Despite these ambiguities, the AL group stands out as markedly different from the life-course–persistent delinquents (Nagin et al., 1995). By the age of 32, those in the West and Farrington sample were indistinguishable from nondelinquent individuals in terms of their attachment to work and family as well as their official crime record. The change in their behavior from that shown in adolescence was marked and important but, despite their generally good adaptive functioning (as judged by their self-reports), they continued to engage in risky behaviors such as illicit drug use, heavy drinking, fighting, and petty theft. The findings underline the importance of the distinction between an antisocial liability (which may persist over time) and engagement in crime that leads to arrest (which may stop in the late teens or at some other age).

Little is known about adult-onset antisocial behavior. Most reviewers, following Robins's (1966) findings from her long-term longitudinal study, have concluded that it is uncommon. Moffitt (1993a) noted that, although some 5% to 15% of men are first convicted as adults, many of them had engaged in antisocial behavior when much younger. The one study with strikingly different findings is that by Kratzer and Hodgins (1996b). Using Swedish data, the authors found that, in both males and females, the adult-onset group was the largest (12.8% of men and 3.5% of women in the cohort studied). The reason for this discrepancy in relation to other studies remains uncertain, but it is probable that one key feature is the higher age of criminal responsibility in Scandinavia (15 years, as compared with 10 years in the United Kingdom). This is likely to mean that a "first" (criminal) arrest after (say) age 18 will carry a different significance in the two countries.

However, it may also be relevant that the Swedish sample had an unusually low rate of adolescent-onset crime and that their measures of antisocial behavior in childhood and adolescence were rather weak. In most respects, their data showed the adult- and adolescent-onset groups to be rather similar in their characteristics. The findings from Hämäläinen and Pulkkinen's (1995) much smaller-scale Finnish longitudinal study are consonant with these inferences. In keeping with the older age of criminal responsibility, they too had a high proportion (12 out of 32) of convicted men whose first recorded crime was not until 21 years. Those in the adult-onset group were less likely to be recidivist. With respect to measures of aggression at age 8, they were intermediate between the groups for juvenile onset (most aggressive) and adolescent onset (least aggressive). Perhaps the most crucial feature of these Scandinavian studies is that, unlike the longitudinal studies that found low rates of adult-onset crime, they placed primary reliance on official crime records rather than self-reports.

The key question is not so much whether there are people whose first *conviction* is in adult life, but rather whether there is a substantial group whose *antisocial behavior* does not begin until after the adolescent years (and, insofar as there is, what causal influences are operative). Clearly, more research is needed into adult-onset crime before any conclusions are warranted. Any such research will have to pay careful attention to possible cohort effects. As discussed in Chapter 4, the rate of crime has risen greatly over the last 50 years. A consequence is that some age groups will have passed through their adolescence during a time of relatively low crime rates but will have spent their early and middle adult life in an era of high crime rates.

Probably Valid Differentiators

Association with Violence

Attempts to determine whether violent crime differs from nonviolent acquisitive crime (i.e. theft) have faced several important methodological difficulties. To begin with, the crimes as officially recorded provide an imperfect index. Individuals who participate in violent crime – through joint planning, or serving as a lookout, or driving a getaway car – even though they do not themselves act violently, are as guilty of violent crime as are the perpetrators of violence. This is legally justifiable, but the inclusion of these participatory (but not themselves personally violent) offenders may interfere with the elucidation of factors that predispose individuals to act violently. A further key problem is that most offenders commit a wide range of offenses; marked specialization is the exception rather than the rule. Violent offenses form part of that pattern. It follows that the greater the number of offenses a person commits, the greater the likelihood that at least one will involve violence. As a consequence, most severely recidivist offenders will have committed a violent offense at some point in their criminal careers, and there will be a necessary (but to some extent artefactual) association between persistent delinquency and violent crime.

Nevertheless, the association both ways is quite strong. Loeber et al. (1998) concluded that 29% of chronic offenders were violent offenders and that 53% of violent offenders were also chronic. Because of the overlap between recidivism and violent crime, any examination of the risk factors for violence needs to control for the number of offenses. Not many studies have done that. A further difficulty is that, because violent crimes are much less frequent than acquisitive crimes, general population samples are likely to include rather few violent offenders. Conclusions from such studies will therefore be based on small numbers. Incarcerated groups will provide much larger numbers, but with the accompanying uncertainty regarding their representativeness. Finally, because violent offenses most often occur in late adolescence or early adult life, the great majority of studies have been based on adult offenders.

With those caveats, we turn to the empirical evidence. Both official statistics and self-report studies agree in showing a greater male preponderance for violent crime than for acquisitive crime (Graham & Bowling, 1995; Home Office, 1996). The possible reasons for this gender difference are considered in Chapter 9.

Farrington (1978), using data from his longitudinal study of inner London boys, compared the 27 with a violent offense (strictly defined) before the age of about 21 with the 98 nonviolent delinquents and with the remaining 283 in his general population sample. Harsh parenting, early separation from parents, aggressiveness at school at age 12–14, and low IQ were the factors that best differentiated violent and nonviolent delinquents. However, parental criminality, poor supervision, marital disharmony, and the characteristics of daring were also important predictors that seemed to operate mainly via the risk for aggressiveness in middle childhood. In short, the personal and family risk factors for violent crime seemed broadly similar to those for nonviolent crime, but the violent offenders tended to show higher-risk features (Farrington, 1991; Lipsey & Derzon, 1998). The Oregon studies have also pointed to the similarities between violent and nonviolent offenders once the frequency of offending is taken into account (Capaldi & Patterson, 1996).

Henry et al. (1996), using data from the Dunedin longitudinal study for ages up to 18, compared the 21 males convicted of at least one violent offense with the 50 with a record of acquisitive crimes only and the 404 who had never been convicted. The violent offenses included, however, seven cases of disorderly behavior likely to cause violence and ten cases of possession of an offensive weapon, so that not all the 21 individuals had engaged in actual assault. The violent and nonviolent crime groups were similar in most respects, but the former differed with respect to the behavioral feature of "lack of control" as observed at ages 3 and 5. This difference held up after controlling for number of offenses.

As already noted, in the Dunedin study, early-onset antisocial behavior that persisted into late adolescence and early adult life seemed to be associated with an increased likelihood that the crimes in the late teenage years would include violence. This was not just a function of the rate of crime at that age, because the early- and late-onset groups did not differ in that respect; rather, by definition, the life-course–persistent group (i.e., those starting early and continuing) had a much longer crime career and had committed far more crimes overall. Accordingly, it remains somewhat uncertain whether the association is with violence as such or rather recidivism.

In the Stockholm Adoptive Study, Bohman (1996) and his colleagues also found that temperamental features (in their case measured at age 11) were more strongly associated with violent crime than acquisitive crime, although the latter group differed in the same way from the no-crime group, albeit to a much lesser extent. The combination of high novelty seeking and low harm avoidance (loosely equivalent to a tendency to seek thrills and to take risks) was associated with the highest risk of violent crime and also with early-onset alcohol abuse.

Because violent crime is associated with recidivism and with a higher level of personal and family risk variables than is acquisitive crime (as well as with multiple other problems – Huizinga & Jacob-Chien, 1998), it might be expected that the genetic influence would be particularly strong. It is striking, therefore, that both the Danish (Brennan et al., 1996) and Swedish (Bohman et al., 1982) studies showed the reverse – that is, a *lack* of any substantial genetic influence. Indeed, the Danish data showed that even the weak genetic effect on violent crime disappeared when the genetic influence on the property crimes committed by the violent offenders was taken into account in the statistical analyses (Brennan & Mednick, 1994).

The Danish register study data (see Chapter 6), based on a very large ($n = 4,269$) cohort, showed that the combination of pregnancy complications and maternal rejection were associated with an increased risk of violent (but not acquisitive) crime. It was argued that the findings represented a biosocial interaction because pregnancy complications, in the absence of maternal rejection, were not associated with an increased risk of violent crime. This interpretation remains a most uncertain one, however, because the interaction arises as a result of a lower risk of crime in the children with pregnancy complications but no maternal rejection, and also because there is no evidence that the obstetric hazards led to any kind of biological damage. The caveat is important because most of the complications were ones that carry a negligible risk of brain damage and because obstetric hazards are more frequent in the pregnancies of socially disadvantaged mothers. In any case, a more intensive study of a subsample of the same cohort (Raine et al., 1996) casts doubt on the earlier claim of a specific association with violence. In this latter study, 397 males were subdivided into three groups: those with psychosocial adversity (as indexed by features such as marital conflict and parental crime) and neurodevelopmental impairment; those with obstetric complications and slow motor development; and those with poverty and *low* levels of both marital conflict and slow motor development. All forms of crime showed a twofold increase in the first group. Interpretation of the findings, however, is much complicated by (a) uncertainty about what causal processes the variables reflect and (b) the fact that the cluster approach used placed everyone in one of three reputedly atypical groups. A further set of analyses (Raine, Brennan, & Mednick, 1997b) has suggested that, after all, the interaction may apply only to violent crime. However, in view of the many uncertainties, the supposed specificity remains in doubt.

Studies of clinical populations have also been used to argue for the importance of neural damage (in conjunction with serious family adversity) in the genesis of violent crime (Lewis et al., 1979, 1989a, 1994). Although this is a possibility, the empirical basis for the claim remains weak and it would be premature to argue that violent crime differs from acquisitive crime with respect to organic brain dysfunction.

Finnish studies of alcoholic, impulsive, habitually violent offenders have found low levels of 5-hydroxyindoleacetic acid (5-HIAA) in the cerebrospinal fluid (CSF), a finding that implies low brain serotonin turnover (Virkunnen, Goldman, & Linnoila, 1996). The concepts and findings are discussed more fully in Chapter 6, but the suggestion is that this is characteristic of violent rather than acquisitive crime. Other research findings point in the same direction (Kruesi et al., 1992; Kruesi & Jacobsen, 1997; Moffitt et al., 1997). It is puzzling, however, that Brunner's (1996) findings with respect to monoamine oxidase A deficiency suggest that *raised* serotonin levels may predispose individuals to impulsive violence. Also, the data so far derive from highly selective samples and include few systematic comparisons between violent and nonviolent offenders.

Although the differentiation between violent and nonviolent crime seems to have some (albeit quite limited) validity, it is important to recognize that violent crime is itself heterogeneous. Perhaps the distinctions between instrumental or assertive aggression (i.e., that which is used to further some other purpose, such as theft), hostile or angry aggression (i.e., that which seems to represent a response to a provoking situation or negative feelings toward the victim), and sadistic aggression (in which the violence seems to be intrinsically rewarding) may be relevant (Buss, 1961; Geen, 1990; Zillman, 1979). Similarly, there may be differences associated with "expressive" violent crime, not particularly directed toward a victim but rather the result of frustration or boredom, such as aggravated forms of burglary and stealing cars, where much violent damage is done but was not necessarily intended.

Psychopathy

In 1941, Checkley put forward the concept of "psychopathy." By this he meant a lack of normal socioemotional responsiveness that resulted in a pattern of social deviance characterized by features such as a lack of remorse, an absence of close relationships, egocentricity, and a general poverty of affect. An association with criminality and violence was noted, but it was not regarded as an essential element. Since then, however, most of the research has been conducted with criminal psychopaths (Hare, 1970; Hare & Schalling, 1978), and the widely used Hare (1991) "psychopathy checklist" includes both an "emotional detachment" factor and an "antisocial behavior" factor (Patrick, 1994). Recent research has shown that the correlates of the two are different (Blair et al., 1995, 1997; Patrick, 1994; Patrick, Zempolich, & Levenston, 1997). Current psychiatric classifications blur somewhat the distinctions between antisocial personality disorder and psychopathy, and this is misleading.

Patrick (1994; Patrick et al., 1997) has used the startle probe reflex to compare the autonomic responsiveness of psychopathic and nonpsychopathic criminals in prison. The presence of emotional detachment (but not antisocial behavior) was found to be associated with decreased startle and autonomic responses to unpleasant stimuli (presented in the form of pictures featuring mutilation or aimed guns) but with no difference in the response to neutral or pleasant stimuli. The emotional detachment component of psychopathy was associated with instrumental aggression involving weapons, but not with assault and other forms of aggression. The emotionally detached offenders differed from other criminals in being *less* likely to have come from a socially disadvantaged background and in being less likely to have experienced abuse.

Blair (1995; Blair et al., 1995, 1997) has used a rather different experimental paradigm but with broadly comparable results. Psychopathic criminals in prison or a special hospital differed from nonpsychopathic criminals in showing a reduced autonomic response to distress cues (color slides of pictures such as a crying face), but not to threatening (e.g. a shark or an angry face) or to neutral stimuli. Psychopaths also differed in their emotional attributions to stories that elicited guilt in other people – being more likely to express happiness or indifference to stories involving someone being hurt. Nonpsychopathic criminals generally show the usual differentiation between conventional transgressions (i.e., those that contravene social conventions or rules) and moral transgressions (i.e., those that involve individual suffering); psychopathic criminals are less likely to do so.

Because the research to date has been conducted almost entirely with incarcerated adults, there must be some caution with respect to conclusions. Nevertheless, the limited available evidence suggests that emotional detachment may constitute a meaningful differentiating feature in childhood as well as adult life (Christian et al., 1997; Frick et al., 1994). Such detachment does not necessarily lead to crime but, when it does, the crime seems to be especially likely to be characterized by instrumental aggression with weapons and a lack of concern for the victim's welfare. The trait is associated with a lack of autonomic response to scenes of extreme distress or suffering, but with no difference in response to neutral or pleasant stimuli (see, however, Newman, Schmitt, & Voss, 1997, for a contrary view) and possibly no difference in response to frightening stimuli. The origins of this trait remain obscure but, unlike violent crimes in antisocial personality disorder, it seems *less* likely to be associated with social disadvantage or adversity. There is some suggestion of an association with neuropsychological impairment on tests thought to reflect the functioning of the frontal lobe of the brain (Lapierre, Braun, & Hodgins, 1995), but the findings in the literature are inconsistent and it is not known whether such deficits as there may be specifically associated with emotional detachment or rather with the antisocial component of psychopathy (Dolan & Coid, 1993).

Association with Serious Mental Disorder

Epidemiologic data (Hodgins, 1993; Hodgins et al., 1996; Hodgins, Coié, & Toupin, in press; Marzuk, 1996; Modestin & Ammann, 1995; Monahan & Steadman, 1994) indicate that alcoholism and drug problems are the psychopathological disorders most strongly associated with crime (although there is some association with a wide range of psychiatric conditions). The same evidence, however, suggests that there is nothing particularly distinctive about the forms of antisocial behavior associated with substance misuse. By contrast, the associations between schizophrenia (and possibly also affective psychoses) may involve rather more specificity. The evidence derives from cohort studies of incident cases of schizophrenia (e.g. Wessely et al., 1994), from studies of mental illness among offenders (e.g. Taylor, 1993), and from general population cohort studies (e.g. Hodgins et al., 1996; Link, Andrews, & Cullen, 1992).

First, there is the small group of crimes that *follow* the onset of psychosis in adult life and in which the antisocial acts seem to have their origin in abnormal mental processes such as distorted perceptions, faulty reasoning, and disordered modulation of affect (Marzuk, 1996; Taylor, 1993; Wessely et al., 1994). The crimes are particularly likely to involve violence that derives directly from delusional thoughts (or, less often, hallucinations). The risk of violence derives from the symptoms and not from the diagnosis as such (Link et al., 1992); there is no increased risk of violence in individuals without active symptoms. The pattern is distinctive in terms of the role of abnormal thought processes, the fact that the increased risk following illness is only for violence (and not theft), and with respect to a high proportion of first convictions that occur well into adult life. Nevertheless, it is important to appreciate that the association is only modest; it accounts for a tiny proportion of crimes, and the great majority of individuals with schizophrenia are neither antisocial nor violent.

The second pattern is quite different in that the antisocial behavior begins in childhood and *precedes* the onset of schizophrenic psychosis in late adolescence or adult life. From Robins's (1966) classic follow-up of Child Guidance clinic attenders, both follow-up and follow-back data have shown that antisocial behavior in childhood (at least in males) is associated with an increased risk of schizophrenia in adulthood (see Rutter & Garmezy, 1983, for a succinct summary of the key research from earlier research findings). Typically, however, the antisocial behavior tends to be solitary, accompanied by social malfunction and odd behavior, often does not result in court appearance, and has a weak association with the usual predictors of crime. The implication is that the antisocial behavior constitutes an intrinsic part of the early manifestations of schizophrenia rather than a separate disorder or behavioral pattern.

The proportion of crimes associated with autism and Asperger's syndrome is even smaller but, again, what is distinctive are the *occasional* unusual qualities (Tantam, 1988; Wolff, 1995). Most individuals with autism show no propensity for antisocial behavior, and the few who are antisocial often are so in a manner broadly comparable with that of any other group of offenders. Nevertheless, in some instances the crimes seem to derive from the insensitivity to social cues that is characteristic of the disorder.

Infanticide also stands out in several key respects, particularly its timing in relation to the period immediately after childbirth, the extent to which it is committed by females (i.e., the mothers), and its lack of strong association with other forms of antisocial behavior (D'Orban, 1979). These distinctive qualities, however, are restricted to killings during the puerperium. Fathers are more often involved in the killing of older infants, although even in this slightly older age group mothers are responsible for nearly half the homicides (Marks & Kumar, 1993).

Special Groups of Uncertain Validity

In addition to the five key differentiating factors that appear to give rise to meaningfully distinctive subgroups, there are several categories that warrant attention because of their apparent "specialness" yet for which the evidence of discriminative validity is weak. In this section we discuss "normal" crime, sexual offenses, juvenile homicide, crime associated with substance abuse, crime associated with somatic medical conditions, and crime associated with emotional disorder.

"Normal" Crime

It is necessary to consider the extent to which some crime may be "normal," meaning that it does not represent any form of either personal psychopathology or social malfunction. The possibility arises in three main ways. First, at some level crime may be seen as *statistically* normative: self-report studies consistently find that the majority of individuals have at some time committed an act for which they could have been prosecuted if caught. However, this should not be taken to mean that their crimes are any different from those committed by the individuals who appear in court. To begin with, although most frequent offenders are caught at some time, not *all* are, and the proportion who escape is bound to be much higher in the case of occasional offenders (because the likelihood of detection and prosecution for any single crime is so low; see Chapter 3). Thus it may be that the self-reported crime that doesn't result in court appearance is simply a milder degree of the same phenomenon. The consistent finding that the risk factors for self-reported delinquency are much the same as those for "official" crime (see Chapter 3) supports this inference.

Second, in the past it has been argued that there is much crime that is viewed as acceptable in particular subcultures and that is not the result of the risk factors operating in the rest of the general population (Cohen, 1956; Mays, 1954). There is no doubt that there are many acts that are technically against the law but which are viewed as noncriminal by many people. Such acts include some minor examples of using work resources (such as telephone or stationery) for personal purposes, inflating travel claims, keeping a mistaken excess of change when shopping, and traveling without paying the fare. On the whole, however, these are viewed as lesser infringements rather than behavior that is outside the law. Moreover, the evidence runs counter to the view that such behavior is restricted to particular social subgroups or that it is not subject to the same risk factors as the rest of crime. As a result, this theoretical view has ceased to have much currency. It is not that subcultural groups do not vary in their attitudes to particular forms of crime (obviously they do), but such variation is pervasive across society and does not serve to pick out meaningfully different antisocial behavior.

Third, some criminal acts represent a highly principled form of civil protest. The suffragettes at the turn of this century, the U.K. pacifists who went to jail during the First World War because of their conscientious objection to killing, and the civil rights activists in the United States who deliberately went into forbidden racially segregated areas all constitute examples of this kind. The reality of highly moral antisocial acts cannot be doubted. The problem, however, is that civil protests (whether for animal rights or Northern Ireland) tend to include a broader range of individuals, some of whom – whatever their views – are at least partially motivated by the excitement of the conflict and also engage in other, less reputable, forms of crime.

The conclusion must be that some criminal acts are indeed normal in the triple sense that their motivation is moral rather than antisocial, that the usual risk factors for crime do not apply, and that they do not reflect either social malfunction or personal psychopathology. Nevertheless, in practice it is by no means straightforward to use this recognition to pick out a distinctive subgroup of either crimes or offenders.

Sexual Offenses

The rise in emphasis on the victims of crime in the 1980s, both in research and in the criminal justice system, has led to an increased awareness of the extent and nature of sex offending. This has included a focus on young people as victims and as perpetrators (Barbaree, Marshall, & Hudson, 1993; Becker & Hunter, 1997; Davis & Leitenberg, 1987; Hagan, King, & Patros, 1994; Vizard et al., 1995; Williams & New, 1996). Most especially, researchers and practitioners in the sexual abuse field have commented on the possibility that the *experience* of sexual abuse in childhood constitutes an important risk factor for being a *perpetrator* later, either in childhood, adolescence, or adult life (Watkins & Bentovim, 1992). This has been associated with a recognition that a substantial number of sex offenses are committed by juveniles – the best available data suggests about a fifth (Barbaree et al., 1993; Home Office, 1996). This proportion is lower than that for other offenses, but it is nevertheless a sufficiently high percentage to warrant serious attention.

Despite a general appreciation of the importance of this subgroup, there have been relatively few attempts to bring together researchers and practitioners from the general sexual deviance field (which usually does not focus on differentiations based on the age of the offender) and those from adolescent psychiatry and psychology (in which sexual offenses tend to be seen as part of a wider range of psychosocial problems rather than as a special group). The book by Barbaree et al. (1993), however, constitutes a notable exception. A recent British review has highlighted the uncertainties regarding definition, the paucity of data on incidence and prevalence, the rarity of systematic comparative studies, and the shortage of follow-up studies (Vizard et al., 1995). All are necessary for firm conclusions on child and adolescent sexual abuse perpetrators, but the available data permit some provisional statements.

It might well seem that sexual crimes should be distinctively different because of the sexual component, but the evidence (in relation to both juveniles and adults) suggests that the similarities are at least as great as the differences. To begin with, to a considerable extent, sexual and nonsexual offenses are committed by the same individuals. About half of sexual offenders are also involved in other types of crime, such as theft and nonsexual violence. The proportion is probably highest with respect to those committing sexual offenses that involve major assault. Researchers and practitioners have also become aware that the main motivation underlying rape is as likely to be the exercise of power or the humiliation of the victim as it is to be sexual gratification per se (Frude, 1980). Most sexual offenses probably derive from general antisocial tendencies rather than any superfluity of sexual drive.

The possible distinctiveness of sexual offenses, or of sexual offenders, needs to be tested through systematic comparisons with respect to risk factors, psychopathology, and to cause and outcome. That is, representative groups of sex offenders need to be compared with other offenders after equating the samples for age, gender, and recidivism. Unfortunately, few such investigations have been undertaken, and nearly all have concerned special groups of one kind or another – usually individuals in custodial or therapeutic facilities (see Barbaree et al., 1993; Becker & Hunter, 1997; Davis & Leitenberg, 1987; and Vizard et al., 1995, for reviews). Most studies have found that sex offenders (particularly where there is violent assault) are overwhelmingly male (95% or more), but the extent to which this reflects recognition rather than true incidence remains uncertain. It seems likely that female sex offenders are underrepresented in official statistics, but it is equally probable that, as with other crimes of extreme violence, sexual assault involving physical attack or coercion differs from theft in showing a much greater male preponderance. Sex offenders show much the same pattern of personal characteristics (poor social competence, high impulsivity, low educational attainment, etc.) and family risk features (physical and/or sexual abuse, family disorganization and breakup, parental neglect, etc.) as those found for serious antisocial behavior more generally. The experience of sexual abuse is quite common for these offenders, but it seems dubious whether it is substantially more frequent than in comparable nonsexual offenders.

The few available data on recidivism are consistent in showing that the likelihood of further *non*sexual crimes is far greater than the risk of further sexual offenses. Hagan et al. (1994), in their two-year follow-up of treated serious sexual offenders, found that 46% were convicted of further nonsexual offenses but only 8% were convicted of further sexual assaults. Other studies have produced broadly comparable results (Becker & Hunter, 1997; Vizard et al., 1995), but little is known about either the features predicting sexual recidivism or the role of treatment in influencing outcome.

Another necessary comparison is that between juvenile and adult sex offenders. Knight and Prentky (1993), in a study of 564 adult male sex offenders, contrasted those with and without a history of sex offenses before the age of 19. The offenders whose history of sex crimes started in adolescence or earlier tended to have more marked personal and family risk factors. This means that an early onset of sex offenses could index greater severity, but it is equally likely that the finding was a consequence of the duration of offending rather than its age of onset. By definition of the sample, those juvenile sex offenders who did not continue to offend in adult life were omitted. The data do not yet allow firm conclusions.

The research undertaken to date has tended to pool all sexual offenses (so that these include both inappropriate fondling and violent rape), and it has not distinguished between those that are and are not accompanied by a history of nonsexual crime. It is possible that offenders who commit *only* nonviolent sexual offenses may be more distinctive than those whose repertoire of antisocial behavior extends much more broadly, but it is not known whether this is so.

Further research into sexual offenses committed by young people is obviously much needed, but the evidence so far does not suggest that juvenile sex offenders constitute a meaningfully separate group. Because sexual offenses (and offenders) are likely to be heterogeneous, it may be that they include distinctive subgroups; if so, they have yet to be identified.

Juvenile Homicide

Juvenile homicide is very rare. In the United Kingdom, the number of cases per year over the last two decades has been of the order of only some two dozen (Justice, 1996). This very low base rate (not only in the United Kingdom, but also in most industrialized countries outside of

North America) inevitably makes it difficult to establish whether juvenile killers constitute a distinct group. The situation in the United States is quite different in that the rate of homicide by young people is some 15 times higher (Snyder et al., 1996). However, this huge national difference in rate raises serious questions on comparability. Such few data as are available suggest that killings by children in the United States may occur more often in the course of acquisitive crime and probably reflect, in part, the much greater availability of guns.

Nevertheless, although there is a paucity of systematic comparative studies of homicide by children or adolescents, there are several reviews of what is known about the characteristics of young people who kill (see Cavadino, 1996; Cornell, Benedek, & Benedek, 1987; Goetting, 1995; Wilson, 1973); one comparative study of adolescents convicted of homicide and those convicted of property offenses (Toupin, 1997); one follow-up of nine delinquents who subsequently killed (Lewis et al., 1985); as well as a number of informative detailed studies of individuals (e.g. Sereny, 1995) and of small groups (Bailey, 1996; Boswell, 1996; Myers et al., 1995).

Considering the evidence as a whole, two conclusions seem reasonably well justified. First, both the nature of the homicidal acts and the characteristics of the young people who commit the acts are quite heterogeneous. Second, the children who kill tend to come from very disturbed (often abusive) family backgrounds and also show a wide range of personal problems. Accordingly, in the great majority of cases, it would seem appropriate to consider the homicide as a result of personal psychopathology and serious psychosocial adversities rather than simply as acts of serious wrongdoing or the consequences of innate evil. At present, that consideration is very poorly represented in the ways in which child killers are dealt with by the British judicial system (Justice, 1996).

Particularly in relation to recent cases that have received extensive media coverage (see e.g. Sereny, 1995), there has been much discussion among professionals on the extent to which juvenile homicide simply reflects the severe end of juvenile delinquent behavior. In terms of both personal and family characteristics, it is apparent that there is much in common between juvenile homicide and the rest of juvenile antisocial behavior, even though serious risk factors tend to be more striking in the former group. However, there is one respect in which the two seem different (at least in the United Kingdom). Over the last 50 years there has been a massive increase in juvenile delinquency in most Western industrialized countries (Rutter & Smith, 1995). This has been accompanied by a similar (although less marked) rise in the rate of other psychosocial disorders in young people, such as drug and alcohol abuse, depression, and suicide. By contrast, the U.K. rate of juvenile homicide does not appear to have risen to any appreciable extent (Justice, 1996; McNally, 1995). The evidence also suggests that a proportion of the killings involve sexual assault and/or extreme repeated violence (Bailey, 1996). It may be inferred tentatively that killings by children or adolescents may be more likely to reflect serious personal psychopathology (but not usually formal mental illness such as schizophrenia) than is the case with most other serious crime by young people. But even this inference has slender empirical support, and this rare but important subgroup of serious offenders warrants further study. That is particularly so with respect to their subsequent careers, about which next to nothing is known.

Crime Associated with Substance Misuse

Drug use and abuse increases in frequency over the same adolescent age period that shows the rise in delinquency (Elliott et al., 1989); it also shows a parallel rise over time during the last 50 years (Rutter & Smith, 1995). Not surprisingly, therefore, the two tended to be associated to a substantially greater extent than would be expected by chance (Swanson, 1994; Thornberry et al., 1995). The key question concerns the mechanisms underlying the association. To a substantial extent, both antisocial behavior and drug problems involve similar risk factors, and it seems reasonable to regard both (at least in part) as reflections of the same broad propensity to engage in socially disapproved behavior (Catalano & Hawkins, 1997; Jessor & Jessor, 1977; Jessor et al., 1991; Robins & Wish, 1977). Nevertheless, there seems to be more to it than that because both prospective and retrospective data suggest that, at all ages throughout adolescence, there is a systematic dose–response relationship between the number of conduct or antisocial problems and the likelihood that the individual will take illicit drugs over the following years (Dobkin, Tremblay, & Sacchitelle, 1997; Hawkins, Catalano, & Miller, 1992a; Hawkins et al., 1992b; McCord, 1988; Robins & McEvoy, 1990). In other words, antisocial behavior seems, in some way, to predispose to illicit drug taking.

Does the converse apply? That is, does drug taking predispose to crime? The evidence suggests that, to some extent, it does. Antisocial peer groups probably provide an ethos in which drug taking is acceptable; moreover, at least with "hard" drugs, stealing may be necessary to finance their purchase (Chaiken & Chaiken, 1991). Also, although the associations between heavy drinking and crime are complex, with both reflecting life-style features, there does seem to be some tendency for alcohol (sometimes with other drugs) to make violent acts more likely (see e.g. Cookson, 1992; Parker, 1996).

However, there is more to the association than that, as four different sorts of study show. First, Cohen and Brook's 20-year longitudinal study of elementary school children in upstate New York (Brook et al., 1996; Cohen & Brook, 1987) showed both that childhood aggression was associated with an increased risk of later drug use and that adolescent drug use was associated with later delinquency over and above the stability of the two behaviors. They suggested that, in addition to shared causal processes that include personal and family risk factors, drug use predisposed to crime by reducing inhibitions, creating a need for money to purchase drugs, causing difficulties in family relationships, interfering with the development of social coping skills, and establishing a peer group culture that fosters both further drug use and delinquent activities. Second, the Tüebingen Criminal Behavior Development Study of prisoners and controls – aged in their 20s and followed until their early 50s – showed that heavy drinking was particularly associated with recidivist serious offending and that both were associated with an antisocial life style involving frequent changes of job, financial difficulties, and loose social contacts (Kerner et al., 1996). Over time, desistance from crime went hand in hand with desistance from alcohol. Third, official statistics for Germany (Kerner et al., 1996) suggested that there was a marked variation among offenses in the likelihood that they would be committed under the influence of alcohol. The likelihood was least for fraud (2%) and simple theft (5%) and greatest for crimes against life (35%) and for violent crimes generally (32%). Fourth, experimental studies have shown that intoxication predisposes to aggression in the presence of frustration (Ito et al., 1996).

The conclusion is that both alcohol and drug abuse show a substantial association with crime, with bidirectional causal processes. The association is strongest with violent crime, but it does not define a distinctive subgroup and it probably reflects several different causal mechanisms (see also the section on drugs and alcohol in Chapter 6).

Medically Caused Crime

Over the years, there have been numerous attempts to identify categories of antisocial behavior directly caused by some medical condition. The XYY chromosomal anomaly was one of the first to hit the headlines with the suggestion that the extra Y chromosome brought about an excess of "maleness" that led to violent crime (Jacobs et al., 1965). Eventually, it became clear that this suggestion derived from the biased samples in the early studies. Epidemiological studies have shown that XYY is associated with an increase in hyperactive behavior and a moderate increase in the risk of crime, but the effects are indirect and not deterministic, and they do *not* particularly apply to violent offenses (see Chapter 6).

More recently, similar claims regarding a predisposition to crime have been made for the hormonal effects associated with premenstrual tension in women (Dalton, 1984). Perhaps surprisingly, these claims have been accepted in law courts as reflecting direct causation (Denno, 1996). Nevertheless, a careful reading of the evidence raises doubts. It seems much more likely that the hormonal effects contribute probabilistically to the risks as part of multifactorial causation but do not in themselves lead directly to crime (see Chapter 6).

The report of a Dutch family with a genetically determined biochemical abnormality associated with impaired intelligence and violence (Brunner, 1996) led to widespread media speculation about the possibility of a "gene for crime." We consider the findings briefly in the next chapter, but the point to be made here is that it is very doubtful that such abnormalities will be of any general relevance for the classification of antisocial behavior.

Medical factors occasionally play a role in individual susceptibility to antisocial behavior, but (with possible rare exceptions) they do not serve as direct causes of criminal acts and do not define a distinctive subgroup of either crimes or offenders.

Crime Associated with Emotional Disorder

In the early days of research into psychological treatments for antisocial behavior, some data suggested that responses to counseling approaches tended to be better in the case of offenders with marked emotional disturbance (see Rutter & Giller, 1983). The classification systems used at that time have fallen out of favor, there are no findings to test the value of the differentiation, and treatment methods have moved in different directions. The notion that psychotherapy or counseling might be more effective when individuals are experiencing emotional distress in relation to their behavior is plausible and it would be wrong to argue that the view is mistaken (Blackburn, 1993), but it continues to lack empirical support.

Although the concept of "neurotic" crime no longer has currency, increasing attention has been paid to the extensive evidence that many individuals showing antisocial behavior also exhibit emotional disturbance (Dishion, French, & Patterson, 1995). Both epidemiological and clinical studies have demonstrated the very high frequency with which individuals tend to have not one but several psychiatric diagnoses when the prevailing systems of diagnostic classification are applied (Achenbach, 1991; Caron & Rutter, 1991; Nottelman & Jensen, 1995; Simonoff et al., 1997). This phenomenon of "comorbidity" (co-occurrence) of two or more supposedly separate disorders is potentially important because of the light it could throw on causal mechanisms. Nevertheless, there are numerous sources of artefact, and systematic research strategies need to be employed in order to test the competing hypotheses on the underlying mechanisms (Caron & Rutter, 1991; Rutter, 1997b). However, the basic question in relation to the heterogeneity of antisocial behavior is whether the causes, correlates, course, and outcome of antisocial behavior differs when it is accompanied by emotional disturbance. Most attention in that connection has been paid to the co-occurrence with depression, focusing on possible differences between comorbid patterns, "pure" antisocial behavior, and "pure" depression. This has been tackled, for example, by examining social cognitions (Garber et al., 1991; Quiggle et al., 1992); genetic influences (Gjone & Stevenson, 1997; O'Connor et al., in press b); temporal interconnections between antisocial behavior symptoms of depression over periods of a few years (Kovacs & Getsonis, 1989); and follow-up into adult life (Harrington et al., 1991; Harrington, Rutter, & Fombonne, 1996; Rutter et al., 1993, 1997b). The findings underline the extent to which antisocial behavior is accompanied by depressive disturbance and also by the much increased risk of suicide and of suicidal behaviors. The issues raised by these findings are discussed in later chapters, but the evidence indicates that such associations probably do not provide a valid means of subgrouping varieties of antisocial behavior. On the other hand, in a single-rater questionnaire study of 5–15-year-olds in Norway, Gjone and Stevenson (1997) found that "externalizing" (disruptive) behavior seemed to involve a stronger genetic component when it occurred in "pure" form than when it was associated with emotional problems. The difference fell short of statistical significance, however, and the matter requires further study before firm conclusions can be drawn.

Other Distinctions

Socialized versus Unsocialized

Numerous studies (reviewed by Asher, Erdley, & Gabriel, 1994; Parker & Asher, 1987) have shown that poor peer relationships tend to be associated with antisocial behavior. Thus, in the West and Farrington longitudinal study of inner London boys, delinquents tended to be unpopular with their peers at 8 to 10 years of age and also more likely to be bullies (Farrington, 1995a,b). On the other hand, it would certainly be misleading to view delinquents as usually social rejects or isolates. Indeed, Farrington (1995a,b) found that being nervous and withdrawn and having no friends was in some circumstances protective against delinquency, despite its association with social malfunction. Much delinquency takes place with other youngsters and, in a real sense, constitutes a group activity. In a descriptive study of adolescents, Giordano, Cernkovich, and Pugh (1986) found that delinquents formed their friendship patterns in much the same way as did other young people; the main difference was that they were more likely to report conflict with friends.

Nevertheless, antisocial individuals vary in the extent to which they form satisfactory peer relationships, and perhaps the longest established subdivision of antisocial behavior is that between "socialized" and "unsocialized" delinquency (Henn, Bardwell, & Jenkins, 1980; Hewitt & Jenkins, 1946). Socialized forms were said to cover activities such as stealing, truancy, and running away but were associated with adequate peer relationships. Unsocialized forms were said to involve more unpopularity, quarreling, and poor peer relationships, and possibly more lying and malicious behavior (Rutter & Giller, 1983). This view has some empirical justification in that the latter group is more likely to involve aggression and to be recidivist. The distinction is still reflected in the ICD-10 subclassification of conduct disorder (World Health Organization, 1992), although it is not part of DSM-IV (American Psychiatric Association, 1994). The reason why it has not become a generally accepted subdivision concerns the difficulties in providing an unambiguous operational differentiation of "socialized" and "unsocialized." Nevertheless, it is evident that the socialized variety has much in common with adolescence-limited delinquency and the unsocialized with life-course–persistent and hyperkinetic varieties.

Overt versus Covert Crime

Loeber and his colleagues (1993, in press) have drawn attention to the possible differences in the developmental pathways associated with overt and covert antisocial behavior. The former is associated with a possible escalation from defiance and confrontation in early childhood to fighting in middle childhood and serious assault in late adolescence or early adult life; the latter deals with different degrees of concealed or surreptitious antisocial behavior. The distinction is not quite synonymous with violence versus nonviolence in that covert crime includes destruction of property and vandalism as well as varieties of theft. The developmental approach is clearly a useful one, but the value of an overt–covert classification scheme remains uncertain, if only because the majority of antisocial youths engage in both types of behavior. The limited attempts so far to determine whether the distinction maps onto genetic influences have also failed to demonstrate discriminative validity (Simonoff et al., 1997).

Recidivist Crime

All studies of antisocial behavior have shown that both personal and family risk factors for crime apply much more strongly for individuals engaging in recidivist crime than to one-time offenders. As viewed from almost any angle, recidivists represent a much more serious subgroup. This is so from a public policy as well as an individual perspective. As discussed in Chapter 3, many commentators have noted that a small proportion of seriously recidivist individuals are responsible for a large proportion of crimes committed. The observation is important in its implication that any effective policy of prevention will have to make a substantial impact on this minority subgroup if it is to succeed. The obvious difficulty, of course, is that recidivism is necessarily defined in terms of patterns over time. If the distinction is to be used for classification, it will be necessary to devise some means of subdividing offenders on the basis of their frequency of offenses as determined at some point in time.

Two remarks need to be made when considering whether recidivists constitute a meaningful subgroup that is different from other offenders. First, the "discovery" that they commit a disproportionate number of offenses says nothing special about crime; it is an inevitable statistical consequence of any J-shaped distribution, in which a high proportion of individuals have just a few episodes or commit just a few acts and in which there is a long diminishing "tail" of a smaller proportion of individuals with many episodes or many acts. Second, if the distribution is J-shaped (which it is with crime), then it is likely to prove quite difficult to pick out a meaningful different group of extreme recidivists. The problem derives from the difficulty of deciding where to place the cutoff point and from the difficulty, at any one point in time, of picking out the offenders who are likely to persist in their criminal activities at a high rate over many years (see Blumstein et al., 1985, 1986). Relying simply on frequency of offending as a distinguishing feature means that, for any given moment during their adolescence, it will be very hard to tell which offenders will be recidivist over long periods of time and which will engage only in a short period of adolescence-limited repeated offending. Yet, society is likely to want to respond differently to the two groups.

The empirical findings from Hagell and Newburn's (1994) English study of frequent offenders well exemplify these points. The proportion of male offenders who have more than one conviction is high. However, within a group of recidivists there is no strong association between number and seriousness of offenses, and different definitions of serious recidivism tend to pick out different individuals. There is no doubt that severely recidivist offenders constitute a particularly important problematic group. But from the point of understanding the causes of crime, a focus on the better validated distinctions is likely to prove more fruitful, although there are some differences in the variables that distinguish offenders from non-offenders and those that distinguish occasional from persistent offenders (Farrington & Hawkins, 1991; Farrington & West, 1993). Equally, from the perspective of those wishing to operate a preventive policy of incapacitation, there are major difficulties in knowing whom to target at the point of conviction (see Chapter 12).

Because our main focus has been on antisocial behavior shown by young people, we have not discussed "white collar" crime in adult life. The topic is an important one, but so far it has attracted little systematic research. Accordingly, we know little about the causes of crime involving financial fraud, embezzlement, and other forms of illegal activity undertaken by people in affluent occupations. The matter warrants investigation.

Psychiatric Diagnoses

Psychiatric classifications, exemplified by the ICD-10 scheme of the international World Health Organization (1992) and the DSM-IV scheme of the American Psychiatric Association (1994), approach the issue of heterogeneity from a different perspective than criminology. For these schemes, the starting point is not antisocial behavior as such but rather personal malfunction that leads to social impairment. The resulting diagnostic categories, however, give rise to three that overlap with antisocial behavior. This is most obviously the case with *conduct disorder*, which is defined in terms of 15 symptoms (at least three of which must be present), some of which explicitly comprise illegal acts (e.g., burglary and rape), some of which do not, although they involve behaviors disapproved of by adults (e.g., staying out late and destructiveness), and some of which may or may not be against the law, depending on circumstances (e.g., cruelty to animals and bullying). The intention is clearly to pick out patterns of social malfunction that are more pervasive than delinquency and yet do not necessarily involve official convictions. Because research into crime has tended to remain rather separate from psychiatric research, the nature and extent of the overlap with delinquency remains uncertain, although it must be very substantial.

Antisocial or dissocial *personality disorder*, generally applied to adults rather than children or adolescents, also overlaps greatly with recidivist crime, but it is defined in terms that extend well beyond illegal acts. Thus,

the criteria in ICD-10 include callous unconcern for the feelings of others
and an incapacity to maintain enduring relationships. These would seem
to involve an overlap with the concept of psychopathy that is unhelpful
because it increases the difficulty of determining whether the origins of
the emotional deficit and of the antisocial behavior are different, as well
as the difficulty of investigating interrelationships between the two. The
DSM-IV uses a somewhat different set of criteria, but they present the
same problem through the inclusion of features such as lack of remorse
and deceitfulness as well as impulsivity and consistent irresponsibility.

The third category, *oppositional/defiant disorder*, has a less direct association with antisocial behavior in that it is primarily targeted at younger
children below the age of criminal responsibility. Nevertheless, there is
overlap both because illegal acts may be involved and because longitudinal studies indicate that often there is progression to conduct disorder
(Hinshaw et al., 1993). The disorder, however, is defined in terms of socially disapproved behaviors that do not involve illegal activities as such
(e.g., "deliberately annoys people" or "is often angry or resentful").

There is one further diagnostic category, hyperkinetic/attention-deficit
disorder, that requires mention – not because its definition includes antisocial behavior but rather because of the associated high risk of antisocial
behavior. As discussed previously, the presence of hyperactivity or inattention as a behavior is of value in defining a meaningful subgroup of antisocial behavior. However, it is less certain whether the particular psychiatric *diagnoses* (as distinct from the behavioral *dimensions*) constitute the
best means of differentiation (see Rutter et al., 1997b).

In the remainder of this volume we consider findings on the diagnostic
categories but only insofar as they appear to increase our understanding
of antisocial behavior; for the most part, we do not use them as organizing constructs. Of course, the diagnostic approach is of proven value in
many areas of psychopathology, and it could yet prove to be so within the
field of antisocial behavior. So far, however, the cutting points or bound-
aries of psychiatric diagnoses have not proved particularly useful with
respect to understanding antisocial behavior.

Conclusions

We have seen in the last few chapters that antisocial behavior by young
people – particularly young men – is common, and that it includes a range
of behaviors and outcomes. It is not surprising, therefore, that it shows a
great deal of heterogeneity. Obviously, many young people who get into
trouble with the police or who show some limited antisocial behavior go

on to be ordinary, reasonably well-functioning adults. However, the further down the continuum we progress, the more obvious are the differences between those with serious or persistent behavior problems and the remainder. It seems clear that, among those who engage in more than one or two antisocial acts in their teens, some subgroups are emerging. A growing body of research, based largely on results from the major longitudinal studies, suggests that subgroups of antisocial behavior based on (i) an overlap with early hyperactivity and/or (ii) age of onset have the greatest validity. However, it may also be useful to pay attention to a propensity to violent crime, an association with psychopathy, and an association with psychosis. These differentiations may not necessarily be mutually exclusive, and several are likely to turn out to be a reworking of earlier distinctions based on (for example) socialized and unsocialized delinquency. The defining characteristics that are the keys to these distinctions are not the fact that young people commit offenses, but how frequently they do so and for how long, and what other problems overlap with the offending behavior.

This chapter has also shown that it is increasingly clear that at least moderate levels of offending by young people are accompanied by a range of different psychosocial problems such as emotional disorder. The last decade has seen a major development in approaches to juvenile delinquency: we have witnessed an increase in the number of researchers and practitioners who advocate a multidisciplinary approach to multiply disadvantaged and troubled young people (e.g., Elliott et al., 1989). The reasons for these overlaps between psychosocial problems (do they play a causal role or are they a consequence of the antisocial behavior?) will be discussed further in Chapters 6, 7, and 8, but it is also important to bear in mind the heterogeneity of offending, as well as the overlaps with other problems, when considering prevention and intervention (Chapters 11 and 12).

CHAPTER 5 – SUMMARY OF MAIN POINTS

Antisocial behavior is very heterogeneous. Two main groups stand out, a further three may well turn out to be important, and nine further proposed subgroups were discussed but rejected.

❑ An *overlap with hyperactivity* implies a small group of people with antisocial behavior that starts earlier, is associated with cognitive and social problems, and persists into adulthood.

❑ A very *early age of onset* also implies a small group of people, over-lapping the first group just described, who show a consistent pattern of antisocial behavior, contrasting with those whose behavior is only *adolescence-limited.*

❑ Three further *potential subgroups* less clearly supported by the litera-ture include violent offenders, psychopathic offenders, and offenders with serious mental disorders.

❑ Nine *groups of uncertain validity* include (a) those whose crime is part of normal subcultural activities, (b) sexual offenders, (c) juvenile murderers, (d) drug offenders, (e) those whose behavior is medically caused, (f) crime associated with emotional disorder, (g) socialized delinquency, (h) unsocialized delinquency, and (i) recidivist offenders.

6 | The Role of Individual Features

Changing Views

Over the course of the last decade or so, there has been a major change in the zeitgeist regarding the possible role of individual characteristics in the liability to antisocial behavior. Rutter and Giller (1983) commented that it had become unfashionable to study such characteristics. This was partly because of the recognition that delinquent acts were so exceedingly common; if most people engaged in antisocial behavior at some time, then it did not seem useful to search for possible biological influences that might have played a role in individual differences in liability. It was also a consequence, however, of the fact that most of the prevailing theories at that time focused on the supposed social causes of crime.

The climate today could scarcely be more different. Scholarly books discuss the genetics of crime (Bock & Goode, 1996), biological risk factors (Mednick, Moffitt, & Stack, 1987; Raine, Brennan, & Farrington, 1997a), neuropsychological features and crime (Milner, 1991), and the links with mental disorder (Hodgins, 1993). Even more strikingly, heavily referenced popular books end with over-the-top deterministic claims that "crime is in large part due to problems in the brain" (Moir & Jessel, 1995, p. 332).

In our discussion of individual risk factors, we must therefore ask how this massive swing in opinion has come about before considering the evidence on the extent to which the current emphasis on the biological basis of antisocial behavior is empirically justified. Rutter and Giller (1983) noted the very substantial body of research showing a consistent association between lower IQ and an increased risk of delinquency (citing the review by Hirschi & Hindelang, 1977). The replicated associations with low autonomic reactivity and with hyperactivity were also noted, and it was suggested that – although individual characteristics might not be very influential in the liability (or propensity) to commit occasional isolated delinquent acts – it was more plausible that these characteristics played a role in repeated and persistent antisocial behavior. The findings were somewhat inconclusive but in future research, it was argued, this highly persistent recidivist subgroup would be an important one on which to focus.

Five factors have probably been critical in bringing about the change in view with respect to antisocial behavior. First, there is the rise in the influence of biological psychiatry in relation to a broad range of mental disorders – a rise that is well justified by research findings (partly stemming from the research possibilities opened up by advances in molecular biology and by technological advances such as brain imaging). However, it must be said that the claims rather outrun the evidence. Eisenberg (1986) put it succinctly in arguing that a "brainlessness" perspective had been replaced by an equally narrow and blinkered "mindlessness" view. In accepting the importance of biological influences, he went on to point to the equally important consideration that *homo sapiens* is a social animal and, moreover, a thinking, talking, and feeling one. It makes no sense to seek to reduce the workings of the mind to cell chemistry alone. As he put it, we must consider "the social construction of brain." The first factor in the change of climate, therefore, is that of scientific fashion, albeit a fashion that has substantial empirical underpinnings (Eisenberg, 1995).

The second factor, discussed explicitly in Chapter 5, has been the much clearer conceptualization of the nature of the heterogeneity in antisocial behavior. The consequence has been research that has sought to determine whether individual characteristics that relate to antisocial behavior operate mainly in subgroups of individuals. Moffitt's (1993a) distinction between life-course–persistent and adolescence-limited antisocial behavior has been particularly important, with the research focus particularly on the latter group.

A third factor has been the increased interest in causal processes and, thereby, in the various ways in which individual features might play a role in the liability to antisocial behavior. One of the important (and valid) blocks to an acceptance of biological influences on crime was the implausibility of deterministic causation of a socially and legally defined behavior. It has been important, therefore, that both genetic and physiological research has been clear-cut in their findings that biological risk factors operate in a probabilistic, not deterministic, fashion. Moreover, it has become evident that there is much more of a dynamic interplay between persons and their environment than the polarization of nature and nurture would seem to imply (see Plomin et al., 1997; Rutter, 1997c; Rutter et al., 1997a).

A fourth factor has been the recognition of the several research steps that are needed to test hypotheses about the causal role of biological risk factors. This has led to a substantial clarification of the correlates that are, and those that are not, likely to be implicated directly in causal processes.

Not surprisingly, this style of research has also led to a better conceptualization of how biological risk factors might operate.

Finally, all of this has been accompanied by a very considerable expansion and strengthening of the empirical research base on individual characteristics as they relate to antisocial behavior. That is particularly striking in relation to genetics, which we consider first because it constitutes the essential backdrop for the discussion of the contribution of individual traits.

Genetic Influences

All studies have found that criminal offending is strongly concentrated in families and strongly transmitted from one generation to the next (Farrington, Barnes, & Lambert, 1996a). Thus, in Farrington's study of inner London boys, if the father had been convicted then 63% of the sons were also convicted, as compared with 30% if the father had not been convicted – an odds ratio (OR) of 3.9 (a statistic that means a 3.9-fold increase in the rate of convictions). The odds ratio was highest (4.4) in relation to the risks associated with conviction of an older sibling and lowest in relation to a conviction of a younger sister (1.9), but it was substantially raised with respect to convictions in all types of family members. Because all odds ratios are raised substantially, not too much should be made of the relatively small differences among odds ratios. Nevertheless, it is perhaps noteworthy that the risk was higher in the case of older siblings (OR = 4.4) than younger siblings (OR = 2.1). The implication is that modeling effects of some kind might be operative. The most marked associations of all, however, were those between the criminality in husband and wife (i.e., the fathers and mothers of the males in the sample) and between the male sample members and their wives (OR = 9.3).

As other studies have also found, criminal parents were less likely to provide adequate supervision ($r = 0.33$ for fathers and 0.40 for mothers) and more likely to show poor child rearing characterized by harsh and erratic discipline, cruel attitudes, and family conflict ($r = 0.11$ and 0.38); they were also more likely to have large families with at least four children ($r = 0.41$ and 0.17). Rowe and Farrington (1997) showed that, although the family environment variables were significantly associated with criminality in the offspring, their effect was weaker than that of parental criminality after controlling for the presence of the other, although both were statistically significant. They concluded that the effects of parental criminality could not be accounted for by the poor rearing environment provided. Taken as a whole, the findings (with respect to crime that included adult as well as child offending) suggested that a genetic component was likely. There was also evidence, however, of some kind of "contagion" effect from criminality in the siblings – an effect not mainly explicable on the basis of co-offending.

Twin and adoptee data, which are now quite extensive (see Bock & Goode, 1996; Carey, 1994; Carey & Goldman, 1997; Eaves et al., 1997; Gottesman & Goldsmith, 1994; Miles & Carey, 1997; Rutter et al., in press b) provide a much more effective separation of genetic and environmental effects. In the past, critics have made much of the limitations of twin and adoptee studies, but the advantages and disadvantages of the two research strategies are quite different. When both give generally comparable answers, there can be reasonable confidence in the conclusions (Rutter et al., 1990a). For the most part, that is the case with respect to antisocial behavior (although the genetic influence appears less in adoptee than in twin studies), and the inference that it involves a significant and important genetic component is solid. In itself that is not a particularly useful finding because it applies to virtually the whole of human behavior (Plomin et al., 1997).

The value and interest come from the evidence on the variations in heritability and on the interplay between nature and nurture. The genetic influence is strongest in the case of hyperactivity, whether considered as a continuously distributed dimension or as a disorder applying only to a small proportion of the population (see Eaves et al., 1997; Goodman & Stevenson, 1989; Levy et al., 1997; Sherman, Iacono, & McGue, 1997; Silberg et al., 1996a,b; Thapar, Hervas, & McGuffin, 1995). The genetic component for this behavior is preponderant, accounting for some 60% to 70% of the variance or possibly even more. It is also apparent that the genetic liability to hyperactivity overlaps greatly with that for antisocial behavior when the two are associated (Silberg et al., 1996a,b).

By sharp contrast, the genetic component is very weak, and environmental influences are preponderant, in the case of antisocial behavior which is *un*associated with hyperactivity or problems in peer relationships and which is reported only by the youths themselves (see Eaves et al., 1997) and not associated with social or behavioral malfunction that is evident to parents (Silberg et al., 1996a). On the face of it, this would seem to suggest that environmental influences are significant only in relation to mild common delinquency that is unaccompanied by other problems. That cannot be the whole story, however, because Simonoff and her colleagues (reported in Rutter et al., 1997b) also found only a weak genetic influence with marked conduct disorders that led to referral to a tertiary referral psychiatric clinic. Clearly, the affected subjects had many problems. It was noteworthy, however, that most of them also came from disorganized families likely to provide a high-risk environment for anti-social behavior.

It should be added that there is a small but growing body of evidence suggesting that – although there is a substantial genetic component in both aggressiveness and disruptive or antisocial behavior – in delinquency as such this component is much weaker (Deater-Deckard & Plomin, in press; Eley, Lichtenstein, & Stevenson, in press; Van der Oord, Boomsma, & Verhulst, 1994).

A further finding is that the genetic component seems to be substantially stronger for the case of antisocial behavior that persists into adult life than when such behavior is confined to childhood and adolescence. This was first noted from comparisons of juvenile and adult twins in relation to crime (DiLalla & Gottesman, 1989), but it has also been found in Miles and Carey's (1997) meta-analysis of twin and adoptee studies of aggression; in Lyons et al.'s (1995) study of antisocial behavior in soldiers, using retrospective data for childhood; and in Simonoff et al.'s longitudinal study of individuals first seen at a psychiatric clinic in childhood (Rutter et al., 1997b). The implication is that environmental factors are very important in relation to transient (but possibly severe and persistent for a while) antisocial behavior that arises during the growing years, but play a much smaller role in relation to the persistence of such behavior into adult life. In what follows we shall consider why this might be so.

The consistent finding (albeit from a small number of studies) that the genetic influence is stronger in twin designs than adoptee designs is important because it suggests that either the genetic effect relies on interactions among genes or that it depends on gene–environment interactions – both of which will affect twin findings but not adoptee findings. We consider the importance of nature–nurture interplay in the next section. A second disparity in the genetic findings is that the genetic component in ratings based on child reports seems to be less than that based on parent reports (Eaves et al., 1997); the explanation seems obscure.

Contrary to popular views, genetic influences on violent crime seem weaker than those on petty acquisitive crime (Bohman, 1996; Brennan et al., 1996; Cloninger & Gottesman, 1987; Lyons et al., 1995). There needs to be some caution in the interpretation of this finding in view of the uncertainties over the definition of "violence." It does not mean that genetic factors are unimportant with respect to aggression because there is good evidence from many studies that this trait shows a heritability of some 40% to 50% (Miles & Carey, 1997), but it does suggest that it would be unwise to assume a strong genetic component in major violent crime.

Some 30 years ago, a study of incarcerated criminals found an excess of the XYY chromosomal anomaly (Jacobs et al., 1965). At first, this led to the popular misconception that XYY individuals were supermasculine sociopaths characterized by extreme violence. General population studies have shown that this supposed association with violence was an artefact (Schiavi et al., 1984, 1988). On the other hand, the major prospective studies (Götz, 1996; Ratcliffe, 1994; Walzer, 1998; Walzer, Bashir, & Silbert, 1991; Witkin et al., 1976) *have* found that XYY individuals have a rate of crime that is several times that in XXY individuals (37.5% versus 13.0%, pooling the three major studies), with the rate in the latter being about the same as the base rate in the general population; the elevated rate is not, moreover, explained by low IQ. Rather, it seems that the raised risk of (mainly acquisitive) antisocial behavior stems from hyperactivity, impulsivity, and other personality features. This risk has not been found with other sex chromosome anomalies (such as XXY). In other words, XYY is a probabilistic, rather than determinative, risk factor for antisocial behavior (along with many other factors). That is to say, the presence of XYY does not cause crime directly but rather (along with other factors) serves as a feature that increases the *probability* of antisocial behavior. It should be noted that about half of XYY individuals have no criminal record and that such individuals cannot sensibly be viewed as "hypermasculine."

The one and only gene that might be considered determinative is that underlying a genetically determined disorder of monoamine oxidase metabolism, described by Brunner et al. (1993). The disorder seems usually to involve violent behavior, but that is only one of many features including cognitive impairment (Brunner, 1996). The affected family is so far the only one reported in the world to have the abnormality, which probably has very little relevance for an understanding of antisocial behavior more generally.

Nature–Nurture Interplay

A key set of findings emphasizes the interplay between nature and nurture; these carry the very important implication that much of the genetic component may operate indirectly rather than directly. Because this makes such a big difference in how genetic influences need to be considered, we must examine how these indirect effects come about. They arise in three main ways: through gene–environment interaction and through passive and active gene–environment correlations (see Plomin, 1994; Plomin et al., 1997; Rutter, 1997c; Rutter et al., 1997a).

(1) *Interaction* means that the genetic effect concerns sensitivity to environmental stressors or adversity. Thus Bohman (1996), in his Swedish

adoptee study, found that the risk of adult criminality in the absence of criminality in the biological parent and with rearing in a low-risk environment was only 3%. In the presence of environmental risk (but not genetic risk) the rate doubled; in the presence of genetic risk (but not rearing risk) the rate rose to 12%, but when there was both genetic and environmental risk the rate was 40%. In other words, the effects of an adverse environment were much greater for individuals with a genetic risk for antisocial behavior. It should be noted that, because adopting parents are chosen on the basis of being likely to provide a good rearing environment, they include few families carrying high environmental risk. For example, the rate of antisocial behavior in adopting parents is low in relation to population norms and much lower than that in the biological parents giving up their children for adoption (O'Connor et al., in press a). Accordingly, adoptee studies are likely to underestimate environmental effects as they operate in the general population (Rutter et al., in press b). Other adoptee studies have also produced similar evidence that genetic factors operate in part through their influence on sensitivity or vulnerability to adverse rearing environments (Cadoret, 1985; Cadoret et al., 1995; Crowe, 1974).

These findings, of course, do not apply particularly to adoptees; it is just that the separation of nature and nurture through the circumstances of adoption makes the interaction between the two easier to study. Most people are reared by their biological parents and this means that nature and nurture will be associated in ways that matter.

(2) A *passive gene–environment correlation* means that the biological parents who pass their genes on to their children are also the people who provide the rearing environment, and that the same parental qualities that index the relevant genes (in this case those that involve susceptibility to antisocial behavior) also index environmental risk. Thus, parental antisocial behavior is associated with a marked increase in the rate of family discord, family breakdown, and hostility to the children (Rutter & Quinton, 1984; Rutter et al., 1997a). Follow-up studies of antisocial children show that they have a much increased likelihood of marrying someone who is also antisocial. Thus, in the Dunedin study, Krueger et al. (in press) found an interpartner correlation of 0.54 for self-reported antisocial behavior. Farrington et al. (1996a) found that, of the 30 males with convicted wives, 25 (83%) were convicted themselves. Antisocial females have a much increased likelihood of becoming a teenage mother, and antisocial individuals of both sexes have a markedly increased rate of serious life stressors (Rutter et al., 1995).

(3) *Active and evocative gene–environment correlations* mean that genetically influenced characteristics affect how people shape and select their

environments and how other people respond to them (Plomin et al., 1997; Rutter, 1997c; Rutter et al., 1997a). Thus, monozygotic (identical) twins are more alike in their experiences than dizygotic (fraternal) twins (Plomin, 1994). This has been found for a range of environmental features including life events, divorce, parent–child relationships, and quality of the home environment. Adoptee studies, too, show genetic effects on the environment. Using data from the Colorado adoption study, O'Connor et al. (in press a) found that the pattern of rearing by the *adoptive* mother was influenced by whether or not the *biological* parent had a crime record. This gene–environment correlation was mediated (i.e., brought about) in part by the children's disruptive behavior. In other words, genes play a contributory role in the development of disruptive behavior, and this behavior by the child has consequent effects on the parents. How mothers and fathers rear their children is partially shaped by the parents' own characteristics and partially by the characteristics of the children that they bring up.

This effect of children's behavior on their parents is by no means confined, however, to genetically influenced characteristics. Indeed, O'Connor et al. (in press a) found that the effect was as great for children who did *not* have an antisocial biological parent. As we discuss further in Chapter 7, this tendency of children to influence the behavior of other people with whom they interact is a general one, and it has implications for the interpretation of studies seeking to assess environmentally mediated psychosocial risks.

It should be noted that the presence of gene–environment correlations and interactions is relevant to the interpretation of heritability figures. That is because genetic analyses attribute these effects to the genes in spite of the fact that their influence on antisocial behavior is contingent upon environmental risks, insofar as the genetic influences operate in this indirect way. It is necessary to recognize the role of genes in influencing individual differences in environmental risk exposure, but equally the role of the environment in these indirect genetic effects provides a further warning against assumptions of genetic determinism.

We have already noted that the genetic component in antisocial behavior continuing into adult life is greater than that confined to childhood. That could arise from genes, so to speak, "switching on" in the transition to adulthood. Although genes are in place at birth, they may not exert their effects until much later. For example, it has been shown that there is a strong genetic influence on the timing of the menarche, and genetic factors are also influential with respect to Alzheimer's disease and its attendant dementia arising in late middle- (or old) age.

In addition, however, genetic effects could come about through three other mechanisms implicit in nature–nurture interplay. Genes that affect behavior only at certain phases of development do exist; but, on the whole, the genes that influence a trait at one age are the same genes that do so at a later age. By contrast, environments (especially those impinging specifically on individuals) show a lesser degree of continuity over time. A consequence is that genetic effects are more likely than environmental ones to shape developmental course. That is, since the genes that influence behavior at one age are the same genes that influence behavior at a later age, their effects will combine in summative fashion. By contrast, if the environmental effects at one age are not the same as those at a later age then they may serve to bring about different effects that pull in different directions. Also, genetic effects will accumulate and become enhanced over time – both through their role in sensitivities to the environment and through shaping of individual differences in environmental risk exposure. These last two considerations may well prove to be the most important of all.

Two important limitations to the genetic findings should be noted (Rutter et al., in press b). First, there are scarcely any data on ethnic minorities. Accordingly, it is unknown how far the pattern of findings is the same in, say, African-Americans or people of Asian origin living in the United Kingdom. Second, both the twin and adoptee samples include a rather small proportion of families whose environmental risks are very high. The role of genetically influenced susceptibilities could be different for children living in very high-risk environments, although in the absence of relevant data it is quite uncertain if this is in fact the case (see Baumrind, 1993; Scarr, 1992).

Routes of Genetic Mediation

It is important to move – from the general finding that there is a substantial genetic component in the liability to at least some forms of antisocial behavior – to the crucial question of how these genetic effects are mediated (meaning how they are brought about). It is, of course, quite implausible that the genetic effects operate on crime directly. There is no gene for crime and it is not at all likely that one could ever be found. Not only is antisocial behavior socially and legally defined but also, as the previous section demonstrated, genetic effects on multifactorially determined behaviors operate probabilistically (i.e., the effects increase the likelihood that these behaviors will occur but whether or not they actually happen will be dependent on a range of other factors). Moreover, molecular genetic research (i.e., that which seeks to identify

actual genes through the analysis of DNA) indicates that most "susceptibility" genes are likely to be normal variations of normal genes and
not abnormal mutations (Plomin et al., 1997; Plomin & Rutter, in press;
Rutter & Plomin, 1997). In other words, the genes that contribute to a
somewhat increased or decreased tendency to engage in antisocial behavior are variations of genes that we all have; they are not "disease"
genes. Also, many will concern risk and protective *dimensions* rather
than any deviant behavior as such. That is, they concern variations in
normal characteristics that we all possess to some degree. Those that
tend to lead to an increased likelihood of antisocial behavior are termed
"risk" dimensions and those associated with a decreased likelihood "protective" ones. Thus, the dimensions might apply to temperamental or
personality characteristics that indirectly involve an increased risk for
antisocial behavior. This consideration is in no way special to crime;
it applies equally to most common medical disorders. Thus, people do
not inherit heart attacks as such. Instead, they have risk characteristics
(such as a high cholesterol level or a tendency to high blood pressure)
that are genetically influenced in part but that are also influenced by the
environment.

In talking about risk characteristics it is necessary to appreciate that
most risks are not inherently bad. Whether a particular trait serves as a
risk or protective factor will often depend on the outcome being considered. Thus, high behavioral inhibition or anxiety is a risk factor for anxiety disorders but a protective factor against antisocial behavior. It follows
that genetic factors may operate protectively as well as through risk features. For example, many Asian individuals have a genetically influenced
flushing response to alcohol; this is quite unpleasant and serves to protect them against alcoholism (McGue, 1993).

A related point is that many genes are involved in susceptibility to
multifactorial traits (i.e., ones due to a combination of many different influences), and that sometimes a particular combination of genes acting
synergistically (i.e., potentiating each other's effects) may be required. It
is sometimes supposed that molecular genetic research will enable identification of people with "bad" genes, and that this will be helpful in the
development of both reproductive control and eugenic policies. The sup-
position is quite wrong. *All* of us are likely to carry susceptibility genes for
some undesirable trait or disorder. We may not have the disorder because
we possess only some of the relevant genes or because we have not experienced the relevant environmental risks. Getting rid of bad genes is not a
practical proposition. The main value of genetics lies in its power to help
elucidate causal mechanisms, including those that mediate environmental

risks, and not in implications for breeding (Plomin & Rutter, in press; Rutter & Plomin, 1997).

We need to return to the topic of routes of genetic mediation. Relatively little is known with any certainty at the moment, but it is clear that this provides the way ahead and that the research means are available to do what is needed. Let us consider some of the possible routes. Attention has been drawn to the strong genetic influence on hyperactivity, and we shall discuss the risks for antisocial behavior associated with hyperactivity. Behavior genetic strategies allow testing of the hypothesis that the genetic risk for antisocial behavior is entirely mediated by hyperactivity. The key statistic concerns the across-twin–across-trait correlation; that is, the extent to which hyperactivity in one twin is correlated with antisocial behavior in the other twin (see Silberg et al., 1996b). The findings suggest that part, but only part, of the genetic influences do operate via this route. The same strategy may be applied to other risk dimensions as considered later in this chapter – autonomic reactivity, IQ, impulsivity, and serotonin metabolism, to mention but a few to illustrate the range. The same strategy (and other, related strategies) may be applied to routes via environmental risk factors (see e.g. Pike et al., 1996a; Rodgers, Rowe, & Li, 1994). For obvious reasons, molecular genetic findings identifying the actual genes that carry susceptibility will be even more helpful in providing an understanding of causal processes – both at the level of neural (brain) mechanisms and the level of nature–nurture interplay (see Plomin & Rutter, in press; Rutter & Plomin, 1997).

Obstetric Complications

There is a long history of research seeking to determine the possible role of obstetric/perinatal complications on children's psychological development (see e.g. Casaer, de Vries, & Marlowe, 1991; Meisels & Plunkett, 1989; Sameroff & Chandler, 1975). There is no doubt that, in certain cases, very low birth weight or an unduly short gestation can be associated with brain damage leading to cerebral palsy or mental retardation (see Casaer et al., 1991). At one time, the damage tended to be attributed to "birth injury" but it has since become clear that, in the great majority of cases, the damage does not arise during the course of birth (see Goodman, 1994). Rather, the damage usually derives either from circumstances in the womb or from bleeding and its sequelae occurring during the neonatal period. Brain imaging studies have shown that the most serious problems do not come from bleeding into the ventricles (the fluid-containing spaces within the brain) but rather from the trauma to the brain substance stemming from either bleeding into the tissues or from secondary vascular shutdown (Casaer et al., 1991). The consequences are to be seen in a leukomalacia of the brain with cyst formation.

Obviously, very few delinquents have overtly handicapping disorders (such as cerebral palsy or mental retardation) that might derive from obstetric/perinatal damage. Why, then, has anyone suggested that such damage might play a role in a biological liability to antisocial behavior in some individuals? The answer is that it has long been known that it is entirely possible to have definite brain damage that does not show up in clinically detectable neurological abnormalities (Rutter, 1983a). This is evident, for example, both from follow-up studies of children with penetrating brain injuries and from brain imaging findings. It was assumed that, if obstetric/perinatal complications lead to definite overt handicapping disorders in some cases, there must be other damage of lesser degree that cannot be detected by a medical examination or by an EEG (brainwave test). This assumption underlay the concepts of a "continuum of reproductive casualty" (Pasamanick & Knobloch, 1966; Sameroff & Chandler, 1975) and of "minimal brain dysfunction" (Rie & Rie, 1980). The basic assumption is doubtless valid, but the concepts have proved troublesome because they involved inferences of brain damage that, prior to brain imaging, could not be tested. The high rate of obstetric complications in normal individuals means that the inference is bound to be wrong much more often than it is right (see Goodman, 1994). A realization that this was so (together with a host of other difficulties) led to the demise of both concepts with respect to their utility in any application to individuals (Rutter, 1983a).

Nevertheless, even if a history of obstetric complications cannot be used to infer minimal brain dysfunction in the individual person, it might be thought that – at least at a group level – if it can be shown that obstetric complications are more common in the background of delinquents, then a contributory role of some form of brain dysfunction in some individuals would seem likely. Unfortunately, that is not a safe inference even at an aggregate level, because it is well established that many obstetric complications are more common in women from psychosocially high-risk backgrounds (Illsley & Mitchell, 1984). Unless the research examines the possible confounding effects of these psychosocial risks, there is a considerable danger that risks that in fact derive from psychosocial adversity may be misattributed to obstetric brain damage.

It might be thought that the universal finding from general population studies (see e.g. Conseur et al., 1997, McGee, Silva, & Williams, 1984; Wadsworth, 1979) that there are at most only extremely weak associations between antisocial behavior or delinquency and either low birth weight, short gestation, or complications (such as toxaemia or bleeding during the pregnancy) would end the matter. Certainly these generally negative findings argue against a major role for obstetric/perinatal complications in the genesis of delinquency. However, two considerations indicate that a contributory causal role cannot be ruled out on that basis. First, most of the negative findings are based on studies of all delinquents. This is a serious limitation in view of the evidence on the heterogeneity of antisocial behavior (see Chapter 5). It is important to consider the possibility that obstetric damage is relevant only in the case of such subgroups as those associated with hyperactivity (although the available evidence suggests that hyperactive or impulsive behavior is only slightly increased in frequency following obstetric complications – Neligan et al., 1976; Nichols & Chen, 1981; Taylor et al., 1991) or with violent crime (as suggested by Lewis et al., 1979). Second, even though brain damage does not lead directly to antisocial behavior, it could still be that such damage increases vulnerability to psychosocial adversities. If this is so, then it will be necessary to determine the risks for antisocial behavior associated with the combination of obstetric complications and psychosocial adversity.

Three influential articles by Raine and his colleagues (1994, 1996, 1997) based on analysis of a very large Danish sample have argued that, although obstetric complications seem to be unassociated with acquisitive crime, they *are* associated with violent crime. Their data also point to an interaction with maternal rejection, with the main risks stemming from the conjunction of obstetric complications and rejection. The suggestion is potentially important, but there are several reasons for questioning the validity of their inference of a causal role mediated via brain dysfunction. First, there was no overall association between obstetric complications and crime; the positive association with violent crime was accompanied by a negative association with nonviolent crime. Second, the details of the findings in their three analyses of the same data set were rather different. Third, most of the complications included in the obstetric risk category were quite minor and not of the kind that often lead to brain damage. Fourth, the supposed biosocial interaction could well mean, instead, that the obstetric complications were mainly indexing psychosocial risk (and not biological damage). Fifth, there were no brain imaging findings to test whether any brain dysfunction had actually occurred.

Data from other studies also raise doubts. Thus, a study by Whittaker et al. (1997) showed no interaction between obstetric damage and psychosocial adversity with respect to psychological sequelae. Antisocial behavior was not assessed, however, and the failure to find an interaction concerned marked damage. Also, the weak associations found inconsistently with obstetric complications are greatly overshadowed by the risks from other sources with which they happen to be associated. For example, Conseur et al. (1997) found that males born to unmarried mothers under the age of 18 had an elevenfold increased risk of chronic offending in adolescence, whereas neither low birth weight nor preterm gestational age carried any increased risk.

No firm conclusions on the postulated causal role of brain damage deriving from obstetric complications are possible. It is certainly clear that such causation is quite unlikely in most cases of delinquency, but the possibility of a potentiating role in the case of some varieties of antisocial behavior (perhaps violent crime) cannot be completely ruled out. On the other hand, there are reasons for scepticism about the claims that a role has been demonstrated.

Intelligence

As we noted in the introduction to this chapter, it has long been known that delinquents, especially recidivist delinquents, tend to have an IQ that is slightly below that of nondelinquents in the general population (Hirschi & Hindelang, 1977). The difference is nontrivial (circa 8 points overall), although the mean IQ of delinquents is nevertheless well within the average range. Empirical findings from more recent epidemiological and longitudinal studies have amply confirmed the reality and robustness of this association (see Hinshaw, 1992; Lynam, Moffitt, & Stouthamer-Loeber, 1993; Maguin & Loeber, 1996; Moffitt, 1990a,b, 1993b; Schonfeld et al., 1988). More importantly, they have taken the issue forward through the testing of possible mechanisms.

For a long time, it was assumed (without testing) that delinquents tended to have a lower IQ because they often came from socially disadvantaged homes. It is now clear that that is not the case. Numerous studies have shown that (lower) IQ is associated with delinquency even after controlling for social background, whereas the reverse does not apply. That is, the association between social class and delinquency is much weakened by controlling for IQ. The same applies to the broader range of associations between IQ and conduct disturbance (Goodman, Simonoff, & Stevenson, 1995; Rutter, Tizard, & Whitmore, 1970). It may safely be concluded that the IQ association is not a function of social class.

A second assumption was that the association represented the effects of poor scholastic achievement rather than low cognitive abilities as such. In other words, the association derived from the psychological and social consequences of educational failure rather than from low IQ per se. There is some evidence that this may be part of the explanation. Maughan et al. (1996), in their longitudinal study of inner London schoolchildren, found that children with severe reading difficulties were much more likely than other children to truant and that the increased risk for antisocial behavior in adolescence arose mainly via that truancy. Strikingly, however, poor reading was not associated with adult crime, suggesting that the effects of educational failure are much less marked after leaving school.

Nevertheless, several findings run counter to the suggestion that the low-IQ–crime association is mainly a consequence of educational failure. Most crucially, measures of language and IQ in the preschool years are associated with a contemporaneous and later increased risk of disruptive and antisocial behavior (Howlin & Rutter, 1987; Richman, Stevenson, & Graham, 1982; Stattin & Klackenberg-Larsson, 1993). Clearly, this could not be mediated by educational failure because the children had not yet started school at the time that language skills or IQ were measured. It has also been found in the Christchurch longitudinal study that conduct problems at age 6 are associated with reading problems at age 8, an association that seems incompatible with any explanation involving educational failure (Fergusson & Lynskey, 1997). In addition, low IQ has been found to be associated with antisocial behavior even after controlling for level of scholastic attainment, although the association may be somewhat reduced (Goodman et al., 1995; Maguin & Loeber, 1996). It is also relevant that the association between either IQ or reading difficulties and conduct disturbance or antisocial behavior largely applies to early-onset varieties and not to those beginning in adolescence (Robins & Hill, 1966; Rutter, 1979; Stattin & Magnusson, 1995; Werner & Smith, 1977). It may be concluded that both low IQ and poor scholastic achievement are associated with antisocial behavior; the low-IQ association is probably stronger, and the poor scholastic achievement effect is not necessarily mediated via children's responses to failing in their schoolwork.

An alternative assumption has been that the association reflects the effect of antisocial behavior *on* cognitive performance, rather than the other way around. Thus, it has been noted that antisocial children are less likely than other children to make scholastic progress because they are disruptive in class and because they truant. Longitudinal data show that antisocial children are much less likely than other children to achieve examination success and are more likely to drop out of school (see Chapter 10). Accordingly, it is clear that antisocial behavior does impede scholastic achievement. Nevertheless, it is equally evident that the lower IQ scores in early childhood cannot be explained in that way.

On the other hand, the effects of IQ on delinquency are closely connected with hyperactivity and attentional problems. For example, in the Pittsburgh Youth Study (Maguin, Loeber, & LeMahieu, 1993), the uncorrected correlation between reading achievement and degree of delinquency for white boys across grades 1 to 7 ranged from −0.16 to −0.31. However, after controlling for attention problems, the range of these correlations was only −0.01 to −0.09; these values do not differ significantly from zero. Similarly, Maughan et al.'s (1996) longitudinal study of London boys showed that the association in middle childhood between reading difficulties and conduct problems was largely a function of inattention. Frick et al.'s (1991) clinic study findings were closely comparable. Maguin and Loeber's (1996) meta-analysis and Hinshaw's (1992) systematic review both showed that this was a general finding; the association between lower IQ and delinquency is closely bound up with hyperactivity and inattention. Farrington (1996) showed that it was also associated with truancy. In a sample that was rather small for the purpose ($n = 213$), Stevenson and Graham (1993) sought to determine whether antisocial behavior and spelling difficulties showed the same genetic liability. The question is clearly important, but the results were inconclusive and the matter needs to be re-examined with both larger numbers and more extensive measures. The findings with respect to the overlap in the genetic liabilities to hyperactivity and spelling difficulties were more clear-cut; the overlap was very substantial (Stevenson & Graham, 1993).

Two further questions arise out of those findings: (1) Is the association with a particular pattern of cognitive functioning? (2) Does the association apply to a particular pattern of delinquency? Moffitt (1993b) has summarized the evidence on the first query and concluded that the cognitive deficit particularly applies to verbal skills and to functions concerned with planning and foresight. It is much less evident with respect to visuospatial or puzzle-type skills. She and her colleagues (Moffitt et al., 1994) have also shown that the association is mainly evident with life-course–persistent antisocial behavior that begins early in childhood. Adolescents with transient antisocial behavior do not differ appreciably in their cognitive scores from the general population. There has been an interest in the extent to which the neuropsychological pattern may be especially associated with violent delinquency (e.g., Seguin et al., 1995), but the data available so far are inconclusive.

In the past, criminologists were concerned with the issue of whether the IQ–crime association reflected a link with conviction or with antisocial behavior. In other words, is it simply that less intelligent offenders are more likely to get caught? It is clear from the extensive evidence of associations between IQ and self-reported offending that the association is with antisocial behavior and not just with being apprehended and convicted (Moffitt, 1993b).

Some commentators (e.g. Hodgins, 1996) have inferred from the data on neuropsychological deficits that they imply "minor brain damage." In the absence of satisfactory biological measures of such postulated minor damage, the hypothesis cannot be put to a decisive test. However, one finding makes it unlikely that the slightly impaired cognitive functioning associated with an increased risk of antisocial behavior is *usually* due to brain damage. Studies from the Isle of Wight survey (Rutter et al., 1970) onward to Goodman et al.'s (1995) careful analysis of twin data have shown that there is a linear relationship between IQ and disruptive behavior within the normal range. That is, other things being equal, a child with (say) an IQ of 100 has a higher likelihood of showing antisocial behavior than one with an IQ of 130. It is implausible that such variations within the normal range are usually due mainly to degrees of brain damage. Quite apart from an absence of positive evidence of such a causal process, there is extensive evidence of a substantial genetic influence on individual variations in IQ (Sternberg & Grigorenko, 1997).

We may conclude, however, that – whatever its origins – neuropsychological impairment closely bound up with attentional problems and hyperactivity is associated with an increased risk of antisocial behavior. The crucial question that follows concerns the route by which this risk is mediated. Several possible mechanisms require consideration. One suggestion (Moffitt, 1990a, 1993b) is that the impairment operates, in large part, through an interplay with psychosocial risk environments. That is, the child's behaviors serve to evoke negative behaviors in other people and also to make the child more vulnerable to environmentally mediated psychosocial risks (such as coercive parenting and ineffective discipline). Insofar as the matter has been examined, it seems that the likelihood of antisocial behavior is greater when neuropsychological impairment is associated with psychosocial risk. However, that isn't quite the same thing as finding that psychosocial risks are *potentiated* by the presence of neuropsychological impairment. Nevertheless, such an interaction was apparent in Moffitt's (1990a) Dunedin study data, where the mean aggression score associated with low neuropsychological functioning combined with family adversity was four times higher than that of boys with either feature on its own. Stattin, Romelsjö, and Stenbacka (1997) similarly found that lower levels of intelligence were associated with a negligible increase in the likelihood of criminality in adult life for individuals without other risks at age 18, but a much larger effect was noted in the presence of other risks. The issue is an important one and needs to be tackled by testing for interactions between neuropsychological impairment and psychosocial risk. The usual multivariate statistics, unfortunately, have notoriously weak power for the detection of interactions (McClelland & Judd, 1993). Often it may be preferable to pose the question in more precise terms and use statistics specifically appropriate for testing the postulated mechanism (Rutter, 1983a; Rutter & Pickles, 1991). Thus, for example, one important issue is whether neuropsychological impairment carries an increased risk for antisocial behavior in the *absence* of psychosocial adversity. It is commonly assumed that a multivariate analysis testing for an effect of neuropsychological impairment after controlling for psychosocial risk does this, but in fact it does not (Rutter, 1983a). It is necessary to focus specifically on the subgroup without psychosocial risk in order to compare rates of antisocial behavior in children with and without neuropsychological impairment. As Pennington and Bennetto (1993) have pointed out, adequate measurement is crucial, but it is also important to determine whether this is a direct effect on antisocial behavior that occurs in the absence of psychosocial adversity or only (or in addition) an indirect effect that is dependent on an interaction with adversity. There are too few published data to justify any firm conclusion, but an interactive potentiating effect seems to constitute part of the mechanism.

A somewhat different mechanism concerns children's social information processing (Coie & Dodge, 1997; Crick & Dodge, 1994; Dodge & Schwartz, 1997). In dealing with all manner of social situations, people need to process social cues and intention and then select appropriate responses. It has been suggested that antisocial children may be less skilled in these aspects of "social intelligence" and hence more likely to behave in inappropriate ways. It is possible (although not demonstrated as yet) that the cognitive impairments that increase the risk do so because they involve some deficit in intention-cue detection or planning ahead in deciding how to respond to social challenges. Alternatively, it could be that the cognitive impairment causes risks, not because it involves any intellectual deficit but rather because lower IQ happens to be associated with impulsivity and hyperactivity; it could be that the real risk mediation lies in these behavioral features rather than the cognitive level as such.

It is evident that no firm conclusions are possible on the route of risk mediation. The issue has nevertheless warranted some discussion because the IQ–crime association has proved so robust. Clearly, it carries a potential for understanding some of the causal mechanisms for antisocial behavior, and research directed at determination of mediating mechanisms would be most worthwhile.

As with other risk factors, it is necessary to ask whether the findings on intelligence have been found to apply across ethnic groups. There are very few data on this matter, although Maguin et al. (1993) and Moffitt et al. (1995) did show broadly similar (although weaker) association in African-Americans compared with whites. However, they did not present their data in a form that allowed testing of whether the higher rate of antisocial behavior in African-Americans was a function of their having, on average, a somewhat lower level of measured intelligence (or whether, for example, the origins of the ethnic difference in antisocial behavior lay in psychosocial adversity).

Temperament and Personality Features

Numerous studies have shown that recidivist delinquents differ from nondelinquents in their personality features, and these differences figure strongly in some psychological theories of crime (e.g., Cloninger, 1987; Cloninger, Svrakic, & Svrakic, 1997; Eysenck, 1977; Quay, 1988; Zuckerman, 1994). Some of the research findings are, however, open to the objection that a number of supposed personality items refer to explicitly antisocial behavior (Farrington, Biron, & LeBlanc, 1982; Tennenbaum, 1977). As a consequence, Rutter and Giller (1983) drew only rather tentative conclusions about the importance of personality features other than hyperactivity. The research since then has mainly focused on four main issues:

(1) whether there are associations between criminality and personality features once this overlap in measurement has been taken care of;
(2) how early in life predictive personality features can be identified;
(3) whether these features tend to be associated with particular varieties of antisocial behavior; and
(4) the degree of specificity in the associations.

Caspi et al. (1994) tackled the first question using data on teenagers from both the Dunedin and Pittsburgh longitudinal studies. In both samples, for both males and females and for both blacks and whites, weak constraint or high impulsivity as well as negative emotionality (meaning a ready tendency to be angry, anxious, or irritable) were associated with crime.

White et al. (1990) found that being disruptive or "difficult to manage" (as reported by mothers in the Dunedin study) at age 3 predicted delinquency at age 11. Caspi et al. (1995), using data from the same study, found that "lack of control" (a factor that combined emotional lability, restlessness, short attention span, and negativism, and which was thought to reflect an inability to modulate impulsive expression) was the dimension most strongly associated with "externalizing" (meaning disruptive and antisocial) behavior as manifest at ages 9–15. This feature showed significant continuity with weak constraint and negative emotionality as assessed in adolescence (Caspi et al., 1995). Tremblay et al. (1994), using data from the Montreal longitudinal study, similarly showed that "impulsivity" (indexed by fidgetiness and overactivity) as measured when the children were in kindergarten was the best predictor of delinquency at age 13. Low anxiety and low reward dependence (indexed by prosocial behaviors) showed weaker associations with delinquency. It seems that behavioral measures reflecting hyperactivity or impulsivity in the preschool years do show a significant, but modest, continuity with later antisocial behavior.

The continuities, as judged by the Dunedin study findings, are strongest with respect to life-course–persistent antisocial behavior (Krueger et al., 1994) and especially violence (Henry et al., 1996). The findings on shyness have tended to be seemingly paradoxical, with shyness on its own a protective factor but, in combination with aggression, a risk factor for antisocial behavior (see Kellam, Simon, & Ensminger, 1983; Moskowitz & Schwartzmann, 1989). Kerr et al. (1997) have recently suggested, based on findings from the Montreal longitudinal study, that the paradox probably arises from using measures that confound social anxiety and social isolation. The former is protective whereas the latter may carry increased risk when in combination with aggression. In the Dunedin study, Krueger et al. (1994) made an interesting comparison between abstainers from delinquency and those engaging in adolescence-limited delinquency. The abstainers stood out in terms of being low in social potency – that is, having a meek, nonaggressive, nonassertive social style as measured in adolescence. Farrington et al. (1988), in their study of inner London boys, looked at the features that seemed to protect boys from high-risk homes from engaging in crime. Social withdrawal (and often social malfunction) seemed to be the key features.

The specificity of personality–crime associations were examined in the Dunedin study by looking at both ends of the link. Impulsivity has long been viewed as a risk factor for antisocial behavior (see Pulkkinen, 1986), but the findings have been contradictory – seemingly a result of differing concepts and methods of measuring impulsivity. In the Pittsburgh study, White et al. (1994) found that *behavioral* impulsivity, as tapped by ratings (of features such as doing things without planning or thinking), was a stronger predictor (0.44 versus 0.16) of delinquency than was *cognitive* impulsivity (as measured by performance on the Stroop, Cognitive

Performance, and other tests of responses to tasks). The former had a weaker association with IQ (0.36 versus 0.52) and continued to predict delinquency after controlling for socioeconomic status and IQ, whereas this was not the case for cognitive impulsivity. Behavioral impulsivity, moreover, showed a stronger association with delinquency than that found for IQ. There is an inevitable concern that the finding simply reflects measurement variance (i.e., there were overlapping sources of ratings for behavioral impulsivity and delinquency, whereas cognitive impulsivity was assessed psychometrically). Nevertheless, there is the suggestion that the risk is for the most part mediated behaviorally rather than cognitively.

Outcome specificity was assessed by determining whether boys who showed difficulty in delaying gratification at age 12 differed from others in their patterns of behavioral disturbance (Krueger et al., 1996). The findings showed that they did; low self-control (vis-à-vis gratification delay) was associated with "externalizing" (disruptive or antisocial) behavior but not with "internalizing" (emotional difficulties). Children with a mixed pattern of behavior, combining internalizing and externalizing dimensions, tended to show the same personality features as those with "pure" externalizing problems.

It should be added that there is continuing uncertainty on the precise nature of the mechanisms involved in a failure to delay gratification (see Schachar et al., 1995; Sonuga-Barke et al., 1992). Whatever its origins, it does seem to be associated with antisocial behavior.

The opposite of impulsivity might be conceptualized as a tendency to plan ahead, although planning or planful competence has been measured in a quite different way. Clausen (1991) defined it as a composite of self-confidence, intellectual involvement, and dependability; he measured it by Q-sort techniques (a card-sorting task designed to identify characteristic profiles of behavior). Quinton and Rutter (1988), by contrast, used interview methods to determine how young people actually dealt with key life decisions such as those involved in work and marriage. Both sets of studies showed that individuals who exhibited planning in adolescence had a better social outcome in adult life and, in Quinton and Rutter's study, this included a lower rate of antisocial behavior (Quinton et al., 1993). The possible mechanisms involved are discussed in Chapter 10 with respect to the issue of life transitions.

The last personality feature to consider is aggressiveness. Traditionally, a distinction has been drawn between hostile or affective (reactive) and instrumental (proactive) aggression (Atkins et al., 1993; Coie et al., 1991; Dodge & Schwartz, 1997; Price & Dodge, 1989), with only the former associated with impulsivity. It seems, too, that reactive aggression tends to be manifest at an earlier age than proactive aggression. Pulkinnen (1987) has also distinguished between offensive (unprovoked) and defensive (provoked) aggression, with only the former associated with later criminality. More recently, Crick (1996; see also Crick & Grotpeter, 1995) has characterized "relational" aggression (excluding friends from the peer group or ignoring them, or saying that they will stop liking them if they don't do something). This form of covert aggression was associated with peer relationship difficulties. Moreover, other children tend to view these negative relational manipulative acts as angry, harmful behaviors – in much the same way as physical aggression is perceived (Crick & Dodge, 1996).

A review of research findings by Parker and Asher (1987) concluded that aggression was established as a predictor of later delinquency. Later studies have confirmed the association with antisocial behavior and have tended to show that the strongest association is found with the combination of peer rejection and aggression (e.g. Coie et al., 1995). Poor peer relationships, however, are much more characteristic of early-onset antisocial behavior than that beginning in adolescence (Stattin & Magnusson, 1995). In Stattin and Magnusson's Swedish longitudinal study, the popularity at age 15 of boys with later-onset offending did not differ from that of nondelinquents.

On the face of it, aggressivity might be thought to be the behavioral feature most likely to be predictive of antisocial behavior, if only because much delinquent activity – even that which does not involve crimes of violence – has an aggressive component. Nevertheless, although aggression is undoubtedly associated with antisocial behavior, surprisingly little is known regarding its role in the developmental processes leading to such behavior. Magnusson and Bergman (1988, 1990) found that aggressivity was associated with crime only when part of a constellation of problem behaviors, suggesting that it was necessary to consider behavior in terms of overall patterns and not only of supposedly separate traits. The suggestion is important but, as yet, data are lacking on the extent to which their finding has general applicability. Similarly, the subdivision of aggression into different types seems potentially very useful, but little is known concerning the validity of the subtypes or their relative importance in relation to antisocial behavior (Vitiello & Stoff, 1997).

Poor Peer Relationships

Numerous studies have shown substantial associations between poor peer relationships and aggression; moreover, longitudinal studies have

shown that poor relationships in early or middle childhood predict social maladaptation (including delinquency) in later childhood and adolescence (Asher & Coie, 1990; Asher et al., 1994; Coie & Dodge, 1997;
Parker & Asher, 1987). There has been a particular research focus on peer
rejection. The evidence from longitudinal investigations indicates that,
although peer rejection and aggression are closely associated, peer rejection at a younger age predicts antisocial behavior and delinquency at a
later age, even after taking into account the children's initial level of aggression (Coie et al., 1992, 1995; Kupersmidt & Coie, 1990; Ollendick et al.,
1992; Patterson & Banks, 1989). The combination of rejection and aggression is particularly likely to be followed by escalating antisocial behavior.

The key question is what these findings mean. Two very different alternatives need to be considered. On the one hand, it could be that the
experience of isolation from the peer group is highly stressful and that
it is the stress that provides the risk. On the other hand, peer rejection
could result from social incompetence, with the risk stemming from the
individual characteristics that make up the incompetence.

Several findings are relevant in deciding between these two broad alternatives. First, it is social rejection, more than social isolation, that is
predictive. Indeed, Farrington et al. (1988) found that isolation provided
some protection against delinquency, even though it was associated with
other indices of maladaptation. Second, by no means does all aggression
receive disapproval from peers. "Standing up for yourself" is in most social contexts viewed positively, especially by boys. Social dominance and
assertiveness are not at all incompatible with peer acceptance or even with
popularity. Social rejection is more often associated with incompetent social functioning, and it is the ineffectual aggressors – who get into lengthy,
hostile, and emotionally charged conflicts (which they often lose) – who
are rejected (Dodge & Coie, 1987; Perry, Perry, & Kennedy, 1992). The
overall pattern of findings, therefore, suggests that the main risk for antisocial behavior resides in social incompetence and not in the experience
of being isolated. The findings also indicate that possibly the main association is with early-onset antisocial behavior rather than that beginning
only in adolescence. Socially incompetent children seek to be involved
with peers, but they do not handle social interactions (and especially lasting friendships) well.

Hyperactivity

Of all the behavioral features that predispose to antisocial behavior, hyperactivity or inattention has the most robust association (Hinshaw, 1987;

Hinshaw et al., 1993). The Cambridge study of inner London boys (Farrington, 1992; Farrington et al., 1990b), the Christchurch longitudinal study (Fergusson & Horwood, 1993; Fergusson, Horwood, & Lloyd 1991; Fergusson et al., 1993), the Pittsburgh study (Loeber et al., 1993), Magnusson's Swedish longitudinal study (Magnusson et al., 1993), the Dunedin study (McGee et al., 1984; Moffitt, 1990a), the Montreal study (Soussignan et al., 1992), Taylor's follow-up of intensively studied subgroups from his epidemiological sample (Taylor et al., 1996), and long-term follow-ups of clinic samples (Satterfield & Schell, 1997) all document the association. We noted in Chapter 5 that the consistency of the association and the distinctiveness of its consequences warranted its consideration as a separate variety of antisocial behavior.

Hyperactivity is evident during the preschool years. It is associated with early-onset antisocial behavior that tends to persist into adult life; some degree of general or specific cognitive impairment is often associated; and generally there is a constellation of other difficulties, including poor peer relationships. The follow-up data suggest that the association tends to be with generalized social malfunction, of which antisocial behavior constitutes a prominent part, rather than with crime per se. The association between hyperactivity and disruptive behavior or conduct disturbance is usually first manifest in early childhood, and the links with later delinquency are entirely through the route of earlier disruptive or antisocial behavior. That is, adolescent or adult crime in individuals who showed hyperactivity has usually been preceded by *some* manifestations of disruptive or antisocial behavior in earlier childhood, although often the severity of such behavioral manifestations falls well short of the usual criteria of a clinically significant conduct disorder.

Because there is such a strong tendency for the associated antisocial behavior to persist into adult life, Lynam (1996) has argued that this combined pattern of hyperactivity and antisocial behavior constitutes the early manifestations of psychopathy. He seems, however, to equate psychopathy with antisocial personality disorder. As discussed in Chapter 5, this may well not be the most appropriate way of conceptualizing psychopathy.

As has been implicit already in our discussions of cognitive impairment and impulsivity, it is far from clear whether these, together with hyperactivity, constitute part of the same risk factor or whether they represent different (albeit intercorrelated) risk features. The empirical findings suggest that hyperactivity needs to be viewed as a risk dimension and not simply as an extreme diagnostic category. Nevertheless, it is quite possible that there may be both a hyperactivity risk dimension (perhaps more appropriately considered as a temperamental characteristic) and a qualitatively different though relatively uncommon clinical disorder (see Eaves et al., 1993; Rutter et al., 1997b).

Biased Cognitive Processing

Dodge (1980, 1986; Dodge & Schwartz, 1997) proposed that aggressive individuals have a distorted style of social information processing characterized, amongst other features, by a tendency wrongly to attribute hostile intent to neutral or ambiguous social approaches, a tendency to make negative misinterpretations (such as perceiving benign teasing as malicious), and a tendency to focus on aggressive social cues to the detriment of nonaggressive ones. The model has generated an immense body of research that is generally supportive of its basic propositions (Coie & Dodge, 1997; Crick & Dodge, 1994; Dodge & Schwartz, 1997; Rubin & Krasnor, 1986). To a significant albeit moderate extent, hostile attributional biases predict later aggressive behavior (Dodge et al., 1995), the association being with angry or reactive aggression and violence rather than with crime generally. In addition, aggressive children have difficulty suppressing aggressive responses (Perry, Perry, & Rasmussen, 1986); they generally hold positive beliefs about aggression and believe that it is socially normative (Dodge & Schwartz, 1997). These positive evaluations tend to be associated with proactive aggression (such as bullying and grabbing other people's belongings) rather than reactive anger (which is more associated with hostile attributional biases; Crick & Dodge, 1996). Also, Waldman (1996) has shown that the associations between aggression and both hostile perceptual biases and aggressive responses to nonhostile identified intentions remained even after controlling statistically for inattention and impulsivity.

The evidence, as a whole, points to the likelihood that these social information processing biases play an important role in many forms of aggression. What is less clear is quite how to conceptualize the feature and what its origins might be. It is a personalized feature (i.e., it comes into play in particular circumstances with specific individuals, rather than existing as a generalized trait), yet its effects are rather pervasive. It represents a *bias* in processing rather than a cognitive deficit as such. On the other hand, it could be that to an important extent the "bias" derives from the reality of the individuals' own experiences (Trachtenberg & Viken, 1994). In other words, they are very ready to attribute hostile intent because they have so often been the target of negative behavior. Nevertheless, the bias seems important in helping shape behavior and hence is likely to be influential in predisposing to the persistence and generalization of aggressive behavior. Whether or not it is as important in the initial genesis of an aggressive style of behavior is less certain, although it could be. The situation is closely parallel to that which applies to the rather different attributional biases found with depression (Teasdale & Barnard, 1993).

From both a theoretical and a practical perspective, the findings are probably most important in relation to two issues. First, they have the potential for providing at least a partial explanation of how the experience of abuse or rejection could be translated into the production of antisocial behavior in the person who suffered the adversities. Dodge et al. (1995) showed in their longitudinal study that social information processing patterns partially mediated the effects of early child abuse in predisposing to later conduct problems (but still in early childhood). The issue of how the effects of adverse early experiences can be carried forward developmentally is one of the major unresolved questions in the area of environmentally mediated risks, and it is possible that effects on cognitive processing might constitute one mechanism. Whether or not there are also genetic influences on social information processing styles has yet to be determined.

The second issue concerns the implications for intervention. If biased cognitive processing plays a part in the persistence of antisocial behavior, it may well be that interventions to prevent or alleviate antisocial behavior should include steps designed to foster more positive and less biased ways of thinking and responding. We return to this possibility in Chapters 11 and 12 when discussing offenders' perceptions of the opportunity to offend.

Drugs and Alcohol

The association between alcohol and/or drug use and crime was discussed in Chapter 5 in relation to the heterogeneity of antisocial behavior. It was concluded that, although there are some differences, to a substantial extent the same risk factors applied to both (see Hawkins, Arthur, & Catalano, 1995, for a systematic review of the empirical findings on predictors of adolescent substance abuse). In addition, however, longitudinal studies have provided good evidence of bidirectional influences that go beyond shared risk factors (Brook et al., 1996; Cohen & Brook, 1987; Kerner et al., 1996). Antisocial behavior at an earlier age increases the risk of alcohol or drug problems at a later age, and vice versa. We need here to consider further what might be involved in this complex pattern of interplay.

Several distinctions need to be made because the use of drugs covers a wide range of behaviors extending from the normative to the very deviant. Many essentially normal children experiment with drugs (Balding, 1994; Graham & Bowling, 1995; Measham, Newcombe, & Parker, 1994; Mott & Mirrlees-Black, 1995), but the extensive use and abuse of drugs remains a minority activity (Shiner & Newburn, 1997). Thus, although the use of marijuana (cannabis) in many countries is illegal, it is very widespread and was even more so during the 1970s. Marijuana is perceived as very different from opiates by most young people – the former being viewed as acceptable and the latter as not (Shiner & Newburn, 1997). The National Commission on Marijuana and Drug Abuse (1973) found that over half of 18–21-year-olds in the United States had used marijuana. That this was a majority behavior, and that in most cases it amounted to no more than occasional recreational use, means that it cannot simply be regarded as a drug abuse disorder. Opiates and hallucinogens were used much less frequently (6% and 15%, respectively), but again most young people took the drugs only occasionally. The rates of drug usage in the United States fell somewhat in the late 1980s (Silbereisen et al., 1995), and U.K. rates have generally been well below those in the United States (Rutter, 1979/80), but there is some evidence that the rates of drug use or abuse by young people in both the United Kingdom and the United States may be increasing again (Robertson & Skinner, 1996; Snyder et al., 1996). Nevertheless, in both countries, it is clear that the great majority of drug users engage in only occasional use of marijuana, stimulants, or hallucinogens, and that escalation to the regular use of multiple "hard" drugs such as heroin or cocaine is confined to quite a small minority (Elliott et al., 1989; South, 1994).

The age trends for drug use differ from those for crime insofar as the peak age tends to be in the early 20s rather than the teens. In the Virginia Twin Study, for example, no children under the age of 12 reported using marijuana; the main rise began at about 14 years and by 16 years some 12% to 14% had used drugs (mostly marijuana) at some time, although the proportion currently doing so was less than half that figure (Maes et al., in press). By contrast, some 4% of boys and 2% of girls aged 8–10 had a conduct disorder involving social impairment; the proportions at 14–16 years were 9% and 5%, respectively (Simonoff et al., 1997). In short, antisocial behavior usually begins several years (often many years) before drug use, and the peak for antisocial behavior occurs earlier. However, except for use of marijuana and tobacco (both of which show little gender difference), drug use is more frequent in males by a factor of about three (South, 1994). *Dealing* in drugs is even more predominantly male.

The role of drugs as a risk factor for crime probably comes about in several different ways (South, 1994; Tonry & Wilson, 1990; Wish & Johnson, 1986). First, regular users of heroin may steal in order to be able to purchase their drugs, or sometimes they may break into pharmacies to obtain their supplies (Chaiken & Chaiken, 1991; Jarvis & Parker, 1989). Such drug-related crime is typically nonviolent and acquisitive. Second, drug trafficking sometimes involves organizations or groups that use violence and firearms to control the drug market. In the past, this has been much more so in the United States than in the United Kingdom, but it is probably increasing in the latter (Pearson, 1991). Third, taking drugs may constitute an element of a deviant life style in which antisocial behavior is part of the ethos and provides some of the excitement. Although these risk mechanisms may be important in some individuals, they apply to only a small minority of drug users (most of whom are not regular heavy users); most drug users engaged in crime started their antisocial activities before they first took drugs.

The role of alcohol is somewhat different in one key respect. Through its direct effects in causing disinhibition (Ito et al., 1996), alcohol is associated with a range of disorderly conduct offenses and with driving offenses (Mott, 1990). Alcohol use is also a factor in some violent crime (Collins, 1986). Even with alcohol, however, some of the effects derive from the impulsive, reckless, aggressive lifestyle of heavy drinkers as much as from the chemical consequences of alcohol. Nevertheless, when considered in population terms, alcohol is a more important risk factor for antisocial behavior than are other drugs (because it is more frequently taken in excess).

The co-occurrence of antisocial behavior and heavy drinking could arise because both reflect a similar set of risk factors. As we have seen, both genetic and environmental factors play a role in the liability to antisocial behavior, the former being particularly important in early-onset varieties associated with hyperactivity and the latter preponderant with adolescence-limited varieties. In the Virginia Twin Study of Adolescent Behavioral Development (VTSABD), shared environmental effects predominated with respect to variations in marijuana use, a finding in keeping with the evidence that it is a common and predominantly social activity. Genetic factors were, however, rather more influential with respect to alcohol use without parental permission. In agreement with other studies, the overlap between alcohol or drug use and antisocial behavior was considerable during adolescence, when both behaviors are common. The findings on the extent to which one behavior in the first twin was associated with the other behavior in the second twin, together with the differences between identical and nonidentical twin pairs in that respect, showed that environmental factors play a major role in the associations (Silberg et al., 1997). There is little firm evidence on which environmental influences are most important in that connection, but it is likely that both earlier family risk factors and contemporaneous peer group influences play a role.

Possible Biological Mediators

The workings of the mind must be based on the functioning of the brain; where else could they reside? Moreover, it is clear that both are influenced by whole body physiology, as indexed by features such as hormone levels or biochemical changes. There is a substantial medical literature documenting the mental sequelae of diseases that involve gross disturbances in body physiology. At a more everyday level, the connections are obvious in the changes that we feel, and see in others, in relation to fever or intoxication with alcohol or use of medication. Given that there are important individual differences in liability to antisocial behavior, it makes sense to consider the possibility that these differences stem from variations in measurable physiological features. Knowledge on this matter is potentially very useful because it might lead to effective means of intervention.

As pointed out in Chapter 2, however, it is crucial to be aware of the pitfalls to be avoided in studies of the associations between soma (bodily functioning) and psyche (mental functioning). Quite definitely, it cannot be assumed that all the causal connections go in the direction of soma to psyche. To begin with, it makes no sense to adopt a dualist position. Changes in the one are necessarily accompanied by alterations in the other. At an everyday level, once more, this is apparent in a wide variety of ways. Thus, it is obvious that when we are severely anxious (as, for example, over exams) we feel tremulous and sweaty, are physically restless, and keep needing to go to the lavatory. Physiological testing at such times will show changes in autonomic functioning and in hormone levels. Anxiety involves physiological and mental aspects both. In a real sense they are part and parcel of the same phenomenon, and it is misleading to ask which causes the other.

Nevertheless, it also follows that stressful experiences will lead to alterations in physiological features. Once more, there is a substantial literature on the topic (see e.g. Garmezy & Rutter, 1983). This is not just something seen in chemical changes. There are also changes in brain structure and function that accompany learning (see Horn, 1990), as well as effects on brain development that stem from deprivation of key experiences in early life (see e.g. Blakemore, 1991; Greenough, Black, & Wallace, 1987). When dealing with findings on statistical associations between biological measures and crime, it is vital to be wary of the trap of inferring that the biological features (whether these concern abnormalities or variations in a normal characteristic) necessarily have caused, or have even predisposed to, the crime.

On the other hand, it is equally important to avoid the opposite assumption. That is, some commentators have sought to dismiss biological findings on the grounds that, because crime is socially and legally defined, it could not have its roots in biology. Sometimes, too, it is presumed that any considerations of possible biological influences necessarily "medicalizes" crime, misleadingly transforming a social phenomenon into a disease. That, too, is quite erroneous. Normal variations in biological features can and do carry implications for individual differences in propensity for different types of social behavior. The parallels with, for example, athletic performance illustrate the point. Differences in (say) physique or physiology do not in themselves cause championship performance. Nevertheless, it would be absurd to suppose that they are completely irrelevant. A very short person will find it much more difficult to succeed as a basketball player, a fat one will struggle to be successful at long-distance running, and it is rare indeed for someone of slender physique to be a weightlifting or shot-put champion. Even so, champions come in an astonishing variety of shapes and sizes, and knowledge about someone's physical make-up provides an extremely weak base for predicting their athletic performance. It provides relevant information on probabilities but, in most cases, the connections will be too weak for strong predictions. Exactly the same applies to biological features and crime.

One further caution needs to be introduced to the discussion of biological findings with respect to crime. Most of the research has involved incarcerated adults or psychiatric patients, in both cases often with a focus on extreme groups of one kind or another – such as murderers or psychopaths. There are two rather separate reasons for being careful about the interpretation (and especially the generalization) of such findings. First, it is quite possible (indeed likely) that biological features will prove to be more important in the propensity to severe and unusual forms of antisocial behavior than to crime as a whole. (This does not mean, of course, that it would not be useful to have a better understanding of the causes of rare and atypical varieties of crime.) Second, it is necessary to bear in mind the possibility that any biological differences that are found apply *not* to the propensity to antisocial behavior but rather to some associated feature (such as mental illness or learning disability or use of drugs or alcohol). The co-occurrence of two separate but interconnected problems is common; the co-occurrence may stem from a number of quite different causal mechanisms, and it is easy to be misled into thinking that findings reflect one problem when in reality they reflect some other associated problem (see Caron & Rutter, 1991; Rutter, 1997b). This issue is a particular concern when studying referred groups (whether referred through judicial or medical processes), since the co-occurrence of two separate problems ("comorbidity" in medical parlance) will always be more common in referred samples (Berkson, 1946). This is because either of the two associated problems can lead to referral; hence, the chances of referral are greater when someone has two problems rather than one.

With these cautions in mind, we turn to the empirical findings on biological features. For reasons arising from the considerations just discussed, we place most weight on epidemiological studies and on longitudinal findings that allow testing of the extent to which differences (or changes) in the biological feature are associated with variations in later antisocial behavior. Unfortunately, such data are thin on the ground.

Toxins and Nutrients

Various claims have been made about the supposed effects of toxins and nutrients on antisocial behavior, usually conceptualized as mediated by hyperactivity. These claims may be considered under the headings of alcohol exposure in utero, lead ingestion, food additives and allergens, and vitamins.

There is good evidence that the children of alcoholic parents have a substantially increased risk of antisocial behavior, as well as other types of psychopathology (see Rutter, 1989a; Steinhausen, 1995), and it appears that part of this risk may be mediated by the damaging effects on fetal development in early pregnancy of high exposure to alcohol consumed by the mother. These may be indexed by certain dysmorphic features, which have been used to diagnose a "fetal alcohol syndrome" (Graham et al., 1988). There is some doubt about the specificity of this syndrome (see Taylor, 1991), and it is not clear what level of alcohol exposure is required to damage fetal development, but it may be accepted that damage can occur. Also, follow-up studies show that babies exposed in the womb to high levels of alcohol show increased levels of problems, including inattention and hyperactivity (Streissguth, 1993; Streissguth et al., 1984). The problem in interpretation lies in the fact that the risks during pregnancy are usually followed by all sorts of adverse experiences after birth, and their relative importance is not at all clear. The same applies to the effects of prenatal cocaine exposure (Mayes & Bornstein, 1997), but again it seems likely that there can be direct neurotoxic effects with persisting behavioral sequelae (Singer, Arendt, & Minnes, 1993; Singer et al., 1997; Volpe, 1992).

The possible effects of lead ingestion on psychological development have been the subject of widely divergent claims (see Rutter, 1980; Rutter & Russell-Jones, 1987; Taylor, 1991). The evidence shows that the moderately raised levels of body lead are associated with slight decrements in cognitive performance, even after controlling for a range of other possible influences (see e.g. Fergusson, Horwood, & Lynskey, 1997a). The effects, however, are quite small and it is uncertain whether there are any measurable effects of the variations in current lead exposure, given the substantial fall in population lead levels in most countries over the last 20 years or so. The evidence regarding possible effects on hyperactivity and antisocial behavior is much more limited. Probably the best evidence is provided by Needleman et al.'s (1996) study of bone lead levels in the Pittsburgh Youth Study sample (see Loeber et al., 1991). Higher lead levels were associated with questionnaire measures of aggressive and delinquent behavior at age 11, but not at age 7. Confounding variables were taken into account, but these mainly concerned broad demographic features (such as socioeconomic status and mother's age at the child's birth) rather than detailed measures of family functioning. Apart from the inevitable uncertainties on possible confounders, there are five main queries. First, the effects concerned most varieties of emotional and behavioral difficulties and not just antisocial behavior. Second, lead levels were unrelated to neurobehavioral and attentional measures. Third, lead levels were assessed with X-ray fluorescence spectroscopy, and it is not known how these relate to more direct measures of blood lead or dental lead. Fourth, some 40% of the children did not participate. Finally, it is unclear why there should be effects at 11 but not at 7. The research findings clearly raise the possibility of lead effects on behavior, but uncertainties remain. It is possible that moderately raised lead levels may slightly increase the risk of antisocial behavior, but it seems unlikely that the effect is other than quite weak, and the mechanisms involved remain unknown.

During the 1970s, strong claims were made that food additives were an important cause of hyperactivity (Feingold, 1975). These claims were not supported by the empirical findings (Mattes & Gittelman, 1981), although very occasional effects may occur in a few individuals (Weiss et al., 1980). Nevertheless, careful studies have shown that some children do respond adversely to elements in their diet, sometimes showing hyperactivity (Carter et al., 1993; Eggar et al., 1985; Kaplan et al., 1989; Schulte-Korne et al., 1996; Taylor, 1991). The foods to which children show intolerance are quite diverse and vary from individual to individual (they include cow's milk, wheat flour, citrus fruits, and food dyes). A restricted diet regimen may be beneficial for the few children with a proven intolerance, but such diets are troublesome to apply and are often rejected by older children. Moreover, a community survey has shown that the majority of children whose parents believe them to be food sensitive are not (Young et al., 1987).

Finally, Schoenthaler (1991) has claimed that vitamin and mineral supplements may reduce antisocial behavior and improve intelligence. There is some evidence that vitamin deficiencies may slightly impair cognitive performance (Eysenck & Schoenthaler, 1997), but the findings are controversial and require replication. The evidence regarding effects on antisocial behavior is almost entirely lacking.

We conclude that the claims regarding the supposed effects of toxins and nutrients on antisocial behavior go far beyond the evidence, and it is not likely that they have major effects. Nevertheless, research findings do confirm that exposure to high levels of alcohol in the early months of pregnancy, moderately increased levels of body lead, and dietary elements do have some effects on behavior in some children. It is not possible to quantify their importance, but it seems likely that they play only a rather minor role in the overall liability to antisocial behavior.

Physique

The early criminological literature argued that recidivist delinquents, perhaps especially those who engage in violent crime, tend to have a mesomorphic (chunky, muscular) build (Sheldon, Stevens, & Tucker, 1940; Glueck & Glueck, 1956). That view is in keeping with what one might expect, but it is important to appreciate that the association is not a strong one; moreover, it does not derive from epidemiological samples. The topic has been re-examined recently by Sampson and Laub (1997), who undertook a detailed statistical analysis of the Gluecks' original data. They confirmed the association with mesomorphy, but they found that the association applied more to convictions than to self-reported delinquency and was largely lost once social background had been taken into account. Also, mesomorphy did not predict longer-term patterns of violence in adult life. Of course, these results could mean that the effects of social adversity on antisocial behavior are mediated by physique. That does not seem very plausible, however. Furthermore, there have been no convincing suggestions of how such a mediating mechanism might operate. As mesomorphy does not appear to have predictive validity, the association also has little practical value. Although it remains plausible that a person's physique may have some effect on how they behave, the effects are too weak and inconsistent to provide any understanding of causal processes.

Androgens

Androgens (the male sex hormones), especially testosterone, would seem to be more promising candidates as a possible biological mediator (Rubinow & Schmidt, 1996). From at least early childhood onward, boys tend to be more physically aggressive than girls (Maccoby & Jacklin, 1980). Antisocial behavior is several times more common in males (see Chapter 9) and tends also to peak in adolescence (see Chapter 10), an age period when there is a huge increase in sex hormone production as part of the physiological changes of puberty. Moreover, there is animal evidence that prenatal sex hormones have an organizing function on brain development (Greenough et al., 1987) and on sex-differentiated behavior. In addition, the experimental administration of testosterone in animals has been shown to increase social dominance and aggression. Nevertheless, despite its plausibility as a biological mediator for antisocial behavior, at least in its aggressive varieties, the empirical evidence in support is inconclusive – especially before adult life (Archer, 1991; Rubinow & Schmidt, 1996).

To begin with, the statistical associations that have been found are inconsistent and relatively weak, despite the fact that most studies have been of extreme groups. The inconsistency may reflect measurement issues. Thus, there is both diurnal and day-to-day variation in testosterone levels; moreover, social context influences levels, and the stage of puberty makes a huge difference. Most studies have been cross-sectional, which makes causal inferences problematic. Perhaps most crucially, both human and animal evidence shows that, just as androgen administration has effects on behavior, so also do social experiences affect androgen level. In particular, success in closely fought competitions increases androgen production whereas failure decreases it.

Tremblay et al.'s (1997) Montreal longitudinal study findings point to the complexities. At the age of 13 years, boys who were rated tough leaders had higher levels of testosterone, but androgen levels were actually somewhat lower in those rated as aggressive. The finding would be in keeping with the view that social rejection reduces testosterone level. The picture, however, was quite different by age 16; over the years, the testosterone levels of the aggressive boys had increased whereas, between 15 and 16, the levels fell in the nonaggressive boys.

The findings run counter to any simple view that individual differences in testosterone levels are "driving" aggressive behavior. On the other hand, they are compatible with the notion that androgens play some mediating role in the causal connections between social experiences, social dominance or rejection, and aggression. It is possible, too, that the enhancing role of high testosterone levels may be greater in late adolescence (when the average levels are much higher) than in the years of childhood or early pubescence.

Autonomic Reactivity

There is extensive evidence from both cross-sectional and longitudinal studies of general population and clinic samples that recidivist delinquents, especially those engaged in aggressive behavior, tend to have lower pulse rates than other young people (Farrington, 1997b; Raine, 1997; Raine, Venables, & Williams, 1995; Raine et al., 1997a). This has usually been interpreted as indicating the mediating effects of low autonomic arousal. The empirical evidence is supportive of this view; other indices (such as skin conductance, cortisol levels, adrenaline excretion, or response to stress stimuli) provide a broadly comparable picture. Low autonomic activity is not only associated with aggression and antisocial behavior contemporaneously but also predicts future crime (see e.g. Lösel & Bender, 1997; Magnusson, af Klinteberg, & Stattin, 1993; McBurnett et al., 1997; Mezzacappa et al., 1997; Raine, Venables, & Williams, 1990; Raine et al., 1997a; Wadsworth, 1976). There are important methodological concerns that need to be considered. For example, autonomic measures are influenced by physical fitness, smoking, drinking alcohol, and attitude of mind at the time of testing. Also, there are only moderate correlations among different measures of autonomic reactivity. Nevertheless, the findings are sufficiently robust (although by no means entirely consistent) to conclude that there is a valid and meaningful association (albeit one of only moderate strength) between low autonomic reactivity and antisocial behavior. Moreover, there are several ways in which this might play a role in causal processes. Venables (1988) has suggested that the key feature is the implied fearlessness. Engaging in crime involves taking risks, and it may be that a diminished level of anxiety under conditions of stress fosters risk taking. Gray (1987) and Quay (1993), on the other hand, place decreased autonomic reactivity within a broader domain of behavioral inhibition thought to characterize one aspect of the neural control of behavior.

Most of the research on autonomic reactivity has dealt with it as an isolated variable, and relatively little is known about the interconnections with other risk and protective features. For example, what are the connections between low autonomic reactivity and sensation seeking or impulsivity? Is low reactivity a risk factor for crime in the absence of other risk factors or, rather, is high reactivity a protective influence for individuals with a high liability for antisocial behavior as a consequence of their temperamental features and adverse psychosocial experiences? What associations are there among possible biological mediators; for example, how does low reactivity relate to the putative mediation of serotonin functioning?

Serotonin Metabolism

There is an extensive research literature, spanning both human and animal studies, indicating that the central serotonergic (5HT) system is involved in the regulation of impulsive aggressive behavior (Coccaro, 1989; Spoont, 1992; van Praag, 1991). Specifically, reduced central serotonergic activity (meaning reduced activity in the chemical processes involved in the transmission of signals in the brain) is associated with suicidal behavior and with irritable impulsive aggression toward other people. The association is with these forms of behavior and not with the particular mental disorders from which they may stem. The idea that serotonin might be implicated is an attractive one because it is known to be a neurotransmitter (a chemical involved in brain activity). Furthermore, the idea fits well with influential theories concerning a postulated behavioral inhibition system in the brain (Gray, 1987; Quay, 1993), the hypothesis being that serotonin operates as a regulator in this system, serving to inhibit impulsive aggressive behavior. Individual variations in serotonin function seem to show a reasonable degree of consistency over time, and both human studies (Oxenstierna et al., 1986; Pedersen et al., 1993) and animal studies (Higley et al., 1993) point to a genetic component (although uncertainty remains regarding its strength). The implication would seem to be that variations in serotonin function might constitute the biological mediator of genetic influences on violent crime.

This could well prove to be the case; however, measurement, conceptual, developmental, and empirical issues complicate the interpretation of findings. The first difficulty is presented by the fact that serotonin in the blood is largely produced in the gut, is wholly contained within platelets, and does not cross the blood–brain barrier. Accordingly, assessments of blood serotonin levels may be completely uninformative about what is going on in the brain. On the other hand, there seem to be parallels between patterns of serotonin re-uptake in platelets and in brain neurons. On this basis, it has been suggested that studies of platelets could offer a convenient window onto neural function. Nevertheless, doubts have led to the development of a range of different indices thought to reflect central serotonergic activity.

The most direct measure is provided by study of the brain after death in suicide victims (Coccaro, 1989). The findings are not wholly consistent, but they point to reduced presynaptic serotonin activity (i.e., at the point just before the cell-to-cell junction), with possibly a compensatory increase at the postsynapse.

Probably, the best index during life of presynaptic central serotonergic activity is provided by the level of 5-hydroxyindoleacetic acid (5HIAA) in the cerebrospinal fluid (CSF), the fluid that bathes the brain. This 5HIAA is the primary metabolite (breakdown product) of serotonin. The findings in adults have been reasonably (but not entirely) consistent in showing lowered CSF levels of 5HIAA in young male personality-disordered subjects with seriously deviant impulsive or aggressive behavior (Tuinier, Verhoeven, & van Praag, 1995) and in violent alcoholic offenders (Virkunnen et al., 1996).

Tapping the CSF is an invasive albeit generally safe procedure; not surprisingly, most of the studies have been undertaken with small atypical samples, mainly adult. Because of the constraints involved in undertaking CSF studies, an alternative approach of using the prolactin response to the "challenge" of fenfluramine administration has been developed. Fenfluramine is a central serotonin agonist that releases stores of presynaptic serotonin and stimulates postsynaptic receptors both directly and indirectly. The enhanced central serotonin activity that is thereby induced is reflected in a dose-related prolactin response. A blunted response is presumed, therefore, to indicate reduced central serotonin activity. Such a blunted response was found by Coccaro (1989) to be associated with impulsive aggression.

Another method is provided by the assessment of monoamine oxidase (MAO) activity in platelets (Schalling et al., 1987). The method is indirect because MAO is implicated in dopamine as well as serotonin metabolism. Nevertheless, the finding of an association between platelet MAO levels and 5HIAA levels, together with psychopathological correlates that are very similar to those found with serotonin, suggests that it may index central serotonergic activity (Oreland et al., 1981). Low MAO activity in platelets has been found to be associated with impulsivity (Schalling et al., 1987), with violent crime (Belfrage, Lidberg, & Oreland, 1992), and with persistent criminality (Alm et al., 1994).

Finally, whole blood serotonin levels have been used as an index – the assumption being that *raised* levels in the blood reflect *reduced* central serotonergic activity (see e.g. Coccaro, 1989; Cook et al., 1995). The empirical basis for this assumption is weak, however. Nevertheless, despite inevitable concerns over what findings mean with respect to brain activity, the ease of study has meant that epidemiological investigation has been possible. In the Dunedin study, Moffitt et al. (1997) examined associations between whole blood serotonin levels at age 21 and violence in 781 individuals, using both court convictions and self-reports. The extensive data set allowed a very thorough examination of confounding variables. The findings showed that the violent men's mean serotonin level was half a standard deviation (the equivalent of some 8 IQ points) above that of nonviolent men, irrespective of whether violence was measured by official records or self-report. The finding is consistent with other methods of measurement in implicating some aspect of serotonin function in violence. It is noteworthy, however, that the association did not hold in women. Possibly this could mean that violence has a different meaning in females, or that impulsive aggression is manifest in women by different behaviors.

Developmental considerations are raised by both the greater inconsistency of findings in children and by the results of several studies showing a pattern opposite to that found in adult life. This has been evident in both CSF 5HIAA findings (Castellanos et al., 1994; Kruesi et al., 1992) and fenfluramine challenge results (Halperin et al., 1994; Pine et al., 1997; Stoff et al., 1992). Pine et al. (1997) have suggested that there may be some kind of developmental switch in the connection between central serotonergic activity and impulsive violence.

Although sufficiently consistent to indicate that serotonin clearly plays some sort of role in impulsive violence (both self-directed and directed against others), there are nevertheless some puzzles that have yet to be explained. The weight of evidence undoubtedly points to the likelihood that serotonin inhibits impulsive violence and that low central serotonergic activity is associated with a lack of such inhibition. But the Dutch family with an MAO deficiency and a pattern of violence seemed to show an *increased* central serotonergic activity (Brunner, 1996). The paradox could simply reflect the complexities involved in the connections between presynaptic and postsynaptic serotonergic activity, but it raises questions that need to be answered.

Supposing, however, that the inconsistencies reflect no more than these complexities, there is still the question of what causal mechanisms are operative (Kruesi & Jacobsen, 1997). The animal data (see Coccaro, 1989) suggest that, although low central serotonergic activity predisposes to violence, the actual commission of antisocial acts is very dependent on social context. An apparently similar finding by Moffitt et al. (1997) is that whole blood serotonin levels were associated with violence mainly in a subgroup of individuals who also experienced psychosocial adversity.

Both animal and human data also indicate that stressful experiences are associated with (and probably lead to) differences in serotonin functioning (e.g. Pine et al., 1997; Raleigh & McGuire, 1991). It seems probable that changes in serotonin functioning, like those of testosterone, both lead to and result from changes in social context and behavior. Any inference of biological determinism would not be warranted, but the evidence is nevertheless persuasive that serotonin probably does act as some kind of mediator in impulsive violence (Kruesi & Jacobsen, 1997).

Overview of Biological Mediators

It is clear from the evidence on all the putative biological mediators considered that bidirectional effects apply throughout. There are effects from physiology to behavior, but it is equally evident that both social experiences and the exertion of behavior have physiological consequences. That is what would be expected from knowledge of biology but, inevitably, it complicates the interpretation of empirical findings. People's biological make-up influences their liability to antisocial behavior – the evidence being strongest in the case of autonomic reactivity and diminished central serotonergic activity – but their biological functioning is not a "given." It is influenced by their experiences. Moreover, even the strongest biological effects are probabilistic, as shown by findings in both humans and animals. Whether or not liabilities are translated into the commission of antisocial acts depends on many other features, as discussed further in the chapters that follow.

Conclusions

Research findings have made it abundantly clear that there are individual characteristics that influence liability to antisocial behavior. However, these characteristics are most strongly operative with respect to the varieties that are first manifest in early childhood, that are accompanied by a range of associated problems and by pervasive social malfunction, and that persist into adult life. Genetic factors are influential in this connection. They do not cause antisocial behavior directly; rather, they constitute one set of influences operating in probabilistic fashion as part of multifactorial causation. There is not, of course, a gene for crime. Although the routes of genetic mediation remain ill-understood, it appears likely that several different genes are involved, that most of the susceptibility genes constitute normal variations of normal genes (and not abnormal mutations), that they operate through dimensions such as hyperactivity or impulsivity or sensation seeking, and that many of the genetic effects are indirect.

That is, some genetic influences operate through effects on vulnerability to environmental adversities and stressors, and some through their role with respect to behaviors concerned with the shaping and selecting of environments.

Many different individual features have been investigated, but those with the best documented involvement in the liability to antisocial behavior are hyperactivity, cognitive impairment (especially with respect to verbal and executive planning skills), temperamental features (especially impulsivity, sensation seeking, lack of control, and aggressivity), and a bias in social cognitive information processing. The biological substrate for these individual risk and protective factors remains uncertain, but autonomic reactivity and central serotonergic functioning have been shown to be involved. It should be added that several of the risk and protective factors seem to operate not on antisocial behavior as a whole but rather on specific facets. Thus, for example, serotonin seems to play a role in impulsive violence but not in crime generally. The findings serve as an important reminder of the need to be concerned with the heterogeneity of antisocial behavior, as discussed in Chapter 5.

CHAPTER 6 – SUMMARY OF MAIN POINTS

Individual characteristics are most likely to influence the development of the types of antisocial behavior described in Chapter 5 as early-onset and life-course–persistent, rather than the more common forms of adolescence-limited behavior. They usually seem to operate not on antisocial behavior as a whole but rather on specific aspects. The individual factors with an established role in the development of antisocial behavior are:

❑ *hyperactivity,* which shows the most robust association with antisocial behavior of all the individual factors, an association that tends to be with generally poor social functioning rather than with crime per se;

❑ *cognitive impairment,* especially verbal and planning skills;

❑ *temperamental features,* especially impulsivity, sensation seeking, lack of control, and aggressivity; and

❑ a distorted style of *social information processing,* including a tendency to wrongly perceive negative intentions in others' behavior, to misinterpret social interactions, and to focus on the aggressive behavior of others.

These well-researched individual features are likely to have *biological* substrates that operate in a probabilistic fashion as part of multifactorial causation. The research evidence is increasingly clear that genes – probably several or many – constitute one set of influences setting up a liability to develop antisocial behavior in childhood through dimensions such as impulsivity and hyperactivity, given the presence of other environmental risk factors.

Estimates for the *genetic component* of hyperactivity are as high as 60%–70% of the variance. Genes may also operate by increasing vulnerability to life experiences and stresses or by very indirect routes such as influencing behaviors that in turn lead to changes in the individual's environment and set up a spiraling cycle of risk factors. The complexity of these processes should not be underestimated.

7 | The Role of Psychosocial Features

Some Concepts and Controversies

Numerous studies of juvenile and adult offenders undertaken over the course of this century have amassed a huge body of evidence that delinquency is statistically associated with a long list of psychosocial risk factors. These span broken homes, single-parent families, teenage parents, family discord, abuse or neglect, coercive parenting, lack of supervision, family criminality, poverty, large family size, delinquent peer groups, poor schooling, and living in a socially disorganized area (Farrington, 1995c, 1996; Hirschi & Gottfredson, 1994; Junger-Tas, 1992; Loeber & Stouthamer-Loeber, 1986). In 1983, Rutter and Giller concluded that the facts of these broad associations were so well established and accepted that it was not necessary to review the empirical evidence in any detail. Controversies centered instead around the interpretation of the findings, rather than the reality of the statistical associations. Attention was drawn to five main issues.

First, it was noted that of all family characteristics, parental criminality showed the strongest and most robust association with delinquency in the offspring (Farrington, Gundry, & West, 1975; Robins & Lewis, 1966), and it was concluded that it was necessary to question whether the associations represented genetic or environmental mediation. The solidity of the associations remains (Farrington et al., 1996a; Rowe & Farrington, 1997), but the necessity of considering the possibility of genetic mediation has become very much clearer (Plomin, 1994; Plomin et al., 1997). There is now extensive evidence that many associations previously attributed to environmental influences are at least partly genetically mediated. Accordingly, we consider that issue more thoroughly.

Second, Rutter and Giller (1983) commented that there was evidence that children can and do have effects on their parents (Bell, 1968; Bell & Harper, 1977), and it was possible that some of the supposed parental "influences" were in fact *consequences* of rearing disruptive and difficult children. Again, there is now much more extensive evidence on child effects, and it is evident that this possibility needs to be considered more seriously than it was in 1983.

Third, as with all statistical correlations, it was crucial to ask whether the association with the putative risk factor was instead due to the operation of some third variable. Were the associations with family discord simply a secondary consequence of the family living in a socially disorganized neighborhood, with the true risk mechanism residing in the community or broader living conditions rather than anything specifically to do with relationships within the family? Quite a lot of evidence was clearly available in 1983 that that was not the case (Robins, 1978; Rutter et al., 1975), but it has been the subject of more detailed study since then. We consider the findings and the inferences to be drawn from them.

Fourth, insofar as the family influences do have a truly causal yet environmentally mediated impact, it is essential to ask about the mechanisms by which the risks operate. This need applies generally to all causal considerations, but it is especially great with respect to psychosocial factors and crime because of the rather strong associations among the various risk factors. At the most basic level, it is necessary to consider whether the risks arise mainly from what families do (e.g., scapegoating, coercive parenting, or abuse) or from what they *fail* to do (e.g., lack of supervision, neglect, or a lack of intimate relationships). This was a feature of much research in the 1970s, but it has come into greater prominence in the 1980s and 1990s as a result of a renewed interest in seeking to move beyond statistical correlations to causal processes (Dishion & Patterson, 1997; Farrington, 1986a, 1992; Loeber et al., 1993; Reiss et al., 1995; Rutter, 1994a; Rutter et al., 1997b). We consider what is known about this difficult issue. In doing so, we highlight a distinction that was not much thought about in 1983 – namely, the extent to which the family risk factors impinge equally on all the children or rather act on just some of the children. The question has important theoretical and practical implications.

Fifth, Rutter and Giller (1983) discussed the evidence on whether the main associations were with antisocial behavior or convictions. We have less to say on this topic because the evidence that the former is the case has become so much more substantial.

In addition, four other issues have come to demand attention. In the past, almost all attention focused on environmental influences stemming from the family of rearing or the social milieu in which it took place. It is now clear that experiences in adult life also play a considerable role in whether or not antisocial behavior continues (Rutter, 1996; Sampson & Laub, 1993). We consider these issues more fully in Chapter 10 when dealing with the broader topic of continuities and discontinuities between childhood and adult life, but it is necessary to make brief mention of them here.

The second new issue is a concern to examine influences on the overall level of crime and not just on individual differences in the liability to engage in antisocial behavior (Rutter & Smith, 1995). The topic of why crime levels have risen so markedly in the last half-century was discussed in Chapter 4, but in Chapter 8 we focus more broadly on the aggregate effects stemming from psychosocial influences. A further issue arising out of influences on overall crime levels, rather than on individual differences in antisocial propensity, is the extent to which situational crime measures are (or can be made) effective. The topic was touched on in Rutter and Giller (1983), but much more evidence is now available. The findings are reviewed briefly in Chapter 12 in the context of discussing a range of approaches to crime prevention.

A further topic that has come to the fore in the last 15 years is the extent to which psychosocial influences operate somewhat differently in different varieties of antisocial behavior. The point was touched on in Chapter 5 when discussing the heterogeneity of antisocial behavior, and it was noted again in Chapter 6 when considering individual risk factors. In this chapter, we need to return to the theme primarily with respect to Moffitt's (1993a) distinction between early-onset, life-course–persistent antisocial behavior and later-onset, adolescence-limited antisocial behavior.

In their 1983 review, Rutter and Giller devoted a separate chapter to protective influences. We do not. This choice reflects the growing attention that is being paid to the potentially important topic of resilience (Hetherington & Blechman, 1996; Rutter, 1995a, in press; Wang & Gordon, 1994). By "resilience" we mean the phenomenon of people functioning well in spite of adverse experiences, of relative resistance to risk factors, or of overcoming stress experiences. Instead of treating this topic separately, we have chosen to consider it in all our discussions of risk and protective influences (although some of the key findings are brought together in a later section of this chapter). In Chapter 6, some attention was paid to individual characteristics that might serve as protective influences. The concept itself, however, is given particular attention in this chapter because its underlying ideas have influenced the ways in which researchers and practitioners have thought about the possible operation of psychosocial influences.

Finally, an awareness has developed that experiences people bring about as a result of their own behavior can exert an important influence on shaping whether or not their behavior persists (Rutter & Rutter, 1993; Rutter et al., 1995). Some of the evidence on how this comes about is considered in Chapter 10, but it is necessary also to discuss the topic in this chapter with respect to some of the psychosocial influences we consider. Also, we examine here the research challenges involved in testing for these effects.

Because of the centrality of these questions on environmental risk mediation, we start with a discussion of what is entailed in the concepts and of which research strategies may be used to test competing hypotheses. In doing so, we will refer to research findings on psychosocial influences on antisocial behavior; but, in order to deal with both the concepts and how they may be tested, we must turn to a rather wider literature. Accordingly, in the second half of this chapter, we bring together some of the key findings on the main psychosocial influences thought to be important with respect to the origins and course of antisocial behavior or its desistance.

Person Effects on the Environment

Up until the late 1960s, statistical associations between psychosocial circumstances (such as maternal deprivation or harsh parenting) and children's behavior were almost always interpreted as a causal effect of the environment on the child. Thus, the finding that parental rejection was associated with delinquency was interpreted as meaning that rejection led to delinquency as part of a causal process. It is now clear that the finding could mean, at least in part, that children who behave in difficult, disruptive, and socially disapproved ways may cause other people to feel rejecting towards them. The New York longitudinal study (Thomas, Chess, & Birch, 1968) raised queries on the basis of its evidence on the role of children's temperamental qualities, and Bell's (1968) critical essay directly questioned the assumption by its challenge of the extent to which the causal arrow ran in the reverse direction. Since then, the evidence on the reality of child influences on other people's behavior has accumulated (Bell & Chapman, 1986; Lytton, 1990; Rutter et al., 1997a; Scarr & McCartney, 1983). In addition, however, it has become evident that the consequences extend much more broadly than the impact on "here and now" interactions (Rutter et al., 1995; see also Chapter 10).

The evidence on the effects of children's behavior on how other people respond to them derives from both experimental and naturalistic studies. For example, Brunk and Henggeler (1984) trained 10-year-old children to behave in compliant or oppositional ways. When placed with an adult who didn't know them and who was instructed to engage them in a task, those behaving in oppositional ways elicited more negative adult behavior and, moreover, did so even when complying. It seemed that expectations and reputations may be created even within the course of less than half an hour! Anderson, Lytton, and Romney (1986) showed much the same thing with an ingenious paradigm comparing the interactions of normal and conduct-disordered children when placed with their own parent, the parent of a normal child, and the parent of a conduct-disordered child. Conduct-disordered children elicited more negative adult behavior both from their own parents and other children's parents. But there were also parental effects; mothers of conduct-disordered children were more negative than mothers of normal children. This parental effect could have derived from either their own personality qualities or their prior experiences in rearing a difficult child. Either way, however, the parental behavior was not brought about by the immediate effects of the conduct-disordered child.

Another research strategy to investigate child effects has been to use the effect of drugs in altering child behavior. Schachar et al. (1987) found that the beneficial effects of stimulant medication on child behavior led to parallel adaptive changes in parental behavior. A fourth tactic has been to use longitudinal data to determine whether differences in child behavior at a given time are followed by later changes in parental behavior (Lee & Bates, 1985). Although there have been relatively few rigorous studies of child effects, the evidence is sufficient to conclude that disruptive behavior in the child does indeed have effects on other people's behavior toward them.

People's behavior influences their experiences in further ways that go beyond evocative effects in interpersonal interactions. By how we act, we shape and select our experiences (Rutter, 1997c; Rutter et al., 1997a; Scarr, 1992; Scarr & McCartney, 1983). Thus, since Robins's (1966) classic follow-up study of child guidance clinic attenders, it has been evident that antisocial children have a much increased likelihood of broken relationships, stressful life events, severe psychosocial adversities, and unemployment – to mention but a few indices of environmental risk (see Rutter et al., 1995). It is clear that any investigation of the effects of these risk factors on the continuation of antisocial behavior must take into account the individual's own role in bringing about these risks.

Three further points, however, need to be made. First, there is equally good evidence on the reality of parental effects on child behavior. To begin with, there is abundant evidence that parenting qualities can derive from the parents' past experiences long before the children were born. This was shown, for example, in Harlow's studies of the effects of early social isolation on the later parenting qualities of rhesus monkeys (Ruppenthal et al.,

1976). In the human arena, too, follow-up studies of institutionally raised girls have shown them to have a much increased rate of serious parenting difficulties when they reach adulthood (Quinton & Rutter, 1988). Research findings have also documented the high rate of family breakdown and parenting difficulties shown by individuals who exhibited antisocial behavior in childhood (Quinton et al., 1993; Robins, 1966) and by people suffering from mental disorders in adult life (Rutter & Quinton, 1984). To a significant (but modest) extent, serious parenting problems are predictable on the basis of knowledge about the parents before the children are born (Altemeier et al., 1984; Quinton & Rutter, 1988). Clearly, in these instances the parenting problems cannot have been brought about by the behavior of the offspring. Moreover, these and other adverse parenting qualities have implications for the children's psychological development. This is evident from their predictive power in longitudinal studies (Henry et al., 1993; Kolvin et al., 1988; Richman et al., 1982). The question that arises, however, is whether some of these effects might be mediated genetically (an issue we discuss in the next section of this chapter).

Second, in most instances it is highly likely that the effects are bidirectional. That is, parents both influence their children and are influenced by them. This has been shown in the here-and-now of family interactions by Patterson and his colleagues (Patterson, 1980, 1982, 1995). Hostile behavior by one family member tends to elicit hostile responses from others, and thereby coercive cycles of interchange are set up. Longer-term effects have been shown through longitudinal studies (Caspi, Elder, & Bem, 1987). For example, Martin, Maccoby, and Jacklin (1981) found that oppositional behavior by toddlers tended to induce mothers to back away, which in turn made it more likely that oppositional behavior would persist.

Third, it is clear that the experiences people bring about by their own behavior may have important consequences for them (Rutter et al., 1993). It is obvious that the origins of a risk factor and its mode of risk mediation have no necessary connection with one another. Thus, people choose to smoke cigarettes for reasons that derive from both their personality and the social context, but the risks for smoking-related diseases stem from carcinogenic tars, carbon monoxide, nicotine effects on blood vessels, and irritants in the smoke – none of which have anything to do with the influences that led the person to smoke in the first place. The same applies to psychosocial influences. Thus, Sampson and Laub (1993) found that, despite the fact that delinquents were incarcerated as a consequence of their own antisocial behavior, the experience of incarceration made it more likely that their antisocial behavior would recur (largely because having been in prison made it more difficult for them to obtain employment).

The research strategies that may be used to test for environmental mediation of risks are discussed in what follows.

Genetic Mediation of Psychosocial Risk Factors

A growing body of evidence has made it clear that measures describing environmental features also involve a genetic component (Plomin 1994, 1995; Plomin & Bergeman, 1991). Three types of findings have been informative on this topic. First, twin studies have been consistent in showing that genetic factors play a significant role in individual differences in most kinds of risk and protective experiences – including stressful life events, divorce, social support, family relationships, and peer groups. This is not surprising, of course, in the light of the evidence that people's behavior to some extent shapes and selects their experiences. Second, adoptee studies have shown that the correlations between family features and child behavior are always much higher in biological families than adoptee families. Plomin (1994) reported correlations ranging from 0.24 to 0.36 between family environment measures and children's behavior at age 7 in biological families but only 0.06 to 0.08 in adoptive families. The difference derives from the facts that (a) biological parents pass on to their children both genes and experiences (a passive gene–environment correlation) whereas adoptive parents provide only experiences, and (b) the parental qualities associated with genetic risk are also the ones that play a role in the type of parenting and family environment they provide for their children. Third, multivariate genetic analyses have shown that the genetic effects associated with risk environments overlap with those associated with children's behavior. This is evident from across-twin, across-trait analyses. Thus, Pike et al. (1996a) found that, in MZ (identical) pairs of twins, mothers' negativity to one twin correlated 0.54 with antisocial behavior in the *other* twin, whereas in DZ (nonidentical) twins the comparable correlation was 0.34. The implication is that much of the apparent environmental effect was actually mediated genetically. However, model fitting indicated that there nevertheless were, in addition, true environmentally mediated effects that operated in both a shared and nonshared fashion.

As noted in Chapter 6, two rather different sorts of genetic mediation of apparently environmental risks need to be considered. First, there are those that stem from *passive* gene–environment correlations – that is, the correlations between the parents' genetic make-up and the environments that they provide for their children. Second, there are those that stem from *active* or evocative gene–environment correlations – correlations between the children's genetic make-up and the environments that they shape or select or evoke with other people's responses to them. The latter constitute one facet of the broader issue of person effects on the environment. These effects derive from people's behavior, regardless of its genetic or environmental origins. Indeed, the limited available evidence suggests that the genetic component in person effects on the environment may sometimes account for only a small proportion of the variance (O'Connor et al., in press a).

The caveat that emerges from these genetic studies is important. Associations between environmental risk factors and antisocial behavior may reflect genetic as well as environmental risk mediation. It is important that research take the steps needed to differentiate the two. On the other hand, it is important not to overreact to this problem in the way that some geneticists have (see e.g. Rowe, 1994). Three main points require emphasis. First, as already noted, most twin and adoptee samples include only a small proportion of environmental high-risk families; accordingly, it is likely that the importance of environmental risk mediation will have been underestimated. Second, multivariate genetic analyses (i.e., those that deal with several variables simultaneously) misleadingly assume that the origins of a risk factor and its mode of risk mediation are synonymous; this means that effects that involve gene–environment correlations or interactions are all attributed to genetics, despite the fact that a degree of environmental mediation must be involved. Third, all the findings refer to individual differences and not to overall level of antisocial behavior. That is a crucial distinction because, as we have noted already, there has been a huge rise in crime over the last 50 years (see Chapter 4), and that rise must be largely attributed to environmental influences of one kind or another.

Tests for Environmental Mediation

Three sets of findings point to the importance of environmental influences on antisocial behavior. First, as just noted, there is the evidence that antisocial behavior has become much more frequent during the last half-century. A rise of such magnitude over such a short period of time could not be due to a changing gene pool. Second, twin studies have been consistent in showing substantial environmental effects of roughly the same strength as genetic effects (see Chapter 6). However, this summary statement conceals major heterogeneity, with environmental influences probably strongest in the case of adolescence-limited crime and weakest in the case of life-course–persistent antisocial behavior associated with an early onset and hyperactivity. Third, adoptee studies have indicated that some of the genetic effects concern an enhanced susceptibility to environmental adversities (see Chapter 6). The main research challenge has concerned the difficulty of translating this general recognition that environmental effects are important into quantification of the environmentally mediated effects of specific risk factors. In that connection, it is necessary to appreciate the distinction between shared and nonshared effects. Shared effects are those that impinge on all children in the same family and thereby serve to make them more alike. Nonshared effects are those that derive either from different children having different experiences (such as experiences outside the family) or from a familywide risk factor (such as family discord or poverty or overcrowding) having a differential impact on the children, with some more affected than others. The latter mechanism is important because of the evidence that most familywide risk factors do impinge differently on different children (Reiss et al., 1995). It is common, when parents quarrel or become stressed, for one child to be a particular target or focus of hostility or criticism, or even scapegoating.

With respect to most psychological characteristics, nonshared effects have been found to be greater than shared ones (Plomin & Daniels, 1987). Care needs to be taken in the interpretation of this finding, for two main reasons. First, in univariate analyses, measurement error is included with (and will therefore artificially inflate) nonshared effects (see Rutter et al., in press b). This is not the case with multivariate analyses because covariance estimates are free of random error (although not of bias). However, there have been very few multivariate analyses dealing with measured environmental risks. Second, longitudinal analyses have shown that nonshared effects are much less important with respect to developmental continuities than they are for behavior at a single point in time (see e.g. Cherny, Fulker, & Hewitt, 1997, in relation to intelligence). That is because the specific environmental risk factors tend to change over time whereas that is less the case with both genetic liabilities and shared environmental effects.

It is crucial also to add the general finding that, to a considerable extent, antisocial behavior constitutes an exception to the "rule" that nonshared environmental effects are stronger than shared ones. It is usual to find that several children in the same family, and not just one, show antisocial behavior (Farrington et al., 1996a). This implies that influences operate similarly on all children and so make them tend to be alike. Twin studies similarly indicate quite high within-pair correlations for both DZ and MZ twins (Carey, 1994). The strong indication, therefore, is that environmental factors are serving to make children in the same family similar with respect to antisocial behavior. On the other hand, there is also evidence that nonshared effects are important. Parental negativity focused

on the individual child seems to be more of a risk factor for antisocial behavior than is general family discord (Pike et al., 1996a; Reiss et al., 1995;
Rutter et al., 1997b). Accordingly, studies of environmentally mediated
risks need to consider both individual-specific and familywide features.

Both genetic and nongenetic designs may be used for this purpose
(Rutter et al., 1997a). The study of family environmental influences within
adoptee families removes the effect of passive gene–environment correlations (provided there has not been selective placement). Accordingly,
associations between parenting qualities and antisocial behavior in the
children provide a better index of environmental risk mediation than that
obtained in biological families (Bohman, 1996; Cadoret et al., 1995; Crowe,
1974; Cutrona et al., 1994). The evidence indicates that substantial risks
for antisocial behavior are associated with features such as family breakdown, family conflict, and institutional care, but that these environmental effects are mainly evident in children who are also genetically at risk
as a result of antisocial behavior in one or both of their biological parents
(who did not rear them).

Adoptee designs have three important limitations, however. First, in
recent years very few children have been adopted in infancy in most
countries (Triseliotis, Shireman, & Hundleby, 1997), so that appropriate
adoptee samples are very difficult to come by (even when access is legally
permitted). Second, adopting parents are selected to provide unusually
low environmental risks. Thus, for example, in the Colorado adoption
study, only 8% of the adopting parents (as compared with some 43% of
the biological parents) showed antisocial behavior (O'Connor et al., in
press a). Third, at least with respect to child-specific environmental risk
factors, the adoptee design does not remove the potential confounding
effects of active person–environment correlations. The solution lies, however, in longitudinal adoptee studies that cover a time span and an age
period in which there are major changes in antisocial behavior (a start in
the preschool period is likely to be necessary).

Twin designs provide an alternative approach. The most straightforward method involves the study of MZ twin differences, as these must
reflect nongenetic influences (Pike et al., 1996b). The problem, however,
has been the difficulty of obtaining satisfactory discriminating measures
of the ways in which identical twins have different experiences within
the same family. Nevertheless, in the Pike et al. (1996b) study there was
some indication of an effect of mothers' self-reported negativity on the
children's antisocial behavior (correlations of between 0.20 and 0.47, depending on the source of the measure of behavior). Alternatively, multivariate analyses using both MZ and DZ twins may be employed for the

same purpose (Pike et al., 1996a). As already noted, they too have shown significant effects of parental negativity on antisocial behavior. Measures to assess the extent to which children within the same family are treated differently have been developed by Daniels and Plomin (1985) and Carbonneau et al. (submitted). Findings show the importance of genetic influences in these differences and emphasize the need to take seriously the fact that, to some extent, disruptive children evoke negative responses from other people.

The methods listed here all focus on nonshared environmental effects, but different tactics are needed to assess shared effects. These are provided by the extended twin–family design, which relies on comparable measures of parent and child behavior to take passive gene–environment correlations into account (Kendler et al., 1996). It is constrained by the difficulties in obtaining comparable measures across generations but, to a reasonable extent, this is possible with antisocial behavior. Using this design, Meyer et al. (submitted; see also Rutter et al., 1997a) showed a significant effect of family maladaptation and lack of cohesion on antisocial behavior. Kendler et al. (1996) similarly showed a significant effect of parental loss on alcoholism in the offspring. An important limitation of this method (as it has been used up to now) is that it fails to assess the differential impact of shared risk factors; however, through a combination with other measurement and analytic strategies, such an assessment should be possible.

Geneticists sometimes seem to imply that only genetic designs can be used to test for environmental effects, but this is not so. Within-individual behavioral change over time can be used equally effectively (Farrington, 1988; Laub, Nagin, & Sampson, 1998; Rutter, 1994a, 1996; Sampson & Laub, 1993), provided certain conditions can be met. The main requirements for such natural experiments are that:

(1) there be a major change in environment that can be measured satisfactorily;
(2) there exist multisource longitudinal data to assess both risk characteristics and individual behavior before and after the change of environment; and
(3) appropriate statistical methods be used to check that the apparent change in behavior is not an artefact resulting from unmeasured aspects of the person's behavior.

The force of the design is also much increased if the environmental change is truly independent of the person's own actions and if there is an environmental change in both directions. The use of reversal effects has been evident, for example, in studies of the effects of unemployment on crime (Farrington et al., 1986) and on emotional disturbance (Banks & Ullah,

1988). Other changes studied in similar fashion include the beneficial effects of moving out of London (Osborn, 1980), of harmonious marriage to a nondeviant spouse (Quinton et al., 1993; Rutter et al., 1997b), and the adverse effects of incarceration (Sampson & Laub, 1993).

Treatment studies can also be helpful in studying environmental risk effects. The demonstration of treatment efficacy in itself is uninformative because it carries no messages regarding causal mechanisms. The key datum is the evidence of a dose–response relationship *within* the treated group between changes in the postulated risk mechanism and changes in child behavior. The evidence (albeit not entirely consistent) from the research of Patterson and his colleagues – that improvements in parental discipline were associated with reductions in antisocial behavior – supports the suggestion that ineffective discipline may play a causal role in the persistence of antisocial behavior (see Chapter 12).

Finally, it should be noted that the study of *extra*familial environments may be informative on possible risk mechanisms that are relevant to family influences as well as to influences outside the home. The key need in all cases is to differentiate, on the one hand, between *selection* into the risk environment as a consequence of the individual's own characteristics and, on the other hand, environmental *causation* (Blane, Davey Smith, & Bartley, 1993; Dohrenwend et al., 1992; Miech et al., submitted; Rowe, Wouldbroun, & Gulley, 1994b). Longitudinal data are crucial, and it is necessary to show that the initial environment is associated with subsequent changes in people's behavior. This has been demonstrated with respect to both school characteristics (see Chapter 8) and the peer group (to be discussed three sections hence).

There have been very few studies that have tested for environmentally mediated risk effects on antisocial behavior, but the scanty evidence that is available has shown significant effects. Clearly, there is a great need for further research of the kind just outlined; in the meanwhile, it may be concluded that it is likely that statistical associations between environmental risk factors and antisocial behavior do, in substantial part, reflect environmental mediation. However, it is equally evident that some of the apparent environmental effects reflect genetic mediation and some the effects of children on their environments. The evidence to date is not sufficient to quantify the relative strength of these mechanisms with respect to individual risk factors.

Third-Variable Effects

All studies of causal hypotheses must deal with possible "third variable" effects, meaning that some third variable might explain the relationship noted between two variables of interest. Genetic mediation and person effects on the environment are third variables of this kind with respect to the assessment of environmental risks. There are, however, many others. One problem with many putative environmental risk mechanisms is that they are indexed by very broad measures that may have only an indirect connection with the proximal risk process itself. Thus, there is a substantial criminological literature on the risks associated with social disadvantage, parental loss, broken homes, and poverty. Each of these indices encompasses a wide range of more specific risk factors, and it is necessary to consider which factor actually mediates the immediate risk process. In all instances, the need is to pit one alternative against another and to undertake appropriate analyses to determine whether each risk factor has effects on antisocial behavior that apply after the effects of other variables have been taken into account. Thus, for example, in the Isle of Wight community epidemiological studies (Rutter et al., 1970) it was found that the weak social class association with deviant behavior was largely lost once IQ had been taken into account, whereas the rather stronger IQ association held across social class groupings. The implication is that, insofar as social class had any causal role, it operated through effects on IQ. Similarly, it was found that the risk of antisocial behavior associated with broken homes largely derived from homes "broken" through divorce or separation rather than parental death (Rutter, 1971): analyses showed that family discord was associated with antisocial behavior even when the home was not broken and that parent–child separation did not carry risks if there was no discord. These early findings (based on statistical analyses that were rather crude by modern-day standards) have been amply confirmed by more recent research. We deal with some of the key findings in individual sections of this chapter, but the general strategy in all cases is broadly similar. The need is to develop competing hypotheses on possible mediating mechanisms and to undertake analyses that effectively pit one against another. Multivariate analyses, in which causal chain processes over time are examined through the use of longitudinal data, are desirable.

One complexity that needs to be recognized is that multivariate analyses that control for other variables are not adequate on their own for determining whether one variable has an effect in the *absence* of other risk factors (Rutter, 1983a). On the whole, single risk factors have rather slight effects if they truly occur in isolation (Kolvin et al., 1990; Rutter, 1979). This means that there must be considerable caution in generalizing from a finding that a risk factor X has an overall significant effect on antisocial behavior (after controlling for other possible confounding variables) to an assumption that factor X carries risks on its own and so reflects a causal mechanism; it may not do so at all if the risks rely on associations with other risk factors. Equally, if the main risks derive from constellations of risk factors (as is generally the case), there will be considerable difficulties in sorting out which risk processes are operating. As we shall discuss, this is indeed a problem with respect to the findings on psychosocial risk factors for antisocial behavior.

Family Influences

Teenage Parents

Conseur et al.'s (1997) analysis of 1974 and 1975 birth certificates from the U.S. state of Washington enabled them to compare offenders (adjudicated between 10 and 17 years of age) and non-offenders. For both males and females, being born to an unmarried mother was associated with over a doubling of the risk of becoming a chronic offender; being born to a mother under the age of 18 was associated with more than a threefold increase in the risk of being a chronic offender. The highest-risk group comprised males born to mothers who were under age 18 at their birth; their risk of being a chronic offender was eleven times that of the lowest-risk group. The findings from other studies are closely comparable (Farrington & Loeber, in press; Furstenberg, Brooks-Gunn, & Morgan, 1987; Kolvin et al., 1990; Maynard, 1997). There is no doubt that being born to an unmarried teenage parent is a good indicator of an increased risk for antisocial behavior. The question is: What risk mechanism does the association represent?

The association could simply reflect the characteristics of women who become teenage parents. Follow-up studies of both institutionally reared and general population samples have shown the high frequency with which antisocial behavior in girls is associated with both teenage motherhood and impulsive liaisons with antisocial men, these features in turn being followed by a high rate of breakdown of the cohabiting relationship together with parenting difficulties and an increased rate of parenting breakdown (Quinton & Rutter, 1988; Quinton et al., 1993). This course of events is less characteristic of antisocial males (Rutter, Quinton, & Hill, 1990b). The Dunedin longitudinal study data similarly showed that individuals who had become parents by the age of 21 had an odds ratio (OR) of 6.3 for official recorded delinquency and 3.2 for domestic violence (Moffitt & Caspi, 1997). The American National Longitudinal Study of Youth and the British national cohort longitudinal studies tell much the same story (Maughan & Lindelow, 1997). Teenage mothers in the British data differed from older mothers most strikingly in terms of a lack of school-leaving qualifications (OR = 3.2) and adolescent antisocial behavior (OR = 2.0).

These characteristics were more strongly evident in those born in 1958 than in those born in 1946. When adult, the teenage mothers experienced a higher rate of marriage breakdown (OR = 2.3) and of domestic violence (OR = 2.0).

Doubtless, much of the risk for the offspring derive from the characteristics of people who become parents at a young age. However, that may not be the whole story because, in the Conseur et al. (1997) study, the risk was greater if the teenage birth concerned the child in question than if it concerned the mother's first birth – irrespective of whether or not this birth was of this particular child. It was found that 4.2% of children became chronic offenders when the mother was unmarried and under 18 at the birth of her first child, but 7.5% became chronic offenders when those conditions applied to their own birth. On the other hand, in the much smaller Farrington sample of inner London boys, the delinquency risk was similar irrespective of whether the early pregnancy applied to that particular child (Nagin, Pogarsky, & Farrington, 1997).

The most thorough analyses were undertaken with the U.S. National Longitudinal Study of Youth (NLSY) data (reported in several chapters of Maynard, 1997). Both within-family comparisons and multivariate analyses taking into account the characteristics and background of the women becoming parents as teenagers showed that a substantial part of the risk derived from the women's characteristics. However, even after these characteristics had been taken into account, the age at which these women gave birth was also a significant risk factor.

Because all the studies show that teenage parenthood is associated with a host of other risk factors – including parenting difficulties, curtailment of education, poverty, being on welfare, and lack of support from a partner – it is likely that much of the risk to the children comes from these associated risk circumstances rather than from the mother's age as such. Thus, Farrington and Loeber (in press), using data from both the London and Pittsburgh studies, found that having a young mother primarily predicted delinquency because it tended to be a precursor of a broken family. The same applies to the risks associated with being a single mother. However – apart from Maynard (1997) and Farrington and Loeber (in press) – the published research does not include the multivariate analyses needed to pinpoint the causal mechanisms that are reflected in the risks associated with being born to an unmarried teenage mother.

Large Family Size

Being reared in a family with at least four children has long been noted as a significant risk factor for delinquency (Rutter & Giller, 1983), and recent research has tended to confirm the association (Farrington & Loeber, in press). Thus, in both the Pittsburgh and London studies, the odds ratio for delinquency as officially recorded exceeded 2. The difficulty has been to determine what mechanism this might reflect. Three main possibilities stand out. First, large family size tends to be associated with less adequate discipline and supervision of the children, and hence the proximal causal process could lie in the parenting difficulties rather than large family size as such, with the latter having an impact only at a more distal level through its role in making good parenting more difficult. The Pittsburgh and London analyses (Farrington & Loeber, in press) suggest that this is the case to an important extent.

Second, it could be, as Offord's (1982) findings suggest, that the risk stems from the influence of delinquent siblings (through some sort of "contagion" effect) rather than from qualities of parenting. He found that the delinquency risk was associated with the number of brothers in the family but not with the number of sisters. The finding, in the London study, that the risk of delinquency was a function of the number of delinquent siblings (Farrington et al., 1996a; Rowe & Farrington, 1997) is in keeping with that suggestion, as is the finding that the association is more with delinquency in older siblings than in younger siblings and more with same-sex than opposite-sex siblings. It may be inferred that a sibling effect is part of the explanation.

A third possibility is that the risk is not environmentally mediated at all but rather that the mechanism derives from a tendency of antisocial individuals to have large families, with the risk genetically mediated in part. Rowe and Farrington's (1997) analysis of the London longitudinal study data set suggests that this may well constitute part of the mechanism. They showed that the effects of large family size on antisocial behavior were greatly reduced when family criminality was taken into account, but that the reverse did not apply. The design did not allow any test of whether the relation was genetic, but it did suggest that the mechanism was much more directly associated with family criminality than with family size.

Although too few studies have undertaken the necessary multivariate analyses for firm conclusions, the weight of evidence suggests that, although large family size is a risk *indicator* for antisocial behavior, it is quite likely that the risk *mechanisms* concern other family features with which large family size happens to be associated.

Broken Homes

Since the very start of criminological research in the last century, "broken homes" have been featured as a risk factor for antisocial behavior

(Rutter & Giller, 1983; Wells & Rankin, 1991; Wilson & Herrnstein, 1985). The effect sizes found have usually been moderate, but the statistical association with delinquency, however assessed, has been reasonably robust. Once more, the issue is what the association means. It has been evident for a long time (Wootton, 1959) that the variable is much too crude, and too wide in its coverage of a heterogeneous range of situations, for it to be viewed as a plausible risk mechanism itself. Nevertheless, multivariate analyses have tended to show effects that remain to some extent after controlling for other risk variables (Farrington & Loeber, in press; Henry et al., 1993), so it is likely to be indexing some feature that is involved in risk mechanisms.

It is necessary to seek to "unpack" broken homes into the various family situations that differ from the traditional, stable, two-parent biological family. Although not usually included in the concept of broken homes, it is instructive to start with adoption because its atypicality is accompanied by, on average, unusually good rearing conditions. Despite this, Fergusson, Lynskey, and Horwood (1995b) found, in the Christchurch longitudinal study, that adopted children have a slightly increased rate of antisocial or disruptive behavior and of self-reported offending as compared with children from ordinary biological two-parent families. The increase was more marked if account was taken of their generally superior social situation. There was no significant increase in emotional difficulties, and the authors concluded it was likely that the slightly elevated risk for antisocial behavior stemmed from genetic factors. The rate was, however, somewhat lower than expected on the basis of the social status of the children's biological parents, suggesting that adoption, with its generally better rearing conditions, may have exerted some protective effect. Maughan and Pickles's (1990) analysis of the British National Child Development Study (NCDS) data found a generally more favorable outcome at 16 years for adoptees, although the pattern was comparable. They lacked measures of criminality, however. Although being adopted has only a very weak association with antisocial behavior, the fact that it has any link serves to alert us to the need to consider possible genetic (or obstetric) influences operating on children being reared in broken homes or other atypical circumstances.

Both the Christchurch and NCDS studies were consistent in showing that the risk of antisocial behavior (and other forms of psychosocial malfunction) was much greater for illegitimate children who were not adopted and who remained with their single mothers. Their rate was about double that of children reared in ordinary biological two-parent families. The illegitimate children in both samples were, however, socially disadvantaged in numerous ways, and it would be unwise to assume that the lack of a father constituted the key risk factor. In the Oregon study, Bank et al. (1993) found that the proximal risk for the children of single mothers stemmed from ineffective discipline and poor monitoring, but that these features were particularly present when the mother showed antisocial behavior herself and was also socially disadvantaged. Moreover, it should be added that the meaning of illegitimacy has changed beyond recognition during the course of the last generation, as an increasing proportion of young people have chosen to live together and have children without getting married (Hess, 1995). As a consequence, some 36% of U.K. children born in 1996 were legally illegitimate, as compared with 6% in 1961 and 8% in 1971 (Office for National Statistics, 1997). The majority of these births are registered in the names of both parents (78% in 1996 as compared with 45% in 1971), and many of the families are not socially disadvantaged. It cannot be assumed that the risks for antisocial behavior (from being born to a single parent) evident in studies of children born several decades ago will apply to the present generation of births.

Many of the early studies focused on parental loss as the key risk factor in broken homes. As already noted, the evidence showed that the main risk did not derive from loss of a parent: although parental divorce or separation was associated with a substantial increase in risk of antisocial behavior, that associated with parental death was minimal (Rutter, 1971; Rutter & Giller, 1983). This conclusion has not been altered by more recent evidence (Farrington, 1996). Thus, the U.S. National Comorbidity Survey (Kessler, Davis, & Kendler, 1997) showed an odds ratio of 3.1 for parental divorce occurring in the absence of other adversities in relation to the risk of conduct disorder in childhood, and 1.9 for adult antisocial personality disorder. The risks were not increased with respect to parental death. There has been one important additional finding, however. Longitudinal studies have shown that many children of divorcing parents showed a raised level of conduct or behavioral disturbance *before* the divorce took place (Block, Block, & Bjerde, 1986; Cherlin et al., 1991). The implication is that much of the risk is likely to stem from chronic family adversities that precede, accompany, and follow divorce, rather than from the event of family breakup as such.

The alternative mechanisms being considered currently are repeated family separations or changes in caregiver (and the disruptions in parental care that this implies) and family conflict and discord. There is plenty of evidence that repeated separations or changes do constitute a substantial risk indicator for antisocial behavior. In the Dunedin study, Henry et al. (1993) found that it was the strongest of all family predictors. Moreover,

its risk association was maintained after controlling for the children's behavior at 5 years, showing that it was most unlikely to have derived
from children's effects on their family environment. It is relevant, however, that the depth of measures of family relationships in the Dunedin
study was fairly limited. In the London study, Farrington and Loeber
(in press) found that the effect of parent–child separation was lost when
child-rearing qualities were taken into account; by contrast, broken families continued to show an effect on antisocial behavior in Pittsburgh. Mc-
Cord (1982) found that the rate of offending was high among boys reared
in an unbroken conflictful home but low in those from a broken home,
provided the mother was affectionate. The most direct test was provided
by Fergusson et al. (1992) in the Christchurch longitudinal study. Considered separately, both family separations and family conflict were accompanied by a substantial increased risk of antisocial behavior. But when
considered together in a multivariate analysis, family conflict continued
to show an increased risk regardless of the number of family separations,
whereas the reverse was not the case. The increased risk for antisocial
behavior that accompanied family separations was accounted for by the
high level of family conflict that tended to characterize families with multiple changes and separations. The Oregon studies undertaken by Patterson and his colleagues, with much more detailed data on family functioning, showed that family transitions tended to disrupt parenting and
that this was especially the case with antisocial mothers (Patterson &
Capaldi, 1991).

When families break up, if the parents are already struggling to cope
then it is quite common for the children to be placed in short-term family
foster care or in residential group care (Quinton & Rutter, 1988; Wolkind
& Rushton, 1994). Numerous studies from Ferguson (1966) onward have
shown that individuals who have experienced periods in such care have
an increased likelihood of being delinquent (Minty & Ashcroft, 1987). It
is evident, however, that in almost all cases the period of being in care is
just one episode in a prolonged series of adversities. That the lack of family support necessitated the use of foster care (either in a family or a children's home) is a strong indication of adversities, but it is doubtful that
the main risk for antisocial behavior stems from the foster care as such.
Nevertheless, Hagell and Newburn's (1994) study of chronic offenders
highlighted the numerous occasions upon which many had experienced
foster care, and almost all the offenders were known to social services.
Also, although group care as such may not constitute the strongest risk
factor for antisocial behavior, adverse experiences in care can exacerbate
risks in a most important way (Utting, 1996).

A few children experience most of their rearing in residential group care as a result of parenting breakdown of some sort. These children show a high rate of antisocial behavior (Quinton & Rutter, 1988; Rutter et al., 1990b). Strikingly, this is so both for those admitted (for their own protection) when young as well as for those who remain in residential care for most of their upbringing. Three possible reasons need to be considered. First, this could reflect genetic risk, despite the finding that parent mental disorder (as assessed from social service records) was not a strong predictor. Second, it could represent the long-term sequelae of adverse family experiences before being admitted into residential care. Third, it could derive from the risks associated with an upbringing that involves an immense turnover of caregivers, although not usually coercive relationships. The last possibility is theoretically important because it implies a risk for antisocial behavior from a *lack* of selective attachment relationships as well as from the pressure of family discord and conflict. In that connection, however, Vorria et al.'s (1998a,b) study of children in Greek institutions may be relevant. They found, in line with other studies, an increase in antisocial behavior (and also emotional disturbance and other difficulties), but this was not the case for the subgroup of children who experienced a stable pattern of early parenting and who were mainly admitted as a result of family poverty. The indication is that the risks associated with institutional rearing may mainly apply to those already at risk because of either their genetic background or adverse early experiences.

Abuse and Neglect

Because seriously delinquent adolescents and adults so frequently report abusive experiences (Boswell, 1995, 1996; Lewis et al., 1989b) – and because follow-up studies have shown the substantial increase in emotional, social, and behavioral problems in children who have experienced serious physical or sexual abuse or parental neglect (Kendall-Tackett, Meyer Williams, & Finkelhor, 1993; Trickett & McBride-Chang, 1995) – much attention has been paid to abuse and neglect as a risk factor for later antisocial behavior. Widom (1989, 1997) found that early childhood victimization increased the risk of later criminality by about 50% – a significant but rather modest effect. It did not appear that the risk for violent crime was any more increased than that for acquisitive crime, but there may have been slightly more of a risk for antisocial personality disorder. This suggestion is supported by the findings from the U.S. National Comorbidity Survey (Kessler et al., 1997). Aggression by the father occurring in the absence of other adversities had an odds ratio of 2.5 for childhood conduct disorder and 4.4 for adult antisocial personality disorder. The evidence, therefore, suggests that abuse or neglect is a risk factor for antisocial behavior and is particularly so when the antisocial behavior is part of a more pervasive personality disorder. The published findings do not allow any differentiation of the effects of the experience of actual abuse from the effects of the chronic psychosocial adversities with which it is often associated. That the increase in risk for antisocial behavior found for more persistent aspects of family life and of parenting seems to be greater than that from abuse per se suggests that the abusive episode itself probably does not provide the main risk.

Coercion and Hostility

There is abundant evidence from numerous studies that a coercive, hostile, critical, punitive parenting style is associated with a substantially increased risk for antisocial behavior (Farrington & Loeber, in press; Loeber & Stouthamer-Loeber, 1986; McCord, 1991; Patterson, 1982, 1995; Patterson, Reid, & Dishion, 1992; Sampson & Laub, 1993). The association is robust and has been found across a diverse range of samples, so there is every reason to suppose that it is likely to be connected in some way with the processes involved in the causation or continuation of antisocial behavior. Nevertheless, four major questions arise with respect to the meaning of the finding. First, it is necessary to ask whether the association may, at least in part, represent genetic mediation. The question arises because of the extensive evidence that many of the parents who behave in coercive or hostile ways have themselves shown antisocial behavior. For example, this has been a consistent finding in the Oregon studies (Bank et al., 1993). Their statistical modeling has suggested that the proximal causal mechanism concerns coercive parenting, with the parental antisocial behavior a more distal causal factor through its role in predisposing to a coercive style. McCord's (1991) analyses of the Cambridge–Somerville study data point to the same conclusion. Neither, however, used genetically sensitive designs. Rowe and Farrington (1997), using data from Farrington's longitudinal study of London boys, found that the mother's convictions correlated 0.38 with coercive child rearing. Their statistical modeling showed that parental convictions carried the main effect but that the rearing environment also contributed (the results varied somewhat across different approaches to data analysis). Again, it was not a genetically sensitive design. Simons et al. (1995) also showed the strong extent to which parents' violence to their children was part of a general antisocial trait. For reasons already considered in relation to evidence of genetic mediation, it is implausible that all the effects of hostile parenting are genetically mediated, but probably some are. The matter clearly warrants further study using appropriate research designs.

The second issue concerns the question of the extent to which the association represents children's influences on their parents rather than the risks associated with hostile parenting. Clearly this cannot be the main explanation, if only because of the evidence on the parental qualities that predict coercive parenting (see e.g. the previous section on teenage parents) as well as the evidence that family circumstances in the preschool years predict later criminality (Kolvin et al., 1988). On the other hand, there is no doubt that child effects exist (see the previous section on person effects). There have been several good attempts to use longitudinal data to sort out the direction of causation. Kandel and Wu (1995) addressed the issue by using two-wave longitudinal measures six years apart on children aged 3–11 on the first occasion. Cross-lagged correlations (i.e., those from parenting at time 1 to child behavior at time 2, and vice versa) showed two-way effects. Harsh parenting predisposed to disruptive behavior, but aggressive behavior by the child tended to make it more likely that mothers would emotionally withdraw, supervise less well, and parent more harshly. A reciprocal dynamic process is suggested. Cohen and Brook (1995) tackled the same issue with a large data set and a more extensive range of measures. The first measures were obtained when the children were aged 1–10, with follow-ups eight and ten years later. Early punishment was associated with later conduct problems, with an odds ratio of over 3 after taking account of confounding variables. In younger – but not older – children, there was also a significant effect of the children's negative behavior on parental punishment. Campbell et al. (1996), in their longitudinal study of "hard to manage" boys, showed much the same. Observed negative maternal control at age 4 predicted antisocial problems at age 9, after controlling for the children's behavior at age 4 and for the stability over time of the two measures (that for child behavior being made greater). The cross-lagged correlation of 0.25 exceeded that (0.14) from child behavior at age 4 to negative control at age 9. Overall, the pattern of findings suggested that the causal effect of punishment was real, that it has most effect on the children already showing problems, and that the likelihood of parents using coercive methods is affected by the child's negative behavior. By later childhood and adolescence, however, antisocial behavior becomes rather stable.

The third question is whether the main effects of coercive hostile parenting are on disruptive behavior in young children (which leads to later delinquency) or on criminal activities as such. The evidence is clear-cut that both are likely to be the case. The studies of younger children show that there are effects long before children reach the age of criminal responsibility. Likewise, the investigations of older children and adolescents show effects that hold up after taking into account the children's earlier behavior (Cohen & Brook, 1995; Deater-Deckard et al., in press; Farrington, 1979, 1986a; Farrington & Loeber, in press). On the whole, however, the effects appear greater for antisocial behavior that begins when the children are young rather than in adolescence (Patterson & Yoerger, 1997).

The fourth issue, and the most difficult to resolve, concerns the nature of the risk processes. Several alternatives need to be considered. During recent years, for example, there has been growing concern both over the high frequency with which parents use physical punishment and over the possible psychological risks associated with slapping and hitting children (Baumrind, 1996; Cohen, 1996; Graziano, 1996; Larzelere, 1996). The question here is whether those corporal methods that do not amount to abuse have risks for antisocial behavior that are not seen with nonphysical methods of punishment and that are not a consequence of more pervasive hostility or coercive styles of interaction. The evidence is not conclusive, but the finding that the risks associated with physical punishment do not seem to apply within African-American samples (Deater-Deckard et al., 1996; Deater-Deckard & Dodge, 1997) necessarily casts doubt on the suggestion that the risks come from the use of physical methods as such. The implication is that the risks occur only when the physical punishment is part of poor parent–child relationships and is not accepted as a reasonable consequence of the child's misdeeds. For a variety of reasons, hitting children seems undesirable, but the main risks for antisocial behavior probably derive from persisting coercive hostile patterns of parenting rather than from whether or not discipline includes slapping or hitting.

Alternatively, it could be that the main risks derive from the poor quality of the parent–child relationship implied by a coercive hostile style of parenting, rather than from the parenting itself. The possibility is suggested by the risks associated with an institutional upbringing (which lacks consistent close caregiver relationships but on the whole also does not involve much coercive hostility) and by the protective effect of a good relationship with one parent (see the section on resilience).

Social control theory (Hirschi, 1969; Sampson & Laub, 1993) argues that bonding to individuals and to their society serves to constrain people from engaging in antisocial behavior. The notion is that social ties foster the development of commitment to shared values and of concern for others. Parent–child relationships may also be important for the rather different reasons that they set the scene for the development of later social functioning and social relationships (Rutter, 1995b,c). In that connection, it is relevant that individuals showing persistent antisocial behavior following earlier psychosocial adversity frequently exhibit a pervasive pattern of social malfunction (Quinton & Rutter, 1988; Robins, 1966; Zoccolillo et al., 1992). Because poor relationships and coercive hostility tend, in practice, to be so closely interwound (Dishion et al., 1995), it has not proved possible so far to separate their efforts satisfactorily.

A third possibility is that coercive acts by parents tend to promote coercive responses from the children (and vice versa). This constitutes one part of Patterson's (1982, 1995) coercive model – a part for which observational data provide empirical support. Chronic exposure to violence, hostility, and coercive styles of interaction may also foster an acceptance of these styles as acceptable means of dealing with problems. As discussed in Chapter 6, there is some evidence that antisocial boys do view the use of aggression more positively than other children. Dodge et al.'s findings (Dodge 1995; Dodge, Bates, & Pettit, 1990) from their multi-site longitudinal study of abused children suggest that this is likely to be part of the mechanism. Observational studies of young children in high-risk families point to the same inference (reviewed by Coie & Dodge, 1997). Abused children seem more likely than other children to respond to distress with aggression.

Alternatively, the mechanism may lie in ineffective parenting that fosters rather than inhibits antisocial behavior. This constitutes the central tenet of Patterson's coercion theory. The suggestion is that a child's counterattacks to parental coercion result in the parent backing off and ceasing to require the child's compliance. When the parent, in effect, gives in, the child stops attacking, so completing a cycle of reinforcement of disruptive behavior. The ineffectiveness of the discipline is increased by the tendency of the parent's coercion to derive more from their own feelings of stress and irritation than from any specific act by the child. Once more, there is evidence in support of this postulated cycle, but the extent to which a coercive relational style and ineffective parenting co-occur has made it impossible to separate the effects of the two.

The pinpointing of the causal mechanisms underlying the risks associated with coercive hostile parenting are potentially important because they imply different models for the processes by which antisocial behavior arises and continues. Three rather different routes seem to be implicated: (i) an impaired social development that involves poor relationships and ineffective social problem solving; (ii) a learning that aggressive behavior pays off; and (iii) a relative failure to develop social bonds and hence a lack of social constraints against behaving in ways that could damage other people. There is evidence in favor of all three processes, and it is likely that coercive parenting is implicated in each of them to some degree.

Ineffective Parenting and Supervision

There is a very extensive literature on what is involved in parenting and on which features are most likely to promote adaptive social functioning (Bornstein, 1995; Maccoby & Martin, 1983). These might seem to be relatively straightforward issues, but several complexities are involved. Thus, it is clear that several rather different needs must be met:

(1) effective monitoring or supervision of the children's activities so that parents can know which behaviors seem likely to lead to trouble;
(2) clear setting of standards with explicit and unambiguous feedback so that children may learn what is expected of them;
(3) skilled diversion or distraction to avoid the development of confrontations and crises;
(4) responsivity to the children's sensitivities and needs;
(5) fostering of prosocial behavior, self-efficacy, and social problem solving; and
(6) encouraging the development of internal controls through open communication, recognition of children's rights, and the taking of responsibility.

Patterson's (1982; Larzelere & Patterson, 1990) studies have clearly shown the extent to which parents of antisocial children tend to fall down on all these facets. They fail to monitor (so that they do not know where their children are or what they are doing); their instructions are ambiguous and unclear; disciplining measures often result from their own mood state as much as from what the child has done; there is neglect of prosocial features; and their coercive style shows little responsivity to children's needs and feelings.

As already noted, numerous studies have documented associations between inept parenting and antisocial behavior. A range of measures – including observations, as well as parental interviews and questionnaires – have been employed, and the association seems robust. In practice, most measures have combined coercion and inept parenting, and it is not possible to assess their relative importance. Hence the methodological issues already discussed in relation to coercion apply, and the conclusions are similar.

There is one possible difference in emphasis, however. Coercion theory focuses mainly on the promotion of antisocial behavior, whereas socialization theories start with a recognition that a degree of stubbornness, defiance, assertiveness, and aggression are normal aspects of children's development of autonomy and independence (Loeber & Hay, 1994). The challenge for parents is to encourage the latter whilst at the same time ensuring that the former elements do not go beyond flexible acceptable limits.

The one element that is most distinctive about a focus on parenting rather than coercion concerns monitoring and supervision, if only because, to a substantial extent (especially with adolescents), it concerns activities both outside and inside the home. Many investigations have shown that the parents of delinquents tend to be less aware than other parents of where their children are and what they are doing (Farrington & Loeber, in press; Graham & Bowling, 1995; Rutter & Giller, 1983; Wilson, 1980, 1987). The assumption that parental supervision is important with respect to antisocial behavior was challenged by Riley and Shaw (1985; Riley, 1987). In a cross-sectional study of adolescents, they found that poor parent–child relationships and being part of a delinquent peer group were more strongly associated with antisocial behavior. Parental supervision did show a significant association in girls, but in boys the association was mediated by the peer group. There are too few data for firm conclusions on the importance of supervision outside of peer group activities. Nonetheless, it is clear (see the next section) that, in adolescence, the peer group is a relevant influence on young people's behavior and hence the parents' role in regulating peer group activities may be important. With girls and with younger boys, monitoring and supervision appear to be important in other contexts as well. Other research, too, has shown the importance of parent monitoring with respect to activities that – although not delinquent in themselves – are associated with antisocial behavior. Thus, Small (1995) found a strong association between a lack of supervision and binge drinking by adolescents.

Peer Groups

It has long been obvious that delinquent individuals tend to have delinquent friends and that many antisocial activities are undertaken together with other people (Reiss, 1988). Opinions on what this means have, however, diverged sharply. At one extreme, the finding has been dismissed as of no consequence for causal mechanisms involved in either the initiation or persistence of antisocial behavior. Sheldon and Eleanor Glueck (1950) summarized the dismissal succinctly in terms of their conclusion that the associations with other delinquents amounted to no more than "birds of a feather flock together." At the other extreme, differential association theorists such as Sutherland and Cressey (1978) have argued that criminal behavior is largely learned through personal interactions in the peer group.

Several key methodological issues have had to be addressed in order to decide between these (and other) alternatives (Thornberry & Krohn, 1997). Most crucially, it has been necessary to determine the relative importance of selection processes and influence processes (Rowe et al., 1994b). Longitudinal data are essential for that purpose, but four somewhat different designs may be employed. First, friendship pairs may be followed over time, as in Kandel's (1978) pioneering study. If friends influence one another then they should become more similar to one another over time. If, on the other hand, there is only a selection effect, then the similarity at the end of a longitudinal study should be no greater than at the beginning. Kandel concluded that about half of friendship similarity was due to influence and about half to selection. The proportion, however, is much affected by the method of analysis employed. Rowe et al. (1994b) argued that selection effects outweighed influence effects. Thus, the intercorrelation for minor delinquency in Kandel's (1978) study was 0.26 at the beginning of the academic year and 0.29 at the end; the comparable figures for frequent marijuana use were 0.45 and 0.51 – in each case an increase of only about 10%. Other studies using the same (or a similar) design have produced much the same picture (Rowe et al., 1994b).

A second approach is to use multiwave panel data to determine the effects of peer group characteristics at time 1 on changes in level of delinquent activities between time 1 and time 2 and vice versa (e.g., to see if delinquent activity at time 1 predicts choice of friends over the subsequent time period). The results from the Rochester Youth Development study (Thornberry et al., 1994), the National Youth Study (Elliott & Menard, 1992; Menard & Elliott, 1994), and other investigations (Thornberry & Krohn, 1997) have been consistent in showing bidirectional effects.

A third design uses statistical modeling or other multivariate methods to examine the direct and indirect effects of peer group characteristics on individual differences in delinquent activity when considered in relation to the person's own prior behavior and family influences (Dishion & Patterson, 1997; Fergusson & Horwood, 1996; Keenan et al., 1995; Patterson, 1993; Patterson & Yoerger, 1997). The findings have been consistent in showing substantial peer group effects. A variant of this design has been to focus on situations that may bring about changes in young people's peer groups. Magnusson, Stattin, and Allen (1986), in their Swedish longitudinal study, focused on the possible effects of unusually early puberty in girls. This was associated with an increase in rule-breaking behavior (playing truant, getting drunk, taking drugs, etc.) and an increased like-lihood of dropping out of education. The effect, however, was evident only in the subgroup of early-maturing girls who joined peer groups of older girls (which included a higher proportion engaging in antisocial be-havior). Caspi and his colleagues (Caspi & Moffitt, 1991; Caspi et al., 1993) took the matter further in the Dunedin study by showing that the effect operated only in coeducational schools and that the main adverse peer group influence brought about by early puberty was on girls who had not previously shown much antisocial behavior.

Finally, longitudinal designs have been used to examine the possible role of the peer group in persistence in or desistance from antisocial behav-ior (Farrington, 1986a; Loeber et al., 1991). The findings indicate that being part of a delinquent peer group is associated with persistence, whereas having few delinquent friends is associated with desistance. The implica-tion is that the peer group was exerting an influence, although the causal influence is less certain than with some other research strategies.

Another methodological issue concerns the fact that most studies relied on self-reports *both* for peer group characteristics and the person's own delinquency. Undoubtedly, this constitutes a serious potential source of bias. There are very few studies that have used peers' own reports about their antisocial behavior, but most that have (e.g., Elliott & Voss, 1974; Esbensen & Huizinga, 1993; Kandel, 1978) produced the same pattern of findings as those relying on just the one informant. Nevertheless, it is important to note that the influence effects have been much smaller when separate informants have been used. It may also be relevant that, using multiple data sources, Tremblay et al. (1995) did not find an ef-fect of best friend's delinquency in middle childhood. This negative find-ing may reflect the exclusive focus on best friends rather than on the peer group as a whole, or the age period studied, or a combination of the two.

Gottfredson and Hirschi (1991) have suggested that the apparent influ-ence effect is an artefact of both variables (i.e., the person's own delin-quency and that of the peers) referring to the same shared delinquent activities. The evidence indicates that this is unlikely to account for the findings, since the same pattern is found if the two measures are designed to exclude this possibility (e.g., by considering drug use rather than delin-quent acts by peers; see Thornberry et al., 1994).

The overall conclusion is the same for each of the research strategies. That is, there are strong selection effects by which antisocial individuals tend to choose friends who are similarly antisocial but, even when this tendency is taken into account, the findings show that the characteristics of the peer group exert an influence on the individual's likelihood of persisting or desisting with their antisocial activities.

A key issue is *how* peer influences exert their effects. Several possibilities need to be considered. Dishion and Patterson (1997) have emphasized the role of differential reinforcement. Their videotape study of interactions showed that dyads of antisocial individuals tend not to respond positively to talk on ordinary topics but laugh approvingly in response to talk about antisocial activities (Dishion, Patterson, & Griesler, 1994; Dishion et al., 1995). It is suggested that these reactions serve to endorse deviant values and norms. Through similar processes, young people in a delinquent peer group may come to perceive the cost and benefits of (and opportunities for) antisocial behavior differently (Gottfredson & Hirschi, 1991). A related possibility is that delinquent activities may serve, within an antisocial peer group, as a source of prestige or esteem (Emler & Reicher, 1995).

On the whole, aggressive and antisocial children are not liked by others (Parker & Asher, 1987), but they do make friendships in much the same way as other children do (Giordano et al., 1986); it may be that, within a deviant peer group, they can achieve the popularity that they lack in other groups. Findings indicate, however, that the effects of delinquent peers are not largely mediated through peer group attitudes; rather, the effects seem to stem from peer behaviors (Warr & Stafford, 1991). There may be direct modeling of behavior, but there may also be implicit pressures as a result of being with peers when the group is engaging in illicit or antisocial activities such as taking drugs, vandalizing property, stealing from shops, and the like. It is not just a matter of peer group pressure, however. Deviant peer groups are likely to be together in situations where there are attractive opportunities for crime, and situational influences may well play a part (Cohen & Felson, 1979; Osgood et al., 1996). In the longer term, the peer group will play a major role in choices of partner. People are likely to marry or cohabit with individuals who are part of their peer group. Longitudinal and cross-sectional studies both show the importance of this in relation to the strong tendency for antisocial individuals to marry and have children by other antisocial individuals (Pawlby, Mills, & Quinton, 1997a; Pawlby et al., 1997b; Quinton et al., 1993). Research findings do not indicate the relative importance of these various mechanisms, but direct and indirect effects both seem to be operative (Thornberry & Krohn, 1997).

A further question concerns the circumstances under which deviant peer group influences are most and least likely to exert their effects. Agnew (1991) found that, on the whole, peer effects were greater when people were closely attached to delinquent peers, when they spent a lot of time with them, when the group was overtly approving of delinquent activities, and where peer group activities served to create pressures to join in antisocial behavior. The National Youth Survey findings (Warr, 1993a) showed that attachment to parents on its own did little to counteract peer group influences. On the other hand, spending much leisure time with the family did reduce, or even eliminate, peer influences. Presumably, it did so both by cutting the amount of time spent with the deviant peer group and by inhibiting the formation of delinquent friendships. Monitoring and supervision by parents is likely also to be important through restriction of young people's activities with antisocial peers that might well create opportunities for illicit or illegal activities (Small, 1995).

The last major issue with respect to peer group influences concerns the age period when they are most strongly operative. The evidence suggests that, although they are operative at all ages, peer influences have the most impact during adolescence (Thornberry & Krohn, 1997). Probably this comes about for three rather different reasons. First, individual characteristics (such as hyperactivity) are most strongly influential in relation to early-onset antisocial behavior (see Chapter 6). Likewise, adverse family features (such as coercive parenting) also make a major impact on this younger onset group. Capaldi and Patterson (1994) found that both individual and family risk factors were much more strongly evident in the case of boys whose first arrest occurred before age 14 than with boys whose first arrest occurred later. The implication is that there is more "room" for antisocial behavior beginning in adolescence to be affected by the peer group simply because other risk factors are less strongly influential.

Second, the nature of peer relationships changes with age (Hartup, 1983). Compared with young children, adolescents spend more time with friends and less time with their families. Friendships in adolescence involve much more sharing of ideas and feelings than is the case in earlier childhood. Also, leisure activities in the teens are both less open to parental supervision and more likely to involve groups (rather than just two children playing together). All these changes make peer group influences more possible.

Third, the marked increase in delinquent activities during adolescence means that a much higher proportion of peers will be engaging in them. It is not that antisocial behavior as a whole increases greatly; rather, there is a shift from disruptive (defiant, aggressive) behavior that operates in interpersonal interactions with peers and elders to actual delinquent acts such as stealing, vandalism, and mugging (Loeber & Hay, 1994). It should be noted, however, that there is a chicken-and-egg problem with these age changes. Menard (1992) and Warr (1993b), using the National Youth Survey data set, found that peer variables largely accounted for the age trends in delinquency and drug use. Taken at face value, the finding is unhelpful because it provides no satisfactory explanation for the marked increase in delinquency over the adolescent age period. It is quite implausible that changes in the peer group could account for it. On the other hand, peer group influences certainly could enhance the age trend.

There is still much to be learned about peer group influences. During the last two decades, though, research findings have indicated that such effects are real and may be particularly important with respect to adolescence-limited antisocial behavior. There is a need now to gain a better understanding of how such influences operate and how their negative effects may be diminished and their positive effects enhanced.

Gangs

There is no sharp dividing line between antisocial peer groups and criminal gangs, but the latter term has usually been restricted to groups with a clear identity and leadership (Klein, 1995, 1996). Although there is an extensive literature on gangs (Cairns et al., 1997; Goldstein, 1991; Klein, 1995), there is a paucity of systematic quantitative studies into their formation or their effects. Cairns et al. (1997), drawing on evidence from the Cairns and Cairns (1994) longitudinal study, argued speculatively for three main routes into gangs. First, they may represent the coming together of aggressive and dominant individuals who have a controlling role in the social networks within which they operate. Second, many individuals who join gangs are disaffiliated and alienated youths who run away from home and become homeless. For them, the gangs are felt to provide the bonds that they lacked in their family life, school, and previous social interactions. Third, some gangs operate as successful businesses built on, or at least heavily engaged in, trade in illegal drugs.

These suggestions focus mainly on individual and family influences, but it is necessary also to consider the extent to which area influences (see Chapter 8) may also play a role. Curry and Spergel's (1988) study in Chicago pointed to a possible role of social disorganization in making gang homicide more likely. The matter warrants further study.

Goldstein (1991) commented that the involvement in drug sales has been one of the biggest changes in the nature of gangs over the last 50 years. Thornberry et al. (1993) found that gang members engaged in more antisocial behavior when associated with a gang and less when they left it. Becoming part of a gang is also accompanied by an increased likelihood of violent offenses (Thornberry, 1987, 1998). Again, leaving the gang was associated with a decrease. These trends derived from longitudinal data, taken in conjunction with the broader set of findings on peer group effects, are likely to reflect causal influences as well as selection effects. Reviewing the evidence, Thornberry (1998) concluded that gangs differed from delinquent peer groups in having a much stronger association with crime. Nevertheless, it has proved quite difficult to determine the extent to which gangs have played a substantial role in the growth of drug trafficking and in the rise in homicides in the United States (Howell, 1997). That both often involve gang members is not in doubt, but the evidence is contradictory on the extent to which the gang as such is influential.

Poverty and Social Disadvantage

Many of the early theories about the causes of crime took as their starting point an assumption that most delinquents came from a socially disadvantaged background (see Rutter & Giller, 1983). Thus, Merton (1938, 1957) postulated that antisocial behavior resulted from the "strain" caused by the gap between cultural goals and the means available for their achievement; Cohen (1956) emphasized the lack of opportunities to acquire social status and prestige; and Mays (1954, 1972) portrayed delinquency as a "normal" way of behaving within a socially disadvantaged subculture. These theories no longer have currency because it became clear that the association between crime and social disadvantage was not as strong or as consistent as assumed, and because the particular mechanisms proposed failed to stand up to empirical testing. Nevertheless, it remains the case that social disadvantage and poverty constitute reasonably robust (although not always strong) indications of an increased risk for delinquency – as assessed both by self-report and by official convictions (Bolger et al., 1995; Farrington & Loeber, in press). What is new in the evidence that has become available during the last 15 years is the set of findings examining alternative causal pathways for this risk association. Conger, Elder, and colleagues, in their longitudinal study of 378 families in rural Iowa, studied the impact of economic pressure on parents and their early adolescent children (Conger et al., 1992, 1993, 1994). The findings are summarized in the path diagram shown in Figure 7.1, where the results for "father" measures are shown above those for "mother" measures (in parentheses). Economic pressure does have an effect on antisocial behavior, but the impact is indirect – it is mediated by parental depression, marital conflict, and parental hostility.

The same approach was adopted with respect to family stress (as indicated by a drop in income or serious illness or injury) in both the Oregon

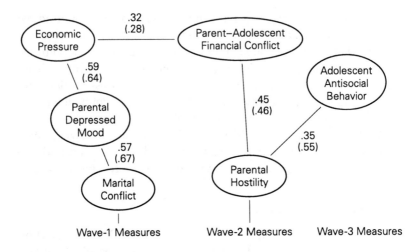

Figure 7.1. Coefficients for economic pressure and related factors. *Note:* Coefficients for father measures above those for mother measures (in parentheses). *Source:* Adapted from Conger et al. (1994).

(Capaldi & Patterson, 1987) and Iowa (Kellam, 1990) longitudinal studies (Conger, Patterson, & Ge, 1995). Despite the fact that the Oregon study was a city sample and the Iowa study a rural one, the results were remarkably similar. In both studies, the effects of family stress was mediated by parental depression and poor parental discipline; see Figure 7.2. It should be noted, however, that in these studies "economic pressure" and "family stress" were rather general concepts and that the basic association between these variables and antisocial behavior (i.e., the association that provided the origins of the more complicated statistical modeling) was quite weak. Nevertheless, Brody et al. (1994) showed much the same (but taking a much broader measure of child behavior) in their study of African-American youths in the rural South of the United States, as did Dodge, Pettit, and Bates (1994) in their three-site longitudinal study and Sampson and Laub (1993) in their reanalysis of the Gluecks' data. Although analyzed somewhat differently, the findings from Farrington's London study and Loeber's Pittsburgh study also showed that much of the risk for antisocial behavior that stemmed from social disadvantage was mediated by poor child rearing. Bolger et al. (1995), in the Charlottesville longitudinal study, also found (with rather weaker measures) that part of the impact of economic hardship was mediated by parental behavior.

Farnworth et al. (1994) used the Rochester Youth Development Study to determine which aspect of social disadvantage was most related to

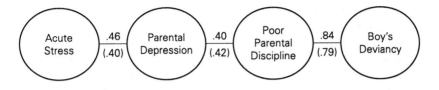

Figure 7.2. Coefficients for family stress and related factors. *Note:* Coefficients for father measures above those for mother measures (in parentheses). *Source:* Data from Oregon study, adapted from Conger et al. (1995).

which types of delinquency. Longitudinal analyses showed that the main effect derived not from social class but rather from continued unemployment and continued dependence on welfare. The strongest associations were with street crime (such as assault, selling drugs, car theft, and purse snatching) rather than with petty theft, property damage, and other types of common delinquency. It was concluded that underclass status was the key risk factor, but its impact was mainly on street crime.

The findings across studies of diverse samples are reasonably consistent in showing that much of the risk for antisocial behavior associated with poverty and social disadvantage is mediated by the adverse effects of prolonged economic (and associated) stresses on family functioning. What none of the studies have examined is the possible role of genetic factors. Follow-up studies of antisocial children into adult life have been consistent in showing that they have a much increased risk of unemployment and of being on welfare (see Chapter 10). It seems that many long-term recipients of welfare have below-average IQ scores. That may be relevant because, in the Oregon study, parental educational background predicted children's academic attainment (Scarr, 1997) and low IQ or poor attainment in the child constitutes a risk factor for antisocial behavior (see Chapter 6). Mednick et al. (1987), using data from their Danish adoptee study, have provided a preliminary test of genetic versus environmental mediation of social status effects. They found that the socioeconomic status (SES) of both biological and adoptive parents was associated with criminality in the offspring, the association being of roughly comparable strength in the two parental types (but marginally stronger in the case of the SES of the adoptive parents). The implication is that, although some of the effect of low SES is genetically mediated, some must be environmentally mediated. To what extent the environmental effect is mediated via the children's IQ and educational attainment is not known, but it seems likely that this is part of the story. As noted in Chapter 6, child IQ is associated with antisocial behavior even after controlling for social status, whereas the effects of social status are largely lost once child IQ is taken into account.

In summary, the weight of evidence suggests that social disadvantage and poverty are involved as distal risk factors in the causal processes that lead to antisocial behavior; however, insofar as the risks are environmentally mediated, the more proximal mechanisms involve the adverse patterns of parenting engendered by parental depression, which in turn derive from the family stresses involved in the broader adverse social situation. It is important to appreciate, however, that the finding that most of the effects of poverty are indirect does not negate its role in the causal chain. The National Youth Survey longitudinal analyses showed that relief of poverty brought benefits in family functioning (Garrett, Ng'andu, & Ferron, 1994).

Unemployment

Numerous studies have shown substantial associations between unemployment and crime. Longitudinal studies in which antisocial children have been followed into adult life have been consistent in showing that they have relatively high levels of unemployment as well as unstable job records (see Chapter 10). In other words, antisocial behavior in childhood (and the psychosocial risk factors with which it is associated) precedes and *predicts* unemployment in adult life (Caspi et al., in press). It is clear, therefore, that part of the explanation for the association between unemployment and crime must be either that committing antisocial acts predisposes to unemployment, or that both crime and unemployment reflect the same underlying risk factors or antisocial life style. At least two causal routes are likely to be implicated. First, antisocial youths have a much increased likelihood of leaving school without educational qualifications; accordingly, an increased proportion will end up in unskilled or semiskilled jobs. That is relevant because many unskilled jobs (such as builder's laborers) have very little job security and are liable to involve recurrent periods of unemployment (Rutter & Madge, 1976). Also, during the last 50 years there has been a marked reduction in the number of unskilled jobs that are available; accordingly, a lack of qualifications has become a greater disadvantage than it used to be. Second, antisocial individuals are liable to behave in ways that lead them to get the sack. This tendency is aggravated by both heavy drinking and periods of incarceration (Sampson & Laub, 1993; see also Chapter 10).

Nevertheless, it is obvious that most unemployment does not arise from antisocial behavior (Petersen & Mortimer, 1994). People of all kinds, in all sorts of jobs, can become unemployed for reasons entirely outside their control. Levels of unemployment all over the world fluctuate widely over time for reasons that are political and economic rather than personal and individual. Numerous studies, both cross-sectional and longitudinal, have shown that involuntary unemployment is associated with a deterioration in mental health and a loss of self-esteem. The improvement that accompanies a return to work (Banks & Ullah, 1988; Patton & Noller, 1984; Warr, 1987) points to a causal effect stemming from unemployment. Several rather different factors are likely to be involved (Rutter & Rutter, 1993). Most obviously, job loss is likely to lead to a marked drop in income. It is also relevant, however, that jobs are important as a source of social interaction that provides people with a source of personal worth (Bolton & Oatley, 1987; Jahoda, 1981). That features other than actual financial strain are influential is shown, for example, by the finding that adverse emotional effects arise *before* people actually lose their jobs – when the overall circumstances make them think that they are likely to be made redundant (Ferrie et al., 1995). On the other hand, Farrington et al.'s (1986) finding that it was only crimes for material gain that increased during periods of personal unemployment indicates that financial issues are not irrelevant. Caution should be exercised, however, in interpreting the apparent specificity of the effect on crimes for material gain; there is a need for replication in other samples.

The possible effects at an individual level of the experience of unemployment on antisocial behavior have been tackled in two rather different ways. First, Fergusson, Lynskey, and Horwood (1997b), in the Christchurch longitudinal study, compared levels of crime in 17–18-year-olds according to their duration of unemployment between the ages of 16 and 18. The two measures were very strongly associated; only 2.2% of those who had never been unemployed had a conviction, compared with 11%–12% of those with less than six months of unemployment and 19.7% of those who had been unemployed for six months or more. The differences on self-reported delinquency were less marked, but there was still in excess of a threefold difference between the two extremes. The findings also showed, however, that unemployment was very strongly associated with all the major risk factors for antisocial behavior. When these risk factors were taken into account statistically, the association between unemployment and antisocial behavior was much diminished (e.g., the adjusted figures for conviction were 3.4% for those without unemployment and 8.3% for those with at least six months unemployment) but remained substantial and statistically significant (except for violent offenses). The adjusted figures for self-reported violent offending still showed a significant difference (a mean score of 0.29 versus 0.47 for the extremes) but less than that for property offending (0.29 versus 0.61). The conclusion is that many of the apparent effects of unemployment on offending are a consequence of shared risk factors but that, even when these are taken into account, some (probably causal) effect remains – especially for property offending.

The second approach has been to examine the effects of unemployment by determining whether the rate of criminal acts goes up within individuals during periods of being out of work. This strategy was employed by Farrington et al. (1986) in their longitudinal study of boys in inner London, which also focuses on individual differences in response to unemployment. Three results stand out. First, youths with at least three months of unemployment committed nearly three times as many offenses *while they were employed* as did the sample as a whole (0.44 per year versus 0.16). This shows a selection effect of antisocial behavior on unemployment. Second, their rate of offenses went up (to 0.62) when they were out of work. This indicates an influence of unemployment on crime. Third, this effect of unemployment on crime was found only in youths with a prior high risk of delinquency, as indexed by their adverse family background, disruptive behavior, and below-average IQ. Similarly, Elder (1974) found that the economic depression in the 1930s has the greatest adverse effect on men who had shown earlier emotional instability; and Caspi and Moffitt (1991) found that early puberty was more likely to lead to an increase in norm-breaking behavior in girls who had already shown behavioral problems before puberty. As Caspi and Moffitt (1993; see also Elder & Caspi, 1990) have argued, life stresses ordinarily tend to accentuate pre-existing behavioral tendencies, rather than completely alter patterns of behavior. They summarized this concept as the "accentuation principle."

With these findings and concepts in mind, we need to return to the questions of whether (and in what circumstances) the experience of unemployment predisposes to antisocial behavior, as well as the possible mechanisms that could be involved. There is a paucity of evidence of a kind that could provide answers to these questions. Nevertheless, what evidence there is indicates that the experience of unemployment may well make it more likely that antisocial individuals will steal more often (Farrington et al., 1986). This probably reflects partly a response to economic loss and partly an increase in the time and opportunities for crime, with perhaps also peer group influences deriving from an increased involvement in a similarly unemployed group of disaffected individuals. As Horney et al.'s (1995) large-scale retrospective study of offenders suggests, rates of offending are likely to be affected by changing life circumstances (but unemployment may well not be the most important of these). These mechanisms suggest a relatively immediate effect.

In addition, Sampson and Laub's (1993) analyses of the Gluecks' data set pointed to the probability of more long-term influences stemming from the effects of job instability on reducing people's bonds to society and to its values. Insofar as that process is operating, one would not necessarily expect to see a close temporal connection between periods of unemployment and rates of crime; rather, a delayed effect that spanned periods of both work and unemployment would be predicted. That is, the postulated mechanism concerns the effects of not having regular work on how people think about themselves and their engagement in society, rather than a response to the immediate stresses of being out of work.

The distinction may be important when turning to the evidence on time trends. These have been approached from two quite different perspectives. Rutter and Smith (1995) started with the factual finding that crime rates had risen greatly over the last 50 years (see Chapter 4) and asked whether this could be due to rising unemployment. The answer was unequivocal that it could not, because the rise in crime was already very marked during the 1950s and 1960s – when the overall levels of unemployment in most countries (especially the United Kingdom) were quite low. Moreover, the gradient of increase in crime did not change appreciably during the 1980s, when unemployment rates rose enormously. Clearly, other factors had to be responsible.

Others have approached the matter from the opposite perspective by focusing on the enormous recent rise in unemployment (NACRO, 1995) or the parallel rise in poverty and social inequality (Field, 1990; Wilkinson, 1995) in order to ask what effects these phenomena may have had on crime. It has been argued that the meaning of unemployment changed during the 1980s, taking on a harsher reality and increasingly becoming a chronic life situation. It is highly likely that this has been the case and entirely plausible that it may have predisposed certain individuals to crime. Nevertheless, the argument that it has led to an increase in crime during the 1980s and 1990s – on the grounds that the two have risen in parallel during this time period and that this period must be considered separately from earlier times (because the meaning of unemployment has changed) – is singularly unconvincing. It does not appear that there has been any substantial change over the recent time period in the slope of increase in crime. Also, a causal connection can only be tested satisfactorily when there are changes in both directions that can be replicated across countries.

There are, however, two other considerations. First, if the main causal mechanism lies in a reduction of ties to society, it is not obvious what time lag there would be in effects. Second, because the main effect may be expected to operate on vulnerable individuals, it is crucial that analyses focus on both the relevant age groups (i.e., adolescents and young adults) and the subgroups most at risk on the basis of their prior disruptive behavior and psychosocial high-risk background. Some of the large-scale cohort longitudinal studies could be used for this purpose but, to date, this has not been done.

We conclude that unemployment does predispose to an increase in criminal activities by individuals already at high risk as a result of their own behavior, characteristics, and psychosocial background. Not much is known about the mechanisms involved, and it is important that they become better understood if appropriate preventative measures are to be developed. It remains completely unclear whether the rise over the last 20 years in long-term unemployment among young people has had effects on overall levels of crime. It may have done so, but the effects have yet to be demonstrated. In order to appreciate the mechanisms involved (which is crucial for policy development), it will be essential to move beyond analyses of overall rates of unemployment to a much more detailed study of key risk groups – and to do so with measures that could tap possible mediating processes.

Resilience

A pervasive finding throughout the literature on psychosocial adversities of all kinds has been that, even with prolonged severely negative experiences, there is huge variation among children in their responses (Garmezy & Rutter, 1983; Hetherington & Blechman, 1996; Rutter, 1981a, 1990; Wang & Gordon, 1994). This has been evident in terms of the development of disorder at the time and also in later recovery. There has been a growing awareness that an understanding of the reasons for this heterogeneity would shed much-needed light on the causal processes involved in psychosocial risk mediation and would also provide invaluable leads on how to develop more effective means of prevention. Accordingly, a growing number of studies have been undertaken whose prime objective is the elucidation of the reasons for resiliency (see Rutter, in press).

One approach, which is useful in generating ideas, is to study individuals who identify themselves as having thrived in spite of extreme early life stresses (Watt et al., 1995). However, the usual – and, in many ways, the strongest – research design has been to focus on children who have had severe high-risk experiences and to compare, within that group, those who have fared well and those with adverse outcomes; Fergusson and Lynskey (1996) did this with the Christchurch longitudinal study data. They used a family adversity index (based on 39 measures) that had proved to be strongly prognostic of antisocial behavior. Outcomes at 15–16 years were assessed using a range of measures including self-reported offending, police contact, parent and youth reports of conduct or oppositional problems, alcohol abuse, and school drop-out. Just over half the sample had low scores on the family adversity index; their rate of multiple antisocial problems was only 0.2%. Three tenths (with moderate scores) had a rate of 2.5%, one tenth (with high scores) a rate of 8.3%, and one twentieth (with the highest scores) a rate of 21.6%. Clearly, the index was a powerful predictor, with a hundredfold difference between the top and bottom risk groups. It was noteworthy, too, that a very high rate of multiple problem behavior required a very high family adversity score; moreover, even in this very high-risk group, many children did *not* show multiple problem antisocial behavior. The top 20 percent on the family adversity index was used as the high-risk group, and the 37 percent without any antisocial problems was taken as the resilient subgroup to be compared with the remainder. Resilience was also dealt with as a dimensional variable.

The first finding was that resilient youngsters had significantly lower adversity scores. In a sense that is not surprising given the steep slope of the risk association, but it is an important reminder that some apparent resilience may represent no more than variations in level of risk. Nevertheless, when this was taken into account statistically, three features stood out. Resilient youngsters (i) tended to have a high IQ at 8 years (a 14-point difference between the top and bottom resilience quintiles), (ii) had lower rates of novelty seeking at age 16, and (iii) were less likely on both maternal and self-reports to have affiliations with delinquent peers. It is of interest that these protective factors spanned individual cognitive and behavioral characteristics and the peer group, and that the main effect on resilience arose from their combination. Just as few individual risk factors carry much risk when they occur in isolation (the main risk coming from multiple adversities), so also do few factors exert much protection on their own. It should be noted, too, that there were some possibly surprising findings: females were no more resilient than males; parental attachments made little difference; and individual features (other than IQ and novelty seeking) were unassociated with variations in resilience once account had been take of the three variables that did index resilience.

This one study has been discussed in some detail because it illustrates well both the analytic approach needed and some of the key methodological issues. Taken in conjunction with a broader literature (Egeland,

Carlson, & Sroufe, 1993; Fonagy et al., 1994; Luthar, 1993; Masten, Best, & Garmezy, 1990; Rolf et al., 1990; Seifer, 1995; Stattin et al., 1997), the latter may be summarized as follows. First, unless care is taken to measure risk experiences both broadly and thoroughly, some apparent resilience will represent nothing more than variations in the degree of risk experienced. The problem will be very much worse if risk is assessed through indicators (such as poverty) that have only rather indirect associations with proximal risk mechanisms. Put more positively, the findings show that, on the whole, the risks for antisocial behavior associated with a single risk experience are quite low. The main risks derive from the cumulative impact of many (often varied) psychological risks. Somewhat similar issues apply to outcome. There are several examples where apparent resilience reflects an unduly narrow focus on one particular domain of functioning. As Luthar, Doernberger, and Zigler (1993) put it, resilience is not a unidimensional construct; individuals may be protected from one sort of adverse outcome whilst remaining vulnerable to others. Luthar et al. (1993) showed this for emotional distress in children who were resilient with respect to behavioral competence, and Farrington et al. (1988) showed the same with respect to social functioning in young people from a high-risk background who did not become criminal.

Third, resilience needs to be considered over time and not just in terms of the situation immediately following the risk experience. Long-term follow-up studies (reviewed in Chapter 10) make clear that experiences even in adult life can make a substantial difference as to whether or not antisocial activities continue. The same studies also emphasize the need to consider risk and protective processes as they operate over time and not just as something that can be assessed in terms of the chemistry of the moment. Thus Quinton et al. (1993 – see also Quinton & Rutter, 1988; Rutter et al., 1990b) found that positive experiences at school made it more likely that youngsters from a high-risk background would plan their lives (assessed in relation to work and marriage), that those who exerted such planning were less likely to become part of a delinquent peer group, that this in turn made it less likely they would marry and have children by someone with antisocial or drug or alcohol problems, that this made it less likely that the partnership would be discordant and break down, and that the experience of a harmonious supportive marriage made discontinuation of antisocial behavior much more likely. The evidence on this process is considered in Chapter 10, but the point to be made here is that the resilience lies in a process that operates over time, often quite a long time.

However, the need to consider processes over time raises a number of further methodological issues. Three are particularly important. First, even individuals with very persistent antisocial behavior do not go on committing criminal acts all the time. Fluctuations over time are to be expected because, in truth, people's behavior varies according to circumstances and also because measurement error will lead to artefactual variations. Multiple measures and appropriate methods of statistical analysis are needed to avoid mistaking fluctuations in behavior for lasting change (Fergusson et al., 1996a,b). Second, when risk and protective processes act over time in ways that are contingent on a multilink chain, a focus on just one variable at one point will hopelessly underestimate cumulative effects (Quinton et al., 1993). This was shown most dramatically in a study of baseball players (Abelson, 1985). The differences between top stars and mediocre players were amazingly small if considered on a single-hit basis, but over the course of a complete game these trivial differences made all the difference between winning and losing. A further consideration is that the proportion of population variance explained will always provide a most misleading underestimate of effects as they operate at an individual level if the relevant protective factors impinge on only a small segment of the population (Rutter, 1987a). This will be the usual situation when dealing with multifactorial behaviors subject to many different influences, as is clearly the case with antisocial behavior. The situation, however, is one that applies very generally – as, for example, with most common medical conditions.

A third methodological issue is that multilink chains or multiphase causal processes imply synergy among risk and protective factors (Pickles, 1993). There is a regrettable and wrong-headed tendency to assume that interactional processes will necessarily result in statistically significant interaction terms in multivariate analyses (Raine et al., 1997a). Quite apart from the formidable problems of the statistical power needed to produce significant interaction terms (McClelland & Judd, 1993), there are many circumstances when other statistical approaches are needed (Rutter, 1983a; Rutter & Pickles, 1991). There is no future in counting up significant interactions; rather, we must pay attention to hypotheses on how protective mechanisms might operate and then use whatever statistical tools are most appropriate for testing the hypotheses put forward.

The final conceptual point that needs to be made concerns the distinction between risk and protective factors. Some investigators (for example, Stouthamer-Loeber et al., 1993) have considered the distinction as the difference between variables that mainly have an effect at the deviant end (i.e., separating the middle of the range from the maladaptive extreme) and those that mainly have an effect at the normal end (i.e., separating the middle of the range from the well-functioning extreme). Not surprisingly, no purely protective variable was found when assessed in this fashion. That is because any dimensional risk or protective factor (and virtually all such factors are dimensional) will operate at both ends. Moreover, any approach on a variable basis must necessarily ignore the fact that the same variable may operate *both* as a risk and as a protective factor, according to circumstances and outcome. The more important need is to focus on risk and protective *processes*, rather than variables, and to consider the circumstances under which protection arises (Fergusson & Lynskey, 1996; Rutter, 1990; Stattin et al., 1997). When approached in this way, there are examples of processes that mainly operate protectively; the issue is considered in more detail in Chapter 10.

We conclude this section with a brief overview of some of the main findings in resilience as assessed in relation to a *lack* of antisocial problems despite high-risk psychosocial experiences. The findings are not discussed in detail because of the paucity of studies that have specifically investigated resilience. First, as discussed in Chapter 6, a lack of genetic vulnerability seems important. Psychosocial adversities have the most impact on those who also carry a genetic risk. Individual differences in susceptibility to psychosocial hazards are by no means entirely due to genetic factors, however; experiences also play an important role. Second, a higher IQ has been found to be protective in several studies of high-risk children (Bender & Lösel, 1996; Dubow & Luster, 1990; Fergusson & Lynskey, 1996; Lösel & Bliesener, 1994; Masten et al., 1988; Moffitt, 1990a; Stattin et al., 1997 – see also the findings discussed in Chapter 6). The effect is not specific to antisocial behavior and applies to some degree to a range of psychosocial and psychopathological outcomes (Cederblad et al., 1994). Third, temperamental and other personality features seem to play a role (Smith & Prior, 1995; Stattin et al., 1997; Werner & Smith, 1982, 1992). The factors associated with resilience seem particularly to involve qualities that elicit positive responses from other people. Fourth, within the family, the maintenance of a stable, warm, harmonious relationship with at least one parent seems protective in the context of overall family discord and conflict (Dubow & Luster, 1990; Egeland et al., 1993; Jenkins & Smith, 1990; Reiss et al., 1995; Rutter et al., 1997b; Werner & Smith, 1982, 1992), although this has not always been found (Fergusson & Lynskey, 1996; Masten et al., 1988). Fifth, parental supervision may be protective, especially in neighborhoods that lack community controls (Small, 1995). Sixth, good experiences at school, perhaps especially when these involve responsibility or success, seem to be helpful – probably through their role in enhancing self-esteem and self-efficacy (Dubow & Luster, 1990; Lösel & Bliesener, 1994; Quinton & Rutter, 1988; Werner & Smith, 1982, 1992).

Seventh, a prosocial peer group seems to help counter other risk processes (Fergusson & Lynskey, 1996; Quinton et al., 1993), although the effects of support in one setting in protecting against adversities in another are limited (Gore & Aseltine, 1995). Eighth, experiences that open up new opportunities through academic advancement or change in peer group or altered social circumstances may provide a turning point (Pickles & Rutter, 1991; Rutter, 1996; Rutter et al., 1997b – see also Chapter 10). Finally, it appears that an attitude of mind that involves a sense of self-efficacy, a positive approach to planning, and social problem solving may be protective (Bandura, 1995; Clausen, 1991, 1993; Connell, Spencer, & Aber, 1994; Quinton & Rutter, 1988; Quinton et al., 1993; Werner & Smith, 1982, 1992).

The findings are too sparse for any firm conclusions, but Rutter (1995a, in press) has suggested that protective processes (in relation to a range of outcomes) may involve eight broad sets of mechanisms:

(1) those that reduce sensitivity to risk (such as by previous successful coping with challenges);
(2) reduction of risk impact (as by parental supervision or monitoring, a positive peer group, avoidance of drawing children into parental conflict, and the child's own distancing from a deviant parent);
(3) reduction of negative chain reactions (e.g., successful handling of family conflict, effective social problem-solving strategies, avoidance of damaging coping strategies such as use of drugs or alcohol);
(4) increasing positive chain reactions (such as through the eliciting of supportive responses from other people);
(5) promotion of self-esteem and self-efficacy (as through secure and supportive personal relationships, responsibility and success in task accomplishments, and successful coping with manageable stresses);
(6) neutralizing or compensatory positive experiences that directly counter the risk effect;
(7) opening up of positive opportunities (as through educational and career opportunities, broadening of marital choice, and change of home environment); and
(8) positive cognitive processing of negative experiences (acceptance rather than denial or distortion, focus on positive aspects, and incorporation into personal schemata).

The supporting evidence for these suggestions is thin, and they should be regarded as no more than leads to follow. What is clear, however, is that the study of resilience and of the processes that foster it is likely to be a growth area of research. The very marked heterogeneity in responses to serious adversity is well documented, and the challenge now is to determine the mechanisms involved.

Conclusions

Research advances during the last 30 years have made it clear that statistical associations between psychosocial adversities and antisocial behavior cannot be assumed necessarily to represent environmental influences on crime. It has been shown that children have effects on how other people respond to them, that some effects that seem to be environmentally mediated actually represent genetic transmission in part, and that some factors are associated with antisocial behavior only because of their indirect connections with proximal causal processes. All of these findings demand caution in the interpretation of research findings on putative psychosocial influences. Nevertheless, there are research designs that can be used to test hypotheses about environmental risk mediation; the findings show that there are important environmental influences on antisocial behavior.

Teenage parenting, large family size, and broken homes have all been found to be robust indicators of an increased risk of antisocial behavior in the offspring. This is especially the case with teenage parenting. In each of these three cases, part of the risk derives from the characteristics of the individuals who end up in these situations and part from the psychosocial risks that follow. Thus, much of the risk seems to come from family discord and ineffective parenting, which tend to be associated. Coercive or hostile parenting, abuse and neglect, ineffective parenting, and poor supervision or monitoring all have quite strong associations with antisocial behavior; they predict future behavior, and their effects remain even after control for other risk factors. The pattern of findings strongly indicates that they are likely to be involved in the proximal processes leading to antisocial behavior, especially that which starts early and tends to persist into adult life.

These different aspects of family life and of parenting are strongly associated with one another and so it has not been possible to separate their individual effects, but the greatest risk effect probably arises from their presence in combination. Circumstantial evidence suggests that four different causal routes are implicated: (i) an impaired social development that involves poor relationships and ineffective social problem solving; (ii) a learning that aggressive behavior pays off; (iii) a relative failure to develop social bonds and hence a lack of social constraints against behaving in ways that could damage other people; and (iv) supervision that makes it less likely that the young people will become part of a delinquent peer group or place themselves in high-risk situations.

It has long been evident that much antisocial behavior takes place in groups and that delinquents tend to associate with other delinquents. Evidence now indicates that, even though antisocial individuals choose to join such groups, their participation in them makes it more likely that they will persist in their antisocial activities.

Poverty and social disadvantage constitute indicators of an increased risk of antisocial behavior, but it appears that the effects are indirect. These effects are mediated by parental depression and family conflict, both of which predispose to suboptimal parenting.

Antisocial individuals have a much increased tendency to have an unstable work record and to experience periods of unemployment. It has also been found that the experience of unemployment predisposes to an increase in acquisitive crime. The risk effects of unemployment are mainly evident in relation to individuals who are already at high risk by virtue of their personal characteristics and psychosocial background.

With all psychosocial risks, there are huge individual differences in response, with some children seriously and lastingly affected and others going on to show normal or near-normal psychological development and social functioning. There are several conceptual and methodological hazards to be dealt with in the study of resilience, but this field of research is growing and is likely to be highly informative in casting light on risk and protective mechanisms.

CHAPTER 7 – SUMMARY OF MAIN POINTS

❑ There are a number of *psychosocial indicators* for the development of antisocial behavior that have long been established as key. What is less clear in almost every case is the nature of the link between indicator and behavior, the role of adult experiences, and the role of the individuals themselves in shaping their own psychosocial environments. These points require a sophisticated approach to the question of putative psychosocial influences, but the field is so enormous that a number of studies do adequately test the principal hypotheses.

❑ Much of the risk associated with *family characteristics* (such as teenage parenting, large family size, and broken homes) seems to arise from the association of these factors with family discord and ineffective parenting, rather than from (for example) large families per se.

❏ Similarly, *poverty and social disadvantage* indicate increased risks, but the research to date suggests that the effects are indirect and are mediated by parental depression and family conflict.

❏ *Parenting* is thus a central and critical risk factor. Coercive or hostile parenting, abuse and neglect, ineffective parenting, and poor supervision or monitoring are all associated with current antisocial behavior, all predict future behavior, and all have a proximal effect on the more serious and persistent forms. The effects could potentially be through attachment processes (implying damage to social development or social bonding with parents and peers) or through learning processes (by rewarding inappropriate behavior and encouraging coercive behavior patterns).

❏ Participation in *delinquent peer groups* will make it more likely that predispositions to act antisocially will be confirmed and that antisocial behavior will persist. These sorts of influences may be particularly important on those for whom antisocial behavior arises in adolescence rather than early childhood.

❏ Not surprisingly, given the increased likelihood of depressed educational achievement, links have been demonstrated between *unemployment* and antisocial behavior. Levels of unemployment fluctuate for reasons beyond the control of individuals, but antisocial people have an increased tendency to have unstable work histories. Moreover, the experience of unemployment can predispose to an increase in acquisitive crime in those already predisposed to theft by other individual characteristics or experiences.

❏ Care must be taken in trying to identify who might be *resilient* to some of these risk factors. Although there are some indicators (e.g., turning points, higher childhood IQ scores, etc.), more work needs to be done on resilience as it unfolds over the life course.

8 | Societywide Influences

In Chapter 7, we discussed a range of psychosocial factors with a main focus on their possible role as risk or protective influences on antisocial behavior in individuals. In this chapter we discuss some societywide factors that might serve to raise or lower overall levels of crime in the community. The distinction is to some extent arbitrary because both sets of variables could influence either individual differences in, or overall levels of, antisocial behavior. Thus, both unemployment and disparities of income could have effects on these levels as well as on individuals' vulnerabilities or individual patterns of behavior. Similarly, exposure to violence in the media, one of the topics we discuss in this chapter, could give rise to individual differences in crime as well as to overall levels of crime in the community. However, the main reason for a focus on the latter is that, whereas there have been major differences over time in people's exposure to the media, individual variations in exposure now tend to be relatively small. Accordingly, it is not to be expected that, say, violence on television will play a major role in determining whether person X rather than Y becomes aggressive or criminal. On the other hand, it might be important as a contributory factor to the rise in crime between 1950 and 1990 (see Chapter 4) because, before 1950, very few people had TV sets whereas nowadays almost everyone watches TV (Wartella, 1995). However, although the distinction between which variables work on individuals and which on overall levels of crime might seem arbitrary at one level, at another it reflects the difference between psychology and sociology; in contrast to some of the preceding chapters, here we draw particularly on the contribution of quantitative sociologists.

As discussed in Chapter 2, even with features that involve strong genetic influences (we used the example of height), a change in environment can still have a major impact on overall trends or levels. Also, the main influences on different varieties of antisocial behavior (as outlined in Chapter 5) may not be the same. Thus, societywide environmental influences might be more influential on adolescence-limited antisocial behavior than on life-course–persistent varieties. Such influences may offer important opportunities for prevention and intervention strategies, even though their effects on individual differences are small.

This focus on aggregate effects on population levels raises three key methodological issues. First, there is a need to use research designs that can test hypotheses about differences in group levels. Second, it is crucial to check whether such differences might simply reflect variations between groups in the characteristics of the individuals they include. Third, it is necessary to consider possible contextual effects – that is, whether the populationwide influences exert their effects mainly on particular subgroups of vulnerable individuals.

Mass Media

There is now a very considerable body of research into the possible effects of watching TV or film violence on aggressive or antisocial behavior. The findings have been reviewed many times (Comstock, 1990; Comstock & Paik, 1991; Huston et al., 1992; Huessman, Moise, & Podolski, 1997; Liebert & Sprafkin, 1988; Livingstone, 1996; Wartella, 1995), and there are also several meta-analyses (Paik & Comstock, 1994; Wood, Wong, & Chachere, 1991). Accordingly, the research findings can be summarized quite briefly.

Several rather different research designs have been used. First, there have been experimental studies in naturalistic settings in which young people's behavior has been assessed before and after viewing violent, prosocial, and neutral films (Berkowitz et al., 1978). The findings have been reasonably consistent in showing small but statistically significant effects of violent films in increasing aggressive behavior. There can be no doubt that viewing violence can make it more likely that children and adolescents will behave aggressively. The fact that the designs have been controlled experiments means that there can be a good deal of confidence in the causal inference. There are, however, two substantial limitations to this research approach: (i) the effects studied have (necessarily) been very short-term; and (ii) there are inevitable uncertainties about the extent to which the changes observed in rather minor aggressive acts can be generalized to violent crime.

An alternative design is provided by naturalistic longitudinal studies in which the extent of viewing violent TV in childhood is correlated with real-life aggressive behavior and violent crime at a later age (Huessman & Eron, 1986). The causal inference in these studies is tested by comparing the predictive correlation from earlier TV viewing to later aggression with that from early aggression to later TV viewing. These cross-lagged comparative findings have been consistent with an effect that derives from viewing violence (although there needs to be some caution in their interpretation because of the possible distorting effects of difference in temporal stability of the measures; Kenny, 1975).

A third approach is afforded by the study of changes over time in areas with and without access to TV (Williams, 1986). Again, the findings are consistent with a modest causal effect of TV viewing on aggressive behavior. Finally, there has been recourse to cross-sectional surveys in which possible confounding variables have been dealt with by statistical manipulation (Belson, 1978). Once more, the pattern of findings have suggested a modest causal effect.

Critics have been quick to seize on the limitations of each of these various sets of findings (Cumberbatch & Brown, 1989). The limitations are real (and indeed are inevitable when dealing with influences of this kind), but any fair appraisal of the evidence must recognize that each of the strategies presents a rather different pattern of advantages and disadvantages and yet almost all of the findings point to the same conclusion – a causal effect that is small but nevertheless big enough to make a difference that matters.

Before considering the implications, we need to note a few important uncertainties. To begin with, people clearly have a degree of choice in the films and TV programs that they watch. It must be expected that children coming from a family background that predisposes to violence, or with personal characteristics that do the same, will be more likely to choose to watch violent films. This consideration is nothing particular to TV; it applies to all activities, as discussed in Chapters 6 and 7. But, as we have pointed out, experiences that we choose can nevertheless have consequent effects on our own behavior. It is necessary to check whether apparent effects of TV could be artefacts of selection, but the mere fact that choice is involved does not in any way invalidate the possibility of a causal effect.

A rather different concern is that what is shown on TV simply reflects what goes on more broadly in society. If there is a lot of violence on TV or in cinema films, then this is likely to be because people are interested in violence and have come to regard its portrayal as acceptable. If that is the case, how can the effects of TV per se be separated from what transpires in society as a whole? This concern is valid. The experimental studies are important in showing that there *can* be an effect when the situation is manipulated to ensure a separation, but of course these studies cannot determine how big that effect is in real life. We conclude that TV or film violence is unlikely to produce effects that are not part of more general features in society, and that it is probable that the effects will be greatest when family, society, and media influences are consonant with one another. This conclusion is in agreement with research into environmental influences on attitudes more generally (Alwin & Krosnick, 1991).

A further reservation is whether the effects stem from viewing violent scenes as such or rather from a family situation in which children are left unsupervised to watch many hours of TV – rather than engaging in constructive activities of their own or participating in shared leisure activities with parents and siblings (Bronfenbrenner, 1976). Again, the question is legitimate, and it could be that this constitutes part of the story. Nevertheless, the experimental evidence is once again relevant in its indication that viewing violence can have effects that derive from the content of what is viewed.

If it is accepted that viewing violence may, in certain circumstances, play a contributory potentiating role in fostering aggressive behavior, three further questions arise: what sorts of violence on film and TV are most likely to have this effect; what kinds of children are most vulnerable to these effects; and by what mechanisms are the effects mediated? The balance of evidence suggests that the potentiating effect on aggression is most likely to occur when the violence that is viewed is of a kind that is close to real life and that is rewarded. The evidence on individual vulnerabilities is more contradictory. It might be supposed that young people who are already predisposed to violence would be the ones most likely to be influenced by portrayals of violence. On the whole, this is probably the case, but the findings are not consistent on this point. Similarly, there is some uncertainty about whether effects are greater or lesser in younger children. Possibly they may be greater, if only because behavior becomes more stabilized as people grow older.

Several different mechanisms could be operative. Public concern following much-publicized crimes of extreme violence has often centered on direct imitation – so-called copycat crimes. Although such effects probably do occur from time to time, it is most improbable that they constitute the main mechanism, other than rarely. Rather, it seems that more long-term processes are influential. Three ideas have come to be seen as the most probable (although the empirical evidence does not adequately differentiate their importance, and it is probable that all three are relevant). First, because viewing violence can be exciting, it serves to disinhibit (and thereby release or potentiate) aggressive tendencies that are present in everyone to some degree (Bandura, 1977). Second, the regular viewing of violence may serve to desensitize people to violence (Donnerstein, Linz, & Penrod, 1987), so that it becomes more acceptable as a means of behaving. Insofar as it is seen to be rewarded, it may indeed be encouraged. Thirdly, the regular viewing of violence may shape and reinforce cognitive scripts, or ways of thinking, about violence (Berkowitz, 1984). That is, violence becomes more incorporated into people's "mental maps" about how challenges or difficulties should be dealt with.

Through these and related mechanisms, it is likely that TV has played a small contributory role in the rise in violence that has occurred over the last half-century. The further question is whether it has been influential with respect to *who* has engaged in violent crime. Hagell and Newburn (1994) found that chronic offenders did not differ from controls in the extent to which they viewed TV violence; however, they did not examine effects on violence as such and did not have data on viewing of violence at an earlier age. The question warrants further study. Nevertheless, because most people watch many hours of TV, and because that is likely to include many scenes of violence, we consider it unlikely that TV viewing will prove to be an important determinant of individual differences in aggression (although it is possible that it could have a very minor effect).

The situation is possibly different with regard to video games or the Internet. On the one hand, there are much greater individual differences in the extent to which young people view violent and pornographic material. On the other hand, this necessarily means that it is more difficult to differentiate between the effects of selection and of environmental influence. The evidence available is much more limited than for TV and films (Griffiths, 1997), although the pattern of findings is broadly similar, and it may be assumed that the effects are similar. However, video games introduce a further dimension insofar as they include an element of gambling. Huff and Collinson (1987), in their survey of 100 trainees in a youth custody center, found that a fifth of those playing video games said they had committed an offense to finance their habit.

Playing computer games and, to a lesser extent, certain uses of the Internet have each been construed as particular forms of gambling behavior, and the question is how far these behaviors relate to impulsivity generally and whether they form part of a more general cluster of addictive and risk-taking behaviors. Persistent gambling may result in physiological arousal, which is then a reinforcer for future behavior, so predisposing to dependence (Griffiths, 1997). Some players of video games engage in a broader range of antisocial behavior. What is not clear is how far impulsive children with existing behavioral difficulties are particularly drawn to these types of gambling, or whether the gambling can in itself lead to delinquency. The opportunities for various forms of adolescent gambling, however, seem likely to become more widespread in the next decade.

Table 8.1. Relative Rates of Crime and Attempted Crime

	Burglary	Auto Crime around Home	Theft from Person
Low risk			
Agricultural areas	2	2	5
Modern family housing	6	7	7
Other middle-status housing	7	10	6
Affluent suburban housing	7	7	7
Better-off retirement areas	7	8	7
Medium risk			
Older terraced housing	12	16	10
Better-off council estates	9	11	12
Less well-off council estates	15	16	10
High risk			
Poorest council estates	28	24	20
Mixed inner metropolitan areas	18	19	34
High-status nonfamily areas	22	15	25
Indexed national average	10	10	10

Source: Mayhew et al. (1993). Crown copyright is reproduced with the permission of the Controller of Her Majesty's Stationery Office.

Area Differences

It is obvious to everyone that there are high- and low-crime areas. Moreover, the differences among areas in rates of crime are very large, as the British Crime Survey (BCS) findings showed (Hope & Hough, 1988; Mayhew et al., 1993). Thus, for example, the rate of burglary in agricultural areas was 20, in relation to an indexed national average of 100, whereas in the poorest council estates it was 280 – a 14-fold difference (see Table 8.1). The rates of crime were found to be especially high in what, on the face of it, would seem to be three rather different kinds of area:

- high-status nonfamily areas in inner cities, including both the homes of the rich and the more "twilight" areas of privately owned buildings in multiple occupation;
- multiracial areas – poor private rentals mixed with owner occupation in inner cities; and

- the poorest council estates, located either in inner cities or on the outer ring of conurbations.

Comparable findings exist for the United States but with a greater emphasis on poor black neighborhoods in the private sector (Massey & Denton, 1993) and somewhat lesser emphasis on public housing, owing to a more limited stock (Holzman, 1996).

Distribution of Offenses

Clearly, there is something important to explain, but the question is what it means (Bottoms & Wiles, 1997; Brantingham & Brantingham, 1991; Bursik, 1986; Farrington, Sampson, & Wikström, 1993; Hope, 1996; Reiss, 1986, 1995; Skogan, 1990). Necessarily, there is a concern that the area differences might reflect no more than variations in police activity (Bottoms, Claytor, & Wiles, 1992; Farrington & Dowds, 1985). The BCS findings (dealing with self-reports of victimization) just noted indicate that this cannot provide an adequate explanation, although it may play a minor role (Jones, Maclean, & Young, 1986; Kinsey, 1985). It is necessary at the outset to distinguish between the spatial distribution of *offenses* and of homes of *offenders*, because the implications of the two are rather different. Of course, to some extent the two are likely to be correlated because delinquents may well choose to commit their crimes in areas near where they live. The limited available empirical findings (Carter & Hill, 1979; Rengert & Wasilchick, 1985) indicate that the choice of targets for crimes is influenced by criminals' familiarity with an area, the attractiveness of the crime opportunities, and the likelihood that they will be noticed and challenged. Familiarity is not necessarily restricted to areas adjacent to where delinquents live; they may well be equally at home in areas on their route into work or near where they go for leisure. These considerations may help to explain why the high-crime areas include some of the more affluent parts of cities as well as the poorest local authority council estates. With respect to findings on the spatial distribution of offenses, the first need is to determine the extent to which this is more than a reflection of where offenders live, work, and have their leisure activities. This is no easy matter, but it is helped by evidence on the extent to which the crime "attractiveness" features of an area are systematically related to the rate of crime in that area.

The rate of violent crime in city centers is highly correlated with locales of public entertainment and public drinking (Hope, 1985; McClintock & Wikström, 1992). Some locations are attractive targets because they contain highly available lucrative rewards. Hence both British (Bennett

& Wright, 1984) and American (Cromwell, Olson, & Avary, 1991) studies have highlighted the active weighing of the opportunity factors by would-be offenders at the potential crime site with respect to residential burglary. The commission of other offenses may be associated with the relative absence of adequate surveillance or other natural guardians (Cohen & Felson, 1979). Studies of car crime (Liddle & Bottoms, 1993) and of vandalism to public payphones (Clarke, 1983) and buses (Mayhew et al., 1976) have all demonstrated the effect that variations in conditions of natural surveillance may produce on the level and location of crime.

A further feature of the spatial distribution of offenses is the extent to which the "hot spots" for crime are ones with an unusually high concentration of households that have been repeatedly victimized (Trickett et al., 1992). The BCS figures show that the rate of repeat victimization is very high; in 1992, some two thirds of crimes were suffered by people who had previously been a victim of crime (Ellingworth, Farrell, & Pease, 1995). This applied to both property and personal crime but was more marked for the latter. This rate of revictimization was especially high in high-crime areas. It has also been evident that the spatial concentration of multiply victimized U.K. households increased during the 1980s (Pease, 1993; Trickett et al., 1995). In order to understand why this might be so, we must consider both the temporal and the spatial distribution of revictimization.

The findings are striking in showing that the great majority of the repeat victimizations take place in the three months following the first incident, with almost one third in the first month (Johnson, Bowers, & Hirschfield, 1997; Polvi et al., 1990, 1991). See Figure 8.1. Research to identify the factors involved in repeat victimization is still at an early stage (see Farrell & Pease, 1993; Johnson et al., 1997; Spelman, 1995), and explanations will need to take account of the fact that, to some extent, the pattern of revictimization varies by offense (Hope, 1995a; Hope & Foster, 1992). In part, it is likely simply to reflect the reason for the area being a high-crime one in the first place: attractive opportunities combined with poor surveillance. It may also be that affluent households are somewhat less likely to be revictimized because they are better able to take swift action on such precautions as fitting burglar alarms. Even so, they are still subject to revictimization. The evidence on the rapid falloff with time in the likelihood of revictimization indicates that the crime potential of the area as a whole cannot constitute a sufficient explanation. Trickett et al. (1992) have suggested that part of the answer may lie in burglars knowing which properties are worth burgling and are reasonably accessible and safe to break into. The reason for the falloff, then, is a function of

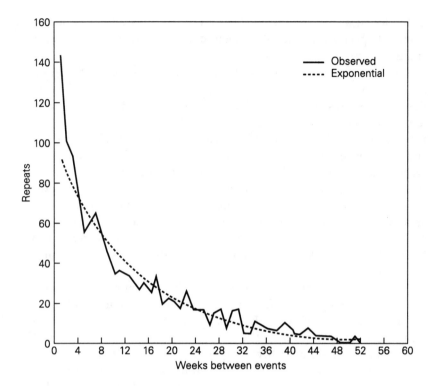

Figure 8.1. Time course of repeat victimization over a twelve-month period. *Source:* S. H. Johnson, K. Bowers, and A. Hirschfield, "New insights into the spatial and temporal distribution of repeat victimization," *British Journal of Criminology* 37 (1997), by permission of Oxford University Press.

a falloff in memory when they are stealing from many different places (Johnson et al., 1997).

The point is that area differences in *offenses* suggest the possibility of influences on people's likelihood of translating whatever antisocial propensity they have into the commission of actual criminal acts. We discuss this issue further in Chapters 11 and 12 in relation to situational influences on crime.

Distribution of Offenders

By contrast, area differences in *offenders* might reflect this likelihood, but they also might be concerned with influences on an antisocial propensity itself. Thus, the area differences in crime are paralleled by somewhat similar differences in rates of mental disorder (Freeman, 1985). The key methodological problem here is the same one discussed in Chapter 7 in relation to peer group effects – namely, distinguishing between selection and influence. In short, do high crime areas arise because (for whatever reason) delinquents move into such areas, or rather because living in such an area makes it more likely that young people will become delinquent? Research findings indicate that there are selection effects (Baldwin & Bottoms, 1976; Bottoms & Wiles, 1997; Reiss, 1995). On the whole, people moving into a high-crime area tend to resemble those already living there, and the same applies to those moving into low-crime areas. To a considerable extent, however, this is a function of market forces and local authority housing policies, rather than personal choice. One other finding also suggests that selection factors are operative: even within high-crime areas, there is considerable heterogeneity. Early studies (Rutter & Giller, 1983) showed that crime rates varied by street and, even within streets, by housing block. More recent studies have shown the same (Bottoms & Wiles, 1997; Hope & Hough, 1988; Reiss, 1995).

Nevertheless, several findings indicate that selection is not likely to constitute the whole story. Three types of research point to the likelihood of some sort of area influence. First, people who move out of a high-crime area tend to show a drop in their delinquent activities (Reiss, 1995). Of course, this could simply reflect the qualities of those who choose to move out and are able to do so, but the data from West and Farrington's longitudinal study (Osborn, 1980) show that this is not the entire explanation. The drop in crime remained even after taking into account the boys' previous rates of self-reported delinquency and official crime records, as well as psychosocial risk characteristics. They continued to show much the same antisocial lifestyle features (such as drinking and risk-taking behavior) but committed less crime. The effect did not derive from moving as such because there was no change in crime for those who moved *within* inner London.

Second, Rutter and Quinton (1977) found that the difference between inner London and the Isle of Wight in emotional or behavioral disorders in young people applied to those born and bred in the area. If selection operated, then it must have done so at least a generation ago.

Third, there are studies that have sought to examine area differences after controlling for the individual and family characteristics of those living in the area (Brooks-Gunn et al., 1993; Brooks-Gunn, Duncan, & Aber, 1997; Massey, Gross, & Eggers, 1992; Peeples & Loeber, 1994). Thus, Brooks-Gunn and her colleagues (1997) analyzed several data sets, including the National Longitudinal Study of Youth, in this manner. The findings showed a significant area effect, even after taking other influences into account. Interestingly, the greatest effects were apparent around the time of school entry (suggesting mediation through the family) and in late adolescence (suggesting more direct effects). The most thorough study of this kind was undertaken by Sampson, Raudenbush, and Earls (1997) in Chicago. It represents several crucial advances: systematic data on a very large sample of individuals (8,782), detailed measures of area characteristics as perceived by the individuals living there as well as by demographic features, control for individual risk characteristics, and the use of analytic techniques to deal with measurement error. The results showed major area effects, with the high–violent crime areas characterized by concentrated disadvantage and residential instability but with these associations largely mediated by collective efficacy. Collective efficacy was assessed by perceived social cohesion and informal social controls. It could be, as always, that the area differences derived from unmeasured individual risk characteristics, but the findings provide a strong case for an area effect and also point to a plausible mode of mediation.

We conclude that the weight of evidence suggests that there are true area effects on crime. Taking this as the starting point, it is necessary to go on to ask three further questions. (i) What is it about the area that provides the risk or protection? (ii) Are the main effects on families (and hence only indirectly on children), or do they operate directly on the young people themselves? (iii) Are the main effects on an antisocial propensity or rather on the translation of such a propensity into the committing of criminal acts?

Some theorists have viewed geographical areas as reflections of community or neighborhood characteristics (see Rutter & Giller, 1983). Communities have been conceptualized as having a social as well as an ecological organization, a collectivity characterized by dominant cultural and normative orientations, formal and informal collective controls, social cohesion, and local networks of various kinds (Reiss, 1995). According to this view, communities are likely to be dynamic and changing and not fixed by geography.

The early thinking about area influences was dominated by Shaw and McKay's (1942) view of the importance of social disorganization and by their focus on particular geographical patterns that persisted over long periods of time. The latter focus has not stood the test of time. High-crime areas are by no means confined to dilapidated inner-city areas. They can also be found in new housing estates (Baldwin & Bottoms, 1976; Bottoms & Wiles, 1986; Wikström, 1991). Also, their distribution no longer fits the concentric pattern put forward by Shaw and McKay. In addition, although there is a substantial degree of consistency over time, major changes occur as the characteristics of neighborhoods alter (Morenoff & Sampson, 1997). For a while, their notion of social disorganization did not fare well either, because of ambiguity about what it quite meant and uncertainty over how to measure it. Recent work has served to put the concept back into the forefront of thinking about how area influences might operate. This shift in thinking has come about because of the positive evidence on social cohesion (Sampson et al., 1997, discussed previously) and because of negative evidence on more structural features of high- and low-crime areas.

Thus, as already noted, although both offenders and offenses tend to be more prevalent in local authority housing estates in the United Kingdom than in middle-class suburbs of owner-occupiers, there is substantial variation among council housing estates. Bottoms et al. (1992) compared two such estates in Sheffield with a threefold difference between them. They were very comparable in demographic characteristics and in housing quality, and neither had a very high population turnover. The differences seemed to lie in three features: a housing allocation policy that meant an influx of both crime-vulnerable and crime-prone individuals to the high-crime area; the effects on residents of a mild criminal culture and negative reputation of the estate; and fewer protective family socialization practices. The other high-crime areas in Sheffield that were studied, together with the findings from other studies (Foster & Hope, 1993; Hope, 1996; Sampson & Groves, 1989), also emphasize the importance of high residential mobility (with a resulting small proportion of residents with a commitment to the area); a high proportion of young people at the age of peak delinquency; a high proportion of unemployed, so that there is not an ethos of legitimate work success; and a population distribution that works against informal community controls (as e.g. from a high proportion of alienated single mothers). In other words, the make-up of the area with respect to the people in it seems to be more important than the physical structure or housing characteristics.

Wilson (1987, 1991) has argued that there is an interactive effect between individuals and the communities in which they live. He suggested that the features just noted create a ghetto concentration of an underclass with a weak labor-force attachment, a collective feeling of low self-efficacy, and – in the face of a paucity of legitimate job opportunities – a tendency to move into illegal activities to earn a living. A lack of trust of neighbors, an unwillingness to intervene in a neighborhood context, and a lack of a sense of control over the social environment all seem to play a part (Sampson et al., 1997).

In essence, the notion has much in common with the social processes considered in Chapter 7 in relation to peer groups. There is, however, one crucial difference in emphasis. Peer groups and communities alike exert part of their effect through the antisocial attitudes they favor. But the evidence on a lack of social cohesion and informal social controls suggests that much of the effect of areas on crime derives from what they are *not*, rather than what they are. In other words, what seems to characterize high-crime areas is that they do not constitute communities in the sense described by Reiss (1995). That is, they lack collectivity, cohesion, and a normative cultural orientation.

Three further points need to be noted. First, although we have emphasized the human features of the environment, physical features may also be influential. Skogan (1990) has emphasized the interconnections between physical disintegration of an area (broken street lights, ill-kept and abandoned buildings, litter, vermin, etc.) and social disorganization (as discussed here). He noted that physical disintegration undermines social cohesion and so fosters a vicious cycle of decline. In addition, physical features will influence crime opportunities (see Chapter 12), so that they are part of what is involved in area influences. Second, areas include schools, and it is necessary to consider how far the effects observed stem from school qualities. We consider the evidence on schools next, but the point to be made here is that it is most unlikely that schools provide a sufficient explanation – if only because the area differences are so marked in relation to adult crime. Nevertheless, it is likely that they contribute. Third, the finding that the population make-up of an area is a prime determinant of its crime propensity does *not* mean that the influences are entirely individual. The key distinction, to which we return when considering schools, is between the influences on individual differences and the influences on overall level. Area effects apply largely to the latter and not to the former. A lot of confusion has been created by misunderstanding of what Robinson (1950) called the "ecological fallacy." He made the very important point that it was invalid to generalize from factors that differentiated between areas to inferences about factors that operated at the individual level. Thus, a finding that high-crime areas often contain a high proportion of single mothers or ethnic minorities does not mean that either of these groups are actually responsible for the crimes. Rather, the finding suggests that they index something about the area that predisposes to a high level of crime; the question of who within the area mainly commits the crime raises an entirely different issue. Even so, the invalidity of generalizing from aggregate to individual correlations does *not* mean that the findings on the characteristics of areas are invalid as a measure of ecological effects.

The final two points to consider regarding area effects are whether such influences operate through the family or directly on the young people themselves, and whether the main effect is on antisocial propensity or rather on the translation of that propensity into actual criminal acts. The evidence on both issues is quite limited, but there are some relevant findings. The inner London–Isle of Wight comparison mentioned earlier showed three important features (Rutter, 1979/80, 1981b; Rutter & Quinton, 1977). First, the proportion of children living in families characterized by psychosocial adversity was much higher in inner London, and taking this difference into account almost removed the area contrast. The implication is that, whatever the influences that stemmed from living in a socially disadvantaged part of inner London, their effects were primarily on parents and families and only indirectly on the children. This finding closely parallels that for poverty discussed in Chapter 7. Second, the area difference applied to a range of emotional and behavioral disturbances that did not necessarily involve delinquent acts (indeed, most did not do so). Third, the area differences were most strongly evident for disturbances that began in early or middle childhood, rather than those with an onset in adolescence. The implication is that the main effect was on emotional and behavioral difficulties that predisposed to delinquency (and hence played a role in the development of an antisocial propensity) rather than on the commission of crimes as such.

On the other hand, the evidence already discussed (indicating substantial effects on adult crime and on victimization, as well as the findings on the benefits of moving out of a high-crime area) means that it is also highly probable that there are some effects on individuals and on the commission of criminal acts.

The final topic to be considered here concerns the processes by which high-crime areas are created and perpetuated. Using the concept of a "community crime career" (Schuerman & Kobrin, 1986), sociologists have asked how particular community structures fail to realize the social values of their residents and fail to maintain effective social control (Sampson & Groves, 1989; Sampson & Wilson, 1995), and how a neighborhood may "tip" into a high-crime area (Skogan, 1990). Four stages have been suggested (Schuerman & Kobrin, 1986). First, there may be a change in land use from owner- to renter-occupied housing and from single to multiple dwelling units. Usually this is accompanied by a decline in commercial and industrial land use, reducing the traditional employment opportunities for local residents. Second, there tends to be a change in the composition of the population, with a departure of capable residents (who are able to promote and sustain local social institutions and social control processes) and an influx of socially disadvantaged residents. Third, a socioeconomic polarization of the area tends to arise, with accelerated levels of poverty and deprivation. Finally, there may be a subcultural change characterized by increased visible signs of disorder and crime that contribute to a "negative coding" of the neighborhood by residents themselves, as well as by agencies and organizations.

Whether neighborhoods become high-crime areas seems to be mediated by what happens with the people in the community (Elliot et al., 1996). In some communities with sparse friendship networks, unsupervised teenage peer groups, and low levels of organized participation, high crime rates develop (Sampson & Groves, 1989). The characteristics of such communities make it difficult for residents to form ties with neighbors or to form organizations that sustain community solidarity and provide effective supervision of local teenagers (Sampson, 1997; Sampson et al., 1997). The findings on the areas in which riots took place in Britain in 1991–92 (Power & Tunstall, 1997), as well as those on European housing estates with a high rate of social problems (Power, 1997), are broadly in keeping with those from North American studies.

Once started, these processes are frequently accompanied by a "velocity," so that tipping may at first begin slowly but then rapidly accelerate (Bottoms & Wiles, 1997), leading to an exponential jump in victimization, poverty concentration, and disorder (Hope, 1996). This velocity seems related to three key aspects of the changing character of the area. First, there is the rate at which unsupervised young people disengage from community sources of conformity (family, schools, employment) and become embedded in crime, with a snowballing of their involvement with delinquency (Hagan, 1994). Second, there is a growth in the number of potentially vulnerable victims – particularly the young and the poor – which raises the chance of multiple victimization (Trickett et al., 1995). Third, there is an extent to which single-adult households reduce the capacity of "guardianship" in the community (Cohen & Felson, 1979) and so constrain the network of people able to provide for the community supervision of the young (Sampson, 1997; Sampson & Groves, 1989).

Whether tipping of a community into a high-crime area takes place, and the extent to which it does take place, both depend upon a complex interplay between social processes and external housing and employment policies (Taub, Taylor, & Dunham, 1984). In principle, the process may be avoided (Hope & Foster, 1992) or reversed (Keeling & Coles, 1996), as indicated by the evidence of change in high-crime areas (Bottoms et al., 1992; Morenoff & Sampson, 1997), but the attempts to bring about change through planned interventions have been rather disappointing so far (see Chapter 12). It should be added that the evidence on community "careers" is fragmentary and the suggestions speculative. It is necessary to put forward testable hypotheses on the mechanisms if effective means of intervention are to be developed.

In our discussion of area differences, we have followed the literature in focusing mainly on variations within urban areas. Much less attention has been paid to the major well-documented differences between urban (especially metropolitan) and rural settings (Bottoms & Wiles, 1997; Weishert & Wells, 1996). This remains a research need.

Previous reviewers (Farrington, 1993b) have noted the inconclusive nature of the evidence that area characteristics do truly influence either the likelihood that young people will become offenders or the overall level of criminal acts in the area. The testing of hypotheses about aggregate causal effects on crime levels is notoriously difficult (Rutter, 1995d), and it cannot be claimed that the matter is settled. Nevertheless, an awareness of what was needed to test the causal inference has led to much more rigorous research (Sampson et al., 1997), and we conclude that it is now reasonable to infer that there are indeed causal effects, although it is not yet possible to gauge their magnitude accurately. Rather more is known on how area influences might operate, but much less on the group most vulnerable to their adverse effects. Thus, Brooks-Gunn et al. (1993) found that white teenagers benefited more than black teenagers from the presence of affluent neighbors, but Peeples and Loeber (1994) found that *not* living in an underclass neighborhood seemed particularly protective for African-American youths. All research is agreed in finding that family influences may greatly increase or decrease the risks associated with living in a high-crime neighborhood (Hagan, 1991; Hagan, MacMillan, & Wheaton, 1996; Richters & Martinez, 1993; Small, 1995), but there is very little solid knowledge on the interplay between family and neighborhood risk and protective features. In many respects, this is now the top priority for research on area effects.

School Effects

As with geographical areas, it is clear to everyone that there are major differences among schools in the rates of delinquency in their pupils, as well as in the rates of vandalism of their premises. The differences among schools with respect to truancy or absenteeism and scholastic achievement are even more obvious and well documented (Maughan, 1994; Mortimore, 1995a; Reynolds et al., 1994, 1996; Rutter, 1983b; Rutter et al., 1979; Rutter, Maughan, & Ouston, 1986; Stringfield & Herman, 1996). As discussed in Chapter 6, low cognitive and educational performance constitutes an important risk factor for crime, and school effects on absenteeism and scholastic achievement could therefore provide indirect risk or protective mechanisms for crime.

Before considering the possible processes involved in school effects, we need to ask whether the observed school *differences* do in fact reflect school *influences*. The alternative to be considered is that the differences simply reflect variations in the intake of pupils to schools. The question is whether the differences in pupil behavior and attainment at the end of their schooling are no more than continuations of the differences already manifest at the time they entered the school. That schools do indeed vary greatly in their intakes is not in doubt; some deliberately select intellectually more able and better-behaved children, whereas others must draw their pupils from socially disadvantaged high-crime areas and have little power to select among them. Nevertheless, as with geographical areas, it is possible that schools can, by the experiences they provide, either enhance or reduce the risks associated with the children's personal characteristics and family background.

Several research strategies have been employed to test for school effects. First, longitudinal studies have followed pupils from the time that they entered the schools being studied to the time they left, and beyond. Three elements are crucial for testing the causal hypothesis: (i) the variations in outcome must remain after taking into account differences in pupil intake; (ii) the outcome variations must be systematically related to qualities of the schools; and (iii) the outcome variations must show a closer association with the school qualities than do the intake variations. Rutter et al.'s (1979) systematic study of children attending secondary schools in inner London (an investigation that met those criteria) showed substantial school effects on children's attendance, attainment, and behavior (Rutter, 1983b). The findings were at first greeted with some scepticism, but subsequent research incorporating several important methodological improvements showed that, in fact, the school effects were probably somewhat greater than those found by Rutter et al. (see Maughan, 1994; Mortimore, 1995a; Mortimore et al., 1988; Reynolds et al., 1994, 1996; Sammons, Nuttall, & Cuttance, 1993; Smith & Tomlinson, 1989). One innovation was to study school effects in relation to the children's *progress* over their time at school, rather than just their outcome at the time they left. The distinction is important because children are already very different at the time they start school, for reasons deriving from both their genetic backgrounds and early family experiences. Of course, schools cannot influence children before they start school, but Mortimore et al. (1988) found that their effects exceeded those of parents with respect to scholastic progress during the school years.

A second strategy has been to examine the effects on pupil behavior and progress when a new principal (head teacher) is appointed to a school that is in serious difficulty. Maughan and Ouston (Maughan et al., 1991; Ouston, Maughan, & Rutter, 1991) showed that a change in regime and approach did in some cases lead to a dramatic improvement in school attendance and scholastic achievement.

A third approach has been to intervene experimentally in order to improve the quality of schooling and then to determine the effects on children's attainment and behavior. There have been some impressive innovations (Comer, 1990), but the evaluations undertaken so far have been somewhat inconclusive (Reynolds et al., 1996; Stringfield & Herman, 1996). In principle, this strategy should provide the best test of school effects but in practice it has proved problematic – both because bringing about effective changes in schools is no easy matter and because of the complex mix of other influences impinging on schools and on pupils.

Another research tactic has been to use large-scale surveys to tap the extent to which schools have reconstructed themselves in ways purported to be beneficial (Lee, Smith, & Croninger, 1995). The findings are consistent with worthwhile school effects, but the evidence is necessarily weak as a test of causal effects.

A further strategy has been to examine the role of good versus poor school attendance or reported good versus bad experiences at school in longitudinal studies extending from childhood to adult life. The findings suggest the benefits of good experiences and the ill effects of poor school attendance as factors leading to a good social outcome (which includes a low rate of antisocial behavior) (Quinton & Rutter, 1988; Rutter et al., 1997b). The limitations of these naturalistic studies, however, is that they do not separate school effects from pupil qualities.

It is clear that the strongest evidence on school effects derives from the first strategy of naturalistic studies relating variations in pupil progress to specific qualities of the schools, but the less conclusive evidence from other research strategies is generally supportive. Almost all findings, however, refer to either pupil attendance or scholastic achievement rather than to disruptive behavior or delinquency as such. Of course, both attainment and attendance are likely to be important through their indirect effects. Numerous studies have shown that truancy constitutes a substantial risk factor for delinquency (Farrington, 1995d; Graham & Bowling, 1995; Robins & Robertson, 1996) although it is less clear whether delinquent acts increase in frequency during the actual period of truancy (Audit Commission, 1996b; Berg et al., 1984; Ekblom, 1979; Graham, 1988). Rather, it seems that truancy is a contributory risk factor facilitating a drift into crime, possibly in part by providing additional opportunities for misconduct. Accordingly, if schools influence truancy (as appears to be the case), then there are likely to be indirect effects on crime. Similarly, as discussed in Chapter 6, low school attainment is a risk factor for delinquency (although uncertainty remains on whether the main risk derives from low cognitive skills or scholastic failure). Hence there is again opportunity for indirect school effects on crime. In addition, there is extensive evidence that disruptive, difficult, or defiant behavior constitutes an important precursor of later antisocial and criminal activities (see Chapters 6 and 10). Insofar as schools can foster more prosocial behavior, there should be protective effects with respect to crime – provided the behavioral gains extend outside the classroom.

The empirical evidence on all these points is decidedly limited, being restricted to the very few studies of school effectiveness that have included relevant measures of behavior. However, what findings there are suggest that there are at least two different types of mechanisms operating. First, there are those that involve the qualities of the school as a social and pedagogic institution operating at the classroom, departmental, and whole school level. Thus, the positive features include such elements as good models of teacher behavior (with respect to time keeping, personal interactions, and responsivity to pupil needs); appropriately high expectation of pupils with helpful feedback; interesting, well-organized teaching; good use of homework and monitoring of progress; good opportunities for pupils to take responsibility and show autonomy, with a wide range of opportunities for all to experience success; an orderly atmosphere with skilled, noncoercive classroom management; and a style of leadership that provides direction but is responsive to the ideas of others and fosters high morale in staff and pupils. The Rutter et al. (1979) findings indicate that features such as these (summarized as representing the school "ethos") were most influential with respect to children's behavior in the classroom and playground, their attendance, and their scholastic attainment. The focus of that study was primarily on schoolwide features, but other research has shown that they may also operate at a departmental or classroom level (Mortimore et al., 1988; Smith & Tomlinson, 1989).

It would seem likely that mutually supportive relationships between home and school would also be important. Certainly, tensions between the two can be a source of difficulty (Graham & Utting, 1996; Lingard & Allen, 1982; Riley & Shaw, 1985). On the other hand, simply seeking to increase parental involvement in school activities may not necessarily be helpful (Hannon, Weinberger, & Nutbrown, 1991). The particular ways in which parent–school interactions are dealt with are probably crucial.

The second broad mechanism concerns the make-up of the pupil body. This is likely to be important in the first instance because children will form many of their friendships from within their peer group at school. As discussed in Chapter 7, the qualities of the peer group will to some extent shape children's behavior in a positive or negative direction. Stattin and Magnusson (1990) showed the importance of this influence in their Swedish longitudinal study; very early–maturing girls tended to show an increase in their norm-breaking behavior and an increased likelihood of stopping education prematurely, but this effect was a consequence of their joining an older peer group. Early-maturing girls who did not affiliate with an alienated older peer group did not change in their behavior. Caspi and Moffitt (1991; Caspi, 1995) showed the same, but also found that the adverse effect on behavior associated with early puberty was not found in all-girl schools, where there was less of an antisocial ethos (presumably because of the lack of male delinquent role models).

The peer group may also be important in a more pervasive fashion that extends beyond particular friendship constellations. That is, the norms of a school will be set by both the staff and the pupils. Rutter et al. (1979) found that the delinquency level in schools was more affected by the composition of the pupil body than by school organizational features. A high preponderance of low-achieving pupils made a high delinquency rate more likely. It should be noted that this constituted a group effect at an aggregate level that went beyond (and was different from) the role of a person's own low achievement in predisposing to antisocial behavior. Being part of a peer group dominated by *other* low-achieving children seemed influential.

A third way in which the composition of the pupil body is important is that the direct interpersonal behavior of other children constitutes part of the proximal social environment of each individual child. Thus, for example, the extent of bullying and of other forms of victimization is likely to matter. As discussed in Chapter 11, this is something that schools can (and should) influence.

The final way in which schools may be important is through their role in the processes leading to a child being proceeded against for a criminal offense (Graham, 1988). In the preprosecution consultation process, interagency panels that make recommendations to the police on whether to caution or prosecute may use a wide range of background information to inform their decision making. Reports from schools on pupils' behavior have been shown to be significantly influential in determining the outcome of this process, including decisions on whether or not to prosecute (Finch, 1986). School reports may also influence sentencing, perhaps particularly with respect to the use of custody (Parker, Casburn, & Turbull, 1981). Juvenile court judges pay attention to reports of poor behavior in school, reports that – although not necessarily connected directly with the offense as charged – may shape judgments on the young person's "moral character" and hence on the penalty deemed appropriate (Morris & Giller, 1987).

As is all too evident, the question of school influences (for better or worse) on young persons' antisocial behavior has received very little systematic attention in school effectiveness studies over the last 15 years. The evidence is sufficient to indicate that schools *do* exert an effect, but much has still to be learned about how the effect operates and the circumstances under which it is most likely to be critical.

One further point requires mention in this connection. As already indicated, there is much that schools can (and should) do to improve their functioning. Even schools with disadvantaged intakes vary greatly in their efficacy, and there are actions within their powers that could be taken to improve their performance. Nevertheless, insofar as the composition of the pupil body exerts an effect above and beyond school organizational features, there are other implications. In many countries, including the United Kingdom, there is a lot of emphasis on assessing the success of individual schools. The current preoccupation with "league tables" based on school performance is a reflection of that emphasis. Two issues need to be highlighted. First, as all the school effectiveness research has shown, it is impossible to assess school success without careful attention to pupil intake. In theory, if there were good measures on intake then a rank ordering of schools with respect to their relative success could be obtained; in practice, however, it would be extremely difficult to do so satisfactorily. Second, owing to the evidence on the importance of intake balance, schools may attempt to minimize the proportion of severely disadvantaged, low-achieving, or behaviorally difficult pupils in their intake. However, the community costs of their doing so are likely to be very negative. There will be an inevitable tendency to create "sink" schools that must cope with the most challenging and difficult pupils, and it may be expected that the operation of a market economy will mean that they will have to do so with less than adequate resources.

Ethnic Variations

Concepts and Methods

There is a large (and often prejudiced and polemicized) literature on the supposed importance of racial differences in crime. Before considering the

empirical evidence, it is necessary to make several basic points. To begin
with, the very term "race" seems to imply a biological basis akin to differences among species of animals. That assumption is completely unwarranted (Hawkins, 1995; Jackson, 1992; Marks, 1995). Genetically speak-
ing, there are far greater differences within so-called races than there are
among them. Of course, this is not to deny the reality of genetic differences. They are real – as shown, for example, in the genetically based
flushing response to alcohol seen in many Japanese (McGue, 1993). However, we must recognize that genetic overlap preponderates. Moreover,
because of past and present intermarriage, few racial groups are "pure"
(whatever that might mean). The recent large-scale Policy Studies Institute (PSI) survey in the United Kingdom dramatically illustrates the extent to which that is so (Modood et al., 1997). Of those with a partner, half
the men from an Afro-Caribbean background had a white partner, and a
third of the Afro-Caribbean women did so. This meant that four out of
ten children from an Afro-Caribbean family had one white parent. It is
necessary to go on immediately to remark that the rate of intermarriage
varies greatly within the United Kingdom by ethnic group; for example, it
is very much lower among Indian and African-Asian people. Thus, only
1% of children from Pakistani or Bangladeshi families had a white parent. The role of intermarriage among ethnic groups in the United States
is also much lower (Small, 1994).

Another important point is that, among groups that appear similar in
physiognomy (and hence of the same inferred race), there are major differences of all kinds. The difference in intermarriage rate between people with "black" skins from Africa and from the West Indies has already
been noted; the same PSI study also revealed major differences in socioeconomic circumstance and education. Within the United States, African-
Americans from the West Indies have been notably more successful than
those who have lived in the United States for generations. Possibly a background of a history of slavery (or perhaps other cultural differences) may
be important.

It should also be noted that, for some ethnic groups, race is not the key
identifying feature. The PSI survey showed that, for many South Asians,
religion was the key characteristic by which they identified themselves in
their own reporting. To be Muslim (rather than Hindu or Sikh) was vi-
tally important, whereas the fact that they were racially heterogeneous
was neither here nor there.

Geography and religion also showed very strong association with living conditions in the PSI study. Those from Bangladesh and Pakistan differed from Indians both in having much larger families and in having (on

average) a much lower income. By their late 30s, half the Pakistani and Bangladeshi women in the PSI survey had four or more dependent children. Families of Caribbean origin stood out with respect to their unusually low rates of marriage: one third of the families with children were headed by a never-married mother. Single parents (including those previously married) accounted for just 6% of Indian families, 15% of white families, 30% of Black African families, and 49% of Black Caribbean families. Educational attainment also varies enormously by ethnic group, with some curious and as yet unexplained differences. For example, the attainments of Turkish Cypriots, on average, are consistently below those of Greek Cypriots.

Immigrant status is also a relevant consideration. Rutter and Giller (1983) made the point that crime rates tended to be low among first-generation immigrants but were higher among some (but far from all) second-generation immigrants. Within the United Kingdom now, almost all children with parents from the West Indies have been born in the United Kingdom.

It is also a grave error to assume homogeneity within ethnic groups. Wilson (1987) has noted that the divergence among African-Americans has grown substantially over time. Simultaneously, there has been a growth in middle-class and professional African-Americans (who have been successful by any criterion) and a worrisome swelling of a severely disadvantaged, unprivileged, African-American ghetto underclass. It makes no sense to treat these two groups as the same. Wilson has made the important point that many of the problems (including high crime) stem from the living conditions of the latter group (especially the chronic lack of employment) and not from the fact that they have a black skin. Of course, racism has played a key role in the course of events that have landed them in that situation, but it does not, Wilson argues, constitute the prime proximal causal process.

Two further features need to be highlighted before turning to the data on ethnic variations in crime. First, almost all ethnic minority groups within the United Kingdom have a substantially younger age structure than the white population; second, they predominantly live in cities and industrial towns where the crime rates are much higher than in rural areas. It is necessary to take both these features into account when examining ethnic variations in crime rates.

Victimization

Before turning to the empirical findings on ethnic variations in crime rate, we need to note the differences among ethnic groups in victimization

Table 8.2. Rates of Victimization by Ethnic Group

Type of Victimization	Ethnic Group		
	White	Asian	Afro-Caribbean
Household vandalism	4.7	7.5	3.6
Burglary with loss	2.7	3.5	6.4
Vandalism to vehicles	9.4	13.7	8.7
All thefts	17.9	19.5	26.3
Bicycle theft (owners)	4.2	3.9	8.4
Assaults or threats	5.5	10.8	9.4
Robbery or theft from person	1.1	3.0	3.3

Note: Values shown are percentage of respective ethnic individuals victimized in the reference period.
Source: Mayhew et al. (1989), from 1988 British Crime Survey. Crown copyright is reproduced with the permission of the Controller of Her Majesty's Stationery Office.

(see Table 8.2). There is an unfortunate tendency to focus on ethnicity in relation to offenders, and it is important to note the striking and parallel variations among ethnic groups in the extent to which they constitute the targets of crime. Both those of Afro-Caribbean and of Asian origin were found, in the British Crime Survey (Mayhew et al., 1989) to have rates of criminal victimization well above those experienced by white groups. For Afro-Caribbeans the excess was greatest with respect to burglary, bicycle theft, personal assaults (both actual and threatened), and robbery or thefts from the person. For South Asians the excess was most marked for household and school vandalism, assaults, and robbery or thefts from the person. Data on identification of assailants was available in only about a third of the cases, but the evidence strongly pointed to a preponderance of attacks *within* rather than between ethnic groups. The proportion of incidents reported to the police does not seem to vary according to the perceived ethnicity of the offender (Shah & Pease, 1992).

These data apply to the United Kingdom, and the U.S. pattern is not quite the same (Sampson & Lauritsen, 1997). There is little variation by ethnicity in personal theft victimization, but blacks are somewhat more likely than whites to experience household victimization (burglary, larceny, and motor vehicle theft); the incident rates are 6.8 versus 4.6 per thousand. The really big difference, however, concerns the experience of personal violence and homicide, both of which are vastly more common among blacks (Kelley et al., 1997). Homicide rates among young black

Table 8.3. Rates of Imprisonment of Males by Ethnic Group in England and Wales, 1991

Offense	Ethnic Group			
	White	**South Asian**	**Black**	**Ratio (Black/White)**
(a) Males aged 17–19 per 10,000 population				
Personal violence	5.8	5.4	35.6	6.1
Rape	0.8	1.8	9.4	11.8
Burglary	10.2	1.8	18.3	1.8
Theft or handling	4.7	1.4	20.0	4.3
Drug offenses	0.7	1.3	7.8	11.1
Total sentences	35.0	36.4	223.3	6.4
(b) Males aged 20–39 per 10,000 population				
Personal violence	7.5	9.0	39.0	5.2
Rape	1.6	2.4	13.9	8.7
Burglary	5.1	1.0	14.7	2.9
Theft or handling	3.0	2.1	13.5	4.5
Drug offenses	2.0	8.5	53.0	26.5
Total sentences	40.4	25.8	213.4	5.3

Source: D. J. Smith, "Race, crime, and criminal justice," in M. Maguire, R. Morgan, and R. Reiner (Eds.), *The Oxford Handbook of Criminology*, 2nd ed. (1997), by permission of Oxford University Press.

males in the early 1990s were *eight* times higher than among young white males. The leading cause of death among black males aged 15 to 24 years is homicide. Accordingly, it has been estimated that a male resident of rural Bangladesh has a greater chance of surviving to age 40 than does a black male in Harlem (McCord & Freeman, 1990).

Crime in the United Kingdom

Because the ethnic mix, historical background, and pattern of crime (especially with respect to homicide) are so different between the United States and the United Kingdom (as well as the rest of Europe), we consider the findings in the two geographical areas separately. Nevertheless, as we shall see, there are some striking similarities.

In both countries, by far the biggest difference among ethnic groups is evident in the prison population (see Table 8.3). In England and Wales,

Table 8.4. Cumulative Participation in Self-Reported Offending between Age 14 and Age 25, by Ethnic Origin

| | Ethnic Group | | | | |
Offense	White	Black	Indian	Pakistani	Bangladeshi
Property	39	38	25	24	12
Violence	19	25	13	18	7

Note: Values shown are percentage of the respective populations.
Source: Graham and Bowling (1995).

young black males are some five to six times as likely as whites to be imprisoned. However, two other features are striking. First, the rate of imprisonment is *not* raised among those originating from South Asia; indeed, for some crimes their rate is lower. The finding is important because the empirical evidence indicates that they are just about as likely as blacks to experience racial discrimination. The implication is that discrimination as such (at least as evident in housing, employment, and the like) is not likely to constitute the key causal influence. Second, the ethnic variations vary greatly by type of offense. They are greatest for drug offenses (black/white ratios of 11 and 27 for males aged 17–19 and 20–39, respectively), rape (ratios of 9 and 12), and personal violence (ratios of 5 and 6); they are least for burglary (ratios of 2 and 3). It follows that any explanation must account for the variations in *pattern* as well as in *level*.

We turn next to the self-report data, where the findings are quite different. Table 8.4 displays findings from Graham and Bowling's (1995) cross-sectional survey. The results are broadly in line with the prison data in showing low rates of crime among people from South Asia, but they are very different from the prison data in showing no increase in property offenses among blacks and only a slight increase in violence. The European self-report data (Junger-Tas et al., 1994a) are similar in showing only rather minor ethnic variations.

At least two very different explanations need to be considered with respect to this disparity between self-report and imprisonment findings. The first possibility is that the self-report data are misleading because ethnic minorities tend to underreport their offenses. This possibility can only be assessed by comparing self-report and official crime data on a person-by-person basis. Amazingly, there are scarcely any studies of this kind, and their results are contradictory and inconclusive. Junger (1989), with respect to Dutch data, found no evidence of underreporting by Surinamese boys, but there was underreporting by Moroccan and Turkish boys. All three ethnic minority groups were visibly different from indigenous Dutch youths, but for the most part the Surinamese were more integrated and had been in the country longer. Earlier U.S. studies showed some tendency for African-American youths to underreport but, overall, this seemed to be influenced by the specifics of the self-report measures used and hence not likely to create a major bias (Elliott & Ageton, 1980; Hindelang et al., 1979, 1981). The most recent findings, based on Loeber's Pittsburgh study, show no substantial tendency for African-Americans to over- or underreport (Farrington et al., 1996b). The evidence is too fragmentary for firm conclusions; it is possible that self-report data may slightly underestimate ethnic variations in crime, but this does not seem likely to constitute a major source of bias.

The other main alternative is that the major ethnic variations at the end of the line – that is, in imprisonment – result from an accumulation of biases in the ways in which possible and actual offenses by people from ethnic minorities are dealt with by the authorities. That there are some differences in handling is clear, although many are relatively small in magnitude.

Evidence of the disproportionate rate at which black people are stopped by the police on suspicion of offending, which originally emerged in the 1970s (Stevens & Willis, 1979) and 1980s (Smith, 1983), continues to be prevalent. Reanalysis of the BCS data, for example, found 14% of South Asians, 15% of whites, and 20% of Black Caribbeans were stopped by the police in a 14-month period (Skogan, 1990). The difference in the stop rate between Black Caribbeans and others remained significant after taking into account differences in age, income, sex, vehicle access, occupation, tenure, urban versus rural location, length of education, marital status, and employment status. Reanalysis of the 1992 BCS data using a wider definition of the term "stop" found 36% of Black Caribbeans stopped compared with 22% of whites or Asians (Skogan, 1994).

Such encounters can significantly contribute to perceived levels of hostility between black people and the police. For example, Smith (1983) reported that Black Caribbeans had twice as many adversarial encounters with the police than whites (28% versus 14%). For young people (aged 15–24), the level of adversarial encounters was significantly greater – 35% for white men and 63% for Black Caribbean men – although the ratio between ethnic groups is similar.

The majority of stops do not produce arrests (Skogan, 1990), and Black Caribbeans are no more likely to be arrested from a stop than their white or Asian counterparts. Nevertheless, the available evidence suggests that blacks (but not Asians) form a much higher proportion of those arrested than of the general population (Smith, 1997a,b; Walker, 1992).† In part this is likely to reflect policing behaviors; stops of black people are more likely to be speculative than stops of white people, and the fact that there are more such stops produces more arrests (Norris et al., 1992; Smith, 1983). However, the scale of the proportion of blacks arrested to their numbers in the general population – for example, three times their population rate in London (Smith, 1997a) and twice their population rate in Leeds (Walker, 1987) – leads to a conclusion that such large differences in per-capita arrests between black and white people is unlikely to be so substantial solely because of biased policing and so must represent a real difference in offending rates.

Once inside the criminal justice system, there is some evidence suggesting that it operates differentially for minority ethnic groups, particularly blacks. Cautioning rates for blacks are lower than for whites, although the evidence for this is somewhat old (Landau, 1981; Landau & Nathan, 1983) and may now be reversed given recent changes in Home Office policy on cautioning, which have reduced the opportunities for diversion for all offenders (see Chapter 3). Blacks are proportionately more likely to be declined bail and remanded into custody, although this is likely to reflect the types of offenses for which they are charged. In youth courts, more cases against black young men than white young men (aged 14–16) are withdrawn for lack of evidence, and acquittal rates are higher for blacks than whites (Walker, 1988). Proportionately more young black people are committed to the Crown Courts for their cases to be dealt with. The evidence is unclear, however, over the extent to which this is due to defendants electing for trial by jury or magistrates disproportionately declining jurisdiction in cases involving black defendants (Fitzgerald, 1993). Hood's (1992) study of five Crown Courts in the West Midlands found that the probability of a custodial sentence was 5% higher for black than for white men, but 5% lower for Asian men. Differences in the use of custody between ethnic groups was greatest where the opportunity to exercise judicial discretion was greatest – that is, for offenses of midlevel seriousness. Similarly, there is some evidence that Black Caribbeans are less likely to receive probation (Fitzgerald, 1993).

The key question is how far these – on the whole, relatively small – differences in processing (which do not always necessarily represent overt

---

† Beginning in April of 1996, all police forces have been required to actively monitor ethnicity data on stops, searches, arrests, and cautions (Audit Commission, 1996b).

discrimination even when they serve to create bias – see Hudson, 1993; Reiner, 1993) could result in a very large artefactual difference in imprisonment rates. Reviewers (Smith, 1997b) have generally argued that they could not. Two points need to be made in relation to that inference. First, as Flynn (1996) has argued persuasively, differential responding can be entirely logical and nondiscriminatory and yet result in a misleading enhancement of group differences. Thus, crimes are much more likely to be committed by young people than old people, and by males than females. Accordingly, it would be entirely logical to stop young males rather than old women walking along a deserted street at night carrying a bag of unknown content. Nevertheless, this policy has the consequence that young men are more likely than old women to feel unreasonably harassed by the police on the basis of their group identity (rather than as a result of their own personal actions). It would not be surprising, therefore, if they built up an attitude of mind and a style of behavior that led them to behave in more defiant ways that, in turn, made it more likely that they would elicit more negative responses from the police. Moreover, although logical and nondiscriminatory, this differential stopping policy would have the net effect that young men who *had* committed an offense would be more likely than older women to be caught with stolen goods in their possession.

The second major point is also a statistical one. In their rather different ways, Abelson (1985) and Pickles (1993) have pointed out that, when causal processes operate over time in a chainlike fashion, multiplicative interactive effects are bound to be operative. As a consequence, quite small differences at any one point in the chain can have much larger cumulative effects if they combine with similar small effects further down the line.

For both of these reasons, we conclude that the cumulative biasing effects in processing are probably rather greater than recognized by previous reviewers. Nevertheless, we must go on to say that it is quite implausible that such effects could account for the huge differences found in imprisonment for serious violent crime, a point to which we return after noting U.S. findings.

Crime in the United States

The U.S. data (Sampson & Lauritsen, 1994, 1997) parallel the U.K. data in two key respects. First, they show a low rate of crime among Asian-Americans, who constitute about 2.9% of the population but only some 1% of arrests. Second, by far the biggest difference between African-Americans and whites concerns violent crime (including homicide), for which the ratio of perpetrators is about six to one. Drug arrests are also much higher, although to a substantial extent this seems likely to be a consequence of targeting policies. African-Americans have been thought to be particularly involved in the local drug distribution economy. The increasing trade in hard drugs – heroin, cocaine, and crack – has been accompanied by violent competition between traders for territory and market share (Williams, 1989). Despite the risks, drug selling and distribution provides a primary route for the young to gain symbols of wealth, success, and the hope of self-determination and economic independence in otherwise hopeless conditions (Hagan, 1994). Such a life style, however, inevitably heightens the exposure of young urban black males to police surveillance and intervention, fueled by the political imperative to wage a "war on drugs" (Tonry, 1995). The main offenses that are *not* substantially more frequent among African-Americans are alcohol-related and runaway offenses.

As with U.K. delinquency findings, we need to consider the extent to which self-report data in the United States provide the same picture as the official statistics. Early studies tended to show rather small differences between African-Americans and Caucasians in self-reported crime rates (Tracy, 1987), and there were concerns that the most delinquent African-Americans had either been missed by the surveys or had underreported their involvement in crime. More recent findings from the Pittsburgh Youth Study tell a somewhat different story (Farrington et al., 1996). To begin with, their self-report findings (from a community sample) showed that the rate of serious offending was substantially greater among African-Americans (33% versus 18% in the older sample; 10% versus 7% in the younger sample). Because official crime data were also available, it was possible to examine the validity of self-reports in the different ethnic groups. A high level of validity was found for both African-Americans and Caucasians. Predictive validity was similar in the two ethnic groups, but concurrent validity was slightly less for African-Americans. Pooling all data sources, serious delinquency was nearly twice as common among African-Americans and an absence of delinquency about half as common. The most systematic self-report data on adult crime are provided by the Epidemiological Catchment Area (ECA) study (Robins et al., 1991). The black/white ratio for reported felonies was 2.6, but the ratio for imprisonment was 6. The findings are in line with those of juveniles in showing a higher rate of antisocial behavior in African-Americans, but also they suggest that the rate of imprisonment is disproportionately high in relation to the level of crime.

Studies of the American juvenile justice process provide evidence that ethnicity is associated with some differences in how offenders are dealt with. African-Americans are more likely to be recommended for formal processing, referred into courts, adjudicated as delinquent, and given harsher penalties than white offenders (Bishop & Frazier, 1988, cited in Sampson & Lauritsen, 1997). The seriousness of the offense and the offender's prior record, however, account for much of the variance in court sentencing. Thereafter, however, the individualized justice philosophy of the juvenile court is associated with racial disparities in sentencing (Feld, 1993). The recent changes in juvenile justice legislation that emphasize consideration of offense seriousness in sentencing decisions (characterized by the expanding use of the waiver of juvenile court jurisdictions to adult courts), when coupled with the impact of race bias factors in screening and processing decisions, exacerbates the overrepresentation of African-Americans in correctional institutions (Krisberg et al., 1987).

There has been a growing disproportion of African-American inmates in the last 20 years. In the late 1970s, 40% of the prison population was nonwhite; by 1989, this had risen to 63%. Incarceration rates for African-Americans are currently six to seven times higher than those for whites (Tonry, 1994, 1995). Blumstein (1982) estimated that 80% of the disproportionality in outcomes could be explained by blacks' differential involvement in serious crime. More recent analyses gave broadly comparable results (Blumstein, 1993; Langan, 1985), although there is some variation among individual states in the extent of racial disproportionality in sentencing (Crutchfield, Bridges, & Pritchford, 1994). Only about a quarter of ethnic variations in imprisonment for homicide and robbery is explicable by factors other than crime seriousness and previous criminal record, but differential processing by ethnicity seems much more influential with respect to drug offenses and other less serious crimes.

It is the response to drug crime, and in particular the "war on drugs" during the Reagan and Bush administrations of the 1980s, that has produced particularly punitive outcomes for young male African-Americans (Hagan, 1994). During the 1960s and 1970s, nonwhite arrest rates per 100,000 of population were double that of white arrests. While the white drug arrest rate remained stable during the 1980s, the rate for nonwhites rose steadily and had risen fivefold by the end of the 1980s. For juveniles, the changing pattern of arrests was even more stark. Whereas white juvenile drug arrests fell by a third in the 1970s and 1980s, nonwhite arrests doubled in that period (Tonry, 1995). Moreover, this changing pattern of arrests and incarceration took place against a background of falling drug use, as measured by household surveys and self-reports of high school seniors (Snyder et al., 1996; Tonry, 1995).

Possible Explanations

In the interests of simplicity of presentation, we have concentrated on U.K. and U.S. findings for evidence on ethnic variations in crime. However, the patterns in other countries present many parallels (with respect to both ethnic differences in rates and to variations in judicial processing according to ethnicity). In the Netherlands, both Moroccans and Antilleans are overrepresented in the crime statistics (Junger-Tas, 1995b). In Australia, Aboriginal and Torres Strait islanders are overrepresented in the youth justice system (Boss et al., 1995). In Canada, "natives" are admitted to prison eight times more frequently than nonnatives (Tonry, 1994). In both France and Germany, foreigners have higher rates of crime (Killias, 1989; Tournier & Robert, 1991, cited by Smith, 1995).

We conclude that there are substantial differences in the rates of crime among ethnic groups. These differences are exaggerated by small (but cumulative) biases in the ways in which judicial processing takes place (this being most evident with respect to imprisonment in the United States for less serious offenses), but major differences remain even when full account is taken of such biasing effects. The differences are most apparent for homicide and other seriously violent offenses in the United States, but the pattern by type of offense is broadly similar in the United Kingdom. The finding that the greatest difference applies to homicide makes it especially implausible that the difference is an artefact, since there is less scope for bias in the ways that such serious offenses are dealt with. Nevertheless, even with these offenses, there are biases. This is perhaps most obvious with respect to the death penalty in the United States (Keil & Vito, 1989). Black offenders who kill white victims are most likely to receive the death penalty, whereas offenders of all ethnic groups who murder black victims are least likely.

The findings also bring out the very important finding that the crime rate is *not* raised in all ethnic minority groups. In particular, the data are consistent in showing that the crime rate tends to be low among people from South Asia. This is particularly striking because in many ways they are among the most disadvantaged of all U.K. ethnic minority groups. In the PSI survey, Modood et al. (1997) found that those from Pakistan and Bangladesh were eight to ten times as likely as whites to have families with at least four children; the proportion of children without substantial educational qualifications at age 16 was twice as high; the unemployment rate among adults was nearly twice as high (in inner cities it was only just below 50%); twice as many were on income support (welfare); the average family income was well below other groups (four times as many were below the low-income threshold); and they were at least as likely as other groups to be subjected to racial harassment. On the other hand, of all population groups the children from Pakistani or Bangladeshi families were the least likely to experience a broken home; nine out of ten were living with formally married parents. Clearly within the United Kingdom, the high crime rate seen in some ethnic minorities cannot be attributed in any straightforward way to poverty, racial discrimination, or low educational attainment. One crucial difference from the United States, however, needs to be mentioned. In the United States, a high proportion of African-Americans live in areas where the majority of other residents are also African-Americans; that is, they reside in black ghettos (Peach, 1996). By contrast, this was infrequently so in the United Kingdom; only one in seven Afro-Caribbeans and one in five Pakistanis and Bangladeshis lived in areas in which nonwhites constituted a majority (Modood et al., 1996).

Children in Afro-Caribbean households in the United Kingdom stand out in two main respects: they were the most likely of all groups to be born to a teenage mother, and they were much the most likely to be brought up by a single never-married mother (this applied to one in three). The rate of poverty among Afro-Caribbeans was less than among Pakistanis and Bangladeshis, but it was above that of whites (41% versus 28%). Strikingly, the educational qualifications of children born in the United Kingdom to Caribbean parents were much the same as whites, although not quite as high at the tertiary educational level (in contrast to the somewhat lower qualifications of the parents).

Before turning to possible explanations for the observed ethnic variations in crime, we need to consider the extent to which higher levels of crime are paralleled by similarly high levels in other forms of psychosocial disturbance or psychopathology. There is remarkably little evidence on this point for ethnic groups in the United Kingdom (see Nazroo, 1997); even in the United States, the findings are less systematic than desirable (Nettles & Pleck, 1994). Clearly, African-American youths have disproportionately high rates of educational difficulties, sexually transmitted diseases, and teenage pregnancy, but probably not of either suicidal behavior or alcohol abuse. In adult life, the ECA findings also (perhaps surprisingly) showed no increase among African-Americans in antisocial personality disorder, despite the substantially higher crime rate (Robins et al., 1991). The data are far too sparse for any firm conclusions other than that the high rate of violent crime stands out in relation to a much more varied picture for other types of both antisocial behavior and psychosocial problems.

The last point to note is the existence of huge variations *within* ethnic groups (Sampson & Wilson, 1995). For example, the black homicide rate in New York was three times that in Chicago in 1980, and that in California three times that in Maryland. Peeples and Loeber (1994) found that the delinquency rate of African-Americans living in areas that were *not* underclass did not differ from that of whites. Brooks-Gunn et al. (1993) similarly found important family and neighborhood effects on the psychological functioning of black children and adolescents. Rowe, Vazsonyi, and Flannery (1994a) have convincingly argued for the importance of taking seriously the likelihood that the same risk factors operate in all ethnic groups and that the differing levels of crime result from variations in exposure to these risk factors.

The evidence is certainly persuasive that living conditions play a major role in accounting for the raised level of violent crime among African-Americans, but there is much less certainty regarding which conditions are most influential and how the effects are mediated. Sampson (1997) used data on intercity U.S. comparisons to argue that a key factor is male joblessness, which leads to economic deprivation and family disruptions, and that it is the resulting disruption that constitutes a key part of the proximal processes leading to violent crime. Wilson (1995) went on to note the extreme concentration effects of these adverse living conditions. The "worst" urban contexts in which whites live are considerably better than the average context of black communities. In 1970, one in five poor blacks lived in ghetto areas, whereas by 1980 two in five did so. Sampson and Lauritsen (1997) suggested that it is this combination of adverse under-the-roof family circumstances *and* living in a ghetto neighborhood without social cohesion or informal controls that provides the main risks.

That may well be so, but there are still some puzzling anomalies. For example, several studies have shown that a single-parent home is less of a risk factor in African-American samples than it is in white ones (Peeples & Loeber, 1994; Smith & Krohn, 1995). We noted, too, in Chapter 7 that physical punishment in African-American families does not seem to be the risk factor that it is in white families (Deater-Deckard & Dodge, 1997). We agree with Sampson and Lauritsen (1997) that a large part of the explanation for ethnic variations in crime is likely to lie in some constellation of family and neighborhood risk factors, but we are quite a long way from understanding just what mechanisms are involved.

It is necessary also to ask whether biological risk factors might be involved. Even less is known about this possibility. As we have noted already (in Chapter 5), there is scarcely any genetic research with ethnic minority groups, and there is no evidence pointing to relevant genetic differences among ethnic groups that might account for variations in crime. It should be added that the crimes (i.e., those involving violence) showing the greatest ethnic variation are the ones with the least evidence for a major genetic contribution. There are other biological risk factors that might conceivably play a contributory role (such as obstetric/perinatal complications or intrauterine exposure to cocaine or heroin), but the suggestion remains highly speculative in the absence of either empirical supporting data or theoretical expectations that there could exist a major effect.

The issue of why violent crime is as high as it is in African-Americans and people from an Afro-Caribbean background living in the United Kingdom is a most important one, because these ethnic groups constitute frequent victims of the violence and also because an understanding of the causal mechanisms would likely cast a broader light on the origins of violent crime generally.

Guns, Drugs, and Contraceptives

The final set of populationwide influences is of a rather different kind but of no less importance. Mention has already been made of the hugely higher homicide rate in the United States as compared with the United Kingdom and other industrialized countries throughout the world. The point to be made here is that this difference is largely confined to killings with firearms (Fingerhut & Kleinman, 1990; Snyder et al., 1996). In 1987, 75% of U.S. homicides committed by 15–24-year-olds involved firearms; the proportion in England and Wales for the same year was only 6%. The figures in other European countries ranged from 0% to 27%, apart from France where it was 54%. It is also striking that the substantial rise in homicides by juveniles in the United States over the last decade is almost entirely due to firearm killings (Howell, 1997; Snyder et al., 1996). It is well known that handguns are much more easily obtained in the United States and that they are owned by a far higher proportion of the general population than in other countries. It may reasonably be inferred that the two statistics reflect some sort of causal connection, although it is difficult to test this directly. Blumstein (1995; Blumstein & Cork, 1996), reviewing the evidence on time trends in the United States, concluded that the major factor in the recent rise in youth homicide (but *not* homicide in older age groups) was the increase in gun availability to young people, combined with the recruitment of youths into drug markets and the neighborhood social disorganization with which this was associated. Of course, the mere possession of guns is not a sufficient explanation on its own; the context of their ownership and the attitudes regarding their use are likely to be crucial as well. Thus, adult men in Switzerland are expected by law to keep a rifle in good working order for use when they are called to the Armed Forces. But this is ritualized and constrained in a way that is utterly different from gun ownership and use in the United States. A discussion of the evidence would take us too far astray from the main themes of this volume, but the importance of the availability of the means of crime does require noting.

We discussed the interconnections between drugs, alcohol, and crime in Chapter 6, but the point to be made here is that there are major variations among countries and among ethnic or religious groups within countries regarding the use of drugs and alcohol. For instance, the use of heroin and cocaine is much higher in the United States than in most European countries. Also, the use of alcohol and of drugs has risen over the last 50 years very much in parallel with the rise in crime (Silbereisen et al., 1995). For reasons discussed in Chapter 6, the two are likely to be interconnected in part.

The third example – use of contraceptives – has a much more indirect connection with crime. Nevertheless, as noted in Chapter 7, being born to a teenage mother does constitute a substantial risk factor for crime (even if its effects are mediated through associated risk processes). American teenagers stand out from the rest of the industrialized world in being less likely to use contraceptives, the major factor being the lack of accessibility and acceptability of family planning services (Hayes, 1987). The pregnancy rate of 15–19-year-olds in the United States during the 1980s (165 per thousand for blacks and 83 for whites) was double that in Canada or the United Kingdom, and the gap has widened in recent years (Forrest & Singh, 1990).

Conclusions

There has been an immense spread in the availability of television since 1950 and, more recently, video games and the Internet have added to mass-media influences. All three include a substantial amount of violence, and there has been public concern over whether this may have fostered aggression and antisocial behavior in the young people who watch the programs – often for several hours a day. Experimental studies have provided evidence that exposure to violence in the media *can* foster aggression in some circumstances, and naturalistic studies suggest that there is a real (albeit small) such effect in real life. The main role of media violence is probably through making violent behavior more acceptable rather than through direct imitation.

Area differences in levels of crime have been obvious for many years, but until recently it has proved difficult to determine whether the differences represented a neighborhood causal influence on antisocial behavior. Research findings suggest that there are causal influences that stem from the areas in which people live; these operate on both offenses and offenders. The former involve mechanisms concerned with crime opportunities and the latter with propensities to engage in antisocial activities. The main risk seems to come more from a *lack* of social cohesion and informal community controls than from the presence of positive pressures to engage in crime. A chronic lack of job opportunities and a collective feeling of low self-efficacy are also important, however. The evidence suggests that, although a run-down physical environment plays some role, it is the human environment that is most influential. Housing policies play a key role in the community processes by which high-crime areas arise.

Longitudinal studies have shown that there are important school influences on children's scholastic achievements, school attendance, and behavior. These operate through both the qualities of the school as a social and pedagogic institution and also through the make-up of the pupil body. There is very little evidence concerning the influence of schools on antisocial behavior as such, but it seems that the former route is most important with respect to children's behavior and attendance and the latter route with regard to delinquent activities.

There are well-demonstrated ethnic variations in levels of antisocial behavior, but the patterns are quite complex. Some ethnic groups, such as those originating from South Asia, tend to have rather low rates of crime despite relatively high levels of social disadvantage and racial discrimination. Others, especially African-Americans in the United States and those of Afro-Caribbean background in the United Kingdom, have relatively high rates of crime – but these are most evident with respect to violent crime and drug offenses and are much less apparent with other offenses. Some of the ethnic variations arise through the cumulative effect of small (sometimes subtle) biases in police practice and judicial processing but, even taking these into account, it is clear that there are real differences among ethnic groups in violent crime. The concept of ethnicity is itself complex and does not equate with distinct biological divisions. For some groups, religious identity is more important than either country of origin or supposed race. The situation in the United Kingdom is changing with high rates of intermarriage for some ethnic groups. The causes of the ethnic variations in antisocial behavior remain poorly understood, but aspects of family and neighborhood living conditions seem likely to be important.

Additional populationwide influences include the availability of guns, drugs, and contraceptives, each of which may influence antisocial behavior in indirect ways.

CHAPTER 8 – SUMMARY OF MAIN POINTS

❏ Research on the *mass media* is methodologically very difficult, but it does suggest a small but statistically significant increase in aggressive behavior after viewing violent films in experimental settings. However, the main role of media violence is probably through making violent behavior more acceptable at a cultural level rather than through direct imitation or learning, and as such may have had a minor contributory role to play in the increase in antisocial behavior by young people since the Second World War.

❏ The debate continues over whether *area differences* are a causal factor in overall levels of antisocial behavior or instead reflect something else, such as policing levels. The make-up of an area in terms of the people residing in it may turn out to be more important in the early development of antisocial behavior than architectural or housing characteristics, although that is not to say that physical features do not have a part to play later in providing opportunities for crime.

❏ The empirical evidence on a causal role for *schools* is limited, but what does exist shows that: (i) the qualities of schools as social institutions are important (ethos, good models of teacher behavior, clear management, etc.); (ii) the make-up of the pupil body is important (presence of male delinquent role models, bullying, etc.); and (iii) both these factors affect antisocial behavior indirectly rather than directly.

❏ The difficulty in establishing the role of *ethnicity* in the development of antisocial behavior stems in part from the lack of congruence between self-report and official statistics. There is no doubt that minority ethnic groups are vastly overrepresented in the prison statistics, and although racism and processing biases can be demonstrated at each stage of the criminal justice system, this probably does not account for all of the overrepresentation. We concluded that there were differences in rates of antisocial behavior (particularly violence) among people from different ethnic backgrounds, exaggerated by processing biases within the system. What causes these underlying differences? Living conditions, joblessness, family risk factors, or some constellation of these are possibilities.

❏ It was important to note that the availability of *guns* (and the context of their ownership) has a significant part to play in overall levels of the most antisocial behavior of all: the substantial recent rise in U.S. homicides by young people can be attributed almost entirely to firearm possession.

❏ That the use of *drugs* by young people has increased in parallel with levels of antisocial behavior must also be considered; the two are likely to be interconnected in part, although the link is unclear.

9 | Gender Differences

We noted in Chapter 3 that a much higher proportion of males than females engage in crime, and that this is so around the world. Indeed, it has been so consistent a feature of criminal statistics over the years that geneticists sometimes jokingly comment that we do not need to search further for a "gene for crime" because we have already identified it – the gene for biological sex found on the Y chromosome! The point that they are seeking to make with this quip, however, is a serious one: the finding of a strong biological risk factor for crime is in itself completely uninformative about mediating mechanisms. Does the male preponderance in crime mean that the risk derives from male sex hormones, from temperamental features that differ between boys and girls, or from variations in the ways in which the two sexes are reared? – to mention just three from a much longer list of alternatives. The issue is an important one because being male is one of the strongest predictors of crime that we have among easily measurable attributes. If we understood *why* it is associated with an increased risk of crime, we might have a valuable lead for the causal processes involved in the underlying liability for antisocial behavior more generally. It is for this reason that we have a whole chapter on the topic, despite the paucity of empirical research.

In Chapter 4, we noted that the sex ratio for crime in England and Wales had fallen from about 11 to 1 in 1957 to just below 4 to 1 in 1995. There is some evidence, too, that the sex ratio varies with ethnicity. Ouston (1984) found that the male preponderance was less among black youths in London than white youths and was substantially greater in those from an Asian background. Accordingly, in seeking to understand why the male crime rate is so consistently higher than the female crime rate, we need to recognize that the ratio is far from fixed. Any adequate explanation for gender differences in crime must account for two facts: (i) the rate is always higher in males; and (ii) the ratio now is only about a third of that observed 40 years ago.

Before proceeding to consider the findings on crime, it is necessary to note that criminality is not a special case. There are marked differences between males and females for a wide range of psychosocial and psychiatric (as well as some medical somatic) disorders (Earls, 1987; Eme, 1979). Thus, almost all early-onset disorders associated with abnormalities of the developmental process (such as autism, hyperkinetic disorder, and developmental disorders of speech and language) are much commoner in boys than girls. The same applies to multiple chronic tics and reading retardation. Although there have been attempts to find a unifying explanation for this widespread greater male vulnerability (Gualtieri & Hicks, 1985), it seems a bit unlikely that the same factor would account for the gender difference in phenomena that seem as disparate as autism and delinquency (Taylor & Rutter, 1986). There are, of course, other disorders that show an equally striking preponderance in females: anorexia and bulimia nervosa provide obvious examples, but so also do depressive disorders in adult life. Interestingly, the range of explanations put forward for the sex difference in depression is as wide as those for crime, and the lack of strong convincing support for any of them is equally frustrating (Bebbington, 1996; Macintyre, Hunt, & Sweeting, 1996).

In considering the possible explanations for the gender difference in crime, three broad alternatives need to be considered. First, it could be that, although crime in males and females looks generally similar, it actually represents two rather different phenomena. Thus, diabetes was formerly seen as one disease; it is now appreciated that, in fact, diabetes can be either insulin-dependent (this variety usually begins in childhood or adolescence) or non–insulin-dependent. The latter variety arises in a somewhat different fashion, being particularly provoked by obesity and usually having an onset later in life. There is no good indication that such a qualitative difference applies to crime generally, although it may be the case with a few specific crimes such as infanticide.

Evidence that would point to a qualitative difference of this kind between males and females would be a contrast between the sexes in the patterns of predictors or correlates of crime. Because there have been so few systematic studies of crime in families, it is difficult to rule out this possibility entirely. Nevertheless, such evidence as there is indicates that the factors associated with offending in girls are generally similar to those found to apply in boys (Graham & Bowling, 1995; Riley & Shaw, 1985; Rowe, Vazsonyi, & Flannery, 1995). In this connection, it should be added that it is crucial to test directly whether the correlates in males differ significantly from those in females – and not to rely simply on whether they are statistically significant for one sex but not the other (Cohen, Cohen, & Brook, 1995).

A second possibility is that the risk factors for crime (such as hyperactivity) are much the same in males and females yet there is a sex difference in their occurrence. This seems likely to be largely the case, for example, with ethnic variations in crime rates (see Chapter 8). In the second half of this chapter we discuss whether this could be the case for gender differences in antisocial behavior.

The third alternative is that the risk factors are the same in the two sexes but that biological sex or psychological gender provides some additional risk or protective factor. Thus, in all societies, women outlive men by several years. The greater longevity of women does not seem to be a function of any sex difference in the role of risk factors for particular diseases or of life circumstances (Madigan, 1957). In a possibly comparable fashion, males seem to be more vulnerable to a wide range of biological hazards spanning malnutrition, obstetric complications, irradiation, and infection (Earls, 1987; Rutter, 1970). Could this apply to crime, possibly in relation to psychosocial hazards?

Rates of Crime in Males and Females

Official statistics from all countries show that more males than females are arrested and are found guilty of offenses (Gottfredson & Hirschi, 1991; Heidensohn, 1997; Kangaspunta, 1995; Loeber & Hay, 1994; Ouston, 1984; Smith, 1995; Stattin et al., 1989; Wikström, 1991; Wilson & Herrnstein, 1985). A comparison of international rates of arrest in the 1960s and 1970s showed that, of those arrested in 25 countries, only some 2% to 21% were female (Wilson & Herrnstein, 1985). The 2%–21% range is, of course, very wide, but it is clear that females always constituted less than a quarter. A survey of European and North American official statistics in the late 1980s reported sex ratios of between 3.4:1 (Germany) to 16.7:1 (Latvia) for arrests of juvenile suspects, and between 5.5:1 (Italy) to 22.7:1 (Scotland) for juvenile prosecutions (Kangaspunta, 1995). The most recent British Home Office figures were cited in Chapter 3, showing that 20% of 10–20-year-old offenders convicted or cautioned in 1995 were female.

Patterns of Offending

Four features immediately stand out when differences between males and females in patterns of offenses are considered: (1) the male preponderance is greatest in early adult life; (2) it is more marked for crimes that involve physical force than for property offenses that do not have that element; (3) females are less likely to be recidivist; and (4) women's criminal careers tend to continue over a shorter time period.

Figure 9.1 shows changes in gender ratio with age using U.K. and U.S. statistics as presented by Farrington (1986b). The U.S. data also illustrate

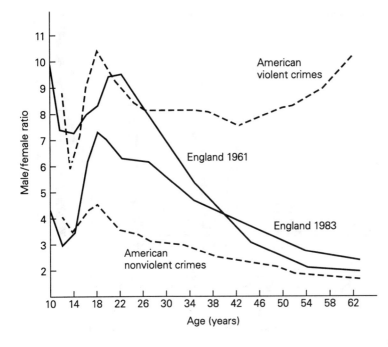

Figure 9.1. The sex difference in crime: male/female ratios at different ages. *Source:* D. P. Farrington, "Age and crime," in M. Tonry and N. Morris (Eds.), *Crime and Justice,* vol. 7. Copyright 1986 by the University of Chicago Press.

the much greater male preponderance for violent crime (although the rise in violent crime has been greater for girls than boys – Kelley et al., 1997). This has generally been evident in other analyses of statistics (Home Office, 1980; McClintock & Avison, 1968; Wadsworth, 1979) and has similarly been the conclusion of recent reviews (Heidenson, 1997; Smith, 1995; Wilson & Herrnstein, 1985). Often the difference has been expressed in terms of the "seriousness" of the crimes, but the use of force of some kind (on persons or property) seems to be the more relevant dimension. In addition, drug crimes are much commoner in males. Thus, the recent British criminal statistics on 10–19-year-olds showed sex ratios ranging from 13.2:1 for burglary, through 10.4:1 for drug offenses, 9:1 for criminal damage, 7.5:1 for robbery, 4:1 for violence, and 2.4:1 for theft (Home Office, 1996).

In addition, sexual assaults of all kinds (whether on adults or children) are largely committed by males (Monck & New, 1996; Vizard et al., 1995). In 1994, for example, it was not possible to estimate ratios for sex crimes

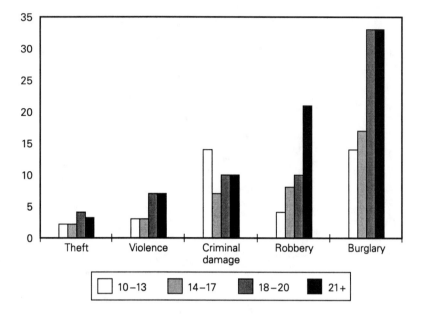

Figure 9.2. Sex ratios by age and crime (all set against 1 for females). *Source:* Data from Home Office (1996).

because there were so few young women between the ages of 10 and 20 who were cautioned or convicted for such crimes (Home Office, 1996).

The age pattern for the sex ratio is evident in both U.K. and U.S. statistics. Thus, the official statistics for England and Wales showed that, in 1994, the sex ratio for 10–13-year-olds cautioned or convicted was 2.4:1, for 14–17-year-olds it rose to 3.5:1, for 18–20-year-olds it was 6.1:1, and for those over age 20 it fell slightly to 4.9:1 (Home Office, 1996). Likewise, U.S. statistics showed the lowest sex ratio in the age-10–14 group and the highest in the late teens (U.S. Department of Justice, 1993).

Breaking down the data according to offense type shows an even more striking pattern. Figure 9.2 shows the sex ratios in the British official statistics (Home Office, 1996) – for convictions or cautions for violence, burglary, and robbery – broken down into four age periods: 10–13, 14–17, 18–20, and 21+.

The figure shows a fairly dramatic increase in the sex ratios for these three more serious offenses over the period between the teens and early 20s. Using a composite ratio across the whole age range shows, for example, that the sex ratio for robbery was 13:1, but this overall figure disguises the fact that it was as low as 4:1 in the early teens. It seems that the differences between women and men in crime are most notable in early adulthood and least marked in early adolescence.

The recent British Home Office (1996, 1997b) figures also highlight the differences between males and females in recidivism and duration of criminal careers. Young women are less likely to have more than one conviction and less likely to be severely recidivist. Thus, analyses of the offender index concluded that, of those born in 1953 who had appeared in court by their early 30s, 78% of the young women did so only once, compared with 55% of the young men. Only 6% of young women offenders, compared with 20% of young male offenders, have at least five convictions. A quarter of young male offenders but only 3% of young female offenders have a criminal career extending over a period of at least ten years. Females are less likely to have more than one offense and less likely to be seriously recidivist; they are also less likely to have been convicted of a serious offense during their offending career, as the sex ratios by offense type indicate. Stattin et al.'s (1989) Swedish study showed much the same. The rate of offending was twice as high for males as females (6.9 versus 3.0), twice as many male offenders had at least ten convictions (11.6% versus 4.9%), and the most active male offenders up to age 30 had committed far more crimes (44.8 versus 13.2) than the most active female offenders.

A further possible point of difference between males and females concerns the peak age of offending, although this has moved in somewhat different directions over the years (see Chapter 4). The peak age for crime in males was 13 years in 1938, 14 in 1961, and 15 in 1983 – somewhat paralleling the rise in the age for the end of compulsory schooling (Farrington, 1986b). The time trend for females moved in the opposite direction over the same time period, dropping from 19 in 1938 to 14 in 1983. More recent (1994) official statistics showed a peak age of offending of 15 for females and 18 for males (Farrington, 1996). It should be noted, however, that the peak age of offending varies by offense (being later for violent crimes), and that this will affect the sex difference (because violent crimes tend to show a greater male preponderance than simple theft).

The findings from official statistics may be summarized as follows:

- more males than females are convicted, the current overall ratio being of the order of 4:1;
- the male preponderance is greatest for sex crimes, drug offenses, and crimes involving force against persons or property;
- the male excess among offenders is least evident in early adolescence and most marked in early adult life;

- female offenders commit fewer crimes than male offenders, they are less likely to be recidivist, and they are less likely to commit really serious crimes;
- women's offending careers tend to be shorter.

There are two varieties of crime that are particularly associated with women. In Chapter 5 we noted that this was true of infanticide, with its highly characteristic timing during the period immediately after childbirth. Physical child abuse also more often involves mothers than fathers. Probably, however, this reflects mothers' greater time with young children rather than any general greater liability to abuse children. To a lesser extent than infanticide, the killing of family members is more characteristic of women than men – at least in the United States (Snyder & Sickmund, 1995). Homicides by women are three times as likely to be of a family member (41% versus 13%) and less likely than in men to be of a stranger (13% versus 34%).

Sociological feminist perspectives have suggested that there may be routes into crime for women that are much less characteristic of men (Daly, 1993; Heidensohn, 1997). Examples put forward include crimes that arise from a relationship with a violent man (in which retaliation or protection might result in killing), crimes that arise through friends or partners who use drugs, and soliciting by prostitutes. Killing of family members as a result of a severe depressive illness might also be more common in women. The empirical data suggest that the similarities in crimes committed by males and females outweigh the differences, and that the notion that crimes by females often represent a "reasonable choice" for a woman placed in an extremely adverse situation is not supported. On the other hand, as we have indicated, it is likely that a few crimes are of this kind.

Judicial Processing

Because (as discussed in Chapter 3) there is substantial discretion at all points in the chain of events by which crimes are dealt with, we need to consider whether the male preponderance in crime could be due to a difference in the ways in which male and female offenders are handled. Rutter and Giller (1983) concluded that, during the 1970s, girls tended to be treated somewhat more harshly than boys by the courts. Thus, they were more likely to be brought before the courts for such noncriminal matters as being "in moral danger" or "beyond control." Although girls were more likely than boys to be cautioned, they tended to be brought to court – and especially to be placed in some form of institutional care – for lesser offenses. If anything, these tendencies would seem likely to lead to an *underestimate* of the true level of male preponderance in crime.

Since then, there appears to have been some alteration in pattern. Recent British Home Office (1996) statistics indicate that young women tend now to be dealt with less harshly than their male counterparts. In 1994, 56% of females who were appearing in court for the first time were given an absolute or conditional discharge, compared with 48% of male first offenders. Turning to the other extreme – individuals aged 21 or more with at least ten convictions – 22% of males but only 13% of females were given immediate imprisonment. This slight differential processing of males and females should tend to lead to an *increase* in the sex ratio over time. In fact, as we have seen, the opposite has taken place. The sex ratio has gradually but steadily diminished over the last 40 years. As measured by official statistics, crimes by females have been increasing at a faster rate than crimes by males. It is clear that the (relatively small) differences in the judicial processing of male and female offenders could not possibly account for the much higher proportion of males with official convictions.

Self-Report Findings

Over the years, self-report studies have consistently agreed with official statistics in showing substantially higher rates of crime in males (Graham & Bowling, 1995; Hindelang et al., 1979, 1981; Junger-Tas et al., 1994; Wilson & Herrnstein, 1985). The first international study (Junger-Tas et al., 1994) showed that this applied in all the participating countries. Graham and Bowling's (1995) study of 1,721 young people aged 14 to 25 also noted that, even among those young women who reported committing offenses, the level of offending was below that in males. On the whole, the sex ratio for offending in self-report studies has been somewhat lower than that in official statistics – for example, 2:1 in Graham and Bowling's (1995) British survey and 4:1 found by Pederson and Wichström (1995) in a Norwegian study of adolescents.

As in the official statistics, the sex ratio has generally been greater for violent crime than property offenses. Thus, in Junger-Tas et al.'s (1994) international survey, the ratio for various violent offenses was in the range of 2:1 to 4:1, whereas for various property offenses it ranged from 1.5:1 to 2:1. Similarly, Graham and Bowling (1995) calculated cumulative participation ratios of 3.5:1 for violent offenses, 2.5:1 for property offenses, and 1.7:1 for "expressive" offenses (criminal damage and arson). Pederson and Wichström (1995), in comparable fashion, found that girls were more likely to admit to oppositional or defiant behavior at school than actual crime, the reverse of the pattern found for boys. The self-report data also agreed with official statistics in showing that the sex ratio was lowest in adolescence and greatest in early adult life. Graham and Bowling (1995) found a sex ratio of 1.4 : 1 at 14–17 years, 4.1 : 1 at 18–21 years, and 11.1 : 1 at 22–25 years. As shown in official statistics, the peak age of offending in females was earlier than in males – 18 years as compared with 21.

In summary, the self-report findings (which on the whole deal with lesser offenses than official statistics) confirm that offending is substantially less prevalent in females. The gender difference is least evident for minor property offenses in adolescence and is most evident for violent offenses in adult life.

Clinical Disorders Involving Antisocial Behavior

Both the official statistics and self-report findings are concerned with acts of offending. Psychiatric assessments differ markedly in their approach because their emphasis is on the qualities of psychological and social functioning rather than on whether the individual has broken the law. Nevertheless, as discussed in earlier chapters, several psychiatric diagnoses include aspects of antisocial behavior, and we need to consider the extent to which their incidence differs between males and females. Four categories require attention: oppositional/defiant disorder, conduct disorder, hyperkinetic or attention-deficit disorders, and antisocial personality disorder.

Oppositional/defiant disorder (ODD) has the least direct connection with overt crime because (i) it is defined in terms of youths' disruptive behaviors that bring them into conflict with adults (rather than illegal acts) and (ii) it is most characteristic of antisocial problems as they occur in young children. Thus, the defining symptoms include angry or resentful behavior, arguing with adults, blaming others, and being spiteful or vindictive. Most general population surveys have shown that such disorders in preschool children occur with approximately the same frequency in boys and girls, although they tend to be very slightly more common in males (Campbell, 1995). In older age groups, too, there is very little gender difference in rates. Thus, Simonoff et al. (1997) found a rate of 29 per thousand in boys and 24 per thousand in girls in the Virginia Twin Study of Adolescent Behavior and Development (VTSABD) sample of 1,412 twin pairs aged 8 to 16. There was, however, a difference between boys and girls in the age trend. The disorder increased in frequency in boys but not in girls, so that ODD was more frequent in the younger girls (as compared with boys) but much more frequent in the older boys (as compared with girls). Costello et al. (1996) similarly found only a small gender difference for ODD in their (American) Great Smoky Mountains study using the same diagnostic instrument; their sex ratio was 1.4 (i.e., 1.4:1). The findings are in good agreement with the self-report data and also with the findings (discussed in Chapter 6) with respect to gender differences in patterns of aggression. It may be concluded that there is little difference between boys and girls in the frequency with which they show oppositional, defiant, and spiteful behavior.

The findings with respect to conduct disorder are different. It is defined in terms of rather more serious behaviors such as fighting, cruelty, and setting fires, as well as by overtly delinquent acts such as stealing and burglary. It does, however, also include lying and truanting. This type of disorder has usually been found to occur in boys at least twice as frequently as in girls. Thus, in the VTSABD study, conduct disorders were found in 59 per thousand boys as compared with 28 per thousand girls (Simonoff et al., 1997). The picture seen in other epidemiological studies is much the same. For example, the sex ratio in the Great Smoky Mountains study was 4.8 (Costello et al., 1996), in the Chartres study it was 2.9 (Fombonne, 1994), in the New York State study it was 2.3 (Cohen et al., 1993), and in the Ontario study it was 2.4 (Offord, Alder, & Boyle, 1986). The gender pattern does, however, vary somewhat according to the details of how the disorders are defined. In the Dunedin study, for example, McGee et al. (1990) found that nonaggressive conduct disorders (mainly comprising truancy and use of alcohol or cannabis) were more frequent in girls whereas aggressive varieties occurred exclusively in males. Zoccolillo (1993) has argued that the prevailing systems of psychiatric diagnosis underestimate the rate of conduct disorder in girls because it is often shown by symptoms that are not included in those used in diagnosis. That may or may not be the case, but what is clear is that disorders characterized by aggressive predatory behavior and accompanied by social impairment are at least twice as common in males.

The third category, attention-deficit or hyperkinetic disorder (ADHD), is defined quite differently, with a focus on inattention, restlessness, overactivity, and impulsiveness. It is first manifest in the preschool years, and it shows a strong tendency to persist and to become associated with overtly antisocial behavior (Taylor, 1994). A recent systematic review of gender differences concluded that it occurred in boys roughly three to six times as often as in girls (Gaub & Carlson, 1997). The overall ratio in the VTSABD study was somewhat lower (2.6), but it increased markedly with age from 2.0 in 8–10-year-olds to 5.6 in 14–16-year-olds (Simonoff et al., 1997). In the Great Smoky Mountains study, the sex ratio for ADHD was 3.1 (Costello et al., 1996).

It has often been found that the sex ratio is least in the preschool period, but that may be in part because measures are picking up milder, more transient, disorders in girls. Thus, for example, Richman et al. (1982) found only minor gender differences for overactivity (as a behavior rather than a diagnosis) at 3 years – 16.1% versus 9.9%. On the other hand, by age 4 the boys with problem behavior were more likely than the girls to have become more difficult to control and to show poor concentration. Moreover, whereas overactivity in boys was a strong predictor of behavioral disturbance that continued to age 8, this was not the case in girls. It may be concluded that disorders characterized by marked and pervasive hyperactivity are several times more common in males, the sex ratio being greater than that found for either ODD or conduct disorder.

Because the gender difference in hyperactivity disorders has generally been considerably greater in clinic samples than in community surveys, it is necessary to consider whether the ratio in girls has been underestimated as a result of referral biases. It is clear that this is unlikely to be the case, because comparisons of girls and boys with ADHD in clinic samples have shown that the girls tend to have milder levels of symptomatology, apart from a possible tendency to be more cognitively impaired (Gaub & Carlson, 1997). It seems that the sex ratio is most marked for the severer varieties of ADHD and for those most associated with antisocial behavior.

Finally, with respect to psychiatric categories, we turn to antisocial personality disorder. This is defined in terms of a pervasive pattern of disregard for, and violation of, the rights of others that has been present from at least as early as mid-adolescence. This is evidenced by such behaviors as illegal acts, deceitfulness, impulsivity, aggressiveness, and consistent irresponsibility. The U.S. Epidemiological Catchment Area (ECA) study showed a lifetime prevalence in males of 4.3% and in females of 0.7% – a ratio of 6.4:1 (Robins et al., 1991). Other surveys have produced broadly comparable pictures, although the ratios range up and down somewhat. Thus the National Comorbidity survey produced figures of 5.8% and 1.2%, with an odds ratio of 5.2 (Kessler et al., 1994). The sex ratio is, however, open to distortion by the requirement in the American system of classification, DSM-IV (American Psychiatric Association, 1994), that the adult pattern must have been preceded by conduct disorder in childhood. It is also relevant that follow-up studies (Zoccolillo et al., 1992) show that the ways in which pervasive social malfunction (or personality disorder) are shown do vary by gender (see Chapter 10). In particular, crime in adult life is a common feature in men but less common in women (who are, however, more likely to show problems in interpersonal relationships and in work). The evidence suggests that there is much less of a gender difference in pervasive social malfunction in adult life than in varieties of such malfunction that include overtly criminal activities.

Kratzer and Hodgins's (1997) analysis of Janson's (1984) Stockholm longitudinal study data adds a further element to the pattern. In childhood, 7.2% of boys showed conduct problems compared with 2.1% of girls – an odds ratio (OR) of 3.4. In adult life, by the age of 30 years, 32.9% of males but only 6.8% of females had an official crime record – an odds ratio of 4.8. Conduct disorder in childhood was a slightly stronger predictor of adult crime in females (an OR of 4.06 versus 2.54), but the absolute rate of adult crime in females who had shown conduct problems in childhood was far below that in a comparable group of males (25.2% versus 75.2%).

Putting the findings together, we may conclude as follows.

- There is very little difference between males and females in rates of oppositional, defiant, or vindictive behavior in childhood.
- There is also little difference between males and females in patterns of pervasive social malfunction that are primarily characterized by major problems in interpersonal relationships.
- On the other hand, conduct disorders occur in males with a frequency about twice that in females.
- Also, pervasive and persistent hyperkinetic disorders are much more frequent in males, with a sex ratio of about 4 : 1.
- Antisocial personality disorders in adult life are some five or six times as frequent in males as in females.
- Conduct problems in childhood are a slightly stronger predictor of adult crime in females, but the absolute rate of adult crime is much lower in females than in males with this pattern of childhood behavior.

If these findings on clinical disorders are combined with official crime statistics and the self-report data, the overall picture with respect to gender differences in antisocial behavior are reasonably clear. Males and females differ little in their tendency to get into interpersonal conflict and to show seriously disturbed interpersonal relationships (although they show these difficulties in slightly different ways); this is so in both childhood and adult life. Males, however, are somewhat more likely than females to engage in theft, particularly frequent theft that persists over many years. Males are much more likely than females to show pervasive and persistent hyperkinetic disorders, to commit seriously aggressive acts and violent crimes, and to make sexual assaults. Those gender differences are least evident in early adolescence and most marked in adult life. Having established (as well as the data allow) the pattern of gender differences in antisocial behavior, we need now to consider the possible explanations for its origins.

Possible Explanations

Same or Different Origins in Males and Females

Because the great majority of studies of crime and delinquency have involved samples that were confined to males or have presented analyses based only on males (because there were too few female delinquents to warrant separate attention), most theories of crime are either very male-oriented or are gender-blind in the sense that there is no consideration of whether or not crime in females might differ in its origin (Gelsthorpe, 1997). Feminist criminologists have rightly highlighted that this is a serious lack, although they have not been notably successful in producing either empirical findings or coherent theoretical formulations to explain why or how crime in females might be different (Gelsthorpe, 1997). We need to begin, therefore, by considering how to tackle the initial question of whether crime in males and females has similar origins.

One approach is to compare the risk and protective factors for crime in males and females. Rowe et al. (1995) did this with a sample of 418 sibling pairs (including 141 of mixed sex). Closely similar correlations between the predictor variables and self-reported delinquency in the two sexes were found. Moreover, much of the difference between males and females in self-reported delinquency was explicable in terms of the higher level of the risk factors in males. Thus, of the factors that showed a correlation with delinquency of 0.25 or greater, all but one (sexual experiences) were greater in males. This applied to lack of maternal affection, low school achievement, impulsivity, deceitfulness, and rebelliousness. Unfortunately, the findings were severely limited by a reliance on cross-sectional self-report data for all variables, introducing the serious problem of lack of independence among measures. Also, because of the nature of the sample, most of the variations in delinquency will have been within the normal range, with very few individuals seriously delinquent. Nevertheless, the research strategy was a good one.

An alternative approach is to determine the extent to which antisocial behavior in one family member is associated with similar behavior in other family members of the same and opposite sex. Farrington et al. (1996a) found substantial associations across the sexes. Twin studies can quantify this more satisfactorily by determining if the correlations for antisocial behavior within opposite-sex pairs are the same as those within same-sex dizygotic pairs. The findings can then be used to test whether the genetic and environmental factors that relate to antisocial behavior in males are the same as those in females. Eaves et al. (1997) did this with conduct disorder symptoms and found no evidence that the origins differed between boys and girls.

A third approach is to consider directly the possibility that an antisocial liability may manifest itself differently in males and females. Thus, Zoccolillo (1993) has drawn attention to the evidence that, in adults, multiple medically unexplained somatic complaints constitute a sequel to conduct problems in childhood, but a sequel that is much more common in females than males. Also, using the retrospective ECA data, Robins (1986) found that conduct problems in childhood showed a somewhat stronger association with depressive disorder in adult life in females (although British longitudinal data did not find this with respect to emotional symptomatology in early adulthood – Rutter, 1991; Rutter et al., 1997b). Could emotional disturbance in females in some way represent an equivalent (meaning that it has the same origins) to antisocial behavior in males? To test that notion, it would be necessary to determine whether the correlates and predictors of depression in females (but not males) are the same as those for antisocial behavior in males. There are few good data on this point and no convincing evidence that it is the case. Alternatively, the across-twin–across-trait approach outlined in Chapter 7 could be used to determine if antisocial behavior in male twins correlated highly with depressive symptomatology in their female co-twins, the correlation being higher than within same-sex dizygotic twin pairs. The point we are seeking to make is that hypotheses on the supposed equivalence of phenomenologically different disorders in males and females are empirically testable, but the necessary tests have yet to be undertaken.

The data base is much too slender for firm conclusions, but what little evidence exists suggests that it would be reasonable to take as a starting point the assumption that there is likely to be a major overlap in the predictors of crime in males and females. It would therefore be useful to consider whether the difference between the two in rates of crime might be due to differences between males and females in the frequency or level of risk and protective factors.

Gender Differences in Individual Risk Factors

We have already seen (in Chapter 6) that hyperactivity is an important major predictor of antisocial behavior, particularly of the variety that begins early in childhood and persists into adult life – the type where the (limited) evidence suggests that the sex ratio is probably most marked. Moreover, we have considered the evidence that hyperactivity, whether dealt with as a risk dimension or as a disorder, is several times more frequent in males than females. It seems highly likely that the gender difference in hyperactivity plays a major role in the parallel difference between males and females in life-course–persistent antisocial behavior.

Of course, in a real sense, that conclusion simply pushes the questions back one step farther. Why is hyperactivity so much more common in males? As discussed in Chapter 6, genetic factors appear particularly important, more so than with antisocial behavior generally. Could males have a quantitatively greater genetic liability than females, or might the genetic basis be qualitatively different in the two sexes? Preliminary findings from the Virginia twin study suggest that, to some extent, the latter may be so (Eaves, 1996), even though no such difference is observed with oppositional/defiant and conduct disorder symptoms (Eaves et al., 1997). The XYY findings (Götz, 1996) discussed in Chapter 6 are also possibly relevant. The extra Y chromosome was associated with a substantially increased risk of antisocial behavior, whereas no risk was found with an extra X or other sex chromosome anomalies. Moreover, the increased risk seemed to be mediated by hyperactivity and other associated behaviors. Considerable caution needs to be exercised in extrapolating from this finding because it concerns a pathological group and also because it is based on a very small sample. Nevertheless, it does raise the speculative possibility that one of the susceptibility genes (there are likely to be several) for hyperactivity may be located on the Y chromosome. The original suggestion that the extra Y led to hyperaggressivity turned out to be mistaken, but possibly it may have something to do with hyperactivity. Be that as it may (and it is but one of many possibilities), we can conclude that hyperactivity is implicated in the gender difference in antisocial behavior and that genetic factors of some kind are likely to play some role in its origins.

It is possible that the temperamental characteristics of novelty seeking and impulsivity may also be implicated. As discussed in Chapter 6, these characteristics constitute reasonably robust predictors of antisocial behavior; they also seem likely to have some biological correlate, probably including neurotransmitter functions (McBurnett, 1992; Quay, 1993). Surprisingly, however, little is known about the extent to which males and females differ on these traits, although such limited evidence as there is suggests that they are more common in males.

There has been more discussion in the literature on the possible role of biologically based gender differences in aggression. That such differences exist is reasonably well documented (Maccoby & Jacklin, 1974, 1980); they are evident from fairly early in childhood, they apply across cultures, and they have also been found in animals. In addition, prenatal androgens have been found to have an organizing function on brain development in animals (Gorski, 1996; Goy, 1996). It remains uncertain whether something similar applies in humans, but there are some indications that it may (Swaab, 1991).

It is necessary, however, to add several important qualifiers to the statement that aggression is more frequent in males. First, in many experimental situations there is little difference between males and females in aggression (Frodi, Macauly, & Thome, 1977), although there must be queries about whether "aggression" in these circumstances has the same meaning as violent behavior in real-life situations outside the laboratory. Males are substantially more physically aggressive than females in most natural settings (Eagly & Steffen, 1986). Although they may not be more likely to show aggression within the family (Magdol et al., in press; Straus & Gelles, 1990; Straus, Gelles, & Steinmetz, 1980), the effects of their violence tend to be greater because of their greater physical strength. Second, the gender difference for physical aggression is substantially greater than that for verbal aggression (Eagly & Steffen, 1986; Hyde & Linn, 1986 – see also Chapter 6 on relational aggression). Third, as argued by Campbell (1993), it may well be that aggression has a somewhat different meaning and purpose in males and females. She suggested that aggression in males largely concerns dominance and power assertion, whereas in females it is more closely associated with the expression of negative feelings (such as anger, frustration, or resentment). There is overlap, of course, but the culturally influenced social representations of aggression differ somewhat between males and females.

As discussed in Chapter 6, male sex hormones also play some role in social dominance, although effects are bidirectional and complex. The implication is that prenatal androgens could play a contributory role in the origins of sex differences in aggressiveness, social assertiveness, and rough-and-tumble play; also, the surge in male sex hormones at puberty could play a role in the increase in violent crime at that time. As well as emphasizing that the causal links implied have yet to be well demonstrated, four further points need to be made. First, the early gender difference in assertiveness and aggression is relatively *small* in comparison with the large variations on these traits within gender. Second, as discussed in Chapter 6, these traits are probably quite weak risk factors for antisocial behavior (as compared, for example, with hyperactivity). Third, so far as hormonal effects in adolescence are concerned, the differences in androgens between males and females are quite *large* compared with the individual differences within gender. Fourth, the factors that account for the relatively small lifelong differences between males and females in antisocial behavior are probably not identical to those that account for the rather larger differences between males and females in violent crime during adult life.

As is all too obvious, the necessary empirical data are extremely thin. No firm conclusions are warranted, but it may be tentatively suggested that androgen differences in the period around birth may play a (probably small) role in the development of gender differences in aggression and assertiveness and that the marked increase in male sex hormone production at puberty may play some contributory role in the male excess in violence (via its impact on dominance; see Chapter 6). Both suggestions, however, need to be viewed as topics for research rather than as firm conclusions. It should be added, too, that the surge in sex hormones in adolescence cannot play much of a role in the gender difference in antisocial behavior in that age period, because the gender difference in crime then is *less* than that found in adult life. Moreover, if sex hormones were responsible, it might be expected that the adolescent peak for criminality would be less evident in females – but such is not the case. Insofar as testosterone plays a role, it is likely to be in violence rather than crime generally, and its effects are likely to be potentiating rather than directly causal.

High physiological reactivity seems to serve as a protective factor against antisocial behavior, and that could be implicated in the gender difference in antisocial behavior. However, high reactivity is probably only slightly commoner in females (Rubin et al., 1997), and it does not seem probable that this constitutes a major factor.

Reading difficulties constitute a risk factor for antisocial behavior, and they are more common in males than females (Maughan & Yule, 1994). Accordingly, they could play a role in the gender difference in crime. But there is a problem with this suggestion: the associations between reading difficulties and antisocial behavior are greatest in childhood and early adolescence, but the differences between males and females are greatest in early adult life, when the association with reading difficulties is minimal (Maughan et al., 1996). On the other hand, the evidence suggests that two rather different processes are operative: first, a more basic association between neuropsychological deficits and hyperactivity (indexed in part by reading difficulties); and second, an antisocial reaction to educational failure. Thus the question is whether the former shows a male : female difference. Clearly there is such a difference with hyperactivity. What remains uncertain is the independent efforts of cognitive impairment.

Finally, with respect to individual risk factors, mention needs to be made of serotonin metabolism, whose possible role in violent crime was discussed in Chapter 6. The only evidence we have on sex differences derives from the Dunedin study (Moffitt, 1997; Moffitt et al., 1997). The findings showed that variations in serotonin level were associated with violent crime in men but not in women. On the other hand, in females there seemed to be some possible effects on other behavior such as risky sex. If this sex difference can be confirmed in other studies, it would suggest that the same biochemical feature might have different effects in the two sexes. This could well be relevant to the gender difference in violence, although it would leave open the question of just why the same underlying biochemical feature had different consequences in males and females.

Gender Differences in Psychosocial Risks

Psychosocial risks could be relevant through three somewhat different routes: (i) a gender difference in the level or frequency of risks encountered; (ii) a gender difference in overall susceptibility or vulnerability to adverse experiences; and (iii) a difference between males and females in the ways in which they usually respond to stress and adversity.

There is surprisingly little evidence on any of these routes, owing to the paucity of research focusing on gender contrasts. Lytton and Romney (1991) concluded in their meta-analysis that there was little difference in the ways in which parents reared sons and daughters. That may well be the case overall, but it must be said that most of the evidence applies to aspects of child rearing that are not likely to have a major influence on antisocial behavior. Questionnaire and interview measures of overall parental warmth or control are not likely to pick up features of differential treatment that could have an impact. The research focus needs to be on questions such as whether – when parents are feeling irritable or low-spirited – they are more likely to get angry with their son or daughter; whether their son or daughter is more likely to have their leisure activities outside the home closely monitored; and whether their son or daughter is more likely to be drawn into family quarrels. *Within*-family comparisons of parental treatment of sons and daughters are required; what the literature provides instead are the much less helpful or informative *between*-family comparisons of parental treatment of sons and daughters.

Riley and Shaw (1985), in their U.K. national household survey of 751 families of 14–15-year-olds, found that boys were more likely than girls to receive low supervision. In both sexes, low supervision was associated with self-reported delinquency, but the association was stronger in girls (because of their lower rate of delinquency under conditions of high supervision: 29% versus 41%, the comparable figures for conditions of low supervision being 56% and 55%, respectively). However, Rowe et al. (1995) found neither a gender difference in supervision nor a risk associated with low supervision. Graham and Bowling (1995) found that poor parental supervision was a significant predictor of delinquency in both males and females. All three studies were cross-sectional, however, and inferences about causation are therefore necessarily quite speculative. It could well be the case that girls are more likely to be more effectively supervised; if so, this could play some role in protecting them against antisocial behavior, but evidence is lacking on the extent to which this is the case.

Boys and girls are likely, at a familywide level, to be equally exposed to parental psychopathology, family discord and violence, and family breakup. They will not necessarily have *completely* equal exposure because there may be differences in the ways that boys and girls are dealt with at times of family breakup (in terms e.g. of which parent has custody and the likelihood of being placed in residential care). To a much greater extent, there may be differences in the extent to which boys and girls are scapegoated at times of family conflict and so become the targets of criticism and hostility. In view of the findings on children's evocative effect on parental behavior and on the role of temperamental differences (see Chapters 6 and 7), it is quite likely that boys could have a greater individualized exposure to coercive negative parenting. It may be relevant, for example, that Harlow's studies of socially isolated monkeys showed that the females tended to become rejecting and indifferent mothers but they were more likely to abuse male infants (Ruppenthal et al., 1976). Once more, however, good data are lacking on the extent to which (in humans) males are more often the target of negative experiences.

As noted in the introduction to this chapter, there is a well-documented sex difference in vulnerability to physical hazards, and it is possible that there could be a parallel greater male susceptibility to psychosocial hazards (Rutter, 1970). There is some (rather inconsistent) evidence that boys may be slightly more vulnerable to the psychological risks associated with family discord (Rutter & Quinton, 1984), but if so, the difference is not marked (Zaslow, 1989; Zaslow & Hayes, 1986) and does not apply to all psychosocial hazards. For example, boys and girls seem equally vulnerable to the ill effects associated with institutional care (Rutter et al., 1990b; Vorria et al., 1998a,b). Indeed, the high rate of crime in women with an institutional upbringing is noteworthy; Quinton and Rutter (1988) found an adult crime rate of 27% (as compared with 2% in their general population comparison group). This difference was greater than that found for males (46% versus 14%) because of the relatively high rate in the male comparison group. Thus, the sex ratio for adult crime (1.7) in this group of institutionally reared individuals was much *lower* than that in the population as a whole. At least with respect to this risk experience, females seemed relatively more vulnerable.

The possibility of a gender difference in psychological vulnerability warrants serious attention, but it has not been easy to investigate. The key statistic is the ratio between males and females with respect to the *increase* in disorder following the experience of some specified psychosocial risk (and not simply the gender difference in overall rate of disorder, because that is what has to be explained). Ideally, this comparison should be based on longitudinal data examining within-individual change. It is crucial to use measures that are equally sensitive to disorders as manifest in males and females, as well as to cover a time period that is sufficient to detect delayed effects. There are far too few data for any firm conclusions, but the available evidence suggests that it is unlikely that there is any substantial difference between males and females in their overall susceptibility to psychosocial risks. However, a gender difference in vulnerability to particular types of adverse experiences is possible. Either way, it seems unlikely that any difference between males and females in psychological vulnerability (if there is one) could play a significant role in accounting for the lower female involvement in crime.

On the other hand, it is possible that a gender difference in *how* children respond to family stresses may be relevant. We have already noted the somewhat greater tendency of boys to show oppositional or defiant behavior, and in Chapter 7 we discussed the evidence that, by their behavior, children evoke and shape other people's responses to them. Children who react in oppositional ways have been found to be more likely to elicit negative critical responses from the people with whom they interact. In a longitudinal study of toddlers, Maccoby and Jacklin (1983) also found that oppositional behavior in boys (but not in girls) tended to lead mothers to back off, which in turn made it more likely that the boy's oppositional behavior would increase. Patterson (1982) and his colleagues have studied in detail how bidirectional effects of negative behavior in parents and children can lead to escalating coercive cycles that serve to reinforce and perpetuate antisocial behavior. Gender differences in these cyclical processes have been very little investigated up until now, but it is plausible that they may exist and play some contributory role in predisposing to the greater persistence of antisocial behavior in boys. It has also been suggested that parents may be less supportive of boys' attempts to cope with changing life circumstances or more likely to respond negatively to their distress reactions (Elder, 1979; Hetherington, 1980); that patterns of interactions are affected by temperamental features that show gender differences (Eme, 1979); and that the salience of some stress events may sometimes be greater for boys (Block, Block, & Morrison, 1981).

Differences in Social Context

In Chapter 7 we drew attention to the role of peer group influences and in Chapter 8 we discussed the importance of the broader social environment. There are probably important gender differences in both. Maccoby (1986, 1988, 1990, 1998) has drawn attention to the evidence from a range of different sources that boys' social groups tend to differ from girls' in several important respects. Six key contrasts may be highlighted. First, boys and girls differ in their styles of interaction with same-sex peers. Boys' interchanges are more domineering and competitive – with bragging, threatening, talking over other people, and ignoring the suggestions of others. By contrast, there is more turn taking and emotional interchange in girls' groups. Second, there is a difference in the content of play, with boys being more likely to engage in challenging, risk-taking, and limit-testing activities. Third, boys' groups are more oriented toward appearing unambiguously male. This tends to mean being tough and nonfeminine. Girls, on the other hand, tend to find it more congenial than boys to show both masculine and feminine qualities. Fourth, boys' groups tend to be larger and more oriented toward activities; girls more often form groupings of dyads and trios, which are identified as friendships. Fifth, boys' groups tend to be more separate from the world of adults and more often explicitly oriented around limit-testing activities that would be disapproved by adults (drinking beer, viewing pornographic pictures, damaging property, and other forms of rule breaking). Sixth, dominance and status are more important within all-male groups than in girls' groups, with both characteristics sometimes defined in terms of daring or illicit activities.

It would be misleading to overemphasize these differences. There is considerable heterogeneity within boys' and girls' peer groups, and most will have a mixture of qualities. Moreover, many groups have some admixture of boys and girls. Nevertheless, the prevailing social cultures of all-male and all-female peer groups do tend to be rather different. The extent to which this has an influence on gender differences in antisocial behavior is not known, but it is highly likely to have some effect (Cairns & Kroll, 1994). Caspi et al. (1993), as discussed in Chapter 7, found different peer group effects on early-maturing girls in coeducational versus all-girl schools.

Four other points need to be made on the social environment of males and females. First, because of gender differences in antisocial behavior, boys will have more delinquent peers in their social groups. This necessarily means that they are likely to be exposed to more peer group influences of an antisocial kind. Second, because drinking alcohol and taking illicit drugs is more frequent in males, boys will be more exposed to the influences of both behaviors at an individual level and more exposed to peer group influences oriented around drugs and alcohol. The two substances with the least gender difference (tobacco and marijuana) are probably the two with least involvement in antisocial subcultures. Thus, adolescent boys and young men are more likely to be involved in the disruptive unruly behavior that is sometimes associated with drinking in public places. Third, at least in some parts of the world, males are much more likely than females to own weapons that could be used in violent encounters. Thus, in Sadowski, Cairns, and Earp's (1989) survey of American teenagers, it was found that a substantial minority of the adolescent males owned guns whereas very few of the females did so.

The fourth point is that antisocial girls are much more likely than other girls to become teenage mothers; the tendency for antisocial boys to become teenage fathers is much less marked (see Chapter 7). This may well predispose such girls to a range of social difficulties (including discordant, broken relationships) and make it more likely that they will experience failures in parenting (see Quinton & Rutter, 1988). As a consequence, they may well have quite a high rate of interpersonal conflict, possibly including violence, with partners and children both. On the other hand, their domestic commitments in late adolescence and early adult life may well make it more difficult for them to be part of a delinquent peer group and to engage in criminal activities outside the home. This is especially likely given the high proportion of unsupportive spouses that they tend to have.

The last 20 years has seen an explosion of writing on gender and crime, particularly by sociologists (Gelsthorpe, 1997; Heidenson, 1997; Messerschmitt, 1993; Newburn & Stanko, 1994). To a considerable extent this has been driven by feminist perspectives, with men constituting the "norms" against which women's behavior is assessed: the main focus is on why women do not get involved in crime, rather than on why men do. It is reasonable – indeed, necessary – to consider the extent to which cultural pressures or expectations play a role in the gender differences in antisocial behavior. Unfortunately, there are few sound data from which to determine their role. Perhaps the main aspect on which it is necessary to bring in broader sociocultural influences is the substantial rise in female crime over recent decades. Thus, in the period between 1985 and 1994, female juvenile violent crime arrests more than doubled (Snyder et al., 1996). Could a change in women's social representations of aggression

(Campbell, 1993) – or the shift in views and expectations that has accompanied the women's rights and feminist movements – be responsible? On the whole, the evidence has tended to be negative. Figuera-McDonough (1984) found no association between feminist orientation and self-reported delinquency. The problem, though, is that feminist movements and feminist orientation provide only rather crude and unsatisfactory indices of what might be involved. Clearly, the rise in the rate of female crime (and the parallel fall in the sex ratio) is likely to be due to some change in the environment, and it is reasonable to view cultural change as one of the possibilities to be considered. This remains a plausible general suggestion, but it needs to be translated into some more specific mechanism if the idea is to be empirically testable.

Conclusions

This chapter, more so than any other in the book, has lacked sound empirical data to support possible causal explanations. The inevitable consequence is that we have had to rely more on speculation about plausible mechanisms than we would have wished. Nevertheless, we make no apology for considering gender differences in some detail. As noted in our introduction, being male is one of the best documented risk indicators for antisocial behavior. It is necessary, therefore, that we seek to understand how the male preponderance in antisocial behavior comes about.

Three main findings require explanation. First, the greater male involvement in crime is a universal finding that applies across cultures and over time, and it is evident on all types of measurement. The ubiquity of the difference makes it likely that some forms of biological influence plays a part. Second, the extent of this gender difference has varied markedly over time and among ethnic groups. At no time and in no group has the ratio approached unity (with the striking exception of shoplifting; see Farrington & Burrows, 1993), but the variations have been large. Thus, over the course of 40 years, the sex ratio for crime in the United Kingdom has fallen from about 11:1 to just below 4:1. This variation alone makes it implausible that the difference between males and females can be wholly attributed to biological factors. Third, the male:female difference varies greatly by both pattern of antisocial behavior and by age. The least difference is to be seen with oppositional or defiant behavior and with minor theft, and the greatest difference with both major violent crime and antisocial personality disorder in adult life and with hyperactive or aggressive disorders in childhood. The implication is that the greatest gender difference is likely to apply to life-course–persistent antisocial behavior.

In view of the paucity of data, no firm conclusions are possible. However, it seems highly probable that the higher frequency of hyperactivity and associated behaviors in males plays a major role in the greater male involvement in crime, and this implicates genetic factors in view of the relatively strong genetic component in individual differences in hyperactivity. Nevertheless, at the moment this remains a strong hypothesis rather than anything that is firmly established.

The effect of prenatal androgens could possibly play a role in the gender differences in aggressivity and dominance, and the surge of androgens at puberty could (via effects on dominance) be involved in the gender difference in violence. Serotonin metabolism differences could similarly play a part. Good data to confirm or refute these suggestions are lacking, however.

In contrast, the variations in sex ratio over time and among ethnic groups would seem to require some more sociocultural explanation. The strongest contender in that connection seems to lie in the gender differences in peer groups and in the cultural meanings attached to aggression for males and females. However, it must be stated that – although this seems the most plausible arena of influence – empirical findings are lacking on whether this actually is the case and (if so) quite how it operates.

Finally, there are some suggestions that within-family psychosocial influences may play a part. It is possible that boys' behaviors make them more likely to be the focus of conflict and discord, and their responses may also make coercive cycles more liable to develop; both could play a contributory role in making antisocial behavior more likely to persist in males.

The topic of gender difference in antisocial behavior should be high on the research agenda. There are a number of useful leads to follow, but currently there is an extreme paucity of solid empirical findings on the causal processes involved in the greater involvement of males in crime.

CHAPTER 9 – SUMMARY OF MAIN POINTS

❑ Young men commit a *higher proportion* of juvenile crime than young women. In the United Kingdom in 1995, young men under the age of 21 accounted for 80% of recorded offenses cleared up and attributed to this age group. Self-report data reflect a lower ratio, but crimes reported by young men still outnumber those reported by young women.

❏ The *sex ratio is falling,* with young women accounting for increasing proportions of officially recorded crimes. Although the rate is always higher for males, the ratio is now only about a third of that observed 40 years ago.

❏ There are *differences in type* of involvement and criminal career, as well as in rates of participation. The male preponderance is greatest in early adult life and is more marked for violent offenses than theft or property offenses; males are more likely to be recidivist; and female offenders have shorter criminal careers that peak earlier.

❏ In terms of the *individual factors* associated with antisocial behavior, rates of almost all other early-onset disorders of development (such as conduct disorder, hyperactivity, specific reading retardation) are also more common in boys. Where these have a part to play, it tends to be for life-course–persistent behavior only. Hormones may also play a small role in gender differences in aggression and dominance, but this is unlikely to be a major part of the explanation.

❏ Not enough is known about whether *psychosocial* factors, such as the significant aspects of parenting, differ by the sex of the child. There is some limited evidence that girls are more effectively supervised, for example. The possibility of a gender difference in psychological vulnerability has not been adequately tested. Girls may likewise respond differently to family stresses. Coercive cycles may be more likely to develop between parents and their sons, but adequate data are simply not yet available.

❏ There is some evidence that social *contextual influences* such as social groups tend to be different for the sexes. In addition, because of the higher base rate of antisocial behavior in boys, boys are more likely to be exposed to more peer group influences of an antisocial kind. Also, antisocial behavior in girls may lead to *increased* domestic bonds through teenage motherhood, whereas the same behavior in boys ends outside the family. Currently these statements can only be given the status of theories in need of rigorous testing.

10 | From Child to Adult

Persistence and Desistance

Analyzing Data from a Life History Perspective

Throughout this book, for the reasons outlined in Chapter 2 (and discussed more fully in Thornberry, 1997), we have placed especial reliance on the findings of longitudinal studies that have spanned many years and that were based on general population samples. Their results have been important in several rather different respects. First, it has become clear that offending, particularly persistent recidivist offending, frequently has its origins in disruptive behavior that may be evident as early as 3 years of age (see Chapter 6). Accordingly, it is necessary to consider how and why early disruptive behavior leads to later criminal acts. The question is important if only because (i) it is obvious that not all troublesome preschoolers become delinquent and (ii) by no means do all delinquents show unusual behavior during the early years. Because we discussed the limited findings in Chapters 5 and 6, we do not reconsider the issue here. The main points that emerged were that the most important early precursor for crime was hyperkinetic behavior; that probably the route to antisocial behavior involved psychosocial risks as well as individual behavior (see Chapter 7); and that these early behavioral features were most strongly associated with violent crime and life-course–persistent antisocial behavior.

Second, longitudinal studies have emphasized the heterogeneity of antisocial behavior and of the individuals who engage in it (see Chapter 5). During recent years, building on earlier work by sociologists and criminologists (Gottfredson & Hirschi, 1991; Hirschi & Gottfredson, 1994), particular attention has come to be paid to the distinction between what Moffitt (1993a) termed adolescence-limited and life-course–persistent antisocial behavior. This is not synonymous with the early distinction between one-time and recidivist offenders, because the adolescence-limited group may have repeated offenses over a number of years and because Moffitt (1993a) has proposed that the two groups differ qualitatively (not just quantitatively) in several key respects. Similarly, Patterson (Patterson & Yoerger, 1997) has argued that research findings point to the need to distinguish between early-onset and later-onset antisocial behavior – groups that roughly coincide with the life-course–persistent and adolescence-limited distinction. Again because these categories were considered in Chapter 5, we do not re-examine them here.

Third, ever since Robins's (1966) pioneering long-term follow-up study of children who attended a child guidance clinic, it has been evident that antisocial behavior in childhood is often a precursor of a much wider spectrum of social maladaptation in adult life. This is evident both in what psychiatrists have regarded as "personality disorder" and in an increased rate of new problems such as depressive conditions and drug or alcohol problems (Blumstein et al., 1986; Kessler et al., 1997; Robins, 1966, 1978, 1986). By "personality disorder," psychiatrists mean a deeply ingrained and enduring pattern of behavior that is deviant for the person's sociocultural milieu, maladaptive and socially dysfunctional, and accompanied by abnormal intraindividual personality traits or psychological characteristics (American Psychiatric Association, 1994; World Health Organization, 1992). Insofar as the concept is valid and the findings robust, it suggests that it may be important to view at least some forms of antisocial behavior as the outcome of a disorder characterized as much by social maladaptation and personal malfunction as by breaking the law. We need to consider the extent to which that may be so.

The association of antisocial behavior with other forms of disturbance (such as depression and alcoholism) also raises the issue of "comorbidity" – the co-occurrence of two or more supposedly separate disorders (Caron & Rutter, 1991; Rutter, 1997b). We need to consider whether such disorders or behaviors are truly separate (rather than different manifestations of the same underlying liability) and, if they are, what causal process might be involved.

Fourth, as argued by Farrington (1988), longitudinal data are invaluable for the testing of causal hypotheses. Within-individual behavioral change over time that can be related to the onset and offset of some risk experience provides a powerful means of determining whether or not the experience truly played a role in the causal processes involved in the change of behavior. Thus, in Chapter 6 we discussed this approach in relation to drugs and alcohol and, in Chapter 7, we did so in relation to peer group experiences and to unemployment. In Chapter 8, we did the same in relation to school influences and geographical factors. The approach has been particularly important in showing the impact of experiences in adult life as factors leading to a desistance from antisocial behavior. Army experiences (Elder, 1986; Sampson & Laub, 1996) and harmonious marriage to a supportive spouse (Farrington & West, 1995; Laub et al., 1998; Quinton & Rutter, 1988; Quinton et al., 1993; Sampson & Laub, 1993) both constitute examples of that kind. Equally, other experiences may make it more likely that antisocial behavior will continue; incarceration and unemployment illustrate this effect (Sampson & Laub, 1993).

This area of research has also served to highlight three other crucial issues: the origins of these influential experiences; the question of the circumstances under which major experiences serve to accentuate or change prior behavioral tendencies; and the extent to which the effects of experiences are dependent on the qualities of the individuals and of their overall life situation. We discussed some aspects of the first and last of these issues in Chapter 6 when considering gene–environment correlations and interactions, and in this chapter we touch on some of the broader aspects of the same topics. In previous chapters we have mentioned accentuation and turning-point effects, but here we discuss the concepts in a little more detail. At first sight the two effects appear to represent conflicting views but, as we indicate, they do not. Caspi and Moffitt (1993) challenged prevailing concepts of stress effects in showing empirically that many adverse experiences served to *accentuate* habitual patterns of behavior and to increase coherence in personality functioning, rather than to change either. Conversely, Pickles and Rutter (1991; Rutter, 1996) and Sampson and Laub (1993) noted that experiences in adult life could sometimes result in a major change in behavior – what they termed "turning point" effects. The issue that requires discussion is just what determines whether accentuation or instead a turning point occurs.

Fifth, longitudinal data have led to a consideration of what have come to be called "criminal careers" (Blumstein et al., 1985, 1986; Blumstein, Cohen, & Farrington, 1988; Loeber & Le Blanc, 1990). There are three basic points that are central to the careers concept. To begin with, there is the distinction between the "participation rate" in crime (i.e., the proportion of a population engaging in crime) and the "frequency" of criminal activities (i.e., the rate of such activities in the subgroup of individuals who are criminally active). Thus, the crime peak in adolescence and the falloff in crime in early adult life could result from changes in either the proportion of the population engaging in crime or in the level of criminal activity in those individuals (Farrington, 1986b). The implications of the two hypotheses are rather different.

In addition, there is the implication that it may be useful to consider whether the factors that influence desistance from crime differ from those that influence initiation into antisocial behavior and also its persistence (Farrington et al., 1990a; Laub et al., 1998). Some criminologists (especially Gottfredson & Hirschi, 1986) have argued that this is a nonissue because age changes in crime are a biological given and because the factors that account for individual differences in antisocial propensity explain every-thing. Those who desist early simply have a weaker propensity. Crimi-nal career investigators have challenged this notion by arguing that – al-though the theory may be true so far as it goes – what happens to people may also influence persistence or desistance. The careers approach seeks to investigate these later experiential effects, as well as the effects of prior propensities (whether originating from biological features or earlier life experiences).

Further, there is the related point of an interest in the overall duration of criminal careers. Thus, in Chapter 9 when discussing gender differences, we noted that males tend to have longer criminal careers than women. Why might this be so?

It will be appreciated that the interest in criminal careers has grown in parallel with the comparable focus in the broader field of behavior and so-cial sciences of life-span and life-course development (Baltes, 1979; Elder, 1995, 1997; Rutter & Hay, 1994; Rutter & Rutter, 1993; Settersten & Mayer, 1997). There has been a major shift away from a concern to quantify con-tinuities in behavior over time and toward a focus on investigating the mechanisms involved in *both* continuities and discontinuities in develop-ment. As part of that movement, psychologists have sought to investi-gate developmental progressions in patterns of antisocial behavior. Thus, Loeber and his colleagues (Loeber & Schmaling, 1985; Loeber et al., 1993, 1997) have proposed three parallel pathways involving "authority con-flict," "covert" antisocial behavior (e.g. theft), and "overt" antisocial be-havior (e.g. violence). It is necessary to consider the extent to which such progressions are consistent features, as well as the processes involved and the factors that lead some individuals to progress up the pathway to more severe forms of criminal behavior and others to stop short at an earlier point.

It will be appreciated that many of the research findings relevant to these issues were introduced in earlier chapters. In this chapter we add some results that apply to adult experiences, but for the most part our aim is to pull together evidence presented earlier in the book in order to highlight some key theoretical and practical implications.

Some Questions about Using Longitudinal Data

Before proceeding further, however, certain methodological considera-tions need to be mentioned. Perhaps our first question should be whether retrospective data from cross-sectional surveys can be used to study life-course developmental questions. Certainly, they have been much used for this purpose – as exemplified by the Epidemiological Catchment Area (ECA) study (Robins & Regier, 1991), to which we have referred several times. Given that there is an interest in time spans that cover several decades, it is obvious that longitudinal methods are bound to be both very expensive and time-consuming. Inevitably, too, the individuals will have gone through their childhoods in a much earlier era, when social circumstances were very different. Also, it must be recognized that longitudinal studies are heavily reliant on retrospective recall. The period of recall may be one year rather than twenty, but still there are similar concerns about reliability and bias. Reviews of research findings (Maughan & Rutter, 1997; Rutter et al., in press a) have shown that people can remember a good deal about their past behavior and major life experiences. Yet there are several problems: (i) accurate recall is dependant on skilled interviewing using personalized time points for dating (Caspi et al., 1996b); (ii) recall is much better for concrete, easily defined behaviors and events than for ones (such as feeling states or parenting qualities) that require relative judgments or that were likely to be less salient at the time (Henry et al., 1994); (iii) errors in the time ordering of happenings include biases that produce sequences that make "most sense" to the individuals in terms of their percepts of themselves – as well as a good deal of random error (Angold et al., 1996); (iv) there is a tendency for individuals who are functioning well in adult life to underreport adversities in their childhoods; (v) poor recall for early childhood is typical; and (vi) subjects will be unable to recall features of which they were unaware at the time (such as physiological measures). All of these considerations mean that there must be considerable caution in the use of retrospective data. They may be satisfactory in providing a reasonably accurate broad picture, but they are prone to important biases and cannot be relied upon for the study of detailed time sequences.

Longitudinal data suffer less from these limitations (although they are not free of them). However, they involve the same set of difficulties deriving from measurement error, the need for independent sources of data as features to be linked, and from differences among informants. We noted in Chapter 7 that errors of measurement may create a picture of change when none has taken place (Fergusson et al., 1996a,b). Multiple measures and multiple data sources provide the protection. We have also commented on the problem of distorting "halo" effects. If information on behavior at two points in time (or on a life experience and a behavior) derive from the same single informant, the associations between them may come about because of the informant's overall percept, which provides a linkage that is at least partially artefactual as a consequence of the informant's own mind-set. The solution lies in using independent sources of information for measures whose association is to be studied. The third problem is far and away the greatest because there is no entirely satisfactory solution. Numerous studies have shown that agreement between informants is typically quite low (see Achenbach et al., 1987; Angold & Costello, 1996; Eaves et al., 1997; Hewitt et al., 1997; Rutter et al., 1970; Simonoff et al., 1995, 1997, in press). Some of the poor agreement reflects measurement error, some reflects the fact that children tend to behave differently in different situations, but some is due to as yet unidentified factors. Whatever its origins, the end result has been that the findings based on different informants are often rather different. This represents a major challenge for research.

Moreover, longitudinal analyses – whether based on retrospective recall or prospective measurement – have a particular problem of their own: the inability to separate age and cohort (or period) effects (Blumstein et al., 1986; Rutter, 1995d). Changes over time could reflect either the fact that the individuals had grown older or that they were living through a different time period. For example, during the 1960s and 1970s there was a massive increase in the use of drugs, and anyone growing up during that period will have been more likely to take drugs – not because they were getting older, but because drug use generally was becoming much more prevalent. Similarly, for someone born in (say) 1940, age changes in offending between the ages of 10 and 20 will inevitably be seriously distorted by the major overall increase in crime between 1950 and 1970. The solution lies in a combination of cross-sectional and longitudinal data, plus the use of mediating variables to test hypotheses about mechanisms. Thus, the finding of a significant age trend between 10 and 20 years does not, in itself, indicate what caused the trend. It could reflect, for example, increased cognitive skills or the hormonal changes of puberty or experience of schooling or exposure to drugs. As Rutter (1989b) put it, age is an "ambiguous variable" that needs unpacking. The requirement is "natural experiments" that pull apart variables that ordinarily go together. Thus, because individuals vary in the timing of reaching puberty, pubertal effects can be contrasted with the other correlates of age (Angold & Rutter, 1992).

A further question with longitudinal data concerns the advantages and disadvantages of official crime records vis-à-vis interviews or other forms of self-report or reports by others (Blumstein et al., 1986). When seeking to study frequency rates of crime over time in offenders, the ways in which crime statistics are dealt with poses a considerable problem (see Chapter 3). A single act of crime may give rise to multiple recorded offenses (because multiple offenders are involved and because a single act may reflect multiple offenses); equally, multiple acts of crime may result in only one recorded offense because of a decision to proceed with charges only on the one major crime most easy to prove. In addition, of course, there are the problems associated with police targeting of known offenders and individual differences in skills in avoiding apprehension. For example, comparing self-reported delinquency and official convictions, Nagin et al. (1995) found a rather low conviction rate at age 14, a much higher one at 18, and a somewhat lower one at 32 in their highest-level recidivist offenders. On the other hand, their lower-level recidivists did not reach their peak conviction rate until age 32. The implication is that, over time, the police get better at picking up chronic offenders but that those who offend at the highest levels (but not the lower-level recidivists) learn something about how to escape detection.

Finally, longitudinal studies are vulnerable to the problem of *attrition*, so that over time an increasing proportion of participants are lost to the study (Junger-Tas & Marshall, in press). Typically, those who cease to participate tend to differ from the remainder in important ways. Fortunately, most of the intensive longitudinal studies on which we have placed greatest reliance in this book (such as the New Zealand studies, Farrington's longitudinal study, and the Pittsburgh study) have been remarkably successful in maintaining their samples over prolonged periods of time.

As we have commented repeatedly, no one method is the best for all purposes. Combinations of research strategies (and of methods of measurement) are always to be preferred. When they all provide basically the same picture, despite having rather different sets of potential biases, there can be reasonable confidence in the validity of the findings. However, when each tells a somewhat different story, there must be great caution with respect to the inferences drawn.

Criminal Careers

The initial research on criminal careers focused on the prediction of recidivism (Rhodes, 1989). Use was made, for example, of the Philadelphia (Wolfgang et al., 1972) and London (Farrington, 1995a) cohorts data (Blumstein et al., 1985). Two findings immediately stood out. First, the recidivism rate rose sharply from the first conviction (just over a third) to the third conviction (about 70%) and thereafter only rose slightly. Second, the data strongly suggested heterogeneity among offenders, with some (desisters) having a low recidivism probability and some (persisters) having a high probability. These two groups differed markedly in their early

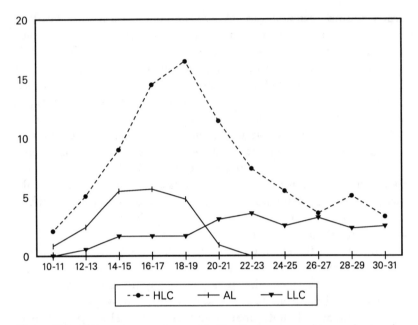

Figure 10.1. Different age patterns of offending: average biannual rate of conviction (tens) by age and offender type. *Notes:* HLC denotes high-level chronic offenders (*n* = 52); AL denotes adolescence-limited offenders (*n* = 51); LLC denotes low-level chronic offenders (*n* = 42). *Source:* D. S. Nagin, D. P. Farrington, and T. E. Moffitt, "Life-course trajectories of different types of offenders," *Criminology* 33 (1995, p. 113), by permission of the American Society of Criminology.

risk factors (both individual and family). Yet because broadly the same features served to distinguish offenders from non-offenders and persisters from desisters, it could be argued that the careers reflected nothing more than differing degrees of liability to crime.

Further analyses have distinguished between frequent and occasional chronic offenders (Barnett, Blumstein, & Farrington, 1987, 1989). The former group had a rather high annual conviction rate (1.14), which remained roughly constant over time, and a low probability of criminal career termination (10%) after each conviction. By contrast, the latter group had a lower annual conviction rate (0.41) and a higher career termination rate (33%). On these bases, Farrington (1986a) argued that the dramatic falloff in crime in early adult life was more a consequence of many individuals ceasing to engage in crime than it was of offenders engaging in less crime.

Nagin et al. (1995; see also Nagin & Land, 1993) have extended the analysis by including data up to the age of 32 and by focusing on further possible subgroup differentiation. Figure 10.1 shows the biannual conviction rates for three subgroups of offenders: high-level chronics, low-level chronics, and those with adolescence-limited antisocial behavior; these subgroups accounted for approximately equal proportions of offenders. Five main findings may be highlighted. First, two of the groups showed the same pattern of peak offending in late adolescence seen in aggregated official crime statistics. Thus, at least as measured by official convictions, part of the rise in adolescence and falloff in early adult life was due to within-individual changes. Second, this pattern did not apply at all to the third of the population of offenders classified as low chronics. They showed only a small rise in crime over the teenage years and no fall at all during the first decade or so of adult life. Clearly, despite Hirschi and Gottfredson's (1983; Gottfredson & Hirschi, 1986) claims of an invariant relationship between age and offending, there is a substantial subgroup to which this does not apply. Third, there is a further substantial subgroup, the adolescence-limited offenders, who cease offending by their early 20s. Accordingly, part of the fall in crime rate in early adult life is a consequence of many individuals ceasing to offend. Fourth, the high-level chronics show a rate of offending in their late 20s that is not much below that of the adolescence-limited group in their teens. Fifth, the peak age of offending of the latter group (14–17 years) is a couple of years below that of the former group (16–19 years).

These data refer to official convictions, and to fill out the picture we turn to self-reports, as illustrated in Figure 10.2. It is evident that the pattern here is very different. To begin with, it is necessary to include a never-convicted group who report a substantial number of antisocial acts at age 14, who show a substantial drop in their delinquent activities by age 18, and who have a very low rate of crime at age 32. Moffitt (1993a) had postulated that adolescence-limited antisocial behavior was very much more common than life-course–persistent antisocial behavior. The official statistics (as shown in Figure 10.1) suggested otherwise. The self-report data, by contrast, are in keeping with Moffitt's postulate; it is just that most of the adolescence-limited offenders never receive an official conviction.

The next point is that there was much less of a difference on self-reports between the high-level and low-level chronics. *Both* showed a substantial falloff in offending in early adult life. The difference was that the low-level group showed a much greater tendency to be caught.

The findings point to the need to consider a broader set of measures dealing both with offender behavior and with risk factors. When Nagin et al. (1995) did this, the risk factors did not differentiate very clearly among the three offender groups (although the high-level chronics were somewhat more likely to show poor concentration and restlessness), but

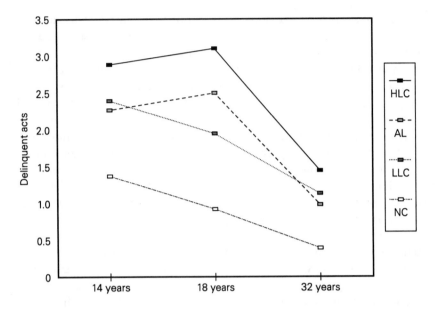

Figure 10.2. Age trends in self-reported delinquency. *Notes:* HLC denotes high-level chronic offenders; AL denotes adolescence-limited offenders; LLC denotes low-level chronic offenders; NC denotes never convicted. *Source:* Nagin et al. (1995), by permission of the American Society of Criminology.

the various risk factors discussed in Chapters 6–8 did differentiate the criminal and noncriminal individuals. The findings, therefore, do not help a great deal in sorting out the sources of heterogeneity among the offenders. Other findings, such as those from Patterson's research group (Patterson & Yoerger, 1997) and from Stattin and Magnusson's (1995) Swedish longitudinal study, suggest that peer group influences may be more important with the adolescence-limited offenders than the early-onset chronics; the family risk factors are somewhat similar, although possibly they may tend to be rather milder in the adolescence-limited group. Clearly, further research is needed to sort out the differences in risk factors between the adolescence-limited and life-course–persistent groups.

What the Nagin et al. (1995) findings did show, however, is an interesting pattern of adult behavior for the adolescence-limited group. Three features stood out. First, at age 18, these offenders appeared very similar in all respects to the high-level chronics. Not only was their level of self-reported offending high, but also they were equally likely to hold unskilled jobs, to be unemployed, and to show emotional instability. Second, by age 32, they were quite different in showing a stable employment record (that did not differ from the unconvicted) and a lack of official convictions. By all accounts, an impressive transformation had taken place. Third, the transformation was strikingly incomplete. Although not resulting in convictions, the adolescence-limited group were still engaging in crime (such as burglary, theft, and drunk driving) as well as such antisocial life-style habits as heavy drinking, using illicit drugs, and brawling. Nagin et al. (1995) interpreted their findings as showing that the adolescence-limited group, although still antisocial in style, were restricting their deviance to forms of behavior least likely to jeopardize their jobs and marriages, and to offenses with a low risk of detection (especially theft from employers). It could be said, flippantly, that it may be safer to marry an adolescence-limited offender than to employ him! (The findings are, so far, entirely restricted to males.)

The type of criminal career about which we know least is the variety that begins in adult life. Most longitudinal studies have shown that this applies to only some 10% of offenders (see Newman et al., 1996, for the Dunedin study findings with respect to the occasional adult onset of antisocial personality disorder); but, as noted in Chapter 5, some Scandinavian studies have found a much higher proportion. Clearly, this is a subgroup that requires more research attention than it has received to date (but see Farrington et al., 1998).

Care needs to be taken not to overinterpret the subgroup differences found in these criminal career studies. To some extent, the subgroup differences in career were built into the findings by the ways in which the subgroups were distinguished. Thus, the adolescence-limited group did not have convictions in adult life because that is how this group was defined. In order to test for true meaningful heterogeneity (as distinct from the variations that are bound to be found within any group), it would be necessary to show that the groups differed in ways *other than* levels of overall risk exposure. There are important indicators that this is probably the case, but the evidence so far is too fragmentary to warrant firm conclusions (see Chapter 5).

A further need is to study the careers of individuals who engage in recurrent major violence. As shown in Figure 10.3, aggravated assault stands out as differing on aggregate arrest data from robbery and burglary with respect to a somewhat older age for the peak and a much later age for the falloff. The general population epidemiological longitudinal studies are of limited value for the study of individual criminal careers of violent offenders, because those for whom violent crimes are a prominent feature are too few in number. Also, there is a problem in deciding whom to include, because so many seriously recidivist offenders commit

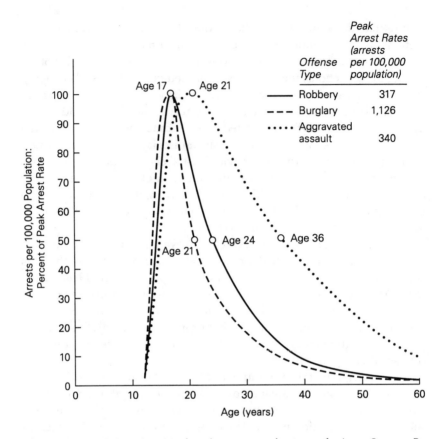

Figure 10.3. Variations in age of peak arrest rate by type of crime. *Source:* Reprinted with permission from A. Blumstein, J. Cohen, J. A. Roth, and C. A. Visher (Eds.), *Criminal Careers and Career Criminals.* Copyright 1986 by the National Academy of Sciences. Courtesy of the National Academy Press, Washington, DC.

some crimes of violence. Nevertheless, the data reviewed in Chapters 5 and 6 suggest that violent crime may to some extent be different in its origins and course. Further research is needed to determine whether, and to what extent, this is actually the case.

Delinquent Pathways

Criminal careers research has focused particularly on the transition from adolescence to adult life, but comparable issues need to be considered in relation to earlier age periods (Farrington, 1986a; Loeber et al., 1993, 1997). Several considerations need attention. Some behaviors involve a necessary series of steps for their progression. For example, with drug dependence it is necessary to start with use; this needs to proceed to regular heavy use; and this must be followed by the acquisition of psychological or chemical dependence. With respect to alcohol abuse, there is also a later stage of physical complications that can arise (cirrhosis of the liver, delirium tremens, etc.). It is not possible to start with the end point, and moreover the factors that influence different steps in the "career" progression are not the same (Robins, 1993; Robins et al., 1977). In the field of somatic disease, there are many progressions of this kind (Hay & Angold, 1993; Rutter et al., in press a).

Antisocial behavior does not fit this model in most respects. There are no crimes that cannot occur without previous offenses of a different kind. Nevertheless, it is possible that particular patterns of progression are characteristic and representative of different mechanisms. Also, there do seem to be some age-dependent (or life-stage–dependent) effects. Thus, although early hyperactivity predisposes to later antisocial behavior, the reverse does not seem to apply (Taylor et al., 1996). Also, family discord in childhood predisposes to antisocial behavior, but it does not lead to the onset of crime in adult life in individuals who have not shown antisocial behavior in childhood. Of course, the discord is not truly comparable at the two life phases; that in childhood concerns the parental home whereas that in adult life concerns the marital relationship. Nevertheless, this is not the whole story, because an unsupportive marriage to a deviant spouse *is* associated with a markedly increased tendency for antisocial behavior to continue (Quinton et al., 1993; Rutter et al., 1997b; Zoccolillo et al., 1992). In other words, marital discord is a risk factor for the perpetuation of antisocial behavior but not for its initiation in adult life. Developmental timing seems crucial.

Loeber and his colleagues (1993, 1997; Loeber & Hay, 1994) have focused on a somewhat different issue – namely, the progression along different pathways from more frequent milder antisocial behavior to less frequent but more severe criminal behavior (see Figure 10.4). Such a progression had been evident in other longitudinal studies, such as the National Youth Study (Elliott, 1994; Huizinga, 1995) and the Quebec longitudinal study (Le Blanc, Cote, & Loeber, 1991). Because meta-analyses had shown that antisocial behavior could be subdivided into overt, covert, and anti-authority problems (Frick et al., 1993; Loeber & Schmaling, 1985), Loeber chose to examine progression along these three supposedly separate pathways. It was argued that the "authority conflict" pathway started earliest and did so with stubborn behavior that was followed by defiance, which in turn led to authority avoidance as exemplified by truancy, staying out late, and running away. The "covert" pathway was said to begin

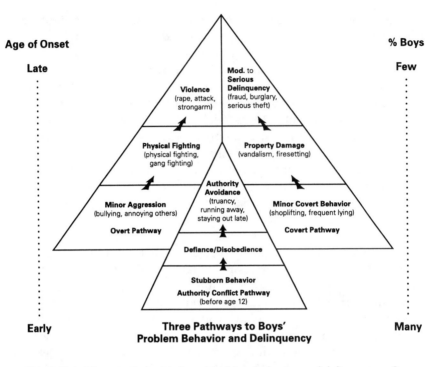

Figure 10.4. Three pathways to boys' problem behavior and delinquency. *Source:* R. Loeber and D. F. Hay, "Developmental approaches to aggression and conduct problems," in M. Rutter and D. F. Hay (Eds.), *Development through Life: A Handbook for Clinicians* (1997), by permission of Blackwell Science Ltd.

with behaviors such as lying and shoplifting, to move on to property damage (vandalism and setting fires), and to end with serious forms of delinquency such as stealing cars, breaking and entering property, selling drugs, and fraud. The "overt" pathway was thought to begin with bullying and annoying others, followed by physical fighting, and ending in violent crime.

Three rather separate issues need to be considered in relation to these ideas. First, the notion of progression derives from cross-sectional data on age trends; hence the first question is whether these progressions are confirmed at an individual level. In other words, what are the transitional probabilities over time of moving up rather than down the pathway, and of doing so to the next step rather than a later one? Also, how often do children enter the pathway in the middle, rather than at the postulated beginning? The findings from the Pittsburgh study are broadly in keeping with the pathways proposed, except that quite a few children entered the authority conflict pathway at what were supposed to be later steps. It was also noteworthy that coherence in progression was less evident with "experimenters" than "persisters," indicating that the pathway applied most clearly to those who continued in crime.

The second issue is whether the timing of the behavior is determined more by age or by prior behavior. Thus, for example, if someone begins to engage in antisocial behavior at age 16, do they enter the postulated pathway with behaviors that are typical of 16-year-olds or with behaviors that are characteristic of an earlier phase on the pathway (which necessarily will equate with those of younger children)? So far, this issue has not been addressed directly, although it is of some importance both theoretically and practically. It is certainly clear that it is possible for younger children to commit criminal acts that are more often undertaken by older individuals. Thus, although very uncommon, preadolescent children do occasionally kill (see Chapter 5). The limited available evidence suggests, however, that the act of homicide has almost always been preceded by other lesser forms of antisocial behavior. To that extent the pathways cannot be related strictly to age, but the role of age has not yet been adequately investigated.

The third issue concerns the extent to which the three proposed pathways are truly separate. The findings indicate that they are not; to a substantial extent, progression on one was accompanied by progression on one or both of the other two. However, overt antisocial behavior (meaning fighting and the like) was more likely to be followed by covert (stealing and property damage) than the other way around. On the whole, authority conflict tended to develop earliest. The implication is that, at least for persistent delinquents, interpersonal clashes with authority and with peers are common precursors of both acquisitive crime and violent crime. This is in keeping with the evidence reviewed in Chapter 6, which points to the role of social maladaptation in the origins of life-course–persistent delinquency. This is less the case with individuals who undergo a temporary phase of delinquency.

It is informative to study the ways in which individuals progress in their patterns of antisocial behavior, but the terminology of overt, covert, and authority conflict pathways suggests much more of a separateness than is the case. The challenge is to delineate the mechanisms that underlie the interconnections between different forms of antisocial behavior to more serious crime. Are the three facets of antisocial behavior outlined by Loeber et al. (1997) simply manifestations of the same underlying liability (the genetic evidence suggests that they may be – see Chapter 6), or are they subject to somewhat different influences, at least initially?

Perhaps the greater need is to focus on the possible differences in origins and course of life-course–persistent versus adolescence-limited antisocial behavior, or between persisters and experimenters (to use Loeber's terminology). As raised in Chapter 5, the question remains as to whether the more important differentiating feature is the degree of persistence or the age of onset of antisocial behavior. The Nagin et al. (1995) findings also force attention on the possible differences between persistence in major offending, persistence in antisocial life style, and persistence in social maladaption. The suggestion that there may be major changes in one of these domains without necessary substantial gains in the others has implications for the goals of intervention (see Chapters 11 and 12).

Socioemotional Functioning in Adult Life

Personality Disorder

The findings on social maladaption also focus attention on the need to consider the adult outcome for young offenders in relation to a broader range of socioemotional features than are encompassed by the concept of antisocial behavior. This need was highlighted more than three decades ago by the findings from Robins's (1966) long-term follow-up of children attending a child guidance clinic. As she commented: "Not only were antisocial children more often arrested and imprisoned as adults, as expected, but they were more mobile geographically, had more marital difficulties, poorer occupational and economic histories, impoverished social and organizational relationships, poor Armed Service records, excessive use of alcohol and, to some extent, even poorer physical health" (p. 68). The key findings are given in Table 10.1 because they illustrate vividly the immense range of difficulties in adult life and the very substantial degree of poor functioning with respect to work, marriage, and social relationships – a constellation of features summarized by Robins (1966) in terms of "sociopathy."

Her sample was based on child guidance clinic attenders, and it could be that the widespread socioemotional malfunction in adult life that she found in ex-patients would not apply to offenders in the general population. That does not, however, seem to be the case. The follow-up of Quinton and Rutter's (1988) sample of children reared in group foster homes ("children's homes," in U.K. terminology) found that those who showed antisocial behavior in childhood had a wide range of socioemotional and behavioral problems in adult life extending across work, marriage, and social relationships (Rutter, Quinton, & Hill, 1990b; Zoccolillo et al., 1992). Indeed, their findings indicate that pervasive social malfunction was more

Table 10.1. Adult Functioning of Individuals Showing Antisocial Behavior in Childhood

	Males		Females	
	Antisocial	**Controls**	**Antisocial**	**Controls**
Practically without friends	29%	7%	31%	8%
Divorced at least twice	15%	2%	23%	4%
Had children placed away from home	19%	0%	26%	11%
Currently unemployed	23%	2%	26%	6%
Alcohol problems in last three years	21%	6%	10%	0%
Received psychiatric in-patient care	17%	1%	14%	0%
Mean number of psychiatric symptoms	6.2	4.6	9.6	6.0

Source: Robins (1966).

often evident in adult life than in Robins's sample; this applied to the majority. What was characteristic was the *pervasiveness* of the malfunction. The antisocial individuals did not show an increase in problems that were confined to just one of these domains (e.g., marriage but not work and social relationships). The findings from other high-risk or socially disadvantaged samples have been closely comparable (Maughan, Pickles, & Quinton, 1995; Quinton et al., 1993). Although not patients, these too have been relatively deprived groups; it remains uncertain whether these findings apply to samples more representative of the general population. The follow-up to age 32 of Farrington's sample of inner London boys suggests that such findings probably do apply to inner-city socially disadvantaged groups, but also that the pervasively poor outcome applies primarily to highly persistent chronic offenders and not to those showing adolescence-limited delinquency (Farrington, 1995a,b; Nagin et al., 1995). Whether similar findings would apply to middle-class groups is more dubious (Jessor et al., 1991). Systematic follow-up studies to age 30 and older of antisocial youngsters living outside deprived inner-city areas are much needed.

In her 1966 book, Robins conceptualized this pattern of pervasive social malfunction as a highly persistent personality disorder that started in childhood and continued through adult life. Of all the diagnostic categories in psychiatry, the concept of "personality disorder" has proved one of the most difficult to pin down (Rutter, 1987b). Follow-up studies of adult psychiatric patients have shown that it exhibits coherence and reliability over time, and that it is not just an equivalent of chronic symptomatology (Quinton, Gulliver, & Rutter, 1995). The concept of personality disorder has considerable predictive validity and is associated with a substantial likelihood of continuing social malfunction. On the other hand, it is not an unchanging feature – despite the connotations of the adjective "personality." We consider next the few findings on factors that seem to bring about change.

Drug and Alcohol Problems

The relatively high frequency in adult life of drug and alcohol problems in individuals who exhibited antisocial behavior or who received criminal convictions in childhood or adolescence does appear to be a general finding (Collins, 1986; McCord & McCord, 1960; Robins, 1986; Robins & McEvoy, 1990; Robins & Price, 1991; Sampson & Laub, 1993; Vaillant, 1983; Wish & Johnson, 1986). Both cross-sectional and longitudinal analyses indicate that about half the variance in alcohol and in illicit drug use derives from an underlying general deviance liability that includes delinquency, but about half stems from more behavior-specific influences (Osgood et al., 1988). As discussed in Chapter 6, one key issue is whether the use of drugs and alcohol plays a role in the perpetuation of antisocial behavior and in the level of generalized social malfunction. We concluded that, to a substantial extent, both derived from the same socially deviant life style but that, after taking this into account, the use of drugs and alcohol did make the continuation in crime somewhat more likely and did predispose to employment instability and to a broader pattern of social difficulties.

Emotional Disturbance

What has been more unexpected in the follow-up findings has been the increased rate in antisocial individuals of emotional disturbance, including anxiety and depressive disorders. This has been found in all the general population epidemiological and longitudinal studies that have examined the matter (Achenbach et al., 1995; Bardone et al., 1996; Feehan, McGee, & Williams, 1993; Ferdinand & Verhulst, 1995; Lewinsohn, Rohde, & Seeley, 1995; Rutter, 1991; Rutter et al., 1997b), as well as in the ECA retrospective study (Robins, 1986; Robins & Price, 1991). Because there is quite a strong association between depression and conduct problems in childhood, it might be supposed that the emotional disturbance in adult life is no more than a reflection of the earlier comorbidity. However, that does not provide the whole explanation. Using data from the British National Child Development Study, Rutter (1991; Rutter et al., 1997b) found that individuals with conduct problems (but no emotional disturbance) in childhood still had an increased rate of anxiety and depressive symptoms at age 23. This was true for both males and females.

Studies of clinic samples have shown the same pattern but have been additionally informative in showing that the main risk is for chronic low-level depressive disorders, often associated with social impairment, but not bipolar features (i.e., not the manic mood swings) or the vegetative symptoms (such as psychomotor retardation) that are characteristic of the most severe forms of affective disorder (Rutter et al., 1994).

The published analyses undertaken so far have not yet determined the causal mechanisms responsible for the increased risk of emotional disturbance in adult life. It is likely, however, that these involve aspects of the antisocial life style and its effects on people's overall social situation. Robins (1978) noted that the job troubles, poor marital relationships, and falling out with friends that were such a prominent part of the circumstances at follow-up could function as stressors or adversities predisposing to further mental disorder. Champion, Goodall, and Rutter (1995) tested this more directly in their follow-up of a community sample first seen at age 10 and then reassessed at age 28. Antisocial behavior in childhood was followed by a severalfold increase in the likelihood of both acute and lasting severely negative events, and in experiences of a kind shown by Brown and Harris (1978) to provoke the onset of depressive disorders. In a real sense, the disturbed interpersonal relationships and unstable work pattern were both part of a continuing pattern of disturbed behavior *and* a source of serious stress. Their role in leading to emotional disturbance in adult life in chronic offenders has not been established, but it seems likely that they are implicated to some degree.

Suicidal Behavior

Follow-up studies have also shown that antisocial behavior in childhood is followed by a substantial increase in the risk for suicidal behavior. Thus, Achenbach et al. (1995) found that aggressive behavior in boys and delinquent behavior in girls were significantly associated with an increased risk for suicidal behavior during the subsequent three years. Harrington et al. (1993), in their follow-up of a child psychiatric clinic sample through the mean age of 32, showed that the increased risk for suicidal behavior was not due to the occurrence in adult life of major depressive disorders (although these were responsible for the increased suicidal risk in individuals who had shown depressive problems in childhood). It seemed that the route to suicidal behavior probably lay in the impulsive, antisocial life style.

It is noteworthy, too, that there is a substantial rate of suicide among offenders within the first month of their going to prison (Liebling, 1992). Ninety percent of these suicides are by hanging.

Cross-sectional data also suggest that drug use may be implicated in part. In their study of Oregon adolescents, Lewinsohn et al. (1995) found that attempted suicide had occurred at some time in the past in only 1.5% of those without disorder but in 4.7% of those with a "pure" disruptive behavior disorder (i.e., with no other associated problems) and in 33.3% of those who had *both* disruptive behavior and substance use problems. Gould, Shaffer, and Davies's (1990) study of 173 suicides in young people (under age 20) similarly showed that – in males but not females – substance abuse and antisocial behavior (particularly substance abuse) were associated. Hawton et al. (1993), in their study of completed suicide, also showed that substance abuse was a strong predictor (within a sample who had previously attempted suicide).

It appears, therefore, that although antisocial behavior is associated with an increased risk of suicidal behavior, probably the risk arises more from the accompanying substance abuse than from the offending per se. However, the matter warrants further study in order to determine the extent to which that is so.

Influential Experiences in Adult Life

Cumulative Continuity and Accentuation Effects

In Chapters 7 and 8 we discussed the evidence that life experiences influenced the development and persistence of antisocial behavior. It was noted that several different kinds of ongoing social experience could serve either to perpetuate or to cut short antisocial behavior. Thus, longitudinal data were instrumental in demonstrating that a radical change in social environment could result in important behavioral changes. This was evident, for example, in the effects of a deviant or prosocial peer group, unemployment, a move away from a high-crime area, the quality of schooling, and taking alcohol or drugs. Three main general points derive from the findings. First, all the effects were found in relation to experiences with quite a pervasive impact. Thus, influences were found for schooling, peer groups, and the areas in which people lived. It is quite unusual for there to be any significant influence on behavioral development from acute, short-lived events or experiences that do not have long-term consequences. A substantial literature has developed on the impact of acute life events as powerful provoking agents for the onset of a psychiatric disorder (Brown & Harris, 1978; Goodyer, 1990). At first sight, this would seem to contradict the statement about the negligible effects of acute events but, in reality, it does not. To begin with, the research evidence has been consistent in showing that the provoking effect requires the event to carry long-term threat. Thus, events such as parental loss or divorce serve to precipitate disorder whereas events such as a dogbite or being involved in an accident rarely do so. Also, the greatest effects seem to derive from acute events that are closely connected with, or derive from, some more chronic psychosocial adversity (Sandberg et al., 1993). In addition, the main evidence concerns effects on the *timing* of onset of disorder rather than its persistence over time or individual differences in lifetime liability.

The importance of long-term implications is well illustrated by the findings on unusually early menarche in females from Stattin and Magnusson's (1990) Swedish longitudinal study. This led to an increase in norm-breaking behavior and in minor alcohol problems (such as drunkenness), which came about as a result of the girls joining an older, more deviant, peer group. The effects at the time were quite substantial but they had entirely dissipated by adult life, presumably because the peer groups and other socializing influences changed over the intervening time period. However, another effect through the same peer group route was an increased likelihood of dropping out of, or failing to continue with, education. Those effects *did* persist, so that early-maturing girls' educational qualifications in early adult life were, on average, lower than those of their normally maturing contemporaries. Having ceased schooling, a positive move in order to obtain later re-entry was required in order to regain their educational position. Although such re-entry was possible, it was not easy and few girls achieved it. The effects persisted, not because of any lasting "internal" change in the girls' personalities, but rather because their ongoing life circumstances and opportunities had been altered.

The second main general point to be derived from examining experiences in childhood and adolescence is that, as discussed in Chapter 6 and earlier in this chapter, many important experiences are influenced by people's own behavior. Antisocial individuals generate and perpetuate coercive cycles of interchange in their own families (see Chapter 7); by falling out with friends they jeopardize the availability of social support; by marrying impulsively someone from their own deviant peer group they make marital discord and breakdown more likely; and by having babies in their teens they cut short their career opportunities.

The third point is that, on the whole, these person–environment effects, when stemming from antisocial behavior, tend to lead to further experiences of an adverse kind that are likely to foster the continuation of the antisocial behavior. This is particularly the case because adverse experiences tend to have their greatest effect on those who are most vulnerable owing to their genetic background, previous adverse experiences, or previously established deviant behavior. In this way, adverse experiences, on the whole, provide an "accentuation effect" that further reinforces and perpetuates pre-existing behavioral deviance (Caspi & Moffitt, 1993). This leads to what Caspi and Moffitt (1995) have termed "cumulative continuity." In other words, the substantial continuity in antisocial behavior that has been found does not necessarily reflect a fixed individual trait; rather, it derives from the cumulative effect of an interplay between predisposing individual characteristics and risk experiences.

In their reanalysis of the Gluecks' (1950) follow-up study data, Sampson and Laub (1993) produced evidence of several experiences that had accentuating or perpetuating effects of this kind. This applied, for example, to incarceration and alcohol abuse – both of which had (adverse) effects on employment and hence on antisocial behavior. It might be assumed, because the antisocial individuals brought about these experiences through their own behavior, that the supposed effects were artefactual and represented no more than unmeasured aspects of their underlying antisocial liability. Undoubtedly, that could be the case with experiences of this kind. Many apparent changes in behavior reflect little more than measurement error (Fergusson et al., 1995a; 1996a,b). Nevertheless, as discussed in Chapter 7, there is a range of statistical techniques available to take account of measurement error and of persistent unobserved (unmeasured) behavioral heterogeneity among individuals (Nagin & Paternoster, 1991; Pickles & Rutter, 1991; Sampson & Laub, 1993; Zoccolillo et al., 1992). These were applied to the Gluecks' data, and it was clear that the experiences had made a difference even when full account was taken of measurement error and of the individuals' previous behavior and prior risk experiences. Adverse experiences can and do accentuate and perpetuate antisocial behavior.

In the past, there has often been an implicit assumption that complete stability in behavior is the norm and that only the changes need to be explained. Of course, this cannot possibly be the case (Rutter, 1994b, 1996; Rutter & Rutter, 1993). Development is all about change; just consider how the physique of an adult differs from that of a baby. *Both* continuity and discontinuity, stability and change, are to be expected, and both must

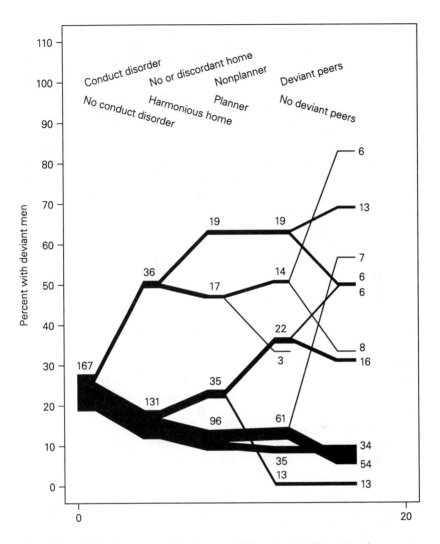

Figure 10.5. Paths of women to deviant men. *Note:* For dividing paths, frequencies are given by numbers and line width. *Source:* D. Quinton, A. Pickles, B. Maughan, and M. Rutter, "Partners, peers and pathways: Assortative pairing and continuities in conduct disorder," *Devlopment and Psychopathology 5* (1993), reprinted with the permission of Cambridge University Press.

be explained (Hagan, 1991; Sampson & Laub, 1993). Moreover, just as experiences may increase stability, so genetic effects may program change.

Indirect chain effects are frequently operative. Figure 10.5 illustrates the point with findings from Quinton et al.'s (1993) follow-up study of girls in inner London. The outcome being considered in the figure is having a deviant marriage partner. Starting from the left of the figure, it is evident that children with conduct problems have a substantially increased risk of having such a partner. Moving to the right, it is evident that this risk is increased if they experience family discord and decreased if they do not. The thickness of the lines on the figure reflects the numbers involved on each path. It is clear that, at each point, the at-risk group is more likely (usually much more likely) to have a further risk experience. Moving again to the right, the role of a "planning" disposition in relation to life choices is evident. As found in other studies (Clausen, 1991, 1993; Shanahan, Elder, & Meich, 1997), a planful and considered approach to decisions on marriage, careers, and so forth made adverse experiences less likely. Antisocial individuals from adverse family backgrounds were particularly unlikely to exhibit planning; on the whole, they felt a lack of control over their lives and so acted impulsively without looking ahead to likely long-term consequences. As a result, amongst other things, they were more likely to become part of a deviant peer group. Being part of such a group in turn made it more likely that they would marry a deviant man (meaning one who showed antisocial behavior and/or substance abuse problems). The cumulative effect of this indirect chain of risk and protective experiences can be great. At one extreme, of those with adversities all along the line, over two thirds had a deviant partner; at the other extreme, of those who had none of the risk factors, only about one in twenty had a deviant partner. It is in this manner that cumulative continuities build up.

Note, however, that there is a reverse side of the same coin. Although, for the most part, one adversity led to another in an accentuating chain effect, some antisocial individuals with high-risk backgrounds had positive experiences. Conversely, some non-antisocial individuals from a low-risk background ended up in a deviant peer group; in the few cases where that happened, there was a much increased chance that they would have a deviant partner. In these circumstances, "turning point" effects could arise (Pickles & Rutter, 1991; Rutter, 1996; Sampson & Laub, 1993); we need now to consider their operation.

Turning-Point Effects

The methodological issues that need attention in testing for turning-point effects are the same as those noted for accentuation effects. It is particularly important to ensure that the apparent changes in behavior are not in reality due to the individuals being less antisocial initially or having less severe or less prolonged risk experiences. That is the first research

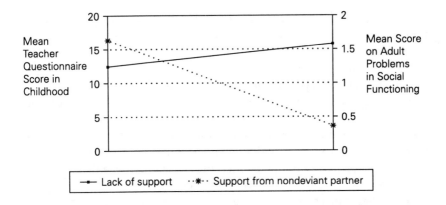

Figure 10.6. Turning-point effect of partner in females with antisocial behavior in childhood. *Source:* 1996 data analysis by Pickles, reported in Rutter et al. (1997b). Reprinted from *Motivation and Delinquency* (volume 44 of the Nebraska Symposium on Motivation). © 1997 by the University of Nebraska Press.

challenge to be met. The second is to account for the occasions by which, against the odds, antisocial individuals had the protective turning-point experiences. The third challenge is to determine the mechanism by which the turning point operated.

There are, as yet, few turning-point experiences that have been investigated in this way, and we lack the data to draw conclusions on their general importance. Still, those that have been studied indicate what can happen and serve to demonstrate the reality of change as a result of experiences in adult life. We first take a supportive, harmonious marriage to a nondeviant spouse and then Army experience as two examples for which effects have been independently replicated.

The longitudinal studies of Quinton and Rutter provide the example of the turning point of a supportive marriage (Pickles & Rutter, 1991; Quinton et al., 1993; Rutter et al., 1997b; Zoccolillo et al., 1992). Figure 10.6 illustrates the effect in a subgroup of individuals who showed antisocial behavior in childhood. Those who did and those who did not have a supportive nondeviant partner (within the antisocial group) did not differ with respect to their antisocial behavior in childhood. They did, however, differ markedly in their level of antisocial behavior in adult life. Those who lacked a supportive partner tended to continue with their antisocial activities, whereas those with marital support showed a marked drop in their level of antisocial behavior. Multivariate analyses that took account of measurement error confirmed the reality of this effect. As already noted, the quality of marriage made no difference to those not already showing antisocial behavior. Marital discord was not a risk factor for the new development of antisocial behavior in adult life, but marital harmony was a protective factor in those already antisocial, making it *less* likely that antisocial activities would continue.

The finding was replicated in Sampson & Laub's (1993) analysis of the Gluecks' data set. Their initial analyses used multivariate approaches in which it was shown that the statistical interaction between a harmonious marriage and nonpersistence of crime through early adult life was *not* a function of the individuals' prior behavior or life circumstances (or measurement error). The finding justified the causal inference that a "good" marriage predisposed to desistance from crime. Laub et al. (1998) then took the testing of a causal effect further by applying a dynamic statistical model developed by Nagin and Land (1993), using yearly longitudinal data to study within-individual change over time. Four main findings provide a compelling case for the validity of the causal inference. First, there was major heterogeneity in pattern of criminal career even within a group of high-risk juvenile offenders. Second, the family and individual variables that predict entry into crime quite well were *not* good predictors of desistance from crime in adult life. Third, desistance was strongly associated with both a cohesive marriage and job stability. This effect was evident both in a comparison with those who had not married and with those whose marriages lacked cohesion or failed to last. Fourth, the magnitude of effects of an early harmonious marriage increased with time.

The finding that a cohesive marriage and stable employment were both associated with desistance from crime was used to argue that the key mediating mechanism might be the informal controls implicit in adult social bonds. Other mechanisms, however, need also to be considered. Both a harmonious marriage and stable employment are likely to involve a change in the person's peer group and social network. As discussed in Chapter 7, such a change may be important. Involvement in work and family activities are likely also to reduce the opportunities for crime. In addition, internal cognition may also play a role. It is possible, for example, that people's images of themselves, their views of life opportunities, and their attitudes and expectations may change as a result of their adult experiences. Whatever the mediating mechanisms prove to be, it would be unwise to assume that the person's underlying antisocial propensities have been permanently altered. The drop in criminal activities associated with a move to somewhere outside inner London (Osborn, 1980), as well as the drop within adult life found with adolescence-limited antisocial behavior (Nagin et al., 1995) in Farrington's (1995a) longitudinal study of inner London boys, took place in the context of a *continuing* antisocial lifestyle. It was also found that marital separations were followed by somewhat increased levels of offending (Farrington & West, 1995), suggesting that the effects may be time-limited and context-dependent.

The question of how it was that some antisocial individuals succeeded in having a harmonious supportive marriage to a nondeviant spouse is an important one. We have already noted the positive effect of a prosocial peer group. Its benefits are likely to come both from the greater availability of nondeviant individuals who constitute possible partners and from changes in attitudes and expectations. Postponing marriage (or cohabitation) until the 20s helped (Pickles & Rutter, 1991), presumably because that, too, increased the range of possible nondeviant partners and because marital breakdown is less likely for marriages made after the teenage years. Positive school experiences were also important in making a planning tendency more likely (Quinton & Rutter, 1988). In short, it was not simply chance that enabled some antisocial individuals to make harmonious marriages to nondeviant individuals. A series of influences along the life course predisposed to developmental continuity.

The second replicated effect is provided by military experiences for youths from a disadvantaged background. This may seem an implausible turning-point experience, but it was shown by Elder (1986) in data from the California longitudinal studies, and it was confirmed by Sampson & Laub (1996) in the Gluecks' longitudinal study data on some 1,000 boys. The findings from these two very different samples are remarkably similar. Sampson and Laub (1996) showed that the benefits particularly applied to delinquents from a high-risk background who entered the Army at an early age, before they had become established in work and marriage. The effects held up in analyses that took into account a wide range of risk features, including childhood antisocial behavior. The reality of the effects is supported by the demonstration that the benefits were largely mediated by on-the-job training and further educational opportunities provided by the GI bill. Sampson and Laub (1996) also suggested that overseas duty may have helped in cutting off past social disadvantages and criminal stigmatization, as well as by the provision of experiences that broadened perspectives and opened up horizons. Elder's (1986) findings also suggested that the postponement of marriage that tended to accompany military service may have been an additional mediator, because it made it more likely that the marriage partner would not be similarly deviant and disadvantaged.

It is evident that it was not going into the Army per se that was important, but rather the benefits that Army service in that era happened to bring to those individuals. As Sampson and Laub (1996) pointed out, it is not likely that the same would apply in the very different circumstances of today. The message does not lie in the specifics but rather in the likely situations in which turning-point effects may occur. Putting together the (rather slender) findings in both childhood and adult life, Rutter (1996) suggested that three broad categories of experience might constitute those that could offer the potential to be beneficial turning points: (i) those that open up new opportunities; (ii) those that result in radical environmental change (perhaps especially in terms of close relationships); and (iii) those that have marked positive effects on self-esteem and self-efficacy or on the views and expectations of others.

Conclusions

Longitudinal studies have been crucially important in showing that:

(1) persistent recidivist offending often has its roots in disruptive behavior first manifest during the preschool years;

(2) there are important differences between adolescence-limited and life-course–persistent antisocial behavior;

(3) persistent antisocial behavior in childhood frequently results in pervasive socioemotional and behavioral malfunction in adult life;

(4) experiences in adult life (as well as in childhood) can make an important impact (for better or worse) on antisocial behavior; and

(5) it is important to distinguish between the proportion of individuals participating in antisocial behavior and the level of offending in those who are engaged in crime.

The adult outcome findings indicate that it is not only crime that may continue from childhood into adult life, but also that this is often accompanied by a wide range of other difficulties in social and occupational functioning and by an increased rate of emotional disturbance, suicidal behavior, and abuse of drugs or alcohol. However, the longitudinal study results also show that people's life experiences play a contributory role in the forces that determine whether problems continue or cease. People's own behavior influences the experiences that they have, and it is usual for these to reinforce and perpetuate pre-existing behavioral tendencies. Stability of behavior is brought about by the cumulative continuity of experiences having accentuating effects, as well as by coherence in individual characteristics and the biological influences on them. Yet development comprises both stability and change, continuity and discontinuity. Positive experiences in childhood and in adult life both can influence social functioning in a beneficial way. Probably, beneficial turning points are most likely to operate when experiences open up opportunities, result in radical environmental change, or bring about major changes in self-concept. The findings have also been consistent in showing that there can be major changes in offending without there necessarily being equally marked changes in overall antisocial lifestyle. Moreover, although the benefits may be marked, they may also be time-limited and context-dependent. This conclusion has implications for the ways in which prevention and intervention are considered – the topic of the next two chapters.

CHAPTER 10 – SUMMARY OF MAIN POINTS

❑ Several of the large longitudinal studies have now collected data beyond the teenage years, which means that important data about *lifespan development and criminal careers* have been collected. These allow us to be a little clearer about persistence and desistance and about different patterns of involvement.

❑ Signals indicating the more serious and persistent forms of antisocial behavior can be detected as early as age 3 in the form of oppositional and hyperactive behavior. This is not so obviously the case for adolescence-limited behavior – indeed, *different risk factors and outcomes* are associated with different types of antisocial behavior.

❑ There are *continuities and discontinuities* in the development of antisocial behavior. The long-term sequelae of early and persistent behavior problems in childhood can be quite broad in adulthood, leading to pervasive difficulties in psychosocial functioning and to criminal offending.

❑ Experiences continue to be important, and *nothing is cast in stone*. Life events, turning points, and transition periods can all play a part in whether antisocial behavior continues or ceases.

11 | Prevention and Intervention I

Principles and Concepts of Application at the Predelinquency Phase

During the last two decades, there has been a sea change in the tone of reviews of what can be achieved by interventions to prevent or reduce crime. During the 1970s there was an atmosphere of pessimism, and rather determined negativity, about the chances of any intervention having any effect (Brody, 1976; Martinson, 1974; Wright & Dixon, 1977). This has now been replaced by an air of cautious optimism (Farrington, 1996; Gendreau & Ross, 1980; Graham & Bennett, 1995; Lipsey, 1992, 1995; Lösel, 1995a,b; McGuire & Priestley, 1995; Mulvey, Arthur, & Reppucci, 1993; Palmer, 1991; Thornton, 1987). In part, this change has derived from more systematic, sophisticated, and quantitative reanalyses of the same early studies that gave rise to the initial despair. To a greater extent, however, it reflects the development of more effective methods of intervention that are closely linked with advances in understanding the complex causal processes that underlie antisocial behavior. Before examining the evidence relevant to the question of the extent to which the present guarded optimism is justified, we need to consider some of the key conceptual and methodological issues. Such background issues as they apply to research into antisocial behavior generally were discussed in Chapters 2 and 3; here we focus on those that apply specifically to evaluations of prevention and intervention strategies.

Concepts and Measures

How Much Is Open to Change?

A range of studies in the 1970s had shown the extent to which individual differences in antisocial behavior persisted from childhood into adult life (e.g., Olweus, 1979; Robins, 1978). The findings tended to create an impression of a highly stable trait or disorder that might well be rather resistant to change. Since then, the evidence in support of strong temporal continuity in individual differences has, if anything, grown stronger (see Chapter 10). It has also been accompanied by a growing appreciation that biological factors may well play an important role in such individual differences in antisocial liability (see Chapter 6). Nevertheless, despite this recognition, several different types of evidence have also led to an acceptance that antisocial behavior *is* modifiable, and that this modifiability is not at all contradicted by evidence on relatively strong consistency over time with respect to individual differences.

First, several studies have shown that individuals may give up crime despite persisting with a life style that reflects an antisocial tendency (see Chapter 10). For example, this was apparent in the case of the inner London boys in West and Farrington's longitudinal study who showed a marked drop in criminal activities when they moved out of the inner city (Osborn, 1980). Second, even with the individuals showing one of the most persistent subtypes of antisocial behavior – namely, that beginning unusually early in childhood – about half do *not* persist (see Chapter 5). The same applies to behavior associated with hyperactivity; the evidence indicates that, to a large extent, the persistence or nonpersistence is a function of parent–child relationships (see Chapters 5 and 6). Third, naturalistic longitudinal studies have shown that the likelihood of individuals continuing to engage in antisocial activities is influenced by their life experiences (see Chapters 7 and 10). This effect has been found with peer group influences in adolescence and also with the stability of employment and the quality of marriage in adult life. If individuals from a high-risk background encounter unusually positive environments, there can be a turning-point effect that makes a real difference (Rutter, 1996). Fourth, as discussed in Chapter 4, the overall rate of crime has risen severalfold over the last 50 years, a rise so marked and rapid that it can only be due to some impact of the environment. Clearly, if society has been so spectacularly successful in causing the level of crime to increase, there must be the potential for the right sort of interventions to be equally effective in causing it to decrease! For all these reasons, there is clear justification for an expectation that crime is modifiable; the challenge is to determine the appropriate means of bringing about the desired changes.

Causal Models

This hopeful expectation has been paralleled by the realization that effective strategies of prevention or remediation need to be developed on the basis of what is known about the causes of crime, both with respect to its initiation and its persistence. That basis was lacking in some of the early programs. For example, some focused almost exclusively on behavioral control in residential settings. It proved possible to achieve success in those settings; the problem lay in the lack of generalization to the communities to which the offenders then returned (Rutter & Giller, 1983).

But, most crucially, developments in preventive and intervention strategies have been accompanied by radical changes in the prevailing models of the causal processes leading to antisocial behavior (see, e.g., Andrews, 1995; Farrington, 1995a,b; Hawkins & Catalano, 1992; Patterson, DeBaryshe, & Ramsey, 1989; Rutter et al., 1997b; Thornberry et al., 1995; Yoshikawa, 1994).

Notions that the origins of crime could be reduced to one basic mechanism have died away as the empirical evidence made it clear that such notions were untenable. As discussed in earlier chapters, multiple factors are involved; they interact in complex ways; and their relative impact varies across different links of the causal chain as well as according to the individual phases of development. On the other hand, it would be quite mistaken to view causation as an unanalyzable "soup" – a mixture of innumerable risk and protective factors in combinations that are unique to each individual.

As discussed in Chapter 5, antisocial behavior is heterogenous; although the same risk and protective factors apply in some degree to most varieties of crime, their relative importance varies considerably. One key shift of emphasis in models of causation concerns the role of individual characteristics. It is now appreciated that criminal acts constitute one set of elements in a broader range of antisocial behaviors that may include (in varying mixtures) risk-taking activities (such as climbing on roofs or playing on railway lines in early childhood and gambling, dangerous driving, or unsafe sex in later adolescence); confrontational aggressive behavior (fighting, bullying, and the like); anti-authority activities (vandalism, defiance, and disruptive behaviors of various kinds); unwise use or abuse of drugs and alcohol; and illegal acquisitive behaviors (stealing, fraud, etc.). It is also recognized that, in many (but far from all) instances, the roots of such behavior lie in early childhood (see Chapter 10) – even though the the age of criminal responsibility in most countries is not until late childhood or early adolescence (in some countries even later – see Chapter 3). The two implications for prevention are obvious: (i) the need to focus on a much broader range of behaviors than illegal acts; and (ii) the desirability of intervening in early childhood, rather than leaving it until adolescence when crime reaches its peak.

It would be wrong, however, to view the causal process as simply the gradual emergence of an antisocial life style. Figure 11.1 presents a schematic representation, derived from Rutter et al. (1997b), of some of the key elements that come together in the various mechanisms involved. The causal chain logically needs to begin with individual liability, in view of the evidence that people vary in their propensity to engage in antisocial

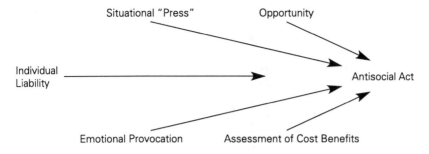

Figure 11.1. Causal scheme for processes leading to crime.

behavior. In part, this liability needs to be considered in terms of behavioral risk characteristics such as impulsivity, novelty seeking, or aggressiveness; of variations in reactivity to environmental adversities; of learned behavioral patterns; of styles in the cognitive processing of experiences (e.g., the tendency to attribute hostile intent); of a lack of status attributes (such as high IQ or educational achievement, an esteemed social position, or admired social qualities); and of a social milieu that provides an acceptability for antisocial activities (as through peer group mores, media influences, and social context). Equally, however, individual liability needs to incorporate what is known about features that inhibit antisocial behavior, because these may serve as positive target features for preventive measures (see Figure 11.2). Such features include overarching values or attitudes (such as a commitment to societal values and to long-term goals); external constraints (such as those provided by a prosocial peer group, parental monitoring, or the availability of nondelinquent rewards); and personal features (high anxiety and responsivity to stress, empathy and concern for others, well-developed internal controls, or effective social problem solving).

This listing of risk and protective factors (see Figure 11.3) serves to emphasize that the domains of influence on an individual's antisocial liability span the external arenas of family, school, and peer group as well as the internal qualities of social problem solving or coping, academic achievement, and the cognitive processing of experiences. Nonetheless, the causal chain leading to the commitment of some antisocial act needs to be extended far beyond individual differences in antisocial liability or propensity. For some sorts of antisocial acts, emotion-provoking features may be influential. These include situations predisposing to feelings of anger, frustration, or resentment – or to a self-perceived need for status, power, or material resources – together with a context that fails to provide alternative means of responding to these emotions or needs.

Values/Attitudes
Commitment to Societal Values
Long-Term Goals & Planning

Personal Features
Anxiety & Responsivity to Stress
Empathy for Others
Internal Controls
Effective Social Problem Solving

External Constraints
Surveillance/Monitoring by Others
Availability of Nondelinquent Rewards
Prosocial Peer Group

Figure 11.2. Features inhibiting antisocial behavior.

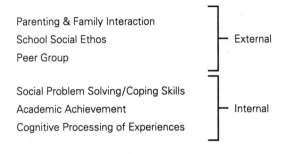

Figure 11.3. Domains of influence on behavior.

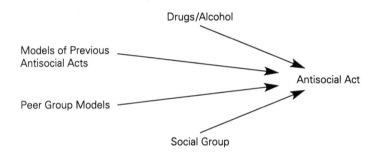

Figure 11.4. Immediate disinhibition effects.

Even given provocation, whether or not antisocial activities occur will be greatly influenced by the extent to which the overall social situation either provides a perceived "press" for antisocial behavior or, alternatively, an inhibiting effect on its occurrence. At an individual level, *disinhi-bition* may be provided by the taking of drugs or alcohol; at a target level, by the evidence of previous antisocial acts (e.g., a building with broken windows is much more likely to be vandalized), by the models of antisocial behavior provided by others in the peer group, and by the mores of the overall social group of which the individual is part – either for the moment (as in a football crowd or a protest rally) or over time (see Figure 11.4).

Opportunities for crime are also critical. As Cohen and Felson (1979) put it, crimes occur when there is the conjunction of a likely offender, a suitable target, and the absence of a capable guardian against crime. This may be summarized (see Figure 11.5) in terms of an accessible target (e.g., goods to steal on display or a car left unlocked and unattended); a lack of

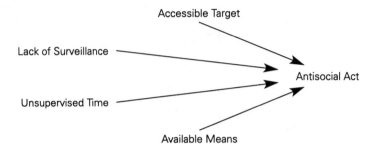

Accessible Target

Lack of Surveillance

Antisocial Act

Unsupervised Time

Available Means

Figure 11.5. Opportunity features.

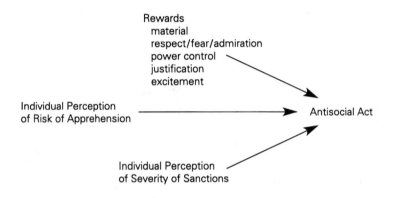

Rewards
  material
  respect/fear/admiration
  power control
  justification
  excitement

Individual Perception
of Risk of Apprehension   Antisocial Act

Individual Perception
of Severity of Sanctions

Figure 11.6. Perception of cost.

surveillance (e.g., nobody in the vicinity or a public area over which no one feels a sense of responsibility); unsupervised time (as when someone is truanting or unemployed); and available means (e.g., knowing how to break into a house and having the implements needed to do so). An appreciation of the importance of opportunities has led to the conceptualization and evaluation of a range of different situational crime prevention measures (Clarke, 1992, 1995).

Finally, whether or not someone commits a crime will be influenced by their *perception* of the costs and benefits involved (see Figure 11.6). Note that the crucial issue is not the *actual* cost–benefit tradeoff but rather the person's own evaluation of that tradeoff – however misguided, mistaken, or biased that may be. On the benefit side there are perceived rewards with respect to material gain, the respect, fear, or admiration of others, exertion of power, excitement of delinquent activities, and feelings of justification.

On the cost side, the individual needs to consider both the likelihood of getting caught and the severity of the likely sanctions if caught.

In this chapter and the next, we examine how these different elements of the causal processes leading to antisocial acts have led to a range of preventive and interventive strategies – in this chapter with respect to those operating at a predelinquent phase, and in Chapter 12 for those impinging on delinquency as such. First, however, it is necessary to consider some of the key advances in the field of evaluation.

Evaluation

Actors or Their Acts

The overall goal, of course, is to reduce crime, but this objective may involve three rather different aims. First, the intention may be to target individuals with the aim of either preventing them from becoming engaged in crime or of causing them to desist from crime. The aim here is thus *within-individual behavioral change* in the targeted persons. Second, the focus may be on groups of people with the hope of reducing the overall level of crime within that group. Thus, the focus might be on school classes. As with the first aim, the target concerns people but the difference lies in the fact that the outcome is concerned with the *aggregate level* of crime, rather than with the actions or behavior of particular individuals. Third, the focus may be on criminal acts rather than offenders. Thus, the target may be a reduction in the vandalism of telephone boxes, or in the frequency of burglary on a particular housing estate. The outcome, in these cases, concerns the *number of criminal acts*, rather than the number of offenders as in the second type of objective.

With both of the first two aims, it has proved important to consider a range of measures of crime. With respect to individuals, many of the earlier studies confined attention to the question of whether or not the individual had committed any crime during the period of follow-up studied. This approach proved to be much too crude, especially given the high base rate of crime in the general population. Measures were therefore extended to cover the time to first crime following the intervention, the frequency of crime per unit time, and the severity of crimes committed. Similarly, the aggregate level measures were extended to the number and severity of crimes.

Reliance on official crime records has all the usual limitations discussed in Chapter 3. In addition, however, there is the possibility that the intervention may have increased police surveillance with the consequence of a greater likelihood of apprehension for the same level of crime. Accordingly, studies have increasingly used self-report measures and, with respect to young people, parent and teacher questionnaires. These assessments have the advantage over official records of covering a wider range of antisocial activities that may well be relevant for the evaluation of the efficacy of interventions. Two tendencies with repeat measures have proved troublesome. First, there is a systematic tendency for questionnaire and interview scores to drop with repeated measures (Boyle et al., 1997). Second, interventions may sometimes lead parents and teachers to be more alert to the young people's disruptive behavior and to monitor their activities more closely (Tremblay et al., 1992) and may also make the children more aware of such behavior in their peers (Smith & Sharp, 1994); this may lead to an artefactual elevation of scores. It is clear from all the evidence that the use of multiple methods of measures is desirable, although there are still unresolved problems on how best to combine them (Rutter, 1997d).

Randomized Controlled Trials

In the medical arena, randomized controlled trials (RCTs) have come to be accepted as providing the best means of evaluating the efficacy of any treatment. Their principles are equally applicable in the field of antisocial behavior (Farrington, 1983, 1997c; Sherman, 1992). The first basic need is for comparison with some group *not* receiving the intervention. This is crucial because human behavior varies for a host of different reasons and, without a comparison, there is no means by which to determine whether or not any changes are a result of the intervention. A key concern, however, must be the comparability of the two groups (i.e., those receiving versus not receiving the intervention). Randomization is the only really satisfactory means of avoiding selective bias deriving from the qualities of the individuals either volunteering for the intervention or being selected for it by those providing the intervention. Nevertheless, on its own, randomization does not guarantee that the groups to be compared will be equivalent. Indeed, it is certain that some differences will arise solely by chance, and this applies both to the preintervention characteristics of the groups and to the results of the intervention. It is inevitable, for example, that one in twenty differences that are statistically significant at the 5% level will arise simply by chance. This is so for all sample sizes. By contrast, true differences that are statistically significant will be more frequent in large samples (because their power will be greater). It follows that the proportion of *false* positive differences will be higher in small samples – a powerful reason for ensuring that samples are of adequate size (Pocock, 1983).

In addition, however, it is necessary to ensure that differences in outcome are not a consequence of preintervention differences between the groups. The requirement is to have high-quality discriminating measures of the characteristics that are known – on the basis of previous research – to predict the course of delinquency. The groups can then, if they happen by chance to differ before the intervention, be statistically equated for these risk characteristics.

The usual procedure in RCTs is to randomize by individual. However, if the intervention is to take place on a group basis (such as by school class, by school, or by neighborhood), then it is equally acceptable to randomize by such groups. But randomization makes sense only if the number is sufficiently large; that will rarely be possible when comparing neighborhoods. A second key feature of RCTs is that evaluation is based on within-individual change. In other words, success or failure is assessed in relation to the effects of the intervention in changing a person's behavior over the course of time. Cross-sectional comparisons provide a very poor alternative to the direct measurement of change over time. The same principle applies to interventions aimed at aggregate levels of crime or at the number of criminal acts. In both cases, the key question is whether these have changed over time in parallel with the timing of the intervention. In all instances, it is highly desirable to have a reasonably prolonged baseline period with*out* the intervention in order to gauge the degree of change that is taking place for reasons unconnected with the intervention.

A further important feature of RCTs is analysis by "intent to treat" (Brent et al., 1997). That is, the comparison is made according to the initial group allocation and not on the basis of compliance with the intervention. This provides a harsh test because the "treated" sample will include some individuals who did not in practice receive the intervention. It is a necessary precaution, however, to ensure that group differences do not come about as a result of a contrast in the characteristics of those who stick with the intervention and those who drop out.

Another key feature of the standard form of RCTs (as originally devised for drug trials) was that evaluation be "double blind" – that is, neither the subjects nor the researchers know whether any individual is receiving the active treatment. This strategy is possible when comparing a drug with a placebo or dummy preparation, but for obvious reasons it is not possible with any form of psychological or social intervention. Accordingly, it is important to be alert to the possibility that changes are attributable not to the specifics of the intervention as such but rather to the knowledge that "something is being done." Likewise, any lack of change (or worsening) in the comparison group may be a consequence of their awareness that they are being denied access to something desirable (see Molling et al., 1962, for an example of just such an effect). Wherever possible, one part of the solution lies in the comparison consisting of something both positive and active but different from the planned intervention. Receiving no intervention *and* being aware that that is the case rarely provides an acceptable control condition.

Because it is so important to determine whether any apparent benefits of an intervention were truly the result of what was done (rather than some adventitious feature), two further steps have increasingly come to be adopted. First, the causal hypothesis can be tested by determining whether there is a dose–response relationship. In other words, were the benefits systematically related to the *degree* of the intervention as indexed by its intensity, frequency, or duration? Ordinarily, if the effects were really a consequence of the intervention, such a relationship would be expected (unless there is reason to anticipate a threshold effect). The second test focuses in a parallel fashion on the postulated mediating variable. That is, if the value of the intervention is thought to lie in its success in raising the child's scholastic achievement (or in reducing family discord, or in increasing community surveillance), are the benefits *within* the group receiving the intervention a function of changes in these hypothesized mediators? If they are, this provides powerful corroborating evidence that the intervention was indeed responsible for the changes that occurred.

Both of these steps require some assessment of the intervention process itself. This requirement applies to any intervention study, but the need is especially great when dealing with psychological or social interventions requiring skills that must be applied by many practitioners with varying degrees of experience and commitment and, most of all, when interventions are being applied in a communitywide setting that is largely (or entirely) outside the control of the "experts" who have devised, developed, and tested the interventions under more tightly controlled conditions. Delinquency intervention studies have been particularly bedeviled by these practical problems.

Some failures to modify delinquent behavior are due to a lack of effective implementation of the interventions rather than to a lack of efficacy of the intervention method itself. The policy (and theoretical) implications are radically different in the two cases, but the reasons for failure can be identified only if there is systematic assessment of the intervention process. A pervasive finding across evaluation studies is that intervention "integrity" is an important ingredient for success; in other words, that the intervention has actually been implemented as intended (Bennett, 1990; Hollin, 1995).

Quasi-Experiments

In the field of delinquency there may be practical difficulties in obtaining randomization, most often because the courts will not accept that judicial decisions may be decided in this way (but see Berg et al., 1978, for a British example of randomization of court procedures in dealing with truancy). In such cases, it may be necessary to conduct quasi-experiments in which either some intervention is introduced in one setting but not others, or in which natural variations in what occurs are used as the basis for comparison. The latter technique is perhaps less problematic than it might first appear, if only because so many decisions seem to include a strong random element. Nevertheless, because of the high probability that the groups to be compared in quasi-experiments will differ in ways that matter for outcome, they are always a second-best alternative to RCTs. Careful measurement of risk characteristics helps minimize the problems (because it allows differences to be taken into account statistically), but its success is reliant on the investigator's ability to measure *all* major risk features (clearly an impossibility because not even all are known).

Nevertheless, despite these problems, it is important not to take a destructively perfectionistic stance. Rather, it is necessary to consider the ways in which the various sources of bias may be minimized (Cook & Campbell, 1979). Although widely employed, simple pre–post designs are the least satisfactory because they provide such weak and unsatisfactory opportunities for testing whether any changes found are due to the intervention (rather than to chance or to the myriad other influences that will have been operating on the individuals who experienced the intervention). Comparative designs in which one intervention is compared with others are much to be preferred. Their strength, however, is dependent on the following four features. First, it is crucial to have longitudinal data so that changes in behavior over time can be examined in relation to the intervention. Second, the groups to be compared must have been broadly similar in their risk characteristics prior to the intervention. Third, the ways in which individuals are selected for each intervention must be reasonably comparable (to avoid the biases created by more cooperative or receptive individuals being chosen for one intervention than the other). Fourth, the interventions to be compared should be defined by practitioners equally skilled in their use. Given these features, quasi-experimental designs may provide an acceptably satisfactory test (see e.g. Bottoms's, 1995a, evaluation of intensive community supervision for young offenders), although inevitably weaker than that provided by RCTs.

Evaluation of Community Interventions

The principles already discussed apply as much to communitywide prevention programs as to individual interventions, but there are some special considerations (see Farrington, 1997c, for a particularly clear discussion). Because the programs are targeted at communities rather than individuals, success needs to be evaluated in relation to changes in the overall level of delinquent activity in the area. This could be measured by victimization surveys, police-recorded crimes, or observation data (e.g. of vandalism), but preferably by a combination of methods. As with individual measures, each is open to bias (as by increases or decreases in police surveillance or recording procedures, or changes in victims' willingness to report), and attention should be paid to their possible operation. As with individuals, it is crucial to compare areas with and without the prevention program; such areas should be broadly comparable prior to the intervention; and it is necessary to be able to examine changes over time. The last, however may be achieved by repeated cross-sectional surveys rather than by prospectively following the same individuals over time. The latter avoids the problem created by sampling variations, but it may be difficult to follow a representative sample and, moreover, longitudinal designs have disadvantages when there is substantial migration in and out of the areas. A combination of repeated surveys and longitudinal data on individuals is ideal, but this is seldom likely to be attainable. Studies of individuals always involve substantial samples because of the need to take account of individual variation. The same applies to community studies although, for obvious reasons, it is more difficult to attain. The important point to recognize, however, is that the relevant statistic is the number of *areas* receiving or not receiving the intervention, and not the number of individuals in the area. Wherever possible, there should be multiple areas in each group.

One special consideration with area studies is the need to examine the possibility that the community intervention has had no effect on the overall level of crime but has instead simply displaced the same level of crime from one community to another. The need is to have measures of delinquent activity in areas adjacent to those involved in the intervention, as well as in the target areas themselves.

Meta-analyses

In recent years, there has been increasing recourse to "meta-analysis," a statistical technique for combining the data from many different studies. This allows the findings from many smaller studies to be put together to create a much larger "mega-study." This has two main advantages. First, it provides a much more satisfactory means of detecting benefits that are real but relatively small. Usually the changes resulting from intervention are expressed in terms of "effect size," a statistic that describes the changes over time in relation to standard deviation (SD) units. Thus, an effect size of 0.33 means that the net change is a third of a standard deviation – a change equivalent to an alteration in IQ of 5 points (since the usual IQ test has an SD of 15). The second advantage is that the effect size can be used to subdivide interventions into those that tend to bring about big changes, those that typically give rise to small benefits only, and those that make little difference. The fact that initially diverse interventions have been pooled is thereby transformed from a limitation to an asset.

Ideally, meta-analyses should include both published and unpublished studies. This is desirable because it is generally easier to get positive findings accepted for publication – a tendency that creates a publication bias in favor of positive effects. On the other hand, there should be a concern about the quality of unpublished studies.

Meta-analyses have provided an undoubted methodological advance and, in our discussion of prevention and intervention strategies, we place weight on their findings. Nevertheless, it is important to appreciate their limitations (Naylor, 1997) as well as the fact that only some sorts of interventions have been included in the published meta-analyses. Most crucially, as compared with drug studies or other forms of medical treatment (for which they were first devised), both the interventions and the groups to which the interventions have been applied tend to be rather heterogeneous, with the nature of the heterogeneity imperfectly assessed in the original studies. Also, the studies vary considerably in their rigor (to some extent this can be taken into account in the meta-analysis), and very few include data on dose–response and mediating variable relationships. Accordingly, in our review of evaluations, we combine attention to meta-analyses with attention to individual studies that are unusually informative either because of their quality or their significance for public policy.

Individual Differences in Response

Most evaluations, whether meta-analyses or individual studies, end up with a conclusion that the intervention involves some reduction in delinquency. Typically, the effects have been rather modest – say, a 12.5% reduction overall. This figure, however, means little without some measure of the spread around it. Figures 11.7(a)–(c) portray this graphically; in all three cases there has been a 12.5% reduction in delinquency following the intervention, from a mean score of 40 to one of 35, but the patterns

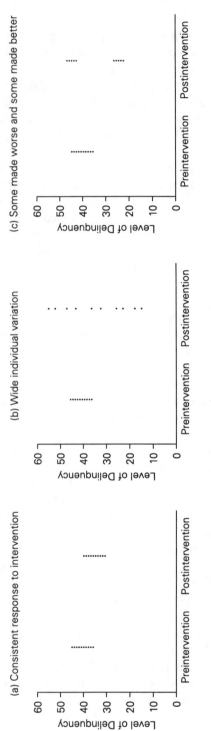

Figure 11.7. Patterns of response to intervention (hypothetical sample).

are widely divergent. For ease of presentation, the simulated data are based on a sample deliberately chosen to be relatively homogeneous. The data for the control group are not shown; it should be assumed that they maintained the same mean 40 score over time.

In Figure 11.7(a), there is very little spread and it may be inferred that, although the benefits were modest, they were consistent. This consistency provides an additional indication that the effect is likely to have been truly brought about by the intervention. In Figure 11.7(b), by contrast, although the average change is the same, there is a huge spread, with some individuals getting worse and others improving. This is a much more typical picture for delinquency studies. The large scatter may mean that the effects of influences outside the intervention vary greatly from person to person and tend to swamp treatment effects. Alternatively, it could indicate true individual differences in response to the intervention. The choice between those alternatives requires further analyses focusing on predictors of outcome. The findings in Figure 11.7(c) are different yet again. In this case, the intervention has clearly had rather marked effects – with half the group benefiting greatly and half being made worse – but with the same net overall effect of a 12.5% reduction in crime. In this instance, the need is to determine what it was about the individuals or about the intervention delivery that made for the difference. As portrayed, the differential effects were dramatic but, in practice, they will rarely be obvious. The expectation that individuals may well vary in their response to interventions is quite reasonable, but identifying the reasons for the variations will usually be difficult. This is because of the paucity of leads on the relevant individual features that give rise to the variations in response, and also because of the statistical difficulties in detecting interaction effects (McClelland & Judd, 1993; Wahlsten, 1990). Of course, given the heterogeneity of antisocial behavior and the varied characteristics and backgrounds of the individuals who exhibit such behavior, it is implausible that the same type of intervention would be equally suitable for everyone. The real need is not to find out which intervention has the greatest efficacy on average, but rather which interventions are most appropriate for which individuals in which circumstances (Rutter, 1982). Throughout this chapter and the one that follows, it should be noted that very few studies have considered the important variations in types of antisocial behavior as discussed in Chapter 5.

Cost–Benefit Analyses

During recent years, increasing attention has been paid to the cost effectiveness of different forms of intervention (see Greenwood et al., 1996,

for a clear and helpful account of the approach and the different considerations that need to be taken into account). In the past this has come about
as a result of an increasing general tendency in many countries to view
everything in terms of economic benefits. However, it also derives in part
from an awareness of the very high costs to the nation that come from
crime, and from evidence that even relatively expensive intensive interventions may save the taxpayer money if they are sufficiently effective
in preventing crime (Schweinhart, Barnes, & Weikart, 1993). In principle,
cost–benefit analyses are very straightforward in that they are based on
calculating the cost per crime prevented for each form of intervention considered. This requires a careful costing of each element in the intervention
program – no easy matter for interventions that involve a multiplicity of
agencies. The benefits are assessed from the effect size of the interventions being compared.

The most obvious complication is that crimes are not equivalent in their
importance. How do you price the comparison between, say, major com-
pany fraud involving the loss of vast sums of money and a brutal assault
on an old woman to rob her of her pitifully small savings? Even putting
those difficulties aside, the cost–benefit analyses need to take account of
issues such as the percentage of the population treated and how much
crime they commit; how much the effectiveness of the intervention will
be reduced if it is expanded from a specialized, small-scale, expert-run
intervention to a communitywide program; how long effects persist after the intervention has ceased; and whether there are benefits from the
intervention apart from crime prevention. Thus, it may be important to
inquire about effects on employment, quality of parenting, and abuse of
drugs or alcohol. It may be equally necessary to consider possible adverse
consequences of interventions – in terms either of limiting individual free-
dom or of effects on fairness and public acceptability. There is no doubt
that cost–benefit analyses can be very informative and may well influence policies regarding which particular large-scale interventions should
be funded. On the other hand, it is necessary to be aware of the many assumptions that must be made in making the calculations and the fragile
empirical base for most of them (e.g., the long-term effects are unknown
for almost all interventions).

Case Studies of Promising Interventions

In any discussion of prevention and intervention, there is a dilemma
in deciding how to deal with the many apparently promising programs
that have not been subjected to systematic quantitative controlled evaluations. Many of these are community programs that have been designed

Table 11.1. Risk Level and Proportion of Potential Criminals Targeted

Risk Level	Increase in Risk	Number in Risk Group	Criminal Proportion	Number of Criminals
Very high	16.7×	10	50%	5
Medium	2.3×	60	7%	4
Very low	1.0×	30	3%	1

to help troubled families, improve parenting, or increase community cohesion and support. Their prime objective has not been the prevention of delinquency and, indeed, the data available on their effects may not even include measures of crime. Nevertheless, in many cases they focus on groups known to have a high risk of delinquency, and we know that gains in social functioning may well be associated with reductions in delinquent behavior. This would seem to apply to the use of home visiting for parent education during pregnancy and infancy, where a randomized trial showed benefits in caregiving and child functioning at age 4 (Olds et al., 1986); to the NEWPIN use of befrienders to help socially isolated mothers who are experiencing difficulties in relationships with their children (Cox et al., 1990; Pound, 1994); and to Home-Start's use of volunteers to help stressed parents of preschool children (Frost et al., 1996) – to give just three examples. Such programs have been well described and documented in reports by Bilchik (1995), Graham and Bennett (1995), Junger-Tas (1996), and Utting (1996). These case studies of approaches that seem possibly useful as part of an overall program to prevent or reduce crime provide valuable leads to follow, but necessarily we place most weight in drawing conclusions regarding efficacy on studies where there are quantitative controlled evaluations.

Targeting High-Risk Groups

Many of the interventions that we discuss in this chapter are focused on high-risk groups. The approach is sound in its assumption that it is likely to be cost-effective to provide preventive services only for those families who most need prevention. However, it is necessary to recognize the inherent limitations, even when it is possible to identify families with an exceptionally high likelihood that the children will become criminal. Table 11.1 illustrates the point by taking a "best case" scenario in which the top 10 percent of the population have a criminality risk nearly 17 times higher than that for the bottom 30 percent with the lowest risk. Members of the middle group, comprising that 60 percent of the population with only some risk factors, have a criminality risk that is just over twice that of the lowest-risk group. In practice, our ability to pick up extremes of risk in this way is far less than assumed by this best-case example. But even with such (hypothetically) powerful risk identification, only half the criminals come from the top-10-percent risk group. In short, a high-risk target strategy will always miss many individuals who will become criminal.

The situation is aggravated by two other considerations. First, if prevention is provided when children are very young (which makes sense in light of evidence that persistent antisocial behavior is rooted in early childhood), then the feasibility of identifying high-risk groups is weaker. This is because some risk factors develop only later (families that initially function well may later run into serious trouble), and also because the indicators of family risk are likely to be somewhat weaker at that stage. Second, the families most at risk may well be less receptive to help than other families.

None of these considerations negates the value of a strategy of focusing services (i) on families for whom the intervention is most needed and (ii) where success would have the greatest benefits in relation to the goal of reducing the most persistent forms of antisocial behavior. However, they do indicate the constraints on what is likely to be achieved.

Relief of Societal Risks

In this chapter we do not discuss prevention in relation to societal risk factors such as poverty, poor housing, unemployment, and racial discrimination. There is no doubt that relief of these adverse features in society is a highly desirable goal. Moreover, in view of the evidence that their presence makes good parenting more difficult (see Chapter 8), reducing such risks would be helpful with respect to preventing delinquency. There are two reasons we do not concentrate on such a strategy: their connections with causal mechanisms seem to be rather indirect; and the social and economic improvements that took place during the 1950s to early 1970s in most industrialized countries did *not* lead to a reduction in crime (see Chapter 4). Indeed, this was the time period during which crime rose greatly.

Neither do we discuss prevention in relation to individual risk factors (such as obstetric complications or institutional care) or parental risk factors (such as teenage parenting or parental drug abuse). There is a clear need for actions to improve obstetric and neonatal care, to improve the care of children when parenting breaks down, to reduce unwanted births (particularly to young girls who are still immature and in the middle of their education), and to prevent substance abuse in young adults. We support steps to take preventive actions in all these domains (see Graham & Bennett, 1995, and Graham & Utting, 1996, for an account of preventive possibilities). However, success along these lines would likely have only modest benefits with respect to crime reduction (because of their weak links with the causal processes), so we do not discuss the evidence on prevention of these risk factors.

Preventive Strategies at a Predelinquency Phase

With these conceptual and methodological considerations in mind, we turn to what is known about prevention at the predelinquency phase – that is, before the police and courts become involved. These strategies have been reviewed by Bilchik (1995), Farrington (1994), Graham and Bennett (1995), Tremblay and Craig (1995), Utting, Bright, and Henricson (1993), and Yoshikawa (1994), and are considered here under the headings of preschool education, improving parenting skills, early treatment of disruptive behavior, schoolwide programs, and multimodal interventions. Findings on the effectiveness of a broader range of early intervention for high-risk groups are well summarized in Guralnick (1997).

Preschool Education

Most preschool education programs were set up with the primary aim of enhancing children's cognitive development and school performance. The U.S. Head Start programs are typical of this form of intervention (Lazar & Darlington, 1982; McKay et al., 1985). The findings showed that, although the IQ gains tended not to persist, there were longer-term benefits on both scholastic progress and broader aspects of social functioning in the best planned and implemented interventions. The intervention most quoted in relation to the prevention of delinquency, however, is the High/Scope Perry Preschool Study, which stands out with respect to its focus on a very high-risk group of poor families, the quality of its program, a low attrition rate, and the length of its follow-up to age 27 (Schweinhart et al., 1993; Weikart & Schweinhart, 1992). The children attended special classes for two and a half hours daily for 30 weeks, and there was a home visit by a teacher once per week. Some of the children attended for one year, but most participated for two years. The focus was on active learning, the encouragement of children's independence, the development of self-esteem, and the teaching of problem solving and task persistence. Emphasis was placed on good home–school integration, small classes, and specially trained and supervised teachers. The results were certainly impressive in several important respects. Two main comparisons were made: first, that between children in the High/Scope program and controls; and second, that among three different preschool intervention programs (High/Scope, a behaviorist programmed learning approach, and a child-centered nursery program). The main focus has been on the first comparison, but the findings up to adolescence were informative in showing that the High/Scope group fared best and the behaviorist group worst in most respects.

The High/Scope group had fewer lifetime arrests (up to age 27) than the no-intervention group (a mean of 2.3 versus 4.6), the difference being most evident for minor offenses and drug-related arrests in adult life and for recidivist crime. One in three of the controls, but only one in fourteen of the High/Scope group, had been arrested five or more times. Teenage pregnancy rates were lower in the High/Scope sample, more children graduated from high school (71% versus 54%), more were homeowners, and fewer had received social services. Nevertheless, it is important to note that the sample size was relatively small (58 in the High/Scope sample and 65 controls); that by age 19, nearly a third of the High/Scope group (31% versus 51% of controls) had been arrested at least once; and that there is no other evaluated intervention of this kind. The results of this high quality intervention are undoubtedly very promising, especially as the findings on educational benefits from the best Head Start programs are broadly comparable. It should be added that although the intervention had by no means prevented delinquency, it did have a major impact in reducing recidivist crime.

Improving the Parenting in High-Risk Families

There are several well-conducted random allocation studies of the effects of intervention in early infancy to improve parenting in high-risk groups of various kinds, especially low–birth-weight infants (Tremblay & Craig, 1995). Typically, home visitor nurses provide guidance on infant development, home care generally, and parenting skills in particular. The findings have been reasonably consistent in showing substantial benefits in relation to the prevention of child abuse and neglect, improved cognitive development, and reduced behavioral difficulties. The findings have obvious implications with respect to the possibility of preventing delinquency in the offspring, but none of the random allocation studies have followed up the children at an age when it can be determined if this potential is actualized. One prevention initiative with adequate follow-up was the Syracuse University program that focused on poor pregnant girls without a high school education (Lally, Mangione, & Honig, 1988), but it lacked randomization. The home and day-care center curriculum that was used sought to foster active initiative and participation together with a sense of self-efficacy. Sensorimotor and language games were also used to promote cognitive development. One hundred and eight pregnant women were recruited into the program, which continued until the offspring were 5 years old. A carefully matched control group was recruited when the project children were aged 3 years, and both groups were followed up to age 15 (with 50%–60% cooperation). As with other interventions, the early IQ gains were not maintained at age 5, but the rate of delinquency (using police data) in the intervention group was substantially lower (6% versus 22%).

Early Treatment of Disruptive Behavior

The third type of intervention differs in that it focuses on the amelioration of disruptive behavior in individual children (Kazdin, 1997; Webster-Stratton, 1991) instead of on early psychosocial development or on parenting. The main concentration has been on the age period of roughly 3–8 years. The pioneering work of Patterson and his colleagues at the Oregon Social Learning Center (Patterson, 1982; Patterson et al., 1992) was particularly influential. They emphasized the value of careful monitoring of the children's behavior at home, the ample use of praise for appropriate behavior, the need for systematic sanctions for disruptive behavior, and the importance of constructive family negotiation and social problem solving. Forehand and McMahon (1981) developed a similar parent training program but with a greater emphasis on playing with children and on fostering prosocial behavior. Webster-Stratton (1984, 1996; Webster-Stratton & Herbert, 1994) has been particularly innovative both in broadening the goals of the intervention and in developing a videotape modeling approach to parent training.

Her studies, like those of others, had shown the high frequency of marital conflict in the families of young children with oppositional and conduct problems. Accordingly, since 1989 her intervention program has added interpersonal skills training for parents to the BASIC parent skills training. The latter focused on how to play with the child, the use of praise and rewards, limit setting, and discipline. The former dealt with problem solving, anger management, communication, depression control, and giving and receiving support. In five RCTs, the BASIC program has been shown to be effective in improving parenting skills and in reducing children's disruptive behavior. There were significant benefits even when the intervention consisted of nothing more than self-administered videotapes. However, follow-up three years later showed that the gains were more likely to persist if there was also therapist-led role playing and group discussion to encourage parents' problem solving. Nevertheless, even with this combined approach, over a quarter of the children showed significant school problems at follow-up.

In order to foster both persistence and generalization of benefits, three further elements have more recently been added. First, parents are helped to aid their children's academic skills through homework support, fostering good learning habits, and liaison with teachers. Second, children are taught social skills, problem solving, and behavioral control in the classroom. Third, teachers are helped with both classroom management and promotion of parent involvement. The combination of parent and child training was found to be more effective than either alone in an RCT involving 97 children (aged 4–8) with conduct problems. The results of teacher training are not yet known, but an RCT is currently underway.

These methods of providing early treatment for young children's disruptive behavior have generated an impressive body of evidence showing their efficacy as compared with either no treatment or family-based psychotherapy. The use of video training and group discussion is also more cost-effective than the traditional individual treatment model as ordinarily applied in clinic settings. However, the benefits in all programs have tended to be less marked and less persistent when there are severe family problems and a lack of social support. Also, the value of these early interventions in the prevention of later delinquency has yet to be assessed.

The extension of the Webster-Stratton program to include child and teacher training as part of a multimodal intervention was designed to deal with the difficulties involved in placing total reliance on parents when they are heavily stressed by their own problems. The combination of parent and child training for kindergarten boys showing disruptive behavior in the Montreal study undertaken by Tremblay and his colleagues (1992) had the same goal. There were 46 families in their treatment group and 84 in a comparison group, both deriving from the same much larger longitudinal study sample. There was also a third control group of 42 not in the longitudinal study. The intervention lasted two years, with one parent training session every two weeks. The children received their social skills training at school; this particularly focused on self-control in the second year.

Three years after completion of the program, when the boys were aged 11–12 years, 22% of the treated group showed serious difficulties in school adjustment compared with 44% of controls; the treated boys were also reported by teachers as fighting less and their school achievement was better. By age 12, they less often engaged in stealing and trespassing (although there was no difference in vandalism). A follow-up at age 15 (Tremblay & Craig, 1995), six years after the end of treatment, showed a fading of the benefits. There was no effect on crime record, but the rate overall (8%) was unusually low. The findings on persistence of benefits for several years are encouraging, but the lack of maintenance of gains during adolescence is a reminder that very few interventions result in long-term prevention if there is no subsequent consolidation of the intervention gains.

The programs described here include several different elements, but parent training constituted the basic component. Other interventions have focused on helping children gain control over anger (Lochman, 1992) or social problem-solving skills (Kazdin, Siegel, & Bass, 1992). The benefits of the former were quite limited, but the combination of social problem solving and parent management training did have a significant effect of diminished (self-reported) delinquency and enhanced social functioning as assessed in a one-year follow-up.

These early treatment studies have not been subjected to meta-analysis, but the overall pattern of findings is reasonably clear in its indication that some combination of intervention with parents and with children is more effective than either on its own. Probably, too, there are advantages of including some intervention at school. In addition, it seems highly desirable to promote effective social problem solving and coping as well as to aid behavioral control. All the successful interventions have been highly focused in their aims and structured in their approach, yet they have all sought to foster independence, initiative, and self-reliance in the children and their parents. For the most part, the interventions have involved therapeutic contact (once per week or two weeks) that continued over a period of at least one year. An encouraging degree of persistence of benefits after the end of treatment has been evident in several of the programs.

Schoolwide Programs

Children spend a high proportion of their waking lives in schools. By their nature, schools constitute social organizations as well as educational establishments. There are major variations among schools in levels of both disruptive behavior and delinquency, and these variations go well beyond those expected on the basis of differences in intake. Children change in their behavior over the course of their schooling, and differences among schools in the patterns of change (worsening or improvement over time) are systematically related to the qualities of schools as social organizations

(Maughan, 1994; Mortimore, 1995b; Rutter, 1983b). The evidence is compelling that, as a consequence of their qualities as organizations, schools have considerable effects on children's behavior and attainments. Taken as a whole, the evidence suggests that effective schooling is characterized by strong positive leadership, high expectations of pupils, systematic monitoring of pupil progress, good opportunities for students to take responsibility and become involved in the life of the school, appropriate use of rewards and incentives, suitable involvement of parents in school activities, the use of joint planning and a consistent approach toward students, an academic emphasis and a focus on learning, and high-quality, purposeful learning (Mortimore, 1995b; Reynolds et al., 1996). On the face of it, it would seem a straightforward matter to use these research findings as the basis for improving schools in ways that should reduce disruptive behavior and truancy and thereby (indirectly) reduce delinquency. In practice, however, their implementation in programs to improve schooling seems to have had only modest success so far (Mortimore, 1995b; Reynolds et al., 1996; Stringfield & Herman, 1996). It has become clear that recognizing your educational aim and knowing how to bring about the desired change involve rather different sets of issues and challenges (Maughan et al., 1991; Ouston et al., 1991). Nevertheless, there are promising leads; this field of work is still at a rather early stage of development, with few systematic evaluations.

The schoolwide interventions that have been evaluated seem to fall into three broad groups: (i) programs to enhance social competence and social problem solving (Beelman, Pfingsten, & Lösel, 1994; Compas, 1995; CSPSC, 1994; Pellegrini, 1994); (ii) programs specifically targeted at the reduction of aggressive behavior (Kellam & Rebok, 1992; Kellam et al., 1994); and (iii) programs to reduce bullying (Farrington, 1993a; Olweus, 1991, 1993; Olweus & Alsaker, 1991; Smith & Sharp, 1994).

A wide range of techniques have been used to enhance social competence and social problem solving. For example, Botvin's Life Skills Training (LST) focuses on the provision of information, fostering social resistance skills, independent decision making, anxiety-coping skills, and self-directed behavior change to prevent substance abuse (Botvin, 1990; Botvin et al., 1984). The approach includes recognition of the role of peer pressure and seeks to help young people deal with it constructively; the results suggest benefits with respect to reduced use of cigarettes, alcohol, and marijuana. The Yale–New Haven program, by contrast, focuses on how to cope successfully with stressful events (Weissberg, Jackson, & Shriver, 1993). Beelman et al.'s (1994) meta-analysis showed that the short-term effects of social competence training were substantial, but the broader benefits with respect to social adjustment were modest and long-term effects were weak.

Kellam et al.'s (1994) program to reduce aggressive behavior in elementary school children used the Good Behavior Game (GBG), a classroom team-based behavioral management strategy. Comparisons were based on (i) schools with and without the intervention and (ii) within-school classes with and without the intervention. The evaluation, which included a six-year follow-up, showed benefits – but these mainly applied to boys who were initially above average in aggression.

In view of the crucial need to determine *which* approaches are most effective, there is much to be said for the comparison of interventions seeking to operate through different mechanisms. Gottfredson and Gottfredson's (1992) contrasting of these secondary school-based programs is potentially informative in that connection. One program, PATHE (Positive Action through Holistic Education), focused on bonding secondary school students to the schools using a range of interventions including counseling, tutoring, and extracurricular activities. The second, STATUS (Student Training through Urban Strategies), placed a greater weight on adolescents' involvement in school and community organizations. The third, PCD (Peer Culture Development), used group methods to alter peer interaction and to foster positive styles of behavior and social interaction. The results with respect to self-reported delinquency and drug involvement favored PCD. Unfortunately, implementation of the random allocation design was less satisfactory in the PCD study, and it remains uncertain whether this played a part in the apparently better results. However, the rather disappointing effects in the PATHE and STATUS projects suggest that a focus only on positive social features may not – at least during adolescence – be effective in preventing delinquency.

Olweus's (1993) Norwegian program to reduce bullying had the goals of increasing awareness of the problem, improving the social milieu of the school, establishing firm limits for acceptable behavior, a degree of monitoring and surveillance, consistent applications of nonhostile and nonphysical sanctions for rule restrictions, and engaging the working together of parents and teachers. The evaluation design used was a cohort longitudinal study in which the difference between an 11-year-old age cohort at time 1 and the same cohort a year later was contrasted with the difference between 11-year-old and 12-year-old age cohorts at time 1 (and so on between adjacent age cohorts). The much greater (former) time effect than (latter) age cohort effect indicates the effect of the school intervention. A causal influence is also suggested by the dose–response finding: school classes that had implemented the program to a greater extent were associated with larger reductions in bullying. The benefits with respect to bullying were accompanied by parallel reductions in such (self-reported) antisocial behavior as vandalism, theft, and truanting. The findings of Smith and Sharp's (1994) U.K. study also showed benefits from a school-based anti-bullying program. However, these effects were most evident at primary school, and there was substantial variation among schools in the degree of change effected.

Multimodal Interventions

As already evident from our discussion of developments in Webster-Stratton's early intervention program, many interventions have moved from single-element to multifaceted interventions. The Seattle Social Development Project (Hawkins et al., 1992b) and the Fast Track Program (Dodge, 1997; Greenberg & CPPRG, 1997; Lochman, Bierman, & McMahon, 1997; McMahon, 1997; McMahon & Greenberg, 1995) provide good examples of well-planned, well-evaluated multimodal approaches. In both cases, the details of the intervention are based on a carefully articulated causal model. Hawkins et al. (1992b) sought to strengthen children's bonds to their family and school and thereby to improve adherence to behavioral standards set by both. Bonds are conceptualized as comprising three elements: "attachment," meaning positive emotional feelings toward others; "commitment," meaning investment in a social unit; and "belief" in the values of that unit. The intervention includes teaching the children social and cognitive problem solving, helping parents to deal more appropriately with their children's behavior and to improve communication with them, and fostering better classroom management by teachers. The experimental design involved a comparison of one experimental and one control school, with random assignment of newly entering pupils to experimental or control groups within the remaining six schools. The findings showed beneficial effects on the targeted postulated mediating variables (such as social bonding and family management and communication) but rather small effects on delinquency.

The Fast Track program constitutes a more ambitious, long-term, multisite intervention in schools serving high-crime areas. The target group is high-risk children in the early years of schooling, with the randomized intervention starting in first grade and continuing through sixth grade. A multiple gating procedure is used to select children in the top-10-percent risk group, the intervention sample of 448 is compared with a similarly sized sample of high-risk controls, plus a normative community sample. The intervention focuses on six domains: scholastic achievement, social coping, peer relations, home–school links, classroom behavior, and parenting. It uses a carefully integrated mix of elements such as home visiting, skills training and academic tutoring with children, parent groups, and peer pairing. A particular strength of the study is the attempt to determine the extent to which changes in the postulated mediating processes account for the beneficial effects on antisocial behavior (see Baron & Kenny, 1986, for the method). The evaluation study is still at an early stage, and it is too soon to assess the outcome. The findings so far are encouraging, but the effects appear modest in relation to the extent and intensity of the intervention. The costs per high-risk child per year are $3,500, which is not high by the standards of other interventions, but the overall costs and benefits have yet to be determined.

Conclusions

Given the extensive evidence that persistent antisocial behavior tends to start early in childhood, that there is continuity between early disruptive behavior and later delinquency, and that maladaptive patterns are likely to be more difficult to alter once well-established, it obviously makes sense to seek effective early preventive measures. This is particularly so when the promising interventions seem likely to have broader benefits and do not appear to have any significant adverse side effects. So far, there have been relatively few systematic evaluations of the effects on delinquency, and it is necessary to be cautious about how much can be achieved. Nevertheless, the findings are encouraging that worthwhile benefits may be attainable, although the extent to which delinquency can be prevented is likely to be modest.

In this chapter we reviewed a number of strategies that can be used and where evaluations exist.

(1) *Preschool education.* The best known of these is the High/Scope Perry Project, which seeks to foster active learning, children's independence, self-esteem and self-efficacy, problem-solving, and task persistence, as well as to form links between the home and school domains.

(2) *Parenting enhancement* in high-risk groups. For example, the Syracuse University program seeks to foster parenting skills and understanding of child development.

(3) *Early treatment* of disruptive behavior, which seeks to train parents, children, and/or teachers in how to prevent the escalation of antisocial behavior once it has begun. For example, the work of the Oregon Social Learning Center focuses on the child and the parent; the

Webster-Stratton program includes teacher training. Strategies include encouraging praise for appropriate behavior alongside the use
of systematic sanctions for disruptive behavior.

(4) *Schoolwide interventions,* such as the PATHE and STATUS programs,
seek to enhance social competence in the school setting as a whole
and to reduce aggressive behavior and bullying. Examples include
Botvin's Life Skills Training, Kellam's "Good Behavior Game," and
the Norwegian anti-bullying program.

(5) *Multimodal invervention,* such as the Seattle Social Development Project and the Fast Track Program, look promising although the effects
on delinquency are as yet unclear. These try to tackle antisocial behavior in all the domains – at home, at school, and with peers.

Eight main issues need highlighting. First, the limited evidence available to date suggests that multimodal intervention that continues for a
prolonged time is likely to be needed. This is to be expected on the basis of what is known about the influences on antisocial behavior. As discussed in earlier chapters, they involve factors in the child, the family,
the school, the peer group, and the community. Changes in any one may
bring benefits, but they are likely to be limited if risk factors remain un-
changed in the others. Second, the call for multimodal intervention does
not mean that diffuse general programs are indicated. To the contrary, all
the successful projects are characterized by well-focused, precisely targeted interventions that are closely linked with what is known about risk
and protective mechanisms for antisocial behavior.

Third, although the necessary planned comparisons have not been undertaken, it seems that the successful interventions involve a combination of means to foster positive social behavior and means to minimize
disruptive behavior. The two are linked but are far from synonymous,
and a focus on just the positive or just the negative seems less satisfactory. Fourth, interventions are more likely to be welcomed by families if
they can see a need for them. The implication is that a focus on families
who are experiencing stress, distress, or other problems may be desirable.
Also, the limited available evidence suggests the possibility that effects
are greater if the children are showing problem behavior at the time of
he intervention. Fifth, there are many practical advantages to interven-
ns that build on services (such as schools or antenatal classes or health
ors) that will be used by participants anyway.

th, benefits are likely to be constrained by the fact that, although it
ly possible to identify high-risk groups for whom the most in-
nterventions can be designed, nevertheless many individuals

(in *absolute* numbers) who subsequently exhibit delinquency will come from lower-risk groups (even though their *relative* risk is less). Seventh, there are very considerable difficulties in ensuring that the quality of interventions remains high when programs are extended on a communitywide basis. The evidence for efficacy derives largely from interventions defined by experts who are convinced of the value of what they are doing. All research points to the importance of maintaining the integrity of interventions. Finally, little is known about the other reasons (beyond program integrity) for individual differences in responses to interventions.

CHAPTER 11 – SUMMARY OF MAIN POINTS

Cautious optimism is the current tone of reviews on prevention and intervention with young people, contrasting with a more determined negativity a couple of decades ago. Some key background issues include the following.

❑ Expectations of modifiability need to be *realistic*. There are clearly grounds for thinking that criminal behavior is open to modification, but indications are that reductions in future offending are likely to be relatively small (e.g., 12%).

❑ *Evaluation* is critical but is often missing. Randomized control trials are the best means of evaluating programs, but are difficult to employ in practice. Other alternatives are quasi-experiments and field evaluations of community interventions. The recent development of meta-analyses of interventions has been helpful.

❑ The prime objective of many studies offered as examples of preventive work has not been to reduce delinquency. Although it is important that a range of different outcomes be considered, *caution* should be employed in assuming that the benefits of some programs will extend to crime.

❑ Intervening at the *predelinquency* stage makes intuitive sense given the research results on the continuity of behavior and the ways in which early predispositions are exaggerated and actualized by later social experiences. Examples of predelinquency interventions include preschool programs such as High/Scope, child-centered work, parent- and teacher-centered training, and schoolwide interventions such as PATHE and STATUS.

❏ *Main issues* in predelinquency interventions include the need for multimodal intervention and precise focusing of projects, combining encouragement with discouragement, involving families, building on existing services, targeting a range of different types of offenders, and ensuring consistency within programs.

12 | Prevention and Intervention II

Applications at the Postdelinquency Phase

In Chapter 11 we considered evidence on the possibility of preventing delinquency at a point before the young people had become involved in official processing, either in terms of contact with the police or appearance in court. In practice, this meant that we discussed measures that were largely focused on children in the first decade of life – a period before the age of criminal responsibility in most countries. In this chapter, we both move up the age range and move into a set of interventions that includes judicial measures of one kind or another. Nevertheless, the distinctions are far from absolute; thus, in this chapter we consider clinical interventions that are based on principles almost identical to those that applied to the early treatment of disruptive behavior discussed in Chapter 11. The differences in this case simply derive from considerations that are introduced by dealing with teenagers rather than young children, and by the fact that the former may be subject to legal sanctions and punishments that cannot be applied before the age of criminal responsibility.

The distinction also cannot be reduced to that between prevention and intervention. Preventive policies come into consideration in this older age group in three different ways. First, there are the interventions that seek to reduce the opportunities for offending either by situational measures, such as making it more difficult for cars to be driven away by thieves, or by better community surveillance, such as by TV monitoring of stores and parking lots or by "Neighborhood Watch" schemes. Second, there are the deterrent effects on the population at large that may derive from either better detection of crimes or heavier penalties when caught. Third, there is the prevention brought about by incapacitation; that is, the removal of opportunities for crime by locking people up. Of course, the latter two interventions need to be considered also in terms of their effects on the individual, but the preventive strategy has the further goal of influencing the behavior of *other* people. This discussion begins, therefore, by summarizing what is known about these different forms of preventive strategy. We then move to an appraisal of the range of interventions designed to prevent offenders from continuing in their antisocial activities. The focus in that section is thus on the effects on the subsequent criminal careers of the

339

individuals experiencing the intervention – be it punitive, therapeutic, or rehabilitative in orientation.

Reducing Opportunities for Offending

The theoretical rationale for situational crime prevention strategies is that, for any given level of individual liability to engage in antisocial behavior, situational factors will influence whether or not that liability is translated into the commission of a criminal act (Rutter et al., 1997b). As discussed in Chapter 11, this is a general proposition with respect to human behavior, both normal and abnormal, and is in no way specific to crime. For example, whether or not people who are feeling suicidal actually attempt to take their life will be influenced in part by the ease of access to effective means of self-destruction. Accordingly, the detoxification of domestic coal gas in the United Kingdom, a very common means of suicide especially in older people, was followed by a fall in suicide rates (Clarke & Mayhew, 1988). Similarly, rates of alcoholism are affected by the cost of alcoholic beverages, and rates of drug abuse by the availability of drugs giving rise to dependence (Rutter, 1979/80; Silbereisen et al., 1995).

With respect to crime, these notions have been developed by Cohen and Felson (1979) in their "routine activities theory," which emphasizes the roles of opportunity (i.e., suitable accessible targets for crime) and surveillance (i.e., the likelihood of offenders being able to commit the crime without being noticed and without anyone in the vicinity who might apprehend them). Somewhat similarly, Clarke (1980), in his "choice" model of crime, emphasized offenders' perceptions of criminal opportunities and their ability to create or take advantage of them, together with their appraisal of the risks of being caught and the consequences that would follow if apprehended. Together with Cornish, Clarke has developed the model into a broader "rational choice" perspective (Clarke, 1995; Clarke & Cornish, 1985; Cornish, 1993; Cornish & Clarke, 1986). This recognizes the somewhat different set of decisions involved in whether or not to continue with antisocial behavior (a multistage process extending over a prolonged period of time) versus those involved in whether or not to commit a particular criminal act in a particular place at a particular time (which is usually a much more immediate decision made on the basis of limited specific information).

In both cases, crime is assumed to be a purposive behavior that serves to meet commonplace needs of money, status, sex, or excitement; it is further assumed that meeting those needs involves decisions. Such decisions, however, will be constrained by the availability of relevant information, by biases in the processing of such information, by individual differences in the extent to which people think about consequences or weigh alternative courses of action, and by the influence of motivational forces. In other words, crime is purposive and is based on choices, but decision making is rudimentary, only semirational, and always based on subjective perceptions rather than a dispassionate objective integration of information about the balance between gains, risks, and adverse consequences. Clarke and Cornish also noted that the decision-making processes and the information used in making choices will vary greatly between different types of offenses. Interviews with criminals confirm both propositions – they do weigh the situational issues, and some crimes are opportunistic whereas others are carefully planned (Bennett & Wright, 1984; Cromwell et al., 1991). There is a difference, too, between affective and acquisitive "opportunity" – that is, between (say) assault during a quarrel and stealing a handbag left exposed by an open window in an unoccupied car.

There is evidence, too, from naturalistic surveys of various kinds that the attractiveness of crime targets and variations in surveillance are associated with parallel variations in rates of criminal acts (Bottoms & Wiles, 1997; Clarke, 1995; Pease, 1997; Rutter, 1979/80; Rutter & Giller, 1983). Damaged or neglected buildings are more often the subject of vandalism than well-maintained buildings. Areas with extensive informal or formal surveillance experience lower rates of burglary and theft than unsupervised areas. For example, Liddle and Bottoms (1993) found that car thefts (and other car crimes) were over three times as frequent per parking space in a long-term parking lot used by commuters in the center of one English town, where by the nature of its use there was little coming and going, than in short-term parking lots in the same vicinity used by shoppers, in which a constant stream of passers-by provided natural surveillance. Similarly, vandalism on buses is less when there is a conductor walking around to issue and check tickets and, on buses where the only surveillance is by the driver, vandalism is less on the lower floor (where the driver sits) than on the upper floor, which is out of view (Mayhew et al., 1976).

Situational Crime Prevention

Situational crime prevention strategies capitalize on these concepts and findings with the development of a wide range of tactics designed to increase the *effort* required in order to commit the offense, to increase the *risks* that attend the criminal act, or to reduce the *rewards* that follow the crime (see Table 12.1).

The list of successes in the use of these situational measures has come to be quite long (Clarke, 1995; Pease, 1997; Poyner, 1993). The evaluation

Table 12.1. Twelve Techniques of Situational Prevention

Technique	Example
Increasing the effort	
Target hardening	Steering locks on cars
Access control	Entry phones to buildings
Deflecting offenders	Street closures
Controlling facilitators	Gun controls
Increasing the risks	
Entry/exit screening	Merchandise tags
Formal surveillance	Burglar alarms
Surveillance by employers	Closed-circuit TV
Natural surveillance	Good street lighting
Reducing the reward	
Target removal	Phone cards
Identifying property	Property marking
Removing inducements	Graffiti cleaning
Rule setting	Banning consumption of alcohol in public spaces

Source: After Clarke (1992, 1995).

of preventive success has typically involved three steps. First, it has been necessary to test for specificity in the causal effect predicted. This requires a comparison with some target or some offense that could not be affected by the situational preventive measure introduced. Thus, the evidence that the introduction of steering-column locks on new vehicles in Britain reduced their theft but not that of older vehicles without them points to a causal connection (Mayhew et al., 1976). The second step requires testing for persistence of specific effects. This is illustrated by the effects of steering-lock legislation in Germany, where (unlike in the United Kingdom and the United States) locks were made compulsory on *all* cars and not just new ones (see Figure 12.1). A striking result is that, over a 30-year period, car thefts remained at a low level despite a massive increase in thefts *from* vehicles (against which steering-wheel locks were no protection). The evidence provides a convincing case for the intended preventive effect but also a warning that crimes may be displaced onto other, more accessible, targets.

The third step is the most challenging: testing for a preventive effect on the *overall* level of crime. The test is an important one because, if crimes

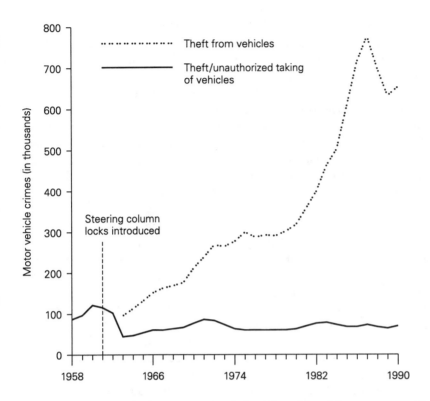

Figure 12.1. Motor vehicle crime in the Federal Republic of Germany, 1958–90. *Source:* Webb and Laycock (1992). Crown copyright is reproduced with the permission of the Controller of Her Majesty's Stationery Office.

are merely displaced, little may have been achieved. Nevertheless, there are formidable problems involved in evaluating whether or not an overall reduction in crime has been achieved (see Ekblom & Pease, 1995, for a constructive critical discussion of the issues). Painter and Farrington's (1997) study of the effects on crime of markedly improving street lighting illustrates one good strategy that may be employed. Two closely similar local authority estates in an industrial town in the Midlands of England were compared using two victimization surveys, twelve months apart, with each covering crimes on the estate only during the preceding year. Markedly improved street lighting was introduced in one estate, but not the other, just after the first survey. No other major changes impinged on either estate. The sample size was large (some 430 in each area), the response rate was good (77%), and the proportion of households reinterviewed in the second survey was also high (83%–86%). Accordingly, there can be some confidence in the findings. However assessed, the overall rate of crime fell substantially (by some 20% to 40%) in the experimental area, whereas it fell only slightly in the control area. Insofar as it could be examined, no crime displacement was found.

Other examples of successful situational crime prevention could be detailed, and there is no doubt that the strategies are well worth pursuing further. Nevertheless, the findings raise several crucial issues. First, there are many instances in which the measures have not proved successful. Clarke (1995) has listed the variety of reasons for failure. These span failures of implementation (e.g., TV screens unmonitored by security guards or carelessness in use of entry control systems), inadequacy of the measures (e.g., early U.S. and U.K. steering locks were easily broken by a heavy blow), and the use of inappropriate measures through failure to analyze the situation properly (e.g., pickpockets stationing themselves near signs that warned of theft on the London Underground to see which pockets were being checked by passengers). Second, there are many examples in which at least some of the crime has been displaced – as in the theft-from-cars example just cited. Moreover, benefits that have been observed have not always persisted.

The question is which features foster continuing generalized benefits. Because it is difficult to make quantified comparisons across studies using different interventions, no definitive conclusions are possible. Nevertheless, a review of the evidence suggests that four main elements are most influential:

(1) the rapidity and pervasiveness of the measure's introduction, which minimizes offenders' opportunities to adapt to or circumvent the measures;
(2) the combining of measures designed to impact related crime targets;
(3) the use of interventions that involve other benefits for the public, so encouraging their acceptability; and
(4) an avoidance of reliance on members of the public taking active responsibility for initiatives.

Thus, the introduction of steering-wheel locks on cars was much more effective in Germany than in the United Kingdom or the United States; Clarke and Harris (1992) suggested that this was because the locks were made compulsory on all cars at once, rather than introducing locks step-by-step. Similarly, target hardening and property marking have sometimes been of limited benefit when thieves have found it easy to switch attention to homes or articles not so protected (Allert, 1984; Gabor, 1981).

Car alarms have not been particularly effective, apparently because people rarely respond to them and instead are merely irritated by the intrusive noise (Clarke & Harris, 1992).

Alongside concerns over possible crime displacement, there has also been evidence of diffusion of benefits – that is, the effects seem to extend beyond the targets involved in the situational prevention steps (Clarke & Weisburd, 1994). For example, the installation of security cameras on some buses and in some parking lots resulted in a reduction in crime even in buses and parking lots not so protected (Clarke, 1995). It seems that this came about because potential offenders were left uncertain as to which ones were and were not protected. Another example is provided by the Kirkholt burglary prevention project (Forrester, Chatteron, & Pease, 1988; Pease, 1992), in which target-hardening measures for repeatedly victimized houses led to a generalized reduction in burglary on the estate. It may be relevant, however, that a series of other measures was also employed. Three elements seem likely to foster diffusion:

(1) an increase in other community initiatives as a result of a feeling that it may now be worthwhile because something effective is being done;
(2) a generalized deterrence of offenders through an alteration in their perception of the risks involved; and
(3) a difficulty in circumvention of the preventive measures because of their multiplicity, together with a lack of ready identification of which targets for crime were less risky.

Increased Community Surveillance and Other Community Initiatives

The general public tend to think of prevention in terms of better neighborhood police patrolling. This may well be desirable but, for fairly obvious practical reasons, the police are unlikely to be in a position to provide sufficient communitywide surveillance to prevent much crime. Moreover, public trust in the police (at least in the United Kingdom) has diminished in recent years as a result of evidence of discriminatory practices and corruption (Reiner, 1997). Such misuse of police powers may well constitute unusual exceptions to generally fair practice, but it does seem that people's attitudes to the police have become more negative in recent years. In any case, even in optimal circumstances, it is clear that most surveillance will have to be provided by the general public.

Accordingly, various Neighborhood Watch schemes were introduced in both the United Kingdom and the United States to encourage community residents to be alert to possible crimes in their area, to take responsibility for the protection of their neighbors as well as themselves, to report

suspicious activities by strangers, and to exercise social control over behavior in public places in their neighborhood. The desirability of better
community surveillance is undeniable, but the evidence to date provides
little indication of success (Bennett, 1990; Hope, 1995b). The reasons appear to lie in the major difficulties in implementation. Anti-crime groups
are least likely to arise in high-crime areas because residents in such areas
are often (with good reason) suspicious of their neighbors and because
there are few obvious personal benefits from participation. Moreover, in
lower-crime areas, where community participation tends to be greater, it
is difficult to maintain participation. As Hope (1995b) put it: "looking
out for crime that does not happen may be nearly as boring as watching
paint dry" (p. 49). We conclude that, on their own, Neighborhood Watch
schemes are unlikely to increase community surveillance (in those areas
where it is most needed) to a sufficient degree to make much impact on
crime level. On the other hand, there is nothing in the research findings to
negate the view that natural surveillance is helpful in countering crime;
accordingly, as part of a broader community strategy, it may well have a
useful contributory role – provided the other measures succeed in changing public attitudes in ways that foster community cohesion and a desire
to act collectively.

Shaw and McKay's (1942, 1969) writings on the role of social disorganization in leading to high-crime inner-city areas were hugely influential in
the interwar years. Although their particular theory on patterns of spatial
distribution of high-crime areas has not stood the test of time, it remains
the case that there are enormous variations in crime rates among areas (see
Chapter 8). By and large, high-crime areas tend to be characterized by low
neighborhood stability, poverty, many single-adult households, high unemployment, a high proportion of young adults, and a high ethnic minority population (Bottoms & Wiles, 1997; Hope, 1995b; Skogan, 1990).
Furthermore, areas of physical decay (abandoned and ill-kept buildings,
litter, lack of maintenance of facilities) tend also to be areas of social problems (prostitution, public drinking, vandalism, etc.) and residential mobility (a high percentage of transients in multiple-occupancy dwellings
and much in- and out-migration).

Nevertheless, it has not proved easy to determine the extent to which
social disorganization (meaning a lack of community cohesion and mu-
tual helpfulness) constitutes a cause, rather than a consequence, of crime.
However, a case can be made that, at the least, its presence fails to prevent
crime and that an increase in social cohesion would be helpful. That view
underlay the Chicago Area Project initiated by Shaw in 1932 (Schlossman,
Zellman, & Shavelson, 1984) and of the much more recent British Priority

Estates Project (Foster & Hope, 1993; Hope, 1995b) and the American Mobilization for Youth initiative (Lavrakis & Bennett, 1989), as well as a variety of other similar schemes. The systematic evaluations have been discouragingly negative in their evidence of a lack of efficacy. It is important, however, to note (as with evaluations of Neighborhood Watch) that the results do *not* show that a diminution in social disorganization is without effects on crime. Rather, what they demonstrate is that it has proved extremely difficult to transform social disorganization into social cohesion. Several factors seem to be important:

(1) the negative impact of housing policies that generate an influx of young, poor, jobless adults with social problems who provide a concentration of both vulnerable victims and individuals likely to engage in crime;
(2) the difficulty of sustaining community initiatives in the face of high population turnover;
(3) a precarious reliance on the organizational and inspirational qualities of key individuals; and
(4) undermining from individuals and groups with vested interests.

A key lesson concerns the need to pay attention to the influence of wider sociopolitical policies, particularly with respect to local authority housing (Hope, 1995b).

Another feature that requires consideration is the possible influence of architectural design. Newman (1973) argued forcefully for its importance, drawing attention to the risks associated with large areas on housing estates for which no individuals had a responsibility, the problems of community surveillance in many estates (e.g., those with tower blocks), the stigma associated with ill-kept public housing, and the difficulties that may stem from a lack of safe leisure areas. Subsequent research has shown that the claims of architectural determinism were markedly excessive and failed to take adequate account of either the characteristics of residents or the quality of social relations on high-risk estates (Bannister, 1991; Mayhew, 1979). Nevertheless, it would be unfortunate if the likely contributory role of the physical environment were to be ignored (Pease, 1997), because it does seem probable that the notions provide useful guides to such practical steps as improved external lighting, avoidance of designs that make surveillance difficult, and the limitation of unassigned open spaces (Rubenstein et al., 1980). There is a lack of evaluated interventions focusing on architectural design features (most programs that have included architectural considerations have been multifaceted, with consequent problems in separating effects; Hope, 1995b) and it is unknown whether improvements would have much effect on crime. The limited available evidence suggests that, on their own, improvements in the design of housing estates would be unlikely to make much difference, but it would seem prudent to avoid obviously undesirable features in future building schemes.

Finally, there have been a variety of projects in which the main target has been the development of schemes to foster young people's constructive use of leisure, to encourage outdoor pursuits, and to use youth workers to aid youths' involvement in constructive activities (Graham & Bennett, 1995; Graham & Smith, 1994; Utting, 1996). In addition, particularly in the United States, there has been an interest in the value of youth organizations such as Scouts (Quinn, 1995). There have been too few evaluations for any general conclusions to be drawn. It seems that youth schemes are usually valued by the young people participating in them, and there is descriptive evidence of probable social benefits. But, on the evidence available to date, it does not appear that they are likely to have a major impact on crime rates, desirable though they may be for other reasons.

Populationwide Deterrent Effects

There is extensive research showing that young people's behavior is influenced by rewards and punishments (Blackburn, 1993; Maccoby & Martin, 1983; Patterson, 1982). It might therefore be expected that an effective means of preventing crime should be provided by steps that increase the likelihood that offenders will be caught and raise the level of punishment if convicted. Several considerations make the latter expectation a very dubious one. To begin with, the evidence that undesired behaviors can be reduced by punishment concerns the effects on the individuals punished. Much less is known about the deterrent effects of an awareness of punishments meted out to *others* for similar acts. Also, the effects are most evident with respect to punitive responses that follow closely in time and that occur with a reasonably high level of consistency.

The situation with respect to crime is quite different. Although the great majority of offenders are convicted at some point, only a tiny proportion (Mayhew et al., 1993, estimated about 3%) of delinquent *acts* result in conviction (see Chapter 3). Accordingly, offenders can have the entirely rational expectation that they are likely to "get away" with the crime without punishment if the likelihood is considered in relation to the decision to commit a particular crime on a single occasion. Moreover, sanctions are far from immediate. The Audit Commission (1996b) reported that, in

England and Wales, there was an average of 121 days from arrest to sentence (the period from the offense would be even longer). If punishment is not seen as an immediate and likely consequence of offending, it is not likely to have a strong deterrent effect (McGuire & Priestley, 1995). Furthermore, the evidence suggests that an awareness of the risk of being caught or imprisoned plays little part in offenders' motivations and decision making with respect to whether or not to commit a particular offense (Light, Nee, & Ingham, 1993).

A further consideration is introduced by the evidence that people's responses to levels of punishment are influenced by their feelings on its fairness and reasonableness (Hart, 1978). If harsh punishments are viewed as discriminatory and unreasonable, the main result may be an increase in resentment and a correspondingly *reduced* general deterrence effect.

It is clear that there can be no strong expectation that increasing the likelihood of conviction following an offense or increasing the severity of punishment will make any major impact on general deterrence. The need is for good empirical studies to test effects. The difficulties in doing that are, however, considerable (Lewis, 1986; Rutter, 1995d). In principle, what are required are time-series analyses comparing changes over time in likelihood of conviction (or severity of punishment) and in levels of crime. The problems arise first from uncertainty over the anticipated time lag in effects: should the general deterrence be seen immediately, a year later, or only several years later? The second need is to have time-series data with trends in both directions for the supposed deterrence measures (either by taking a sufficiently long time period or by using comparisons across countries). Even given adequate time-series data, there are still hazards from measurement artefacts (such as changes in police procedures or recording practices), from the possible confounding of deterrence and incapacitation effects, from difficulties identifying the direction of any causal effect, and from difficulties in taking account of other possible influences on crime levels.

Farrington and Langan's (1992) analysis of changes in crime and punishment in England and America in the 1980s went some way toward dealing with these issues (but the data do not apply specifically to young people). They were able to use contrasts between the two countries and between trends for violent and for acquisitive crime as tests; they also used both victim-reported and police-recorded offenses. The findings are, however, constrained by the fact that only two time points were compared, by reliance on data from just two countries, and by a lack of control for possible confounding factors. Nevertheless, the data are consistent with a possible general deterrence effect by which the decreased risk of conviction and custody for property offenders may have played a contributory role in the rise over the same time period for property offenses. This conclusion is strengthened by the addition of data from Sweden and from a further time point in 1991 (Farrington, Langan, & Wikström, 1994). The findings showed a high negative correlation between changes in the crime rate and changes in the probability of an offender being convicted. However, the data (Snyder et al., 1996) showing a rise in violent crime by U.S. juveniles during the last decade would seem to cast doubt on the inference that an effective general deterrence was operating.

Currie (1996) has also questioned the validity of general deterrence effects on the basis of intercity comparisons in the United States with respect to homicide rates and rates of imprisonment over a much longer time period. It is clear that the associations are highly inconsistent, but caution is called for both because homicide may be atypical and because U.S. homicide rates are so extremely high compared with the rest of the industrialized world.

In many respects, the clearest test of a general deterrence effect is provided by the British experience with the introduction of the use of "breathalyser" testing as a means of reducing alcohol-impaired driving (Ross, 1984). It led to an immediate and marked reduction of fatal and serious crash-related injuries on weekend nights (but not during the week, when alcohol was less likely to have been consumed). Unfortunately, however, the accident rate started rising again almost immediately, with most of the benefit lost after a couple of years. The experience in other countries is similar. The findings also show that the deterrence effect does not seem to be increased by the perceived severity of the penalty. The benefits derive from the increased likelihood of being caught and receiving some punishment of a severity that matters. Of course, the breathalyser results largely concern adults, not young people, but the conclusion may well be applicable more generally to deterrence effects.

Systematic analyses of British delinquency data for juveniles over a long time period have yet to be undertaken, but the overall trends are inconsistent with a strong deterrence effect. Thus, during the 1950s and 1970s, there was no appreciable change in the proportion of crimes cleared up (Rutter & Giller, 1983; Tarling, 1993) but there was a marked rise in crime rate (see Chapter 4). The data on severity of sentencing are more complicated. During the 1950s and 1960s there was no marked change, but during the 1970s three shifts occurred in parallel. First, there was a marked increase in the arrest rate of adolescents (which seems to have resulted from a widening of the net so that offenses that would previously have been dealt with informally came to be dealt with by arrest; Farrington & Bennett, 1981). Second, sentencing became more punitive, with a rise in the proportion of offenders given custodial penalties (Gelsthorpe & Morris, 1994). Third, there was a massive rise in the proportion of offenses dealt with by cautioning (Gelsthorpe & Morris, 1994). It is not self-evident whether these trends should be viewed as an overall increase or decrease in severity of punishment. Either way, there was no obvious change in the trend for crimes to rise.

During the 1980s and early 1990s, through developments in social work–led community services and diversionary arrangements, there was a substantial reduction in the use of custody by U.K. youth courts and a concomitant increase in the use of community sentences (Allen, 1991; Gelsthorpe & Morris, 1994; Morris & Giller, 1987). During the mid-1990s there was a return to a greater emphasis on punishment, and changes in legislation (the Criminal Justice Act of 1991) encouraged an increase in coercive approaches by increasing the number of components that could be combined (e.g., a supervision order with compulsory activity program participation and a curfew; Ashworth et al., 1992) and by imposing more stringent requirements within existing orders (such as financial penalties on parents). It has been noted that fines and curfews may exacerbate family conflicts, with a consequent negative effect on individual outcomes (Drakeford, 1996). Crime clear-up rates have fallen over the 1980s and 1990s. None of these various changes has had an obvious effect on overall crime levels.

More detailed analyses are called for in view of the fact that findings on general deterrence are so inconclusive at the moment. In principle, it seems desirable to increase the likelihood that crimes will result in apprehension of the offender; in practice, it is probable that the increase would have to be much greater than is likely to be feasible if there is to be any substantial effect on individual offenders' judgments about their own risks of being caught. The situation with respect to severity of punishment is more complicated. There is no convincing evidence that an increase in severity of punishment would have any major general deterrence effect, although a small effect cannot be ruled out. Decisions on the wisdom of a policy of increasing incarcerations, however, need to take into account incapacitation effects and effects on the individual offender.

Incapacitation

There has been a renewed interest in recent years in the incapacitation effects of custody, that is, of taking offenders out of circulation (Spelman,

1994; Zimring & Hawkins, 1995). Thus, the notion of automatic custody for repeat offenders – "three strikes and you're out" – has seemed to many people as obviously beneficial. After all, while offenders are in custody they cannot commit crimes in the community. Also, as numerous studies have shown, a high proportion of crimes are committed by a small number of seriously recidivist offenders (see Chapter 5). If this small number could be safely locked away, it would seem that the result must be a substantial reduction in the overall level of crime.

Nevertheless, the issue is not quite so straightforward as it seems at first sight. Tarling (1993) suggests that three main questions need to be posed. (i) How many crimes are prevented by current or past levels of imprisonment? (ii) What would be the effects on levels of crime if the use of imprisonment were increased or decreased? (iii) Can imprisonment be used in a selective way to control crime? A further query, of course, must concern the costs involved to achieve worthwhile benefits.

Answers necessarily depend on various assumptions (regarding e.g. the rate of offending of known offenders and who commits unsolved or unreported crimes). Nevertheless, Tarling's (1993) analyses, using British data, provide well-based and carefully quantified estimates of the approximate size of effect that may be achieved. Current sentencing policy probably reduces recorded crime by no more than 9% – a figure broadly in line with earlier American figures. In order to reduce crime by a further 1%, there would need to be a 16% increase in the prison population. The introduction of an 18-month mandatory prison sentence for second or subsequent convictions would have prevented 26% of offenders from committing further offenses (although the effects would vary by offense). Greenwood et al.'s (1994) estimate that California's "three strikes" law will reduce serious adult crimes by 21% is of the same order. The cost, however, would be more than $5.5 billion per year – a doubling of the California criminal justice system operating costs. Stolzenberg and D'Alessio (1997) have undertaken the one empirical examination of the effect of the three-strikes approach as applied in California. A time-series analysis showed little effect on crime levels that was not due to a pre-existing trend. It would be premature to argue that there is no effect of the approach through either deterrence or incapacitation, but the results so far do not suggest that this is likely to be an effective method of reducing crime.

A concern over costs, as well as over the acceptability of a massive increase in the prison population, has led to analyses of what might be achieved by a selective approach to incapacitation (Greenwood & Abrahamse, 1982; Greenwood et al., 1994; Spelman, 1994). It was estimated that, for California, a doubling of the sentences of high-rate robbery offenders while limiting sentences for low- and medium-rate offenders would reduce robbery offenses by 20% without any overall increase in the prison population. Estimates for other sites and for other crimes varied, but the overall conclusion was that modest reductions in crime (10% to 15%) were achievable by selective incapacitation with only modest (10% to 30%) increases in the prison population.

It may or may not be desirable to be much more selective in the use of long prison sentences, but the claims on what could be achieved by such policy are questionable (Tarling, 1993). The first limitation is provided by the prediction instrument used, which was largely based on self-report data, had a substantial misclassification rate (Visher, 1986), and was not cross-validated on a different sample (a crucial need when considering predictive accuracy). Prediction is not so satisfactory using official records (Farrington, 1997a) and, as Tarling (1993) noted, offenders are scarcely likely to be forthcoming and truthful if they are aware that the information they provide may be used to lengthen their sentences. Le Blanc (1998), too, concluded that there was no really satisfactory measure for picking out serious and violent offenders.

So far as young people are concerned, there is the additional problem of identifying the persistent offenders who should be incapacitated (it is somewhat easier in adult life when there is a longer crime record on which to make assessments). Thus, Hagell and Newburn (1994), in testing different definitions of persistence, found little overlap in the individuals selected by different methods and no consistent association between persistence and seriousness of offenses. There is no doubt that a small number of offenders are responsible for a large proportion of offenses. The problem is that, while it is straightforward to identify these individuals after the fact (i.e., after they have committed a large number of offenses), it is not nearly as easy to do so earlier in their criminal careers. We conclude that the potential of selective incapacitation to reduce the overall level of crime is quite limited, and that the limitations are most marked with regard to young people. It should be added that there are also ethical concerns over the justifiability of sentencing people on the basis of crimes they might commit rather than those they have committed; such concerns are that much greater in the light of findings that the predictability of future crime careers is a shaky business, rife with false positives.

Spelman (1994) noted that selective police targeting of persistent offenders could be more effective than selective incarceration. Such targeting would not carry the same ethical objections in that the courts would still have to decide whether or not the individuals were in fact guilty of the charged offenses and since sentencing would be on the basis of crimes actually committed rather than ones that might be committed in the future. Nevertheless, as Spelman pointed out, there is the same problem of deciding which offenders to target as well as of deciding what targeting would be both effective and acceptable.

Different Responses to Delinquency

Diversionary Policies

The impetus for the development of diversionary approaches in the early 1970s came from several rather different sources. These included an awareness of the very high frequency of minor delinquent behavior (see Chapter 2), with the implication that – if it were almost normative and likely to prove transient in many instances – neither therapeutic interventions nor punitive responses would likely be needed for first offenders. In addition, labeling theorists (Becker, 1963) in the 1960s had suggested that taking young people to court at an early stage might accelerate them into a criminal career by encouraging the offenders to be viewed as delinquents by themselves and others. There was a concern that people would thereby behave according to this reputation. Some empirical support for this postulated process became available in the 1970s (see Rutter & Giller, 1983), indicating that – for first (but not subsequent) offenses – court processing made continuation in crime more, rather than less, likely (Farrington, 1977; Farrington, Osborn, & West, 1978).

Official U.K. policies came to place a much increased emphasis on cautioning (allowable only if the person admitted the offense). This involved a formal warning by a uniformed senior police officer, a warning that indicated that further offending would lead to prosecution. The idea was to provide a firm and unambiguous expression of official disapproval linked with an explicit reminder that more unpleasant sanctions would follow if there were persistence in antisocial activities. The policy was followed by a massive increase in the use of cautioning in the United Kingdom, especially for older adolescents (see Gelsthorpe & Morris, 1994). During the 1970s, it became clear that, as implemented, there were disadvantages to this scheme. Evidence indicated both a net-widening effect (with consequent *extension* of official sanctions to behaviors that would not previously have resulted in police action) and discriminatory application, with cautions more likely to be used with girls than boys and less likely to be employed with black youths (Gelsthorpe & Morris, 1994; Rutter & Giller, 1983; Smith, 1997a). The situation during the 1980s seems to have improved, with avoidance of net-widening effects (Morris & Giller, 1987).

Table 12.2. Reconviction Rates for Offenders Cautioned in 1991

Criminal History before Sample Caution	Portion of Offenders Subsequently Convicted within 2 Years
No previous court appearance and	
no previous cautions	11%
one previous caution	22%
two or more previous cautions	45%
Previous court appearances and	
no previous cautions	24%
one previous caution	33%
two or more previous cautions	46%

Source: Home Office (1995b, p. 93). Crown copyright is reproduced with the permission of the Controller of Her Majesty's Stationery Office.

The empirical data provide support for the appropriateness of cautioning for first offenses (see Table 12.2). Almost nine out of every ten offenders remain without conviction two years later. The findings are much less positive, however, for the use of cautions when the individual has had a previous caution or court appearance. Of course, youngsters who are being cautioned for their first offense are a low-risk group for recidivism. Also, styles of cautioning vary (Audit Commission, 1996b) and many offenders seem to see the caution as "getting away with it" (Light et al., 1993). Even so, it is not likely that any other response could improve greatly on an 11% reconviction rate, and Whitehead and Lab's (1989) meta-analysis supports the inference that cautioning has results for reconviction that are better than the alternatives. Their findings, however, also show that the same benefits do not apply to "nonsystem" diversionary approaches (informal reprimands and the like).

Consideration needs to be given to the appropriateness of repeated cautions when, as Table 12.2 indicates, the reconviction rate increases markedly. Not only is the base rate expectation of reconviction likely to be high for these repeat offenders, but two further aspects of the situation suggest that repeated cautions are probably undesirable. First, a reconviction rate of nearly 50% would seem to argue that cautioning is not an effective response and that some form of more intensive intervention needs to be considered. Second, if repeated offenses keep resulting in cautions, it would seem highly probable that this will reinforce offenders' views that they are "getting away with it" and that no change in their behavior is needed. In appropriate circumstances, a second caution may sometimes be justifiable, but a third would seem definitely unhelpful.

In some diversionary arrangements, other elements may be added – for example, befriending schemes (Giller, 1983), compensation schemes (Marshall, 1992), and reparation programs (Audit Commission, 1996b). Systematic evaluations are lacking, but the available evidence suggests that they probably do not improve reconviction rates. On the other hand, there may be gains to the victim or to the local community that justify their use.

There are other forms of diversion apart from official cautions, of which the most obvious is provided by prosecutor discretion on whether or not to proceed with prosecution (Gelsthorpe & Giller, 1990). In England and Wales, the prosecutor does not have the power to use alternatives to court procedures, but broader powers are available in Scotland (Moody & Tomas, 1982), many countries in mainland Europe (Dunkel, 1991; Van der Laan, 1988), and the United States (Feld, 1993). The advantages and disadvantages of such broadening do not seem to have been subjected to systematic evaluation.

Community "Alternatives to Custody" Schemes

At about the same time as the increased use of cautioning (1970s), and for broadly similar reasons, there evolved a range of community schemes (Junger-Tas, 1994b). These first developed in the 1970s in the United Kingdom and United States but are now available in most countries, with the main growth having taken place in the 1980s. The schemes were quite varied in their components and in their orientations (Bottoms et al., 1990). The aim of the schemes as a whole was to provide an alternative to custody that combined supervision of the offender (through involvement in a recreational and work program), support in relation to home stresses, rehabilitation, and penalties or punishment (primarily through demands and controls on the offenders' time). The active programs entailed in these approaches came to be termed "intermediate treatment" (IT) in the United Kingdom, and their development during the 1980s was indeed accompanied by a reduced use of custodial sentences – perhaps because they provided courts with an alternative that previously had not been perceived as credible (Allen, 1991; Rutherford, 1992b). At first, IT was mainly focused on relatively minor offenders, but later it came also to be used with more serious recidivist offenders.

The most extensive evaluation of IT is that undertaken by Bottoms (1995b) in the United Kingdom during the period between 1987 and 1990. Most of the IT programs were undertaken at dedicated central premises;

they included a mixture of group and individual work, the teaching of social skills, and various constructive activities. All tended to share a relatively ordered approach and authoritative leader style coupled with a strongly caring orientation. Four groups were compared: "heavy end" IT (HEIT) received compulsorily; those receiving custodial sentences (CUS); other IT (OIT) for offenders on supervision orders; and young offenders on supervision (SUP) orders without IT. These numbered respectively 103, 141, 40, and 142 (with complete data on 78, 83, 26, and 83) individuals. The main comparisons of interest were those between the first pair and those between the second pair, as these constituted practical alternatives to one another. Random allocation was not considered feasible, so a quasi-experimental design was employed that made use of wide sources of data to ensure statistical comparability. Data were obtained at three time points: soon after sentence, one month after treatment, and one year after treatment. Outcome was assessed from both official crime records and self-reports. The reconviction rates 14 months after the end of treatment were 74% for HEIT versus 81% for custody and 65% for OIT versus 61% for supervision. None of the differences was statistically significant. The nonsignificant advantage of HEIT over custody nevertheless produced an effect size of 0.14 for officially recorded crime and of 0.24 for self-reported crime. Some caution, however, must be exercised in placing weight on this small difference, since the custody group had a slightly worse prior crime record. This was taken into account statistically, probably adequately, but there must be some slight uncertainty. The effect size of the difference between OIT and supervision was both trivial and nonsignificant. The costs of supervision, however, were substantially less (Knapp & Fenyo, 1995), and supervision without IT may well be preferable on those grounds in view of the finding that IT did not seem to bring any additional benefits. Interestingly, there was no cost difference between HEIT and custody. The authors suggest that (because custodial costs are higher per week but custodial sentences tended to be slightly shorter) the policy implication could be to try using somewhat shorter durations of IT for heavy-end offenders, as this would be cheaper and might well be more cost-effective (because variations in the length of IT were said not to be associated with outcome – details not published). Bottoms (1995a) also suggested that IT might be made more effective when there was work with parents as well as offenders, more attention to posttreatment social adjustment, and more of a behavioral focus on key problems.

Restorative Justice

Restorative justice is a collective term for approaches that seek resolution by having the offender confront the victim and make good the losses (material, mental, or social) caused (Bazemore & Umbreit, 1995; Consedine, 1995). Victims may be individuals, groups, or even whole communities. The focus is problem solving: making offenders aware of their liabilities and obligations in order to develop plans to ameliorate the harm brought about by their delinquent acts. It constitutes an alternative sanctioning model for juveniles that aims to be more closely engaged with the real problems of victims, offenders, and communities than is the case with traditional retributionist and rehabilitation models. The tactics used include: making amends (Wright, 1982), reconciliation (Marshall, 1985), reintegrative shaming (Braithwaite, 1989; Braithwaite & Mugford, 1994), and relational justice (Schluter, 1994). Each seeks to emphasize how victims can contribute to the social re-integration of the offenders.

The techniques that may be employed include:

- *mediation* – structured communication between the victim, offender, and impartial intermediary to identify how the offense can be remedied;
- *reparation* – "making good" the damage or injury by undertaking an act of reparation for the victim of their offenses or of other people's;
- *compensation* – redressing the loss by financial payment to the victim;
- *community service* – undertaking tasks for the benefit of individuals or social institutions as recompense for the crime;
- *victim confrontation* – confronting the offender with the pain, loss, or suffering of the victim; and
- *shaming and reintegration* – shaming of the offender by the victim (and their family and friends), identifying the harm experienced, and negotiating with the offender for acts of recompense.

Several of these practice methods have recently come together under the concept of the Family Group Conference (FGC) (Jackson, forthcoming). Originally developed in New Zealand as a way of providing indigenous Maori people with a culturally appropriate form of dispute resolution, the FGC is now enshrined in law (The Children, Young Persons and Their Families Act of 1989) as the main forum for resolving offenses that cannot be dealt with by police warning (Morris, Maxwell, & Robertson, 1993). The FGC consists of the offender, their immediate and extended family (and whomever else they wish to involve), the victim and the victim's representative(s), the police, and social workers (where previously involved). The aim of the conference is for the offender and their family group to come up with an appropriate plan that will meet the needs of the victim. This can involve an apology to the victim, work in the community or for the victim, making reparation, or a donation to charity. A key practitioner in the FGC is the coordinator, who acts as an intermediary between the victim, the offender, the family, and the other agencies. How truly victim-oriented the FGC is can be significantly influenced by who acts as coordinator – police officers, social workers, or independent intermediaries (Braithwaite, 1989).

There is a growing literature on the processes involved in running FGCs (Alder & Wundersitz, 1994; Braithwaite, 1989; Brown & Polk, 1996; Consedine, 1995; Jackson, forthcoming), but there has been no systematic evaluation of its outcomes in terms of the effect on reoffending. In New Zealand, an evaluation of the views of victims who have been through the FGC process suggests that a substantial minority are dissatisfied with its operation and that the interests of the offender are promoted over those of the victim (Morris et al., 1993). The FGC has now been extended into Australia (Brown & Polk, 1996), and several European jurisdictions are experimenting with it both for criminal matters and for issues such as child protection and child care more generally (Jackson, forthcoming).

The general notion that it may be helpful for offenders to be more aware of the personal and social impact of their crimes, and that restorative approaches may be constructive, is an attractive one. But, clearly, net-widening effects need to be avoided, and there are numerous practical issues that will need to be dealt with (Walgrave, 1995). These include the definition and measurement of harm and the selection of compensatory actions, not to mention the issues of due procedure, relations with insurers, and development of suitable techniques for bringing about mediation and restoration. An increasing interest in restorative approaches is likely; they will need to be accompanied by appropriate evaluations.

Punishment

The research on specific deterrent effects (i.e., the effects on the individual offender) of punishment is inconclusive (Brennan & Mednick, 1994; Rutter & Giller, 1983). Brennan and Mednick (1994) used data from a very large ($n = 28,879$) Danish general population sample to examine the effects of sanctions on recidivism in males committing crimes after the age of 15. Approximately a third of offenders (for all arrest levels from first to fifth offense) were released without any kind of sanction. Their rate of recidivism was significantly higher than those who received some form of sanction (probation, fine, or imprisonment). The authors argued that the findings suggest that punishment reduces the rate of reoffending.

There are three main problems with this suggestion. First, although the data set is very large, the inevitable drawback is that the available measures were extremely limited – so much so that it must remain uncertain whether the finding is valid. Second, no one would seriously suggest that "doing nothing" (i.e., release without any kind of sanction) is appropriate for older offenders. The query is not whether some sanction is desirable (which clearly it is) but instead whether increasing the severity of punishment reduces recidivism. "Sanctions" in the Brennan and Mednick study spanned probation to prison, so their findings do not help on that question. Third, they argue that their findings fit in with learning theory. This seems a rather dubious claim. As they point out, both theory and research findings indicate the importance of immediacy and high probability of punishment. And as already discussed, neither is the case in the way that the criminal justice system operates. We conclude that the evidence on the specific deterrent effects of punishment is no more satisfactory now than it was when the evidence was reviewed over a decade ago (Rutter & Giller, 1983). Some form of sanction is desirable to indicate society's disapproval, but it seems unlikely that increasing the severity of punishment would make much difference to the deterrent effect on the individual offender.

"Short Sharp Shock" Approaches

In the mid-1980s, "shock incarceration" or "boot camp" programs were introduced in the United States. The rationale was that prisons were becoming increasingly overcrowded, that the general conditions in prisons did not foster rehabilitation, that it was necessary to be "tough" on crime, that a more arduous military-style regime might be capable of combining a greater deterrent effect with more appropriate social training, and that with this approach a shorter period in custody might lead to both a reduction in overcrowding and a reduced reconviction rate. The main intended target group for this approach were males aged roughly 17–25 years who had committed nonviolent crimes (MacKenzie & Souryal, 1994). The programs were modeled after military boot-camp training and incorporated military-style drills, physical training, mandatory hard labor, and structured activities throughout the day. Initially, rehabilitation programs played a minor role but in recent years they have come to have a more prominent place. MacKenzie and Souryal (1994) undertook a major multisite evaluation in which comparisons were made with a sample who underwent ordinary prison experiences and with a sample who dropped out of the boot-camp regimes (and with other smaller groups). The modal duration of the boot-camp programs studied was 80 to 120 days. All samples were followed for either one or two years. The groups were chosen to be comparable though random assignment was not employed, and statistical adjustment was made for relevant risk variables.

There was no consistent effect, either positive or negative, of shock incarceration on reconviction rates. There was also no consistent effect on adjustment during community supervision after release. However, the boot-camp participants, compared with prison inmates, were more likely to develop positive attitudes toward their experience. Participants commented on the benefits in terms of physical fitness and a drug-free environment. There were also adverse comments, however, about harsh treatment by staff, verbal abuse, and the amount of yelling and screaming. The work experiences did not seem to be of much value in that most involved very menial activities of little use in obtaining later employment.

No entirely straightforward conclusions are possible. The lack of any consistent effect on crime after release argues against the notion that a short sharp shock would have a useful specific deterrent effect on participants in boot-camp programs. Internal comparisons, however, showed substantial variations among programs in both their quality and their effects. The data did not allow systematic analysis of the links between the two, but there was some suggestion that the rehabilitation elements may be important. As MacKenzie and Souryal (1994) have hypothesized: "A non-military program with a strong rehabilitative component followed by intensive supervision might be just as effective as one with the boot camp atmosphere" (p. 42). The suggestion sounds reasonable and seems worthy of further exploration. Other work indicates that attempts to introduce tougher regimes in custodial institutions are not likely to be helpful; they may even be counterproductive (Fickenauer, 1992; Thornton et al., 1984).

Custodial Care

As we have noted already, until very recently in the United Kingdom there has been a declining use of custodial sentences for juveniles, so that the figure in 1995 was roughly half that in 1985. In the United States, the picture is more diverse across the different states (McGarrell, 1991). In both countries, however, youths discharged from custodial institutions continue to exhibit very high reconviction rates. The British Home Office (1995c) gave a figure of 89% reconviction within two years for 14–16-year-olds released from custody.

The fall in custodial sentences has been paralleled by a reduction in the number of children in group foster care, but all the evidence indicates that those children (and especially adolescents) in such care are a particularly troubled and troublesome group (Bullock, Little, & Milham, 1993; Sinclair & Gibbs, 1996; Utting, 1991). Typically, about a half of the residents have had formal contact with the criminal justice system, and most have engaged in substantial antisocial behavior. Also, many have suffered sexual or physical abuse before entering the institution, and some experience further abuse while in care (Support Force for Children's Residential Care, 1996; Utting, 1991). The adversities suffered by section-53 offenders (those with particularly severe offenses) seem unusually great, although systematic comparisons with other offenders are lacking (Boswell, 1995).

The issues involved in custodial care have not gone away with the reduction in the proportion of young people in residential settings. Indeed, they may well have been heightened, although efforts have shifted slightly toward more particular focus on those who seem in need of secure accommodation. In 1983, Rutter and Giller concluded, on the basis of research findings, that institutions did have a quite important and substantial effect on the behavior of young people in them. Variations in effect were not coincident with the theoretical orientation of the institutions, but those with the best results seemed to combine firmness, warmth, harmony, high expectations, good discipline, and a practical approach to training. Yet it was also found that the effects of institutional care on young people's behavior *after* their return to the community were much weaker. It was argued that more attention should be paid to the environments to which these youths return. Research since 1983 is broadly supportive of those conclusions, but what is new is the evidence on secure institutions.

In 1992, Ditchfield and Catan made a systematic comparison of section-53 offenders (those with very serious offenses such as murder, manslaughter, and serious wounding) in youth offender institutions (YOIs) and a similar group in local authority community homes (LACHs). There were 119 males in YOIs and 54 in LACHs. The two types of institutions were similar with respect to their need to maintain security and to their strong emphasis on rehabilitation. They differed, however, in that the LACHs strove to maintain contact with families and involve them in their activities (39% of LACH boys had family visits at least three times per month versus 1% of YOI boys); also, there was much more contact with the external community as provided by frequent trips outside (69% of LACH boys had these at least weekly versus 1% of YOI boys) and by progression to open accommodation. Educational and work training activities were also much better in LACHs. In most respects the boys in the two types of institutions were similar: half had been in residential group care at some time, about half came from homes headed by a single parent, three fifths had a father who was unemployed, and they all had similar crime records. The YOI boys were, however, somewhat older on average; they were also more likely to have had troubled school careers (43%

having been expelled compared with 25% of LACH boys). On the other hand, the LACH boys were more likely to have experienced child abuse (41% versus 21%).

The better educational opportunities with LACH were reflected in the much higher proportion who attained educational qualifications while in the institution. Two years after discharge, 53% of YOI boys had been reconvicted compared with 40% of LACH boys, and more had committed violent offenses (43% versus 28%). The pattern of findings as a whole strongly suggested that the characteristics of the regimes in the two types of institutions had played a role in the relatively better outcome for LACH boys.

The average costs per resident week in YOIs (£426) were substantially less than those for LACH (£564–£892) but both were much lower than therapeutic youth treatment centers (£1,231–£1,421), which also accommodate a high proportion of section-53 offenders.

One of the reasons for initiating the study in the first place had been a concern over abscondings from LACHs. During the four-year period of the study, they were more frequent in LACHs (27) than in YOIs (8), but they were relatively infrequent in both. The higher rate of absconding for LACHs must also be interpreted within the context of the much greater openness in (and hence opportunities for absconding from) LACHs.

Another relevant comparison is that between young people in secure versus open institutions. It might be assumed that the former would necessarily be populated by much more serious offenders. Certainly, they include many young people with long histories of serious behavioral and emotional disturbance (Bailey, Thornton, & Weaver, 1994; Bullock et al., 1993). Also, many have committed serious offenses. Nevertheless, they are more heterogeneous than one might think. Nearly half of Ditchfield and Catan's (1992) sample's current offenses involved nonviolent property crime. Curran et al.'s (1995) comparison of young offenders in open and secure custody following a period in training schools for delinquents in Northern Ireland showed even less serious crime. Those in secure custody were there primarily because they had proved unmanageable in open settings (often through absconding) rather than because of the seriousness of their offenses.

Three years following discharge, the reconviction rates were very high for both groups, but they were somewhat worse for those who had been in secure custody (86% versus 72%). The secure group also accumulated higher cumulative sentences (57 months versus 41 months). About a fifth received adult convictions for a violent offense, but this was not higher in the secure group.

In view of the difficulties in taking account of likely differences in the characteristics and background of offenders in the two groups, not too much should be made of the slightly higher reconviction rate in the secure group. After all, it was extremely high in both. Nevertheless, the authors' conclusion – that open custody should be the preferred option unless there is clear evidence that the offender is unmanageable (or that the offenses were particularly serious) – seems reasonable.

In seeking to draw some general conclusions about custodial care, it is necessary to note the wide variety of residential institutions involved – spanning group foster homes, therapeutic institutions, community homes, and secure custody. Many of the early studies reviewed by Rutter and Giller (1983) had assumed that the main impact of residential care would come via some change in the young people themselves and hence that therapeutic approaches would be more successful. That turned out not to be the case. Moreover, even marked changes in young people's behavior whilst in institutions usually failed to persist if they returned, as they usually did, to the same adverse environments from whence they had come. In order to draw conclusions, we therefore need to turn to a wider literature – one that explores which experiences are likely to have lasting benefits as well as which institutional features are likely to provide such experiences.

The possibly relevant experiences were discussed in Chapters 7 and 8, the individual factors that may influence people's abilities to profit by their experiences in Chapter 6, and the ways in which it may be possible to have a turning point from a maladaptive to a positive life trajectory in Chapter 10. With respect to beneficial turning points, it was noted that three features stood out: a change in social group to one that involved more appropriate mores and values; a change in skills or qualifications likely to open up advantageous new opportunities; and a change in mental set that provided a concept of self-efficacy and control over one's destiny. The institutional features likely to foster such features were considered in Chapters 8 and 11 in relation to findings on schools; many of the results probably apply also to other institutions.

Institutions are more likely to have beneficial effects, it would seem, if the overall ethos is prosocial; if educational and work training activities are good; if they facilitate development of a more positive and supportive social group; and if there are opportunities to exercise responsibilities and personal decision making in ways that foster self-efficacy. Many prisons stand out as particularly likely to be damaging as judged by these criteria. The rate of drug abuse is high in the prison population (a quarter of males and nearly one third of females in Gunn, Maden, & Swinton's 1991 survey);

there is ready availability of drugs in prisons (Home Office, 1995a); family ties are fragile (Walmsley, Howard, & White, 1992); there is a prison culture that is anti-staff (see Morgan, 1994); and ties with the outside world are weak. The implication is that the peer group pressures are likely to be antisocial, that there is a risk of increasing involvement with drugs, and that prisons' social ties are likely to become more oriented to others chronically engaged in antisocial behavior. It is also relevant that Sampson and Laub's (1993) analysis of the Gluecks' longitudinal data showed that imprisonment made it more likely that criminal activities would persist or recur, and that this negative effect mainly stemmed from the adverse effects of prison on the prospects of employment after leaving prison.

Conversely, the limited data from the few comparative studies of custodial institutions that have been undertaken suggest the probable benefits associated with: (i) the provision of education and work training that is likely to improve chances of employment; (ii) a drug-free environment and help for individuals to deal with their drug problems; (iii) a prosocial ethos that is fostered by good staff–inmate relationships and good models of behavior; (iv) opportunities for taking responsibilities and exercising personal autonomy and decision making; and (v) links with families that both maintain ties and seek to improve the family circumstances to which the inmates will return.

There have not been sufficient comparative studies for these suggestions to be more than inferences derived from limited empirical data, but the evidence does point to the probable importance of the nature of people's experiences in institutions with respect to their later behavior. Most of the public debate on custody has been on the supposed deterrent effects (which seem to be quite limited) or incapacitation effects (which are greater but still decidedly modest). More attention needs now to be paid to the consequences of the content and nature of people's experiences in institutions.

Psychological Treatments

A recent Home Office Research Study report (Vennard, Sugg, & Hedderman, 1997) concluded that programs using cognitive–behavioral methods had the greatest effects in reducing antisocial behavior in both juveniles and adults. They concluded that results were best when: (i) factors contributing to the genesis of offending behavior were targeted; (ii) active, participatory, problem-solving methods of working were used; (iii) the intensity and duration of intervention were well matched to the likely future risk of offending; and (iv) steps were taken to ensure that therapeutic programs did actually run in the way intended. In his thoughtful review of promising psychosocial treatments for conduct disorder, Kazdin (1997) came up with similar conclusions. He emphasized the value of four steps: (i) a clear conceptualization of the hypothesized causal mechanisms; (ii) research showing that the mechanism can be measured and that, irrespective of treatment, it is related to antisocial behavior; (iii) empirical evidence that the treatment approach does lead to the desired change; and (iv) that changes in the proposed causal processes do play a major role in the changes in antisocial behavior that come about through treatment.

Kazdin concluded that parent management training (PMT), as first developed by Patterson and his colleagues (Dishion, Patterson, & Kavanagh, 1992; Kavanagh & Dishion, 1990; Patterson, 1982) is the best established effective treatment, with the additional merit of treatment manuals and training materials for professionals and parents (e.g., Forehand & McMahon, 1981; Forgatch & Patterson, 1989; Patterson & Forgatch, 1987). In addition, however, there is similar evidence showing the benefits of cognitive problem-solving skills training (PSST), functional family therapy, and multisystematic therapy – all of which have many elements in common. However, PMT and PSST differ in that the former focuses on parenting and the latter on children's problem-solving skills. In a randomized controlled trial, Kazdin et al. (1992) compared the effects (on 7–13-year-olds attending an outpatient psychiatric clinic) of PMT and PSST given separately with the effects of the two treatments in combination. At a one-year follow-up, the combined group showed the greatest reduction in self-reported delinquency and in antisocial behavior as reported by parents.

Parent management training uses Patterson's (1982) coercion model as its theoretical basis, and it focuses treatment on four main targets: effective monitoring of children's behavior, prosocial fostering, well-focused discipline, and good social problem solving. Scores of controlled trials have shown worthwhile reductions in antisocial behavior, which are often maintained for one to three years (Kazdin, 1992; Miller & Prinz, 1990; Patterson, Dishion, & Chamberlain, 1993). Furthermore, the findings for the most part are in line with the postulated parental mediating mechanism. Thus, several studies have shown substantial correlations between inept maternal discipline and antisocial children's behavior, and have found that changes in the former correlate with changes in the latter (Forgatch, 1991). The most stringent test was provided by Dishion et al. (1992), who compared a behavioral approach focused on parenting with one focused on the 10–14-year-olds themselves. The latter approach focused on self-monitoring, prosocial goal setting, peer relationships, and problem-solving and communication skills. Both approaches were followed by reductions in antisocial behavior, but there was only a marginally significant overall effect for parent training (although there was a significant parenting effect on teacher ratings of the children's antisocial behavior). The findings are supportive of the focus on parenting; but, like the parallel findings in Kazdin et al.'s (1992) study, they also point to the somewhat comparable value of child-focused approaches. That there has been therapeutic efficacy from PMT is shown by the follow-up findings with respect to delinquency. Home observation posttreatment ratings of antisocial behavior were better predictors of later delinquency than were pretreatment ratings; similarly, the amount of change in parental problem solving and monitoring were better predictors than the baseline measures (Patterson & Forgatch, 1995).

The results of PMT are highly encouraging, but there are several important limitations. The demands on parents are quite high and, as with other methods, drop-out from treatment is a significant concern (with about a half terminating prematurely). On the whole, it seems that results may be better with younger children (Dishion & Patterson, 1992), although there are few systematic comparisons of possible age effects. Families characterized by social disadvantage, parental psychopathology, and marital discord tend to do less well (Dadds & McHugh, 1992) – a crucial limitation in view of the extensive evidence that these constitute a high-risk group most in need of intervention.

Patterson and his colleagues, however, have been pioneering in their study of treatment resistance directly (Patterson & Chamberlain, 1994; Stoolmiller et al., 1993). They have found that negative parental reactions to therapy relate to their disciplinary practices at home, that changes in parental resistance during therapy predict changes in parenting at home, and that specific therapist techniques serve to either overcome or exacerbate resistance.

Clearly, a lot of progress has been made with PMT, but the benefits are least evident with the most disturbed families. As with all treatments, they provide modest rather than dramatic gains in most instances; by no means do all youngsters respond. Other limitations are that treatment needs to be intensive and the drop-out rate is substantial.

One finding with respect to less promising treatments requires note. There is much evidence on the importance of deviant peer groups in antisocial behavior (see Chapter 7), and it would seem to be an important target for interventions. Undoubtedly, reducing negative peer group influences should be helpful (see Feldman, 1992), but several studies have found that placing antisocial adolescents in a deviant peer group (albeit with therapeutic intentions) can exacerbate their problems in some

Treatment modality

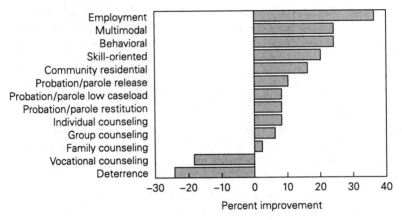

Figure 12.2. Juvenile justice treatments: percentage improvement over control group by modality. *Source:* M. Lipsey, "What do we learn from 400 research studies on the effectiveness of treatment with juvenile delinquents?" In J. McGuire (Ed.), *What Works: Reducing Reoffending* (1995). Copyright John Wiley & Sons Limited. Reproduced with permission.

circumstances (Dishion & Andrews, 1995), particularly in the case of non-delinquents treated as part of mixed groups (O'Donnell, 1992).

Meta-analyses

Finally, it is necessary to turn attention to the multiple meta-analyses that have been undertaken. Up to this point, we have largely relied on good-quality evaluations of individual types of intervention, but it is necessary now to seek to compare across different types of intervention. As numerous reviewers have pointed out (see e.g. Lösel, 1995a,b, 1996), this must be done with caution in view of the many conceptual and methodological hazards to be circumvented. Nevertheless, the findings are informative and sufficiently consistent in their broad trends to provide some guidelines for policy and practice (Sheldon, 1994). The findings are generally quite close to the inferences already drawn from individual studies (see Figures 12.2 and 12.3).

Little weight should be attached to the completely discrepant findings on the effects of employment approaches in judicial and nonjudicial settings, because they are based on quite small numbers. Possibly, the findings mean that an emphasis on job training and opportunities within

Treatment modality

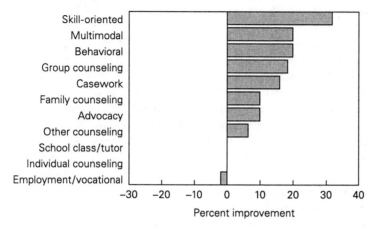

Figure 12.3. Nonjuvenile justice treatments: percentage improvement over control group by modality. *Source:* Lipsey (1995). Copyright John Wiley & Sons Limited. Reproduced with permission.

broader-based programs *is* beneficial but that, when provided on its own without judicial constraints, such emphasis is of little use. However, the evidence is inconsistent and inconclusive (Lipsey & Wilson, 1998). Otherwise, in both sorts of settings, it is clear that the best results derive from behavioral, skill-oriented, and multimodal methods, with deterrence approaches doing particularly badly (although this last conclusion is also based on small numbers). Nevertheless, the efficacy of even the best treatments should not be overstated. The remediation of antisocial behavior continues to present major challenges and difficulties, and the efficacy of interventions to reduce crime has been estimated as only about half that of interventions to deal with other psychosocial or psychiatric problems (Lipsey & Wilson, 1993). It should be added that the best results tend to derive from research interventions, the effects from more ordinary clinical interventions being less impressive (Weisz, 1997; Weisz et al., 1995).

Elements of Effective Programs of Intervention

Using the findings of meta-analyses (Andrews et al., 1990; Gottschalk et al., 1987; Lipsey, 1992; Lipsey & Wilson, 1998; Lösel, 1995a,b; Whitehead & Lab, 1989), McGuire and Priestley (1995) have identified six principles underpinning the design and delivery of effective programs of intervention in offending behavior.

(1) *Risk classification* – A matching between offender risk levels and the degree of intervention, so that higher-risk individuals receive more intensive services and lower-risk ones minimal intervention.

(2) *Responsivity* – An appropriate matching between styles of worker and styles of clients, but the learning styles of most offenders require active participatory methods of working rather than either didactic methods or loose, unstructured experiential methods.

(3) *Community base* – On the whole, programs in the community or having close links with the community tend to be more effective.

(4) *Treatment modality* – Effective programs tend to be multimodal (seeking to impact several different types of problems) and social-skills oriented; they tend to use methods drawn from behavioral and cognitive–behavioral sources.

(5) *Program integrity* – The stated aims are closely linked to the methods to be used; adequate resourcing is provided; and there is staff training, systematic monitoring, and evaluation (Hollin, Epps, & Kendrick, 1995).

(6) *Criminogenic needs* – A focus on problems or features that contribute or are conducive to offending rather than those only distantly related to it.

With respect to the identification of criminogenic needs, Andrews (1989; Andrews & Bonton, 1994) has distinguished between two groups of (more or less) promising targets. The more promising targets include:

- changing antisocial attitudes;
- changing antisocial feelings;
- reducing antisocial peer associations;
- promoting familial affection and communication;
- promoting familial monitoring and supervision;
- promoting identification and association with anticriminal role models;
- increasing self-control, self-management, and problem-solving skills;
- replacing the skills of lying, stealing, and aggression with more prosocial alternatives;
- reducing chemical dependencies;
- shifting the density of the personal, interpersonal, and other rewards and costs for criminal and noncriminal activities in familial, academic, vocational, recreational, and other behavioral settings, so that the noncriminal alternatives come to be favored;
- providing the chronically psychiatrically troubled with low-pressure, sheltered, supportive living arrangements;

- changing other attributes of clients and their circumstances that, through individualized assessments of risk and need, have been linked reasonably with criminal conduct;
- ensuring that clients are able to recognize risky situations and have concrete and well-rehearsed plans for dealing with those situations.

Less promising targets include:

- increasing self-esteem (without simultaneous reductions in antisocial thinking, feeling, and peer associations);
- focusing on vague emotional or personal complaints that have not been linked with criminal conduct;
- increasing the cohesiveness of antisocial peer groups;
- improving neighborhoodwide living conditions without touching the criminogenic needs of higher-risk individuals;
- showing respect for antisocial thinking on the grounds that the values of one culture are equally valid to the values of another culture;
- increasing conventional ambition in the areas of school and work without concrete assistance in realizing these ambitions;
- attempting to turn the client into a "better person" when the standards for becoming so do not link with recidivism.

Even taken as a whole, it could not be claimed that these suggestions provide a detailed and exact template for effective treatment. Nevertheless, the field has moved on considerably over the last 15 years, and it is now possible to differentiate between approaches that are likely to be helpful and those that seem to carry a very limited potential for benefits with respect to reducing antisocial behavior.

Conclusions

There are good reasons for supposing that interventions designed to reduce the opportunities for offending should be helpful. A wide range of situational crime prevention strategies has been developed for this purpose. They aim to increase the *effort* required to commit offenses, as well as to increase the attendant *risks* and reduce the *rewards* that result from crime. There are many situational measures that have been shown to bring about useful benefits, but there also are failures. Comparative studies are lacking, but four main elements seem to predispose to success: (i) rapid pervasive introduction of the measures; (ii) combinations of measures to impact related crime targets; (iii) use of interventions with other public benefits; and (iv) an avoidance of reliance on individual responsibility and initiative.

On the whole, community initiatives to increase public surveillance or social cohesion have been less successful. The available evidence suggests that the problem is not that the goals are inappropriate, but rather that successful implementation in high-risk communities is extremely difficult.

The findings on the general and specific deterrent effects of severe punishments for crime are inconclusive. It seems unlikely that this provides a useful way forward in view of the facts that most crimes do not result in convictions and that, even when they do, there is a long delay between committing the crime and being punished for it. Theory and experimental studies indicate that both considerations are likely to severely reduce the deterrent effects of punishments.

Incapacitation – that is, taking offenders out of circulation by locking them up – has received increasing attention in recent years. It is undeniable that offenders cannot commit crimes in the community while they are in custody. Nevertheless, it is clear that there would have to be a massive increase in the prison population in order to bring about much reduction in the crime rate, unless offenders who will be markedly recidivist can be identified early in their criminal careers. The evidence suggests that such identification is quite difficult to achieve without an unacceptably high error rate. The potential of selective incapacitation to reduce crime is quite limited, and is especially so with young people.

Current policies with respect to young offenders place an emphasis on the use of cautioning for first offenses. The evidence supports the value of this approach; the reoffense rate for first offenders who receive cautions is very low. On the other hand, the findings also indicate that cautions are not likely to be effective with recurrent offenders.

Various "alternatives to custody" community schemes have been developed during the last 20 years or so. There have not been many systematic evaluations, but the findings suggest that such schemes have few advantages over supervision in the case of minor offenses. Their results with serious offenders are no worse than custody and may possibly be marginally better if implemented well with work involving both parents and offenders (although this has yet to be established).

Restorative justice, with its focus on making offenders aware of their liabilities and obligations, is a relatively new approach, and evidence on its efficacy is still lacking. The general notion is an attractive one, and appropriate evaluations are much needed.

Shock incarceration or "boot camp" programs have been introduced in the last decade. The evidence does not suggest that the particularly tough regimes are helpful, but it may be that nonmilitary programs with a strong rehabilitative element could be more promising.

Custodial measures are neither good nor bad in themselves; much depends on the qualities of the custodial institutions. The limited available evidence suggests that benefits are more likely when there is: (i) provision of education and work training; (ii) a drug-free environment; (iii) a prosocial ethos; (iv) opportunities for taking responsibility; and (v) links with families that both maintain ties and improve family circumstances.

During the last 15 years, there has been a great increase in the quality of psychological interventions and in their evaluation. Training in parent management and in cognitive problem solving skills seem the most effective approaches bringing worthwhile benefits. The main challenge remains that of engaging high-risk families in treatment, and the chief limitation is the intensity of intervention required to bring about worthwhile change. Nevertheless, detailed individual studies and meta-analyses both indicate that there is a range of promising interventions, even though their efficacy is modest rather than dramatic.

CHAPTER 12 – SUMMARY OF MAIN POINTS

❏ *Situational crime prevention* may work to prevent the translation of a liability to be antisocial into an actual criminal act. A number of successful techniques have now been documented, and the reasons (e.g., failure of implementation, displacement of crime, etc.) why some do not succeed have been identified. With careful implementation, this can be a useful crime prevention strategy.

❏ Problems of implementation seem to be the reason why *community initiatives* have been rather less successful. Researching their effectiveness is very difficult, resulting in a shortage of good evaluations.

❏ Likelihood of conviction is very small for young people, and it is not clear whether *populationwide deterrence* – such as increasing the chances of conviction or the seriousness of punishments – will make much difference.

❏ There has been a range of *different responses to delinquency* over the last few decades, including diversionary policies, community schemes, restorative and retributional justice, short sharp shock regimes, and so forth. The elements that contribute to the success or failure of such schemes are becoming clearer (e.g., including positive experiences as well as negative, addressing cognitive as well as behavioral elements, etc.).

❏ *Meta-analyses* have identified a long list of promising targets for use in building effective programs, as well as less promising or distracting targets. Even if taken as a whole, these do not provide a template for the perfect program, but they do suggest that advances have and can be made.

13 | Conclusions

In this book we sought to provide an up-to-date account of the state of the international research literature on antisocial behavior shown by young people. We focused on three main aspects of this behavior: what it is like in descriptive and historical terms, what causes it, and whether interventions or preventive strategies can be helpful in ameliorating it. The twelve chapters that formed the main body of the volume were designed to be relatively self-contained. Each had a stand-alone conclusion section bringing together the main findings, and rather than repeat these at this point, we bring the review to a close by highlighting particular findings and setting a series of broader questions. These are intended to open up discussion about antisocial behavior rather than prescribe the answer.

Our starting point was a fairly broad definition of antisocial behavior. We have concentrated on acts that involve breaking the law and may result in prosecution, and also on antisocial behavior that is not necessarily illegal but involves similar qualities of aggression and disruptiveness. The breadth of antisocial behavior, so defined, is such that it operates as a dimensional feature that most people show to a greater or lesser degree. One way of delineating the review was by age; most of the research considered concentrated on the age period between 10 and 19 years, although we have taken a broader age range where this is useful – down to the preschool years and up into the mid-20s.

In What Ways Has This Review Shed Any New Light on Antisocial Behavior?

The research literature on antisocial behavior is much more extensive than it was 15 years ago, when two of us conducted a similar review. Classification and understanding of antisocial behavior have developed considerably, fueled largely by the development of a number of large-scale, prospective, longitudinal studies of general populations spanning the age period from childhood to adolescence or adult life. We have made particular use of those from the United Kingdom, the United States, Canada,

New Zealand, Germany, Sweden, and Finland. What are the "new" findings that this review has highlighted? Rather than present a comprehensive list of details, we have selected six broad areas to highlight: (i) evidence on the heterogeneity of antisocial behavior; (ii) understanding of causal processes and the interrelationship between different levels of explanation; (iii) understanding of the concept of a *liability* to become antisocial; (iv) antisocial behavior over the life course; (v) changes in time trends; and (vi) gender differences.

Heterogeneity

One of the most significant conclusions of this review has been that substantial progress has been made in delineating and understanding the heterogeneity of antisocial behavior. This relates to the pervasiveness, persistence, severity, and pattern of such behavior. We conclude that it is quite simply meaningless to talk of, try to explain, or treat antisocial behavior as if it were of only one "type." It is different in different people, in different situations, and at different times in the life history. In Chapter 5 we saw that there was enough evidence in the research literature to be reasonably certain about two key differentiators – antisocial behavior that overlaps with hyperactivity and antisocial behavior with a very early onset. There was also enough evidence to conclude that three further differentiators are likely to turn out to be important: antisocial behavior that is violent, antisocial behavior that is associated with psychopathy, and antisocial behavior associated with serious mental disorder. Finally, a set of nine further proposed subgroups were discussed where the necessary evidence is equivocal or lacking. These included (among others) sexual offenders, juvenile murderers, and crimes associated with drug use and abuse. Key criteria for establishing a valid classificatory subdivision of antisocial behavior include the establishment of different causal influences, epidemiological correlates, and response to treatment or long-term outcomes; this is the type of information lacking with respect to the groups of uncertain validity.

Looking simply at the subgroups about which the literature allows confidence, it seemed that an *overlap with hyperactivity* implies antisocial behavior that starts earlier, is associated with cognitive and social problems, is more likely to persist into adulthood, and shows a beneficial response to medication – at least in the short term. There is also an increasing body of evidence pointing to a particularly strong genetic influence; moreover, where genes are implied in a predisposition to antisocial behavior, it seems to be mainly for this type and less so for types without accompanying hyperactivity.

Antisocial behavior that has a very *early age of onset* is also more likely to persist into adolescence and adulthood, and has thus earned the term "life-course–persistent" to distinguish it from antisocial behavior that arises in the teenage years and is often referred to as "adolescence-limited." One difficulty with these developmentally defined subtypes is that the longitudinal studies on which they are based have not yet followed up their samples to a sufficiently old age to be certain of identifying all the age patterns. For example, it has been suggested that there is a group of people whose antisocial behavior does not start until they are adults; this may turn out to be a very important subgroup, but there is a lack of information on the topic at the moment. Similarly, there is some limited evidence that there is a group who follow a "stop and start" pattern of discontinuous offending. Several longitudinal studies have shown that the life-course–persistent group resembles the group with overlapping hyperactivity in many ways – for example, showing more cognitive deficits and higher rates of individual and family problems. Those with adolescence-limited delinquency tend to have more normal peer group relationships, although their peer group is often antisocial in orientation.

Despite being relatively confident that these subgroups are meaningful, there are still some uncertainties concerning the heterogeneity of antisocial behavior.

- The size of the more definite subgroups is not clear. The early-onset, life-course–persistent group is a small one, but estimates of its size still vary considerably, from a few percent of males to a fifth.
- Do the distinctions between these types of antisocial behavior actually pick out valid and meaningful subcategories, or do the differentiating characteristics rather operate as dimensional risk characteristics? Is it whether or not children are hyperactive that is important or instead the *degree* to which they are hyperactive? Where is the cutoff?
- Will all or any of the distinctions turn out to be mutually exclusive?
- Do the patterns of heterogeneity described fit as well for antisocial behavior by young women as they do for behavior by young men? Because of the relative rarity of antisocial behavior in young women, many of the longitudinal studies either concentrate on males or do not have enough females to subdivide them by type of antisocial behavior.

Acknowledging the heterogeneity of antisocial behavior has obvious consequences for the way it is studied and dealt with. Different causal pathways may relate to different subgroups, and different interventions will be appropriate depending on what we know about the alternative pathways in and out of such behavior.

Notions of Causality

This may seem a rather odd item to include in this list of key conclusions from the review, but from the very start we have tackled the question of how causal influences might be revealed; it is clear that this is an area where there have been significant recent developments. Obviously, not all the research reviewed was equally sophisticated, but it is fair to say that a number of studies can now distinguish between, for example, different types of cause and can also make distinctions between risk indicators and risk mechanisms.

For example, in Chapter 2 we noted that there were at least *five different types of cause*, including those responsible for individual differences in liability to offend (e.g., early-onset hyperactivity), those involved in translating liabilities into acts (e.g., peer group influences), those accounting for changes in differences in overall levels of crime (e.g., cultural change and availability of guns), those leading to situational variations in delinquency (e.g., environmental and architectural differences in the local area), and those responsible for the persistence of behavior over time in an individual's life (e.g., an unsupportive marriage to a deviant spouse).

It is also evident that *what works in one of these categories may not be a factor in another.* Thus, for example, marital discord is a risk for the perpetuation of antisocial behavior, but not for its initiation. A potential cause of antisocial behavior should not be thrown out simply because it works as an explanation of one aspect of antisocial behavior but not another – this is, after all, just what we would expect. This is perhaps easier to demonstrate in other fields than it is in the field of human behavior. One of the clearest examples is that of height. Although height has a heritability of approximately 90%, it is obvious that genes were not responsible for the fact that the average height of London schoolboys rose by about 12 cm over the first half of the twentieth century; this can be almost entirely attributed to improved nutrition.

The research shows that many causal processes are neither simple nor unidirectional. They involve *indirect chain effects* rather than one basic cause, and they can also reflect a *two-way interplay* between underlying biological features and behavior. This leads to two further points. First, it is important to analyze causal processes one link at a time rather than by attempting to find a set of factors that operate similarly throughout the causal chain. Second, if biological correlates of behavior are found then it should not be assumed that the former caused the latter, since the opposite is possible. Thus, for example, it has been shown that the winner of a tightly fought tennis or chess match will show a consequent rise in sex hormones, and it would be wrong to assume that it was the higher levels of sex hormones that led to the success.

Liability

It is not really new to stress the role of psychosocial factors (such as antisocial peer groups) in the development of antisocial behavior, despite the fact that this is where much recent research has been concentrated. This important body of work has already been the focus of several recent reviews. Similarly, research on area and environmental factors (such as housing, schools, and the mass media) has continued over the last two decades and receives widespread attention, but in a cumulative rather than startling fashion. However, in Chapter 6 we noted a marked swing in opinion about the role of individual characteristics in the liability to antisocial behavior as research on their influence has grown. This development has been less widely welcomed, and its importance warrants inclusion as a key conclusion of our review.

The importance of this new conclusion does not relate to exactly which characteristics are important – although these include hyperactivity, cognitive impairment, temperamental features, and styles of information processing. Rather, the important points are: (i) that these factors relate mainly to a certain subgroup of antisocial behavior – namely, to the life-course–persistent type rather than to the more common form of adolescence-limited behavior; and (ii) that these well-researched individual features are likely to have biological substrates that operate in a probabilistic fashion as part of multifactorial causation.

Thus, the research evidence is increasingly clear that genes – probably several or many – constitute one set of influences setting up a liability to develop antisocial behavior in childhood through dimensions such as impulsivity and hyperactivity, given the additional presence of other environmental risk factors. Estimates for the genetic component of hyperactivity are as high as 60%–70% of the variance. Genes may also operate by increasing vulnerability to life experiences and stresses, or by very indirect routes such as influencing behaviors that themselves then lead to changes in the individual's environment and so set up a spiraling cycle of risk factors. The question is not which of (a) individual factors, (b) psychosocial factors, or (c) other environmental factors are the most important influences; the question is how these interact. How is the child who is born with a tendency to be rather overactive, oppositional, and impulsive subsequently trained by the world to behave well or, alternatively, coerced into behaving badly? The complexity of these processes should not be underestimated, and criminological research should not shy away from addressing the issue.

Antisocial Behavior over the Life Course

One way of clarifying the complexity of some of these relationships between factors is to study people over time, as well as to compare between groups. That several of the large longitudinal studies have now collected data beyond the teenage years means that important data about life-span development and criminal careers have been collected, and this has constituted a major advance in the field. These studies have generated numerous findings as follows.

- Persistent recidivist offending often has its roots in disruptive behavior that can be detected as early as 3 years of age.
- Different patterns of offender behavior, risk factors, and adult outcomes stand out for the offenders who are life-course–persistent and those whose behavior is adolescence-limited.
- The effects of early and persistent antisocial behavior in childhood are wider than simply an increased propensity to offend: such behavior patterns often result in pervasive socioemotional and behavioral malfunction in adult life.
- Life experiences continue to be important in the course of a criminal career after childhood. Life events play a contributory role in determining whether antisocial behavior will persist or desist. Pre-existing dispositions and later experiences will work on each other in a cyclical and cumulative way, but people can also break out of patterns as a result of beneficial turning points.
- It is important to distinguish between the proportion of individuals participating in antisocial behavior and the level of offending in those who are engaged in crime. Although it is true that participating in offending is highest in teenage years (as this is when the greatest proportion of the population are offending), some offenders will keep up consistently high (or low) levels of offending for years without this obvious peak.

Time Trends

Levels of participation in antisocial behavior are not static over time, and there is evidence that the last 50 years have seen a significant increase in juvenile crime throughout the Western world. There is little doubt, from official statistics, that crime rates have been on a steady rise over the last half of the twentieth century, with few national exceptions (e.g., Japan). It is a little less clear what part juveniles have had to play in this pattern because in some countries fewer juveniles were processed at times of great crime increases. However, the balance of the evidence from different sources led us to the conclusion that underlying trends in behavior problems have shown a concomitant (albeit perhaps less sharp) rise. Time will tell whether recent falls in some countries turn out to be part of a leveling off in crime rates. In any event, the international rise between the 1950s and the 1970s was extremely dramatic and surely has something important to say about the causes of antisocial behavior. As part of these trends, violence by young people has been on the increase, particularly in the United States, and the ratio between male and female young offenders has fallen considerably.

Setting these trends in the broader picture of trends in both (i) juvenile justice and (ii) rates of other types of psychosocial disorders in young people reveals that, although increased juvenile crime may be partly the result of the former, this cannot be the entire explanation because the latter also rose. The rise in crime and other psychosocial disorders since the Second World War must have a largely environmental explanation because of the speed of the changes. Research findings give us no more than plausible leads at this stage, but the most likely explanations include demographic and social changes such as increases in family breakdown, changes in the meaning and experiences of adolescence, and situational changes in surveillance and opportunities for crime. It is important to note that these leads do not contradict what has been suggested already about the causal factors that are important in the development of an individual's liability to antisocial behavior. Recall the height example – even with high heritability, overall heights of populations can change rapidly owing to environmental factors. Why this is the case with crime is the sort of question that opens up areas of research requiring rather different strategies.

Gender Differences

The important feature of the research on gender differences in antisocial behavior was not the new conclusions that were reached but rather the opposite. Research has had much difficulty in moving forward in this area. The international statistics on officially recorded offenses have always demonstrated a clear variation in offending by gender, despite differences in criminal process and the age of criminal responsibility. That men commit more crime is one of the few universally accepted facts of criminology. All the evidence supports the conclusion that women participate less, commit different crimes, and follow different offending careers. In addition, underlying conduct and hyperkinetic disorders are much more common in boys. Although there has been evidence over the years that young men and women are treated differently by the criminal justice system once they offend, this cannot be held responsible for the overall differences in the statistics. Hence we can be certain that some real difference in behavior exists and needs explaining. There is limited evidence that some of the major known risk factors for antisocial behavior vary by sex, but there are simply too few data to allow firm conclusions on any of the possible explanations. This topic should remain high on the research agenda, as it could potentially elucidate much about how antisocial behavior develops.

Research and Methodological Advances

The conclusions reached in this review have been facilitated by a number of advances in the research literature, relating to (i) the quality and quantity of official statistics, (ii) the development of longitudinal studies, and (iii) meta-analyses of evaluations of preventive and intervention programs.

First, although official statistics seem to offer a concrete measure, in truth crime is a moving target. Establishing definitions, overall levels, and historical trends all involve estimates rather than facts. To start with, whether something is defined as criminal depends on legislation concerning the age of criminal responsibility, which varies enormously from one country to another and even *within* countries, making international comparisons very difficult. There is no foolproof source of information concerning levels of antisocial behavior, since all sources are open to (different) biases and methodological limitations. Instead, a patchwork must be constructed from official statistics, scans of criminal records, victim surveys, and self-report data. However, the quality and variety of the data available from various sources has improved over time, and these frequently supplement each other and converge in a number of respects. For example, the development of repeated victimization surveys on both sides of the Atlantic has been a useful complement to police statistics, helping us to track the underlying trends.

Second, as we have indicated, one of the main methodological advances in the field has been the development and enhancement of *longitudinal studies* – for example, the Cambridge Study in Delinquent Development, the Pittsburgh Youth Study, the Christchurch and Dunedin Health and Development studies, and the National Youth Study, to name but a few. Several of these now have sample members in early adulthood, allowing for an analysis of "criminal careers" against a backdrop of a wide range of information about life histories and experiences. Innovative designs, such as accelerated longitudinal studies (e.g., the Pittsburgh Youth Study and the Chicago study) have speeded up the years that can be tracked within the life of a project. In addition, the development of a multidisciplinary, international community of researchers working on these studies has led to a sharing of measures and analyses, strengthening the conclusions that can be reached. In a major way, the longitudinal studies have facilitated a coming together of psychological, psychiatric, criminological, and sociological perspectives on deviance – which, until recently, was somewhat lacking from the study of antisocial behavior.

Third, some major advances have also been made in *prevention and intervention research,* leading to a tone of cautious optimism that such programs have a part to play in reducing antisocial behavior. In the first place, expectations of the modifiability of behavior have become more realistic. There are good grounds for thinking that criminal behavior *is* modifiable, but researchers and practitioners also need to be practical about what is possible to achieve given the multiplicity of causes and the complexity of human behavior. Typically the effects on delinquency in successful interventions have been in the order of a 12% reduction, with considerable variation between studies and among individuals.

Evaluation is absolutely critical in the field of prevention and intervention, and the development of meta-analyses of evaluations has aided interpretation of the data. At the *predelinquency stage,* evaluations and meta-analyses have revealed that:

- the need is for multimodal intervention over long periods of time;
- projects should be focused, precisely targeted, and based on a causal model;
- combining the encouragement of prosocial behavior with discouragement of antisocial behavior may work best;
- families need to be included and convinced;
- building on existing services is likely to be easier and more effective than developing entirely new services;
- focusing only on high-risk samples will miss a substantial number of offenders;
- ensuring consistency of application and adherence to the original design is important when programs are expanded into new settings;
- we do not know enough about why programs work for some people and not others.

Interventions at the *postdelinquency stage* are complicated by the fact that they often occur within the context of the youth justice system; evaluation can be very difficult to design given the needs and momentum of the law. One major category of postdelinquency interventions is that focused on reducing the opportunities for offending: making it more difficult to steal items, increasing surveillance, and mobilizing neighborhoods. Examples of successful situational crime prevention do exist. A second category of intervention is populationwide deterrence, the main strategy employed by the law. It is assumed that increasing the chances of conviction and the severity of punishments will deter even those who do not receive a conviction or punishment themselves. However, this notion has rarely been tested, and the evidence that does exist is equivocal. It seems more desirable to increase the likelihood that crimes will result in the apprehension of the offender, but this may not be feasible within the resource constraints of the criminal justice system. Incapacitation is not as effective as is popularly assumed: for example, it has been estimated that reducing crime by 1% would require a 16% increase in the prison population.

Different responses to delinquency have included:

(1) diversion policies (where the evidence suggests that they work well at early stages of a criminal career);

(2) community schemes designed to offer alternatives to custody (which may be more cost effective but which need to be carefully designed to include multimodal work and posttreatment follow-up that involves behavioral elements);

(3) restorative justice (having the victim confront the offender and allowing the offender to make good the losses, which has not been systematically evaluated but is proving very popular in a number of jurisdictions around the world);

(4) short, sharp, shock regimes (where the evidence is slim for a value-added component from the shock elements over and above the effectiveness of less-tough rehabilitative regimes);

(5) custodial care (which is most likely to be effective if the ethos is prosocial and if both positive and negative experiences are offered); and

(6) psychosocial treatments (which may work best if they combine cognitive–behavioral methods).

On the basis of the evidence reviewed, it has been possible to conclude that considerable advances have been made in identifying the elements of success.

What Is the Relationship between the Research Conclusions and Policy?

In the arena of criminal justice policy, the past 15 years has marked a serious reversal of fortunes for the role of research. While research-based policy making has never constituted the entire tradition of U.K. and U.S. approaches (cf. the role of research in policy making in Northern Europe and Scandinavian countries), it clearly enjoyed a higher status in the immediate postwar period and up until the 1970s. As we have noted (see Chapter 3), since that time the politicization of law and order and an appeal to populist punitiveness has prevailed. Indeed, such has been the forcefulness of this movement that there are now few significant differences among the major political parties in the overall thrust of criminal justice policy. The predominant philosophy is that characterized as "bifurcation" – prevention and diversion for those at risk or on the border of the criminal justice system, and intensive community supervision or custody for those who cross that border. This philosophy had its origins in the postwar policy agenda, but the definition of what constitutes misbehavior that places an individual over the border has broadened over time.

Despite the growing rhetoric of punitive law-and-order politics since the 1980s, substantive research-based practice developments mediating excessive intervention continue. In England and Wales in the mid-1980s, juvenile justice practitioners were able to influence the courts' use of public care and custody for offenders and to persuade magistrates to pass sentences of community supervision instead. To a large extent, this initiative relied upon labeling theory and the evidence of delinquency amplification associated with early intervention. The impact of this development in turn led to legislation that formally restricted the courts' access to custodial institutions for young offenders and that expanded the resources locally available to provide community-based supervised activity programs. Similar theory-based practice approaches have been observed in the United States with respect to the deinstitutionalization of status offenders within a contrary policy context of the "war against crime." Likewise, the current emergence of restorative-justice approaches demonstrates the continued potency of a practice base to be innovative and inclusive.

It would be naive to assume a direct and linear relationship between theory, research, and policy, or between research and practice. The alignment of the spheres of influence may always be an exceptional event. Policy making is not first and foremost a rational enterprise, and "events" are usually a more significant fulcrum for policy change than are "findings." Similarly (as we have seen in Chapter 12), whereas practitioners may be attracted to theoretical schools and practice methodologies, they can be selective in their interpretation and implementation and neglectful in their monitoring and evaluation. Researchers themselves often neglect to address and promulgate the policy implications of their work, or to translate its relevance for an emerging policy agenda that "events" otherwise dictate. Likewise, researchers often provide insufficient detail of their program requirements and evaluation methodologies to enable practitioners to replicate their findings, restricting their applicability for the development of robustly tested policy platforms. For each point in the triad, therefore, some key messages need to be distilled if there is to be a closer alignment of influence.

(1) For *researchers,* there is a need to be clearer in their statements of findings and the implications that they may hold for policy makers and practitioners alike. This should include not only a routine addressing of the policy and practice messages from research, but greater caution in drawing conclusions from findings that are provisional, speculative, or in need of further testing.

(2) For *practitioners,* there is a need to be more evidence-based in their practice approaches and to develop practice networks that can exchange and replicate methodologies and findings. An orientation toward outcomes (rather than process) continues to be the exception rather than the rule, and an inability to validate practice remains too common.

(3) For *policy makers,* there is a need for more openness toward research findings, against a backdrop that such findings are unlikely to provide a "magic bullet" – a panacea for crime and social problems. Indeed, recent research evidence reinforces the message that changes in criminal justice policy alone are unlikely to have a significant impact on criminal behavior and may, in fact, unintentionally exacerbate its associated consequences. Hence, consideration of the implications of crime research for allied policy arenas – the family, education, housing, and health – is likely to be equally if not more important than the implications it may have for criminal justice policy. A closer cross-referencing of policy agendas may thus be required, despite the absence of such a tradition in many Western democratic countries.

A Research Agenda for the Future

Any research review inevitably makes a case for further research, and this one is no exception. Despite the enormous amount of work that has been done over the last couple of decades, there are still gaping holes in the literature as well as bits where the thread is rather thin. In 1983, a long list of research needs in this area was provided, and we can say that a number have indeed been partly met. Thus, we have witnessed the increased use of repeated special surveys such as victimization studies; work on historical trends has advanced considerably; there has been more experimental comparison of different forms of intervention and prevention; the study of individual differences has advanced; we know more about the importance of hyperactivity and educational failure; and peer group effects and the role of area differences have been at least partly clarified. However, in no case is the work in any of these areas complete. The most obvious gap still concerns the causes of gender differences. Other areas where more research is needed to complete an already sketchy outline include: gene–environment interactions; continuities and discontinuities in antisocial behavior over the whole life-span; the heterogeneity of antisocial behavior; and, at every point, the *mechanisms* involved.

References

Abelson, R. P. (1985). A variance explanation paradox: When a little is a lot. *Psychological Bulletin*, *97*, 129–33.

Achenbach, T. M. (1991). "Comorbidity" in child and adolescent psychiatry: Categorical and quantitative perspectives. *Journal of Child and Adolescent Psychiatry*, *1*, 271–8.

Achenbach, T. M., Howell, C. T., McConaughy, S. H., & Stanger, C. (1995). Six-year predictors of problems in a national sample: III. Transitions to young adult syndromes. *Journal of the American Academy of Child and Adolescent Psychiatry*, *34*, 658–69.

Achenbach, T. M., McConaughy, S. H., & Howell, C. T. (1987). Child/adolescent behavioral and emotional problems: Implications of cross-informant correlations for situational specificity. *Psychological Bulletin*, *101*, 212–32.

Agnew, R. (1991). The interactive effects of peer variables on delinquency. *Criminology*, *29*, 47–87.

Alder, C., & Wundersitz, J. (1994). *Family Group Conferencing in Australia*. Canberra: Australian Institute of Criminology.

Allen, F. A. (1981). *The decline of the rehabilitative ideal: Penal policy and social purpose*. New Haven, CT: Yale University Press.

Allen, R. (1991). Out of jail: the reduction in the use of penal custody for male juveniles 1981–88. *Howard Journal of Penal Reform*, *30*, 30–53.

Allert, P. (1984). Residential security: Containment and displacement of burglary. *Howard Journal of Criminal Justice*, *23*, 99–116.

Alm, P. O., Alm, M., Humble, K., Leppert, J., Sörensen, S., Lidberg, L., & Oreland, L. (1994). Criminality and platelet monoamine oxidase activity in former juvenile delinquents as adults. *Acta Psychiatrica Scandinavica*, *89*, 41–5.

Altemeier, W. A., O'Connor, S., Vietze, P., Sandler, H., & Sherrod, K. (1984). Prediction of child abuse: A prospective study of feasibility. *Child Abuse and Neglect*, *8*, 393–400.

Alwin, D. F., & Krosnick, J. A. (1991). Aging, cohorts, and the stability of sociopolitical orientations over the life span. *American Journal of Sociology*, *97*, 169–95.

American Psychiatric Association (1994). *Diagnostic and statistical manual of mental disorders: DSM–IV*, 4th ed. Washington, DC: American Psychiatric Association.

Anderson, K. E., Lytton, H., & Romney, D. M. (1986). Mothers' interactions with normal and conduct-disordered boys: Who affects whom? *Developmental Psychology*, *22*, 604–9.

Anderson, S., Kinsey, R., Loader, I., & Smith, C. (1990). *Cautionary tales: A study of young people and crime in Edinburgh.* Edinburgh: University of Edinburgh Centre for Criminology.

Andrews, D. A. (1989). Recidivism is predictable and can be influenced: Using risk assessments to reduce recidivism. *Forum on Corrections Research, 1,* 11–18.

(1995). The psychology of criminal conduct and effective treatment. In J. McGuire (Ed.), *What works: Reducing reoffending,* pp. 35–62. Chichester: Wiley.

Andrews, D. A., & Bonton, J. (1994). *The psychology of criminal conduct.* Cincinnati, OH: Anderson.

Andrews, D., Zinger, I., Hoge, R., Bonta, J., Gendreau, P., & Cullen, F. (1990). Does correctional treatment work? A clinically relevant and psychologically informed meta-analysis. *Criminology, 28,* 369–404.

Angold, A., & Costello, E. J. (1996). The relative diagnostic utility of child and parent reports of oppositional defiant behaviors. *International Journal of Methods in Psychiatric Research, 6,* 253–9.

Angold, A., Erkanlis, A., Costello, E. J., & Rutter, M. (1996). Precision, reliability and accuracy in the dating of symptom onsets in child and adolescent psychopathology. *Journal of Child Psychology and Psychiatry, 37,* 657–64.

Angold, A., & Rutter, M. (1992). Effects of age and pubertal status on depression in a large clinical sample. *Development and Psychopathology, 4,* 5–28.

Archer, J. (1991). The influence of testosterone on human aggression. *British Journal of Psychology, 82,* 1–28.

Asher, S. R., & Coie, J. D. (1990). *Peer rejection in childhood.* New York: Cambridge University Press.

Asher, S. R., Erdley, C. A., & Gabriel, S. W. (1994). Peer relations. In M. Rutter & D. Hay (Eds.), *Development through life: A handbook for clinicians,* pp. 456–87. Oxford: Blackwell Scientific.

Ashworth, A. (1997). Sentencing. In M. Maguire, R. Morgan, & R. Reiner (Eds.), *The Oxford handbook of criminology,* 2nd ed., pp. 1095–1135. Oxford: Clarendon.

Ashworth, A., Cavadino, P., Gibson, B., Harding, J., Rutherford, A., Seago, P., & Whyte, L. (1992). *Criminal Justice Act 1991: Legal points.* Winchester: Waterside.

Ashworth, A., & Hough, M. (1996). Sentencing and the climate of opinion. *Criminal Law Review* (November), 776–87.

Atkins, M. S., Stoff, D. M., Osborne, M. L., & Brown, K. (1993). Distinguishing instrumental and hostile aggression: Does it make a difference? *Journal of Abnormal Child Psychology, 21,* 355–65.

Audit Commission. (1996a). *Streetwise: Effective police patrol.* London: Audit Commission.

(1996b). *Misspent youth: Young people and crime.* London: Audit Commission.

Aye Maung, N. (1995). *Young people, victimisation and the police. British Crime Survey findings on experiences and attitudes of 12 to 15 year olds.* London: HMSO.

Bailey, S. (1996). Adolescents who murder. *Journal of Adolescence, 19,* 19–39.

Bailey, S. M., Thornton, L., & Weaver, A. B. (1994). The first 100 admissions to an adolescent secure unit. *Journal of Adolescence, 17,* 207–20.

Baker, A. W., & Duncan, S. P. (1985). Child sexual abuse: A study of prevalence in Great Britain. *Child Abuse and Neglect, 9,* 457–67.

Balding, J. (1994). *Young people in 1993.* Exeter: Exeter University Schools Health Education Unit.

Baldwin J., & Bottoms, A. E. (1976). *The urban criminal.* London: Tavistock.

Baltes, P. B. (1979). Life-span developmental psychology: Some converging observation on history and theory. In P. B. Baltes & O. G. Brim, Jr. (Eds.), *Life-span development and behavior,* vol. 2, pp. 256–81. New York: Academic Press.

Bandura, A. (1977). *Social learning theory.* Englewood Cliffs, NJ: Prentice-Hall.
   (Ed.) (1995). *Self-efficacy in changing societies.* Cambridge: Cambridge University Press.

Bank, L., Forgatch, M. S., Patterson, G. R., & Fetrow, R. A. (1993). Parenting practices of single mothers: Mediators of negative contextual factors. *Journal of Marriage and the Family, 55,* 371–84.

Banks, M. H., & Ullah, P. (1988). *Youth unemployment in the 1980s: Its psychological effects.* London: Croom Helm.

Bannister, J. (1991). *The impact of environmental design upon the incidence and type of crime.* Edinburgh: Scottish Office.

Barbaree, H. E., Marshall, W. L., & Hudson, S. M. (1993). *The juvenile sex offender.* New York: Guilford.

Bardone, A. M., Moffitt, T. W., Caspi, A., Dickson, N., & Silva, P. A. (1996). Adult mental health and social outcomes of adolescent girls with depression and conduct disorder. *Development and Psychopathology, 8,* 811–29.

Barnett, A., Blumstein, A., & Farrington, D. P. (1987). Probabilistic models of youthful criminal careers. *Criminology, 25,* 83–107.
   (1989). A prospective test of a criminal career model. *Criminology, 27,* 373–88.

Baron, R. M., & Kenny, D. A. (1986). The moderator–mediator variable distinction in social psychological research: Conceptual, strategic, and statistical considerations. *Journal of Personality and Social Psychology, 51,* 1173–82.

Baumrind, D. (1993). The average expectable environment is not good enough: A response to Scarr. *Child Development, 64,* 1299–1317.
   (1996). Response: A blanket injunction against disciplinary use of spanking is not warranted by the data. *Pediatrics, 98,* 828–31.

Bazemore, G., & Umbreit, M. (1995). Rethinking the sanctioning function in juvenile court: Retributive or restorative responses to youth crime. *Crime and Delinquency, 41,* 296–316.

Bebbington, P. (1996). The origins of sex differences in depressive disorder: Bridging the gap. *International Review of Psychiatry, 8,* 295–332.

Becker, H. (1963). *Outsiders: Studies in the sociology of deviance.* New York: Free Press.

Becker, J. V., & Hunter, J. A. (1997). Understanding and treating child and adolescent sexual offenders. In T. O. Ollendick & R. J. Prinz (Eds.), *Advances in clinical child psychology,* vol. 19, pp. 177–98. New York: Plenum.

Beelman, A., Pfingsten, U., & Lösel, F. (1994). Effects of training social competence in children: A meta-analysis of recent evaluation studies. *Journal of Clinical Child Psychology, 23,* 260–71.

Belfrage, H., Lidberg, L., & Oreland, L. (1992). Platelet monoamine-oxidase activity in mentally disordered violent offenders. *Acta Psychiatrica Scandinavica, 85,* 218–21.

Bell, R. Q. (1968). A reinterpretation of the direction of effects in studies of socialization. *Psychological Review, 75,* 81–95.

Bell, R. Q., & Chapman, M. (1986). Child effects in studies using experimental or brief longitudinal approaches to socialization. *Developmental Psychology, 22,* 595–603.

Bell, R. Q., & Harper, L. V. (1977). *Child effects on adults.* Hillsdale, NJ: Erlbaum.

Belson, W. A. (1978). *Television violence and the adolescent boy.* Westmead: Saxon House, Teakfield.

Bender, D., & Lösel, F. (1996). *Effects of intelligence on the development of antisocial behavior: Results from a study of high-risk adolescent boys.* Poster presented at the XIVth Biennial ISSBD Conference, Québec City, Canada, August 12–16.

Bennett, T. (1990). *Evaluating neighbourhood watch.* Aldershot: Gower.

Bennett, T., & Wright, R. (1984). *Burglars on burglary.* Aldershot: Gower.

Berg, I., Consterdine, M., Hullin, R., McGuire, R., & Tyrer, S. (1978). The effect of two randomly allocated court procedures on truancy. *British Journal of Criminology, 18,* 323–44.

Berg, I., Goodwin, A., Hullin, R., & McGuire, R. (1984). Juvenile delinquency and failure to attend school. *Educational Research, 27,* 226–9.

Berk, R. A. (1983). An introduction to sample selection bias in sociological data. *American Sociological Review, 48,* 386–98.

Berkowitz, L. (1984). Some thoughts on anti- and prosocial influence of media events: A cognitive-neoassociation analysis. *Psychological Bulletin, 95,* 410–27.

Berkowitz, L., Parke, R. D., Leyens, J. P., West, S., & Sebastian, J. (1978). Experiments on the reactions of juvenile delinquents to filmed violence. In L. A. Hersov, M. Berger, & D. Shaffer (Eds.), *Aggression and antisocial behavior in childhood and adolescence,* pp. 59–71. Oxford: Pergamon.

Berkson, J. (1946). Limitations of the application of four-fold table analysis to hospital data. *Biometrics, 2,* 47–53.

Bilchik, S. (1995). *Delinquency prevention works* (Program Summary for Office of Juvenile Justice and Delinquency Prevention). Washington, DC: Department of Justice.

Bishop, D. M., & Frazier, C. S. (1988). The influence of race in juvenile justice processing. *Journal of Research in Crime and Delinquency, 25,* 242–63.

Blackburn, R. (1993). *The psychology of criminal conduct: Theory, research and practice.* Chichester: Wiley.

Blair, R. J. R. (1995). A cognitive developmental approach to morality: Investigating the psychopath. *Cognition, 57,* 1–29.

Blair, R. J. R., Jones, L., Clark, F., & Smith, M. (1997). The psychopath: A lack of responsiveness to distress cues? *Psychophysiology, 34,* 192–8.

Blair, R. J. R., Sellars, C., Strickland, I., Clark, F., Williams, A. O., Smith, M., & Jones, L. (1995). Emotion attributions to the psychopath. *Personality and Individual Differences, 19*, 431–7.

Blakemore, C. (1991). Sensitive and vulnerable periods in the development of the visual system. In G. R. Bock & J. Whelan (Eds.), *The childhood environment and adult disease* (Ciba Symposium no. 156), pp. 129–54. Chichester: Wiley.

Blane, D., Davey Smith, G., & Bartley, M. (1993). Social selection: What does it contribute to social class differences in health? *Sociology of Health and Illness, 15*, 1–15.

Blau, Z. S., & Hagan, J. (1995). *Current perspectives on aging and the life cycle.* Greenwich, CT: JAI.

Block, J. H., Block, J., & Gjerde, P. F. (1986). The personality of children prior to divorce: A prospective study. *Child Development, 57*, 827–40.

Block, J. H., Block, J., & Morrison, A. (1981). Parental agreement–disagreement on childbearing orientations and gender-related personality correlates in children. *Child Development, 52*, 965–74.

Blumstein, A. (1982). On the racial disproportionality of the U.S. states' prison population. *Journal of Criminal Law and Criminology, 73*, 1259–81.

  (1993). Racial disproportionality of U.S. prison populations revisited. *University of Colorado Law Review, 64*, 743–60.

  (1995). Youth violence, guns, and the illicit-drug industry. *Journal of Criminal Law and Criminology, 86*, 10–35.

Blumstein, A., Cohen, J., & Farrington, D. P. (1988). Criminal career research: Its value for criminology. *Criminology, 26*, 1–34.

Blumstein, A., Cohen, J., Roth, J. A., & Visher, C. A. (Eds.) (1986). *Criminal careers and career criminals.* Washington, DC: National Academy Press.

Blumstein, A., & Cork, D. (1996). Linking gun availability to youth gun violence. *Law and Contemporary Problems, 59*, 5–24.

Blumstein, A., Farrington, D. P., & Moitra, S. (1985). Delinquency careers: Innocents, desisters, and persisters. In M. Tonry & N. Morris (Eds.), *Crime and justice,* vol. 6, pp. 187–220. Chicago: University of Chicago Press.

Bock, G. R., & Goode, J. A. (Eds.) (1996). *Genetics of criminal and antisocial behaviour* (Ciba Foundation Symposium no. 194). Chichester: Wiley.

Bohman, M. (1996). Predisposition to criminality: Swedish adoption studies in retrospect. In G. R. Bock & J. A. Goode (Eds.), *Genetics of criminal and antisocial behaviour* (Ciba Foundation Symposium no. 194), pp. 99–114. Chichester: Wiley.

Bohman, M., Cloninger, C. R., Sigvarsson, S., & Von Knorring, A.-L. (1982). Predisposition to petty criminality in Swedish adoptees. I. Genetic and environmental heterogeneity. *Archives of General Psychiatry, 39*, 1233–41.

Bolger, K. E., Patterson, C. J., Thompson, W. W., & Kupersmidt, J. B. (1995). Psychosocial adjustment among children experiencing persistent and intermittent family economic hardship. *Child Development, 66*, 1107–29.

Bolton, W., & Oatley, K. (1987). A longitudinal study of social support and depression in unemployed men. *Psychological Medicine, 17*, 453–60.

Bornstein, M. H. (Ed.) (1995). *Handbook of parenting*, vols. 1–4. Mahwah, NJ: Erlbaum.

Boss, P., Edwards, S., & Pitman, S. (1995). *Profile of young Australians*. Melbourne: Churchill Livingstone.

Boswell, G. (1995). *Violent victims: The prevalence of abuse and loss in the lives of Section 53 offenders*. London: The Prince's Trust.

(1996). *Young and dangerous*. Aldershot: Avebury.

Bottomley, K., & Pease, K. (1993). *Crime and punishment: Interpreting the data*. Milton Keynes, UK: Open University Press.

Bottoms, A. E. (1995a). The philosophy and politics of punishment and sentencing. In C. Clarkson & R. Morgan (Eds.), *The politics of sentencing reform*, pp. 17–49. Oxford: Clarendon.

(1995b). *Intensive community supervision for young offenders: Outcomes, process and cost*. Cambridge: Institute of Criminology Publications.

Bottoms, A. E., Brown, P., McWilliams, B., McWilliams, W., & Nellis, M. (1990). *Intermediate treatment and juvenile justice: Key findings and implications from a national survey of intermediate treatment policy and practice*. London: HMSO.

Bottoms, A. E., Claytor, A., & Wiles, P. (1992). Housing markets and residential community crime careers: A case study from Sheffield. In D. J. Evans, N. R. Fyfe, & D. T. Herbert (Eds.), *Crime, policing and place: Essays in environmental criminology*, pp. 118–44. Chicago: University of Chicago Press.

Bottoms, A. E., Knapp, M., & Fenyo, A. (1995). *Intensive community supervision for young offenders: Outcomes, process and cost*. Cambridge: Institute of Criminology Publications.

Bottoms, A. E., & Wiles, P. (1986). Housing tenure and residential community crime careers in Britain. In A. J. Reiss & M. Tonry (Eds.), *Communities and crime*, pp. 101–62. Chicago: University of Chicago Press.

(1997). Environmental criminology. In M. Maguire, R. Morgan, & R. Reiner (Eds.), *The Oxford handbook of criminology*, 2nd ed., pp. 305–59. Oxford: Clarendon.

Botvin, G. J. (1990). Substance abuse prevention: Theory, practice and effectiveness. In M. Tonry & J. Q. Wilson (Eds.), *Drugs and crime*, pp. 461–519. Chicago: University of Chicago Press.

Botvin, G. J., Baker, E., Renick, N. L., Filazzola, A. D., & Botvin, E. M. (1984). A cognitive–behavioral approach to substance abuse prevention. *Addictive Behaviors, 9*, 137–47.

Boyle, M. H., Offord, D. R., Racine, Y. A., Szatmari, P., Sinford, M., & Fleming, J. E. (1997). Adequacy of interviews versus checklists for classifying childhood psychiatric disorder on parent reports. *Archives of General Psychiatry, 54*, 793–9.

Braithwaite, J. (1989). *Crime, shame and reintegration*. Cambridge: Cambridge University Press.

Braithwaite, J., & Mugford, S. (1994). Conditions of successful reintegration ceremonies. *British Journal of Criminology, 34*, 139–71.

Brantingham, P. J., & Brantingham, P. L. (1991). *Environmental criminology*. Beverly Hills, CA: Sage.

Brennan, P. A., & Mednick, S. A. (1994). Learning theory approach to the deterrence of criminal recidivism. *Journal of Abnormal Psychology, 103,* 430–40.

Brennan, P. A., Mednick, S. A., & Jacobsen, B. (1996). Assessing the role of genetics in crime using adoption cohorts. In G. R. Bock & J. A. Goode (Eds.), *Genetics of criminal and antisocial behaviour* (Ciba Foundation Symposium no. 194), pp. 115–28. Chichester: Wiley.

Brent, D. A., Holder, D., Kolko, D., Birmaher, B., Baugher, M., Roth, C., Iyengar, S., & Johnson, B. A. (1997). A clinical psychotherapy trial for adolescent depression comparing cognitive, family, and supportive therapy. *Archives of General Psychiatry, 54,* 877–85.

Brody, G. H., Stoneman, Z., Flor, D., McCrary, C., Hastings, L., & Conyers, O. (1994). Financial resources, parent psychological functioning, parent co-caregiving and early adolescent competence in rural two-parent African-American families. *Child Development, 65,* 590–605.

Brody, S. (1976). *The effectiveness of sentencing* (Home Office Research Study no. 35). London: HMSO.

Brogden, M., Jefferson, T., & Walklate, S. (1988). *Introducing policework.* London: Unwin.

Bronfenbrenner, U. (1976). Who cares for America's children? In V. C. Vaughan & T. B. Brazelton (Eds.), *The family – Can it be saved?* pp. 3–32. Chicago: Year Book Medical.

Brook, J. S., Whiteman, M., Finch, S. J., & Cohen, P. (1996). Young adult drug use and delinquency: Childhood antecedents and adolescent mediators. *Journal of the American Academy of Child and Adolescent Psychiatry, 35,* 1584–92.

Brooks-Gunn, J., Duncan, G. J., & Aber, J. L. (1997). *Neighborhood poverty, vol. 1: Context and consequences for children.* New York: Russell Sage Foundation.

Brooks-Gunn, J., Duncan, G. J., Klebanov, P. K., & Sealand, N. (1993). Do neighborhoods influence child and adolescent development? *American Journal of Sociology, 99,* 353–95.

Brown, G. W., & Harris, T. O. (1978). *Social origins of depression: A study of psychiatric disorder in women.* London: Tavistock.

Brown, M., & Polk, K. (1996). Taking fear of crime seriously: The Tasmanian approach to community crime prevention. *Crime and Delinquency, 42,* 398–420.

Brunk, M. A., & Henggeler, S. W. (1984). Child influences on adult controls: An experimental investigation. *Developmental Psychology, 20,* 1074–81.

Brunner, H. G. (1996). MAOA deficiency and abnormal behaviour: Perspectives on an association. In G. R. Bock & J. A. Goode (Eds.), *Genetics of criminal and antisocial behaviour* (Ciba Foundation Symposium no. 194), pp. 155–67. Chichester: Wiley.

Brunner, H. G., Nelen, M., Breakefield, X. O., Ropers, H. H., & van Oost, B. A. (1993). Abnormal behaviour associated with a point mutation in the structural gene for monoamineoxidase A. *Science, 262,* 578–80.

Bullock, R., Little, M., & Millham, S. (1993). *Residential care for children: A review of the research.* London: HMSO.

Burney, E. (1985). *Sentencing young people.* Aldershot: Gower.

Bursik, R. J. (1986). Delinquency rates as sources of ecological change. In J. M. Byrne & R. J. Sampson (Eds.), *The social ecology of crime*, pp. 63–74. New York: Springer-Verlag.

Buss, A. H. (1961). *The psychology of aggression*. New York: Wiley.

Cadoret, R. J. (1985). Genes, environment and their interaction in the development of psychopathology. In T. Sakai & T. Tsuboi (Eds.), *Genetic aspects of human behavior*, pp. 165–75. Tokyo: Igaku-Shoin.

Cadoret, R. J., Yates, W. R., Troughton, E., Woodworth, G., & Stewart, M. A. (1995). Genetic–environmental interaction in the genesis of aggressivity and conduct disorders. *Archives of General Psychiatry, 52,* 916–24.

Cairns, R. B., Cadwallader, T. W., Estell, D., & Neckerman, H. J. (1997). Groups to gangs: Developmental and criminological perspectives and relevance for prevention. In D. Stoff, J. Breiling, & J. Maser (Eds.), *Handbook of antisocial behavior*, pp. 194–205. New York: Wiley.

Cairns, R. B., & Cairns, B. D. (1994). *Lifelines and risks: Pathways of youth in our time*. Cambridge: Cambridge University Press.

Cairns, R. B., & Kroll, A. B. (1994). Developmental perspective on gender differences and similarities. In M. Rutter & D. F. Hay (Eds.), *Development through life: A handbook for clinicians*, pp. 350–72. Oxford: Blackwell Scientific.

Campbell, A. (1993). *Men, women, and aggression*. New York: Basic Books.

Campbell, S. B. (1995). Behavior problems in preschool children: A review of recent research. *Journal of Child Psychology and Psychiatry Annual Research Review, 36,* 113–49.

(1997). Behavior problems in preschool children: Developmental and family issues. In T. O. Ollendick & R. J. Prinz (Eds.), *Advances in clinical child psychology*, vol. 19, pp. 1–26. New York: Plenum.

Campbell, S. B., & Ewing, L. J. (1990). Hard-to-manage preschoolers: Adjustment at age nine and predictors of continuing symptoms. *Journal of Child Psychology and Psychiatry, 31,* 871–89.

Campbell, S. B., Pierce, E. W., Moore, G., Marakovitz, S., & Newby, K. (1996). Boys' externalizing problems at elementary school age: Pathways from early behavior problems, maternal control, and family stress. *Development and Psychopathology, 8,* 701–19.

Cantwell, D. P., & Rutter, M. (1994). Classification: Conceptual issues and substantive findings. In M. Rutter, E. Taylor, & L. Hersov (Eds.), *Child and adolescent psychiatry: Modern approaches*, pp. 3–21. Oxford: Blackwell Scientific.

Capaldi, D. M., & Patterson, G. R. (1987). An approach to the problem of recruitment and retention rates for longitudinal research. *Behavior Assessment, 9,* 169–77.

(1994). Interrelated influences of contextual factors on antisocial behavior in childhood and adolescence for males. In D. Fowles, P. Sutker, & S. Goodman (Eds.), *Psychopathy and social personality: A developmental perspective*, pp. 165–98. New York: Springer.

(1996). Can violent offenders be distinguished from frequent offenders: Prediction from childhood to adolescence. *Journal of Research in Crime and Delinquency, 33,* 206–31.

Carbonneau, R., Eaves, L. J., Silberg, J. L., Meyer, J. M., Maes, H. H., Rutter, M., Simonoff, E., & Hewitt, J. K. (submitted). *Longitudinal assessment of non-shared environmental experiences in twins: Psychometric properties and multiple ratings of the Twin Inventory of Relationships and Experiences (TIRE).*

Carey, G. (1994). Genetics and violence. In A. J. Reiss, Jr., K. A. Miezek, & J. A. Roth (Eds.), *Understanding and preventing violence, vol. 2: Behavioral influences,* pp. 21–58. Washington, DC: National Academy Press.

Carey, G., & Goldman, D. (1997). The genetics of antisocial behavior. In D. M. Stoff, J. Breiling, & J. D. Maser (Eds.), *Handbook of antisocial behavior,* pp. 243–54. New York: Wiley.

Caron, C., & Rutter, M. (1991). Comorbidity in child psychopathology: Concepts, issues and research strategies. *Journal of Child Psycholoy and Psychiatry, 32,* 1063–80.

Carter, C. M., Urbanowicz, M., Hemsley, R., Mantilla, L., Strobel, S., Graham, P. J., & Taylor, E. (1993). Effects of a new food diet in attention deficit disorder. *Archives of Disease in Childhood, 69,* 564–8.

Carter, R. L., & Hill, K. Q. (1979). *The criminal's image of the city.* New York: Pergamon.

Casaer, P., de Vries, L., & Marlowe, N. (1991). Prenatal and perinatal risk factors for psychosocial development. In M. Rutter & P. Casaer (Eds.), *Biological risk factors for psychosocial disorders,* pp. 139–74. Cambridge: Cambridge University Press.

Caspi, A. (1995). Puberty and the gender organization of schools: How biology and social context shape the adolescent experience. In L. Crockett & A. Crouter (Eds.), *Pathways through adolescence: Individual development in relation to social contexts,* pp. 57–74. Hillsdale, NJ: Erlbaum.

Caspi, A., Elder, G. H., Jr., & Bem, D. J. (1987). Moving against the world: Life course patterns of explosive children. *Developmental Psychology, 23,* 308–13.

Caspi, A., Entner Wright, B. R., Moffitt, T. E., & Silva, P. A. (in press). Early failure in the labor market: Childhood and adolescent predictors of unemployment in the transition to adulthood. *American Journal of Sociology.*

Caspi, A., Henry, B., McGee, R. O., Moffitt, T. E., & Silva, P. A. (1995). Temperamental origins of child and adolescent behavior problems: From age 3 to age 15. *Child Development, 66,* 55–68.

Caspi, A., Lynam, D., Moffitt, T. E., & Silva, P. A. (1993). Unraveling girls' delinquency: Biological, dispositional, and contextual contributions to adolescent misbehavior. *Developmental Psychology, 29,* 19–30.

Caspi, A., & Moffitt, T. E. (1991). Individual differences are accentuated during periods of social change: The sample case of girls at puberty. *Journal of Personality and Social Psychology, 61,* 157–68.

(1993). When do individual differences matter? A paradoxical theory of personality coherence. *Psychological Inquiry, 4,* 247–71.

(1995). The continuity of maladaptive behavior: From description to understanding in the study of antisocial behavior. In D. Cicchetti & D. Cohen (Eds.), *Developmental Psychopathology,* vol. 2, pp. 472–511. New York: Wiley.

Caspi, A., Moffitt, T. E., Newman, D. L., & Silva, P. A. (1996a). Behavioral observations at age 3 years predict adult psychiatric disorders: Longitudinal evidence from a birth cohort. *Archives of General Psychiatry, 53,* 1033–9.

Caspi, A., Moffitt, T. E., Silva, P. A., Stouthamer-Loeber, M., Krueger, R. F., & Schmutte, P. S. (1994). Are some people crime-prone? Replications of the personality–crime relationship across countries, genders, races, and methods. *Criminology, 32,* 163–95.

Caspi, A., Moffitt, T. E., Thornton, A., Freedman, D., Amell, J. W., Harrington, H. L., Smeijers, J., & Silva, P. A. (1996b). The Life History Calendar: A research and clinical assessment method for collecting retrospective event-history data. *International Journal of Methods in Psychiatric Research, 6,* 101–14.

Castellanos, F. X., Elia, J., Kruesi, M. J., Gulotta, C. S., Mefford, I. N., Petter, W. Z., Ritchie, G. S., & Rapoport, J. L. (1994). Cerebrospinal fluid monamine metabolites in boys with attention-deficit/hyperactivity disorder. *Psychiatry Research, 52,* 305–16.

Catalano, R. F., & Hawkins, J. D. (1997). The social development model: A theory of antisocial behavior. In J. D. Hawkins (Ed.), *Delinquency and crime: Current theories,* pp. 149–77. New York: Cambridge University Press.

Cavadino, P. (1996). *Children who kill: An examination of the treatment of juveniles who kill in different European countries.* Winchester: Waterside.

Cederblad, M., Dahlin, L., Hagnell, O., & Hansson, K. (1994). Intelligence and temperament as protective factors for mental health: A cross-sectional and prospective epidemiological study. *European Archives of Psychiatry and Clinical Neuroscience, 245,* 11–19.

Central Statistical Office (1994). *Social focus on children.* London: HMSO.

Cernkovich, S. A., Giordano, P. C., & Pugh, M. D. (1985). Chronic offenders: The missing cases in self-report delinquency research. *Journal of Criminal Law and Criminology, 76,* 705–32.

Chaiken, J., & Chaiken, M. (1991). Drugs and predatory crime. In M. Tonry & J. Wilson (Eds.), *Drugs and crime,* pp. 203–40. Chicago: University of Chicago Press.

Champion, L. A., Goodall, G. M., & Rutter, M. (1995). Behavioural problems in childhood and stressors in early adult life: A 20-year follow-up of London school children. *Psychological Medicine, 25,* 231–46.

Cherlin, A. J., Furstenberg, F. F., Jr., Chase-Lansdale, P. L., Kiernan, K. E., Robins, P. K., Morrison, D. R., & Teitler, J. O. (1991). Longitudinal studies of effects of divorce on children in Great Britain and the United States. *Science, 252,* 1386–9.

Cherny, S. S., Fulker, D. W., & Hewitt, J. K. (1997). Cognitive development from infancy to middle childhood. In R. J. Sternberg and E. L. Grigorenko (Eds.), *Intelligence, heredity, and environment,* pp. 463–82. Cambridge: Cambridge University Press.

Christian, R. E., Frick, P. J., Hill, N. L., Tyler, L., & Frazer, D. R. (1997). Psychopathy and conduct problems in children: II. Implications for subtyping children with conduct problems. *Journal of the American Academy of Child and Adolescent Psychiatry, 36,* 233–41.

Clarke, R. V. (1980). Situational crime prevention: Theory and practice. *British Journal of Criminology, 20,* 136–47.

(1983). Situational crime prevention: Its theoretical basis and practical scope. In M. Tonry & N. Morris (Eds.), *Crime and justice,* vol. 4, pp. 225–56. Chicago: University of Chicago Press.

(1992). *Situational crime prevention: Successful case studies.* Albany, NY: Harrow and Heston.

(1995). Situational crime prevention. In M. Tonry & D. P. Farrington (Eds.), *Crime and justice,* vol. 19, pp. 91–149. Chicago: University of Chicago Press.

Clarke, R. V., & Cornish, D. B. (1985). Modelling offenders' decisions: A framework for research and policy. In M. Tonry & N. Morris (Eds.), *Crime and justice: An annual review of research,* vol. 6, pp. 147–85. Chicago: University of Chicago Press.

Clarke, R. V., & Harris, P. M. (1992). Auto theft and its prevention. In M. Tonry (Ed.), *Crime and justice: A review of research,* vol. 16, pp. 1–54. Chicago: University of Chicago Press.

Clarke, R. V., & Hough, J. M. (1984). *Crime and police effectiveness* (Home Office Research Study no. 79). London: HMSO.

Clarke, R. V., & Mayhew, P. (1988). The British gas suicide story and its criminological implications. In M. Tonry & N. Morris (Eds.), *Crime and justice,* vol. 10, pp. 79–116. Chicago: University of Chicago Press.

Clarke, R. V., & Weisburd, D. (1994). Diffusion of crime central benefits: Observations on the reverse of displacement. In R. V. Clarke (Ed.), *Crime prevention studies,* vol. 2, pp. 165–83. Monsey, NY: Criminal Justice Press.

Clausen, J. S. (1991). Adolescent competence and the shaping of the life course. *American Journal of Sociology, 96,* 805–42.

(1993). *American lives: Looking back at the children of the Great Depression.* New York: Free Press.

Cloninger, C. R. (1987). A systematic method for clinical description and classification of personality variants. *Archives of General Psychiatry, 44,* 573–88.

Cloninger, C. R., & Gottesman, I. I. (1987). Genetic and environmental factors in antisocial behavior disorders. In S. A. Mednick, T. E. Moffitt, & S. A. Stack (Eds.), *Causes of crime: New biological approaches,* pp. 92–109. Cambridge: Cambridge University Press.

Cloninger, C. R., Svrakic, D. M., & Svrakic, N. M. (1997). A multidimensional psychobiological model of violence. In A. Raine, P. Brennan, D. P. Farrington, & S. A. Mednick (Eds.), *Biosocial bases of violence,* pp. 39–54. New York: Plenum.

Coccaro, E. F. (1989). Central serotonin and impulsive aggression. *British Journal of Psychiatry, 155* (Suppl. 8), 52–63.

Cohen, A. K. (1956). *Delinquent boys: The culture of the gang.* London: Routledge & Kegan Paul.

Cohen, P. (1996). Response: How can generative theories of the effects of punishment be tested? *Pediatrics, 98,* 834–6.

Cohen, P., & Brook, J. S. (1987). Family factors related to the persistence of psychopathology in childhood and adolescence. *Psychiatry, 50,* 332–45.

(1995). The reciprocal influence of punishment and child behavior disorder. In J. McCord (Ed.), *Coercion and punishment in long-term perspectives*, pp. 154–64. Cambridge: Cambridge University Press.

Cohen, P., Cohen, J., & Brook, J. S. (1995). Bringing in the sheaves, or just gleaning? A methodological warning. *International Journal of Methods in Psychiatric Research, 5*, 263–6.

Cohen, P., Cohen, J., Kasen, S., Velez, C. N., Hartmark, C., Johnson, J., Rojas, M., Brook, J., & Streuning, E. L. (1993). An epidemiological study of disorders in late childhood and adolescence: I. Age and gender-specific prevalence. *Journal of Child Psychology and Psychiatry, 34*, 851–67.

Cohen, L. E., & Felson, M. (1979). Social change and crime rate trends: A routine activities approach. *American Sociological Review, 44*, 588–608.

Coie, J. D., & Dodge, K. A. (1997). Aggression and antisocial behavior. In W. Damon & N. Eisenberg (Eds.), *Handbook of child psychology, vol. 3: Social, emotional, and personality development*, 5th ed., pp. 779–862. New York: Wiley.

Coie, J. D., Dodge, K. A., Terry, R., & Wright, V. (1991). The role of aggression in peer relations: An analysis of aggression episodes in boys' play groups. *Child Development, 62*, 812–26.

Coie, J. D., Lochman, J. E., Terry, R., & Hyman, C. (1992). Predicting early adolescent disorder from childhood aggression and peer rejection. *Journal of Consulting and Clinical Psychology, 60*, 783–92.

Coie, J. D., Terry, R., Zakriski, A., & Lochman, J. E. (1995). Early adolescent social influences on delinquent behavior. In J. McCord (Ed.), *Coercion and punishment in long-term perspectives*, pp. 229–44. New York: Cambridge University Press.

Coleman, C., & Moynihan, J. (1996). *Understanding crime data: Haunted by the dark figure*. Buckingham: Open University Press.

Collins, J. J. (1986). The relationship of problem drinking to individual offending sequences. In A. Blumstein, J. Cohen, J. A. Roth, & C. A. Visher (Eds.), *Criminal careers and career criminals*, pp. 89–120. Washington, DC: National Academy Press.

Comer, J. (1990). *School power: Implications of an intervention project*. New York: Collier Macmillan.

Compas, B. E. (1995). Promoting successful coping during adolescence. In M. Rutter (Ed.), *Psychosocial disturbances in young people*, pp. 247–73. Cambridge: Cambridge University Press.

Comstock, G. (1990). Deceptive appearances: Television violence and aggressive behavior. *Journal of Adolescent Health Care, 11*, 31–44.

Comstock, G., & Paik, H. (1991). *Television and the American child*. San Diego, CA: Academic Press.

Conger, R. D., Conger, K. J., Elder, G. H., Jr., Lorenz, F. O., Simons, R. L., & Whitbeck, L. B. (1992). A family process model of economic hardship and adjustment of early adolescent boys. *Child Development, 63*, 526–41.

(1993). Family economic stress and adjustment of early adolescent girls. *Developmental Psychology, 29*, 206–19.

Conger, R. D., & Elder, G. (1994). *Families in troubled times: Adapting to change in rural America*. Hillsdale, NJ: Aldine.

Conger, R. D., Ge, X., Elder, G. H., Jr., Lorenz, F. O., & Simons, R. L. (1994). Economic stress, coercive family process, and developmental problems of adolescents. *Child Development, 65,* 541–61.

Conger, R. D., Patterson, G. R., & Ge, X. (1995). It takes two to replicate: A mediational model for the impact of parents' stress on adolescent adjustment. *Child Development, 66,* 80–97.

Connell, J. P., Spencer, M. B., & Aber, J. L. (1994). Educational risk and resilience in African-American youth: Context, self, action, and outcomes in school. *Child Development, 65,* 493–506.

Consedine, J. (1995). *Restorative justice.* Lyttleton, New Zealand: Ploughshares Publications.

Conseur, A., Rivara, F. P., Barnoski, R., & Emanuel, I. (1997). Maternal and perinatal risk factors for later delinquency. *Pediatrics, 99,* 785–90.

Consortium on the School-based Promotion of Social Competence [CSPSC] (1994). The school-based promotion of social competence: Theory, research, practice, and policy. In R. J. Haggerty, L. R. Sherrod, N. Garmezy, & M. Rutter (Eds.), *Stress, risk, and resilience in children and adolescents: Processes, mechanisms, and interventions,* pp. 268–316. Cambridge: Cambridge University Press.

Cook, E. H., Jr., Stein, M. A., Ellison, T., Unis, A. S., & Leventhal, B. L. (1995). Attention deficit hyperactivity disorder and whole-blood serotonin levels: Effects of comorbidity. *Psychiatry Research, 57,* 13–20.

Cook, T. D., & Campbell, D. T. (1979). *Quasi-experimentation: Design and analysis issues for field settings.* Chicago: Rand McNally.

Cookson, H. M. (1992). Alcohol use and offence type in young offenders. *British Journal of Criminology, 32,* 352–60.

Cornell, D. G., Benedek, E. P., & Benedek, B. A. (1987). Juvenile homicide: Prior adjustment and a proposed typology. *American Journal of Orthopsychiatry, 57,* 383–93.

Cornish, D. B. (1993). Theories of action in criminology: Learning theory and rational choice approaches. In R. V. Clarke & M. Felson (Eds.), *Routine activity and rational choice: Advances in criminological theory,* vol. 5, pp. 351–82. New Brunswick, NJ: Transaction Publishers.

Cornish, D. B., & Clarke, R. V. (1986). *The reasoning criminal.* New York: Springer-Verlag.

Costello, E. J., Angold, A., Burns, B., Stangl, D., Tweed, D., & Erkanli, A. (1996). The Great Smokey Mountain Study of Youth, I: Prevalence and correlates of DSM-III-R disorders. *Archives of General Psychiatry, 53,* 1137–43.

Council of Europe. (1995). *Draft model of the European Sourcebook on Criminal Justice Statistics.*

Cox, A. D., Puckering, C., Pound, A., Mills, M., & Owen, A. L. (1990). *The evaluation of a home-visiting and befriending scheme: NEWPIN* (Final Research Report to the Department of Health). London.

Crick, N. B. (1996). The role of overt aggression, relational aggression, and prosocial behaviour in the prediction of children's future social adjustment. *Child Development, 67,* 2317–27.

Crick, N. B., & Grotpeter, J. K. (1995). Relational aggression, gender, and social-psychological adjustment. *Child Development, 66,* 710–22.

Crick, N. R., & Dodge, K. A. (1994). A review and reformulation of social information-processing mechanisms in children's social adjustment. *Psychological Bulletin, 115,* 74–101.

(1996). Social information-processing mechanisms in reactive and proactive aggression. *Child Development, 67,* 993–1002.

Cromwell, P. F., Olson, J. N., & Avary, D. W. (1991). *Breaking and entering: An ethnographic analysis of burglary.* Newbury Park, CA: Sage.

Crowe, R. R. (1974). An adoption study of antisocial personality. *Archives of General Psychiatry, 31,* 785–91.

Crutchfield, R., Bridges, G., & Pritchford, S. (1994). Analytical and aggregation biases in analyses of imprisonment: Reconciling discrepancies in studies of racial disparity. *Journal of Research in Crime and Delinquency, 31,* 166–82.

Cumberbatch, G., & Brown, N. (1989). Violence to television: Effects research in context. *British Journal of Social Psychology, 31,* 147–64.

Curran, D., Kilpatrick, R., Young, V., & Wilson, D. (1995). Longitudinal aspects of reconviction: Secure and open intervention with juvenile offenders in Northern Ireland. *The Howard Journal, 34,* 97–123.

Currie, E. (1996). *Is America really winning the war on crime and should Britain follow its example?* London: National Association for the Care and Rehabilitation of Offenders.

Curry, G. D., & Spergel, I. A. (1988). Gang homicide, delinquency, and community. *Criminology, 26,* 381–405.

Curtis, S. (1989). *Juvenile offending: Prevention through intermediate treatment.* London: Batsford.

Cutrona, C. E., Cadoret, R. J., Suhr, J. A., Richards, C. C., Troughton, E., Schutte, K., & Woodworth, G. (1994). Interpersonal variables in the prediction of alcoholism among adoptees: Evidence for gene–environment interactions. *Comprehensive Psychiatry, 35,* 171–9.

Dadds, M. R., & McHugh, T. A. (1992). Social support and treatment outcome in behavioral treatment of child conduct disorders. *Journal of Consulting and Clinical Psychology, 60,* 252–9.

Dalby, J. T. (1985). Criminal liability in children. *Canadian Journal of Criminology, 27,* 137–45.

Dalton, K. D. (1984). *The premenstrual syndrome and progesterone therapy.* London: Heinemann.

Daly, K. (1993). *Gender, crime, and punishment.* New Haven, CT: Yale University Press.

Daniels, D., & Plomin, R. (1985). Differential experiences of siblings in the same family. *Developmental Psychology, 21,* 747–60.

Davis, G. E., & Leitenberg, H. (1987). Adolescent sex offenders. *Psychological Bulletin, 101,* 417–27.

Deater-Deckard, K., & Dodge, K. A. (1997). Externalizing behavior problems and discipline revisited: Nonlinear effects and variation by culture, context, and gender. *Psychological Inquiry, 8,* 161–75.

Deater–Deckard, K., Dodge, K. A., Bates, J. E., & Pettit, G. S. (1996). Physical discipline among African American and European American mothers: Links to children's externalizing behaviors. *Developmental Psychology, 32,* 1065–72.

(in press). Multiple risk factors in the development of externalizing behavior problems: Group and individual differences. *Development and Psychopathology.*

Deater–Deckard, K., & Plomin, R. (in press). An adoption study of the etiology of teacher reports in externalizing problems in middle childhood: Comparing individual differences and extreme groups. *Child Development.*

Denno, D. W. (1996). Legal implications of genetics and crime research. In G. R. Bock & J. A. Goode (Eds.), *Genetics of criminal and antisocial behaviour* (Ciba Foundation Symposium no. 194), pp. 248–56. Chichester: Wiley.

Dent, H., & Flin, R. (1992). *Children as witnesses.* Chichester: Wiley.

Diekstra, F. W., Kienhorst, C. W. M., & de Wilde, E. J. (1995). Suicide and suicidal behaviour among adolescents. In M. Rutter & D. J. Smith (Eds.), *Psychosocial disorders in young people: Time trends and their causes,* pp. 686–761. Chichester: Wiley.

DiLalla, L. F., & Gottesman, I. I. (1989). Heterogeneity of causes for delinquency and criminality: Lifespan perspectives. *Development and Psychopathology, 1,* 339–49.

Dishion, T. J., & Andrews, D. W. (1995). Preventing escalation in problem behaviors with high-risk young adolescents: Immediate and 1-year outcomes. *Journal of Consulting and Clinical Psychology, 63,* 538–48.

Dishion, T. J., French, D. C., & Patterson, G. R. (1995). The development and ecology of antisocial behavior. In C. Cicchetti & D. Cohen (Eds.), *Manual of developmental psychopathology, vol. 2: Risk, disorder and adaptation,* pp. 421–71. New York: Wiley.

Dishion, T. J., & Patterson, G. R. (1992). Age effects in parent training outcomes. *Behavior Therapy, 23,* 719–29.

(1997). The timing and severity of antisocial behavior: Three hypotheses within an ecological framework. In D. Stoff, J. Breiling, & J. Maser (Eds.), *Handbook of antisocial behavior,* pp. 206–18. New York: Wiley.

Dishion, T. J., Patterson, G. R., & Griesler, P. C. (1994). Peer adaptation in the development of antisocial behavior: A confluence model. In L. R. Huesmann (Ed.), *Current perspectives on aggressive behavior,* pp. 61–95. New York: Plenum.

Dishion, T. J., Patterson, G. R., & Kavanagh, K. A. (1992). An experimental test of the coercion model: Linking theory, measurement and intervention. In J. McCord & R. E. Tremblay (Eds.), *Preventing antisocial behavior: Intervention from birth through adolescence,* pp. 253–82. New York: Guilford.

Ditchfield, J., & Catan, L. (1992). *Juveniles sentenced to serious offences: A comparison of regimes in young offender institutions and local authority community homes.* London: Home Office.

Dobkin, P. L., Tremblay, R. E., & Sacchitelle, C. (1997). Predicting boy's early onset substance abuse from father's alcoholism, son's disruptiveness, and mother's parenting behavior. *Journal of Consulting and Clinical Psychology,* 65, 86–92.

Dodge, K. A. (1980). Social cognition and children's aggressive behavior. *Child Development, 51,* 162–70.

—— (1986). A social information processing model of social competence in children. In M. Perlmutter (Ed.), *The Minnesota symposium on child psychology,* vol. 18, pp. 77–125. Hillsdale, NJ: Erlbaum.

—— (1997). Testing developmental theory through prevention trials. Paper presented at the Society for Research in Child Development Biennial Meeting, Washington, DC, April 1997.

Dodge, K. A., Bates, J. E., & Pettit, G. S. (1990). Mechanisms in the cycle of violence. *Science, 250,* 1678–83.

Dodge, K. A., & Coie, J. D. (1987). Social information-processing factors in reactive and proactive aggression in children's peer groups. *Journal of Personality and Social Psychology, 53,* 1146–58.

Dodge, K. A., Pettit, G. S., & Bates, J. E. (1994). Socialization mediators of the relation between socioeconomic status and child conduct problems. *Child Development, 65,* 649–65.

Dodge, K. A., Pettitt, G. S., Bates, J. E., & Valente, E. (1995). Social information-processing patterns partially mediate the effect of early physical abuse on later conduct problems. *Journal of Abnormal Psychology, 104,* 632–43.

Dodge, K. A., & Schwartz, D. (1997). Social information processing mechanisms in aggressive behavior. In D. Stoff, J. Breiling, & J. D. Maser (Eds.), *Handbook of antisocial behavior,* pp. 171–80. New York: Wiley.

Dohrenwend, B. P., Levav, I., Shrout, P., Schwartz, S., Naveh, G., Link, B., Skodol, A., & Stueve, A. (1992). Socioeconomic status and psychiatric disorders: The causation–selection issue. *Science, 255,* 946–52.

Dolan, B., & Coid, J. (1993). *Psychopathic and antisocial personality disorders: Treatment and research issues.* London: Gaskell / Royal College of Psychiatrists.

Donnerstein, E., Linz, D., & Penrod, S. (1987). *The question of pornography: Research findings and policy implications.* New York: Free Press.

Donovan, J., Jessor, R., & Costa, F. (1988). Syndrome of problem behavior in adolescence. *Journal of Consulting and Clinical Psychology, 56,* 762–5.

D'Orban, P. T. (1979). Women who kill their children. *British Journal of Psychiatry, 134,* 560–71.

Downes, D. (Ed.) (1992). *Unravelling criminal justice: Eleven British studies.* Basingstoke: Hamps / London: Macmillan.

Drakeford, M. (1996). Parents of young people in trouble. *The Howard Journal, 35,* 242–55.

Dubow, E. F., & Luster, T. (1990). Adjustment of children born to teenage mothers: The contribution of risk and protective factors. *Journal of Marriage and the Family, 52,* 393–404.

Dunhill, C. (Ed.) (1989). *The boys in blue: Women's challenge to policing.* London: Virago.

Dunkel, F. (1991). Legal differences in juvenile criminology in Europe. In T. Booth (Ed.), *Juvenile justice in the new Europe,* pp. 1–29. Sheffield: Sheffield University Press.

Eagly, A., & Steffen, V. (1986). Gender and aggressive behavior: A meta-analytic review of the social psychological literature. *Psychological Bulletin, 100,* 309–30.

Earls, F. (1987). Sex differences in psychiatric disorders: Origins and developmental disorders. *Psychiatric Developments, 1,* 1–23.

(1994). Oppositional-defiant and conduct disorders. In M. Rutter, E. Taylor, & L. Hersov (Eds.), *Child and adolescent psychiatry: Modern approaches.* Oxford: Blackwell Scientific.

Eaves, L. J. (1996). Patterns, problems, and possibilities in the developmental genetic analysis of adolescent psychopathology. Paper presented at the XIVth Biennial ISSBD Conference, Québec City, Canada, August 12–16.

Eaves, L. J., Silberg, J., Hewitt, J. K., Meyer, J., Rutter, M., Simonoff, E., Neale, M., & Pickles, A. (1993). Genes, personality, and psychopathology: A latent class analysis of liability to symptoms of attention-deficit hyperactivity disorder in twins. In R. Plomin & G. E. McClearn (Eds.), *Nature, nurture and psychology,* pp. 285–303. Washington, DC: American Psychological Association.

Eaves, L., Silberg, J., Meyer, J., Maes, H., Simonoff, E., Pickles, A., Rutter, M., Neale, M. C., Reynolds, C. A., Erikson, M. T., Heath, A. C., Loeber, R., Truett, T. R., & Hewitt, J. K. (1997). Genetics and developmental psychopathology: 2. The main effects of gene and environment on behavioral problems in the Virginia Twin Study of Adolescent Development. *Journal of Child Psychology and Psychiatry, 38,* 965–80.

Egeland, B., Carlson, E., & Sroufe, L. A. (1993). Resilience as process. *Development and Psychopathology, 5,* 517–28.

Eggar, J., Carter, C. M., Graham, P. J., Gumley, D., & Soothill, J. F. (1985). Controlled trial of oligoantigenic treatment in the hyperkinetic syndrome. *Lancet, 1,* 540–5.

Eisenberg, L. (1986). Mindlessness and brainlessness in psychiatry. *British Journal of Psychiatry, 148,* 497–508.

(1995). The social construction of the human brain. *American Journal of Psychiatry, 152,* 1563–75.

Ekblom, P. (1979). Policy truancy patrols. In R. V. G. Clark & P. Mayhew (Eds.) *Designing out crime,* pp. 18–33. London: HMSO.

Ekblom, P., & Pease, K. (1995). Evaluating crime prevention. In M. Tonry & D. P. Farrington (Eds.), *Crime and justice,* vol. 19, pp. 585–662. Chicago: University of Chicago Press.

Elder, G. H., Jr. (1974). *Child of the Great Depression: Social change in life experience.* Chicago: University of Chicago Press.

(1979). Historical change in life patterns and personality. In P. B. Baltes & O. G. Brim (Eds.), *Life span development and behavior,* vol. 2, pp. 117–59. New York: Academic Press.

(1986). Military times and turning points in men's lives. *Developmental Psychology, 22,* 233–45.

(1994). Time, human agency and social change: Perspectives on the life course. *Social Psychology Quarterly, 57,* 4–15.

(1995). The life course paradigm: Social change and individual development. In P. Moch, G. H. Elder, Jr., & K. Luscher (Eds.), *Examining lives in context:*

Perspectives on the ecology of human development, pp. 101–39. Washington, DC: APA Press.

(1997). The life course and human development. In R. M. Lerner (Ed.), *Handbook of child psychology*, vol. 1, pp. 939–91. New York: Wiley.

Elder, G. H., Jr., & Caspi, A. (1990). Studying lives in a changing society: Sociological and personological explorations. In A. L. Rabin, R. A. Zucker, S. Frank, & R. A. Emmons (Eds.), *Studying persons and lives*, pp. 276–322. New York: Springer.

Eley, T. C., Lichtenstein, P., & Stevenson, J. (in press). Sex differences in the aetiology of aggressive and non-aggressive antisocial behavior: Results from two twin studies. *Child Development*.

Ellingworth, D., Farrell, G., & Pease, K. (1995). A victim is a victim? *British Journal of Criminology, 35*, 360–5.

Elliott, D. S. (1994). Serious violent offenders: Onset, developmental course, and termination – The American Society of Criminology 1993 Presidential Address. *Criminology, 32*, 1–21.

Elliott, D. S., & Ageton, S. (1980). Reconciling race and class differences in self-reported and official estimates of delinquency. *American Sociological Review, 45*, 95–110.

Elliott, D. S., Huizinga, D., & Menard, S. (1989). *Multiple problem youth: Delinquency, substance use, and mental health problems*. New York: Springer-Verlag.

Elliott, D. S., Huizinga, D., & Morse, B. (1986). Self-reported violent offending: A descriptive analysis of juvenile violent offenders and their offending careers. *Journal of Interpersonal Violence, 1*, 472–514.

Elliott, D. S., & Menard, S. (1990). Conventional bonding, delinquent peers, and delinquent behavior. Paper presented at the annual meeting of the American Sociological Association, Washington, DC, August.

Elliott, D. S., & Voss, H. (1974). *Delinquency and dropout*. Lexington, MA: Heath.

Elliott, D., Wilson, D., Huizinga, R., Sampson, A., & Rankin, B. (1996). The effects of neighborhood disadvantage on adolescent development. *Journal of Research in Crime and Delinquency, 33*, 389–426.

Eme, R. F. (1979). Sex differences in childhood psychopathology: A review. *Psychological Bulletin, 86*, 574–95.

Emler, N., & Reicher, S. (1995). *Adolescence and delinquency: The collective management of reputation*. Oxford: Blackwell.

Esbensen, F. A., & Huizinga, D. (1993). Gangs, drugs, and delinquency in a survey of urban youth. *Criminology, 31*, 565–89.

Evans, R. (1992a). Cautioning: Counting the cost of retrenchment. *Criminal Law Review* (August), 566–75.

(1992b). *The conduct of police interviews with juveniles* (Royal Commission on Criminal Justice Research Study no. 8). London: HMSO.

Evans, R., & Wilkinson, C. (1990). Variations in police cautioning policy and practice in England and Wales. *Howard Journal for Penal Reform, 29*, 155–76.

Eysenck, H. J. (1977). *Crime and personality*. London: Paladin.

Eysenck, H. J., & Schoenthaler, S. J. (1997). Raising IQ level by vitamin and mineral supplementation. In R. J. Sternberg & E. L. Grigorenko (Eds.),

Intelligence, heredity and environment, pp. 363–92. Cambridge: Cambridge University Press.

Farnworth, M., Thornberry, T. P., Krohn, M. D., & Lizotte, A. J. (1994). Measurement in the study of class and delinquency: Integrating theory and research. *Journal of Research in Crime and Delinquency, 31*, 32–61.

Farrell, G., & Pease, K. (1993). *Once bitten: Repeat victimization and its implications for crime prevention* (Crime Prevention Unit Paper no. 46). London: Home Office.

Farrington, D. P. (1977). The effects of public labelling. *British Journal of Criminology, 17*, 112–25.

(1978). The family backgrounds of aggressive youths. In L. A. Herzov, M. Berger, & D. Shaffer (Eds.), *Aggression and anti-social behaviour in childhood and adolescence*, pp. 73–94. Oxford: Pergamon.

(1979). Longitudinal research on crime and delinquency. In N. Morris & M. Tonry (Eds.), *Criminal justice: An annual review of research*, vol. 1, pp. 289–348. Chicago: University of Chicago Press.

(1981). Prevalence of convictions. *British Journal of Criminology, 21*, 173–5.

(1983). Randomized experiments on crime and justice. In M. Tonry & N. Morris (Eds.), *Crime and justice*, vol. 4, pp. 257–308. Chicago: University of Chicago Press.

(1986a). Stepping stones to adult criminal careers. In D. Olweus, J. Blockand, & M. R. Yarrow (Eds.), *Development of antisocial and prosocial behaviour*, pp. 359–84. New York: Academic Press.

(1986b). Age and crime. In M. Tonry & N. Morris (Eds.), *Crime and justice*, vol. 7, pp. 189–250. Chicago: University of Chicago Press.

(1988). Studying changes within individuals: The causes of offending. In M. Rutter (Ed.), *Studies of psychosocial risk: The power of longitudinal data*, pp. 158–83. Cambridge: Cambridge University Press.

(1989). Self-reported and official offending from adolescence to adulthood. In M. W. Klein (Ed.), *Cross-national research in self-reported crime and delinquency*, pp. 339–423. Dordrecht: Kluwer.

(1991). Childhood aggression and adult violence: Early precursors and later life outcomes. In D. J. Pepler & K. H. Rubin (Eds.), *The development and treatment of childhood aggression*, pp. 5–29. Hillsdale, NJ: Erlbaum.

(1992). Explaining the beginning, progress and ending of antisocial behavior from birth to adulthood. In J. McCord (Ed.), *Advances in criminological theory, vol. 3: Facts, frameworks and forecasts*, pp. 253–86. New Brunswick, NJ: Transaction Publishers.

(1993a). Understanding and preventing bullying. In M. Tonry & N. Morris (Eds.), *Crime and justice*, vol. 17, pp. 381–458. Chicago: University of Chicago Press.

(1993b). Have any individual, family or neighbourhood influences on offending been demonstrated conclusively? In D. P. Farrington, R. J. Sampson, & P.-O. H. Wikström (Eds.), *Integrating individual and ecological aspects of crime*, pp. 7–39. Stockholm: National Council for Crime Prevention.

(1994). Early developmental prevention of juvenile delinquency. *Criminal Behaviour and Mental Health, 4*, 209–27.

(1995a). The Twelfth Jack Tizard Memorial Lecture: The development of offending and antisocial behaviour from childhood: Key findings from the Cambridge Study in Delinquent Development. *Journal of Child Psychology and Psychiatry, 36,* 929–64.

(1995b). Key issues in the integration of motivational and opportunity-reducing crime prevention strategies. In P. H. Wikstrom, R. V. Clarke, & J. McCord (Eds.), *Integrating crime prevention strategies: Propensity and opportunity,* pp. 333–57. Stockholm: National Council for Crime Prevention.

(1995c). The challenge of teenage antisocial behavior. In M. Rutter (Ed.), *Psychosocial disturbances in young people: Challenges for prevention,* pp. 83–130. New York: Cambridge University Press.

(1995d). Later life outcomes of truants in the Cambridge Study. In I. Berg & J. Nursden (Eds.), *Unwillingly to school,* pp. 96–118. London: Gaskell.

(1996). *Understanding and preventing youth crime. Social policy research 93.* York: Joseph Rowntree Foundation.

(1997a). Human development and criminal careers. In M. Maguire, R. Morgan, & R. Reiner (Eds.), *The Oxford handbook of criminology,* 2nd ed., pp. 361–408. Oxford: Clarendon.

(1997b). Resting heart rate and violent crime: A biosocial perspective. In A. Raine, P. Brennan, D. P. Farrington, & S. A. Mednick (Eds.), *Biosocial bases of violence,* pp. 89–106. New York: Plenum.

(1997c). Evaluating a community crime prevention program. *Evaluation, 3,* 157–73.

Farrington, D. P., Barnes, G. C., & Lambert, S. (1996a). The concentration of offending in families. *Legal and Criminological Psychology, 1,* 47–63.

Farrington, D. P., & Bennett, T. (1981). Police cautioning of juveniles in London. *British Journal of Criminology, 21,* 123–35.

Farrington, D. P., Biron, L., & Le Blanc, M. (1982). Personality and delinquency in London and Montreal. In J. Gunn & D. P. Farrington (Eds.), *Abnormal offenders: Delinquency and the criminal justice system,* pp. 153–201. Chichester: Wiley.

Farrington, D. P., & Burrows, J. N. (1993). Did shoplifting really decrease? *British Journal of Criminology, 33,* 57–69.

Farrington, D. P., & Dowds, E. A. (1985). Disentangling criminal behaviour and police reaction. In D. P. Farrington and J. C. Gunn (Eds.), *Reactions to crime: The public, the police, courts, and prisons,* pp. 41–72. Chichester: Wiley.

Farrington, D. P., Gallagher, B., Morley, L., St. Ledger, R. J., & West, D. J. (1986). Unemployment, school leaving and crime. *British Journal of Criminology, 26,* 335–56.

(1988). Are there any successful men from criminogenic backgrounds? *Psychiatry, 51,* 116–30.

Farrington, D. P., Gundry, G., & West, D. J. (1975). The familial transmission of criminality. *Medicine, Science and the Law, 15,* 177–86.

Farrington, D. P., & Hawkins, J. D. (1991). Predicting participation, early onset and later persistence in officially recorded offending. *Criminal Behaviour and Mental Health, 1,* 1–33.

Farrington, D. P., Lambert, S., & West, D. J. (1998). Criminal careers in two generations of family members in the Cambridge Study of Delinquent Development. *Studies on Crime and Crime Prevention, 7,* 1–22.

Farrington, D. P., & Langan, P. A. (1992). Changes in crime and punishment in England and America in the 1980s. *Justice Quarterly, 9,* 5–46.

Farrington, D. P., Langan, P. A., & Wikström, P.-O. H. (1994). Changes in crime and punishment in America, England and Sweden between the 1980s and the 1990s. *Studies on Crime and Crime Prevention, 3,* 104–31.

Farrington, D. P., & Loeber, R. (1989). Relative improvement over chance (RIOC) and phi as measures of predictive efficiency and strength of association in 2 × 2 tables. *Journal of Quantitative Criminology, 5,* 201–13.

(in press). Transatlantic replicability of risk factors in the development of delinquency. In P. Cohen, C. Slomkowski, & L. N. Robins (Eds.), *Where and when: The influence of history and geography on aspects of psychopathology.* Mahway, NJ: Erlbaum.

Farrington, D. P., Loeber, R., Elliott, D. S., Hawkins, J. D., Kandel, D. B., Klein, M. W., McCord, J., Rowe, D. C., & Tremblay, R. E. (1990a). Advancing knowledge about the onset of delinquency and crime. In B. B. Lahey & A. E. Kazdin (Eds.), *Advances in clinical child psychology,* vol. 13, pp. 283–342. New York: Plenum.

Farrington, D. P., Loeber, R., Stouthamer-Loeber, M., Van Kammen, W. B., & Schmidt, L. (1996b). Self-reported delinquency and combined delinquency seriousness scale based on boys, mothers, and teachers: Concurrent and predictive validity for African-Americans and Caucasians. *Criminology, 34,* 501–25.

Farrington, D. P., Loeber, R., & Van Kammen, W. B. (1990b). Long-term criminal outcomes of hyperactivity-impulsivity-attention deficit and conduct problems in childhood. In L. Robins & M. Rutter (Eds.), *Straight and devious pathways from childhood to adulthood,* pp. 62–81. New York: Cambridge University Press.

Farrington, D. P., & Morris, A. M. (1983). Sex, sentencing and reconviction. *British Journal of Criminology, 33,* 57–69.

Farrington, D. P., Osborn, S., & West, D. J. (1978). The persistence of labelling effects. *British Journal of Criminology, 18,* 277–84.

Farrington, D. P. Sampson, R. J., & Wikström, P.-O. H. (Eds.) (1993). *Integrating individual and ecological aspects of crime.* Stockholm: National Council for Crime Prevention.

Farrington, D. P., & West, D. J. (1993). Criminal, penal and life histories of chronic offenders: Risk and protective factors and early identification. *Criminal Behavior and Mental Health, 3,* 492–523.

(1995). Effects of marriage, separation, and children on offending by adult males. In Z. Smith Blau & J. Hagan (Eds.), *Current perspectives of aging and the life cycle: Delinquency and disrepute in the life course,* pp. 249–381. Greenwich, CT: JAI.

Featherstone, M. (1991). *Consumer culture and postmodernism.* London: Sage.

Federal Bureau of Investigation (1993). *Uniform crime reports for the United States 1993.* Washington, DC: FBI, U.S. Department of Justice.

Feehan, M., McGee, R., & Williams, S. M. (1993). Mental health disorders from age 15 to age 18. *Journal of the American Academy of Child and Adolescent Psychiatry, 32,* 1118–26.

Feeney, F. (1985). Interdependence as a working concept. In D. Moxon (Ed.), *Managing criminal justice,* pp. 8–17. London: HMSO.

Feingold, B. F. (1975). Hyperkinesis and learning disabilities linked to artificial food flavors and colors. *American Journal of Nursing, 75,* 797–803.

Feld, B. C. (1993). Criminalizing the American juvenile court. In M. Tonry (Ed.), *Crime and justice: A review of research,* vol. 17, pp. 197–280. Chicago: University of Chicago Press.

Feldman, R. A. (1992). The St. Louis Experiment: Effective treatment of antisocial youths in prosocial peer groups. In J. McCord & R. E. Tremblay (Eds.), *Preventing antisocial behvior: Interventions from birth through adolescence,* pp. 233–52. New York: Guilford.

Feldman-Summers, S., & Norris, J. (1984). Differences between rape victims who report and those who do not report to a public agency. *Journal of Applied Social Psychology, 14,* 562–73.

Ferdinand, R. F., & Verhulst, F. C. (1995). Psychopathology from adolescence into young adulthood: An 8-year follow-up study. *American Journal of Psychiatry, 152,* 1586–94.

Ferguson, T. (1966). *Children in care – and after.* Oxford: Oxford University Press.

Fergusson, D. M., & Horwood, L. J. (1993). The structure, stability and correlations of the trait components of conduct disorder, attention deficit and anxiety/withdrawal reports. *Journal of Child Psychology and Psychiatry, 34,* 749–66.

(1995). Predictive validity of categorically and dimensionally scored measures of disruptive behavioral adjustment and juvenile offending. *Journal of the American Academy of Child and Adolescent Psychiatry, 34,* 477–85.

(1996). The role of adolescent peer affiliations in the continuity between childhood behavioral adjustment and juvenile offending. *Journal of Abnormal Child Psychology, 24,* 205–21.

Fergusson, D. M., Horwood, L. J., Caspi, A., Moffitt, T. E., & Silva, P. A. (1996a). The (artefactual) remission of reading disability: Psychometric lessons in the study of stability and change in behavioral development. *Developmental Psychology, 32,* 132–40.

Fergusson, D. M., Horwood, L. J., & Lloyd, M. (1991). Confirmatory factor models of attention deficit and conduct disorder. *Journal of Child Psychology and Psychiatry, 32,* 257–74.

Fergusson, D. M., Horwood, L. J., & Lynskey, M. T. (1992). Family change, parental discord and early offending. *Journal of Child Psychology and Psychiatry, 33,* 1059–75.

(1993). The effects of conduct disorder and attention deficit in middle childhood on offending and scholastic ability at age 13. *Journal of Child Psychology and Psychiatry, 34,* 899–916.

(1995a). The stability of disruptive childhood behaviors. *Journal of Abnormal Child Psychology, 23,* 379–96.

(1997a). Early dentine lead levels and educational outcomes at 18 years. *Journal of Child Psychology and Psychiatry, 38*, 471–8.

Fergusson, D. M., & Lynskey, M. T. (1996). Adolescent resiliency to family adversity. *Journal of Child Psychology and Psychiatry, 37*, 281–92.

(1997). Early reading difficulties and later conduct problems. *Journal of Child Psychology and Psychiatry, 38*, 899–908.

Fergusson, D. M., Lynskey, M. T., & Horwood, J. (1995b). The adolescent outcomes of adoption: A 16-year longitudinal study. *Journal of Child Psychology and Psychiatry, 36*, 597–615.

(1996b). Factors associated with continuity and changes in disruptive behavior patterns between childhood and adolescence. *Journal of Abnormal Child Psychology, 24*, 533–54.

(1997b). The effects of unemployment on juvenile offending. *Criminal Behaviour and Mental Health, 7*, 49–68.

Ferrie, J. E., Shipley, M. J., Marmot, M. G., Stansfeld, S., & Davey Smith, G. (1995). Health effects of anticipation of job change and non-employment: Longitudinal data from the Whitehall II study. *British Medical Journal, 311*, 1264–9.

Fickenauer, J. O. (1992). *Scared straight! and the panacea phenomenon.* Englewood Cliffs, NJ: Prentice-Hall.

Field, S. (1990). *Trends in crime and their interpretation: A study of recorded crime in post-war England and Wales.* London: HMSO.

Figuera-McDonough, J. (1984). Feminism and delinquency. *British Journal of Criminology, 24*, 325–34.

Finch, J. (1986). Pastoral care, juvenile justice and the welfare network. *Journal of Education Policy, 1*, 133–47.

Fingerhut, L. A., & Kleinman, J. C. (1990). International and interstate comparisons of homicide among young males. *Journal of the American Medical Association, 263*, 3292–5.

Finkelhor, D., & Dziuba-Leatherman, J. (1994). Victimization of children. *American Psychologist, 49*, 173–83.

Fitzgerald, M. (1993). *Ethnic minorities and the criminal justice systems* (Royal Commission on Criminal Justice Research Study no. 20). London: HMSO.

Fleiss, J. L. (1981). *Statistical methods for rates and proportions*, 2nd ed. New York: Wiley.

Flynn, J. R. (1996). Group differences: Is the good society impossible? *Journal of Biosocial Science, 28*, 573–86.

Fombonne, E. (1994). The Chartres study: I. Prevalence of psychiatric disorders among French school-aged children. *British Journal of Psychiatry, 164*, 69–79.

(1995a). Depressive disorders: Time trends and possible explanatory mechanisms. In M. Rutter & D. J. Smith (Eds.), *Psychosocial disorders in young people: Time trends and their causes*, pp. 544–615. Chichester: Wiley.

(1995b). Eating disorders: Time trends and possible explanatory mechanisms. In M. Rutter & D. J. Smith (Eds.), *Psychosocial disorders in young people: Time trends and their causes*, pp. 616–85. Chichester: Wiley.

Fonagy, P., Steele, M., Steele, H., Higgitt, A., & Target, M. (1994). The Emanuel Miller Memorial Lecture 1992: The theory and practice of resilience. *Journal of Child Psychology and Psychiatry, 35,* 231–57.

Forehand, R. L., & McMahon, R. J. (1981). *Helping the non-compliant child: A clinicians guide to parent training.* New York: Guilford.

Forgatch, M. S. (1991). The clinical science vortex: A developing theory of antisocial behavior. In D. J. Pepler & K. H. Rubin (Eds.), *The development and treatment of childhood aggression,* pp. 291–315. Hillsdale, NJ: Erlbaum.

Forgatch, M. S., & Patterson, G. R. (1989). *Parents and adolescents living together, part 2: Family problem solving.* Eugene, OR: Castalia.

Forrest, J. D., & Singh, S. (1990). The sexual and reproductive behavior of American women, 1982–1988. *Family Planning Perspectives, 22,* 206–14.

Forrester, D., Chatteron, M., & Pease, K. (1988). *The Kirkholt Burglary Prevention Project, Rochdale* (Crime Prevention Unit Paper no. 13). London: Home Office.

Foster, J., & Hope, T. (1993). *Housing, community and crime: The impact of the Priority Estates Projects* (Home Office Research Study no. 131). London: HMSO.

Freeman, H. L. (1985). *Mental health and the environment.* London: Churchill Livingstone.

Frick, P. J., Kamphaus, R. W., Lahey, B. B., Loeber, R., Christ, M. A. G., Hart, E. L., & Tannenbaum, L. E. (1991). Academic underachievement and the disruptive behavior disorders. *Journal of Consulting and Clinical Psychology, 59,* 289–94.

Frick, P. J., Lahey, B. B., Loeber, R., Tannenbaum, L., Van Horn, Y., Christ, M. A. G., Hart, E. A., & Hanson, K. (1993). Oppositional defiant disorder and conduct disorder: A meta-analytic review of factor analyses and cross-validation in a clinic sample. *Clinical Psychology Review, 13,* 319–40.

Frick, P. J., O'Brien, B. S., Wootton, J. M., & McBurnett, K. (1994). Psychopathy and conduct problems in children. *Journal of Abnormal Psychology, 103,* 700–7.

Frodi, A., Macaulay, J., & Thome, P. (1977). Are women always less aggressive than men? A review of the experimental literature. *Psychological Bulletin, 84,* 634–60.

Frost, N., Johnson, L., Wallis, L., & Stein, M. (1996). *Negotiated friendships: Home Start and family support.* London: Home Start.

Frude, N. (Ed.) (1980). *Psychological approaches to child abuse.* London: Batsford.

Furstenberg, F. F., Jr., Brooks-Gunn, J., & Morgan, S. P. (1987). *Adolescent mothers in later life.* New York: Cambridge University Press.

Gabor, T. (1981). The crime displacement hypothesis: An empirical examination. *Crime and Delinquency, 26,* 390–404.

Garber, J., Quiggle, N. L., Panak, W., & Dodge, K. A. (1991). Aggression and depression in children: Comorbidity, specificity, and social cognitive processing. In D. Cicchetti & S. L. Toth (Eds.), *Internalizing and externalizing expressions of dysfunction* (Rochester Symposium on Developmental Psychopathology), vol. 2, pp. 225–64. Hillsdale, NJ: Erlbaum.

Garmezy, N., & Rutter, M. (Eds.) (1983). *Stress, coping, and development in children.* New York: McGraw–Hill.

Garrett, P., Ng'andu, N., & Ferron, J. (1994). Poverty experiences of young children and the quality of their home environment. *Child Development, 65,* 331–45.

Gaub, M., & Carlson, C. L. (1997). Gender differences in ADHD: A meta-analysis and critical review. *Journal of the American Academy of Child and Adolescent Psychiatry, 36,* 1036–45.

Geen, R. G. (1990). *Human aggression.* Milton Keynes, UK: Open University Press.

Gelsthorpe, L. (1997). Feminism and criminology. In M. Maguire, R. Morgan, & R. Reiner (Eds.), *The Oxford handbook of criminology,* 2nd ed., pp. 511–33. Oxford: Clarendon.

Gelsthorpe, L., & Giller, H. (1990). More justice for juveniles: Does more mean better? *Criminal Law Review* (March), 153–64.

Gelsthorpe, L., & Morris, A. (1994). Juvenile justice 1945–1992. In M. Maguire, R. Morgan, & R. Reiner (Eds.), *The Oxford handbook of criminology,* pp. 949–93. Oxford: Clarendon.

Gelsthorpe, L., & Raynor, P. (1995). Quality and effectiveness in probation officers: Reports to sentencers. *British Journal of Criminology, 35,* 188–200.

Gendreau, P., & Ross, R. R. (1980). Effective correctional treatment: Bibliotherapy for cynics. In R. R. Ross & P. Gendreau (Eds.), *Effective correctional treatment,* pp. 13–36. Toronto: Butterworths.

Giller, H. J. (1983). The Cheshire juvenile volunteer schemes. *Journal of Social Welfare Law,* 283–95.

Gilling, D. (1997). *Crime prevention: Theory, policy and politics.* London: UCL Press.

Giordano, P. C., Cernkovich, S. A., & Pugh, M. D. (1986). Friendships and delinquency. *American Journal of Sociology, 91,* 1170–1202.

Gjone, H., & Stevenson, J. (1997). The association between internalizing and externalizing behavior in childhood and early adolescence: Genetic or environmental common influences? *Journal of Abnormal Child Psychology, 25,* 277–86.

Glueck, S., & Glueck, E. T. (1950). *Unraveling juvenile delinquency.* New York: Commonwealth Fund.

(1956). *Physique and delinquency.* New York: Harper & Row.

Goetting, A. (1995). *Homicide in families and other special populations.* Berlin: Springer-Verlag.

Goldstein, A. P. (1991). *Delinquent gangs: A psychological perspective.* Champaign, IL: Research Press.

Goodman, R. (1994). Brain disorders. In M. Rutter, E. Taylor, & L. Hersov (Eds.), *Child and adolescent psychiatry: Modern approaches,* 3rd ed., pp. 172–90. London: Blackwell Scientific.

Goodman, R., Simonoff, E., & Stevenson, J. (1995). The relationship between child IQ, parent IQ and sibling IQ on child behavioural deviance scores. *Journal of Child Psychology and Psychiatry, 36,* 409–25.

Goodman, R., & Stevenson, J. (1989). A twin study of hyperactivity: II. The aetiological role of genes, family relationships and perinatal adversity. *Journal of Child Psychology and Psychiatry, 30,* 691–709.

Goodyer, I. (1990). *Life experiences, development and childhood psychopathology.* Chichester: Wiley.

Gore, S., & Aseltine, R. J., Jr. (1995). Protective processes in adolescence: Matching stressors with social resources. *American Journal of Community Psychology, 23,* 301–27.

Gorski, R. A. (1996). Gonadal hormones and the organization of brain structure and function. In D. Magnusson (Ed.), *The lifespan development of individuals: Behavioral, neurobiological, and psychosocial perspectives,* pp. 315–40. Cambridge: Cambridge University Press.

Gottesman, I. I., & Goldsmith, H. H. (1994). Developmental psychopathology of antisocial behavior: Inserting genes into its ontogenesis and epigenesis. In C. A. Nelson (Ed.), *Threats to optimal development: Integrating biological, psychological, and social risk factors,* pp. 69–104. Hillsdale, NJ: Erlbaum.

Gottfredson, D. C., & Gottfredson, G. D. (1992). Theory-guided investigation: Three field experiments. In J. McCord & R. E. Tremblay (Eds.), *Preventing antisocial behaviour: Interventions from birth through adolescence,* pp. 311–29. New York: Guilford.

Gottfredson, M. (1984). *Victims of crime: The dimension of risk.* London: HMSO.

Gottfredson, M., & Hirschi, T. (1986). The true value of lambda would appear to be zero: An essay on career criminals, criminal careers, selective incapacitation, cohort studies, and related topics. *Criminology, 24,* 213–34.

(1991). *A general theory of crime.* Stanford, CA: Stanford University Press.

Gottschalk, R., Davidson, W. S., Mayer, J., & Gensheimer, L. K. (1987). Behavioural approaches with juvenile offenders: A meta-analysis of long-term treatment efficiency. In E. K. Morris & C. J. Braukmann (Eds.), *Behavioral approaches to crime and delinquency,* pp. 399–422. New York: Plenum.

Götz, M. (1996). The psychiatric consequences of sex chromosome abnormalities: A cohort study. M.Phil. thesis, University of Edinburgh, July.

Gould, M. S., Shaffer, D., & Davies, M. (1990). Truncated pathways from childhood to adulthood: Attrition in follow-up studies due to death. In L. N. Robins & M. Rutter (Eds.), *Straight and devious pathways from childhood to adulthood,* pp. 3–9. Cambridge: Cambridge University Press.

Goy, R. W. (1996). Patterns of juvenile behavior following early hormonal interventions. In D. Magnusson (Ed.), *The lifespan development of individuals: Behavioral, neurobiological, and psychosocial perspectives,* pp. 296–314. Cambridge: Cambridge University Press.

Grace, L., Lloyd, C., & Smith, L. (1992). *Rape, from recording to conviction.* London: HMSO.

Graham, J. (1988). *Schools, disruptive behavior and delinquency: A review of research* (Home Office Research Study no. 96). London: HMSO.

(1994). Recent developments in SRD research: A commentary. Paper presented at the Colloquium on Crime and Criminal Policy in Europe, Romainmotier, Switzerland, September.

Graham, J., & Bennett, T. (1995). *Crime prevention strategies in Europe and North America.* Helsinki: HEUNI.

Graham, J., & Bowling, B. (1995). *Young people and crime* (Home Office Research Study no. 145). London: HMSO.

Graham, J. M., Hanson, J. W., Darby, B. L., Barr, H. M., & Streissguth, A. P. (1988). Independent dysmorphology evaluations at birth and 4 years of age for children exposed to varying amounts of alcohol in utero. *Pediatrics, 81,* 772–8.

Graham, J., & Smith, D. I. (1994). *Diversion from offending – The role of the Youth Service.* Swindon: Crime Concern.

Graham, J., & Utting, D. (1996). Families, schools and criminology prevention. In T. Bennett (Ed.), *Preventing crime and disorder,* pp. 385–416. Cambridge: Cambridge University Press.

Gray, J. A. (1987). *The psychology of fear and stress.* Cambridge: Cambridge University Press.

Graziano, A. M. (1996). Presentation: Middle class families and the use of corporal punishment. *Pediatrics, 98,* 845–8.

Greenberg, M. T., & Conduct Problems Prevention Research Group [CPPRG] (1997). Improving peer relations and reducing aggressive behavior: The classroom level effects of the PATHS curriculum. Paper presented at the Society for Research in Child Development Biennial Meeting, Washington, DC, April.

Greenough, W. T., Black, J. E., & Wallace, C. S. (1987). Experience and brain development. *Child Development, 58,* 539–59.

Greenwood, P. W., & Abrahamse, A. F. (1982). *Selective incapacitation.* Santa Monica, CA: RAND.

Greenwood, P. W., Model, K. E., Rydell, P., & Chiesa, J. (1996). *Diverting children from a life of crime: Measuring costs and benefits.* Santa Monica, CA: RAND.

Greenwood, P. W., Rydell, P., Abrahamse, A., Caulkins, J., Model, K. E., & Kelin, S. P. (1994). *Three strikes and you're out: Estimated benefits and costs of California's new mandatory sentencing laws.* Santa Monica, CA: RAND.

Griffiths, M. D. (1997). Video games and aggression. *The Psychologist, 10,* 397–401.

Gualtieri, C. T., & Hicks, R. E. (1985). An immunoreactive theory of selective male affliction. *Behavioral and Brain Sciences, 8,* 427–77.

Gudjonsson, G., & Clark, N. (1986). Suggestibility in police interrogation: A social psychological model. *Social Behaviour, 1,* 88–104.

Gudjonsson, G., & MacKeith, J. (1988). Retracted confessions: Legal, psychological and psychiatric aspects. *Medicine, Science and the Law, 28,* 187–94.

Gunn, J., Maden, A., & Swinton, M. (1991). *The mentally disordered offender.* London: Institute of Psychiatry.

Guralnick, M. J. (1997). *The effectiveness of early intervention.* Baltimore: Brookes.

Hagan, J. (1991). Destiny and drift: Subcultural preferences, status attainments and the risks and rewards of youth. *American Sociological Review, 56,* 567–82.

(1994). *Crime and disrepute.* Thousand Oaks, CA: Pine Forge Press.

Hagan, J., MacMillan, R., & Wheaton, B. (1996). New kid in town: Social capital and the life course effects of family migration on children. *American Sociological Review, 61,* 368–85.

Hagan, M. P., King, R. P., & Patros, R. L. (1994). Recidivism among adolescent perpetrators of sexual assault against children. *Journal of Offender Rehabilitation, 21,* 127–37.

Hagell, A., & Newburn, T. (1994). *Persistent young offenders.* London: Policy Studies Institute.

Hagell, A., & Shaw, C. (1996). *Opportunity and disadvantage at age 16.* London: Policy Studies Institute.

Halperin, J. M., Sharma, V., Siever, L. J., Schwartz, S. T., Matier, K., Wornell, G., & Newcorn, J. H. (1994). Serotonergic function in aggressive and nonaggressive boys with attention deficit hyperactivity disorder. *American Journal of Psychiatry, 151,* 243–8.

Hämäläinen, M., & Pulkkinen, L. (1995). Aggressive and non-prosocial behaviour as precursors of criminality. *Studies on Crime and Crime Prevention, 4,* 6–20.

(1996). Problem behaviour as a precursor of male criminality. *Development and Psychopathology, 8,* 443–55.

Hannon, P., Weinberger, J., & Nutbrown, C. (1991). A study of work with parents to promote early literacy development. *Research Papers in Education, 6,* 77–98.

Harada, Y. (1995). Adjustment to school, life course transitions, and changes in delinquent behavior in Japan. In Z. S. Blau & J. Hagan (Eds.), *Current perspectives on aging and the life cycle: Delinquency and disrepute in the life course,* pp. 35–60. Greenwich, CT: JAI.

Hare, R. D. (1970). *Psychopathy: Theory and research.* New York: Wiley.

(1991). *The Hare psychopathy checklist – revised.* Toronto: Multi-Health Systems.

Hare, R. D., & Schalling, D. (Eds.) (1978). *Psychopathic behavior: Approaches to research.* New York: Wiley.

Harrington, R., Fudge, H., Pickles, A., & Hill, J. (1991). Adult outcomes of childhood and adolescent depression: II. Links with antisocial disorders. *Journal of the American Academy of Child and Adolescent Psychiatry, 30,* 434–9.

Harrington, R. C., Fudge, H., Rutter, M., Bredenkamp, D., Groothues, C., & Pridham, J. (1993). Child and adult depression: A test of continuities with data from a family study. *British Journal of Psychiatry, 162,* 627–33.

Harrington, R., Rutter, M., & Fombonne, E. (1996). Developmental pathways in depression: Multiple meanings, antecedents, and endpoints. *Development and Psychopathology, 8,* 601–16.

Hart, R. J. (1978). Crime and punishment in the Army. *Journal of Personality and Social Psychology, 36,* 1456–71.

Hartless, J. M., Ditton, J., Nair, G., & Phillips, S. (1995). More sinned against than sinning: A study of young teenagers' experience of crime. *British Journal of Criminology, 35,* 114–33.

Hartup, W. W. (1983). Peer relations. In P. H. Mussen and E. M. Hetherington (Eds.), *Handbook of child psychology, vol. 4: Socialization, personality and social development,* pp. 103–96. New York: Wiley.

Hawkins, D. (1995). Ethnicity, race and crime: A review of selected studies. In D. Hawkins (Ed.), *Ethnicity, race and crime*, pp. 11–45. Albany: State University of New York Press.

Hawkins, D. J., Arthur, M. W., & Catalano, R. F. (1995). Preventing substance abuse. In M. Tonry & D. P. Farrington (Eds.), *Building a safer society: Strategic approaches to crime prevention*, pp. 343–428. Chicago: University of Chicago Press.

Hawkins, J. D., & Catalano, R. F. (1992). *Communities that care*. San Francisco: Jossey-Bass.

Hawkins, J. D., Catalano, R. F., & Miller, J. Y. (1992a). Risk and protective factors for alcohol and other drug problems in adolescence and early adulthood: Implications for substance abuse prevention. *Psychological Bulletin, 112,* 64–105.

Hawkins, J. D., Catalano, R. F., Morrison, D. M., O'Donnell, J., Abbott, R. D., & Day, L. E. (1992b). The Seattle Social Development Project: Effects of the first four years on protective factors and problem behaviors. In J. McCord & R. E. Tremblay (Eds.), *Preventing antisocial behaviour: Intervention from birth through adolescence*, pp. 139–61. New York: Guilford.

Hawton, K., Fagg, J., Platt, S., & Hawkins, M. (1993). Factors associated with suicide following parasuicide in young people. *British Medical Journal, 306,* 1643–4.

Hay, D. F., & Angold, A. (Eds.) (1993). *Precursors and causes in development and psychopathology*. Chichester: Wiley.

Hayes, C. D. (1987). *Risking the future: Adolescent sexuality, pregnancy, and childbearing*, vol. 1. Washington, DC: National Academy Press.

Heidensohn, F. (1997). Gender and crime. In M. Maguire, R. Morgan, & R. Reiner (Eds.), *The Oxford handbook of criminology*, 2nd ed., pp. 761–98. Oxford: Oxford University Press.

Henn, F. A., Bardwell, R., & Jenkins, R. L. (1980). Juvenile delinquents revisited: Adult criminal activity. *Archives of General Psychiatry, 37,* 1160–3.

Hennessey, J. W., & Levine, S. (1979). Stress, arousal and the pituitary-adrenal system: A psychoendocrine hypothesis. In J. M. Sprague & A. N. Epstein (Eds.), *Progress in psychobiology and physiological psychology*, pp. 133–78. New York: Academic Press.

Henry, B., Caspi, A., Moffitt, T. E., & Silva, P. A. (1996). Temperamental and familial predictors of violent and non-violent criminal convictions: From age 3 to age 18. *Developmental Psychopathology, 32,* 614–23.

Henry, B., Moffitt, T. E., Caspi, A., Langley, J., & Silva, P. A. (1994). On the "Rememberance of things past": A longitudinal evaluation of the retrospective mind. *Psychological Assessment, 6,* 92–101.

Henry, B., Moffit, T., Robins, L., Earls, F., & Silva, P. (1993). Early family predictors of child and adolescent antisocial behavior: Who are the mothers of delinquents? *Criminal Behaviour and Mental Health, 3,* 97–118.

Hess, L. E. (1995). Changing family patterns in Western Europe: Opportunity and risk factors for adolescent development. In M. Rutter and D. J. Smith (Eds.), *Psychosocial disorders in young people: Time trends and their causes*, pp. 104–93. Chichester: Wiley.

Hetherington, E. M. (1980). Children and divorce. In R. Henderson (Ed.), *Parent–child interaction: Theory, research and prospects*, pp. 33–58. New York: Academic Press.

Hetherington, E. M., & Blechman, E. A. (Eds.) (1996). *Stress, coping, and resiliency in children and families.* Mahwah, NJ: Erlbaum.

Hewitt, J. K., Silberg, J. L., Rutter, M., Simonoff, E., Meyer, J. M., Maes, H., Pickles, A., Neale, M. C., Loeber, R., Erickson, M. T., Kendler, K. S., Heath, A. C., Truett, K. R., Reynolds, C. A., & Eaves, L. J. (1997). Genetics and developmental psychopathology: I. Phenotypic assessment in the Virginia Twin Study of Adolescent Behavioral Development. *Journal of Child Psychology and Psychiatry, 38,* 943–64.

Hewitt, L. E., & Jenkins, R. L. (1946). *Fundamental patterns of maladjustment.* Michigan, IL: Michigan Child Guidance Institute.

Higley, J. D., Thompson, W. W., Champoux, M., Goldman, D., Hasert, M. F., Kraemer, G. W., Scanlan, J. M., Suomi, S. J., & Linnoila, M. (1993). Paternal and maternal genetic and environmental contributions to cerebrospinal fluid monamine metabolites in rhesus monkeys (Macaca mulatta). *Archives of General Psychiatry, 50,* 615–23.

Hindelang, M., Hirschi, T., & Weis, J. (1979). Correlates of delinquency: The illusion of discrepancy between self-report and official delinquency. *American Sociological Review, 44,* 995–1014.

(1981). *Measuring delinquency.* Beverly Hills, CA: Sage.

Hinshaw, S. P. (1987). On the distinction between attentional deficits/hyperactivity and conduct problems/aggression in child psychopathology. *Psychological Bulletin, 101,* 443–63.

(1992). Externalizing behavior problems and academic underachievement in childhood and adolescence: Causal relationships and underlying mechanisms. *Psychological Bulletin, 111,* 127–55.

Hinshaw, S. P., Lahey, B. B., & Hart, E. L. (1993). Issues of taxonomy and comorbidity in the development of conduct disorder. *Development and Psychopathology, 5,* 31–49.

Hirschi, T. (1969). *Causes of delinquency.* Berkeley: University of California Press.

Hirschi, T., & Gottfredson, M. (1983). Age and the explanation of crime. *American Journal of Sociology, 89,* 552–84.

(1994). *The generality of deviance.* New Brunswick, NJ: Transaction Publishers.

Hirschi, T., & Hindelang, M. T. (1977). Intelligence and delinquency: A revisionist review. *American Social Review, 42,* 571–87.

Hoddinott, J. (1994). Public safety and private security. *Policing, 10,* 158–65.

Hodgins, S. (Ed.) (1993). *Mental disorder and crime.* Newbury Park, CA: Sage.

(1996). Biological factors implicated in the development of criminal behaviors. In R. Linden (Ed.), *Criminology: A Canadian perspective*, pp. 199–235. Toronto: Harcourt Brace.

Hodgins, S., Coié, G., & Toupin, J. (in press). Major mental disorder and crime: An etiological hypothesis. In D. Cooke, A. Forth, & R. D. Hare (Eds.), *Psychopathy: Theory, research and implications for society.* Dordrecht: Kluwer.

Hodgins, S., Mednick, S. A., Brennan, P. A., Schulzinger, F., & Engberg, M. (1996). Mental disorder and crime: Evidence from a Danish birth cohort. *Archives of General Psychiatry, 53,* 489–96.

Hofer, H. V. (1995). Violence and youth in Sweden in a long-term perspective. Paper presented at the Xth International Workshop for Juvenile Criminology, Siena, May 18–21.

Hollin, C. R. (1995). The meaning and implications of "programme integrity." In J. McGuire (Ed.), *What works: Reducing reoffending,* pp. 195–208. Chichester: Wiley.

Hollin, C. R., Epps, K. J., & Kendrick, D. J. (1995). *Managing behavioural treatment: Policy and practice with delinquent adolescents.* London: Routledge.

Holzman, H. R. (1996). Criminological research on public housing: Toward a better understanding of people, places and space. *Crime and Delinquency, 42,* 361–79.

Home Affairs Committee (1993). *Juvenile offenders.* London: HMSO.

Home Office (1980). *Criminal statistics England and Wales 1979.* London: HMSO.

(1986). *Criminal statistics England and Wales 1985.* London: HMSO.

(1988). *Criminal statistics England and Wales 1987.* London: HMSO.

(1995a). *Prison statistics England and Wales 1994* (Cm. 3087). London: HMSO.

Home Office, Department of Health, Welsh Office (1995b). *National Standards for the Supervision of Offenders in the Community.* London: HMSO.

Home Office, Research and Statistics Department (1995c). *Cautions, court proceedings and sentencing England and Wales 1994.* London: Government Statistical Service.

Home Office, Statistical Bulletin (1995d). *Criminal careers of those born between 1953–1973.* London: Home Office.

Home Office (1996). *Criminal statistics England and Wales 1995.* London: HMSO.

(1997a). *Aspects of crime – Gender.* London: Home Office Research and Statistics Directorate.

(1997b). *Criminal statistics England and Wales 1996.* London: HMSO.

Hood, R. (1992). *Race and sentencing: A study in the Crown Court.* Oxford: Clarendon.

Hope, T. (1985). *Implementing crime prevention measures* (Home Office Research Study no. 86). London: HMSO.

(1995a). The flux of victimization. *British Journal of Criminology, 35,* 327–42.

(1995b). Community crime prevention. In M. Tonry & D. Farrington (Eds.), *Crime and justice,* vol. 19, pp. 21–89. Chicago: University of Chicago Press.

(1996). Communities, crime and inequality in England and Wales. In T. Bennett (Ed.), *Preventing crime and disorders,* pp. 165–94. Cambridge: Cambridge University Institute of Criminology.

Hope T., & Foster, J. (1992). Conflicting forces: Changing the dynamics of crime and community on a "problem" estate. *British Journal of Criminology, 32,* 488–504.

Hope, T., & Hough, M. (1988). Area, crime and incivilities: A profile from the British Crime Survey. In T. Hope & M. Shaw (Eds.), *Communities and crime reduction,* pp. 30–47. London: HMSO.

Horn, G. (1990). Neural bases of recognition memory investigated through an analysis of imprinting. *Philosophical Transactions of the Royal Society, 329,* 133–42.

Horney, J., Osgood, D. W., & Marshall, I. H. (1995). Criminal careers in the short-term: Intra-individual variability in crime and its relation to local life circumstances. *American Sociological Review, 60,* 655–73.

House of Commons Select Committee on Juvenile Offending (1993). *Juvenile offenders,* 6th report. London: HMSO.

Howell, J. C. (1997). *Juvenile justice and youth violence.* Thousand Oaks, CA: Sage.

Howlin, P., & Rutter, M. (1987). The consequences of language delay for other aspects of development. In W. Yule & M. Rutter (Eds.), *Language development and disorders,* pp. 271–95. London: MacKeith.

Hudson, B. (1993). Penal policy and racial justice. In L. Gelsthorpe & W. McWilliam (Eds.), *Minority ethnic groups and the criminal justice system,* pp. 154–71. Cambridge: Cambridge University Institute of Criminology.

Huessman, L. R., & Eron, L. D. (1986). *Television and the aggressive child: A cross-national comparison.* Hillsdale, NJ: Erlbaum.

Huessman, L. R., Moise, J. F., & Podolski, C.-L. (1997). The effects of media violence on the development of antisocial behavior. In D. Stoff, J. Breiling, & J. Maser (Eds.), *Handbook of antisocial behavior,* pp. 181–93. New York: Wiley.

Huff, G., & Collinson, F. (1987). Young offenders, gambling and video game playing: A survey in a youth custody centre. *British Journal of Criminology, 27,* 401–10.

Huizinga, D. (1995). Developmental sequences in delinquency: Dynamic typologies. In L. J. Crockett & A. C. Crouter (Eds.), *Pathways through adolescence,* pp. 15–34. Mahwah, NJ: Erlbaum.

Huizinga, D., & Elliot, D. P. (1986). Reassessing the reliability and validity of self-report delinquency measures. *Journal of Quantitative Criminology, 24,* 293–327.

Huizinga, D., & Jacob-Chien, C. (1998). The contemporaneous co-occurrence of serious and violent juvenile offending and other problems. In R. L. Loeber & D. P. Farrington (Eds.), *Serious and violent juvenile offenders: Risk factors and successful interventions,* pp. 47–67. Thousand Oaks, CA: Sage.

Huston, A. C., Donnerstein, E., Fairchild, H., Feshbach, N. D., Katz, P. A., Murray, J. P., Rubinstein, E. A., Wilcox, B. L., & Zuckerman, D. (1992). *Big world, small screen: The role of television in American society.* Lincoln: University of Nebraska Press.

Hyde, J. S., & Linn, M. C. (1986). *The psychology of gender: Advances through meta-analysis.* Baltimore: Johns Hopkins University Press.

Illsley, R. & Mitchell, R. G. (1984). *Low birthweight: A medical, psychological and social study.* Chichester: Wiley.

Institute for the Study of Drug Dependency. (1994). *Drug misuse in Britain 1994.* London: Institute for the Study of Drug Dependency.

Ito, T., Miller, N., & Pollock, V. E. (1996). Alcohol and aggression: A meta-analysis on the moderating effects of inhibitory cues, triggering events, and self-focused attention. *Psychological Bulletin, 120,* 60–82.

Jackson, F. L. C. (1992). Race and ethnicity as biological constructs. *Ethnicity and Disease, 2,* 120–5.

Jackson, S. (forthcoming). *Family group conferencing in youth justice: Issues for implementation in England and Wales.*

Jacobs, P. A., Brunton, M., Melville M. M., Brittain, R. P., & McClermont, W. F. (1965). Aggressive behavior, mental subnormality, and the XYY male. *Nature, 208,* 1351–2.

Jahoda, M. (1981). Work, employment, and unemployment: Values, theories, and approaches in social research. *American Psychologist, 36,* 184–91.

Janson, C. G. (1984). Project Metropolitan: A presentation and progress report. Department of Sociology, University of Stockholm, Sweden.

Jarvis, G., & Parker, H. (1989). Young heroin users and crime: How do the "new users" finance their habits. *British Journal of Criminology, 29,* 175–85.

Jenkins, J. M., & Smith, M. A. (1990). Factors protecting children living in disharmonious homes: Maternal reports. *Journal of the American Academy of Child and Adolescent Psychiatry, 29,* 60–9.

Jessor, R., Donovan, J. E., & Costa, F. (1991). *Beyond adolescence: Problem behavior and young adult development.* Cambridge: Cambridge University Press.

Jessor, R., & Jessor, S. L. (1977). *Problem behavior and psychosocial development: A longitudinal study of youth.* New York: Academic Press.

Johnson, S. H., Bowers, K., & Hirschfield, A. (1997). New insights into the spatial and temporal distribution of repeat victimization. *British Journal of Criminology, 37,* 224–41.

Jolin, A., & Stipak, B. (1992). Drug treatment and electronically monitored home confinement: An evaluation of a community-based sentencing option. *Crime and Delinquency, 38,* 158–70.

Jones, T., Maclean, B., & Young, J. (1986). *The Islington Crime Survey.* Aldershot: Gower.

Junger, M. (1989). Discrepancies between police and self-report data for Dutch racial minorities. *British Journal of Criminology, 29,* 273–84.

Junger-Tas, J. (1992). Changes in the family and their impact on delinquency. *European Journal of Criminal Policy and Research, 1,* 27–51.

(1994a). *Delinquent behaviour among young people in the Western world.* Amsterdam: Kugler.

(1994b). *Alternatives to prison sentences: Experiences and developments.* Amsterdam: Kugler.

(1995a). *Youth and violence in Europe: A quantitative review.* Leyden: Institute of Criminology.

(1995b). *Ethnic minorities and the criminal justice system in the Netherlands.* Leyden: University of Leyden.

(1996). *Youth and family: Crime prevention from a judicial perspective.* Amsterdam: Ministry of Justice.

Junger-Tas, J., & Block, R. (1988). *Juvenile delinquency in the Netherlands.* Amsterdam: Kugler.

Junger-Tas, J., & Marshall, I. H. (in press). The self-report methodology in crime research: Strengths and weaknesses. In M. Tonry (Ed.), *Crime and justice,* vol. 20. Chicago: University of Chicago Press.

Junger-Tas, J., Terlouw, G.-J., & Klein, M. W. (1994). *Delinquent behavior among young people in the Western world: First results of the international self-report delinquency study.* Amsterdam: Kugler.

Justice (1996). *Children and homicide: Appropriate procedures for juveniles in murder and manslaughter cases.* London: Justice.

Kandel, D. B. (1978). Homophily, selection and socialization in adolescent friendships. *American Journal of Sociology, 84,* 427–36.

Kandel, D. B., Simcha-Fagan, O., & Davies, M. (1986). Risk factors for delinquency and illicit drug use from adolescence to young adulthood. *The Journal of Drug Issues, 16,* 67–90.

Kandel, D. B., & Wu, P. (1995). Disentangling mother–child effects in the development of antisocial behavior. In J. McCord (Ed.), *Coercion and punishment in long-time perspectives,* pp. 106–23. Cambridge: Cambridge University Press.

Kangaspunta, K. (1995). *Crime and criminal justice in Europe and North America 1986–1990.* Helsinki: European Institute for Crime Prevention and Control.

Kaplan, B. J., McNicol, J., Conte, R. A., & Moghadam, H. K. (1989). Dietary replacement in preschool-aged hyperactive boys. *Pediatrics, 83,* 7–17.

Kaplan, H. B. (1995). *Drugs, crime, and other deviant adaptations: Longitudinal studies.* New York: Plenum.

Kavanagh, K., & Dishion, T. J. (1990). *Parent Focus: A skill enhancement curriculum for parents of young adolescents.* Eugene, OR: Independent Video Services.

Kazdin, A. E. (1992). Treatment of conduct disorder: Progress and directions in psychotherapy research. *Development and Psychopathology, 5,* 277–310.

(1997). Psychosocial treatments for conduct disorder in children. *Journal of Child Psychology and Psychiatry, 38,* 161–78.

Kazdin, A. E., Siegel, T. C., & Bass, D. (1992). Cognitive-problem-solving skills training and parent management training in the treatment of antisocial behaviour in children. *Journal of Consulting and Clinical Psychology, 60,* 733–47.

Keating, D. P. (1990). Adolescent thinking. In S. S. Feldman & G. R. Elliott (Eds.), *At the threshold: The developing adolescent,* pp. 54–89. Cambridge, MA: Harvard University Press.

Keeling, G. L., & Coles, C. M. (1996). *Fixing broken windows.* New York: Free Press.

Keenan, K., Loeer, R., Zhang, Q., Stouthamer-Loeber, M., & van Kammen, W. B. (1995). The influence of deviant peers on the development of boys' disruptive and delinquent behavior: A temporal analysis. *Development and Psychopathology, 7,* 715–26.

Keil, T., & Vito, G. (1989). Race, homicide severity, and application of the death penalty. *Criminology, 27,* 511–31.

Kellam, S. G. (1990). Developmental epidemiological framework for family research on depression and aggression. In G. R. Patterson (Ed.), *Depression and aggression in family interaction,* pp. 11–48. Hillsdale, NJ: Erlbaum.

Kellam, S. G., & Rebok, G. W. (1992). Building developmental and etiological theory through epidemiologically based preventive intervention trials. In J. McCord & R. E. Tremblay (Eds.), *Preventing antisocial behavior: Interventions from birth to adolescence,* pp. 162–95. New York: Guilford.

Kellam, S. G., Rebok, G. W., Ialongo, N., & Mayer, L. S. (1994). The course and malleability of aggressive behavior from early first grade into middle school: Results of a developmental epidemiologically-based preventive trial. *Journal of Child Psychology and Psychiatry, 35,* 259–81.

Kellam, S. G., Simon, M. B., & Ensminger, M. E. (1983). Antecedents in first grade of teenage substance use and psychological well-being: A ten-year community-wide prospective study. In D. F. Ricks & B. S. Dohrenwend (Eds.), *Origins of psychopathology,* p. 17–42. Cambridge: Cambridge University Press.

Kelley, B. T., Huizinga, D., Thornberry, T. P., & Loeber, R. L. (1997). *Epidemiology of serious violence.* Washington, DC: Department of Justice.

Kendall-Tackett, K. A., Meyer Williams, L., & Finkelhor, D. (1993). Impact of sexual abuse on children: A review and synthesis of recent empirical studies. *Psychological Bulletin, 113,* 164–80.

Kendler, K. S., Neale, M. C., Prescott, C. A., Kessler, R. C., Heath, A. C., Corey, L. A., & Eaves, L. J. (1996). Childhood parental loss and alcoholism in women: A causal analysis using a twin-family design. *Psychological Medicine, 26,* 79–95.

Kenny, D. A. (1975). Cross-lagged panel correlation: A test for spuriousness. *Psychological Bulletin, 82,* 887–903.

Kerner, H.-J., Weitekamp, E., & Stelly, W. (1995). From child delinquency to adult criminality: First results of the follow-up of the Tübingen criminal behavior development study. *EuroCriminology, 8,* 127–62.

Kerner, H.-J., Weitekamp, E., Stelly, W., & Thomas, J. (1996). Patterns of criminality and alcohol abuse: Results of the Tübingen Criminal Behavior Study. Paper presented at the Life History Research Society Meeting, London, October.

Kerr, M., Tremblay, R. E., Pagani–Kurtz, L., & Vitaro, F. (1997). Boys' behavioral inhibition and the risk of later delinquency. *Archives of General Psychiatry, 54,* 809–16.

Kessler, R. C., Davis, C. G., & Kendler, K. S. (1997). Childhood adversity and adult psychiatric disorder in the U.S. National Comorbidity Survey. *Psychological Medicine, 27,* 1101–19.

Kessler, R. C., McGonagle, K. A., Zhao, S., Nelson, C. B., Hughes, M., Eshleman, S., Wittchen, H. U., & Kendler, K. S. (1994). Lifetime and 12-month prevalence of DSM-III-R psychiatric disorders in the United States: Results from the National Comorbidity Survey. *Archives of General Psychiatry, 51,* 8–19.

Killias, M. (1989). *Les Suisses face au crime.* Grusch, Switzerland: Ruegger.

Kinsey, L. (1985). *Merseyside crime survey: First report.* Liverpool: Merseyside County Council.

Klein, M. W. (1994). Epilogue. In J. Junger-Tas (Ed.), *Delinquent behaviour among young people in the Western world,* pp. 381–5. Amsterdam: Kugler.

(1995). *The American street gang.* New York: Oxford University Press.

(1996). Gangs in the United States and Europe. *European Journal of Criminal Policy and Research, 4,* 63–80.

Klinteberg, B. A., Andersson, T., Magnusson, D., & Stattin, H. (1993). Hyperactive behavior in childhood as related to subsequent alcohol problems and violent offending: A longitudinal study of male subjects. *Personality and Individual Differences, 15,* 381–8.

Knapp, M., & Fenyo, A. (1995). The cost and cost-effectiveness of intermediate treatment. In A. E. Bottoms, *Intensive community supervision for young offenders: Outcomes, process and cost,* pp. 53–70. Cambridge: Cambridge University Press.

Knight, R. A., & Prentky, R. A. (1993). Exploring characteristics for classifying juvenile sex offenders. In H. E. Barbaree, W. L. Marshall, & S. M. Hudson (Eds.), *The juvenile sex offender,* pp. 45–83. New York: Guilford.

Kolvin, I., Miller, F. J. W., Fleeting, M., & Kolvin, P. A. (1988). Social and parenting factors affecting criminal-offence rates: Findings from the Newcastle Thousand-Family Study (1947–1980). *British Journal of Psychiatry, 152,* 80–90.

Kolvin, I., Miller, F. J. W., Scott, D. M., Gatzanis, S. R. M., & Fleeting, M. (1990). *Continuities of deprivation? The Newcastle Thousand-Family Survey.* Aldershot: Avebury.

Kovacs, M., & Getsonis, C. (1989). Stability and change in childhood-onset depressive disorders: Longitudinal course as a diagnostic validator. In L. N. Robins & J. E. Bennett (Eds.), *The validity of psychiatric diagnosis,* pp. 27–55. New York: Plenum.

Kratzer, L., & Hodgins, S. (1996a). Childhood factors and adult criminality among women. Paper presented at the XIVth Biennial ISSBD Conference, Québec City, Canada, August 12–16.

(1996b). A typology of offenders: A test of Moffitt's theory among males and females from childhood to age 30. Paper presented at the Life History Research Society meeting, London, October 3–5.

(1997). Adult outcomes of child conduct problems: A cohort study. *Journal of Abnormal Child Psychology, 25,* 65–81.

Krisberg, B., & Austin, J. F. (1993). *Reinventing juvenile justice.* Newbury Park, CA: Sage.

Krisberg, B., Schwartz, I., Fishman, G., Eisikovits, Z., Guttman, E., & Joe, K. (1987). The incarceration of minority youth. *Crime and Delinquency, 33,* 173–205.

Krueger, R. F., Caspi, A., Moffitt, T. E., & White, J. (1996). Delay of gratification, psychopathology, and personality: Is low self-control specific to externalizing problems? *Journal of Personality, 64,* 107–29.

Krueger, R. F., Moffitt, T. E., Caspi, A. C., & Bleske, A. (in press). Assortative mating for antisocial behavior: Developmental and methodological implications. *Behavior Genetics.*

Krueger, R. F., Schmutte, P. S., Caspi, A., Moffitt, T. E., Campbell, K., & Silva, P. A. (1994). Personality traits are linked to crime among males and females: Evidence from a birth cohort. *Journal of Abnormal Psychology, 103,* 328–38.

Kruesi, M. J., Hibbs, E. D., Zahn, T. P., Keysor, C. S., Hamburger, S. D., Bartko, J. J., & Rapoport, J. L. (1992). A 2-year prospective follow-up study of children and adolescents with disruptive behavior disorders: Prediction by cerebrospinal fluid 5–hydroxyindoleacetic acid, homovanillic acid, and autonomic measures. *Archives of General Psychiatry, 49,* 429–35.

Kruesi, M. J., & Jacobsen, T. (1997). Serotonin and human violence: Do environmental mediators exist? In A. Raine, D. Farrington, P. Brennan, & S. A. Mednick (Eds.), *Biosocial bases of violence*, pp. 189–207.

Kupersmidt, J. B., & Coie, J. D. (1990). Preadolescent peer status, aggression, and school adjustment as predictors of externalizing problems in adolescence. *Child Development, 61,* 1350–62.

Kyvsgaard, B. (1991). The decline in child and youth criminality: Possible explanations of an international trend. In A. Snare (Ed.), *Youth, crime and justice: Scandinavian studies in criminology,* vol. 12, pp. 26–41. Oslo: Norwegian University Press.

Lahey, B. B., & Loeber, R. (1994). Framework for a developmental model of oppositional defiant disorder and conduct disorder. In D. Routh (Ed.), *Disruptive behaviour disorders in childhood: Essays in honor of Herbert C. Quay,* pp. 139–80. New York: Plenum.

Lally, J. R., Mangione, P. L., & Honig, A. S. (1988). The Syracuse University Family Development Research Program: Long-range impact of an early intervention with low-income children and their families. In D. R. Powell (Ed.), *Parent education as early childhood intervention: Emerging directions in theory, research, and practice,* pp. 79–104. Norwood, NJ: Ablex.

Landau, S. F. (1981). Juveniles and the police. *British Journal of Criminology, 21,* 27–46.

Landau, S. F., & Nathan, G. (1983). Selecting delinquents for cautioning in the London Metropolitan Area. *British Journal of Criminology, 23,* 128–49.

Langan, P. A. (1985). Racism on trial: New evidence to explain the racial composition of prisons in the United States. *Journal of Criminal Law and Criminology, 76,* 666–83.

Lapierre, D., Braun, C. M. J., & Hodgins, S. (1995). Ventral frontal deficits in psychopathy – Neuropsychological test findings. *Neuropsychologia, 33,* 139–51.

Larzelere, R. E. (1996). Presentation: Implications of the strongest studies for discriminating effective vs counterproductive corporal punishment. *Pediatrics, 98,* 824–8.

Larzelere, R. E., & Patterson, G. R. (1990). Parental management: Mediator of the effect of socioeconomic status on early delinquency. *Criminology, 28,* 301–23.

Laub, J. H., Nagin, D. S., & Sampson, R. J. (1998). Trajectories of change in criminal offending: Good marriages and the desistance process. *American Sociological Review, 63,* 225–38.

Lavrakis, P. J., & Bennett, S. F. (1989). A process and impact evaluation of the 1983–1986 Neighbourhood Anti-Crime Self-Help program: Summary report. Center for Urban Affairs and Policy Research, Northwestern University, Evanston, IL.

Laycock, G., & Tarling, R. (1985). Police force cautioning: Policy and practice. *Howard Journal of Criminal Justice, 24,* 81–92.

Lazar, I., & Darlington, R. (1982). The lasting effects of early education. A report from the consortium of longitudinal studies. *Monographs of the Society for Research in Child Development, 47,* 9–151.

Le Blanc, M. (1998). Screening of serious and violent offenders: Identification, classification and prediction. In R. L. Loeber & D. P. Farrington (Eds.), *Serious and violent juvenile offenders: Risk factors and successful interventions*, pp. 167–93. Thousand Oaks, CA: Sage.

Le Blanc, M., Cote, G., & Loeber, R. (1991). Temporal paths in delinquency: Stability, regression and progression analyzed with panel data from an adolescent and a delinquent male sample. *Canadian Journal of Criminology, 33*, 23–44.

Lee, C. L., & Bates, J. E. (1985). Mother–child interaction at age two years and perceived difficult temperament. *Child Development, 56*, 1314–25.

Lee, V. E., Smith, J. B., & Croninger, R. G. (1995). Another look at high school restructuring. In *Issues in restructuring schools*, pp. 6–10. Madison, WI: Center on Organization and Restructuring of Schools.

Levy, F., Hay, D. A., McStephen, M., Wood, C., & Waldman, I. (1997). Attention-deficit hyperactivity disorder: A category or a continuum? Genetic analysis of a large-scale twin study. *Journal of the American Academy of Child and Adolescent Psychiatry, 36*, 737–44.

Lewinsohn, P. M., Rohde, P., & Seeley, J. R. (1995). Adolescent psychopathology: III. The clinical consequences of comorbidity. *Journal of the American Academy of Child and Adolescent Psychiatry, 34*, 510–19.

Lewis, D. E. (1986). The general deterrent effect of longer sentences. *British Journal of Criminology, 26*, 47–62.

Lewis, D. O., Lovely, R., Yeager, C., & Femina, D. D. (1989a). Toward a theory of the genesis of violence: A follow-up study of delinquents. *Journal of the American Academy of Child and Adolescent Psychiatry, 28*, 431–6.

Lewis, D. O., Mallouh, C., & Webb, V. (1989b). Child abuse, delinquency, and violent criminality. In D. Cicchetti & V. Carlson (Eds.), *Child maltreatment: Theory and research on the causes and consequences of child abuse and neglect*, pp. 707–21. Cambridge: Cambridge University Press.

Lewis, D. O., Moy, E., Jackson, L., Aaronson, R., Restifo, N., Serra, S., & Simos, A. (1985). Biopsychosocial characteristics of children who later murder: A prospective study. *American Journal of Psychiatry, 142*, 1161–7.

Lewis, D. O., Shanok, S. S., Pincus, J. H., & Glaser, G. H. (1979). Violent juvenile delinquents: Psychiatric, neurological, psychological and abuse factors. *Journal of the American Academy of Child and Adolescent Psychiatry, 18*, 307–19.

Lewis, D. O., Yeager, C. A., Lovely, R., Stein, A., & Cobham-Portorreal, C. S. (1994). A clinical follow-up of delinquent males: Ignored vulnerabilities, unmet needs, and the perpetuation of violence. *Journal of the American Academy of Child and Adolescent Psychiatry, 33*, 518–28.

Liddle, M., & Bottoms, A. E. (1993). *The five towns crime prevention initiative: Key findings and implications from a retrospective research analysis*. London: Home Office.

Liebert, R. M., & Sprafkin, J. (1988). *The early window: Effects of television on children and youth*. New York: Pergamon.

Liebling, A. (1992). *Suicides in prison*. London: Routledge.

Light, R., Nee, C., & Ingham, H. (1993). *Car theft: The offender's perspective* (Home Office Research Study no. 130). London: HMSO.

Lingard, A., & Allen, J. (1982). *Parent–teacher relations in secondary schools*. Gravesend: Gravesend School Council.

Link, B. G., Andrews, H. A., & Cullen, F. T. (1992). The violent and illegal behavior of mental patients reconsidered. *American Sociological Review, 57,* 275–92.

Lipsey, M. (1992). Juvenile delinquency treatment: A meta-analytic inquiry into the variability of effects. In T. D. Cook, H. Hooper, D. S. Cordray, H. Hartmann, L. V. Hedges, R. L. Light, T. A. Louis, & F. Mosteller (Eds.), *Meta-analysis for explanation*, pp. 83–127. New York: Russell Sage Foundation.

(1995). What do we learn from 400 research studies on the effectiveness of treatment with juvenile delinquents? In J. McGuire (Ed.), *What works: Reducing reoffending*, pp. 63–78. Chichester: Wiley.

Lipsey, M. W., & Derzon, J. H. (1998). Predictors of violent or serious delinquency in adolescence and early childhood. In R. L. Loeber & D. P. Farrington (Eds.), *Serious and violent juvenile offenders: Risk factors and successful interventions*, pp. 86–105. Thousand Oaks, CA: Sage.

Lipsey, M., & Wilson, D. B. (1993). The efficiency of psychological, educational and behavioural treatment. *American Psychologist, 48,* 1181–1209.

(1998). Effective intervention for serious juvenile offenders. In In R. L. Loeber & D. P. Farrington (Eds.), *Serious and violent juvenile offenders: Risk factors and successful interventions*, pp. 313–45. Thousand Oaks, CA: Sage.

Littlechild, B. (1995). Reassessing the role of the appropriate adult. *Criminal Law Review* (July), 540–5.

Livingstone, S. (1996). On the continuing problem of media effects. In J. Curran & M. Gurevich (Eds.), *Mass media and society*, pp. 305–24. London: Arnold.

Lochman, J. E. (1992). Cognitive–behavioural intervention with aggressive boys: Three-year follow-up and preventive effects. *Journal of Consulting and Clinical Psychology, 60,* 426–32.

Lochman, J. E., Bierman, K. L., & McMahon, R. J. (1997). Predictors of outcome: Family, neighborhood, and child characteristics. Paper presented at the Society for Research in Child Development Biennial Meeting, Washington, DC, April.

Loeber, R., De La Matre, M., Keenan, K., & Zhang, Q. (in press). A prospective replication of developmental pathways in disruptive and delinquent behavior. In R. Cairns (Ed.), *The individual as a focus in developmental research*. Thousand Oaks, CA: Sage.

Loeber, R., & Farrington, D. P. (1994). Problems and solutions in longitudinal and experimental treatment studies of child psychopathology and delinquency. *Journal of Consulting and Clinical Psychology, 62,* 887–900.

Loeber, R. L., Farrington, D. P., & Waschbusch, D. A. (1998). Serious and violent juvenile offenders. In R. L. Loeber & D. P. Farrington (Eds.), *Serious and violent juvenile offenders: Risk factors and successful interventions*, pp. 13–29. Thousand Oaks, CA: Sage.

Loeber, R., Green, S. M., Lahey, B. B., Christ, M. A. G., & Frick, P. J. (1992). Developmental sequences in the age of onset of disruptive child behaviors. *Journal of Child and Family Studies, 1*, 21–41.

Loeber, R., & Hay, D. F. (1994). Developmental approaches to aggression and conduct problems. In M. Rutter & D. F. Hay (Eds.), *Development through life: A handbook for clinicians*, pp. 488–516. Oxford: Blackwell Scientific.

Loeber, R., Keenan, K., & Zhang, Q. (1997). Boys' experimentation and persistence in developmental pathways toward serious delinquency. *Journal of Child and Family Studies, 6*, 321–57.

Loeber, R. L., & Le Blanc, M. (1990). Towards a developmental criminology. In M. Tonry & N. Morris (Eds.), *Crime and justice: A review of research*, vol. 12, pp. 375–473. Chicago: University of Chicago Press.

Loeber, R., & Schmaling, K. (1985). Empirical evidence for overt and covert patterns of antisocial conduct problems. *Journal of Abnormal Child Psychology, 13*, 337–52.

Loeber, R., & Stouthamer-Loeber, M. (1986). Family factors as correlates and predictors of juvenile conduct problems and delinquency. In N. Morris & M. Tonry (Eds.), *Crime and justice*, vol. 7, pp. 29–149. Chicago: University of Chicago Press.

Loeber, R., Stouthamer-Loeber, M., Van Kammen, W., & Farrington, D. P. (1991). Initiation, escalation and desistance in juvenile offending and their correlates. *Journal of Criminal Law and Criminology, 82*, 36–82.

(1996). Are more recent generations of juvenile boys worse off than past generations? Paper presented at the 6th Biennial Meeting of the Society for Research in Adolescence, Boston, March 7–10.

Loeber, R., & Waller, D. (1988). Artefacts in delinquency: specialisation and generalisation studies. *British Journal of Criminology, 28*, 461–77.

Loeber, R., Wung, P., Keenan, K., Giroux, B., Stouthamer-Loeber, M., Van Kammen, W. B., & Maughan, B. (1993). Developmental pathways in disruptive and child behavior. *Development and Psychopathology, 5*, 103–33.

Lösel, F. (1995a). Increasing consensus in the evaluation of offender rehabilitation? Lessons from recent research synthesis. *Psychology, Crime and the Law, 2*, 19–39.

(1995b). The efficacy of correctional treatment: A review and synthesis of meta-evaluations. In J. McGuire (Ed.), *What works: Reducing reoffending*, pp. 79–111. Chichester: Wiley.

(1996). Working with young offenders: The impact of meta-analysis. In C. R. Hollin & K. Howells (Eds.), *Clinical approaches to working with young offenders*, pp. 57–82. Chichester: Wiley.

Lösel, F., & Bender, D. (1997). Heart rate and psychosocial correlates of antisocial behavior in high-risk adolescents. In A. Raine, P. Brennan, D. P. Farrington, & S. A. Mednick (Eds.), *Biosocial bases of violence*, pp. 321–4. New York: Plenum.

Lösel, F., & Bliesener, T. (1994). Some high-risk adolescents do not develop conduct problems: A study of protective factors. *International Journal of Behavioral Development, 17*, 753–77.

Luthar, S. S. (1993). Annotation: Methodological and conceptual issues in research on childhood resilience. *Journal of Child Psychology and Psychiatry, 34,* 441–53.

Luthar, S. S., Burack, J. A., Cicchetti, D., & Weisz, J. R. (1997). *Developmental psychopathology: Perspectives on adjustment, risk, and disorder.* New York: Cambridge University Press.

Luthar, S. S., Doernberger, C. H., & Zigler, E. (1993). Resilience is not a unidimensional construct: Insights from a prospective study of inner-city adolescents. *Development and Psychopathology, 5,* 703–17.

Lynam, D. R. (1996). Early identification of chronic offenders: Who is the fledgling psychopath? *Psychological Bulletin, 120,* 209–34.

Lynam, D., Moffitt, T. E., & Stouthamer-Loeber, M. (1993). Explaining the relation between IQ and delinquency: Class, race, test motivation, school failure, or self-control? *Journal of Abnormal Psychology, 102,* 187–96.

Lyons, M. J., True, W. R., Eisen, S. A., Goldberg, J., Meyer, J. M., Faraone, S. V., Eaves, L. J., & Tsuang, M. J. (1995). Differential heritability of adult and juvenile antisocial traits. *Archives of General Psychiatry, 52,* 906–15.

Lytton, H. (1990). Child and parent effects in boys' conduct disorder: A reinterpretation. *Developmental Psychology, 26,* 638–97.

Lytton, H., & Romney, D. (1991). Parents' differential socialization of boys and girls: A meta-analysis. *Psychological Bulletin, 109,* 267–96.

Maccoby, E. E. (1986). Social groupings in childhood: Their relationship to prosocial and antisocial behavior in boys and girls. In D. Olweus, J. Block, & M. Radke-Yarrow (Eds.), *Development of antisocial and prosocial behavior,* pp. 263–84. Orlando, FL: Academic Press.

(1988). Gender as a social category. *Developmental Psychology, 24,* 755–65.

(1990). Gender and relationships: A developmental account. *American Psychologist, 45,* 513–20.

(1998). *The two sexes: Growing up apart, coming together.* Cambridge, MA: Belknap.

Maccoby, E. E., & Jacklin, C. N. (1974). *The psychology of sex differences.* Stanford, CA: Stanford University Press.

(1980). Sex differences in aggression: A rejoinder and reprise. *Child Development, 51,* 964–80.

(1983). The "person" characteristics of children and the family as environment. In D. Magnusson & V. Allen (Eds.), *Human development: An interactional perspective,* pp. 75–91. New York: Academic Press.

Maccoby, E. E., & Martin, J. A. M. (1983). Socialization in the context of the family: Parent–child interaction. In P. H. Mussen & E. M. Hetherington (Eds.), *Handbook of child psychology,* vol. 4, pp. 1–101. New York: Wiley.

Macintyre, S., Hunt, K., & Sweeting, H. (1996). Gender differences in health: Are things really as simple as they seem? *Social Science and Medicine, 42,* 617–24.

MacKenzie, D. L., & Souryal, C. (1994). *Multisite evaluation of shock incarceration* (National Institute of Justice Research Report). College Park: University of Maryland Press.

Madigan, F. C. (1957). Are sex mortality differentials biologically caused? *Millbank Memorial Fund Quarterly, 35,* 202–23.

Maes, H. H., Woodard, C. E., Murelle, L., Meyer, J. M., Silberg, J. L., Hewitt, J. K., Rutter, M., Simonoff, E., Pickles, A., Neale, M. C., & Eaves, L. J. (in press). Tobacco, alcohol and drug use in 8–16 year old twins: The Virginia Twin Study of Adolescent Behavioral Development (VTSABD). *Journal of Studies on Alcohol.*

Magdol, L., Moffitt, T. E., Caspi, A., & Silva, P. A. (in press). Developmental antecedents of partner abuse: A prospective-longitudinal study. *Journal of Abnormal Psychology.*

Magnusson, D. (1988). *Paths through life: A longitudinal research programme.* Hillsdale, NJ: Erlbaum.

Magnusson, D., af Klinteberg, B., & Stattin, H. (1993). Autonomic activity/reactivity, behavior, and crime in a longitudinal perspective. In J. McCord (Ed.), *Facts, frameworks and forecasts,* pp. 287–318. New Brunswick, NJ: Transaction Publishers.

(1994). Juvenile and persistent offenders: Behavioral and physiological characteristics. In R. D. Ketterlinus & M. E. Lamb (Eds.), *Adolescent problem behaviors: Issues and research,* pp. 81–91. Hillsdale, NJ: Erlbaum.

Magnusson, D., & Bergman, L. R. (1988). Individual and variable-based approaches to longitudinal research on early risk factors. In M. Rutter (Ed.), *Studies of psychosocial risk: The power of longitudinal data,* pp. 45–61. Cambridge: Cambridge University Press.

(1990). A pattern approach to the study of pathways from childhood to adulthood. In L. Robins & M. Rutter (Eds.), *Straight and devious pathways from childhood to adulthood,* pp. 101–15. New York: Cambridge University Press.

Magnusson, D., Stattin, H., & Allen, V. L. (1986). Differential maturation among girls and its relation to social adjustment: A longitudinal perspective. In P. B. Baltes, D. Feathermanand, & R. M. Lerner (Eds.), *Life-span development,* vol. 7, pp. 136–72. New York: Academic Press.

Maguin, E., & Loeber, R. (1996). Academic performance and delinquency. In M. Tonry & D. P. Farrington (Eds.), *Crime and justice,* vol. 20, pp. 145–264. Chicago: University of Chicago Press.

Maguin, E., Loeber, R., & LeMahieu, P. G. (1993). Does the relationship between poor reading and delinquency hold for males of different ages and ethnic groups? *Journal of Emotional and Behavioral Disorders, 1,* 88–100.

Maguire, M. (1997). Crime statistics, patterns and trends: Changing perceptions. In M. Maguire, R. Morgan, & R. Reiner (Eds.), *The Oxford handbook of criminology,* pp. 135–88. Oxford: Clarendon.

Maguire, M., & Norris, C. (1992). *The conduct and supervision of criminal investigations* (Royal Commission on Criminal Justice Research Study no. 5). London: HMSO.

Mair, G., & Nee, C. (1990). *Electronic monitoring: The trends and their results* (Home Office Research Study no. 120). London: HMSO.

Marks, J. (1995). *Human biodiversity: Genes, race, and history.* Hawthorne, NY: de Gruyter.

Marks, M. N., & Kumar, R. (1993). Infanticide in England and Wales. *Medicine, Science and the Law, 33,* 329–39.

Marshall, T. E. (1985). *Alternatives to criminal courts: The potential for non-judicial dispute settlement.* Aldershot: Gower.

(1992). Restorative justice on trial in Britain. In H. Messner & H. V. Otto (Eds.), *Restorative justice on trial.* Dordrecht: Kluwer.

Martin, J. A., Maccoby, E. E., & Jacklin, C. N. (1981). Mothers' responsiveness to interactive bidding and nonbidding in boys and girls. *Child Development, 52,* 1064–7.

Martinson, R. (1974). What works? Questions and answers about prison reform. *The Public Interest, 10,* 22–54.

Marzuk, P. M. (1996). Violence, crime, and mental illness: How strong a link? *Archives of General Psychiatry, 53,* 481–6.

Massey, D. S., & Denton, N. (1993). *American apartheid: Segregation and the making of the underclass.* Boston: Harvard University Press.

Massey, D. S., Gross, A. B., & Eggers, M. L. (1992). Segregation, the concentration of poverty and the life chances of individuals. *Social Science Research, 20,* 397–420.

Masten, A. S., Best, K. M., & Garmezy, N. (1990). Resilience and development: Contributions from the study of children who overcome adversity. *Development and Psychopathology, 2,* 425–44.

Masten, A. S., Garmezy, N., Tellegen, A., Pellegrini, D. S., Larkin, K., & Larsen, A. (1988). Competence and stress in school children: The moderating effects of individual and family qualities. *Journal of Child Psychology and Psychiatry, 29,* 745–64.

Mattes, J. A., & Gittelman, R. (1981). Effects of artificial food colorings in children with hyperactive symptoms. *Archives of General Psychiatry, 38,* 714–18.

Maughan, B. (1994). School influences. In M. Rutter & D. Hay (Eds.), *Development through life: A handbook for clinicians,* pp. 134–58. Oxford: Blackwell Scientific.

Maughan, B., & Lindelow, M. (1997). Secular change in psychosocial risks: The case of teenage motherhood. *Psychological Medicine, 27,* 1129–44.

Maughan, B., & Pickles, A. (1990). Adopted and illegitimate children growing up. In L. Robins & M. Rutter (Eds.), *Straight and devious pathways from childhood to adulthood,* pp. 36–61. Cambridge: Cambridge University Press.

Maughan, B., Pickles, A., Hagell, A., Rutter, M., & Yule, W. (1996). Reading problems and antisocial behaviour: Developmental trends in comorbidity. *Journal of Child Psychology and Psychiatry, 37,* 405–18.

Maughan, B., Pickles, A., & Quinton, D. (1995). Parental hostility, childhood behavior and adult social functioning. In J. McCord (Ed.), *Coercion and punishment in long term perspectives,* pp. 34–58. New York: Cambridge University Press.

Maughan, B., Pickles, A., Rutter, M., & Ouston, J. (1991). Can schools change? I. Outcomes at six London secondary schools. *School Effectiveness and School Improvement, 1,* 188–210.

Maughan, B., & Rutter, M. (1997). Retrospective reporting of childhood adversity: Some methodological considerations. *Journal of Personality Disorders, 11,* 19–33.

Maughan, B., & Yule, W. (1994). Reading and other learning disabilities. In M. Rutter, E. Taylor, & L. Hersov (Eds.), *Child and adolescent psychiatry: Modern approaches,* 3rd ed., pp. 647–65. Oxford: Blackwell Scientific.

Mawby, R., & Walklate, S. (1994). *Critical victimology.* London: Sage.

Mayes, L. C., & Bornstein, M. H. (1997). The development of children exposed to cocaine. In S. S. Luthar, J. A. Burack, D. Cicchetti, & J. R. Weisz (Eds.), *Development psychopathology: Perspectives on adjustment, risk, and disorder,* pp. 166–88. Cambridge: Cambridge University Press.

Mayhew, P. (1979). Defensible space: The current status of a crime prevention theory. *Howard Journal of Penology and Crime Prevention, 18,* 150–9.

(1993). *Findings from the International Crime Survey.* London: Home Office.

Mayhew, P., Aye Maung, N., & Mirrlees-Black, C. (1993). *The 1992 British Crime Survey.* London: HMSO.

Mayhew, P., Clarke, R. V. G., Sturman, A., & Hough, J. M. (1976). *Crime as opportunity* (Home Office Research Unit Study no. 34). London: HMSO.

Mayhew, P., & Elliott, D. P. (1990). Self-reported offending, victimization and the British Crime Survey. *Victims and Violence, 5,* 83–96.

Mayhew, P., Elliott, D., & Dowds, L. (1989). *The 1988 British Crime Survey* (Home Office Research Study no. 111). London: HMSO.

Maynard, R. A. (1997). *Kids having kids: Economic costs and social consequences of teen pregnancy.* Washington, DC: Urban Institute Press.

Mays, J. B. (1954). *Growing up in the city.* Liverpool: University Press.

(Ed.) (1972). *Juvenile delinquency: The family and the social group; A reader.* London: Longmans.

Mazur, A., Booth, A., & Dabbs, J. M. (1992). Testosterone and chess competition. *Social Psychology Quarterly, 55,* 70–7.

Mazur, A., & Lamb, T. (1980). Testosterone, status and mood in human males. *Hormones and Behaviour, 14,* 236–46.

McBurnett, K. (1992). Psychobiological approaches to personality and their applications to child psychopathology. In B. B. Lahey & A. E. Kazdin (Eds.), *Advances in clinical child psychology,* vol. 14, pp. 107–64. New York: Plenum.

McBurnett, K., Lahey, B. B., Capasso, L., & Loeber, R. (1997). Aggressive symptoms and salivary cortisol in clinic-referred boys with conduct disorder. *Annals of the New York Academy of Sciences, 794,* 169–78.

McClelland, G. H., & Judd, C. M. (1993). Statistical difficulties of detecting interactions and moderator effects. *Psychological Bulletin, 114,* 376–90.

McClintock, F. H., & Avison, N. H. (1968). *Crime in England and Wales.* London: Heinemann.

McClintock, P. H., & Wikström, P.-O. H. (1992). The comparative study of urban violence: Criminal violence in Edinburgh and Stockholm. *British Journal of Criminology, 32,* 505–20.

McConville, M., Sanders, A., & Leng, R. (1991). *The case for the prosecution.* London: Routledge.

McCord, J. (1982). A longitudinal view of the relationship between paternal absence and crime. In J. Gunn & D. P. Farrington (Eds.), *Abnormal offenders, delinquency, and the criminal justice system*, pp. 113–28. Chichester: Wiley.

(1988). Identifying developmental paradigms leading to alcoholism. *Journal of Studies in Alcoholism, 49*, 357–62.

(1991). The cycle of crime and socialization practices. *Journal of Criminal Law and Criminology, 82*, 211–28.

McCord, C., & Freeman, H. (1990). Excess mortality in Harlem. *New England Journal of Medicine, 322*, 173–5.

McCord, W., & McCord, J. (1960). *Origins of alcoholism*. Stanford, CA: Stanford University Press.

McGarrell, E. (1991). Differential effects of juvenile justice reform on incarceration rates of the States. *Crime and Delinquency, 37*, 262–80.

McGee, R., Feehan, M., Williams, S., Partridge, F., Silva, P. A., & Kelly, J. (1990). DSM-III disorders in a large sample of adolescents. *Journal of the American Academy of Child and Adolescent Psychiatry, 29*, 611–19.

McGee, R., Silva, P. A., & Williams, S. (1984). Perinatal, neurological, environmental and developmental characteristics of seven-year-old children with stable behaviour problems. *Journal of Child Psychology and Psychiatry, 25*, 573–86.

McGue, M. (1993). From proteins to cognitions: The behavioral genetics of alcoholism. In R. Plomin & G. E. McClearn (Eds.), *Nature, nurture and psychology*, pp. 245–68. Washington, DC: American Psychological Association.

McGuire, J., & Priestley, P. (1995). Reviewing "what works": Past, present and future. In J. McGuire (Ed.), *What works: Reducing reoffending*, pp. 3–34. Chichester: Wiley.

McKay, R. H., Candelli, L., Granta, H., Barrett, B., McConkey, C., & Plantz, M. (1985). *The impact of Head Start on children, families and communities*. Washington, DC: CRS.

McMahon, R. J. (1997). Prevention of antisocial behavior: Initial findings from the Fast Track Project. Paper presented at the Society for Research in Child Development Biennial Meeting, Washington, DC, April.

McMahon, R. J., & Greenberg, M. T. (1995). The FAST Track Program: A developmentally focused intervention for children with conduct problems. *Clinician's Research Digest* (Supplemental Bulletin 13).

McNally, R. B. (1995). Homicidal youth in England and Wales 1982–1992: Profile and policy. *Psychology, Crime and Law, 1*, 333–42.

Measham, F., Newcombe, R., & Parker, H. (1994). The normalisation of recreational drug use amongst young people in North West England. *British Journal of Sociology, 45*, 287–312.

Mednick, S., Moffitt, T., & Stack, S. (Eds.) (1987). *The causes of crime: New biological approaches*. Cambridge: Cambridge University Press.

Meisels, S. J., & Plunkett, J. W. (1989). Developmental consequences of pre-term birth: Are there long-term effects? In P. B. Baltes, D. L. Featherman, & R. M. Lerner (Eds.), *Life-span development and behavior*, vol. 9., pp. 87–128. Hillsdale, NJ: Erlbaum.

Menard, S. (1992). Demographic and theoretical variables in the age-period-cohort analysis of illegal behavior. *Journal of Research in Crime and Delinquency, 29,* 178–99.

Menard, S., & Elliott, D. S. (1994). Delinquent bonding, moral beliefs and illegal behavior: A three-wave panel model. *Justice Quarterly, 11,* 173–88.

Merton, R. K. (1938). Social structure and anomie. *American Sociological Review, 3,* 672–82.

(1957). *Social theory and social structure.* New York: Free Press.

Messerschmitt, J. (1993). *Masculinities and crime.* Lanham, MD: Rowman & Littlefield.

Meyer, J. M., Rutter, M., Simonoff, E., Shillady, C. L., Silberg, J. L., Pickles, A., Hewitt, J. K., Maes, H. H., & Eaves, L. J. (submitted). Familial aggregation for conduct disorder symptomatology: The role of genes, marital discord and family adaptability.

Mezzacappa, E., Tremblay, R. E., Kindlon, D., Saul, J. P., Philip J. P., Arseneault, L., Séguin, J., Pihl, R. O., & Earls, F. (1997). Anxiety, antisocial behavior and heart rate regulation in adolescent males. *Journal of Child Psychology and Psychiatry, 38,* 457–70.

Miech, R. A., Caspi, A., Moffitt, T. E., Wright, B. E., & Silva, P. A. (submitted). Low socio-economic status and mental illness: A longitudinal study of causation and selection.

Miles, D. R., & Carey, G. (1997). The genetic and environmental architecture of human aggression. *Journal of Personality and Social Psychology, 72,* 207–17.

Miller, G. E., & Prinz, R. J. (1990). Enhancement of social learning family interventions for child conduct disorder. *Psychological Bulletin, 108,* 291–307.

Milner, J. S. (1991). *Neuropsychology of aggression.* Boston: Kluwer.

Minty, E. B., & Ashcroft, C. (1987). *Child care and adult crime.* Manchester: Manchester University Press.

Mirrlees-Black, C., Mayhew, P., & Percy, A. (1996). *The 1996 British Crime Survey England and Wales.* London: Home Office Research and Statistics Directorate.

Modestin, J., & Ammann, R. (1995). Mental disorders and criminal behaviour. *British Journal of Psychiatry, 166,* 667–75.

Modood, T., Beishon, S., & Virdee, S. (1994). *Changing ethnic identities.* London: Policy Studies Institute.

Modood, T., Berthoud, R., Lakey, J., Nazroo, J., Smith, P., Virdee, S., & Beishon, S. (1997). *Ethnic minorities in Britain: Diversity and disadvantage.* London: Policy Studies Institute.

Moffitt, T. E. (1990a). Juvenile delinquency and attention deficit disorder: Developmental trajectories from age 3 to 15. *Child Development, 61,* 893–910.

(1990b). The neuropsychology of juvenile delinquency: A critical review. In M. Tonry & N. Morris (Eds.), *Crime and justice,* vol. 12, pp. 99–169. Chicago: University of Chicago Press.

(1993a). Adolescence-limited and life-course–persistent antisocial behavior: A developmental taxonomy. *Psychological Review, 100,* 674–701.

(1993b). The neuropsychology of conduct disorder. *Development and Psychopathology, 5,* 135–52.

(1997). Personal communication.

Moffitt, T. E., & Caspi, A. (1997). Personal communication.

Moffitt, T. E., Caspi, A., Dickson, N., Silva, P., & Stanton, W. (1996). Childhood-onset versus adolescent-onset antisocial conduct problems in males: Natural history from ages 3 to 18 years. *Development and Psychopathology, 9,* 399–424.

Moffitt, T. E., Caspi, A., Fawcett, P., Brammer, G. L., Raleigh, M., Yuwiler, A., & Silva, P. A. (1997). Whole blood serotonin and family background relate to male violence. In A. Raine, P. Brennan, D. P. Farrington, & S. A. Mednick (Eds.), *Biosocial bases of violence,* pp. 231–50. New York: Plenum.

Moffitt, T. E., Caspi, A., Silva, P. A., & Stouthamer-Loeber, M. (1995). Individual differences in personality and intelligence are linked to crime: Cross-context evidence from nations, neighborhoods, genders, races, and age-cohorts. *Current Perspectives on Aging and the Life Cycle, 4,* 1–34.

Moffitt, T. E., Lynam, D., & Silva, P. A. (1994). Neuropsychological tests predict persistent male delinquency. *Criminology, 32,* 101–24.

Moir, A., & Jessel, D. (1995). *A mind to crime: The controversial link between the mind and criminal behavior.* London: Michael Joseph.

Molling, P., Lockner, A., Sauls, R. J., & Eisenberg, L. (1962). Committed delinquent boys: The impact of perphenazine and of placebo. *Archives of General Psychiatry, 7,* 70–6.

Monahan, J., & Steadman, H. (Eds.) (1994). *Violence and mental disorder: Developments in risk assessment.* Chicago: University of Chicago Press.

Monck, E., & New, M. (1996). *Report of a study of sexually abused children and adolescents, and of young perpetrators of sexual abuse who were treated in voluntary agency community facilities.* London: HMSO.

Moody, S. R., & Tomas, J. (1982). *Prosecution in the public interest.* Edinburgh: Scottish Academic Press.

Morenoff, J. D., & Sampson, R. J. (1997). Violent crime and the spatial dynamics of neighbourhood transition: Chicago, 1970–1990. *Social Forces, 76,* 31–64.

Morgan, J., & Zedner, L. (1992). *Child victims: Crime, impact and criminal justice.* Oxford: Oxford University Press.

Morgan, R. (1994). Imprisonment. In M. Maguire, R. Morgan, & R. Reiner (Eds.), *The Oxford handbook of criminology,* pp. 889–948. Oxford: Clarendon.

Morgan, R., McKenzie, I., & Reiner, R. (1990). *Police powers and policy: A study of custody officers.* Unpublished final report to the ESRC.

Morris, A., & Giller, H. (1987). *Understanding juvenile justice.* London: Croom Helm.

Morris, A., Maxwell, G., & Robertson, J. P. (1993). Giving victims a voice: A New Zealand experiment. *The Howard Journal, 32,* 304–21.

Mortimore, P. (1995a). Effective schools: Current impact and future potential. Inaugaral address given at the Institute of Education, London, February.

(1995b). The positive effects of schooling. In M. Rutter (Ed.), *Psychosocial disturbances in young people: Challenges for prevention,* pp. 333–63. Cambridge: Cambridge University Press.

Mortimore, P., Sammons, P., Stoll, L., Lewis, D., & Ecob, R. (1988). *School matters: The junior years.* Wells: Open Books.

Moskowitz, D. S., & Schwartzmann, A. E. (1989). Painting group portraits: Studying life outcomes for aggressive and withdrawn children. *Journal of Personality Disorders, 57*, 723–46.

Mott, J. (1990). Young people, alcohol and crime. *Home Office Research Bulletin, 28,* 24–8.

Mott, J., & Mirrlees-Black, C. (1995). *Self-reported drug misuse in England and Wales: Findings from the 1992 British Crime Survey.* London: Home Office.

Moxon, D., Jones, P., & Tarling, R. (1985). *Juvenile sentencing: Is there a tariff?* (Home Office Research and Planning Unit Paper no. 32). London: Home Office.

Mulvey, E. P., Arthur, M. W., & Reppucci, N. D. (1993). The prevention and treatment of juvenile delinquency: A review of the research. *Clinical Psychology Review, 13,* 133–67.

Myers, W. C., Scott, K., Burgess, A. W., & Burgess, A. G. (1995). Psychopathology, biopsychosocial factors, crime characteristics, and classification. *Journal of the American Academy of Child and Adolescent Psychiatry, 34,* 1483–9.

Nagin, D. S., Farrington, D. P., & Moffitt, T. E. (1995). Life-course trajectories of different types of offenders. *Criminology, 33,* 111–39.

Nagin, D. S., & Land, K. C. (1993). Age, criminal careers, and population heterogeneity: Specification and estimation of a nonparametric, mixed Poisson model. *Criminology, 31,* 327–62.

Nagin, D. S., & Paternoster, R. (1991). On the relationship of past and future participation in delinquency. *Criminology, 29,* 163–90.

Nagin, D. S., Pogarsky, G., & Farrington, D. P. (1997). Adolescent mothers and the criminal behavior of their children. *Law and Society Review, 31,* 137–62.

National Association for the Care and Resettlement of Offenders [NACRO] (1987). *Diverting juveniles from custody.* London: NACRO.

(1995). *Facts about young offenders in 1993.* London: NACRO.

National Commission on Marihuana and Drug Abuse (1973). *Drug use in America: Problems of perspective* (Second Report of the Commission). Washington, DC: U.S. Government Printing Office.

Naylor, C. D. (1997). Meta-analysis and the meta-epidemiology of clinical research. *British Medical Journal, 315,* 617–19.

Nazroo, J. Y. (1997). *Ethnicity and mental health: Findings from a national community survey.* London: Policy Studies Institute.

Needleman, H. L., Riess, J. A., Tobin, M. J., Biesecker, G. E., & Greenhouse, J. B. (1996). Bone lead levels and delinquent behavior. *Journal of the American Medical Association, 275,* 363–9.

Neligan, G. A., Kolvin, I., Scott, D. M., & Garside, R. F. (1976). *Born too soon or too small: A follow-up study to 7 years of age.* London: Heinemann.

Nettles, S. M., & Pleck, J. H. (1994). Risk, resilience and development: The multiple ecologies of black adolescents in the United States. In R. J. Haggerty, L. R. Sherrod, N. Garmezy, & M. Rutter (Eds.), *Stress, risk and resilience in children and adolescents,* pp. 147–82. Cambridge: Cambridge University Press.

Newburn, T., & Stanko, E. A. (1994). *Just boys doing business? Men, masculinities and crime*. London: Routledge.

Newman, D. L., Moffitt, T. E., Caspi, A., Magdol, L., & Silva, P. A. (1996). Psychiatric disorder in a birth cohort of young adults: Prevalence, comorbidity, clinical significance, and new case evidence from ages 11 to 21. *Journal of Consulting and Clinical Psychology, 64*, 522–62.

Newman, J. P., Schmitt, W. A., & Voss, W. D. (1997). The impact of motivationally neutral cues on psychopathic individuals: Assessing the generality of the response modulation hypothesis. *Journal of Abnormal Psychology, 106*, 563–75.

Newman, O. (1973). *Defensible space*. London: Architectural Press.

Nichols, P. L., & Chen, T.-C. (1981). *Minimal brain dysfunction: A prospective study*. Hillsdale, NJ: Erlbaum.

Norris, C., Fielding, N, Kemp, C., & Fielding, J. (1992). Black and blue: An analysis of the influence of race on being stopped by the police. *British Journal of Sociology, 43*, 207–24.

Northcott, J. (1995). *The future of Britain and Europe*. London: Policy Studies Institute.

Notteleman, E. D., & Jensen, P. S. (1995). Comorbidity of disorders in children and adolescent: Developmental perspectives. In T. H. Ollendick & R. J. Prinz (Eds.), *Advances in clinical child psychology*, vol. 17, pp. 109–55. New York: Plenum.

O'Connor, T. G., Deater-Deckard, K., Fulker, D., Rutter, M., & Plomin, R. (in press a). Genotype–environment correlations in late childhood and early adolescence: Antisocial behavioral problems and coercive parenting. *Developmental Psychology*.

O'Connor, T. G., McGuire, S., Reiss, D., & Plomin, R. (in press b). Co-occurrence of depressive symptoms and antisocial behavior in adolescence: A common genetic liability. *Journal of Abnormal Psychology*.

O'Donnell, C. R. (1992). The interplay of theory and practice in delinquency prevention: From behavior modification to activity settings. In J. McCord & R. E. Tremblay (Eds.), *Preventing antisocial behavior*, pp. 209–32. New York: Guilford.

Office for National Statistics (1997). *Social Trends 27*. London: The Stationery Office.

Offord, D. R. (1982). Family backgrounds of male and female delinquents. In J. Gunn & D. P. Farrington (Eds.), *Abnormal offenders: Delinquency and the criminal justice system*, pp. 129–51. Chichester: Wiley.

Offord, D. R., Alder, R. J., & Boyle, M. H. (1986). Prevalence and sociodemographic correlates of conduct disorder. *American Journal of Social Psychiatry, 6*, 272–8.

Olds, D. L., Henderson, C. R., Chamberlin, R., & Teitelbaum, R. (1986). Parenting child abuse and neglect: A randomized trial of nurse home visitation. *Pediatrics, 78*, 65–78.

Ollendick, T. H., Weist, M. D., Borden, M. C., & Greene, R. W. (1992). Sociometric status and academic, behavioral, and psychological adjustment: A five-year longitudinal study. *Journal of Consulting and Clinical Psychology, 60,* 80–7.

Olweus, D. (1978). *Aggression in the schools: Bullies and whipping boys.* Washington, DC: Hemisphere.

——— (1979). Stability of aggressive reaction patterns in males: A review. *Psychological Bulletin, 86,* 852–75.

——— (1991). Bully/victim problems among schoolchildren: Basic facts and effects of a school based intervention program. In D. Pepler & K. Rubin (Eds.), *The development and treatment of childhood aggression,* pp. 411–48. Hillsdale, NJ: Erlbaum.

——— (1993). *Bullying at school: What we know and what we can do.* Oxford: Blackwell.

Olweus, D., & Alsaker, F. D. (1991). Assessing change in a cohort-longitudinal study with hierarchical data. In D. Magnusson, L. R. Bergman, G. Rudinger, & B. Törestad (Eds.), *Problems and methods in longitudinal research: Stability and change,* pp. 107–32. Cambridge: Cambridge University Press.

Oreland, L., Wiberg, A., Asberg, M., Traskman, L., Sjostand, L., Thorn, P., Bertilson, L., & Tybring, G. (1981). Platelet MAO activity and monoamine metabolites in cerebrospinal fluid in depressed and suicidal patients and in healthy controls. *Psychiatric Research, 4,* 21–9.

Osborn, S. G. (1980). Moving home, leaving London and delinquent trends. *British Journal of Criminology, 20,* 54–61.

Osgood, D. W., Johnston, L. D., O'Malley, P. M., & Bachman, J. G. (1988). The generality of deviance in late adolescence and early adulthood. *American Sociological Review, 53,* 81–93.

Osgood, D. W., Wilson, J. K., O'Malley, P. M., Bachman, J. G., & Johnston, L. D. (1996). Routine activities and individual deviant behavior. *American Sociological Review, 61,* 635–55.

Ouston, J. (1984). Delinquency, family background and educational attainment. *British Journal of Criminology, 24,* 2–26.

Ouston, J., Maughan, B., & Rutter, M. (1991). Can schools change? II. Practice at six London secondary schools. *School Effectiveness and School Improvement, 2,* 3–13.

Oxenstierna, G., Edman, G., Iselius, L., Oreland, L., Ross, S. B., & Sedvall, G. (1986). Concentrations of monamine metabolites in the cerebrospinal fluid of twins and unrelated individuals – A genetic study. *Journal of Psychiatric Research, 20,* 19–29.

Paik, H., & Comstock, G. A. (1994). The effects of television violence on antisocial behavior: A meta-analysis. *Communication Research, 21,* 516–46.

Painter, K., & Farrington, D. P. (1997). The crime reducing effect of improved street lighting: The Dudley Project. In R. V. Clarke (Ed.), *Situational crime prevention: Successful case studies,* 2nd ed., pp. 209–26. Albany, NY: Harrow and Heston.

Palmer, T. (1991). The effectiveness of intervention: Recent trends and current issues. *Crime and Delinquency, 37,* 330–46.

Parker, H. (1996). Young adult offenders, alcohol and criminological cul-de-sacs. *British Journal of Criminology, 36,* 282–98.

Parker, H., Casburn, M., & Turbull, D. (1981). *Receiving juvenile justice.* Oxford: Blackwell.

Parker, H., Measham, F., & Aldridge, J. (1995). *Drugs futures: Changing patterns of drug use amongst English youth.* London: Institute for the Study of Drug Dependence.

Parker, H., Sumner, M., & Jarvis, G. (1994). *Unmasking the magistrates: The "custody or not" decision in sentencing young offenders.* Milton Keynes, UK: Open University Press.

Parker, J. G., & Asher, S. R. (1987). Peer relations and later personal adjustment: Are low-accepted children at risk? *Psychological Bulletin, 102,* 357–89.

Pasamanick, R., & Knobloch, H. (1966). Retrospective studies on the epidemiology of reproductive casualty: Old and new. *Merrill-Palmer Quarterly, 12,* 7–26.

Patrick, C. J. (1994). Emotion and psychopathy: Startling new insights. *Psychophysiology, 31,* 319–30.

Patrick, C. J., Zempolich, K. A., & Levenston, G. K. (1997). Emotionality and violent behavior in psychopaths: A biosocial analysis. In A. Raine, P. Brennan, D. P. Farrington, & S. A. Mednick (Eds.), *Biosocial bases of violence,* pp. 145–63. New York: Plenum.

Patterson, G. R. (1980). Mothers: The unacknowledged victims. *Monographs of the Society for Research in Child Development, 45* (5, Serial no. 186), 1–64.

(1982). *Coercive family process.* Eugene, OR: Castalia.

(1993). Orderly change in a stable world: The antisocial trait as a chimera. *Journal of Consulting and Clinical Psychology, 61,* 911–19.

(1995). Coercion as a basis for early age of onset for arrest. In J. McCord (Ed.), *Coercion and punishment in long-term perspectives,* pp. 81–105. Cambridge: Cambridge University Press.

(1996). Some characteristics of a developmental theory for early onset delinquency. In M. Lenzenweger & J. J. Haugaard (Eds.), *Frontiers of developmental psychopathology,* pp. 81–124. New York: Oxford University Press.

Patterson, G. R., & Bank, C. L. (1989). Some amplifying mechanisms for pathologic processes in families. In M. Gunar & E. Thelen (Eds.), *Minnesota symposia on child psychology, vol. 22: Systems and development,* pp. 167–209. Hillsdale, NJ: Erlbaum.

Patterson, G. R., & Capaldi, D. M. (1991). Antisocial parents: Unskilled and vulnerable. In P. A. Cowan & E. M. Hetherington (Eds.), *Family transitions,* pp. 195–218. Hillsdale, NJ: Erlbaum.

Patterson, G. R., & Chamberlain, P. (1994). A functional analysis of resistance during parent training therapy. *Clinical Psychology and Scientific Practice, 1,* 53–70.

Patterson, G. R., DeBaryshe, B. D., & Ramsey, E. (1989). A developmental perspective on antisocial behavior. *American Psychologist, 44,* 329–35.

Patterson, G. R., Dishion, T. J., & Chamberlain, P. (1993). Outcomes and methodological issues relating to treatment of antisocial children. In T. R. Giles (Ed.), *Handbook of effective psychotherapy,* pp. 43–87. New York: Plenum.

Patterson, G. R., & Forgatch, M. S. (1987). *Parents and adolescents living together. Part 1: The basics.* Eugene, OR: Castalia.

(1995). Predicting future clinical adjustment from treatment outcome and process variables. *Psychological Assessment, 7,* 275–85.

Patterson, G. R., Reid, J. B., & Dishion, T. J. (1992). *Antisocial boys: A social interactional approach.* Eugene, OR: Castalia.

Patterson, G. R., & Yoerger, K. (1997). A developmental model for late-onset delinquency. In R. Dienstbier & D. W. Osgood (Eds.), *The Nebraska symposium on motivation, vol. 44: Motivation and delinquency,* pp. 119–77. Lincoln: University of Nebraska Press.

Patton, W., & Noller, P. (1984). Unemployment and youth: A longitudinal study. *Australian Journal of Psychology, 36,* 399–413.

Pawlby, S. J., Mills, A., & Quinton, D. (1997a). Vulnerable adolescent girls: Opposite sex relationships. *Journal of Child Psychology and Psychiatry, 38,* 909–20.

Pawlby, S. J., Mills, A., Taylor, A., & Quinton, D. (1997b). Adolescent friendships mediating childhood adversity and adult outcome. *Journal of Adolescence, 20,* 633–44.

Payne, J. (1995a). *Routes beyond compulsory schooling* (Youth Cohort Report no. 31). London: Employment Department Research Series.

(1995b). *Qualifications between 16 and 18: A comparison of achievement on routes beyond compulsory schooling* (Youth Cohort Report no. 32). London: Employment Department Research Series.

Peach, C. (1996). Does Britain have ghettos? *Transactions of the Institute of British Geographers, 21,* 216–35.

Pearson, G. (1991). Drug control policies in Britain. In M. Tonry & N. Morris (Eds.), *Crime and justice: A review of research,* vol. 14, pp. 167–227. Chicago: University of Chicago Press.

Pease, K. (1992). Preventing burglary on a British public housing estate. In R. V. Clarke (Ed.), *Situational crime prevention: Successful case studies,* pp. 223–9. Albany, NY: Harrow and Heston.

(1993). Individual and community influences on victimization and their implications for crime prevention. In D. P. Farrington, R. J. Sampson, & P.-O. H. Wikström (Eds.), *Integrating individual and ecological aspects of crime,* pp. 323–38. Stockholm: National Council for Crime Prevention.

(1997). Crime prevention. In M. Maguire, R. Morgan, & R. Reiner (Eds.), *The Oxford handbook of criminology,* 2nd ed., pp. 963–95. Oxford: Clarendon.

Pease, K., & Tseloni, A. (1996). Juvenile–adult differences in criminal justice: Evidence from the United Nations Crime Survey. *The Howard Journal, 35,* 40–60.

Pedersen, N. L., Oreland, L., Reynolds, C., & McClearn, G. E. (1993). Importance of genetic effects for monamine oxidase activity in thrombocytes in twins reared apart and twins reared together. *Psychiatry Research, 46,* 239–51.

Pedersen, W., & Wichström, L. (1995). Patterns of delinquency in Norwegian adolescents. *British Journal of Criminology, 35,* 543–62.

Peeples, F., & Loeber, R. (1994). Do individual factors and neighbourhood context explain ethnic differences in juvenile delinquency? *Journal of Quantitative Criminology, 10,* 141–57.

Pellegrini, D. (1994). Training in interpersonal cognitive problem-solving. In M. Rutter, E. Taylor, & L. Hersov (Eds.), *Child and adolescent psychiatry: Modern approaches,* pp. 829–43. Oxford: Blackwell Scientific.

Pennington, B. F., & Bennetto, L. (1993). Main effects or transactions in the neuropsychology of conduct disorder? Commentary on "The Neuropsychology of conduct disorder." *Development and Psychopathology, 5,* 153–64.

Perkins, C., Klaus, C., Bastian, L., & Cohen, R. (1996). *Crime victimization in the United States 1993.* Washington DC: U.S. Department of Justice, Bureau of Justice Statistics.

Perry, D. G., Perry, L. C., & Kennedy, E. (1992). Conflict and the development of antisocial behavior. In C. U. Shantz & W. W. Hartup (Eds.), *Conflict in child and adolescent development,* pp. 301–29. New York: Cambridge University Press.

Perry, D. G., Perry, L. C., & Rasmussen, P. (1986). Cognitive social learning mediators of aggression. *Child Development, 57,* 700–11.

Petersen, A. C., & Mortimer, J. T. (1994). *Youth unemployment and society.* New York: Cambridge University Press.

Petersilia, J., & Turner, S. (1993). Intensive probation and parole. *Crime and Justice, 17,* 281–335.

Pickles, A. (1993). Stages, precursors and causes in development. In D. F. Hay and A. Angold (Eds.), *Precursors and causes in development and psychopathology,* pp. 23–49. Chichester: Wiley.

Pickles, A., & Rutter, M. (1991). Statistical and conceptual models of "turning points" in developmental processes. In D. Magnusson, L. R. Bergman, G. Rudinger, & B. Törestad (Eds.), *Problems and methods in longitudinal research: Stability and change,* pp. 133–65. Cambridge: Cambridge University Press.

Pike, A., McGuire, S., Hetherington, E. M., Reiss, D., & Plomin, R. (1996a). Family environment and adolescent depressive symptoms and antisocial behavior: A multivariate genetic analysis. *Developmental Psychology, 37,* 590–603.

Pike, A., Reiss, D., Hetherington, E. M., & Plomin, R. (1996b). Using MZ differences in the search for nonshared environmental effects. *Journal of Child Psychology and Psychiatry, 37,* 695–704.

Pine, D. S., Coplan, J. D., Wasserman, G. A., Miller, L. S., Fried, J. E., Davies, M., Cooper, T. B., Greenhill, L., Shaffer, D., & Parsons, B. (1997). Neuroendocrine response to fenfluramine challenge in boys: Associations with aggressive behavior and adverse rearing. *Archives of General Psychiatry, 54,* 839–46.

Plomin, R. (1994). *Genetics and experience: The interplay between nature and nurture.* Thousand Oaks, CA: Sage.

(1995). Genetics and children's experiences in the family. *Journal of Child Psychology and Psychiatry, 36,* 33–8.

Plomin, R., & Bergeman, C. S. (1991). The nature of nurture: Genetic influence on "environmental" measures. *Behavioural and Brain Sciences, 14,* 373–427.

Plomin, R., & Daniels, D. (1987). Why are children in the same family so different from one another? *Behavioral and Brain Sciences, 10,* 1–15.

Plomin, R., De Fries, J. C., McClearn, G. E., & Rutter, M. (1997). *Behavioral genetics*, 3rd ed. New York: Freeman.

Plomin, R., & Rutter, M. (in press). Child development, molecular genetics and what to do with genes once they are found. *Child Development*.

Pocock, S. J. (1983). *Clinical trials: A practical approach*. Chichester: Wiley.

Polvi, N., Looman, T., Humphries, C., & Pease, K. (1990). Repeat break and enter victimisation: Time course and crime prevention opportunity. *Journal of Police Science and Administration, 17*, 8–11.

(1991). The time course of repeat burglary victimisation. *British Journal of Criminology, 31*, 411–14.

Pound, A. (1994). *NEWPIN: A befriending and therapeutic network for careers of young children*. London: HMSO / National NEWPIN.

Power, A. (1997). *Estates on the edge: The social consequences of mass housing in Northern Europe*. London: Macmillan.

Power, A., & Tunstall, R. (1997). *Dangerous disorder: Riots and violent disturbances in thirteen areas of Britain 1991–92*. York: Joseph Rowntree Foundation.

Poyner, B. (1993). What works in crime prevention: An overview of evaluations. In R. V. Clarke (Ed.), *Crime prevention studies*, vol. 1, pp. 7–34. Monsey, NJ: Criminal Justice Press.

Pratt, J. (1985). Delinquency as a scarce resource. *The Howard Journal, 24*, 93–107.

Price, J. M., & Dodge, K. A. (1989). Reactive and proactive aggression in childhood: Relations to peer status and social context dimensions. *Journal of Abnormal Child Psychology, 17*, 455–71.

Pulkkinen, L. (1986). The role of impulse control in the development of antisocial and prosocial behavior. In D. Olweus, J. Block, & M. Radke-Yarrow (Eds.), *Development of antisocial and prosocial behavior*, pp. 149–63. Orlando, FL: Academic Press.

(1987). Offensive and defensive aggression in humans: A longitudinal perspective. *Aggressive Behavior, 13*, 197–212.

Pulkkinen, L., & Pitkänen, T. (1994). A prospective study of the precursors to problem drinking in young adulthood. *Journal of Studies on Alcohol, 55*, 578–87.

Quay, H. C. (1988). The behavioral reward and inhibition system in childhood behavior disorder. In L. M. Bloomingdale (Ed.), *Attention deficit disorder*, pp. 176–86. Oxford: Pergamon.

(1993). The psychobiology of undersocialized aggressive conduct disorder: A theoretical perspective. *Development and Psychopathology, 5*, 165–80.

Queloz, N. (1991). Protection, intervention and the rights of children and young people. In T. Booth (Ed.), *Juvenile justice in the new Europe*, pp. 30–45. Sheffield: Sheffield University Press.

Quiggle, N. L., Garber, J., Panak, W. F., & Dodge, K. A. (1992). Social information processing in aggressive and depressed children. *Child Development, 63*, 1305–20.

Quinn, J. (1995). Positive effects of participation in youth organizations. In M. Rutter (Ed.), *Psychosocial disturbances in young people: Challenge for prevention*, pp. 274–304. Cambridge: Cambridge University Press.

Quinton, D., Gulliver, L., & Rutter, M. (1995). A 15–20 year follow-up of adult psychiatric patients: Psychiatric disorder and social functioning. *British Journal of Psychiatry, 167,* 315–23.

Quinton, D., Pickles, A., Maughan, B., & Rutter, M. (1993). Partners, peers and pathways: Assortative pairing and continuities in conduct disorder. *Development and Psychopathology, 5,* 763–83.

Quinton, D., & Rutter, M. (1988). *Parenting breakdown: The making and breaking of inter-generational links.* Aldershot: Avebury.

Raine, A. (1997). Antisocial behavior and psychophysiology: A biosocial perspective and a prefrontal dysfunction hypothesis. In D. Stoff, J. Breiling, & J. D. Maser (Eds.), *Handbook of antisocial behavior,* pp. 289–304. New York: Wiley.

Raine, A., Brennan, P., & Farrington, D. P. (1997a). Biosocial bases of violence: Conceptual and theoretical issues. In A. Raine, P. Brennan, D. P. Farrington, & S. A. Mednick (Eds.), *Biosocial bases of violence,* pp. 1–20. New York: Plenum.

Raine, A., Brennan, P., & Mednick, S. A. (1994). Birth complications combined with early maternal rejection at age 1 year predispose to violent crime at age 18 years. *Archives of General Psychiatry, 51,* 984–8.

(1997b). Interaction between birth complications and early maternal rejection in predisposing individuals to adult violence: Specificity to serious, early-onset violence. *American Journal of Psychiatry, 154,* 1265–71.

Raine, A., Brennan, P., Mednick, B., & Mednick, S. A. (1996). High rates of violence, crime, academic problems, and behavioral problems in those with both early neuromotor deficits and negative family environments. *Archives of General Psychiatry, 53,* 544–9.

Raine, A., Venables, P. H., & Williams, M. (1990). Relationships between central and autonomic measures of arousal at age 15 years and criminality at age 24 years. *Archives of General Psychiatry, 47,* 1003–7.

(1995). High autonomic arousal and electrodermal orienting at age 15 years as protective factors against criminal behavior at age 29 years. *American Journal of Psychiatry, 152,* 1595–1600.

Raleigh, M., & McGuire, M. T. (1991). Bidirectional relationships between tryptophan and social behavior in vervet monkeys. *Advances in Experimental Medicine and Biology, 294,* 289–98.

Ramsay, M., & Percy, A. (1996). *Drug misuse declared: Results of the 1994 British Crime Survey* (Home Office Research Study no. 151). London: HMSO.

Ratcliffe, S. G. (1994). The psychosocial and psychiatric consequences of sex abnormalities in children based on population studies. In F. Poutska (Ed.), *Basic approaches to genetic and molecular biological developmental psychiatry,* pp. 99–122. Berlin: Quintessatz Verlag.

Reiner, R. (1985). *The politics of the police.* Brighton: Harvester Wheatsheaf.

(1992). *The politics of the police,* 2nd ed. Hemel Hempstead, Hertss: Harvester Wheatsheaf.

(1993). Race, crime and justice: Models of interpretation. In L. Gelsthorpe & W. McWilliam (Eds.), *Minority ethnic groups and the criminal justice system,* pp. 1–25. Cambridge: Cambridge University Institute of Criminology.

(1997). Policing and the police. In M. Maguire, R. Morgan, & R. Reiner (Eds.), *The Oxford handbook of criminology,* 2nd ed., pp. 997–1049. Oxford: Clarendon.

Reiss, A. J. (1986). Why are communities important in understanding crime? In A. J. Reiss & M. Tonry (Eds.), *Communities and crime,* pp. 1–33. Chicago: University of Chicago Press.

(1988). Co-offending and criminal careers. In M. Tonry & N. Morris (Eds.), *Crime and justice: A review of research,* vol. 10, pp. 117–70. Chicago: University of Chicago Press.

(1995). Community influences on adolescent behavior. In M. Rutter (Ed.), *Psychosocial disturbances in young people: Challenges for prevention,* pp. 305–32. Cambridge: Cambridge University Press.

Reiss, D., Hetherington, M., Plomin, R., Howe, G. W., Simmens, S. J., Henderson, S. H., O'Conner, T. J., Bussell, D. A., Anderson, E. R., & Law, T. (1995). Genetic questions for environmental studies: Differential parenting and psychopathology in adolescence. *Archives of General Psychiatry, 52,* 925–36.

Rengert, G., & Wasilchick, J. (1985). *Suburban burglary.* Springfield, IL: Thomas.

Reynolds, D., Creemers, B., Nesselrod, P., Schaffer, E., Stringfield, S., & Teddlie, C. (1994). *Advances and school effectiveness practice and research.* Oxford: Pergamon.

Reynolds, D., Sammons, P., Stoll, L., Barber, M., & Hillman, J. (1996). School effectiveness and school improvement in the United Kingdom. *School Effectiveness and School Improvement, 7,* 133–58.

Rhodes, W. (1989). The criminal career: Estimates of the duration and frequency of crime commission. *Journal of Quantitative Criminology, 5,* 3–32.

Richardson, N. (1990). *Justice by geography.* Manchester: Social Information Systems.

Richman, N., Stevenson, J., & Graham, P. J. (1982). *Pre-school to school: A behavioural study.* London: Academic Press.

Richters, J. E., & Martinez, P. E. (1993). Violent communities, family choices, and children's chances: An algorithm for improving the odds. *Development and Psychopathology, 5,* 609–27.

Rie, H. E., & Rie, E. D. (Eds.) (1980). *Handbook of minimal brain dysfunction: A critical view.* New York: Wiley.

Riley, D. (1986). *Demographic changes and the criminal justice system* (Home Office Research and Planning Unit Research Bulletin no. 20), pp. 30–3. London: HMSO.

(1987). Parental supervision re-examined? *British Journal of Criminology, 27,* 421–4.

Riley, D., & Shaw, M. (1985). *Parental supervision and juvenile delinquency.* London: HMSO.

Robertson, L., & Skinner, M. (1996). Trends in adolescent drug use: Comparisons of metropolitan and non-metropolitan areas of the United States. Paper presented at the 6th Biennial Meeting of the Society for Research in Adolescence, Boston, March 7–10.

Robins, L. N. (1966). *Deviant children grown up: A sociological and psychiatric study of sociopathic personality.* Baltimore: Williams & Wilkins.

(1978). Sturdy childhood predictors of adult antisocial behaviour: Replications from longitudinal studies. *Psychological Medicine, 8,* 611–22.

(1986). The consequences of conduct disorder in girls. In D. Olweus, J. Block, & M. Radke-Yarrow (Eds.), *Development of antisocial and prosocial behaviour: Research, theories, and issues,* pp. 385–414. Orlando, FL: Academic Press.

(1993). Vietnam veterans' rapid recovery from heroin addiction: A fluke or normal expectation? *Addiction, 88,* 1041–54.

Robins, L. N., Davis, D. H., & Wish, E. (1977). Detecting predictors of rare events: Demographic family and personal deviance as predictors of stages in the progression toward narcotic addiction. In J. S. Strauss, H. M. Babigian, & M. Roff (Eds.), *The origins and course of psychopathology,* pp. 379–406. New York: Plenum.

Robins, L., & Hill, S. Y. (1966). Assessing the contributions of family structure, class and peer groups to juvenile delinquency. *Journal of Criminal Law, Criminology and Police Science, 57,* 325–34.

Robins, L. N., & Lewis, R. G. (1966). The role of the antisocial family in school completion and delinquency: A three-generation study. *Sociology Quarterly, 7,* 500–14.

Robins, L. N., & McEvoy, L. (1990). Conduct problems as predictors of substance abuse. In L. Robins & M. Rutter (Eds.), *Straight and devious pathways from childhood to adulthood,* pp. 182–204. Cambridge: Cambridge University Press.

Robins, L. N., & Price, R. K. (1991). Adult disorders predicted by child conduct problems: Results from the NIMH Epidemiological Catchment Area project. *Psychiatry, 54,* 116–32.

Robins, L. N., & Regier, D. A. (Eds.) (1991). *Psychiatric disorders: The Epidemiological Catchment Area Study.* New York: Free Press.

Robins, L. N., & Robertson, J. (1996). Truancy and later psychiatric disorder. In I. Berg & J. Nursden (Eds.), *Unwillingly to school,* pp. 119–28. London: Gaskell.

Robins, L. N., & Rutter, M. (Eds.) (1990). *Straight and devious pathways from childhood to adulthood.* Cambridge: Cambridge University Press.

Robins, L., Tipp, J., & Przybeck, T. (1991). Antisocial personality. In L. Robins & D. A. Regier (Eds.) *Psychiatric disorders in America: The Epidemiological Catchment Area Study,* pp. 258–90. New York: Free Press.

Robins, L. N., & Wish, E. (1977). Child deviance as a developmental process: A study of 223 urban black men from birth to 18. *Social Forces, 56,* 448–73.

Robinson, W. S. (1950). Ecological correlations and the behavior of individuals. *American Sociological Review, 15,* 351–7.

Rodgers, J. L., Rowe, D. C., & Li, C. (1994). Beyond nature and nurture: DF analysis of nonshared influences on problem behaviors. *Developmental Psychology, 30,* 374–84.

Rolf, J., Masten, A., Cicchetti, D., Nuechterlein, K., & Weintraub, S. (1990). *Risk and protective factors in the development of psychopathology.* New York: Cambridge University Press.

Rosenthal, R., & Rubin, D. B. (1982). A simple, general purpose display of magnitude of experimental effect. *Journal of Educational Psychology, 74,* 166–9.

Ross, H. L. (1984). Social control through deterrence: Drinking-and-driving laws. *Annual Review of Sociology, 10,* 21–35.

Rowe, D. C. (1994). *The limits of family influence: Genes, experiences, and behavior.* New York: Guilford.

Rowe, D. C., & Farrington, D. P. (1997). The familial transmission of criminal convictions. *Criminology, 35,* 177–201.

Rowe, D. C., Vazsonyi, A. T., & Flannery, D. J. (1994a). No more than skin deep: Ethnic and racial similarity in developmental process. *Psychological Review, 101,* 396–413.

(1995). Sex differences in crime: Do means and within-sex variation have similar causes? *Journal of Research in Crime and Delinquency, 32,* 84–100.

Rowe, D. C., Wouldbroun, E. J., & Gulley, B. L. (1994b). Peers and friends as nonshared environmental influences. In E. M. Hetherington, D. Reiss, & R. Plomin (Eds.), *Separate social worlds of siblings,* pp. 159–73. Hillsdale, NJ: Erlbaum.

Rubenstein, H., Murray, C., Motoyama, T., Rouse, W. V., & Titus, R. M. (1980). *The link between crime and the built environment: The current state of knowledge.* Washington, DC: National Institute of Justice.

Rubin, K. H., Hastings, P. D., Stewart, S. L., Henderson, H. A., & Chen, X. (1997). The consistency and concomitants of inhibition: Some of the children, all of the time. *Child Development, 68,* 467–83.

Rubin, K. H., & Krasnor, L. R. (1986). Social cognitive and social behavioral perspectives on problem solving. In M. Perlmutter (Ed.), *The Minnesota symposium on child psychology,* vol. 18, pp. 1–68. Hillsdale, NJ: Erlbaum.

Rubinow, D. R., & Schmidt, P. J. (1996). Androgens, brain, and behavior. *American Journal of Psychiatry, 153,* 974–84.

Ruppenthal, G. C., Arling, G. L., Harlow, H. F., Sackett, G. P., & Suomi, S. J. (1976). A 10-year perspective of motherless-mother monkey behavior. *Journal of Abnormal Psychology, 85,* 341–9.

Russell, D. E. H. (1983). The incidence and prevalence of intrafamilial and extrafamilial sexual abuse of female children. *Child Abuse and Neglect, 7,* 133–46.

Rutherford, A. (1992a). *Growing out of crime: The new era.* Winchester: Waterside.

(1992b). *Criminal justice and the pursuit of decency.* Oxford: Oxford University Press.

(1996). *Transforming criminal policy.* Winchester: Waterside.

Rutter, M. (1970). Sex differences in children's responses to family stress. In E. J. Anthony & C. Koupernik (Eds.), *The child in his family,* vol. 1, pp. 165–96. New York: Wiley.

(1971). Parent–child separation: Psychological effects on the children. *Journal of Child Psychology and Psychiatry, 12,* 233–60.

(1979). Protective factors in children's responses to stress and disadvantage. In M. W. Kent and J. E. Rolf (Eds.), *Primary prevention of psychopathology, vol. 3: Social competence in children,* pp. 49–74. Hanover, NH: University Press of New England.

(1979/80). *Changing youth in a changing society: Patterns of adolescent development and disorder.* London: Nuffield Provincial Hospitals Trust / Cambridge, MA: Harvard University Press.

(1980). Raised lead levels and impaired cognitive/behavioural functioning: A review of the evidence. *Developmental Medicine and Child Neurology, 22* (Suppl. 42).

(1981a). *Maternal deprivation reassessed,* 2nd ed. Harmondsworth: Penguin.

(1981b). The city and the child. *American Journal of Orthopsychiatry, 51,* 610–25.

(1982). Psychological therapies: Issues and treatments. *Psychological Medicine, 12,* 723–40.

(1983a). Statistical and personal interactions: Facets and perspectives. In D. Magnusson & V. Allen (Eds.), *Human development: An interactional perspective,* pp. 295–319. New York: Academic Press.

(1983b). School effects on pupil progress: Research findings and policy implications. *Child Development, 54,* 1–29.

(1987a). Continuities and discontinuities from infancy. In J. Osofsky (Ed.), *Handbook of infant development,* 2nd ed., pp. 1256–9. New York: Wiley.

(1987b). Temperament, personality and personality disorder. *British Journal of Psychiatry, 150,* 443–58.

(1988). Longitudinal data in the study of causal processes: Some uses and some pitfalls. In M. Rutter (Ed.), *Studies of psychosocial risk: The power of longitudinal data,* pp. 1–28. Cambridge: Cambridge University Press.

(1989a). Psychiatric disorder in parents as a risk factor for children. In D. Shaffer, I. Philips, N. B. Enzer, M. M. Silverman, & V. Anthony (Eds.), *Prevention of mental disorders, alcohol and other drug use in children and adolescents* (OSAP Prevention Monograph no. 2), pp. 157–89. Rockville, MD: Office for Substance Abuse Prevention, U.S. Department of Health and Social Services.

(1989b). Age as an ambiguous variable in developmental research: Some epidemiological considerations from developmental psychopathology. *International Journal of Behavioral Development, 12,* 1–34.

(1990). Psychosocial resilience and protective mechanisms. In J. Rolf, A. Masten, D. Cicchetti, K. Nuechterlein, & S. Weintraub (Eds.), *Risk and protective factors in the development of psychopathology,* pp. 181–214. New York: Cambridge University Press.

(1991). Childhood experiences and adult psychosocial functioning. In G. R. Bock & J. A. Whelan (Eds.), *The childhood environment and adult disease* (CIBA Foundation Symposium no. 156), pp. 189–200. Chichester: Wiley.

(1994a). Beyond longitudinal data: Causes, consequences, changes and continuity. *Journal of Consulting and Clinical Psychology, 62,* 928–40.

(1994b). Continuities, transitions and turning points in development. In M. Rutter & D. Hay (Eds.), *Development through life: A handbook for clinicians,* pp. 1–25. Oxford: Blackwell Scientific.

(1995a). Psychosocial adversity: Risk, resilience and recovery. *Southern African Journal of Child and Adolescent Psychiatry, 7,* 75–88.

(1995b). Clinical implications of attachment concepts: Retrospect and prospect. *Journal of Child Psychology and Psychiatry, 36,* 549–71.

(1995c). Maternal deprivation. In M. H. Bornstein (Ed.), *Handbook of parenting, vol. 4: Applied and practicel parenting. Part I: Applied issues in parenting,* pp. 3–31. Mahwah, NJ: Erlbaum.

(1995d). Causal concepts and their testing. In M. Rutter & D. J. Smith (Eds.), *Psychosocial disorders in young people: Time trends and their causes*, pp. 7–34. Chichester: Wiley.

(1996). Transitions and turning points in developmental psychopathology: As applied to the age span between childhood and mid-adulthood. *International Journal of Behavioral Development, 19*, 603–26.

(1997a). Individual differences and levels of antisocial behavior. In A. Raine, P. A. Brennan, D. P. Farrington, & S. A. Mednick (Eds.), *Biosocial bases of violence*, pp. 55–68. New York: Plenum.

(1997b). Comorbidity: Concepts, claims and choices. *Criminal Behaviour and Mental Health, 7*, 265–85.

(1997c). Nature–nurture integration: The example of antisocial behavior. *American Psychologist, 52*, 603–26.

(1997d) Commentary: Child psychiatry disorder: Measures, causal mechanisms and interventions. *Archives of General Psychiatry, 54*, 785–9.

(in press). An update on resilience: Conceptual considerations and empirical findings. In J. Schonkof & S. Meisels (Eds.), *Handbook of early childhood intervention*. New York: Cambridge University Press.

Rutter, M., Bolton, P., Harrington, R., Le Couteur, A., MacDonald, H., & Simonoff, E. (1990a). Genetic factors in child psychiatric disorders I. A review of research strategies. *Journal of Child Psychology and Psychiatry, 31*, 3–37.

Rutter, M., Champion, L., Quinton, D., Maughan, B., & Pickles, A. (1995). Understanding individual differences in environmental risk exposure. In P. Moen, G. H. Elder, Jr., & K. Luscher (Eds.), *Examining lives in context: Perspectives on the ecology of human development*, pp. 61–93. Washington, DC: American Psychological Association.

Rutter, M., Dunn, J., Plomin, P., Simonoff, E., Pickles, A., Maughan, B., Ormel, J., Meyer, J., & Eaves, L. (1997a). Integrating nature and nurture: Implications of person–environment correlations and interactions for developmental psychopathology. *Development and Psychopathology, 9*, 335–64.

Rutter, M., & Garmezy, N. (1983). Developmental psychopathology. In E. M. Hetherington (Ed.), *Socialization, personality, and child development, vol. 4: Mussen's handbook of child psychology*, 4th ed., pp. 775–911. New York: Wiley.

Rutter, M., & Giller, H. (1983). *Juvenile delinquency: Trends and perspectives*. Harmondsworth: Penguin.

Rutter, M., Harrington, R., Quinton, D., & Pickles, A. (1994). Adult outcome of conduct disorder in childhood: Implications for concepts and definitions of patterns of psychopathology. In R. D. Ketterlinus & M. Lamb (Eds.), *Adolescent problem behaviors: Issues and research*, pp. 57–80. Hillsdale, NJ: Erlbaum.

Rutter, M., & Hay, D. F. (Eds.) (1994). *Development through life: A handbook for clinicians*. Oxford: Blackwell Scientific.

Rutter, M., & Madge, N. (1976). *Cycles of disadvantage: A review of research*. London: Heinemann.

Rutter, M., Maughan, B., Meyer, J., Pickles, A., Silberg, J., Simonoff, E., & Taylor, E. (1997b). Heterogeneity of antisocial behavior: Causes, continuities, and consequences. In R. Dienstbier & D. W. Osgood (Eds.), *Nebraska symposium on motivation, vol. 44: Motivation and delinquency.* Lincoln: University of Nebraska Press.

Rutter, M., Maughan, B., Mortimore, P., Ouston, J., & Smith, A. (1979). *Fifteen thousand hours: Secondary schools and their effects on children.* London: Open Books / Cambridge, MA: Harvard University Press.

Rutter, M., Maughan, B., & Ouston, J. (1986). The study of school effectiveness. In J. C. van der Wolf & J. J. Hox (Eds.) *Kwaliteit van onderings in het geding,* pp. 32–43. Lisse: Swetsand Zeitlinger.

Rutter, M., Maughan, B., Pickles, A., & Simonoff, E. (in press a). Retrospective recall recalled. In R. B. Cairns & P. C. Rodkin (Eds.), *The individual in developmental research: Essays in honor of Marian Radke-Yarrow.* Thousand Oaks, CA: Sage.

Rutter, M., & Pickles, A. (1991). Person–environment interactions: Concepts, mechanisms, and implications for data analysis. In T. D. Wachs & R. Plomin (Eds.), *Conceptualization and measurement of organism–environment interaction,* pp. 105–41. Washington, DC: American Psychological Association.

Rutter, M., & Plomin, R. (1997). Opportunities for psychiatry from genetic findings. *British Journal of Psychiatry, 171,* 209–19.

Rutter, M., & Quinton, D. (1977). Psychiatric disorder – Ecological factors and concepts of causation. In H. McGurk (Ed.), *Ecological factors in human development,* pp. 173–87. Amsterdam: North-Holland.

(1984). Parental psychiatric disorder: Effects on children. *Psychological Medicine, 14,* 853–80.

Rutter, M., Quinton, D., & Hill, J. (1990b). Adult outcome of institution-reared children: Males and females compared. In L. Robins & M. Rutter (Eds.), *Straight and devious pathways from childhood to adulthood,* pp. 135–57. Cambridge: Cambridge University Press.

Rutter M., & Russell–Jones, R. (1987). *Lead versus health: Sources and effects of low level lead exposure.* Chichester: Wiley.

Rutter, M., & Rutter, M. (1993). *Developing minds: Challenge and continuity across the lifespan.* Harmondsworth: Penguin / New York: Basic Books.

Rutter, M., Silberg, J., O'Connor, T., & Simonoff, E. (in press b). Genetics and child psychiatry. *Journal of Child Psychology and Psychiatry.*

Rutter, M., Silberg, J., & Simonoff, E. (1993). Whither behavior genetics? A developmental psychopathology perspective. In R. Plomin and G. E. McClearn (Eds.), *Nature, nurture and psychology,* pp. 433–56. Washington, DC: American Psychological Association.

Rutter, M., & Smith, D. J. (1995). *Psychosocial disorders in young people: Time trends and their causes.* Chichester: Wiley.

Rutter, M., Tizard, J., & Whitmore, K. (1970). *Education, health and behaviour.* London: Longmans.

Rutter, M., Yule, B., Quinton, D., Rowlands, O., Yule, W., & Berger, M. (1975). Attainment and adjustment in two geographical areas: III. Some factors accounting for area differences. *British Journal of Psychiatry, 126,* 520–33.

Sadowski, L. S., Cairns, R. B., & Earp, J. A. (1989). Firearm ownership among nonurban adolescents. *American Journal of Diseases of Children, 143,* 1410–13.

Sagel-Grande, I. (1991). Looking for one age. In T. Booth (Ed.), *Juvenile justice in the new Europe*, pp. 66–74. Sheffield: Sheffield University Press.

Sameroff, A. J., & Chandler, M. J. (1975). Reproductive risk and the continuum of caretaking casualty. In F. D. Horowitz (Ed.), *Review of child development research*, vol. 4, pp. 187–244. Chicago: University of Chicago Press.

Sammons, P., Nuttall, D., & Cuttance, P. (1993). Differential school effectiveness: Results from a reanalysis of the Inner London Education Authority's Junior School Project data. *British Educational Research Journal, 19*, 381–405.

Sampson, R. J. (1997). Collective regulation of adolescent misbehavior: Validation results from eight Chicago neighborhoods. *Journal of Adolescent Research, 12*, 227–44.

Sampson R. J., & Groves, W. B. (1989). Community structure and crime: Testing social-disorganization theory. *American Journal of Sociology, 94*, 774–802.

Sampson, R. J., & Laub, J. H. (1993). *Crime in the making: Pathways and turning points through life.* Cambridge, MA: Harvard University Press.

(1996). Socioeconomic achievement in the life course of disadvantaged men: Military service as a turning point, circa 1940–1965. *American Sociological Review, 61*, 347–67.

(1997). Unraveling the social context of physique and delinquency: A new, long-term look at the Gluecks' classic study. In A. Raine, P. Brennan, D. P. Farrington, & S. A. Mednick (Eds.), *Biosocial bases of violence*, pp. 175–88. New York: Plenum.

Sampson, R. J., & Lauritsen, J. L. (1994). Violent victimization and offending: Individual, situational, and community-level risk factors. In A. J. Reiss & J. Roth (Eds.), *Understanding and preventing violence*, pp. 1–114. Washington, DC: National Academy Press.

(1997). Racial and ethnic disparities in crime and criminal justice in the United States. In M. Tonry (Ed.), *Crime and justice*, vol. 21, pp. 311–74. Chicago: University of Chicago Press.

Sampson, R. J., Raudenbush, S. W., & Earls, F. (1997). Neighborhoods and violent crime: A multilevel study of collective efficacy. *Science, 277*, 918–24.

Sampson, R. J., & Wilson, W. J. (1995). Toward a theory of race, crime, and urban inequality. In J. Hagan & R. Peterson (Eds.), *Crime and inequality*, pp. 37–54. Stanford, CA: Stanford University Press.

Sandberg, S., Rutter, M., Giles, S., Owen, A., Champion, L., Nicholls, J., Prior, V., McGuinness, D., & Drinnan, D. (1993). Assessment of psychosocial experiences in childhood: Methodological issues and some illustrative findings. *Journal of Child Psychology and Psychiatry, 34*, 879–97.

Sanders, A. (1997). From suspect to trial. In M. Maguire, R. Morgan, & R. Reiner (Eds.), *The Oxford handbook of criminology*, 2nd ed., pp. 1051–93. Oxford: Clarendon.

Satterfield, J. H., & Schell, A. (1997). A prospective study of hyperactive boys with conduct problems and normal boys: Adolescent and adult criminality. *Journal of the American Academy of Child and Adolescent Psychiatry, 36*, 1726–35.

Scarr, S. (1992). Developmental theories for the 1990s: Development and individual differences. *Child Development, 63*, 1–19.

(1997). Behavior-genetic and socialization theories of intelligence: Truth and reconciliation. In R. J. Sternberg and E. L. Grigorenko (Eds.), *Intelligence, heredity, and environment*, pp. 3–41. Cambridge: Cambridge University Press.

Scarr, S., & McCartney, K. (1983). How people make their own environment: A theory of genotype → environment effects. *Child Development, 54*, 424–35.

Schachar, R., Rutter, M., & Smith, A. (1981). The characteristics of situationally and pervasively hyperactive children: Implications for syndrome definition. *Journal of Child Psychology and Psychiatry, 22*, 375–92.

Schachar, R., Tannock, R., Marriott, M., & Logan, G. (1995). Deficient inhibitory control in attention deficit hyperactivity disorder. *Journal of Abnormal Child Psychology, 23*, 411–37.

Schachar, R., Taylor, E., Wieselberg, M., Thorley, G., & Rutter, M. (1987). Changes in family function and relationships in children who respond to methylphenidate. *Journal of the American Academy of Child and Adolescent Psychiatry, 26*, 728–32.

Schalling, D., Asberg, M., Edman, G., & Oreland, L. (1987). Markers for vulnerability to psychopathology: Temperamental traits associated with platelet MAO activity. *Acta Psychiatrica Scandinavica, 76*, 172–82.

Schiavi, R. C., Theilgaard, A., Owen, D. R., & White, D. (1984). Sex chromosome anomalies, hormones, and aggressivity. *Archives of General Psychiatry, 41*, 93–9.

(1988). Sex chromosome anomalies, hormones, and sexuality. *Archives of General Psychiatry, 45*, 19–24.

Schlossman, S., Zellman, G., & Shavelson, R. (1984). *Delinquency prevention in south Chicago: A fifty-year assessment of the Chicago Area Project.* Santa Monica, CA: RAND.

Schluter, M. (1994). What is relational justice? In J. Burnside & N. Baker (Eds.), *Relational justice: Repairing the breach*, pp. 17–27. Winchester: Waterside.

Schneider, A. L. (1988). A comparative analysis of juvenile court responses to drug and alcohol offences. *Crime and Delinquency, 34*, 103–24.

Schoenthaler, S. J. (1991). Abstracts of early papers on the effects of vitamin and mineral supplementation on I.Q. and behavior. *Personality and Individual Differences, 12*, 335–41.

Schonfeld, I. S., Shaffer, D., O'Connor, P., & Portnoy, S. (1988). Conduct disorder and cognitive functioning: Testing three causal hypotheses. *Child Development, 59*, 993–1007.

Schuerman, L., & Kobrin, S. (1986). Community careers in crime. In A. J. Reiss & M. Tonry (Eds.), *Communities and crime*, pp. 67–100. Chicago: University of Chicago Press.

Schulte-Korne, G., Deimel, W., Gutenbrunner, C., Hennighausen, K., Blank, R., Reiger, C., & Remschmidt, H. (1996). Effect of an oligo-antigen diet on the behaviour of hyperkinetic children. *Zeitschrift fur Kinder und Jugenpsychiatrie, 24*, 176–83.

Schumann, K. F. (1995). The deviant apprentice: The impact of the German dual system of vocational training on juvenile delinquency. In Z. S. Blau &

J. Hagan (Eds.), *Delinquency and disrepute over the life course*, pp. 91–104. Greenwich, CT: JAI.

Schwartz, J. M., Stoessel, P. W., Baxter, L. R., Martin, K. M., & Phelps, M. E. (1996). Systematic changes in cerebral glucose metabolic rate after successful behaviour modification treatment for obsessive compulsive disorder. *International Journal of Behavioral Development, 53,* 109–16.

Schweinhart, L. J., Barnes, H. V., & Weikart, D. P. (1993). *The High/Scope Perry Preschool Study through age 27.* Ypsilanti, MI: High/Scope Educational Foundation.

Seguin, J. R., Pihl, R. O., Harden, P. W., Tremblay, R. E., & Boulerice, B. (1995). Cognitive and neuropsychological characteristics of physically aggressive boys. *Journal of Abnormal Psychology, 104,* 614–24.

Seifer, R. (1995). Perils and pitfalls of high-risk research. *Developmental Psychology, 31,* 420–4.

Sereny, G. (1995). *The case of Mary Bell: A portrait of a child who murdered.* London: Pimlico.

Settersten, J. R. A., & Mayer, K. U. (1997). The measurement of age, age structuring, and the life course. *Annual Review of Sociology, 23,* 233–61.

Shah, R., & Pease, K. (1992). Crime, race and reporting to the police. *The Howard Journal, 31,* 192–9.

Shanahan, M. J., Elder, G. H., & Meich, R. A. (1997). History and agency in men's lives: Pathways to achievement in cohort perspective. *Sociology of Education, 70,* 54–67.

Shapland, J., & Vagg, J. (1988). *Policing by the public.* London: Routledge.

Shaw, C. R., & McKay, H. D. (1942). *Juvenile delinquency and urban areas.* Chicago: University of Chicago Press.

    (1969). *Juvenile delinquency and urban areas,* rev. ed. Chicago: University of Chicago Press.

Sheldon, B. (1994). Social work effectiveness research: Implications for probation and juvenile justice services. *The Howard Journal, 33,* 218–35.

Sheldon, W. H., Stevens, S., & Tucker, W. B. (1940). *The varieties of human physique.* New York: Harper.

Sherman, D. K., Iacono, W. G., & McGue, M. K. (1997). Attention-deficit hyperactivity disorder dimensions: A twin study of inattention and impulsivity–hyperactivity. *Journal of the American Academy of Child and Adolescent Psychiatry, 36,* 745–53.

Sherman, L. W. (1992). *Policing domestic violence: Experiments and dilemmas.* New York: Free Press.

Shiner, M., & Newburn, T. (1997). Definitely, maybe not? The normalisation of recreational drug use among young people. *Sociology, 31,* 511–29.

Silbereisen, R. K., Robins, L., & Rutter, M. (1995). Secular trends in substance abuse: Concepts and data on the impact of social change on alcohol and drug abuse. In M. Rutter & D. J. Smith (Eds.), *Psychosocial disorders in young people: Time trends and their causes,* pp. 490–543. Chichester: Wiley.

Silberg, J., Eaves, L., Simonoff, E., Maes, H., Murrelle, L., Pickles, A., & Rutter, M. (1997). Substance use and antisocial behavior: Comorbidity of two separate traits or two facets of the same underlying liability. (1997). Paper presented at the World Congress of Psychiatric Genetics, Santa Fe, CA, October 19–23.

Silberg, J., Meyer, J., Pickles, A., Simonoff, E., Eaves, L., Hewitt, J., Maes, H., & Rutter, M. (1996a). Heterogeneity among juvenile antisocial behaviours: Findings from the Virginia Twin Study of Adolescent Behavioral Development. In G. R. Bock & J. A. Goode (Eds.), *Genetics of criminal and antisocial behaviour* (Ciba Foundation Symposium no. 194,) pp. 76–85. Chichester: Wiley.

Silberg, J., Rutter, M., Meyer, J., Maes, H., Hewitt, J., Simonoff, E., Pickles, A., Loeber, R., & Eaves, L. (1996b). Genetic and environmental influences of the covariation between hyperactivity and conduct disturbance in juvenile twins. *Journal of Child Psychology and Psychiatry, 37*, 803–16.

Simonoff, E., Pickles, A., Hewitt, J., Silberg, J., Rutter, M., Loeber, R., Meyer, J., Neale, M., & Eaves, L. (1995). Multiple raters of disruptive child behavior: Using a genetic strategy to examine shared views and bias. *Behavior Genetics, 25*, 311–26.

Simonoff, E., Pickles, A., Meyer, J., Silberg, J. L., & Maes, H. H. (in press). Genetic and environmental influences on subtypes of conduct disorder behavior in boys. *Journal of Abnormal Child Psychology.*

Simonoff, E., Pickles, A., Meyer, J., Silberg, J. L., Maes, H. H., Loeber, R., Rutter, M., Hewitt, J. K., & Eaves, L. J. (1997). The Virginia Twin Study of Adolescent Behavioral Development: Influences of age, gender and impairment on rates of disorder. *Archives of General Psychiatry, 54*, 801–8.

Simons, R. L., Wu, C.-I., Johnson, C., & Conger, R. D. (1995). A test of various perspectives on the intergenerational transmission of domestic violence. *Criminology, 33*, 141–72.

Sinclair, I., & Gibbs, I. (1996). *Quality of care in children's homes.* York: University of York.

Singer, L., Arendt, R., Farkas, K., Minnes, S., Huang, J., & Yamashita, T. (1997). Relationship of prenatal cocaine exposure and maternal postpartum psychological distress to child developmental outcome. *Development and Psychopathology, 9*, 473–91.

Singer, L., Arendt, R., & Minnes, S. (1993). Neurodevelopmental effects of cocaine. *Clinics in Perinatology, 20*, 245–62.

Skogan, W. G. (1990). *Disorder and decline: Crime and the spiral of decay in American neighbourhoods.* New York: Free Press.

 (1994). *Contacts between police and public: Findings from the 1992 British Crime Survey* (Home Office Research Study no. 134). London: HMSO.

Small, S. A. (1994). *Racialised barriers: The black experience in the United States and England in the 1980s.* London: Routledge.

 (1995). Enhancing contexts of adolescent development: The role of community-based action research. In L. J. Crockett & A. C. Crouter (Eds.), *Pathways through adolescence: Individual development in relation to social contexts,* pp. 211–34. Mahwah, NJ: Erlbaum.

Smith, C., & Krohn, M. D. (1995). Delinquency and family life among male adolescents: The role of ethnicity. *Journal of Youth and Adolescence, 24*, 69–93.

Smith, D. A., Visher, C. A., & Davidson, L. A. (1984). Equity and discretionary justice: The influence of race on police arrest decisions. *Journal of Criminal Law and Criminology, 75,* 234–49.

Smith, D. J. (1983). *Police and people in London.* London: Policy Studies Institute.

(1994). Race, crime and criminal justice. In M. Maguire, R. Morgan, & R. Reiner (Eds.), *The Oxford handbook of criminology,* 1st ed., pp. 1041–1118. Oxford: Clarendon.

(1995). Youth crime and conduct disorders: Trends, patterns and causal explanations. In M. Rutter & D. J. Smith (Eds.), *Psychosocial disorders in young people: Time trends and their causes,* pp. 389–489. Chichester: Wiley.

(1997a). Race, crime and criminal justice. In M. Maguire, R. Morgan, & R. Reiner (Eds.), *The Oxford handbook of criminology,* 2nd ed., pp. 703–59. Oxford: Clarendon.

(1997b). Ethnic origins, crime and criminal justice in England and Wales. In M. Tonry (Ed.), *Ethnicity, crime and immigration: Comparative and cross-national perspectives,* pp. 101–82. Chicago: University of Chicago Press.

Smith, D. J., & Tomlinson, S. (1989). *The school effect: A study of multi-racial comprehensives.* London: Policy Studies Institute.

Smith, J., & Prior, M. (1995). Temperament and stress resilience in school-age children: A within-families study. *Journal of the American Academy of Child and Adolescent Psychiatry, 34,* 168–79.

Smith, L. (1989). *Concerns about rape* (Home Office Research Study no. 106). London: HMSO.

Smith, P. K., & Sharp, S. (1994). *School bullying: Insights and perspectives.* London: Routledge.

Snyder, H. N., & Sickmund, M. (1995). *Juvenile offenders.* Washington, DC: National Institute of Justice.

Snyder, H. N., Sickmund, M., & Poe-Yamagata, E. (1996). *Juvenile offenders and victims: 1996 update on violence.* Washington, DC: Office of Juvenile Justice and Delinquency Prevention.

Sonuga-Barke, E. J. S., Taylor, E., Sembi, S., & Smith, J. (1992). Hyperactivity and delay aversion: I. The effect of delay on choice. *Journal of Child Psychology and Psychiatry, 33,* 387–98.

Soussignan, R., Tremblay, R. E., Schaal, B., Laurent, D., Larivee, S., Gagnon, C., Le Blanc, M., & Charlebois, P. (1992). Behavioural and cognitive characteristics of conduct disorder–hyperactive boys from age 6 to 11: A multiple informant perspective. *Journal of Child Psychology and Psychiatry, 33,* 1333–46.

South, N. (1994). Drugs: Control, crime and criminological studies. In M. Maguire, R. Morgan, & R. Reiner (Eds.), *The Oxford handbook of criminology,* pp. 393–440. Oxford: Clarendon.

Spelman, W. (1994). *Criminal incapacitation.* New York: Plenum.

(1995). Once bitten, then what? Cross-sectional and time-course explanations of repeat victimization. *British Journal of Criminology, 35,* 366–83.

Spencer, J. R., & Flin, R. (1990). *The evidence of children.* London: Blackstone.

Spoont, M. R. (1992). Modulatory role of serotonin in neural information processing: Implications for human psychopathology. *Psychological Bulletin, 112,* 330–50.

Stattin, H., & Klackenberg-Larsson, I. (1993). Early language and intelligence development and their relationship to future criminal behaviour. *Journal of Abnormal Psychology, 102,* 369–78.

Stattin, H., & Magnusson, D. (1990). *Pubertal maturation in female development.* Hillsdale, NJ: Erlbaum.

—— (1995). Onset of official delinquency: Its co-occurrence in time with educational, behavioural, and interpersonal problems. *British Journal of Criminology, 35,* 417–49.

Stattin, H., Magnusson, D., & Reichel, H. (1989). Criminal activity at different ages: A study based on a Swedish longitudinal research population. *British Journal of Criminology, 29,* 368–85.

Stattin, H., Romelsjö, A., & Stenbacka, M. (1997). Personal resources as modifiers of the risk for future criminality: An analysis of protective factors in relation to 18-year-old boys. *British Journal of Criminology, 37,* 198–222.

Steinhausen, H. P. (1995). Children of alcoholic parents: A review. *European Journal of Child and Adolescent Psychiatry, 4,* 419–32.

Stephenson, G. (1992). *The psychology of criminal justice.* Oxford: Blackwell.

Sternberg, R. J., & Grigorenko, E. L. (Eds.) (1997). *Intelligence, heredity and environment.* Cambridge: Cambridge University Press.

Stevens, P., & Willis, C. (1979). *Race, crime and arrests* (Home Office Research Study no. 58). London: HMSO.

Stevenson, J., & Graham, P. (1993). Antisocial behaviour and spelling disability in a population sample of 13 year old twins. *European Child and Adolescent Psychiatry, 2,* 179–91.

Stewart, G., & Tutt, N. (1987). *Children in custody.* Aldershot: Avebury.

Stoff, D. M., Pasatiempo, A. P., Yeung, Y., Cooper, T. B., Bridger, W. H., & Rabinovich, H. (1992). Neuroendocrine responses to challenge with *dl*-fenfluramine and aggression in disruptive behavior disorders of children and adolescents. *Psychiatric Research, 43,* 263–76.

Stolzenberg, L., & D'Alessio, S. J. (1997). "Three strikes and you're out": The impact of California's new mandatory sentencing law on serious crime rates. *Crime and Delinquency, 43,* 457–69.

Stoolmiller, M., Duncan, T., Bank, L., & Patterson, G. R. (1993). Some problems and solutions in the study of change: Significant patterns in client resistance. *Journal of Consulting and Clinical Psychology, 61,* 920–8.

Stouthamer-Loeber, M., Loeber, R., Farrington, D. P., Zhang, Q., Van Kammen, W., & Maguin, E. (1993). The double edge of protective and risk factors for delinquency: Interrelations and developmental patterns. *Development and Psychopathology, 5,* 683–701.

Straus, M. A., & Gelles, R. J. (1990). *Physical violence in American families: Risk factors and adaptations to violence in 8,145 families.* New Brunswick, NJ: Transaction Publishers.

Straus, M. A., Gelles, R. J., & Steinmetz, S. K. (1980). *Behind closed doors: Violence in the American family.* New York: Doubleday.

Streissguth, A. P. (1993). Fetal alcohol syndrome in older patients. *Alcohol, 2,* 209–12.

Streissguth, A. P., Martin, D. C., Barr, H. M., & MacGregor Sandman, B. (1984). Intrauterine alcohol and nicotine exposure: Attention and reaction time in 4 year old children. *Developmental Psychology, 20,* 533–41.

Stringfield, S., & Herman, R. (1996). Assessment of the state of school effectiveness research in the United States of America. *School Effectiveness and School Improvement, 7,* 159–80.

Sumner, M., & Parker, H. (1995). *Low in alcohol: A review of international research into alcohol's role in crime causation.* London: The Portman Group.

Support Force for Children's Residential Care. (1996). *Report to the Secretary of State for Health.* London: Department of Health.

Sutherland, E. H., & Cressey, D. R. (1978). *Criminology,* 10th ed. Philadelphia: Lippincott.

Swaab, D. F. (1991). Relation between maturation of neurotransmitter systems in the human brain and psychosocial disorders. In M. Rutter & P. Casaer (Eds.), *Biological risk factors for psychosocial disorders,* pp. 50–66. Cambridge: Cambridge University Press.

Swanson, J. W. (1994). Mental disorder, substance abuse, and community violence: An epidemiological approach. In J. Monahan & H. Steadman (Eds.), *Violence and mental disorder: Developments in risk assessment,* pp. 101–36. Chicago: University of Chicago Press.

Tantam, D. (1988). Lifelong eccentricity and social isolation: I. Psychiatric, social and forensic aspects. *British Journal of Psychiatry, 153,* 777–82.

Tarling, R. (1979). *Sentencing practice in magistrates' courts* (Home Office Research Study no. 56). London: HMSO.

(1993). *Analysing offending: Data, models and interpretation.* London: HMSO.

Tarling, R., & Dowds, L. (1997). Crime and punishment. In R. Jowell, J. Curtice, A. Park, L. Brook, K. Thomson, & C. Bryson (Eds.), *British social attitudes: The 14th report. The end of Conservative values?* Aldershot: Ashgate.

Taub, R., Taylor, D. G., & Dunham, J. D. (1984). *Paths of neighbourhood change.* Chicago: University of Chicago Press.

Taylor, E. (1991). Toxins and allergens. In M. Rutter & P. Casaer (Eds.), *Biological risk factors for psychosocial disorders,* pp. 199–232. Cambridge: Cambridge University Press.

(1994). Syndromes of attention deficit and overactivity. In M. Rutter, E. Taylor, & L. Hersov (Eds.), *Child and adolescent psychiatry: Modern approaches,* 3rd ed., pp. 285–308. Oxford: Blackwell Scientific.

Taylor, E., Chadwick, O., Heptinstall, E., & Danckaerts, M. (1996). Hyperactivity and conduct problems as risk factors for adolescent development. *Journal of the American Academy of Child and Adolescent Psychiatry, 35,* 1213–26.

Taylor, E., & Rutter, M. (1986). Sex differences in neurodevelopmental and psychiatric disorders: One explanation or many? *Behavioral and Brain Sciences, 8,* 460–1.

Taylor, E., Sandberg, S., Thorley, G., & Giles, S. (1991). *The epidemiology of childhood hyperactivity.* Oxford: Oxford University Press.

Taylor, E., Schacher, R., Thorley, G., Wieselberg, H. M., Everitt, B., & Rutter, M. (1987). Which boys respond to stimulant medication? A controlled trial of methylphenidate in boys with disruptive behaviour. *Psychological Medicine,* 17, 121–43.

Taylor, P. J. (1993). Schizophrenia and crime: Distinctive patterns in association. In S. Hodgins (Ed.), *Mental disorder and crime,* pp. 63–85. Newbury Park, CA: Sage.

Teasdale, J. D., & Barnard, P. J. (1993). *Affect, cognition and change: Re-modelling depressive thought.* Hove: Erlbaum.

Tennenbaum, D. J. (1977). Personality and criminality: A summary and implications of the literature. *Journal of Criminal Justice,* 5, 225–35.

Thapar, A., Hervas, A., & McGuffin, P. (1995). Childhood hyperactivity scores are highly heritable and show sibling competition effects: Twin study evidence. *Behavior Genetics,* 25, 537–44.

Thapar, A., & McGuffin, P. (1994). A twin study of depressive symptoms in childhood. *British Journal of Psychiatry,* 165, 259–65.

Thomas, A., Chess, S., & Birch, H. (1968). *Temperament and behavior disorders in children.* New York: New York University Press.

Thornberry, T. P. (1987). Toward an interactional theory of delinquency. *Criminology,* 25, 863–91.

(Ed.) (1997). *Developmental theories of crime and delinquency: Advances in criminological theory,* vol. 6. New Brunswick, NJ: Transaction Publishers.

(1998). Membership in youth gangs and involvement in serious and violent offenders. In R. L. Loeber & D. P. Farrington (Eds.), *Serious and violent juvenile offenders: Risk factors and successful interventions,* pp. 147–66. Thousand Oaks, CA: Sage.

Thornberry, T. P., Huizinga, D., & Loeber, R. (1995). The prevention of serious delinquency and violence: Implications from the program of research on the causes and correlates of delinquency. In J. C. Howell, B. Krisberg, D. Hawkins, & J. J. Wilson (Eds.), *Sourcebook on serious, violent, and chronic juvenile offenders,* pp. 213–37. Thousand Oaks, CA: Sage.

Thornberry, T. P., & Krohn, M. D. (1997). Peers, drug use, and delinquency. In D. Stoff, J. Breiling, & J. D. Maser (Eds.), *Handbook of antisocial behavior,* pp. 218–33. New York: Wiley.

Thornberry, T. P., Krohn, M. D., Lizotte, A. J., & Chard-Wiershem, D. (1993). The role of juvenile gangs in facilitating delinquent behavior. *Journal of Research in Crime and Delinquency,* 30, 55–87.

Thornberry, T. P., Lizotte, A. J., Krohn, M. D., Farnworth, M., & Jang, J. S. (1994). Delinquency peers, beliefs, and delinquent behavior: A longitudinal test of interactional theory. *Criminology,* 32, 47–83.

Thornton, D. (1987). Treatment effects on recidivism: A reappraisal of the "nothing works" doctrine. In B. J. McGurk, D. M. Thornton, & M. Williams (Eds.), *Applying psychology to imprisonment: Theory and practice,* pp. 181–9. London: HMSO.

Thornton, D., Curran, L., Grayson, D., & Holloway, W. (1984). *Tougher regimes in detention centres.* London: HMSO.

Tizard, J. (1975). Race and IQ: The limits of probability. *New Behaviour,* 1, 6–9.

Tolan, P. H., & Thomas, P. (1995). The implications of age of onset for delinquency risk. II: Longitudinal data. *Journal of Abnormal Child Psychology,* 23, 157–81.

Tonry, M. (1994). Racial disproportion in U.S. prisons. *British Journal of Criminology, 34,* 97–115.

(1995). *Malign neglect: Race, crime and punishment in America.* New York: Oxford University Press.

Tonry, M., & Farrington, D. P. (1995). Strategic approaches to crime prevention. In M. Tonry and D. P. Farrington (Eds.), *Crime and justice,* pp. 1–26. Chicago: University of Chicago Press.

Tonry, M., Ohlin, L. E., & Farrington, D. P. (1991). *Human development and criminal behavior: New ways of advancing knowledge.* New York: Springer-Verlag.

Tonry, M., & Wilson, J. Q. (1990). Drugs and crime. In *Crime and justice, a review of research,* vol. 13. Chicago: University of Chicago Press.

Toupin, J. (1997). Adolescent murderers: Validation of a typology and study of their recidivism. In A. V. Wilson (Ed.), *Homicide: The victim/offender connection,* pp. 135–56. Cincinnati, OH: Anderson.

Tournier, P., & Robert, P. (1991). *Étrangers et délinquances: Les chiffers du débat.* Paris: Harmattan.

Trachtenberg, S., & Viken, R. J. (1994). Aggressive boys in the classroom: Biased attributions or shared perceptions? *Child Development, 65,* 829–35.

Tracy, P. E. (1987). Race and class differences in official and self-reported delinquency. In M. E. Wolfgang, T. P. Thornberry, & R. M. Figlio (Eds.), *From boy to man, from delinquency to crime,* pp. 87–121. Chicago: University of Chicago Press.

Tracy, P. E., Wolfgang, M. E., & Figlio, R. M. (1990). *Delinquency careers in two birth cohorts.* New York: Plenum.

Tremblay, R. E., & Craig, W. (1995). Developmental crime prevention. In M. Tonry & D. P. Farrington (Eds.), *Building a safer society: Strategic approaches to crime prevention,* vol. 19, pp. 151–236. Chicago: University of Chicago Press.

Tremblay, R. E., Mâsse, L. C., Vitaro, F., & Dobkin, P. L. (1995). The impact of friends' deviant behavior on early onset of delinquency: Longitudinal data from 6 to 13 years of age. *Development and Psychopathology, 7,* 649–67.

Tremblay, R. E., Pihl, R. O., Vitaro, F., & Dobkin, P. L. (1994). Predicting early onset of male antisocial behavior from preschool behavior. *Archives of General Psychiatry, 51,* 732–9.

Tremblay, R. E., Schall, B., Boulerice, B., & Perusse, D. (1997). Male physical aggression, social dominance and testosterone levels at puberty: A developmental perspective. In A. Raine, P. Brennan, D. P. Farrington, & S. A. Mednick (Eds.), *Biosocial bases of violence,* pp. 271–92. New York: Plenum.

Tremblay, R. E., Vitaro, F., Bertrand, L., Le Blanc, M., Beauchesne, H., Boileau, H., & David, H. (1992). Parent and child training to prevent early onset of delinquency: The Montreal Longitudinal-Experimental Study. In J. McCord & R. E. Tremblay (Eds.), *Parenting antisocial behaviour: Interventions from birth through adolescence,* pp. 151–236. New York: Guilford.

Trickett, A., Ellingworth, D., Hope, T., & Pease, K. (1995). Crime victimization in the eighties: Changes in area and regional inequality. *British Journal of Criminology, 35,* 343–59.

Trickett, A., & McBride-Chang, C. (1995). The developmental impact of different forms of child abuse and neglect. *Developmental Review, 15,* 311–37.

Trickett, A., Osborn, D. R., Seymour, J., & Pease, K. (1992). What is different about crime areas? *British Journal of Criminology, 32,* 81–9.

Triseliotis, J., Shireman, J., & Hundleby, M. (1997). *Adoption: Theory, policy and practice.* London: Cassell.

Tuinier, S., Verhoeven, W. M. A., & van Praag, H. M. (1995). Cerebrospinal fluid 5-hydroxyindolacetic acid and aggression: A critical reappraisal of the clinical data. *International Clinical Psychopharmacology, 10,* 147–56.

U.S. Department of Justice. (1993). *Uniform crime reports for the United States.* Washington, DC: U.S. Department of Justice.

Utting, D. (1996). *Reducing criminality among young people: A sample of relevant programmes in the United Kingdom.* London: Home Office.

Utting, D., Bright, J., & Henricson, C. (1993). *Crime and the family: Improving child-rearing and preventing delinquency.* London: Family Policy Studies Centre.

Utting, W. (1991). *Children in the public care: A review of residential child care.* London: HMSO.

(1997). *People like us: The report of the review of the safeguards for children living away from home.* London: HMSO.

Vaillant, G. E. (1983). *The natural history of alcoholism: Causes, patterns and paths to recovery.* Cambridge, MA: Harvard University Press.

Van der Laan, P. H. (1988). Innovations in the Dutch juvenile justice system – Alternative sanctions. In J. Junger-Tas & R. Black (Eds.), *Juvenile delinquency in the Netherlands,* pp. 203–19. Amsterdam: Kugler.

Van der Oord, E. J. C. G., Boomsma, D. I., & Verhulst, F. C. (1994). A study of problem behaviors in 10- to 15-year-old biologically related and unrelated international adoptees. *Behaviour Genetics, 24,* 193–205.

van Dijk, J., Mayhew, P., & Killias, M. (1990). *Experiences of crime across the world.* Deventer: Kluwer.

Van Praag, H. M. (1991). Serotonergic dysfunction and aggression control. *Psychological Medicine, 21,* 15–19.

Venables, P. H. (1988). Psychophysiology and crime: Theory and data. In T. E. Moffitt & S. A. Mednick (Eds.), *Biological contributions to crime causation,* pp. 3–13. Dordrecht: Martinus Nijhoff.

Vennard, J., Sugg, D., & Hedderman, C. (1997). Part I: The use of cognitive–behavioural approaches with offenders: Messages from the research. In *Changing offenders' attitudes and behaviour: What works?* (Home Office Research Study no. 171), pp. 1–35. London: HMSO.

Verhulst, F. C., & Koot, H. M. (1992). *Child psychiatric epidemiology: Concepts, methods and findings.* Newbury Park, CA: Sage.

Virkunnen, M., Goldman, D., & Linnoila, M. (1996). *Serotonin in alcoholic violent offenders.* In G. R. Bock & J. A. Goode (Eds.), *Genetics of criminal and antisocial behaviour* (Ciba Foundation Symposium no. 194), pp. 168–82. Chichester: Wiley.

Visher, C. A. (1986). The Rand inmate survey: A reanalysis. In A. Blumstein, J. Cohen, J. A. Rother, & C. A. Visher (Eds.), *Criminal careers and "career criminals,"* vol. II, pp. 161–212. Washington, DC: National Academy of Sciences.

Vitiello, B., & Stoff, D. (1997). Subtypes of aggression and their relevance to child psychiatry. *Journal of the American Academy of Child and Adolescent Psychiatry, 36,* 307–15.

Vizard, E., Monck, E., & Misch, P. (1995). Child and adolescent sex abuse perpetrators: A review of the research literature. *Journal of Child Psychology and Psychiatry, 36,* 731–56.

Volpe, J. (1992). Effects of cocaine on the fetus. *New England Journal of Medicine, 327,* 399–405.

Vorria, P., Rutter, M., Pickles, A., Wolkind, S., & Hobsbaum, A. (1998a). A comparative study of Greek children in long-term residential group care and in two-parent families: I. Social, emotional, and behavioural differences. *Journal of Child Psychology and Psychiatry, 39,* 225–36.

(1998b). A comparative study of Greek children in long-term residential group care and in two-parent families: II. Possible mediating mechanisms. *Journal of Child Psychology and Psychiatry, 39,* 237–45.

Wadsworth, M. E. J. (1976). Delinquency, pulse rates, and early emotional deprivation. *British Journal of Criminology, 16,* 245–56.

(1979). *Roots of delinquency: Infancy, adolescence and crime.* Oxford: Martin Robertson.

(1991). *The imprint of time: Childhood, history and adult life.* Oxford: Clarendon.

Wahlsten, D. (1990). Insensitivity of the analysis of variance to heredity–environment interaction. *Behavioral and Brain Sciences, 13,* 109–61.

Waldman, I. D. (1996). Aggressive boys' hostile perceptual and response biases: The role of attention in impulsivity. *Child Development, 67,* 1015–34.

Walgrave, L. (1995). Restorative justice for juveniles: Just a technique or a fully fledged alternative? *The Howard Journal, 34,* 228–49.

Walker, M. A. (1987). Interpreting race and crime statistics. *Journal of the Royal Statistical Society, 150,* 39–56.

(1988). The court disposal of young males, by race, in London in 1983. *British Journal of Criminology, 28,* 441–59.

(1992). Arrest rates and ethnic minorities: A study in a provincial city. *Journal of the Royal Statistical Society, 155,* 259–72.

(1995). Statistics of offences. In M. A. Walker (Ed.), *Interpreting crime statistics,* pp. 4–23. Oxford: Clarendon.

Walker, N. (1991). *Why punish?* Oxford: Oxford University Press.

Walker, N., & Hough, M. (Eds.) (1988). *Public attitudes to sentencing: Surveys from five countries.* Aldershot: Gower.

Walmsley, R., Howard, L., & White, S. (1992). *The National Prison Survey 1991: Main findings* (Home Office Research Study no. 128). London: HMSO.

Walzer, S. (1998). Personal communication.

Walzer, S., Bashir, A. S., & Silbert, A. R. (1991). Cognitive and behavioral factors in the learning disabilities of 47 XXY and 47 XYY boys. *Birth Defects Original Article Series, 26,* 45–58.

Wang, M. C., & Gordon, E. W. (1994). *Educational resilience in inner-city America: Challenges and prospects.* Hillsdale, NJ: Erlbaum.

Warr, M. (1993a). Parents, peers, and delinquency. *Social Forces, 72,* 247–64.

(1993b). Age, peers and delinquency. *Criminology, 31,* 17–40.

Warr, M., & Stafford, M. (1991). The influence of delinquent peers: What they think or what they do. *Criminology, 29,* 851–65.

Warr, P. (1987). *Work, unemployment and mental health.* Oxford: Clarendon.

Wartella, E. (1995). Media and problem behaviours in young people. In M. Rutter & D. J. Smith (Eds.), *Psychosocial disorders in young people: Time trends and their causes,* pp. 296–323. Chichester: Wiley.

Watkins, B., & Bentovim, A. (1992). The sexual abuse of male children and adolescents: A review of current research. *Journal of Child Psychology and Psychiatry, 33,* 197–248.

Watt, N. F., David, J. P., Ladd, K. L., & Shamos, S. (1995). The life course of psychosocial resilience: A phenomenological perspective on deflecting life's slings and arrows. *Journal of Primary Prevention, 15,* 209–46.

Webb, B., & Laycock, G. (1992). *Tackling car crime: The nature and extent of the problem.* London: Home Office.

Webb, B., & Marshall, I. H. (1989). Response to criminal victimization by older Americans. *Criminal Justice and Behaviour, 16,* 236–59.

Webster-Stratton, C. (1984). Randomized trial of two parent-training programs for families with conduct-disordered children. *Journal of Consulting and Clinical Psychology, 52,* 666–78.

(1991). Annotation: Strategies for helping families with conduct disordered children. *Journal of Child Psychology and Psychiatry, 32,* 1047–62.

(1996). Early intervention with videotape modeling: Programs for families of children with oppositional defiant disorder or conduct disorder. In E. H. Gibbs & P. S. Jensen (Eds.), *Psychosocial treatments for child and adolescent disorders,* pp. 435–74. Washington, DC: American Psychological Association.

Webster-Stratton, C., & Herbert, M. (1994). *Troubled families – Problem children.* New York: Wiley.

Weikart, D. P., & Schweinhart, L. J. (1992). High/Scope preschool progam outcomes. In J. McCord & R. E. Tremblay (Eds.), *Preventing antisocial behavior: Interventions from birth through adolescence,* pp. 67–86. New York: Guilford.

Weishert, R. A., & Wells, L. E. (1996). Rural crime and justice: Implications for theory and research. *Crime and Delinquency, 42,* 379–97.

Weiss, B., Williams, J. H., Margen, S., Abrams, B., Caan, B., Citron, L., Cox, C., McKibben, J., Ogar, D., & Schultz, S. (1980). Behavioral response to artificial food colors. *Science, 207,* 1487–9.

Weissberg, R. P., Jackson, A. S., & Shriver, T. P. (1993). Promoting positive social development and health practices in young urban adolescents. In M. J. Elias (Ed.), *Social decision making and life skills development: Guidelines for middle school educators,* pp. 45–77. Gaithersburg, MD: Aspen.

Weisz, J. R. (1997). Effects of interventions for child and adolescent psychological dysfunction: Relevance of context, developmental factors, and individual differences. In S. S. Luthar, J. A. Burack, D. Cicchetti, & J. R. Weisz (Eds.), *Developmntal psychopathology: Perspectives on adjustment, risk, and disorder,* pp. 3–23. Cambridge: Cambridge University Press.

Weisz, J. R., Donenberg, G. R., Han, S. S., & Weiss, B. (1995). Bridging the gap between laboratory and clinic in child and adolescent psychotherapy. *Journal of Consulting and Clinical Psychology, 63,* 688–701.

Weitekamp, E., Kerner, H.-J., Schubert, A., & Schindler, V. (1996). Multiple and habitual offending among young males: Criminology and criminal policy lessons from a re-analysis of the Philadelphia Birth Cohort Studies. *International Annals of Criminology, 12,* 9–52.

Wells, L. E., & Rankin, J. H. (1991). Families and delinquency: A meta-analysis of the impact of broken homes. *Social Problems, 38,* 71–93.

Werner, E. E., & Smith, R. S. (1977). *Kauai's children come of age.* Honolulu: University of Hawaii Press.

(1982). *Vulnerable but invincible: A longitudinal study of resilient children and youth.* New York: McGraw-Hill.

(1992). *Overcoming the odds: High risk children from birth to adulthood.* Ithaca, NY: Cornell University Press.

Wessely, S. C., Castle, D., Douglas, A. J., & Taylor, P. J. (1994). The criminal careers of incident cases of schizophrenia. *Psychological Medicine, 24,* 483–502.

West, D. J., & Farrington, D. P. (1973). *Who becomes delinquent?* London: Heinemann.

White, J. L., Moffitt, T. E., Caspi, A., Jeglum, D., Needles, D., & Stouthamer-Loeber, M. (1994). Measuring impulsivity and examining its relationship to delinquency. *Journal of Abnormal Psychology, 103,* 192–205.

White, J. L., Moffitt, T. E., Earls, F., Robins, L., & Silva, P. A. (1990). How early can we tell? Predictors of childhood conduct disorder and adolescent delinquency. *Criminology, 28,* 507–33.

Whitehead, J. T., & Lab, S. P. (1989). A meta-analysis of juvenile correctional treatment. *Journal of Research in Crime and Delinquency, 26,* 276–95.

Whittaker A. H., Van Rossem, R., Feldman, J. F., Schonfeld, I. S., Pinto-Martin, J. A., Torre, C., Shaffer, D., & Paneth, N. (1997). Psychiatric outcomes in low birthweight children at age six: Relation to neonatal cranial ultrasound abnormalities. *Archives of General Psychiatry, 54,* 847–56.

Widom, C. S. (1989). The cycle of violence. *Science, 244,* 160–6.

(1997). Child abuse, neglect, and witnessing violence. In D. M. Stoff, J. Breiling, & J. D. Maser (Eds.), *Handbook of antisocial behavior,* pp. 159–70. New York: Wiley.

Wikström, P.-O. H. (1990). Age and crime in a Stockholm cohort. *Journal of Quantitative Criminology, 6,* 61–83.

(1991). *Urban crime, criminals and victims.* New York: Springer-Verlag.

Wilkinson, R. G. (1995). *Unequal shares: The effects of widening income differentials on the welfare of the young.* Ilford: Barnardos.

Williams, B., & New, M. (1996). Developmental perspective on adolescent boys who sexually abuse other children. *Child Psychology and Psychiatry Review, 1,* 122–30.

Williams, T. M. (Ed.) (1986). *The impact of television: A natural experiment in three communities.* New York: Academic Press.

(1989). *The cocaine kids.* New York: Addison-Wesley.

Wilson, H. (1980). Parental supervision: A neglected aspect of delinquency. *British Journal of Criminology, 20,* 203–35.

(1987). Parental supervision re-examined. *British Journal of Criminology, 27,* 275–301.

Wilson, J. Q., & Herrnstein, R. J. (1985). *Crime and human nature.* New York: Simon and Schuster.

Wilson, P. (1973). *Children who kill.* London: Michael Joseph.

Wilson, W. J. (1987). *The truly disadvantaged: The inner city, the underclass, and public policy.* Chicago: University of Chicago Press.

(1991). Studying inner-city social dislocations: The challenge of public policy research. *American Sociological Review, 56,* 1–14.

(1995). Jobless ghettos and the social outcome of youngsters. In P. Moen, G. Elder, Jr., & K. Luscher (Eds.), *Examining lives in context: Perspectives on the ecology of human development,* pp. 527–43. Washington, DC: American Psychological Association.

Winkel, F. W. (1991). Interaction between the police and minority group members: Victimization through the incorrect interpretation of nonverbal behaviour. *International Review of Victimology, 2,* 15–27.

Wish, E. D., & Johnson, B. D. (1986). The impact of substance abuse on criminal careers. In A. Blumstein, J. Cohen, J. A. Roth, & C. A. Visher (Eds.), *Criminal careers and career criminals,* pp. 52–88. Washington, DC: National Academy Press.

Witkin, H. A., Mednick, S. A., Schulsinger, F., Bakkestrom, E., Christianse, K. O., Goodenough, D. R., Hirschhorn, K., Lundsteen, C., Owen, D. R., Philip, J., Rubin, D. B., & Stocking, M. (1976). Criminality in XYY and XXY men. *Science, 193,* 547–55.

Wolff, S. (1995). *Loners: The life path of unusual children.* London: Routledge.

Wolfgang, M. E., Figlio, R. M., & Stelim, T. (1972). *Delinquency in a birth cohort.* Chicago: University of Chicago Press.

Wolfgang, M. E., Thornberry, T. P., & Figlio, R. M. (1987). *From boy to man, from delinquency to crime.* Chicago: University of Chicago Press.

Wolkind, S., & Rushton, A. (1994). Residential and foster family care. In M. Rutter, E. Taylor, & L. Hersov (Eds.), *Child and adolescent psychiatry: Modern approaches,* 3rd ed., pp. 252–66. Oxford: Blackwell.

Wood, W., Wong, F. Y., & Chachere, G. (1991). Effects of media violence on viewers' aggression in unconstrained social interaction. *Psychological Bulletin, 109,* 371–83.

Wootton, B. (1959). *Social science and social pathology.* London: Allen & Unwin.

World Health Organisation (1992). *The ICD-10 classification of mental and behavioural disorders: Clinical descriptions and diagnostic guidelines.* Geneva: WHO.

Wright, M. (1982). *Making good: Prisons, punishment and beyond.* London: Hutchinson.

Wright, W. E., & Dixon, M. C. (1977). Community prevention and treatment of juvenile delinquency: A review of evaluation studies. *Journal of Research in Crime and Delinquency, 14,* 35–67.

Wundersitz, J. (1993). Some statistics on youth offending: An inter-jurisdictional comparison. In F. Gale, N. Naffine, & J. Wundersitz (Eds.), *Juvenile justice: Debating the issues*, pp. 18–36. London: Allen & Unwin.

Yoshikawa, H. (1994). Prevention as cumulative protection: Effects of early family support and education on chronic delinquency and its risk. *Psychological Bulletin, 115*, 28–54.

Young, E., Patel, S., Stoneham, M., Rona, R., & Wilkinson, J. D. (1987). The prevalence of reaction to food additives in a survey population. *Journal of the Royal Colege of Physicians of London, 21*, 241–7.

Zaslow, M. J. (1989). Sex differences in children's responses to parental divorce: II. Samples, variables, ages and sources. *American Journal of Orthopsychiatry, 59*, 118–41.

Zaslow, M. J., & Hayes, C. D. (1986). Sex differences in children's response to psychosocial stress: Toward a cross-context analysis. In M. E. Lamb, A. L. Brown, & B. Rogoff (Eds.), *Advances in developmental psychology*, vol. 4, pp. 285–337. Hillsdale, NJ: Erlbaum.

Zillman, D. (1979). *Hostility and aggression*. Hillsdale, NJ: Erlbaum.

Zimring, F., & Hawkins, G. (1995). *Incapacitation: Penal confinement and the restraint of crime*. Oxford: Oxford University Press.

Zoccolillo, M. (1993). Gender and the development of conduct disorder. *Development and Psychopathology, 5*, 65–78.

Zoccolillo, M., Pickles, A., Quinton, D., & Rutter, M. (1992). The outcome of childhood conduct disorder: Implications for defining adult personality disorder and conduct disorder. *Psychological Medicine, 22*, 971–86.

Zuckerman, M. (1994). *Behavioral expressions and biosocial bases of sensation seeking*. Cambridge: Cambridge University Press.

Index

Claude Monet:
Impressions
of France